1,000,000 Books

are available to read at

www.ForgottenBooks.com

Read online
Download PDF
Purchase in print

ISBN 978-1-332-23568-1
PIBN 10302344

This book is a reproduction of an important historical work. Forgotten Books uses state-of-the-art technology to digitally reconstruct the work, preserving the original format whilst repairing imperfections present in the aged copy. In rare cases, an imperfection in the original, such as a blemish or missing page, may be replicated in our edition. We do, however, repair the vast majority of imperfections successfully; any imperfections that remain are intentionally left to preserve the state of such historical works.

Forgotten Books is a registered trademark of FB &c Ltd.
Copyright © 2018 FB &c Ltd.
FB &c Ltd, Dalton House, 60 Windsor Avenue, London, SW19 2RR.
Company number 08720141. Registered in England and Wales.

For support please visit www.forgottenbooks.com

1 MONTH OF FREE READING

at

www.ForgottenBooks.com

By purchasing this book you are eligible for one month membership to ForgottenBooks.com, giving you unlimited access to our entire collection of over 1,000,000 titles via our web site and mobile apps.

To claim your free month visit:
www.forgottenbooks.com/free302344

* Offer is valid for 45 days from date of purchase. Terms and conditions apply.

English
Français
Deutsche
Italiano
Español
Português

www.forgottenbooks.com

Mythology Photography **Fiction**
Fishing Christianity **Art** Cooking
Essays Buddhism Freemasonry
Medicine **Biology** Music **Ancient Egypt** Evolution Carpentry Physics
Dance Geology **Mathematics** Fitness
Shakespeare **Folklore** Yoga Marketing
Confidence Immortality Biographies
Poetry **Psychology** Witchcraft
Electronics Chemistry History **Law**
Accounting **Philosophy** Anthropology
Alchemy Drama Quantum Mechanics
Atheism Sexual Health **Ancient History**
Entrepreneurship Languages Sport
Paleontology Needlework Islam
Metaphysics Investment Archaeology
Parenting Statistics Criminology
Motivational

SMITHSONIAN INSTITUTION
BUREAU OF AMERICAN ETHNOLOGY
BULLETIN 99

THE SWIMMER MANUSCRIPT

CHEROKEE SACRED FORMULAS AND MEDICINAL PRESCRIPTIONS

BY

JAMES MOONEY

REVISED, COMPLETED, AND EDITED BY

FRANS M. OLBRECHTS

UNITED STATES
GOVERNMENT PRINTING OFFICE
WASHINGTON : 1932

FOR SALE BY THE SUPERINTENDENT OF DOCUMENTS, WASHINGTON, D. C.

LETTER OF TRANSMITTAL

Smithsonian Institution,
Bureau of American Ethnology,
Washington, D. C., May 29, 1929.

Sir: I have the honor to submit the accompanying manuscript, entitled "The Swimmer Manuscript: Cherokee Sacred Formulas and Medicinal Prescriptions," by James Mooney, revised, completed, and edited by Frans M. Olbrechts, and to recommend its publication, subject to your approval, as a bulletin of this bureau.

Respectfully,

M. W. Stirling, *Chief.*

Dr. C. G. Abbot,
Secretary of the Smithsonian Institution.

CONTENTS

	Page
Bibliography	XIII
Acknowledgments	XV
In memoriam—James Mooney	XVII
Introduction	1
Material and method	1
The writer of the manuscript	7
General background—Informants used	7
Linguistic notes	10
Phonetic symbols and abbreviations	11
Disease, its nature and its causes	14
Nature of disease	14
General semeiology	16
Disease causes	17
Natural causes	17
Supernatural causes	18
Spirits	19
The Sun	19
The Fire	21
The Moon	22
The River	22
Thunder—Red Man—Two Little Red Men	23
Purple Man, Blue Man, Black Man, etc	24
Various Little People	25
Animal Spirits	25
Ghosts	26
Human ghosts	26
Animal ghosts	26
Preternatural causes	29
Witches	29
"Man-killers"	33
ayɛ́"lıGɔ"Gi diseases	33
"Mulier menstruans"	34
Dreams	35
Omens	37
Neglected taboos; disregarded injunctions	38
Causes of contagious disease	39
Disease and its treatment	39
Diagnosis and prognosis	39
List of spirits	42
Color symbolism—Sacred numbers	51
Materia medica	52
Paraphernalia used in the treatment	58
Curing methods	60
Prescriptions as to diet, taboos, etc	64
A typical curing procedure	67
Surgery	68

Disease and its treatment—Continued.
    Prophylaxis 73
    Change from within—Influence from without 77
    Attitude of the community toward the sick 80
    Efficacy of treatment 81
The medicine man 83
    Different classes 84
    Scope of knowledge 88
    Social status 91
    Professional ethics 93
    The medicine man's fee 95
    Mutual relations 97
    Initiation 99
    Diffusion of knowledge 104
    Succession and inheritance 105
    Skepticism 106
    Attitude toward white culture 107
    Personalities—Individual differences 109
Birth 116
    Sexual life 116
    Conception 116
    Abortus—Contraceptives 117
    During pregnancy 118
        Pregnant woman's taboos 120
        Husband's taboos 121
    Partus 122
    Afterbirth 126
    Care for child—Child life 128
    Raising the child to become a witch—Twins 129
Death and afterlife 131
    Death 131
    Between death and burial 134
    Burial 136
    After burial 138
    Afterlife 140
        The soul 141
        Survival of the soul 142
    Suicide 144
    Tragical deaths 144
The formulas 144
    Name 144
    Origin 146
    Kinds 146
        Prayers 149
            For protection 149
            For long life 150
            For gathering medicine 150
        Conjurations 151
            For curing 151
            For using tobacco 151
            For examining with the beads 152
            Against witches 152
            Agricultural 152
            For hunting and fishing 153

CONTENTS

The formulas—Continued.
  Kinds—Continued.

	Page
Incantations	153
"To change"	153
To kill	154
For love attraction	154
For making unattractive	155
For separating	155
How the formulas are recited or sung	155
How the formulas are considered by the laity and by the medicine men	156
Technique of writing the formulas	157
Structure of the formulas	159
The ritual language	160

CHEROKEE TEXTS

1. (For) the big chill this is the medicine _____ 167
2. And this is (for) when their heads are ill _____ 170
3. This is the medicine when they are sick with sharp pains _____ 171
4. This is to cure with, when they have them itching _____ 173
5. If snakes have bitten them, this is the medicine _____ 175
6. This is to cure with, to give it to them to drink when they are sick with "eaters" _____ 178
7. This is when they are sick with the "yellow" _____ 180
8. This is the medicine for their navel _____ 182
9. This (is for) when they have them drooping _____ 184
10. When they have them drooping, this is the medicine _____ 185
11. (For) their navel, this is the medicine _____ 186
12. This is the medicine (if) simulators have made it resemble it (i. e., a real sickness) _____ 187
13. This (is for) when they have their heads aching _____ 188
14. Their navel, this is the medicine (for) _____ 189
15. This is the medicine for their navel _____ 190
16. This is to treat (them) with if the raccoon causes them to be ill _____ 192
17. And another one if the little ones have diarrhea _____ 193
18. This is to take people to the water with _____ 193
19. This is to treat (them) with (when) he habitually breaks them (i. e., rheumatism) _____ 196
20. This (is) to treat (them) with when they have dreamed of snakes; (what) to give them to drink, and (how) it is to be said _____ 196
21. This (is) to cure (them) with whenever they have lost their voice _____ 198
22. And this (is) for the purpose (of treating them) when they urinate (like) milk _____ 199
23. This (is) to blow their heads with; the medicine (which is) to be used with it is told below _____ 200
24. This (is) the treatment for their breast _____ 201
25. This (is) for using the snake tooth at the scratching of them _____ 202
26. This is the treatment whenever they are ill with the "yellow" _____ 204
27. This (is) for when they become ill suddenly _____ 205
28. This is to scratch them; a brier should be used with it _____ 205
29. This is the medicine (for) when their breast swells _____ 208
30. This is to treat them with when they have blisters _____ 210
31. (This is) for the purpose of scratching people, using the snake tooth with it _____ 212

CONTENTS

	Page
32. This (is) to treat them with (for) worms	213
33. This (is) the medicine, if they have (pains) appearing about in different places	215
34. This (is) to make them vomit bile	217
35. (This is) the treatment when they have them drooping	219
36. This (is) for the purpose of it, whenever they have pain in different places	219
37. This tells (about) what to treat (them) with if they urinate yellow	221
38. (This is) to treat (them) with, if they have their urinary passages stopped up	222
39. This (is) the medicine (for) the black "yellow"	222
40. This (is) the medicine whenever they have them shaking	225
41. This is the medicine for the chill	226
42. This is the medicine when they attack him suddenly	229
43. This is to take those that have been left (alive) to the water with	232
44. When they have pains appearing about in different places	235
45. This is the medicine for their sides	236
46. This (is) to treat (them) with when "it affects them in such a way," as they usually call it	239
47. This is the medicine if snakes have bitten them	240
48. This is the medicine when they have it hot	241
49. This (is) when they are ill (by) those living in the forest	243
50. This (is) to treat (them) with (when) they have inhaled bad (odors)	245
51. And (this is for) when they are under restrictions (and) they dream of all sorts (of things)	246
52. This is the medicine for worms	247
53. This is the medicine when they have blisters	250
54. This is the medicine for their breast, when the terrapin affects them as they go about	251
55. This is to cure (them) with, if what they urinate is yellowish	253
56. This is the medicine for their throat	254
57. This (for) their head (is) the medicine	255
58. This is the medicine when they have become as though (they were really ill)	256
59. This, whenever their feet are frost bitten, (is) the treatment	257
60. This is the medicine when their feet are frost bitten	258
61. This is the medicine when their mouths are sore	259
62. This is the medicine for the insects living in the water	260
63. This is the medicine when their teeth ache	262
64. This is the medicine when their breast aches	263
65. This is the medicine for their navel	264
66. This is the medicine when they have pains (shifting) about	265
67. This is the medicine whey they have it along both sides	267
68. This is the medicine whenever their breast aches	269
69. To cure them with, when they have been shot	271
70. This is to make (the) little ones jump down from them, for their (mothers)	273
71. And this (is for) when they discharge slimy (matter) from their bowels	274
72. (This is) the medicine when they discharge blood from their bowels	275
73. Also a medicine when they discharge blood from their bowels	275
74. Also a medicine when they discharge pale blood (and) slimy matter from their bowels	276

CONTENTS

	Page
75. To cure the chill with	276
76. This is to make the small ones jump down from them for their (mothers)	277
77. This is the medicine when their food is changed	279
78. This is to cure (them) with, when they let them down from their stomach, (and) they do not recover	281
79. This is for the purpose of (curing) children when they constantly cry	283
80. This is the medicine when they have the itching	285
81. This is the medicine to give them to drink when they urinate yellowish (urine)	287
82. This is the medicine (for) their head	288
83. This is to examine with the beads	289
84. This is the medicine (when) it breaks them	291
85. This is for the purpose of (curing) the "yellow" of their navel	294
86. This is (for) when they are sick with a swelling	297
87. To cure them when they have their feet frost bitten	298
88. This is the medicine (for) what they call "cocoons"	299
89. This is the medicine for their head	300
90. This is the medicine for a beanlike (boil)	300
91. This is (for) what they call "it causes them to be broken"	301
92. This is (for) when they have bad dreams	302
93. This is to take oneself to the water with, to help oneself	305
94. This is the medicine when they urinate white (matter)	307
95. This is the medicine when they urinate milky (substance)	307
96. This is, when a tooth comes out, to throw it away with	308
Index	311

ILLUSTRATIONS [1]

PLATES

1. James Mooney--- XVII
2. Facsimile page of the reconstituted text--------------------------- 2
3. Facsimile page of the aʻʻyŏⁿʼɩ·ʼni manuscript---------------------- 2
4. aʻʻyŏⁿʼɩ·ʼni ("Swimmer"), the writer of the manuscript------------ 8
5. W., main informant and interpreter-------------------------------- 8
6. *a*, The root of an inverted raspberry branch. *b*, Bark from the sunny side of a tree. *c*, He then wraps the simples in his white cloth--- 54
7. *a–h*, Surgical instruments. *i*, The "ḳʻanu·ɢa" scarification instrument--- 54
8. *a*, Ts., the oldest of the medicine men. *b*, seʻʻlɩyɛ·ʼni a medicine woman-- 84
9. *a*, Og., two days before he died. *b*, The corpse is put down on wooden boards--- 84
10. *a*, Jud., the Cherokee Rabelais. *b*, The chief of the coffin makers. *c*, T., the unofficial chief medicine man--------------------- 114
11. *a*, J., One of the lesser stars. *b*, Del., descendant of an old lineage of medicine men--- 114
12. *a*, Je., a prominent midwife. *b*, O., Del.'s mother; midwife---- 116
13. Cherokee dance mask-- 116

[1] Plate 4 is from a photograph taken by James Mooney in 1888. Plates 1, 2, 3, and 7, *i*, are from the collections of the Bureau of American Ethnology. The other illustrations are from photographs taken in the field by the editor (1926–27).

BIBLIOGRAPHY

ADAIR, JAMES. The history of the American Indians. London, 1775.
ADMINISTRATIVE REPORT. Thirty-seventh Ann. Rept. Bur. Amer. Ethn., pp. 1–31. Washington, 1923.
BERGEN, FANNY D. Current superstititions. Mem. Amer. Folk-Lore Soc., vol. IV. Boston and New York, 1896.
——— Animal and plant lore. Ibid., vol. VII, 1899.
CHAMBERLAIN, A. F. Disease and medicine (American). Hastings' Encyclopædia of Religion and Ethics, vol. IV, pp. 731–741. New York and Edinburgh, 1914.
CULIN, STEWART. Games of the North American Indians. Twenty-fourth Ann. Rept. Bur. Amer. Ethn. Washington, 1907.
DODONAEUS, REMBERTUS. Cruydt-Boeck. Leyden, 1608.
HAYWOOD, JOHN. The natural and aboriginal history of Tennessee. Nashville, 1823.
KLEIWEG DE ZWAAN, J. P. Die Heilkunde der Niasser. Haag, 1913.
LEMERY, NICOLAS. Dictionnaire ou Traité Universel des Drogues simples. Amsterdam, 1716.
LUDEWIG, HERMANN E. The literature of American aboriginal languages. London, 1858. (Trübner's Bibliotheca Glottica. I.)
MACCAULEY, CLAY. The Seminole Indians of Florida. Fifth Ann. Rept. Bur. Ethn., pp. 469–531. Washington, 1887.
MACGOWAN, D. J. Indian secret societies. A paper read before the American Ethnological Society, March, 1866. Historical Magazine and Notes and Queries, vol. X, pp. 139–141. Morrisania, N. Y., 1866.
MOONEY, JAMES. The sacred formulas of the Cherokee.[1] Seventh Ann. Rept. Bur. Ethn., pp. 301–397. Washington, 1891.
——— Myths of the Cherokee. Nineteenth Ann. Rept. Bur. Amer. Ethn., pt. 1. Washington, 1900.
——— The Cherokee River cult. Journ. Amer. Folk-Lore, vol. XIII, pp. 1–10. Boston and New York, 1900.
——— The Cherokee ball play. Amer. Anthrop., vol. III, pp. 105–132. Washington, 1890.
PICKERING, JOHN. A grammar of the Cherokee language. [Boston, 1830.] (Four printed sheets only; n. p., n. d.)
PILLING, JAMES C. Bibliography of the Iroquoian languages. Bull. 6, Bur. Ethn. Washington, 1888.
PUCKETT, NEWBELL NILES. Folk beliefs of the southern Negro. Chapel Hill, N. C., 1926.
ROTH, WALTER E. An inquiry into the animism and folk-lore of the Guiana Indians. Thirtieth Ann. Rept. Bur. Amer. Ethn., pp. 103–386. Washington, 1915.
STEVENS, W. B. A history of Georgia. Vol. I. New York, 1857.
TIMBERLAKE, HENRY. Memoirs of Lieut. Henry Timberlake. London, 1765.
VON DER GABELENTZ, HANS GEORG CONNOR. Kurze Grammatik der Tscherokesischen Sprache. In Zeitschrift fur die Wissenschaft der Sprache, III (1852), 257–300.
VON HOVORKA and KRONFELD. Vergleichende Volksmedizin, II vol. Stuttgart, 1908.
WOOD, GEORGE B., and BACHE, FRANKLIN. The Dispensatory of the United States. Nineteenth Edition. Philadelphia, 1907.

---

[1] Usually cited as SFC.

ACKNOWLEDGMENTS

I take this opportunity to extend my sincere thanks to those who have in many ways assisted me in completing this task.

To Dr. Franz Boas, of Columbia University, to whom I am not only indebted for my ethnological training and for many personal favors, but who has been directly responsible for my being intrusted with the editing of the present manuscript.

To the late and the present chiefs of the Bureau of American Ethnology, Dr. J. Walter Fewkes and Mr. M. W. Stirling; to the ethnologists of the bureau, especially to Dr. John R. Swanton; and to the officers of the Smithsonian Institution.

To the C. R. B. Educational Foundation (Inc.), New York, to whom I owe the great benefit of two years' study and research in the United States. I want to thank especially Dr. P. C. Galpin, secretary, and Mr. Millard K. Shaler, the foundation's representative in Brussels.

To Mrs. Allan Watson, of the Office of Indian Affairs, Washington, D. C., and to Mr. J. Henderson, superintendent of the Yellowhill Government Boarding School, as well as to the members of his staff, especially to Mr. Jessie Lambert.

More than to any other of the white residents in the Cherokee country I feel indebted to Mr. and Mrs. J. R. Edmunds, jr., teachers of Big Cove Day School, Ravensford, N. C., who by their cordial hospitality of the first two weeks and by their repeated proofs of sympathy during the rest of our stay have greatly facilitated the field work.

To Mr. Paul C. Standley, of the United States National Museum, Washington, D. C., I am greatly obliged for the identification of the botanical specimens, as well as for valuable hints and instructions.

Thanks are due also to Mr. F. W. Hodge, of the Museum of the American Indian, Heye Foundation, and to Dr. Frank G. Speck, of the University of Pennsylvania, who both gave me valuable information and advice before I started on the trip.

To all of the Cherokee informants with whom I worked I feel a great debt of gratitude. I especially want to remember W., Del., and Og., since deceased.

To Margriet Olbrechts, my wife, who cheerfully shared all the joys and troubles of the trip with me, much credit is due for invaluable assistance in practical as well as in ethnological matters.

F. M. O.

JAMES MOONEY

IN MEMORIAM—JAMES MOONEY
(Pl. 1)

I consider it an obvious act of piety to dedicate this paper to the memory of the scientist who devoted so much of his erudition and enthusiasm to the ethnological study of the North American Indians, and particularly of the Cherokee; to a man without whose previous intelligent research and publications the following pages could not now be offered to the public.

The glowing tribute paid to him in the name of his colleagues and friends by Dr. John R. Swanton in the American Anthropologist, volume 24, No. 2, April-June, 1922, pages 209–214, has done him justice from one quarter only. Doctor Swanton was the eloquent spokesman of James Mooney's white friends. When I went to live with the Cherokee of the Great Smoky Mountains to continue the work of Mooney I found that his departure had been felt as cruelly by his Indian friends as by his white colleagues. The mere statement that I came to stay with them with the same purpose in view as had nǫ'ⁿdɔ' (Mooney's Cherokee name, meaning "moon") served as the best introduction I could have desired. People who looked askance, and medicine men who looked sullen when first approached, changed as if touched by a magic wand as they heard his name and as I explained my connection with his work.

From all that I heard I concluded that his life and his dealings with our mutual friends, the Cherokee, were a stimulating example for me, and I was well satisfied whenever I heard my conduct and my person not too unfavorably compared with that of my sympathetic predecessor.

The line of research which Mooney had started in the Cherokee field was too interesting not to be followed up; the results he had obtained demanded still a considerable amount of further study, both in the field and at the desk. It is sad indeed that he did not have the satisfaction of seeing this manuscript published before he passed away from his beloved Cherokee studies. But the life of a scientist and a pioneer like Mooney is not of threescore and ten only. He continues to live for generations in his splendid and altruistic work, in monuments more durable than stone.

I consider it a great honor and an enviable privilege to link my name with his, and at the same time to be able to contribute something more to the memory of James Mooney, by offering to the public the results of our joint work contained in the following pages.

Frans M. Olbrechts.

Kessel-Loo, Belgium,
Christmas, 1928.

THE SWIMMER MANUSCRIPT

CHEROKEE SACRED FORMULAS AND MEDICINAL PRESCRIPTIONS

By JAMES MOONEY

REVISED, COMPLETED, AND EDITED BY
FRANS M. OLBRECHTS

INTRODUCTION

MATERIAL AND METHOD

Cherokee manuscripts and material on the Cherokee language have a most uncanny propensity to get lost.

The "dictionary" of Christian Priber has never been heard of since it reached Frederica, Ga., probably in 1741.[1]

The bulky material of the Rev. S. A. Worcester, including a grammar and a dictionary, went down on the *Arkansas* about 1830.[2]

The manuscript contributions to Cherokee linguistics by Col. W. H. Thomas have "unfortunately (been) mislaid."[3]

The manuscript of John Pickering's grammar of the Cherokee language, the printing of which was interfered with, or was thought to have been interfered with, by the invention of the Sequoya syllabary,[4] has never been found.

To reach a climax: The manuscript which is edited in the following paper has been true to the tradition, and has disappeared without leaving a clue. The manuscript is described by Mooney, who discovered it and brought it to Washington, as "a small daybook of about 240 pages, . . . about half filled with writing in the Cherokee characters,"[5] and elsewhere as "an unpaged blank book of 242 pages, 3½ by 12 inches, only partially filled; 137 (formulas) in all."[6]

Mooney started work on it in 1888; he transliterated and translated the formulas with the assistance of native informants, a'yö"ɩ·ni', the writer, himself taking a conspicuous part in the work.

---

[1] Stevens, Hist. of Georgia, vol. I, p. 165; Adair, Hist. Amer. Inds., p. 243.
[2] Pilling, Bibliography of the Iroquoian Languages, p. 174.
[3] Mooney, Myths of the Cherokee, p. 162, note.
[4] Ludewig, Literature of Amer. Aboriginal Languages, p. 38.
[5] Seventh Ann. Rept. Bur. Ethn., p. 312.
[6] Thirty-seventh Ann. Rept. Bur. Amer. Ethu., p. 8.

Of the 137 formulas, Mooney edited 14 in SFC.[7] Four only of these 14 formulas he intended to incorporate in the final edition of the Ay. book,[8] viz, Nos. 1, 3, 29, and 70 of the present collection, which were tentatively edited in SFC., pages 359, 366, 365, and 363, respectively. I have respected Mr. Mooney's intention and conserved these four formulas in the present paper.

Of three more formulas, Nos. 43, 83, and 93 of the present paper, a translation without the Cherokee text was published by Mooney in The Cherokee River Cult; the phonetic texts have now been incorporated in this paper, as Mooney intended. The manuscript as Mooney planned to hand it to the printer consisted of the texts and translations, together with explanatory notes, of 96 formulas, including, as just stated, the 4 formulas published with texts, translations, and notes in the SFC., and the 3 formulas of which a translation and the accompanying notes were published in The Cherokee River Cult. The remaining formulas that are left unaccounted for were not included by Mooney in those intended for publication, possibly on account of their being incomplete, or because they were for some reason deemed unfit for publication. The explanation which seems most probable is that Mooney intended to edit in this paper only the formulas that were of a strictly medicinal character, and that he withheld all other formulas, such as love-attraction formulas, incantations, hunting songs, etc., for publication at some future time.

Indeed, not one of the many Cherokee manuscripts that I have seen contained such a homogeneous collection as is here presented, so much so that this homogeneity can only be explained by its being artificial. The true character of a Cherokee book of formulas and prescriptions does not therefore appear from the manuscript now published to the same extent as it will from the other manuscripts, the publication of which is under consideration.

The 96 formulas here published had furthermore been arranged by Mooney in a systematic sequence, in a logical order, "logical" from the white man's point of view, classifying the various formulas as those "against genito-urinary disorders," "against indigestion," "against bowel troubles," etc. This classification is quite foreign to Cherokee knowledge and use, and I have considered that it diminished the value of the manuscript as an aboriginal document.

The original of the manuscript not being available for comparison, I went through a tedious process of comparing various notes and cross references found in Mooney's manuscript notes. By so doing I have been able to reconstitute the original sequence of the manuscript as faithfully as this could be done by the means available [9]; it is, of

---

[7] Sacred Formulas of the Cherokees, Seventh Ann. Rept. Bur. Ethn.

[8] For the abbreviations of the names of medicine men as Ay., W., etc., see p. 9.

[9] The sequence as given by Mooney is shown in the Appendix, p. 167.

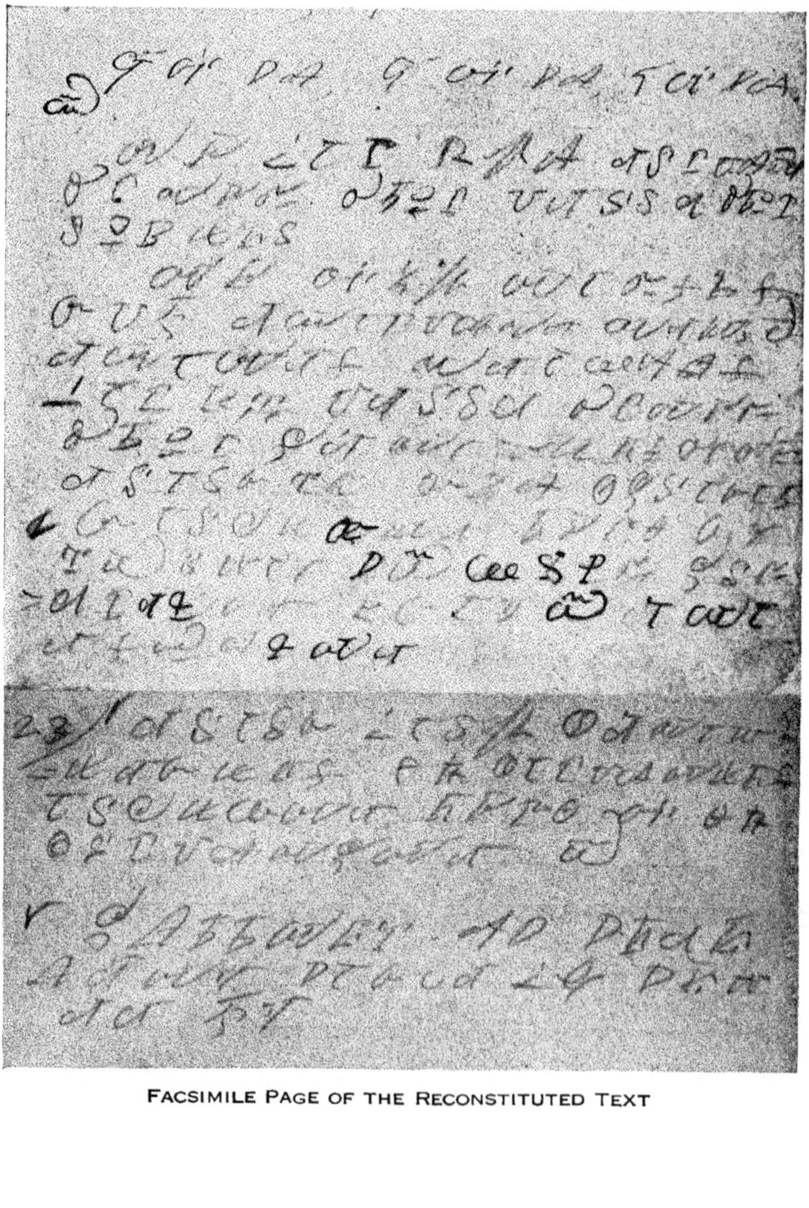

FACSIMILE PAGE OF THE RECONSTITUTED TEXT

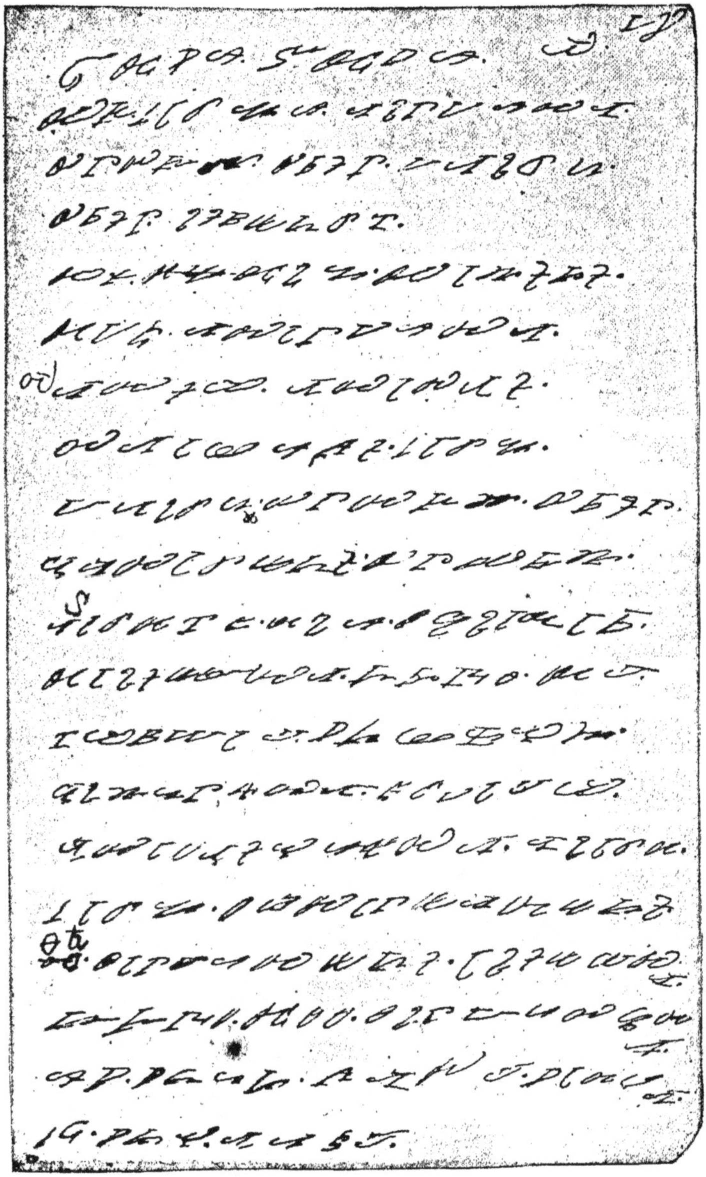

Facsimile page of the a'yūn'i'ni manuscript

course, not possible to say which place was taken in this sequence by the formulas which had been discarded by Mooney.

Another fact to which attention should be called is that this manuscript contains 13 formulas which were obtained by Ay. from another medicine man, vʻtłanö·ʻⁿDə, who had died when Mooney started working on the manuscript. Ay. himself was unable to give Mr. Mooney much information on these formulas and the data we have on them have mainly to be gathered by analogy with what we know of the other formulas. This vʻtłanö·ʻⁿDə must have been rather generous with his knowledge, as this collection of formulas is also found in the compilation of wɩlnɔ·ti' (Ms. II),[10] another of the reputed medicine men of Ay.'s time.

So as to be able to complete the work on the manuscript with the best results possible the following method was adopted:

The original manuscript having been lost, Mooney's transliteration was taken along when I went on the Cherokee field trip. After contacts were made with the people, and especially with some of the more prominent medicine men, efforts were made to acquire a sound knowledge of Cherokee phonetics, as well as pronunciative facilities. The transliteration of Mooney was then read aloud to a medicine man, who wrote the text in the Sequoya syllabary. This text was then read aloud by the medicine man and was taken down phonetically by me. On this latter text the work was done.

This may seem to be a very artificial way of reconstituting the text but I can vouch for its accuracy. Until the original manuscript comes to light again—which I sincerely hope it will—there is only one proof to test the accuracy of the texts acquired in this way: Mooney, in his SFC., gives an illustration (Pl. XXVI) of a page of the Ay. manuscript (Formula 29); with this illustration the text obtained by me was compared after I came back to Washington and it was found that there were no real discrepancies. The two texts are given on opposite pages. (Pls. 2 and 3.)

From a careful investigation of them, and after due allowance is made for the variants resulting from the difference between the magistral, calligraphic writing of Ay. in the one, and the current, almost stenographic scribble of my informant (W.) in the other, it appears that there is really no discrepancy that could in any way interfere with the meaning. Such differences as there seemingly are, are merely matters of orthography, or show that one individual is more slave to "sandhi" laws than the other. The words that

---

[10] In the course of this paper the manuscript here edited will usually be referred to by an abbreviation: the Ay. Ms. By Ms. II, I refer to Wɩlnɔ·ti's manuscript, which will soon be ready for publication; and by Ms. III to a manuscript by the latter's father, Gaʻᴅɩɢwanaʻʻsti.

differ in the two versions are listed below, followed by an explanation of each fact:[11]

Ay.	W.
Line 1. yu'a·.a'i (written twice)	Line 1. yu'a·.a'i (written three times) (1)
Line 2, 8. ö̧`·ⁿDaletGwɔ'ʻi.	Line 3, 9. ö̧·'ⁿDali ɛ·Gwɔ'ʻi (2)
Line 4. dʋnʋ`·y'tanɩ·le·.i`	Line 5. dʋnʋ`·y'tanɩle·' (3)
Line 12. nö̧·ⁿdadu`·gta'ö̧·ⁿsti'	Line 12. nö̧·ⁿtadu`·kta'ö̧·ⁿsti' (4)
Line 14. de·`·du·dö̧·ne·li`se·sti'	Line 14. de·`·du·dö̧·ne·lidi`se·sti' (5)
Line 14. gö̧·ⁿtsa`d(ɔ)tagɩ·ya'	Line 14. gö̧·ⁿtsa`tagɩ·ya' (6)
Line 16. widistötł(i)tadinö̧tanɩga	Line 16. widistötł(a)tadi ... (7)
Line 20. atsɩ·lö̧ⁿ'	Line 21. atsɩ·la' (8)

(1) Whereas Ay. has written the song-word twice, W. writes it three times; neither of them is right, since, strictly speaking, it should be written seven times; but it is very rare that this is done; often we even find these song-words written only once, since every medicine man knows that they are to be repeated four or seven times anyhow.

(2) It is customary for the Cherokee who write a great deal in the Sequoya syllabary to adhere to a "sandhi"-law of the spoken language, and to drop a final vowel before a word beginning with a vowel, linking the consonant of the first word with the vowel of the second as in this case: (ö̧·Da) li + ɛ·(gwɔ) > -lɛ·-

It will be noticed that Ay. conforms to this use in every one of the three cases where the word occurs (Ay. lines 2, 8, 16), whereas W. does it only in the last case (W. line 16). This discrepancy is to be explained by the fact that I read out the text in slow tempo, and by so doing no "sandhi" phenomenon was heard by my informant.

(3) In the written as well as in the spoken language the -i, at the end of the -lɛ·i, -nɛ·i, -sɛ·i and similar tense-suffixes is written and pronounced when the sentence is considered as finished; if more words follow in the sentence, however, it is generally dropped. It is a mere matter of euphony, to which W. has in this case not conformed, probably because I may have led him to believe by the intonation of my voice that the sentence was not finished.

(4) In the Cherokee syllabary the system of the surd and sonant velars and dentals is very imperfectly worked out. As a result, the Cherokee themselves are quite inconsistent in using the symbols for g, k and d, t. The matter is made more complicated by the actual existence of the so-called "intermediates" in their phonetics. This discrepancy is an illustration of this state of affairs.

(5) Ay. omitted the symbol for the -di- syllable here, without which the word has no meaning. W. consequently interpolated it.

(6) Although such phonetic phenomena as breath, stops, etc., are quite frequent in Cherokee linguistics, the syllabary very imper-

---

[11] The figures in parentheses following the words as written by W. refer to the explanations in the following paragraphs.

fectly provides for the representation of the former; the latter are disregarded completely. In the written documents they are therefore left to the reader to discover, as in W.'s text here; or else they are represented by various very clever but inadequate, and especially quite uncoordinated, devices, as in Ay.'s text, where the stop following the t is indicated by writing the -d(o)- syllable for it.

(7) The -tɫ- phonem, which is so common in Cherokee, has no specific symbol. It is usually represented by the complex: -(d)a-l(i)-, as by Ay.; more rarely by: -(d)a-l(a)-, the symbols used in this instance by W. (W. line 16). In lines 17 and 19, however, W. conforms to the general usage.

(8) The word as written by Ay. is the nearest approach to the spoken language; it is, however, commonly written as in W.'s version.

It appears from the foregoing notes that, as I said, the few and slight differences that can be found are mainly phonetic. These are not of a nature to invite skepticism as to the accuracy of the texts. Moreover, since writing them, it has been possible, by further research, to discover additional texts and to obtain from other medicine men copies of separate formulas. Some of these are identical with those in the Ay. manuscript. They must be either later copies or earlier predecessors, if not the actual originals, from which some of the Ay. formulas were copied.

Comparing two versions wherever this was possible has again proved that the method used in reconstituting the texts is flawless.

In order not to commit Mr. Mooney's name, and to take my own responsibility, I have thought it advisable to make a definite statement as to what part of this paper is Mooney's and how much of it is my work.

As has already been clearly stated, the credit for the discovery of the manuscript and for the first work on it is Mooney's. I am also very much indebted to his former publications on the Cherokee tribe and to many items of interest found in his manuscript notes. Wherever I have made use of this material this has been explicitly stated.

Mooney transliterated and translated the formulas (free translations) and wrote explanatory comments, some of them quite lengthy, to accompany them. It should be borne in mind that this work was done by Mooney about 40 years ago, at a time when methods for studying the native languages and the phonetic notations to record them had not attained the same degree of perfection they now boast of. That is the reason why it has been deemed expedient to take down the texts anew, as has already been explained in detail.

I have, moreover, considered that the value of the texts would be considerably enhanced by an interlinear translation, which I have consequently added. The accurate analysis and the grammatical work necessary to obtain the data for these interlinear translations have in some cases considerably influenced the free translations, so that, in the second part of this paper, viz, the texts, all responsibility for the phonetic texts, and the interlinear and free translations rests with the editor.

As for the explanatory notes and comments which Mooney had written for every formula, these could not possibly be improved upon. In some cases, however, I was able to collect items of information that cast an additional light on the subject; sometimes I was able to actually catch a belief or a practice in the process of change and evolution; or again, I got the individual point of view of different medicine men. All this was carefully noted and is added to Mr. Mooney's explanations, inclosed in brackets.

I have furthermore collected all the botanical specimens of which mention is made in the manuscript. For the identification of these I am obliged to Mr. Paul C. Standley of the United States National Museum.

Finally I wrote an introduction which gives as extensive a survey of Cherokee beliefs and practices with regard to disease and medicine as is necessary to fully understand the formulas and prescriptions of the Ay. manuscript. Although every formula contains a few elements that inherently belong to it, and may not be met with in any of the others, yet there is in all of the formulas an underlying complex of ideas that is basically the same. Whereas those elements that specifically belong to a given formula are better explained in a short note commenting on them, and affixed to that particular formula, it has been thought advisable, in order to avoid constant repetitions, and also in order to present a more synthetic picture of the whole, to give a broadly sketched and general outline of the subjects treated: Disease, its nature and its causes; the means by which disease is diagnosed and cured; the materia medica and the curing methods; of the person who is constantly associated with all of this, the medicine man. Short chapters on birth and death have been added, as well as a general introduction to the formulas.

Lengthy as these introductory notes may seem, yet they have been strictly limited to the subject matter contained in the Ay. manuscript. I have modified my first intention, which was to append in copious notes any parallels with which I am acquainted. However, the time for a comparative work of wide scope on primitive medicine has not yet come, our special knowledge being far too inadequate to justify generalizations. I have therefore considered that it would be better to give as exhaustive a survey as possible of Cherokee medical lore and custom; a collection of monographs of this kind will be the material from which once a comparative study of the medicine and of the science of "primitive" peoples, will be compiled. The only parallels I have drawn attention to are such as may shed light on questions of origin and diffusion, influence from missionary activities, from the white mountaineers, or even from the negro slaves of the region.

The Writer of the Manuscript

α'‛yŏⁿ'‛ι·ni′, i. e., "he is swimming (habitually)", "he is a swimmer," (pl. 4), is the writer, or as might be more fit to state it, the compiler of the present manuscript. (On the Cherokee method of compilating manuscripts of this description, see pp. 157–159.)

He died in 1899, at 65 years of age. He was Mooney's main informant on the history, mythology, and later especially on the medicine and botany of the Cherokee. On his personality, see what Mooney says about him in his Myths, pp. 236–237. The lucky chance by which Mooney got scent of the existence of the manuscript, and how he ultimately obtained it, are related by him in his SFC., pages 310–312.

The son, t‛a·mi (i. e., Tom), and a grandson, αltαsɢι·ski (Dancer), of Ay. are still living on the reservation, but neither of them has succeeded him in his medical practice.

The memory of Ay. is still treasured by the Cherokee of the present generation. He is looked upon as one of the last old, wise men, such as there are now none left.

General Background—Informants Used

The territory of the Cherokee that once covered the better part of three States (see map in Mooney Myths, pp. 22–23) has been reduced to a small reserve that can be crossed from end to end in a day's walk.

For ample details regarding the historic past of the Cherokee, and especially of the present reservation of the Eastern Band, the reader is referred to the excellent historical sketch by James Mooney in his Myths, pages 14–228.

Of the seven villages of the reserve, k‛ɔ·‛lɑnǫ·yi′ (i. e. "the Raven's place," generally called Big Cove or Swayney by the whites) was selected for our stay. There were many reasons that all but enforced this choice: Lying in a secluded cove, of difficult and at some times of the year of impossible access, with a population of far more conservative people than that of the villages lying nearer the boarding school and the Government offices, tribal life has conserved much of its aboriginal flavor in Big Cove. Especially the beliefs and practices relating to medicine are still rampant in this community to such an extent that of the 15 families that constituted the population of the cove 10 people were avowed medical practitioners, whereas three or four more occasionally took up the practice of medicine as a side line.

The people are mostly agriculturists, and very primitive tillers of the soil, and turn to fishing and to what little hunting there is still to be done as the seasons and the white man's law allows! They live as a rule in 1-room log cabins, covered with hewn boards, although five or six families live in frame houses built by natives or half bloods that have learned the art in the Government schools. The cabins are scattered about the two slopes of the cove, at least 500 to 600 yards, often a mile and more, from each other. This does not prevent the inmates from knowing all that happens in the valley. Even if Cherokee eyes are no longer trained on the warpath, they are still annoyingly keen!

There is quite a remarkable spirit of tribal and social solidarity reigning among the people (cf. pp. 80–81); against a white intruder, whether he be a Government official or not, a glacial reserve is observed, and it takes weeks and months in some cases to break down this inhibition against the whites. These people have known abominable treatment and tyrannic oppression at our hands, and they know how to remember. Their only word by which they can refer to a white man is identical with their expression for "(he is) a mean fellow."

It was quite difficult to coax the only man who had a spare room— a dilapidated attic, used as a storeroom for all nondescript scraps and heaps of filth and rubbish—into allowing us to live in it. Finally, the almighty dollar scored a victory over his patriotic tribal feelings, and we were indifferently, if not reluctantly, admitted to share his leaky roof. This attic was the best post of observation one could have wished for: not only did it from three sides command a view of the most important section of the valley, but also the "ball ground" near the river, and the five main trails of the cove could be leisurely observed without any one suspecting it. But the facilities these quarters afforded us for studying the home life of the family we lived with were an even greater advantage; the floor of rough-hewn rafters had cracks in different places; this exposed our landlord underneath us to a shower of boiling coffee whenever our primitive stove toppled over, but also afforded us the immense pleasure of listening at nights to the conversation, the songs, and the other manifestations of family life going on round the hearth fire.

The very fact that we had come from so far, and from the east (the direction of favor, luck, and fortune), "to learn their language, and to listen to their beautiful stories," that we lived with one of their own people in his house, that we cut our own wood, carried our own supplies, etc., gradually smoothed the frown from many faces and softened the scowling look in many eyes. Soon we had progressed so far that we knew the joy of being looked upon, if not as one of them, at least as congenial neighbors.

aʻyo͞nʻtsʻni ("Swimmer"), the writer of the manuscript

W., MAIN INFORMANT AND INTERPRETER

On account of the special nature of the work it was not easy to find the right sort of informants. As a whole only medicine men could be used. Some of these, even if they were good practitioners were but poor informants; others as a matter of principle refused for many months to give information. Some of them, however, were ideal collaborators, and for such of them as W., Del., and Og., one is at a loss what to praise most in them—their immense fund of knowledge or the keenness and the interest they manifested in the work.

The following is a list of the informants and medicine men cited in these pages. Those the names of whom are preceded by two asterisks are the medicine men who worked with Mooney and who died between his visits and mine; the names preceded by one asterisk are those of the medicine men I worked with, but who died during or since my stay; the medicine men whose names are not preceded by an asterisk are those I worked with, and who are, so far as I know, still alive at the time of writing. Since some of the latter are depicted in these pages in terms that are not always complimentary, and also because much of their activity as described in this paper might bring upon them the wrath of people who believe it their duty to stamp out all vestiges of aboriginal belief and practice, it is deemed best to cite them by their initials only. I have deposited a detailed list in the archives of the Bureau of American Ethnology by which these individuals can be identified by any ethnologist who may desire to make investigations in that quarter of the world in the future.

Abbreviation used	Refers to—
**Ay	a'yŏⁿ''ɩ·ni', writer of the manuscript (cf. p. 7).
**Ayɔ	Ayɔsta, W.'s mother (see Mooney Myths, Pl. xiv) (cf. p. 67).
Del	See this paper, pl. 11, *b*; cf. also pp. 115–116.
**Gad	ɢaDɩɢwaɳa'sti, the writer of manuscript III (cf. SFC., 312).
*J	Jukias (pl. 11, *a*), died 1928 (cf. p. 115).
*Je	W.'s half-sister; medicine woman and midwife (see pl. 12, *a*; cf. p. 116).
Jo	Cf. p. 113 et seq.
Jud	See pl. 10, *a*; cf. p. 114 et seq.
O	Del.'s mother, Climbing Bear's widow, W.'s and Og.'s sister-in-law (see pl. 12, *b*; cf. p. 116).
*Og	Died spring 1927; W.'s half-brother, Del.'s uncle (see pl. 9, *a*; cf. p. 112 et seq.).
T	Del.'s brother-in-law (see pl. 10, *c*; cf. p. 111).
*Ts	J.'s father (see pl. 8, *a*; cf. p. 115).
**Ut	Cf. p. 3.
W	My main informant and interpreter (see pl. 5; cf. p. 109 et seq.).
**Wil	The writer of manuscript II, Gad.'s son (cf. SFC., p. 312).

Linguistic Notes

The Cherokee language (Iroquoian stock) has often been studied, but through various vicissitudes only very few of the results have been published. But two attempts to publish a grammar of it have been made—one by J. Pickering (cf. p. 1), another by Von der Gabelentz. (See Bibliography.)

Pickering's attempt was not any better than could be expected at a time when so little of American Indian linguistics was known, and Von der Gabelentz's sketch, though interesting, is based on material gleaned from very inadequate sources. Neither of the two have found, for example, the typical Iroquoian system of pronominal prefixes in the Cherokee verbal series, nor the difference between the static and active verbs.

There are still two Cherokee dialects extant—the Western (often called "Upper") dialect, spoken by the majority of the Cherokee in Oklahoma and by a few families in Graham County, N. C., and the Central (often called "Middle") dialect, spoken by the Cherokee on the Qualla Reservation, where these investigations were made. There is historic evidence of a third dialect, which may be called the Eastern (it has sometimes been referred to as the "Lower") dialect; the last Indian, as far as we know, who spoke this dialect died in the beginning of this century.

There is a possibility that one (or two?) more dialects existed in the past, but there is very scant and inadequate evidence of this.

The differences existing between the two dialects that are still spoken are small indeed, nor does the extinct dialect seem to have diverged much from the two others. Allowing for such phonetic shifts as West. Dial. -tł-> Cent. D. -ts-; W. D. aGi-> C. D. ɛ-; C. D. -W. D. -l-> East. D. -r-, the vocabulary is practically the same; in the morphology there do not seem to be other differences than can be explained by these phonetic shifts; the syntaxis can not yet be compared as our knowledge of the Eastern dialect is so scanty; nor has the Western dialect been adequately studied.

The formulas as written in the Ay. manuscript and in the majority of the other manuscripts that have since been collected are mostly written in the Central dialect. Still, a lot of Western dialect forms are to be found in them and there are also a great many archaic, ritualistic expressions the meaning of which is rapidly disappearing. (Cf. Ritual Language, p. 160 et seq.)

I have given in the interlinear analysis a translation as correct and conveying the Cherokee meaning as faithfully as was found possible. Rather than speculate on probabilities or advance conjectures that can not be proved, I have indicated by a query mark those elements that can not be satisfactorily analyzed. If query marks are met with more often than either the reader or the editor likes, it should be borne in mind that the language in which the formulas are couched is a ritualistic idiom, often very different from the ordinary language, both as regards vocabulary and grammar, and abounding in expressions which even the initiated do not always understand.

As for this analysis, I have always given in the interlinear translation the original meaning as far as this could be ascertained, giving the semasiological evolution in footnotes to the free translation. Thus, Ga⁽ᴰ⁾ni' will be rendered by "arrow" in the interlinear translation, as this was its original meaning. In the free translation it will be rendered by "bullet," which is its meaning in the context, a footnote explaining the evolution in meaning: "arrow" > "bullet" > "lead." The same applies to such words as: aDɛ·'lŏⁿ that has gone through the following evolution in meaning: "seed(?)" > "bead" > "money" > "dollar"; or to: k'a'lɔ·Gwɛ·'kt'i "locust tree" > "bow" (because locust wood was used to make bows) > "gun" (the modern successor of the bow).

It is hoped that a paper on Cherokee linguistics, on which the present writer is working, will soon be ready for publication.

PHONETIC SYMBOLS AND ABBREVIATIONS

The following list will serve the double purpose of explaining the phonetic symbols and the abbreviations used in the texts, and of presenting a summary description of the Cherokee phonetic system as I heard it.

PHONETICS

Vowels—Oral:
  Long or short—
    Open—
      a, as in Engl. far, Gm. Band.
      ɔ, as in Engl. not, nought; Gm. Gott.
      v, as in Engl. spoon, you.
      ɛ, as in Engl. air; Gm. Wählen; French scène.
      ι, as in Engl. seat.
    Closed—
      a, as in Gm. einmal; Gm. wahl.
      u, as in Engl. nook.
      e, as in Engl. baby, stain (this sound is very rarely heard in Cherokee, and then always finally; where it occurs at all it seems to be a contraction of ɛ· (nasalized long ɛ)+i).
      o, only occurs in songs.
      i, as in Engl. pin.
    Short—
      ŏ, as in Engl. bird, but very short; Gm. Götter.
      ŭ, a sound between a and ŏ.
      ə, vowel of indefinite quality, as in Engl. father, believe.
  Parasitical—
    Phonems that are scarcely audible and occur frequently as weakly articulated vowels are indicated by small superior characters: ɔ·ᵘ, ɛ·ⁱ, ᵘw, ⁱy, etc.

Vowels—Oral—Continued.
  Voiceless—
    a, i, u, ɔ—
      Voiceless vowels, as they are paradoxically called, are phonems produced by lips and tongue taking the position to pronounce a vowel (a, i, u, or ɔ, as the case may be); there may be—and there usually is—a strong emission of breath, but as the vocal cords are not brought in action, the phonem is voiceless.
  Nasalized—
    ą, ą̊, but more commonly with less pronounced nasalization, thus: aⁿ, aⁿ.
    ǫ·, (usually long) as in Fr. bon; as in Engl. don, but longer and nasalized.
    ę·, (usually long) as in Fr. pain, dessin.
    ǫ̈·, (usually long) as in Fr. un.
    ɔ̈ⁿ, (very short) as in Engl. bird, Gm. Götter, Fr. bœuf, but always short and nasalized.
      When only a slight degree of nasalization is heard, this is shown by writing a small -ⁿ after the vowel, instead of writing a hook under it, as is done in cases where nasalization is more pronounced.
Semiconsonants:
  y, w, may be strongly aspirated, when they are written yʻ, wʻ; may also be voiceless, when they are rendered ʏ, ᴡ. The w is often preceded by a barely audible u sound; in this case the phonem is written ᵘw.
Consonants:
  Stops—
    Dental—
      d, voiced, as in Engl. dawn.
      ᴅ, intermediate sound between voiced and unvoiced dental.
      t, unvoiced, as in Engl. hit.
      tʻ, unvoiced and aspirated, as in Engl. tin, tan, but with aspiration more emphatic.
    Velar—
      g, voiced, as in Engl. go, dog.
      ɢ, intermediate sound between voiced and unvoiced velar.
      k, unvoiced, as in Engl. back.
      ḵ, unvoiced, but pronounced farther back than previous sound.
      kʻ, unvoiced and aspirated, as in Engl. come, can, but with more emphatic aspiration.
  Nasals—
    Dental—
      n, voiced nasal, as in Engl. can, near.
      ᴰn, the same nasal, but preceded by a hardly audible d. The tongue takes the dental position as if about to pronounce d (implosion), but immediately the uvula is lowered and the breath escapes by the nose passage, without having occasioned the explosion usually accompanying the d phonem.
      ɴ, voiceless nasal; always followed by a strong nasal aspiration
    Bilabial—
      m, voiced as in Engl. mother.
    Velar—
      ŋ, voiced, as in Engl. sing, rang.
  Spirants—
    Dental—
      s, unvoiced fricative as in Engl. race, sing.
      z, voiced fricative as in Engl. gaze, doze.

Consonants—Continued.
  Prepalatal—
    c, unvoiced, as in Engl. shut, fish.
    j, voiced, as in Fr. jambe, genou.
  Palatal—
    x̣, unvoiced, as in Gm. ich, nicht.
  Laterals—
    l, voiced, as in Engl. lid, rill.
    ᴅl, the same voiced sound, but preceded by the dental element described s. v. Nasals, ᴅn.
    ł, unvoiced l.
  Affricatives—
    Dental—
      dz, voiced, as in Engl. hands up.
      ts, unvoiced, as in Engl. bits, ants.
    Prepalatal—
      dj, voiced, as in Engl. George.
      tc, unvoiced, as in Engl. China.
    Lateral—
      tł, unvoiced l, preceded by unvoiced dental stop.

Diacritical Marks

-ʽ-, the Greek "spiritus asper" indicates breath, aspiration.
-ʼ-, the Greek "spiritus lenis" indicates glottalization.
ą, a hook, turned to the right, under a vowel indicates nasalization.
-ʽ̨-, a combination of the "spiritus asper" with the nasalization hook indicates a strong nasal aspiration.
-ⁿ-, a small superior n indicates slight nasalization.
-·, a dot after a vowel, above the line, indicates long quantity of the vowel.
-:, a colon after a vowel indicates very long quantity.
-˘-, a breve over a vowel indicates abnormally short duration.
-., a dot after a vowel or consonant on the line indicates a very slight pause.
-´, the "acute accent," following a phonem, indicates primary stress.
-`, the "grave accent," following a phonem, indicates secondary stress.
´, the "acute accent" printed over a vowel indicates rising pitch.
`, the "grave accent" printed over a vowel indicates falling pitch.
  The two latter can be combined to `´, i. e., "falling-rising," or to ´`, i. e., "rising-falling" pitch.

Abbreviations Used in the Texts (Interlinear Translation)

App.=apparently.
Dir.=direction.
(2)=dual.
E.=emphatic.
Excl.=exclamation.
H., Hab.=habitually.
kn.=kneadable.

l.=liquid.
L.=limitative.
L (=E.)=limitative, used as emphatic.
Loc.=locative.
On.=onomatop.
sol.=solid.
T. L.=temporal-locative.

Words or parts of words between brackets [ ] in the texts were written by the native compiler of the manuscript by mistake.

Words or parts of words between parentheses ( ) had been omitted by him but have been interpolated by J. Mooney, by W., my interpreter, or by myself. In every case the interpolation is accounted for in a footnote.

Words or sentences between brackets, in the explanatory notes following every one of the formulas, are by the editor. All the rest in these explanatory notes is the work of James Mooney.

DISEASE—ITS NATURE AND ITS CAUSES

Nature of Disease

Many of the facts contained in this paper are bound to remain unintelligible if no sound understanding is gained into the Cherokee conceptions of disease.

These are not by any means so simple or uniform as many theorists are wont to ascribe to peoples at this stage of culture.

Disease in general is commonly referred to by the word: u‘yu′ɢi, which is no doubt related with the stem √-yuɢ- "resentment" (cf. ɢǫ̈yu′ɢa—"I have resentment toward thee.")

In the ritualistic language of the formulas, however, this expression never occurs, ulsɢɛ·′dȫⁿ always being used in its stead. The original meaning of this word has now been lost, even by the medicine men, who always claim it merely means "the disease present in the body," and Mooney accordingly invariably translated it as "the intruder." Although this way of translating it conveys its general meaning, there is cause to discuss it somewhat further. It appears from various expressions that can be compared with the one under discussion that the meaning would be "that which is important." Although this concept is usually rendered ɢalǫ̈·ⁿkw‘tɩ·yu′ in the ordinary language, yet such expressions as the following are still in constant use:

ulsɢɛ·′dȫⁿ dzɩ·‘lu‘ɢi′, "I came on important business."

(ɢa)do·‘iyulsɢɛ·′dȫⁿ ‘ǫ̈·lu·ɢi′, "What on earth didst thou come in here for?" (implied: It must be very important, else thou wouldst not have come).

ɩ·ɢǫ̈·‘wulsɢɛ·′dȫⁿ "of but trivial worth; not important."

These expressions clearly prove what the true meaning of the term is. It would thus appear that it is one of the many "euphemistic terms" which the Cherokee, as so many other tribes and peoples, use, and the object of which is to allude to a dreaded concept by a (respectful) circumlocution, so as not to offend it, or so as not to bring about its appearance, its "materialization," we might say, by calling it by its common name.

The ulsɢɛ′dȫⁿ is the disease as it is present in the body of the sufferer. Although it is invisible, intangible, and in all other respects immaterial, it very often may manifest its presence by material means, as swellings, protuberances, or even by worms and insects.

It does not as a rule torment a person of its own free will; it is inert of itself, but is subdued to the will of more powerful agents, spirits, ghosts, or even human beings, who may cause it to enter the body of those persons whom they wish to harm.

The idioms of the formulas seem to imply that the ʋlsGɛ‧′Dö^n is not so much put into the victim, as under him; the expression: Dʋnʋ‧`y‛tanʋlɛ‧^{n}i′ "he (the disease causer) has put it (the disease) under him, it appears," always being used. How the disease then finally enters the victim under whom it has been put is not clear. There is a consensus of opinion among the medicine men that it enters the body somehow, but on the question as to whether this introduction takes place by way of a natural orifice or whether it is possible for a disease to enter the body anywhere, not one of the medicine men cared to commit himself.

From the fact that an ʋlsGɛ‧′Dö^n is present in a person's body it by no means follows that an illness is the instantaneous result: the disease may be present in a dormant, latent condition, and often months, or even years after the revengeful animal-ghost or spirit has "inoculated" the person the malady may become "virulent." It is easy to see how powerful a means this conception must be toward consolidating the prestige of the medicine man, enabling him as it does to explain many diseases, for which there is no evident cause, by events and dreams of many months or years ago, and to explain how it is that certain acts and infractions of taboos that, according to the general belief ought to be followed by the contraction of a disease, apparently remain without any immediate results.

The presence of an ʋlsGɛ‧′Dö^n, however, does not account for all the cases of sickness. There are, for example, the ailments due to "our saliva being spoiled." The Cherokee believes that the saliva is located in the throat and that it is of capital importance in human physiology; as a matter of fact, the physiologic rôle they ascribe to the saliva would lead us to believe that they consider it as important as the blood and the gall. When the saliva is "spoiled" the patient becomes despondent, withers away, and dies.

The most frequent causes of this state of affairs are dreams, especially the dreams caused by the ghost people (see p. 26), but also those caused by snakes and fish. The belief is based no doubt on the feeling of oppression and anguish that accompanies many dreams, especially those of the "nightmare" variety.

A state of ill health very much akin to the one just mentioned, and where no ʋlsGɛ‧′Dö^n is believed to be present, is caused by an enemy of ours feeling ʋ‧′ya uDa‧′N‛tɔ, "of a different mind" toward us, "different" here again being a euphemistic term for "bad" or "worse."

This is usually ascribed to the activities of a human enemy and refers to a psychopathological state rather than to any other disorders. The victim is utterly despondent and dejected and seems to be the victim of a severe case of chronic melancholy.

Another explanation that is offered in some cases, and one which is more apt to cause surprise, as it is not common to the Indians of the eastern United States, is that the illness is caused by the action of a human being who has ravished the soul of the patient. The fact that one's soul has been buried does not result in instant death: one may live without it for six or eight months, or even for a year. But if the party working on behalf of the victim is not successful in ultimately removing the ban, death is inevitable. The symptoms ascribed to an illness of this order do not differ materially from those belonging to "having one's saliva spoiled" or to the illness caused by some one "having his mind different toward us." This makes it the easier for a medicine man who does not succeed in curing a patient to make a new diagnosis, and to change his treatment from one, the object of which was to dislodge the spoiled saliva, to a new one aiming at removing the ban from the buried soul of the patient.

The way in which the medicine man finds out what is actually the cause of a given disease will be discussed under the caption of Diagnosis (p. 39). Sometimes, however, a diagnosis, however accurate, will fail to disclose the actual cause of the ailment. A favorite explanation in such a case is to ascribe the evil to the fact that the patient "has dreamed of different things." It is implicitly understood that this means "different, or all sorts of bad things." Since in this case the causes are complex, it is considered that the treatment must be the same, and a medicine is prescribed consisting of a decoction of as many as 24 different plants.

Nobody ever becomes ill without a cause. And with very few exceptions every individual is responsible and blamable for the diseases he contracts.

A distinction is made between dangerous and less serious diseases, but even the latter have to be adequately cared for and attended to; for disease senders and causers, whether human or nonhuman, have a predilection for sending disease to a person when he is already in a weakened condition; they know that then they stand a far better chance to be successful and attain their ends.

General Semeiology

Although very little value is attached to what might be called a scientific symptomatology by the Cherokee, a few remarks about the subject are not out of place here.

As will soon appear from a glance at the titles of the formulas, the different ailments themselves are usually called by names that refer to one or to several of the more striking symptoms; as "when they have a headache," "when their eyes droop," "when they have a dry cough," "when they discharge slimy matter from their bowels," etc.

As a rule, only the main symptom—that is, the phenomenon which the patient or the medicine man considers as the main symptom—is considered to be of any importance, and as a result of this many ailments that are of an entirely different pathological nature are classed as one and the same disease, because headache, for example, is the most impressive symptom.

Yellowness of the skin, black rings round the eyes, headache, swellings, and the nature of the feces and of the urine are practically the only general signs which the medicine men consider as being of any importance.

Some may be impressed by the rationality of this symptomatology; but it should be borne in mind that the deductions made from it, and the treatment followed as a result of it, are by no means as rational as we are led to expect.

Headache is not so much a symptom as a proof that a group of birds have invaded the patient's head, and are there carrying on in a way which is not conducive to the rest of the victim. A swelling or a dilatation of the stomach in no way indicates a trouble of the digestive tract, but is merely the outward evidence of the ʋlsGɛ·Dȫⁿ. Diarrhea in children is evidenced by the nature of the feces, but is explained by the fact that two rival teams of "Little People" are playing a ball game in the child's stomach.

More of the symptoms that are known and that are occasionally mentioned and taken into consideration will be discussed with the relevant formulas.

Disease Causes

Natural Causes

However primitive and unsophisticated may be the views of a tribe on disease and its causes, and however great may be the share of mysticism and occultism in its explanation of the events of daily life, yet there is almost everywhere a recognition of natural agency if not for some of the ailments, at least for some accidents.

A Cherokee, wounded by falling with his hand on the cutting edge of his ax, or breaking his leg when sliding off a foot log when crossing the river, may, if he has a turn of mind given to the mysterious and the occult, explain those accidents by the machinations of an enemy, but the chances are that he will look upon them in a very fatalistic way, and will search for no hidden cause to explain so obvious a fact.

But one should never be too sure. If the same Cherokee slides down a precipice through a lump of rock crumbling away beneath his foot, or if he is wounded by a stray arrow, or by a tree branch falling on his head, his imagination forthwith finds cause for speculation, and he may come to the conclusion that the "Little People," or the "Mountain People" have become angry at him and have taken vengeance by the means just stated.

SUPERNATURAL CAUSES

If even in cases where the natural course and cause of events seems evident and obvious, a mythologic explanation may be advanced, what are we to expect when it becomes necessary to account for such mysterious, unexplainable, insidious changes of condition to which disease subjects our body and mind?

The man who but two or three days ago was a living image of both Hercules and Adonis, and who came home from the mountain carrying on his shoulder a tree trunk of formidable weight and dimension as lightly as if it were but a bark canoe, to-day lies prostrate, pain and terror stricken, with haggard looks and sallow complexion, suffering, panting, and gasping. . . .

The buxom woman, from whom last week a chubby, healthy baby boy "jumped down," as the Cherokee express it, is now suffering more than ever she did, and feels herself as being burned by a scorching internal fire . . .

The sprightly baby, which ever since it moved was as alert and bustling as a young chipmunk or a scampering squirrel, suddenly lapses into spasmodic convulsions, or lies motionless with haggard eyes wide open, as those of a terror-stricken rabbit . . .

Why? For what reason?

When we think of how, in a civilized community, as soon as anything uncanny happens, as soon as the Awful Incomprehensible makes its presence felt, even the sophisticated lose their reasoning faculties and grasp at ridiculous explanations and at impossible hopes, how can we scoff at the conclusions these poor people reach?

The man who became ill so suddenly has had a quarrel a week or so ago with an ill-reputed medicine man, who told him, as they separated, that he would hear about him again. The wizard has shot an invisible flint arrowhead into his bowels.

The woman who had known the joys of such a happy delivery had not heeded the subsequent taboo, prohibiting all warm food to any one in her condition. That is why she is now being consumed by an internal fire.

The baby is now paying the penalty of his mother having partaken of rabbit meat during her pregnancy, six months or so ago. And that is why it is now assuming the cramped position, so reminiscent of the hunchback position of a squatting rabbit, or why its eyeballs are so dilated.

These are but some instances taken at random; but let us in a systematic and methodical way make a survey of the different disease causes and we will be the better prepared to comprehend the Cherokee way of treating them.

Spirits

As will readily be seen from the "List of spirits" on pages 44–50, the Cherokee believe in quite a remarkable collection of beings whose major occupation seems to be to pester the inhabitants of this planet with all possible and impossible varieties of ailments.

The motives of these spirits, whether they be of an anthropomorphic or of a zoomorphic type, are mostly very human and justifiable— they take revenge for slights, lack of respect, abuses, etc., of which they have been the subject at the hands of the human beings. This holds especially for the animal spirits, the Little Deer, the White Bear, etc., who are all the tireless and valiant defenders of their particular animal clan and who mete out justice and take vengeance for the conduct of neglectful and disrespectful hunters.

There are hardly any spirits that are, per se, benevolent or nefarious; they may be one or another, according to circumstances. One spirit may send a disease as a punishment, and yet may on another occasion help the same individual to overcome another spirit.

As a rule the spirit who has caused a disease is never prevailed upon to take the disease away; the office of another, rival, spirit is called upon to do this.

Spirits do not merely send disease of their own initiative; they may be prevailed upon to do so by human agency, by witches (see p. 29) or by man killers (see p. 33), for instance.

According to some informants it would seem that spirits may exercise their nefarious power quite arbitrarily; the sun may cause a headache without any apparent reason, or without any plausible cause. This is, however, so exceedingly rare that it is quite possible that this view is foreign to earlier Cherokee conceptions, and that such an allegation is now made simply because the earlier explanation has been lost.

Let us now pass in review the more important of these anthropomorphic spirits. By far the most important is

The Sun.—In everyday language there is no distinct word for "sun" or "moon." This is a common feature of all the Iroquoian dialects and of many other North American Indian languages; nǫ·ⁿDo' conveys the meaning of "luminary"; if the distinction has to be expressed the locutions used are:

nǫ·ⁿDo' ɩ·'Ga ɛ'ⁿi "The luminary that is (that lives) in the daytime," viz, the sun.

nǫ·ⁿDɔ' sǫnɔ·'yi ɛ'ʃi "The luminary that is (that lives) in the nighttime," viz, the moon.

In the ritualistic language, however, the sun is always referred to either as unɛ`·tɬanɔ̈'ʃi or Gɛ`'yaGʋ·'Gǝ.

The first of these expressions means: "He has apportioned, allotted, divided into equal parts," doubtlessly referring to the time-dividing rôle of the sun. The same stem is used to express the allotting of the tribal territory to the individuals that are entitled to a part, "an allotment," of it.

Since this unɛ`·tɬanɔ̈'ʃi has always been looked upon as their most powerful spirit by the Cherokee, the missionaries have read into his name the meaning of "Great Spirit," "Creator," and hence the verb-stem $\sqrt{\text{-nɛtɬ-}}$ is now gradually acquiring the meaning of "to create," a concept absolutely foreign to its primary meaning.

It is now well-nigh impossible to gain a clear conception of the part which this spirit must have once played in Cherokee religion. Only a very few of the older people can shed any light on his true nature. Some who have been missionized to some extent identify this spirit with the God of the Christians; others, even if they do not go quite so far, have absolutely forgotten that unɛ`·tɬanɔ̈'ʃi is identical with the sun, and have even no idea of the sex of this spirit.

Although this spirit was not considered responsible for the origin of things (see Mooney, Myths, pp. 239, 248), yet he must once have had the reputation of a most eminent spirit, if not of the preeminent deity. When such very important tribal or ritualistic events take place as the ball game, or the search for medicine, he is always invoked in a very humble and propitiating way. He and the Fire (they are still by a few of the oldest informants felt to be one and the same person) are the only spirits to which prayers, in the true meaning of the term, are ever offered; of them things are asked, while other spirits are merely commanded to do things.

If it were not for the fortunate fact that another ritualistic name of this important spirit has been preserved it might not now be possible to definitely identify the sex of this spirit; the name Gɛ`'yaGʋ·'Gǝ, however, makes it clear that a feminine person is meant (aGɛ`'ya "woman"); -Gʋ·Gǝ can not be identified with certainty; probably it is a dialectical variant of the suffix -Gɔ·Ga "very important"; "primus inter pares"; "par excellence" (cf. 'ɩDa·'ᵘwɛ'ɩ`Gɔ·Ga' "thou most powerful wizard"; ayɔ̈ⁿ`Gɔ·Ga' "but I myself indeed").

Another proof is found in the etiological myth explaining the black spots on the "face" of the moon as a result of the love affair of the moon with the sun, his sister. (See Mooney, Myths, pp. 256–257.)

Only rarely do we find evidence that the sun sends disease, although a couple of cases have come to my attention where she is alleged to have caused headache (insolation?). No one could give the reason why the sun causes disease. An explanation is found in a myth where it is stated that the sun causes fever because she hates to see her grandchildren (the human beings) screw up their faces when they look up at her. (Mooney, Myths, p. 252.)

As unɛ'́tɬanöṣ́i the sun is often called upon to cure disease, however, and she is invariably addressed in the prayers that are recited to ask permission to gather plants and simples.

The Fire.—We find the fire so closely associated with the sun that their identity could plausibly be surmised, even if there were no actual and definite proof of it.

The fire but rarely sends disease, and then only because of our disrespectful conduct; throwing the offal of anything we have chewed into the fire results in our being visited with toothache; urinating on the ashes that have been thrown outside exposes us to a disease as the one referred to in Formula No. 4.

It is often addressed as "our grandparent," opening his (her?) sheltering arms in affection, and surrounded by us, his (her?) grandchildren. Epithets, as "Ancient white," "Ancient red," are often bestowed upon it. The hunter, when returning from a successful trip, never neglected to offer a particle of meat, usually the liver of the animal, to it, but this custom is now well-nigh obsolete. It is unfortunately not now possible to ascertain whether this offer was intended for the fire, in its capacity as emanation of unɛ'́tɬanöṣ́i, or simply as a recompense for the fire's divinatory offices, as the hunter usually consults the fire prior to his departure as to where he will be able to locate and kill game.

There is only one instance of the fire curing an ailment by its own virtue, viz, where burns and scalds caused by flames are exposed to the fire, "so that the fire should take the pain back," but there are a great many instances where the curing virtue of the fire is relied upon as an additional element in the cure. In all the cases, viz, where the patient has "to be hit" (see p. 62), the medicine man, prior to this operation, warms his hands near the fire. Usually a few live coals are taken from the hearth on a shovel, in a dish, or a flat vessel, and put near the patient; the medicine man warms his hands over these coals before he starts "rubbing the disease away."

The fire is also generally invoked against all disease caused by "cold-blooded" animals, as the terrapin, snakes, fish, etc. (Mooney, Notes), and also often against complaints caused by Frost, Cold, the Blue Man, etc.

Another case where the curing virtue of the fire is resorted to is when an infusion, prior to being drunk by the patient, or to being rubbed on his body, is "strengthened" by dropping four or seven live coals into it.

The considerable rôle the fire plays in divination ceremonies is retained for discussion in a future paper dealing with that subject, when also the use made of the fire in a "man-killing" ceremony will be amply described.

The Moon.—The moon, although he is the brother of the sun (see p. 20), is not very prominent in the tribal mythology, nor does he play a part of any importance in the folklore.

It would appear, however, that this loss of popularity is of rather recent date, since very old customs, such as the "going to water" (see p. 150), with every new moon seem to indicate that the moon cult must once have been of far greater importance than it is now.

The diseases held to be caused by the moon are very scarce; blindness is one of them. It is furthermore believed that if, at new moon, a person sees the luminary for the first time through the trees he will be ill all the following month. It may be that originally this illness was considered to be caused by the moon, but such a belief does not exist now; it is now merely looked upon as an omen. (See p. 37.)

The moon is never appealed to with a view to dispelling disease. This offers the more cause for surprise, as the moon must once have been the object of great respect. It is still occasionally addressed as "grandparent," the only spirit to share this honor with the Sun and the Fire.

The Cherokee believe that when a person sees the new moon of the month the first time he must look at him and say:

Gǫ·yɔ·ˈlɩ·Ga´	ɛDʋ·´Dʋ	ě´ti	skɩˈᴰnʋ.stɛ·sti´
I greet thee	maternal grandfather	long time	this like it will be

ɩ·yǫⁿDə	kʼɩla·ˀi·´	DɩˋGɩndaGɔ´´wa.tö ⁿ.tiˋ	ˋɩGɛˋˈsɛ·sti´
over there	continually	thou and I to be seeing one another	it will be

("How do, Grandpa! At the time when it will be like this again (i. e., next month) we will still be seeing each other." (i. e., I will still be alive.)

Pronouncing this salutation formula is a sure means of safeguarding against all sickness or accidents throughout the ensuing month.

The River.—The River cult of the Cherokee has formed the object of a paper read by James Mooney before the Columbus meeting of the American Association for the Advancement of Science, in August, 1899, and which has been reprinted.[12] This paper is practically exhaustive, and what small additional points of information have been obtained subsequently by Mooney or by me will be found in their relevant places in these pages.

---

[12] The Cherokee River Cult, in JAFL., January–March, 1900, pp. 1–10.

The river, usually addressed in the ritualistic language as—

yŏ·ⁿwi′   Gaʻnəʻɩ·′Dŏⁿ   "Long Human Being,"
aʻskŭ′ya Gaʻnəʻɩ·′Dŏⁿ   "Long Man,"
ɩ·na′Dŏⁿ Gaʻnəʻɩ·′Dŏⁿ   "Long Snake,"

continues to enjoy a great deal of credit and is still an object of sincere respect to the more traditionalist of the Cherokee. The rite of going to water, however, is rapidly disappearing from the tribal life, and after another couple of generations all that will probably subsist of the river cult will be a few survivals, unintelligible even to those who practice them.

The river sends disease to those who insult it by such actions as throwing rubbish into it, by urinating into it, etc. As a vengeance for the latter act it causes a disease from a description of the symptoms of which it appears that enuresis is meant.

The use of river water in the preparation of medicine is discussed under Materia Medica (p. 52 et seq.).

Apart from the rites that are performed at the river's edge in such ceremonies as "going to water," "for long life," in divination and incantation ceremonies, which are all described in the notes appended to the relevant formulas, attention should here be called to the custom of vomiting into the river to get rid of diseases, especially of those in which the patient's "saliva has been spoiled." (See p. 63.)

The patient drinks the emetic at home, while still fasting, and then hurries to the river's edge, where he vomits into the water, thereby "throwing off the spoiled saliva," and, with it, the disease. If the emetic itself does not have the desired result mechanical means are resorted to (irritating the uvula with finger, grass stalk, etc.). A formula is usually recited at the same time by the medicine man accompanying the patient, by which the water is commanded to carry the disease down the stream, "to the settlements where (other) people live." "In every case where a ceremony is performed at the water side, either by a number of persons or by a single individual, it must be at daybreak, while the participants are still fasting, and the spot chosen for the performance of the rite is at a bend of the river where the supplicants can face the east while looking upstream." (Mooney, Notes.)

Thunder—Red Man—Two Little Red Men.—The Thunder is referred to by these three different names. The two former refer to the Thunder himself; the latter to his two sons. Often in the formulas the Thunder is spoken of as surrounded by a host of Little Red Men, all Thunderers.

The heavy rolling crashes of thunder are said to be the voice of Thunder himself, whereas the lighter, metallic peals of thunder are ascribed to the Little Red Men.

The Cherokee pretend that the Thunder is the friend of all Indians, and that he never kills one; not one case can be cited, they say, of a Cherokee having been "struck by the Thunder," whereas white people have frequently been killed on the reservation, and scores of trees are struck every year.

The Thunder's rôle is that of a disease expeller rather than that of a disease causer. He and his two sons are the enemies of the Black Man and of anything and anybody having his abode in the "Black Land," in the "Evening Land," in the "Dark Land," or in the West.

The only case, it seems, where the Thunder gets angry is when we do not observe the taboo relating to him, and which prohibits referring to him as "Red" in the everyday language. The epithet "Red" should only be bestowed on him in the ceremonial language, whereas in everyday speech he is to be referred to as "White."

The Two Little Red Men (the Cherokee never explicitly call them "Thunder Boys") always rove about together; they are reputed to be about 60 centimeters high and to wear a cap, half red, half purple, surmounted by a peak, the whole looking "like a German military helmet," which some of the Cherokee have seen or have heard described. $s^u w\epsilon\cdot'$ɢi and tsɑ·'ni (John), both now dead, claim to have seen the Thunder Boys; they looked exactly as they had always heard them described; which does not surprise us.

According to Og., the Two Little Red Men are to be identified with the two sons of k'ɑnɑ·'ti (cf. Mooney, Myths, p. 242); k'ɑnɑ·ti himself being no one else than the Thunder in person.

Purple Man, Blue Man, Black Man, etc.—There is not much definite information to be gathered about these spirits, neither from the texts themselves nor from oral information.

Possibly they owe their existence merely to the desire to oppose to the Red Man corresponding men of the different colors, to conform to the color symbolism.

The Black Man, living in the West, seems in many cases to be identical with a ghost. (See p. 26 et seq.). The diseases they cause, the nature of their activities, their opponents and antagonists, all this supports this impression, and many informants explicitly and spontaneously state that this identity exists.

The Purple Man is generally called upon to assist in nefarious machinations, such as incantations, love conjurations, etc. That purple is the color of witchcraft will appear from other facts listed in these pages.

The Blue Man, living in the North, is called upon to act as an antagonist in diseases sent by the scorching sun (insolation, blisters, etc.). He himself causes such pains and ailments as usually follow in the wake of severe frost.

Dαwi′skŭlŏⁿ‵, or Flint, does not play so important a part in Cherokee medicine as he does in the mythology. To his reputation of being an ogrelike being he owes the appeal made to him to come and frighten the little girls at birth, thus enticing them "to jump down" from their mothers. (See texts, p. 277.)

Various Little People.—Finally there are to be mentioned the various kinds of "Little People," yǫ·′ⁿwi tsu·nsti′′ fairylike beings of either sex, very small (about 40 cm. high, informants say) with long hair falling down to their heels.

They very seldom are mentioned as individuals, and usually act as a group. There are colonies of Little People in the mountains, in the rocks, in the water, and in the forests. They live in settlements just as usual human beings, have clans, town houses, hold dances and councils, etc., and frequently their music and dancing can be heard at night by lonely travelers. As a rule they are invisible, but there are a few cases on record where some rarely gifted individuals (e. g., twins that are being brought up to be witches, cf. p. 129) can see them and talk with them. They can speak Cherokee.

They are as a rule kindly inclined toward mankind and may help a hunter to find his arrows, or they may care for and feed a lost and spent traveler. But they are also feared as disease causers and are believed to especially choose children as their victims.

Animal Spirits

The animal spirits so frequently mentioned in the Cherokee formulas are by no means to be thought of as identical with the specimens of our earthly fauna. They are the prototypes of our common animals and are far more considerable in size, power, swiftness, and all other qualities than their earthly successors. They can not be seen or heard, nor can their presence be felt by any of our senses; yet we know what they are like, and how they behave; we know even of what color they are, White, Red, Blue, etc., "because the old people have always addressed them by those epithets."

It is needless to say that these colors are mainly imaginary; there is not only a Brown Otter, but also a Red one, a Blue one, etc. The same applies to all other animal spirits, as Deer, Bear, Dog, Weasel, Raven, Eagle, Frog, Leech, etc. The same remarks we made with regard to the colors of the Purple, Blue, etc., Men (p. 24) no doubt also hold here; we have only the color symbolism (p. 51) to blame—or to thank—for the existence of this multicolored spirit fauna.

The motives of these animal spirits in sending disease are mainly dictated by considerations of self-defense, or in a spirit of vengeance for the wrong done and the relentless warfare waged against them and their species by the human race. This is lucidly shown by the myth explaining the "Origin of Disease," collected by Mooney (Myths, pp. 250–252). Mooney has also described the rôle of such animal spirits as Little Deer, White Bear, etc., so thoroughly that it is superfluous to duplicate those descriptions here.

For further details regarding the animal spirits the reader is referred to the "List of Spirits," pages 44–50.

For a discussion of the animal ghosts, as distinct from animal spirits, see pages 26–28.

Ghosts

To the spirits and animal spirits as discussed in the preceding paragraphs should be added "ghosts," i. e., according to the Cherokee views, the immaterial, spiritual, immortal part of human beings and animals that have lived the life and died the death of commonplace creatures.

The motives that entice human ghosts, aʻnɪsɢɪ"na (sgl. asɢɪ'na) and animal ghosts 'ɔⁿʻta'li (sing. and pl.) to visit mankind with disease and death are quite different and will be treated separately.

Human ghosts (aʻnɪsɢɪ'na).—When people who have died go to tsùʻsɢɪnɔ'ⁱi "(the place) where the (human) ghosts (are)" (see p. 142), the place out West where they stay, they feel lonesome and homesick and want the company of their friends and relatives. They therefore make them sick and suffering, so that they may die and come and join them in the Ghost Land.

It was emphatically stated to me by informants that there is not a shadow of malignity or jealousy about this activity of the ghosts of the departed; they act out of pure love, devotion, affection, and all other commendable motives. Yet the living are not quite bent on this mode the ghosts indulge in of showing their affection, and they leave no means untried to escape from the ghosts' influence. I have been able to observe real poignant cases, where filial affection forced a person's attention again and again on the memory of a dearly beloved parent, so much so that he would brood and pine away and languish, but at the same time he felt that he must at all costs make efforts to forget and to make merry, as thinking and dreaming about the departed ones is the very first symptom of a disease sent by the aʻnɪsɢɪ'na.

Animal ghosts ('ɔⁿʻta'li).—With the diminishing curve the importance of hunting has made with the Cherokee, they are not now ascribing so much power to the animal ghosts as they once did. The references to them have to be gleaned chiefly from the formulas, as there is now no Cherokee medicine man living who can give any satisfactory information on the subject. Mooney had already to cope with the same difficulty, and translated 'ɔⁿʻta'li as "after-ghost," or "secondary ghost," basing his conclusion on the following facts:

"Most diseases are ascribed to the influence of ghosts, usually the revengeful ghosts of slain animals. But there are two classes of these ghosts, the 'anɩsgi'na' (singular 'asgi'na') and the "ᵘⁿtali" (the ûⁿ- being an almost inaudible grunt), and it was only after long inquiry that it was possible to learn the distinction between them. It is held by the shaman that an animal killed by the hunter or otherwise is again revived in the same form, and enters upon a new lease of life, to be again killed, or to die naturally, as the case may be. This may recur an indefinite number of times, probably four or seven, the shamans questioned not being able to state. At the final death, the animal ceases to exist in the body, and its ghost goes to join its comrades in Usûhi'yi, the night land. One doctor (Ayûⁿ'ini) stated that the deer had seven lives or successive animations, each in the same deer shape, after which came annihilation. He was unable to say whether other animals were reanimated in the same way, but such seems to be the belief from the evidence afforded by the formulas. An example of this reincarnation occurs in the story of the 'Bear Man'.[13] The belief differs from the ordinary doctrine of metempsychosis in that the animal is reincarnated in its original form, instead of becoming an animal of another kind.

"'Asgi'na' is the name applied to the ghost of the original animal (or person) after the first death, while the "ᵘⁿtali" is the ghost of the successive reincarnations, or as the doctor explained, 'the ghost of an animal that has been killed more than once,' the "ᵘⁿtali" being the more dreaded of the two.

"The old religion of the Cherokees is now so beclouded and corrupted by the influence of missionary ideas that it is extremely difficult to get an intelligent statement of such points, but it seems possible that the original belief assigned to every animal a definite life period, which could not be curtailed by violent means. When an animal lived out this allotted period it died and its body decayed, while its spirit became an 'asgi'na' and went to join the other ghosts in the night land. If killed before the expiration of the allotted time, the death was only temporary, the body took shape again from the blood drops (see the story of the "Bear Man") and was reanimated by the spirit, now called "ᵘⁿtali'.' This new existence continued, unless again interrupted and again renewed, until the end of the predestined period, when the body was finally dissolved and the liberated spirit took up its journey to the night land, there to remain with its kindred shades." (Mooney, Notes.)

Moreover, Mooney based his conclusions on a belief of his according to which 'Ŏⁿ'ta'li was etymologically related with t'aᵖli' "two" (his transcription being, respectively, ᵘⁿtali' and tali').

---

[13] See Mooney, Myths, pp. 327–329.

This is, however, not the case, as will appear from my texts, there being two important phonetic differences:

(1) The surd dental is not aspirated in 'ŏⁿʽta'li whereas it is most decidedly so in tʽαᴾli'.

(2) In 'ŏⁿʽta'li the liquid is not preceded by a dental implosion as it is in tʽαᴾli'.

As for the successive incarnations of the animals, according to Og., the only one of my informants who had ever heard of it, this was only the case for the bears (as is indeed confirmed by Mooney's story of the "Bear Man" (Mooney, Myths, pp. 327–329) and by several stories collected by me); neither the deer nor any other animals, Og. states, had the benefit of a second or of any subsequent lives after having once been killed.

I have found evidence, moreover, that the term 'ŏⁿʽta'li was also used by the hunter, referring to the particle of meat of a killed animal which he offered to the fire to return thanks for his luck. (See p. 21.)

Finally, by several medicine men still living, 'ŏⁿʽta'li is felt to mean "the decayed thing," i. e., the offal of a piece of game. The disrespectful treatment extended to their bones and bowels, now, is exactly what makes the animals so revengeful toward the neglectful hunter.

From all this I am inclined to believe that 'ŏⁿʽta'li does not mean "after-ghost" or "secondary ghost," nor that it specifically refers to the ghost of an animal that has been killed before its "lease of life" had been completed. Nor did I find the term asGɩ'ʽna ever used with reference to animal ghosts.

To come to a conclusion, I think that I am entitled to adhere to my explanation, and to my distinction between asGɩ'ʽna "human ghost" and 'ŏⁿʽta'li "animal ghost."

The diseases sent by these human and by the animal ghosts are so multifarious as to include practically the whole of known illnesses and ailments.

Commonly, however, the human ghosts act by "spoiling the saliva" of the victim, whereas the activity of the animal ghosts results in troubles that are not so much of a psychopathological order. Rheumatism and dysentery, swellings in the cheek, and violent headaches may all be caused in different patients by one and the same animal ghost, e. g., a deer's. On the other hand, several different kinds of animal ghosts may all manifest their ill will and take vengeance on the human race by inflicting one and the same disease, as rheumatism which can be caused by the measuring worm, the rabbit, or the buffalo.

A species of animal ghosts to which many ailments are ascribed are the various kinds of tcsGɔ'ʽya or insects.

"'Tsgâya' is a generic term for all small insects, larvæ, and worms, excepting intestinal worms. These 'tsgâya' are very numerous, having colonies in the water, in the earth, on the foliage of trees, and in every decaying log, and as they are constantly being crushed, burned, or otherwise destroyed by the human race, they are constantly actuated by a spirit of revenge. To accomplish their purpose the ghosts of the slain 'tsgâya' 'form settlements' in the bodies of their victims, usually just under the skin, and thus cause malignant ulcers, watery blisters and swellings, all of which are generally ascribed to the 'tsgâya.' The 'tsgâya' doctrine of the Indian practitioner is thus the equivalent of the microbe theory of the white physician." (Mooney, Notes.)

PRETERNATURAL CAUSES

Not only natural and supernatural causes are active night and day to shower disease and death on the poor humans; as many, if not more, of the calamities of life are to be laid at the door of fellow human beings, who through preternatural means have the power of sending mysterious diseases into the bodies and limbs of their neighbors.

WITCHES

The most dreaded of these human disease causers are the witches. Not that their activities and the results of these are very much different from those of the "man-killers" (see p. 33); the latter, however, only "work against us" for very sound and obvious reasons, e. g., because we have insulted them, poked fun at them, quarreled with them, or have given them offense in one way or another; at worst, when trying to kill us, they may act as agents of some enemy of ours, but at any rate there is usually this "comforting" consideration about it, that we are aware and conscious of the motives of their activities, and that usually we have only ourselves and our conduct to blame. Being careful and courteous in our dealings with "man-killers" may considerably diminish the risk of being harmed from their quarter. Moreover, counteracting their evil machinations is not so hopeless a task as to fight witchcraft.

The witches are usually referred to as tsɪkɪli' or as sǫ·nɔ·'yi aˋnɛˤDɔ·ˊïi "they walk about during the night." The meaning of tsɪkɪli' is literally "hooting owl," but since this night bird is considered as a bird of ill omen, and because of the mysterious occult power ascribed to it, moreover because it indulges in its activities only during the night as the witches do, the word has been extended to mean "witch."

A witch is held to be a human being, male or female, who is a "powerful wizard" (aDa·ˋᵘwɛˋi', aDa·ˋᵘwɛˋiˊyu') such as a medicine man may become who has "got the utmost" (see p. 87), but the semantic, and especially the emotional value given to the word, always conveys concepts expressing baseness, meanness, slyness, an activity of an insidious, nefarious, deleterious nature.

These activities are not subject to the same "reasonable" motives as are those of the "man-killers"; whereas the latter harm to take (just) revenge for some (uncalled-for) offense, the witch harms simply because it is an inherent trait of his or her wicked nature.

Moreover, whatever the witch can steal of the life, and therefore of the vital principle, of the animus, the power, the "orenda" of his victim, he adds to his own, and this is the reason why witches are always hovering about the sick, the feeble, the moribund people; invisible as they can make themselves, they put their mouths over those of the victims, and steal their breath; according to some informants "because they like the taste of sick people's breath; it is so sweet"(!); according to others, because stealing their breath comes to the same as securing for themselves the victim's vitality, which they add to their own. At the time the moribund expires, especially, the witch is careful not to miss his chance.

Although, as a rule, to become a witch one has to be "brought up" for the profession (see p. 129), it is possible to become one, even if one's parents neglected to go through the necessary ritual and prescriptions. A peculiar root, that of the scarce a'ɔ·'tɫyɛ'ɔⁿ'ski "it (the root) has it (the stalk) growing from its mouth" (*Sagittaria latifolia* Willd.?),[14] looks like a beetlelike insect, with the stem of the plant growing from its mouth. It has to be steeped and drunk, the usual fast being observed. If the infusion is drunk and the fasting prolonged for four days, you will be able to metamorphose yourself into any person or animal living on the surface of the ground; i. e., a man can take the shape of a woman, and vice versa; they can also take the form of a dog, a deer, an opossum, etc.

If, however, the treatment is prolonged for seven days you will have power to take the shape of animals flying in the air or living under the ground; you will be able to fly in the air or to dive under a mountain; you can at will put on the appearance of an eagle, an owl, a raven, a mole, an earthworm, etc.

The metamorphosis into a raven is one of the most common, and a witch traveling about in this garb is referred to as k'ɔ·'lanɔ̈ⁿ a'yɛ·lɪ'ski "he (is) a raven imitator."

When traveling about at night a witch of this "degree" very frequently travels through the air as a flame, a spark, or a light. Some informants pretend to have seen that the "medicine" previously referred to, and which the witches have to drink, has at certain times of the year—some say in spring and early summer—a purplish fire droop-

---

[14] This same medicine is given to a dog to make it a sure tracker of game. The animal must drink the infusion for four consecutive mornings. It must not fast.

ing from its stem. I have not been able to ascertain whether this belief is a mere phantasy or whether it might have its base in the phosphorescent qualities of certain plants. Be that as it may, a purple flame, a reddish-blue spark is usually associated with witchcraft, so much so that even sporadic flames of that color in the hearth fire are believed to forebode the visit of a witch.

The visit of a witch to a house where one of the inmates is ill is countenanced with frantic fright. That is why a number of relatives and friends are always watching through the night, "guarding (the patient) against witchcraft." While a couple of them may be asleep two or three more keep awake, "working" near the fire. This work consists in smoothing a small heap of ashes, about 20–25 centimeters in diameter, aside from the hearth, and occasionally dropping a tiny pinch of finely crushed tsɔ·'laɢayǫ·'ⁿli ("old tobacco," *Nicotiana rustica* L.) on it; the center of the hot ashes are thought of as representing the patient's cabin; any particle of the tobacco dust catching fire, to the right or to the left of the center, indicates the position from where the witch is approaching. If the dust alights on the center of the ashes it is a sign that the witch is right overhead, and should the tobacco, as it drops on the center, take fire with a crack or a burst, it shows that the witch has already entered the room. In this case the burst will cause the death of the witch within four days, if she is one of the kind that has fasted for four days to attain her occult power; within seven days if she is one of the kind that "has got the utmost."

Another method to prevent the witch from approaching is to direct the smoke of "old tobacco" against the several points of the compass, as will be found described on page 75.

But the most drastic means of all is to simply shoot the witch with a gun; a certain medicine, obtained from a plant (not one of the informants could tell me exactly from which plant), has to be mixed with the powder, and a hair taken from the crown of the head has to be wound round the bullet (many of the Cherokee still use muzzle-loading guns); in this practice we find, no doubt, the beliefs of the Cherokee blended with those of the white mountaineers.

In order to shoot the witch, however, we must be able to see him in his regular human form. This can be attained by fasting until sunset for seven days, drinking an infusion of the same root to which the witches owe their power: a'ɔ·'tɫiyɛ'ɔ̃ⁿ'ski (see p. 30).

There are dozens of anecdotes on this subject circulating on the reservation, three of which will here be inserted as illustrations.

I. A long time ago somebody was ill. The people came and sat up with him, guarding against witchcraft. They built a fire outdoors, and when some of them became sleepy they went outside, and stood by the fire, while others continued to watch inside.

Those who were standing by the fire outside all of a sudden saw a purple fire up in the air; it went toward a house; after a few minutes it rose up again, and came back, and dropped on the house of the sick person; as soon as the fire fell inside, the person died. This fire was a tsɪkɪli'.

II. Once a man was very ill, caused by witchcraft. Two friends of his decided to fast and drink the medicine by which they could see witches.[15] The seventh day they hid themselves outside the house. They heard the witch coming,[16] and he alighted in the yard, and there took his human shape and walked toward the house. These two men had a gun with them, loaded for the purpose of killing a witch;[17] they fired and hit him, but instead of blood, fire spouted forth from the wound. The witch disappeared.

III. About 25 or 26 years ago[18] T. (pl. 10, c; see p. 111) was ill. His friends were summoned to guard against witchcraft, as he[19] had found out that he was ill by ayeʻlɪɢɔ·'ɢi .[20]

yɔ·'nɔ̃ⁿɢaᴅlɛ·'ɢi[21] examined by putting tobacco on the fire, but he found out that the witch was stronger than he, as the tobacco sparkled like a star, but no burst was heard. The next day he tried again, but again he found that the witch was stronger than he. So he instructed all the attendants as well as the patient to fast and to drink the medicine by which you can see witches. He himself did the same. At night he told the attendants to stay inside; he took a burning branch from the fire and went out.

Outside, he saw a man standing near the chimney; he was intently gazing at T. through the wall. Climbing Bear could see him because he had drunk the medicine. He passed near by the man, and as he passed him, touched the witch with his burning switch. When he looked back the witch had disappeared.

Now, since the witch had been recognized, he was sure to die within four or seven days. T. told W., from whom I have the account, that the witch was J. B. of a near-by settlement. And sure enough, the third day after the event here related, J. B. died. T. recovered.

Powerful though witches are, they evidently believe in obtaining the greatest results with the smallest exertions, and that is why they make it a point to attack individuals that are feeble and decrepit, as they know that these will far more readily fall a prey to their activities than would the more healthy and robust individuals of

---

[15] Vide supra.
[16] In the shape of some bird.
[17] Cf. p. 31.
[18] This was told me in the spring of 1927.
[19] T. being a medicine man could discover this for himself.
[20] Cf. p. 33.
[21] Climbing Bear, now deceased; O.'s husband, Del.'s father, W. and Og.'s half-brother.

the tribe. This also explains the exertions of witches against women in labor and newly born infants. (See p. 123.)

Although witches are most strenuously active when death is imminent, they are constantly on the lookout to cast a spell, a disease, on an unsuspecting individual, and particularly to aggravate the complaints of the stricken. This reputation they share with those other human disease causers, the "man-killers."

"Man-Killers"

This knack which witches and "man-killers," Dɩ`ᴅa·nɛ`·səGɩ´·ski, have to aggravate disease, explains the generic name given to complaints for the origin of which these disease causers are held responsible. These names can all be shown to be related with the stems $\sqrt{}$-yaḵt'- "change," and $\sqrt{}$-yɛ'l- "likeness." (If a thing, a disease, etc., is made to look *like* another, its original condition is *changed*.)

Whereas the process by which a witch manages to "change the condition" of a victim for the worse is rather obscure, and can not be definitely elucidated, the means by which a "man-killer" attains this object is well known and vividly described. He may, by his occult power, "change the food" in the victim's stomach, or "cause the food to sprout." He may "change our mind to a different condition," or make a given disease we are afflicted with "as if it were like" a more serious ailment. But above all, he may use the most orthodox manner of disposing of an enemy, viz, by shooting an invisible arrowhead into his body. In a forthcoming paper, in which Cherokee incantations and man-killing ceremonies will be described, this subject will be dealt with in detail.

ayɛ`·lɩGɔ·´Gi Diseases

Under this name is known a group of diseases that are held to be caused by the machinations of a human agent. They are the most dreaded of the many complaints the Cherokee knows.

The term, which is strictly ceremonial, can not be analyzed but has $\sqrt{}$-yɛ'l- "likeness" as its root. Mooney has usually translated it as "simulators," and this translation is correct in so far as the term refers to the action of deluding the vigilance of the patient and medicine man by sending a disease which looks like another one which it really is not. For example, the victim falls ill with indigestion; the medicine man ascribed it, according to the current views, to the insects, or to animal ghosts, or to some similar cause. But he is wrong. He is led astray by the sorcerer who sent the disease, and who "made it resemble some such ailment as found by the medicine man in his diagnosis"; but the disease is of a totally different nature.

Even now there are often cases where two parties are waging a battle, often lasting weeks and months, pestering each other with various ayɛ`·lɩGɔ·´Gi-diseases.

According to information collected by Mooney, these diseases were even sent to each other by friends and relations "as a joke" to mutually test their knowledge and aptitude to ward off such attacks. I did not find this view confirmed.

"MULIER MENSTRUANS" [22]

Again and again in these pages proofs will be found of the nefarious influence ascribed to a woman during her catamenial period. This influence she exercises involuntarily; it is inherent to her condition at that time.

Eating the food she has prepared, touching whatever object she has used, even walking along a trail by which she has traveled, may cause a painful and obstinate malady. Up to two or three generations ago this belief was far more pronounced, and practices with regard to it were observed much more strictly than is the case now. As soon as the first signs of her condition manifested themselves, the woman repaired to the ɔ·′si, a small low hut set apart for people "under restrictions," as menstruating women, women in labor, and probably also for patients suffering from certain diseases; the ɔ·′si was also reserved for certain acts of a ceremonial nature, as the instruction of aspirant medicine men, the recitation of certain myths, etc.

There is not one ɔ·′si left on the reservation, and not even the oldest persons remember ever having seen one. The women, therefore, nowadays no longer leave the common dwelling place during their periods, but abstain from cooking meals, or from any other duties pertaining to the household. The meals are cooked by other female members of the household or prepared by the men.

The Cherokee medicine men are considerably at odds as to the actual way in which menstruating women exercise their disease-causing influence. According to the view that commonly prevails, the mere presence of such a person is sufficient to cause disease, and this I consider to be the primary form of the belief. Others, Og. among them, held that especially the look of her was nefarious; this would indicate a belief that is intimately related with the "evil eye" superstition, and may possibly be of foreign (white?) origin, as the Cherokee do not seem to attach any importance to this mode of bewitching. The only other instance that can be cited is that of the fascinating look of the ukt'ɛ·′na: "if he even looked at a man, this man's family would die." (Mooney, Myths, p. 253.)

It is of import to note that not only the presence of the woman is held to be dangerous, but even that of her husband. I have myself

---

[22] Under this caption only the "disease-causing" influence of a mulier menstruans is considered. The taboos she has to observe herself are mentioned (p. 120) and will be discussed at greater length in a forthcoming paper, in which the sexual life of the Cherokee will be more adequately described.

had the experience that when I visited sick members of the tribe I was not granted admission to the cabin until I had been subjected from inside, by the patient himself, to a very meticulous and an annoyingly intimate cross-examination. (See p. 66.)

Not only in the domain of sickness does a woman in this condition exert this unfortunate influence, but even on growing plants and crops her presence is equally pernicious, whereas if she were to wade through a river where a fish trap is set she would spoil the catch.

Pregnant women are considered only slightly less dangerous, and the harm and havoc they may cause is combated by the same means as that of the menstruantes. (See p. 120; also Mooney, Myths, p. 442.)

For further facts relating to these subjects, the reader is referred to Childbirth, page 116 et seq.

Dreams

The importance the Cherokee ascribe to dreams as causes of disease is quite remarkable.

Whereas it appears from the more archaic data available that some dreams are the actual cause of many diseases, there is now in this very generation an evolution to be observed from "dream = disease-cause"; to "dream = omen of disease." [23] In either of those two cases it is still possible for the dream to play an active part as symptom.

The Cherokee, especially those that have kept intact their allegiance to the aboriginal gastronomical ways and manners, dream frequently, and their dreams are often of the "nightmare" variety. Hearing them relate a dream of this sort, and their comments upon it, makes one more than ever inclined to accept Höfler's theory according to which the conception and the visualization of disease-demons have their origin in nightmare dreams.

Dreams, as a rule, affect the dreamer only, but in a few cases the person dreamed about may be the future sufferer. Certain types of dreams may occur more frequently at a certain time than at another; a woman during her catamenial period often dreams of "all sorts of things" (i. e., of unnatural intercourse, of giving birth to animals, etc.). Dreams may vary also according to the sphere of interest of the individual: dza·'dzi (George), a powerful Nimrod before the Lord, dreamed of negroes more than W. did, the latter being given to dreams of the medicine man's type: Thunder, train, burning house, etc. Attention should also be called to the psychological shrewdness of considering "rheumatism" a result of dreams with sexual contents.

One individual had to some extent formed his own exegesis: If he dreams during winter of a nice summer day, it is going to be

---

[23] "Fish dreams is a sign our appetite is going to be spoiled," an informant told me. From the older texts, however, it appears that it is the very fact of dreaming of fish that causes the disease.

bitterly cold, he says; if in summer he dreams of a cold winter day, it is going to be a nice day.

As a whole there is a definite rule as to which diseases are caused by certain dreams. It is even very probable that at a time when their culture was still uncontaminated there was a very elaborate and definite dream-exegesis.

I have found it most advisable to list the dreams under three headings:
1. Dreams that cause definite ailments or death.
2. Dreams that cause complaints that are not specifically indicated.
3. Dreams that do not belong to the domain of medicine.

1.—DREAMS CAUSING DEFINITE AILMENTS OR DEATH

Dreams about—	Cause
"Little People" (see p. 25)	"Our mind is going to be changed" (i. e., insanity).
All kinds of birds	Do.
Sun	Fever.
Moon	Do.
Meat ("lean meat," some say)	Toothache.
Being in deep water	Do.
Rattlesnake or copperhead	Toothache; also swelling of the body and cancer.
Persons of opposite sex; sexual intercourse	Rheumatism.
To wrestle with fat person of opposite sex	Do.
Sexual-pathological (incest, vice, etc.)	Do.
Bees, wasps, yellow jackets, and similar insects	Blindness.
To burn foot, hand, or finger	Snake bite.
A ball game; the dreamer's team wins	A member of the dreamer's settlement will die soon.
A train rushing to a cabin	One of the inmates will die within 6–12 months.
A train journey with a companion	The companion will die within 6–12 months.
A cabin of the settlement burns completely	One of the inmates will die soon.
A member of the family is leaving	The one who leaves will die after 2–3 years.

2.—DREAMS THAT CAUSE COMPLAINTS THAT ARE NOT SPECIFICALLY INDICATED

Dreams about—	Cause
Fish	Illness.
Snakes	Do.
"Impure water" (i. e., rapids bringing snow from the mountains; the river flooding the country, etc.).	Do.
"Inverted dreams" (when a man dreams about women's utensils (mortar, pestle, sieve, etc.), or a woman about men's utensils (bow, ax, etc.).	Do.
Many people gathering	Do.

Dreams about—	Cause
Many visitors at a house (not necessarily the dreamer's house).	Illness.
"Invisible people"	Do.
To lose small personal belonging (coat, ax, kerchief, etc.).	Do.
Drowning	Do.
Eagle	Do.
"tcgɔ·'ya" (see p. 28)	Do.
To walk with a deceased person	Do.
A deceased person is calling us or beckoning	Do.
A cabin of the settlement is on fire (but does not burn completely).	One of the inmates will fall ill; if we dream that the fire is extinguished by somebody, this person is the one who will be able to cure the case.
"Little Men" (Thunder Boys)	ayɛ·'lɪgɔ·'gi
Thunder	Do.
A dog approaching from distance	Witchcraft.
A mad bull rushing wildly all over the settlement	An epidemic.
A windstorm rushing wildly all over the settlement	Do.

3.—Dreams Without Relation to Medicine

Dreams	Cause
About white people	It is going to snow.
About Indians	It is going to rain.
About negroes	We will kill game.

Omens [24]

If the family dog howls all the time and acts "as if he were homesick" somebody of the family is going to fall ill. The dog should be killed "so as to make an exchange." Ayo., W.'s mother, told him many years ago that the dog should be addressed and commanded to die itself, instead of the member of the household whose death the dog's howling announced. (See p. 62.)

A hen that crows like a rooster should be killed forthwith; else disease will befall the household. If the hen is killed the misfortune is averted. (See p. 78.)

When the "thunder" strikes a tree near the cabin, there is some trouble in store for the inmates.

If a fox (tsʋ'la) howls near a cabin one of the household is going to be ill; the same result follows the hooting of the night owl. The cry of the whippoorwill is believed to forebode not only disease but even death.

If we see a shooting star we are going to be ill.

---

[24] All the following "omens" are in a stage where it is not possible to class them definitely as disease causes or as signs of future illness.

Neglected Taboos; Disregarded Injunctions

As if the formidable force of disease causes which we have now passed in review were not sufficient to soon rob the earth in general and the Cherokee country particularly of every living mortal, there is yet a complex of causes arrayed against the unsuspecting creature who has successfully run the gantlet of spirits, ghosts, witches, and dreams: the neglected taboos and the disregarded injunctions.

In a way these work in an even more insidious and surreptitious way than any of those that have until now come to our attention. For in a good many instances we may avoid diseases if only we adhere strictly to certain rules of conduct: carefully ask the bear's pardon after having killed it, making a point of burning the entrails of a slain deer, not spit into the fire, not urinate into the river, not offend "man-killers," etc. We can avoid violating these taboos; but others there are which we may violate however carefully we try to avoid doing so, and however honest our intentions are. It makes no difference whether we violate them purposely or inadvertently, the results are the same.

Some of these taboos that now seem unintelligible, not only to us but to the Cherokee themselves, are undoubtedly survivals of an earlier age, where certain phenomena were the object of a cult which has in later days been neglected and forgotten, such as is illustrated in "One must not point at the rainbow, or one's finger will swell at the lower joint." (Mooney, Myths, p. 257.)

"Sourwood . . . is never burned, from an idea that the lye made from its ashes will bring sickness to those who use it in preparing food." (l. c., p. 422.)

Others of these taboos are very probably (unconscious?) attempts at laying down rules for moral and even hygienic conduct. For example, one should never do one's needs in the yard or in a trail, i. e., in public; this would result in diseases of the urinary system. It may be mentioned in this place how extremely carefully and considerately the Cherokee observe this taboo. Likewise, the entrails and offal of all small game, the water in which it is washed and with which some of its blood may be mixed, and the blood itself, should never be disposed of by throwing or pouring it away in the yard or in a trail, etc., but should be carefully taken to a secluded place and disposed of.

The diseases that may result from the neglect of these taboos are varied and multifarious; they may in fact be almost anything. If toothache "results" it will be blamed on the "animal's insects"; if rheumatism, the explanation may be found in the fact that the particular piece of game was a rabbit; if Dᴜ·lɛ·′dzi because it was a turkey, etc.

CAUSERS OF CONTAGIOUS DISEASE

To close this review of disease causers, there is a last category to be briefly mentioned, viz, the white people, and especially the white physicians. These cause one kind of disease only, but they are the very diseases the Cherokee stand in most frantic fear of—epidemics.

A. F. Chamberlain, in his article on Disease and Medicine—American, in Hastings's Encyclopedia of Religion and Ethics, III, page 732, draws attention to the fact that many North American Indian tribes ascribe epidemics to the evil influence or activities of the white people, and has illustrated his statement by an interesting citation from Winslow's Good News from New England (1624); cf. also Dr. H. U. Williams, The Epidemic of the Indians of New England, 1616–1620, with Remarks on Native American Infections, in Johns Hopkins Hospital Bulletin (Baltimore), XX (1909), pages 340–349.

The Cherokee medicine men are at odds when it comes to state which motives drive white physicians when they let loose epidemics to ravage the Cherokee settlements. According to some informants, they do it simply because they hate the Indians; according to others, in order to enrich themselves at the expense of their victims.

It is not known exactly in what ways and by what methods the white physician attains his ends, but at least one case is known, the Cherokee claim, where it is clearly shown what means were used.

"Toward the close of the Civil War two Cherokee (one of them was called Isaac) were captured by Union troops and kept prisoners of war at Knoxville, Tenn. When, after the war, they were released they were called into a room and shown a red fish (swimming in a bowl). After they had looked at it the fish was put away again. They came back to where they lived, and three or four days after they got home they became feverish, and their whole body became covered with sores; they had smallpox." (W., Og., T.)

In this case it is emphatically stated by present informants that it was the mere looking at the fish that caused the disease and that it was purposely shown them by the white people to bring affliction and death on the two Cherokee and their people.

There is a generic name for contagious disease: a⸍⸌yɛlɩ⸍ᴅɔⁿ:a′ i. e. "he (the disease causer?) drives it (the disease) about."

As for the means used to cure or prevent it, see "Prophylaxis," p. 73 et seq.

DISEASE AND ITS TREATMENT

Diagnosis and Prognosis

We now have a pretty sound and tolerably complete idea of the Cherokee views on disease and are equipped with the indispensable elements to understand their practices with regard to the treatment of diseases.

We may at first be shocked by the "unreasonable," the "preposterous," etc., in these practices. If, however, on second thought, we endeavor to make an honest effort to understand them, we will soon see how remarkably logical they are, if only we bear the premises in mind. For whatever there has been said about "the primitive mind," there is at least this tribute to be paid to it, that it invariably gives proof of a most rigorous congruency and a perfect harmony in its reasoning.

The first thing the medicine man endeavors to find out, when he calls on a patient, is the seat of the pain. Since Cherokee medical art does not aim so much at "curing a disease" or "allaying pain" as at removing the cause of the ailment, of the agent causing the pain, the medicine man forthwith sets out upon his quest after the cause of the ailment. In this he is actively seconded by the patient, whose aid may prove the more efficacious the more he is versed in the traditional lore.

If we are not dealing with one of the very few cases where a natural cause is accepted (see p. 17) the medicine man inquires whether the patient has by any chance infringed upon a taboo (see p. 38) or whether the patient has had any dreams or omens (see p. 36). The patient is, of course, but rarely sufficiently versed in this body of lore to be able to answer in a satisfactory manner, and the medicine man usually has to go over with the patient the very extensive collection of dreams and omens that may affect the particular situation. The patient, being only too anxious to find relief, would not think of withholding any information of a nature to help the final discovery of "the important thing."

The dreams investigated may go back several months, or even as much as two or three years; there is no definite rule as to this, and it rests with the personal opinion of every individual medicine man how deeply into the past he chooses to probe to find the dream that would plausibly explain the "case." Similarly, the very emphasis on dreams as diagnostic means varies more or less with individual conceptions. It appears, for example, from Mr. Mooney's notes that Ay. held dreams of secondary importance, and that he gave primary attention to such symptoms as headache, lividness in the face, blue-black rings round the eyes, etc. This point of view does not seem to predominate with the average Cherokee medicine man, as, indeed, it hardly could, if we bear in mind this very important axiom of Cherokee medical practice, that whatever the ailment in question may seem to be, we must be sure to hit upon the real disease causer, so as to be able to "work" against him, and to force him "to let go his hold" on the patient. The identity of the disease causer is found out much more readily and far more accurately by the patient's dreams and experiences than by such symptoms as described above, which the Cherokee medicine men, as well as Mr. Mooney and I, have noticed are identically the same for a score and more of radically different diseases.

As soon as the medicine man, by this pseudo "psychoanalytical" method has found out which dream has caused the ailment he is able to prescribe the treatment and to go on his quest for herbs and roots.

There are cases, however, where by this method no result is obtained, and the medicine man's exertions remain unrewarded. One individual dreams less frequently than another and the few dreams he can recall may not contain sufficient elements to form a conclusion. In these cases there is still the ever-useful and never-failing method of "examining with the beads" to resort to; the procedure is virtually the same as described (p. 132), only changing in this respect, that the medicine man names a disease or a disease causer and asks of the bead whether his statement is right. The brisk movements of the right-hand bead gives an affirmative answer; its sluggish movements, or its remaining motionless, a negative answer.

A couple of unusual facts on the score of diagnosis have come to my attention. When in the summer of 1926 W. was suffering from a severe attack of toothache, that could not be cured by any of the "usual" means, he was soon convinced that it could not be "just a usual toothache" he was suffering from, but that it must have been sent to him by a witch. One evening as he was sitting by the fire and gazing into the fantastically leaping flames, he suddenly saw, grinning at him from the glowing embers, the face of an old woman; the face of a woman he knew. She was living in another settlement, and had the reputation of being a witch. So W. forthwith concluded that she was the one who had "worked" against him and who had sent him the toothache. According to the rules of the art, at which he was a full-fledged adept, he did not lose time in launching his counterattack as a result of which the witch died before the sun had set seven times.

As far as I could find out, W. is the only individual who ever had experiences in this domain that emerged from the banal, the everyday, and the common conceptions. I am quite confident that he was quite sincere and honest about them, and I am anxious to point out that, even if they are unknown to other members of the tribes, or of the profession for that matter, still they absolutely conform in form and in content to the pattern and the structure of the more common Cherokee beliefs.

The Cherokee do not pay much attention to prognosis. A patient should officially show signs of improvement after four or seven days of treatment. If the ailment refuses to be impressed by the Cherokee belief in sacred numbers, and the seventh day brings no relief, an expectant attitude may be taken by the patient, his medicine man and his friends for two or three days, during which there are animated discussions as to what might have been wrong with the treatment or with the diagnosis. Maybe the diagnosis was not absolutely wrong, but was not sufficiently right; the patient may have been suffering from more than one disease; he may have infracted more than one taboo; he may have offended more than one animal spirit. At the time of the diagnosis the medicine man was satisfied when he had found one cause, whereas there were two. Hence repetition of the diagnosis and beginning of another treatment. There may be yet other explanations—a complication may have set in, in that the ailment was due to a mere breach of taboo at its outset, but has since been aggravated by the machinations of an enemy or a witch. Or, again, maybe the patient has not paid heed to the taboos while under treatment. Maybe a change of medicine man would do no harm?

It is possible that the changes that are expected in the patient's condition after a set number of days (officially four or seven, according to the Cherokee sacred number) coincide with the crisis of certain ailments. Some such facts the Cherokee have not been slow to observe, although their explanation of them is, of course, always in keeping with the general trend of their beliefs. I feel sure, for instance, that it is the phenomenon of the rising temperature of certain patients toward nightfall that has contributed considerably toward the clever explanation of the "witches walking round at night," tormenting the sick and the feeble. Hence the special care with which a patient is surrounded after dusk by his friends and relatives.

The favorite phrase used when prognosticating is that the patient "will soon be able to walk about"; but "soon" and "walk about" as used by the Cherokee medicine man are both very vague and elastic expressions. Occasionally the death of a patient may be predicted, but this in no way influences the treatment. Even in the face of a losing battle the medicine man bravely and pluckily sticks to the job.

After all, the most common and the most "efficacious" means of prognosis is the one by the beads, the beads being the instruments "par excellence" for discovering the truth, in prognosis as in diagnosis, as they are, indeed, in all ceremonies of a divinatory nature. (See p. 132.)

List of Spirits

The Cherokee pantheon of disease-causing spirits is quite considerable and the number of spirits that are called upon to eat, pull out, carry away, destroy, or in any other way eliminate disease is even greater.

Since in the aboriginal belief as well as in the formulas these spirits always appear and behave according to most rigidly circumscribed patterns, a complete survey can best be given in an index, in which the particular traits of each of these beings are listed analytically.

As for the method of finding out which particular spirit or what agent has caused the disease, see Diagnosis, p. 139.

As will be noticed in the formulas, the same spirit that causes a given disease is never appealed to to eliminate it; Cherokee medicine men constantly put into practice a "policy of equilibrium" as did the European diplomats of pre-war days, and according to which every spirit has one or more antagonists that are appealed to in order to undo the work and to combat the nefarious activities of their opponents. The application of this theory is best studied in the formulas. A glance at the following table will also be found instructive in this regard. If a disease is held to be caused by worms, various kinds of birds that are known as worm eaters are called upon to wage the fight. If the disease is thought to be of an unusually tenacious and obstinate nature, such animals as beavers, rats, weasels, the dogged stubbornness of which is proverbial, are commanded to gnaw and tug at it until no trace of it is left. Should the most striking feature of the "important thing" be its cunning, its evasiveness, such a sly and wary individual as the otter is commandeered to effect the relief.

It has been deemed expedient to use some abbreviations in the following table, the meanings of which are given below. The analysis of the traits of each spirit has been effected under eight headings.

Under the first the name is given. These names have been put into alphabetical sequence, in order to make the list the more serviceable. The Cherokee names of the spirits will be found without difficulty by looking up the formula in which they occur. This formula is referred to in the last column, under the caption "Reference."

The second column mentions the color of the spirit. Abbreviations used:

W	White.	P	Purple.
Br	Brown.	R	Red.
Bl	Blue.	Y	Yellow.
B	Black.		

The third column lists the location, the place of residence, of the spirits. Abbreviations used:

H	On high.	E	In the east.
C	In the center.	N	In the north.
Ab	Above.	S	In the south.
W	In the west.		

The fourth column lists the diseases caused; the fifth, the ailments cured by the spirit. It is obvious that a spirit who is listed under the fourth caption will be found wanting under the fifth, and vice versa.

The sixth column lists eventual helpers or collaborators of the spirit and the seventh his eventual antagonists.

Only rarely is a spirit appealed to who is not sufficiently described in the formulas to make his identification possible; such is the case in the formulas Nos. 26 and 39.

Name	Color	Location	Causes	Cures	Collaborators	Antagonists	Reference
Apportioner		H. C.		When they urinate yellowish.			81
Do		H		"Scratching"			25
Do		H		do			31
Beaver	W.	Headwaters of stream		Tooth comes out			96
Do	Br.			Bad dreams	Brown beaver		92
B tåh (big)	W.	Night land		do	White beaver		92
Bittern	W.	H	Have them shaking				40
Do	Bl.	Ab		Worms	Old white One, White sandpiper, White mud snipe.	Two Red men	32
Do	Bl.	Ab		do	Little flint, Bl. flint, Bl. goose, W. swan, Bl. Sandpiper.		52
Buzzard	B.	Night land		Yellow of their navel	B. raven, Br. eagle		85
Blue catfish	P.	Middle of water		Purple insects (living in water).	Br. red horse		62
Chat	Y.		"Eaters"		Y. frog	R. kingfisher	6
Deer	B.			Frost-bitten feet	Wolf, fox, opossum		87
Dog	B.	H. W		When their food is changed	Br. dog, Bl. dog, little R. dogs.		77
Do	Bl.	H. N		do	Br. dog, B. dog, little R. dogs.		77
Do	Br.	H. E		do	Bl. dog, B. dog, little R. dogs		77
Dogs (two little)	R.	H. Ab		do	Br. dog, Bl. dog, B. dog		77
Dog	Br.	C		When they have been shot			69
Do	Y.	E		Simulators have made it bite it.		Purple man	12
Eagle	Br.	H		Yellow of their and	B. raven, B. buzzard		85
Do	B.	Tree tops		Pain in different places	Br. eagle, Bl. eagle, W. eagle		36
Do	Bl.	do		do	Br. eagle, B. eagle, W. eagle		36
Do	Br.	do		do	Bl. eagle, B. eagle, W. eagle		36
Do	W.	do		do	Br. eagle, Bl. eagle, B. eagle		36
Enemy			When they have drooping				9
Do			Drooping				35
Fawn	W.			Snake bite	W. lizard		47

Fire	Y.			Itching	Y. rabbit	80
Fox	P.			Frost-bitten feet	Wolf, deer, opossum	87
Human being					Bl. water snake	58
Do	B.		As though (they were really ill)		Ghost, speaker of incantations	67
		W		Important thing (they have it along both sides)	Two little R. Men	83
Long human being		Right here		To examine with the beads		15
Do		Right here		"Yellow" navel	Y. goldfinch, Y. pigeon, W. kingfisher, R. fish hawk	93
Do				To take oneself to the water with		
Fish	W.	E		Heats (fish)	Bat Bl. Man	48
Fish (small)	Y.	Where the great swamp is		The "Yellow"	Y. killdee bird	7
Fish hawk	Bl.	H		(Pains shifting) about	Bl. toter, W. mk, W. kingfisher	66
Do	R.			"Yellow" navel	Y. fish, Y. pigeon long human being, W. kingfisher	15
Flint	Bl.	The big swampy laurel thicket		Worms	Lile flint, Bl. goose, W. swan, Bl. bittern, Bl. sandpiper	52
Do		W		To make the girl jump down from them		76
Flint (little)		Where the little mountains are		Worm	Bl. flint, Bl. goose, W. swan, Bl. bittern, Bl. sandpiper	52
Flint		W		To make the boy jump down from them		76
Fog (little)				Blisters	Little frost	30
Forest dwellers		Forest				49
Frog	Bl.	Great lake. N		Diarrhea	Br. frog	56
Do	Y.			Throat	Y. chat	6
Do	Br.	Great lake. E		Throat	Bl. frog	56
Frost (little)		H		Blisters	Little fog	30
Ghost			As though (they were really ill)	Navel	Speaker of incantations, P. human being	58
Goldfinch	Y.	Where the great swampy thicket is		do	Y. pigeon	11
Do	Y.	do				14

46 BUREAU OF AMERICAN ETHNOLOGY [BULL. 99

Name	Color	Location	Causes	Cures	Collaborators	Antagonists	Reference
Goldfinch	Y.	Great swampy thicket		"Yellow" navel	Y. pigeon long, human being, W. kingfisher, R. fishhawk.		15
Goose	Bl.	Ab		Worms	Little flint, Bl. flint, W. swan, Bl. bittern, Bl. sandpiper.		52
Grandfather (maternal).				Make little ones jump down from them.			70
Grannie (old)				do			70
Heat			Breast ache			R. man	64
Do			Mouths sore			Little snow	61
Important thing	P.	Great lake	When their breast swells			Two little men	29
Insects	Br.		Insects (living in water)		Br. insects	P. Bl. catfish	62
Do	Y.		do		P. insects	Br. r. horse	62
Killdee bird	Y.	Great water. W. Where foam is piled.		"Yellow" navel			65
Do	Y.	Where the great swamp is		The "Yellow"	Y. small fish		7
Kingfisher	W.	Near edge of water		(Pains shifting) about bak.	Bl. otter, W. mink, Bl. fish hawk	Speaker of evil	66
Do	W.			Naval "yellow"	Y. goldfinch, Y. pigeon, long human being, R. fish hawk.		15
Do	R.	Tree top		"Eaters"			6
Leech	Bl.			Breast aches	R. mk, R. otter, terrible o tér, eel.		68
Lizard	W.			Snake bite	W. fawn	Heat	47
Man	R.	H		(Breast ache)		Heat	64
Man (great)	Bl.	N		Head	W. fish	Heats (fish)	48
Man (little)	Bl.	N		Blisters (sum)		Heat	57
Do	R.	Ab		Children when they constantly cry.		Heat	53
Do	Bl.			(It causes them to be broken).	Two R. men	Heat	79
Do	B.	W	The "yellow"			Killdee bird, Y. small fish	91
							7

Do	P.	W	Made it resemble		Y. dog	12
Do	B.	W	Sharp pains in breast		Two R. men, two Bl. men	24
Do	W.	E		To make the little ones jump down from		76
Do	B.	See: Bitch, big				
Do	R.	E		Chill	Bl. man, B. man, W. man	40
Do	Bl.	N		do	R. man, B. man, W. man	41
Do	W.	S		do	R. man, Bl. man, B. man	41
Bun (little)		Sunny side of mountain slope		When they attack him suddenly		42
Ma	R.	E		Their sides	Two little R. men, two little Bl. men	45
h fare worm			When it breaks them	They have it along both sides	B. human being	84
Men (to little)	R.				Important thing	67
Men	P.			Head	Men, R. men	8
Do	R.			Their head	Men, P. men	82
Men (two)	R.			do	R. men, P. men	82
Do	R.			It causes them to be broken	Bl. man	91
Men				Headache		2
Men (two little)		W		They have dreamt of snakes		20
Men (to)	Bl.	N		Breast	Two R. men	24
Do	R.	E		do	Two Bl. men	24
Men (two little)	R.	E		When their breast swells	Important thing	29
Men	R.			Purpose of scratching, using the snake tooth		31
Men (two)	R.	E		They have tirn shaking	Big bitch	40
Men (two little)	R.			Snake bi		5
Do	R.	E		Their sides	R. man, two little Bl. men	45
Do	Bl.	N		do	R. man, two little R. men	45
Mer	W.	H		When they have drooping		10
Mink	W.	Great water		Pains (shifting about)	Bl. otter Bl. fish hawk, W. kingfisher	66
Do	R.			Breast aches	R. ottter, terrible otter, weasel, Bl. leech	68
Moth			Boil		Speaker of evil	88
Mountain lion	R.			Frostbite		59

7548°—32——5.

Name	Color	Location	Causes	Cures	Collaborators	Antagonists	Reference
Mud snipe	W.			Worms	Old W. owl, W. bittern, W. sandpiper.		32
Old One	W.			do	W. sper, W. bittern, W. mud sipe.		32
Do	W.					Terrapin	54
Opossum				Frostbitten feet	Fox, wolf, deer		87
Otter (terrible)				Breast aches	R. ink, R. teer, weasel, Bl. edn.		68
Otter	R.			do	R. ink, male otter, weasel, Bl. deh.		68
Otter (fearful)	R.	Great lake in mid-heaven		Navel	R. otter		8
Otter	R.	Great lake		do	Fearful do		8
Do	Bl.	Great water		Pains (shifting) about	W. mink, Bl. fish hak, W. kingfisher.	Speaker of evil	66
Do	Br.	N		If they have (pains) appearing about in different places.			33
Do	R.	E., beyond great water		Pains appearing about in different places.	Br. otter, Bl. otter, B. otter		44
Do	Br.	E., this side of the great lake.		do	R. otter, Bl. otter, B. otter		44
Do	Bl.			do	R. otter, Br. otter, B. otter		44
Do	B.			do	R. otter, Br. otter, Bl. otter		44
Pain			Throat				56
Pigeon	Y.	Great swamp		"Yellow" navel	Y. goldfinch, long human being, W. kingfisher, R. fish hawk.	Br. frog, Bl. frog	15
Do	Y.	Where the great swamp thicket is.		Navel	Y. goldfinch		11
Do	Y.	do		do			14
Rabbit	Y.	Under the broom sedge		Itching	Y. fire		80
Do	Br.	do		Frost-bitten feet	Bl. rabbit, B. rabbit		60
Do	Bl.	do		do	Br. rabbit, B. rabbit		60
Do	B.			do	Br. rabbit, Bl. rabbit		60
Raccoon			Fainting spell				16

Raven	B.	W	"Yellow" navel	B. buzzard, Br. eel	85
Do	Bl.	Ab	Sick with sharp pains	B. raven, R. mn, W. raven	3
Do	R.	Ab	do	Bl. ravn, B. raven, W. raven	3
Do	B.	Ab	do	R. mn, Bl. raven, W. raven	3
Do	W.	Ab. toward the S	do	B. ravn, Bl. raven, R. raven	3
Do	Bl.	H. N	To scratch them	R. raven	28
Do	R.	E	do	Bl. raven	28
Red Horse	Br.	dle of water	Brown insects (living in water)	P. blue catfish	62
Sandpiper	Bl.	Ab	Worms	Little flint, Bl. flint, Bl. goose, W. swan, Bl. bittern	52
Do	W.		do	Old W. one, W. bittern, W. mud snipe	32
Snake	B.	In the path	Snake bite	Two little men	5
Do			do		47
Do			Dream of snakes	Two little men	20
Snow				Heat	61
Speaker			Pains (shifting) about	Bl. otter, W. mink, Bl. fish hawk, W. kingfisher	66
Do			As though (they were really ill)	Bl. water snake	58
Spirits			Headache	Ghost, P. human being	89
Squirrel	W.	E	Pain (tooth)		63
Sun			(Blisters) heat	Bl. man	53
Swan	W.	Ab	Worms	Little flint, Bl. flint, Bl. goose, Bl. bittern, Bl. sandpiper	52
Terrapin		Little mountain. W	Breast	Old W. one	54
Do			Breast ache		29
Water snake	Bl.	Head of the streamlet		Ghost, speaker of incantations, P. human being	58
Weasel			To make them vomit bile	R. mink, R. otter, terrible otter, Bl. leech	34
Do			Breast aches		68

Name	Color	Location	Causes	Cures	Collaborators	Antagonists	Reference
Whirlwind (little)		Small branches			Big whirlwind	Big chill	1
Whirlwind (big)		Stretched-out tree branches of the big mountains.			Little whirlwind	do	1
Wolf				Frost-bitten feet	Fox, deer, opossum		87
Do				Headache			13
Woman		E	Feverish condition				23
Woman (old)			Their food is changed			Br. dog, Bl. dog, B. dog, two little R. dogs.	77
Yellow	Br.		"Yellow"			B. raven, B. buzzard, Br. eagle.	85
Do			Navel			Y. goldfinch, Y. pigeon, long human being, W. kingfisher, R. fish hawk.	15

Color Symbolism—Sacred Numbers

There is but little to be added to what Mooney (SFC., p. 342) says about the Cherokee color symbolism, unless it be this, that the distinction is not always made quite so definitely as would appear from Mooney's tabulation. It is, of course, possible that 40 to 50 years ago the people's ideas were still less vague and fleeting on this score than they are now, but the formulas' evidence does not indicate that even quite a few generations back the color symbolism was much more definite. This will readily appear upon consulting the analytical table, Disease spirits (pp. 44–50).

A couple of facts are established beyond doubt—red and white can not possibly be associated with the west, nor with anything unsuccessful; black can only be associated with the west, and blue with the west or the north; neither of these latter colors can under any circumstances be symbolic of success. Apart from this it is not possible to be dogmatic: Red may be used in connection with the south as well as with the east and the zenith, whereas white is no more the inalienable color of the south than red is the one of the east.

Whether this phenomenon has any correlation with the defective power of discrimination between colors of the Cherokee I hesitate to say. However that may be, it is a fact that even the Cherokee who have known the joys of a Government school education do not score much better, according to our standards, when it comes to discriminating between colors than did the Seminoles of MacCauley.[25]

To gain some more definite data on this I asked the informant who was the least hopeless in this respect (W.) to pick out from a color chart, showing 95 colors in all possible shades and nuances, those "which the Cherokee know and have a name for." The following is the result of this experiment:

Usual name of color	Cherokee name	Translation
Canary	Daloˑ'nɪˑGɛˑⁿ'	Yellowish.
Pea green	ɪtsɛ'i ɪyʋ'ˑsti	Like green.
Maroon	ʋˑ'nɪGwu'tłi	(Like) clotted blood.
Myrtle green	ɪtsɛ'ˑi	Green.
Oxide red	wɔˑ'DɪGɛˑⁿ'	Like hematite.
Buff	ʋ'dzat'i' Dalɔˑ'ni	Extremely yellow.
Maroon	ʋ'lɔˑsöⁿ'st Gɪˑ'GaGɛˑⁿ'	Beyond red.
Ivory	Gaˑyɔˑ'tłi Dalɔ'nɪGɛˑⁿ'	Feebly yellowish.
Lead color	ʋ'wɛˑ'tɪGɛˑⁿ'	(Dusty gray.)
Holland blue	saˑ'kˑ'ɔˑ'nɪGɛˑⁿ'	Bluish.
Tuscan red	Gɪˑ'GaGɛˑⁿ'	Bloody (i. e., "red").
Light gray	Gaˑyɔˑ'tłi ʋnɛˑ'Göⁿ ɪˑyʋ''sti saˑ'-kˑ'ɔˑ'nɪGɛˑⁿ'.	Feebly white like bluish.
Dark blue	Dɛˑ'aᴰlʋGɛˑⁿ'	Purple.

---

[25] Cf. Fifth Ann. Rept. Bur. Ethn., p. 525.

As with the majority of the North American Indians, color symbolism is intimately associated with the rite of circumambulation, of which further mention is made (p. 63).

Sacred numbers.—Four is the fundamental sacred number in Cherokee ritual and seems always to have been. Although seven is also frequently met with, it would seem that this number has no claim to as venerable an age as has four.

Seven may have grown in importance by such outside and accidental influences as the 7-day week and by the reduction to seven of the number of Cherokee clans.

There are traces of the significance of another number, viz, 12 (and also of its multiple 24) as evidenced by—

The 12 runs in the ball game.

The 24 days' taboo of a woman after her delivery (this 24 days can be reduced to 12 by using an appropriate medicine).

The 24 different plants used against anisgı·na diseases.

The formulas and the notes appended to them simply teem with illustrations of the importance of the sacred numbers, especially of 4 and 7. I therefore considered it superfluous to multiply the examples here. Attention has been called on page 122 to the interesting process of rationalization by which a sanction of the use of the number 4 is alleged to be found in a (nonexisting) North Carolina State law.

Materia Medica

In this section I endeavor to give a summary description of Cherokee materia medica. I would have very much preferred to incorporate in this paper a detailed Cherokee "pharmacopœia," but the Cherokee botanical materia medica is so extensive as to command separate treatment. It is considered best to withhold this material, and to publish it, probably in the form of a paper on Cherokee ethnobotany, in the near future.

As a general and preliminary consideration it may be stated that although the Cherokee believe to a limited extent in the therapeutic value of certain matters of animal and vegetal origin, their materia medica consist primarily of botanical elements. It is happily ignorant of any human ingredients, the use of which is so conspicuous in the primitive medicine of numerous tribes, nay, in the folk medicine of so many civilized countries; even the belief in the curative power of saliva (cf. our "fasting spittle") is found wanting; stercoraria are never used, and as a whole, their materia medica is very much cleaner than, for instance, that of the rural communities of Europe.

The generic name for any particle possessing medicinal properties is nǫ·'wo·t'i', the meaning of which is literally "to treat with," but the emotional value of which had better be rendered "to cure with."

Although Cherokee possesses words to express such concepts as "herbs (in general)" or that refer to certain definite families of plants ("families" to be taken here from the Cherokee point of view, as "those that grow in the mountains," "those that are ever green," "those that grow near the river," etc.), these are but rarely heard, and as a rule the specific names of the plant are used.

Although some of the simples used are undeniably of officinal value, this would seem in the majority of cases to be a mere matter of accident, rather than evidence of conscious experiment or even of fortunate experience. The rule underlying the choice of a certain plant as an antidote against a given ailment is of a mythological and an occult rather than of a natural nature.

The chemical properties of the herbs, roots, barks, etc., used may in some cases happen to be appropriate to the result to be obtained, but that this is merely a matter of coincidence and chance is proved by many practices, a few of which are:

The outer appearance of the plants is of tremendous value in determining their efficacy against certain given diseases, as, "a thimbleberry shrub growing high up (in the cavity) of a hollow (tree)" is used against "painful remembrance of the dead" (see p. 233), because the medicine man said, "when we tear away the roots, deeply buried and stubbornly clinging to the tree, we will, when we drink a decoction of the roots, also be able to pull the remembrance out of our mind that makes us sick."

Plants that have a pungent smell are great favorites in many ailments. The Cherokee have no explanation to offer. The same fact, observed times without number elsewhere, has usually been explained, "the pungent smell puts the disease demon to rout."

Trees and plants, the sap and the juice of which are of a mucilaginous nature, as that of Da·'ᵘwədzɩ·'la (*Ulmus fulva* Michx., "slippery elm") are used in cases where something is to be ejected out of the body, as in childbirth—"the inside is to be made slippery."

Plants that show certain peculiar characteristics, identical to those shown by the disease, are used as antidote: the "milky discharge" common to certain maladies of the urinary system is thought to be efficaciously combated by administering plants that contain a milky juice; as if, by showing to the ailment that there is plenty of the milky, juicy matter at hand, there is hope of convincing it of the futility of staying.

Or the contrary may be the case: Plants and fruits that contain great quantities of juice must by no means be used by the patient when he is suffering from a complaint, one of the symptoms of which is the presence of a lot of "juicy matter," as in blisters, boils, etc.

Mooney in his notes has left us a typical illustration of this mode of reasoning; against rheumatism "the plants used in the preparation are all ferns . . . The doctor explained that the fronds of the young fern are coiled up, but unroll and straighten out as the plant grows; ergo, a decoction of ferns will give to the rheumatic patient the power to straighten out the contracted muscles of his limb."

Not only is there great importance attached to this symbolism of the outward appearance, also due regard is to be paid to the sacred numbers; in scores of cases the medicine is only effective if four or seven of the plants (usually of the same "family") are used, and thus it often happens that the actual officinal value of one plant is absolutely neutralized, to say the least, by three or five others.

Another consideration that is not of a nature to stimulate our faith in the efficacy of Cherokee materia medica is the tremendous importance laid on the use of certain plants that are not held to have any inherent curative properties but that are considered to possess remarkable power in virtue of a mysterious way of behavior—an uncommon way of growing, a quaint inclination of their branches, grotesque parasitical excrescences, or that show any other evidence of so-called freaks of nature, as the roots of an "inverted raspberry branch," i. e., the branch of a raspberry shrub that has come back to the soil and taken roots again (pl. 6, *a*) is often used in cases where the Cherokee consider the roots of the "parent plant" as being destitute of any curative properties. Or it will be specified that the roots used must be those of a plant that has only one stalk, even if the plant named has usually several stalks. Or again, it will be prescribed that the bark has to be stripped from a "crippled" tree, i. e., a tree that has been broken by some accident while it was still young, but that has nevertheless continued its growth in its "crippled" condition.

The curious, the unusual, that which is rare and difficult to find, have always and everywhere played a considerable rôle in the materia medica of all times and of all peoples, and we here find ourselves confronted with these same considerations.

The same trend of thought is no doubt also responsible for the remarkable properties ascribed to lightning-struck wood, especially of a tree that has continued to live after the accident, although this belief may have to be explained partly by an additional element, the respect for thunder and its "emissary," lightning. (Cf. Mooney, Myths, p. 422.) Also the mysterious power ascribed to the root that looks like an insect, "that has (a stalk) growing from its mouth" (see p. 30) is no doubt to be explained by this belief in the uncanny properties of the unusual.

Finally, such prescriptions as are made with regard to the time of collecting a plant (during a storm), or the mode of selecting a particular part of it (the bark on the "sunny side" of trees (pl. 6, *b*) the roots running out to the east, etc.), prove again to what an extent the materia medica of the tribe is influenced by mythological conceptions.

BUREAU OF AMERICAN ETHNOLOGY　　　　　　　　　　　　　　　　　　　BULLETIN 99　PLATE 6

a, THE ROOT OF AN INVERTED RASPBERRY BRANCH

b, BARK FROM THE SUNNY SIDE OF A TREE

c, HE THEN WRAPS THE SIMPLES IN HIS WHITE CLOTH

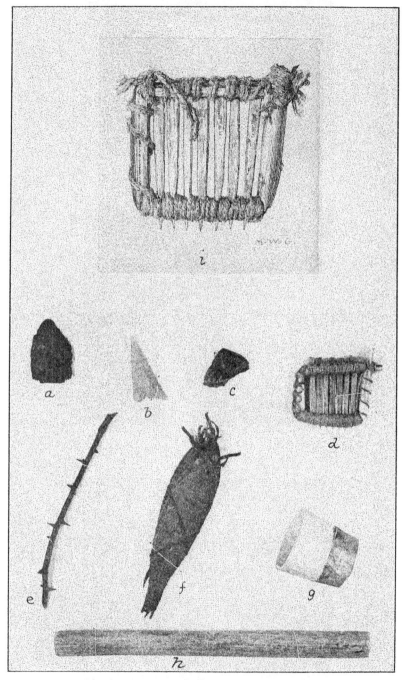

a–h, Surgical instruments. *i*, The "K'anv'ga" scarification instrument

Collection.—As a rule simples are never collected and kept ready for emergency in a dried or prepared state. Only those needed in case of childbirth are gathered during the summer, so as to be available in wintertime (see p. 91). It is just as rare to find medicine men endowed with enough foresight to lay out a garden of medicinal plants as did the European monks in the Middle Ages. (See p. 90.)

The rules for collecting the plants are as follows: As soon as the medicine man has made his diagnosis he tells the patient and the latter's household that he will have to go and collect simples. He usually does not tell him what kinds he will need, but if he is a greedy and a "businesslike" individual, he may tell them how great a trouble it will mean to him, how far he will have to walk through the pouring rain or the scorching sun; to how many places he may have to go in vain; how often he will probably have to retrace his steps and start the search all over again, etc.; all this to induce the people to give him a considerable fee. (See p. 95.) He invariably tells them what kind of cloth (what color, and dimensions) he will need to gather the plants in. This is given to him; if the people do not have the cloth available they have to borrow it from neighbors or buy it from the trader. Then the medicine man starts on his quest for the simples.

He usually knows where to find the specimens he needs—in the woods, along the mountain side, near the river, on marshy ground, etc. He also knows that some plants have a tendency to grow near certain trees, as oaks, in apple orchards, on moist, shady rocks, etc.

To gather certain plants, such as ginseng, he must first recite a prayer asking ʋnɛ·ˋtłanȫ́ˈⁱi (see p. 20) for permission to pluck them. Or he is not allowed to pluck them without dropping a bead in the earth where they stood.

Sometimes (in times gone by this was probably a strict and general rule) when his bundle is complete he takes it to the river and puts it in the water; if it floats it is a sign that all the prescriptions have been duly followed and that the eventual taboos have not been violated; it is a sign, moreover, that the bundle of medicine is all right, and that its use will be followed by the results that are expected of it.

He then wraps up the simples in the cloth (pl. 6, *c*) and returns to the cabin of the patient, where he hands the bundle to one of the household. The roots are unwrapped and the cloth is handed back to the medicine man as his fee. The medicine is then steeped, boiled, or prepared as the medicine man directs and in due course of time is administered to the patient, either by a relative or by the medicine man himself, again according to the prescription of the formula.

Preparation.—There are three major modes of preparing the medicine; it is either: (*a*) pounded and steeped in cold or warm water, (*b*) boiled, or (*c*) boiled down.

Pounding the roots and barks is still occasionally done with a stone, but a hammer is now more generally used. Leaves that are to be steeped are, prior to being put into the infusion vessel, crushed or crumpled in the hand. The different ingredients that are to be boiled or steeped are usually tied together in a bundle, by means of a strip of hickory bark.

"Boiling down" is a mode of preparing the medicine which is prescribed with many formulas. It consists in boiling the medicine and drinking part of it the first day, boiling the same decoction over again and drinking another part of it the second day, and so on, usually, for four consecutive days. The fourth day the decoction is often a thick treaclish sirup. Sometimes, however, water from the river is added every day to the decoction.

Occasionally poultices are made of large leaves of mullein and held by the hand against the affected part for a few minutes.

Black pine wax (a·tsaʹ) is used, and also the use of bear grease (yɔ·ʹnŏⁿ Gɔ.iʹ) and eel oil (tŏ·ⁿtɛ·ʹGa Gɔ.iʹ) is occasionally met with.

In some cases, when the decoction is so bitter as to be very disagreeable to swallow, it is sweetened by adding honey or the pods of honey locust to it. This procedure is especially frequent when the decoction is to be administered to children. The custom of adding whisky to certain decoctions has been taken over from the white mountaineers.

Mode of administering.—This is as a rule fairly simple. Usually a member of the patient's household gives him the medicine to drink; in a few cases it is specified that an aboriginal gourd dipper be used for this purpose. These dippers are not used so extensively as household utensils now as they used to be, metal spoons and ladles having gradually replaced them, but it is an often observed fact that in primitive and folk medicine, as in ritual, objects are retained that have passed out of existence as everyday utensils hundreds of years ago. (See p. 58.)

In some cases, however (all this is invariably and minutely laid down in the prescriptions appended to the formulas, p. 158), the medicine has to be administered by the medicine man himself. In doing this he observes certain ceremonies, as standing with his back toward the east, so that the patient opposite him faces the "sun land," lifting the dipper containing the medicine high up, and bringing it down in a spiral or swooping movement, imitating by so doing certain birds of prey that may have been mentioned in the formulas he has recited prior to giving the patient his medicine to drink.

Not the slightest attention is paid to dosing the patient nor, it is superfluous to state, to his idiosyncrasy. If any question is asked, as to the amount of the decoction or of the infusion to be taken, the answer is invariably "Just as much as he can hold." This I found upon observation is very elastic and fluctuating from one individual to another; it may mean anything from a minimum of 2 to a maximum of 6 to 7 liters a day. This appalling amount of liquid by itself is often sufficient to account for the emetic results the Cherokee obtain by the use of simples that are devoid of emetic properties.

A few words remain to be said about the animal and mineral materia medica in use in Cherokee therapeutics.

Against rheumatism and stiffness in the joints eel oil (tö·ⁿtɛ·'Ga Gɔ.i') is used. The oil is fried out of the animal in a frying pan. The eel owes the honor of thus being admitted into the Cherokee pharmacopœia to its considerable suppleness and litheness.

Bear grease (yɔ·'nö'ⁿ Gɔ.i'), known to most of the North American Indian tribes and extensively used in the Southeast, is likewise known to the Cherokee. The rapidly progressing extinction of the bear in the Great Smokies will, however, soon account for the untimely end of this popular article.

A prescription against a disease that can only be identified as tuberculosis specifies among other ingredients the brains of an otter, mixed with "rock treacle," i. e., the moisture oozing out of the natural fissures of a mossy rock.

Stones, especially worked and fashioned arrowheads, may be added to the water in which roots and stems are put to boil, but they owe their therapeutic value chiefly to the belief that "they will cut the disease to pieces" in the patient's body. The stones and flints are, of course, removed before the decoction is drunk.

Water enters into practically every remedy, in so far as it is used to boil the other ingredients in. It usually has to be dipped out of the river, to where, in some cases, it has to be taken back after use. (See p. 68.) There are no specific instructions as to whether the water has to be dipped "with the stream" or "against the stream" as is so frequent in primitive medicine. One instance has come to my knowledge where the water has to be taken from a cataract.

The use of snow water and of ice is common in treating cases of frostbite.

"Stumpwater" is but rarely referred to, and its use, together with the belief in its marvelous properties, may have been borrowed from the whites.

Disposing of used ingredients.—As a rule proper care is taken to dispose of the materia medica after its use; it is never carelessly thrown away, but is usually kept on outside shelves, with at least two of which every cabin is provided. It is quite likely that formerly there was a proper ceremony to dispose of these decocted barks and herbs, but although this has been lost, enough of the custom is remembered to prevent the used ingredients from being thrown away as refuse. A few formulas have directions appended to them, which direct that the medicine, after its use, has to be "stored in a dry place," or has to be placed in a rock fissure with an appropriate formula.

Paraphernalia Used in the Treatment

The list of paraphernalia used by the Cherokee medicine man is not extensive; it may be conveniently classed under three headings:

(1) Objects used in divinatory ceremonies. These will be amply described when the formulas relating to divination are published.

(2) The instruments used in surgical or pseudosurgical operations; a description of these will be found under the caption of surgery (p. 68).

(3) Finally there are the objects used in treating disease. These include blowing tube, gourd dipper, terrapin shell, persimmon stamper, beads, rattle.

The blowing tube (pl. 7, *h*) is a portion of the stem of a'maɒi'ʻtɔ.ʻtiʻ v'ʻtʻanô", *Eupatorium purpureum* L., joe-pye-weed, trumpet weed. Usually it is about 20–25 centimeters long, with an outside diameter of about 15 millimeters and an inside diameter of 10–12 millimeters.

It is used to blow or spray the medicine, which the medicine man has previously sipped from a dipper, over the patient's temples, the crown of his head, his breast, or whatever part of his body is "under treatment."

Only in one case did I find a much longer blowing tube of the same provenance used. It measures 50–60 centimeters and is the means by which a decoction has to be sprayed on the body of a parturient woman; the medicine man, while doing this, for propriety's sake stands 3 or 4 yards behind the semireclined woman (see p. 125) and blows the medicine in a jet over her head. This procedure makes it imperative that the blowing reed be of the length described so as to be the better able to direct the jet of medicine.

There is a faint indication that until about 40 years ago occasionally a grass stalk was used to blow a decoction of plants into the urethra, but nothing more definite could be learned about the procedure, which is now completely discontinued and almost forgotten, even by the oldest of the medicine men.

Although gourd dippers are still used to some extent in the Cherokee household they tend to disappear and to be replaced by more modern utensils introduced by the whites, metal spoons, ladles, etc.

For use in medicine, however, it is always implicitly understood and often explicitly stated that the dipper used to administer the medicine must be the good old aboriginal gourd dipper Gaʻᴅluneʻ-Gwôⁿ; so much so that this object is gradually becoming, from a common kitchen utensil which it still wasʻone or two generations ago, a true component of the medicine man's paraphernalia.

This tendency of less civilized communities to cling not only to their archaic practices but also to retain certain material objects associated with them, is very frequent and common, and parallels of it could be cited by the dozen. To give a couple of instances only:

In the folk medicine of many rural communities of western Europe it is often specified that the medicine be prepared, steeped, or boiled in an earthen vessel; this in spite of the fact that the use of earthen vessels for everyday purposes was dropped centuries ago.[26]

Some of the Morocco Mohammedans who have known and used for centuries metal daggers and knives that are the pride of museum collections still use a stone knife for such a delicate, but ritual and archaic operation as circumcision.[27]

A consideration of the same order as the one commented upon under gourd dippers is no doubt partly responsible for the use of a terrapin shell (tū'ksi v'ya'ska) to keep the medicine in. (Cf. Mooney, SFC., p. 345.)

The persimmon-wood stamper is an object that has fallen into complete desuetude. It was used in certain manipulations closely related to, if not identical with, massage. Mooney, as appears from his notes, found it mentioned during his first visit, but even then the object was no longer in actual use; after repeated vain efforts he was able to locate a man who was still able to nake a specimen, which now forms part of the collections of the Division of Medicine, United States National Museum, Washington, D. C.

If I had not found the reference to this object in Mooney's notes I would not have suspected that it was ever in use, as only a couple of the oldest medicine men could painstakingly recall it—its name is completely lost—but no one could be found who was able to carve a specimen. Neither of the two medicine men who vaguely remembered its having been in use could describe the procedure; they could not tell me whether it was used to rub, to stamp, or to press the sore spot.

The beads (aDɛ·'lōⁿ) belong, properly speaking, not so much to the medicine man's paraphernalia as to those of the divinator. Since, however, these two arts are very often pursued by one and the same individual, and especially since the divination with the beads is so often inextricably fused with a curing procedure, they can not very well be left outside of this enumeration.

Finally the rattle calls for a few comments in this connection. Nowadays there is no medicine man, as far as I know, who still uses the rattle (i. e., the gourd rattle, Gandzɛ'ti) when singing medicine songs; its use is entirely restricted to the accompanying of dance songs. The terrapin-shell rattles were apparently never used in medicine.

There are some indications, however, that would lead us to believe that the gourd rattle must once have been extensively used in medicine and must once have been practically the emblem of the medicine man's profession.

---

[26] "Troost der Armen" Gent (n. d.), p. 9.

[27] Rohlfs, "Mein erster Aufenthalt in Marokko," ap. von Hovorka and Kronfeld, vol. II, p. 492.

Curing Methods

As we have seen in our paragraph on materia medica, the Cherokee do not only attach officinal value to the intrinsic properties of the simples used, but they expect as much, if not more, curing power from observing and complying with sundry regulations when selecting, picking, preparing, and administering them.

We are again faced with conceptions of the same order, when it comes to the actual use of the plants or of the other materia medica—not only the object used is of importance, but the method of using it is of great consequence. A short description of these modes and methods will form the object of the following paragraphs.

Whatever be the method used, the act of treating a patient is usually referred to as Dɩ`Galô$^{n}$'ᶜ wɩsta`Nːti` "to work for him" (DaGɩlô`^{n}ᶜ-wɩsta`nɛ́a' "I work for him"). This expression is also frequently used when referring to "examining with the beads" or to the nefarious machinations of an enemy. It is also used by the people in everyday language to render "to work for (someone)," i. e., to do manual labor, and only when it is used in the medical jargon does it have this restricted meaning of "treating a patient."

It will be superfluous to state that the enumeration as well as the description of the different methods as they appear in the following pages are the result of patient observation and of information from many different sources, both oral and as written in the sundry manuscripts; not one Cherokee medicine man realizes that his science can boast of such a wealth of curing methods.

Some of the methods have no specific name in Cherokee. The names of those that do have one will be found in the relevant formulas.

Administering the medicine.—A given disease may be cured by merely administering the decoction or the infusion of the medicine prescribed. This procedure has been amply described on page 56 and does not here call for any further comment.

Often the root or the bark of the simple prescribed is chewed by the patient, instead of being drunk by him in a decoction or in an infusion.

Blowing the medicine.—In certain diseases, even if the ailment is held to be of an internal order, the medicine is not taken internally at all, but is sprayed over the patient, either over the whole of his body or only over parts of it (e. g., over his head, his breast, etc.). This is usually done by means of the blowing tube (p. 58). The medicine man takes a long draught of medicine, without swallowing it, and then blows it with one continued jet over the patient.

Often, instead of blowing the medicine over the patient the medicine man merely *blows his breath.* This may be done again by means of the blowing tube, but this instrument is often dispensed with. It could not be ascertained whether the use of the blowing tube **is of** any particular ritualistic meaning. The general feeling among the medicine men is that the blowing tube is used so as to be better able to direct the liquid or the air. If one feels that this effect is attained without the aid of the tube the latter is not used.

As is customary when he is having medicine administered to him, the patient should face the east when the liquid or the medicine man's breath is being blown over him.

Again, instead of being blown over the patient the medicine may be *sprinkled* over him; a small pine branch is used for this purpose.

In a few cases the cure is expected from an *inunction* with the liquid of the parts affected. This procedure is especially frequently associated with the "scratching" of the patient. (See p. 68.)

Another method which can boast of all but intertribal reputation is to spray or pour the decoction on previously heated stones and to *expose the patient to the vapors* thus obtained.

A practice which is very much related to the one just mentioned is *the sweat bath,* hardly less popular with the majority of the North American aborigines. The difference between the sweat bath and the vapor bath described seems to be that in the latter the curing power is expected from the ingredients of the decoction sprinkled on the stones, whereas in the sweat bath the object is primarily to cause the patient to profusely perspire.

This custom is another one that has been discontinued, and it would not be possible now to obtain such a vivid description of it as Mooney has left us in his notes: "The operation was formerly performed in the â′sĭ or 'hothouse,' a small low hut, intended for sleeping purposes, in which a fire was always kept burning. It has but one small door, which was closed during the operation, in order to confine the steam. The patient divested himself of all clothing, and entered the â′sĭ, when the doctor poured the liquid over the heated stones already placed inside, then retired and closed the door, leaving the patient to remain inside until in a profuse perspiration from the steam which filled the hothouse. The door was then opened and the man came out, naked as he was, and plunged into the neighboring stream. The sweat bath, with the accompanying cold plunge bath, was a favorite part of Indian medical practice as far north as Alaska, so much so that it was even adopted in cases of smallpox epidemics, when it almost invariably resulted fatally. The East Cherokee lost 300 souls in consequence of pursuing this course of treatment for smallpox in 1865. The sweat bath is still in use among them,[28] but as the â′sĭ is no longer built, the patient is steamed in his own house, and afterwards plunges into the nearest stream, or is placed in the open doorway and drenched with cold water over his naked body."

---

[28] This was written by Mooney about 40 years ago.

Massage plays a considerable part in Cherokee curing methods and is frequently mentioned. Although they use it in some cases where it is unquestionably of a nature to bring relief, as in painful menstruation, spraining, etc., it is resorted to in many other cases—as a rule as soon as there is evidence of any kind of swelling, whether of the stomach or of the knee—where it lacks the least degree of efficacy. The underlying principle is invariably that the swelling is the material evidence of an immaterial agent (the "important thing," the disease) and that this can be eliminated, expelled, ejected out of the affected part of the body by pressing and rubbing.

Previous to starting the massaging, the medicine man always warms his hands near some live coals taken by his assistant—who is usually a member of the patient's household—from the hearth, and that are put down near the medicine man on a shovel, on the lid of a pot, a flat pan, or some other such receptacle. The medicine man warms his hands while he recites the first part of the formula, and then rubs the affected part, eventually under the clothes of the sufferer. The massage is done by the whole right hand, the palm effecting most of the pressure, and a circle of 6–7 centimeters from the center being described. Starting from the right, he moves upward, comes down to the left, continuing the motion for a few minutes, from 2 to 3 or 6 to 7 times, as he sees fit.

He then warms his hands again, reciting meanwhile the second part of the formula, and the whole treatment is continued until the (usually) four parts of the formula have been recited and followed by the rubbing.

Mooney, SFC., p. 335, has drawn attention to the rubbing for treating snake bites. In this case the "operator is told to rub in a direction contrary to that in which the snake coils itself, because 'this is just the same as uncoiling it'."

A practice that was still faintly remembered when Mooney visited the tribe is the massage by means of a stamper made of the wood of persimmon. (See p. 59.)

I have been surprised to find that the Cherokee all but ignore the elsewhere so popular and common method of *transferring disease* to other creatures—to fellow human beings, dead or alive, to animals, to trees even, and to rocks, rivers, etc.

Of the two only instances of this kind which I found—and I am pretty sure that no other varieties exist—one has very probably been borrowed from the whites, if not in its actual form, at least in certain of its aspects. I am referring to the following practice on which only one informant (W.) could give me full particulars: A howling dog forebodes illness or death; the only way to avoid its prophecy being fulfilled is to command it to die itself, instead of the person, or the member of the household who is the object of its evil warning. (See p. 37.)

The claim to aboriginality of the other instance, however, rests on a sound and solid basis: In some Dalɔ·'ni diseases (see p. 63) the sufferer goes to the river and there vomits. The formula recited on this occasion sends the illness, along with the vomit, floating down the river, to "the settlements where (other) people live," and transfers the ailment to them (see p. 23).

This practice is so reminiscent of other Cherokee incantation ceremonies that there is no doubt about its being indigenous.

Vomiting into the river is also very common with merely the object in mind to get rid of the disease, without the intention being explicitly present of transferring it to the people living in other settlements along the river. Whether this intention ever implicitly belonged to this practice it is not now possible to ascertain.

A method that is again very frequently met with in various countries and among different tribes is one based on the belief that the ailment can be banished, the *pain diminished*, by symbolic means, as by gradually diminishing the number of ingredients in a decoction, by calling the disease by a series of names or objects of diminishing size, etc. (Compare German "abzählen.")

This practice is found in the Cherokee custom of curing certain ailments by drinking medicine all day long the first day, until noon the second day, until about 10 a. m. the third day, and until breakfast the fourth day.

Scratching, sucking, and *burying* the disease are methods that are being discussed with reference to the "chirurgical" methods of curing. (See p. 68.)

If none of the multifarious methods described above brings any relief to the patient, and if it is deemed that no chances for his recovery exist, a last effort is made: The patient, called, let us say, Climbing Bear, is abandoned to the disease, but a *new name* is bestowed upon the sufferer; henceforth, he will be called, let us say, Cutting Ax; and, while the disease spirit may temporarily be deluded and gloat over his success in bringing Climbing Bear to his doom, a new series of treatments is inaugurated by the concerted action of the medicine man and the patient's relatives to save Cutting Ax. A man who owes his name, Alick, to such a procedure is now living on the reservation, not far from Big Cove. (See the description of the event by W., p. 67.)

A mode of curing is to be mentioned finally which may not effect a cure by its sole power, yet is found associated so often with other curing methods that it should not be passed over in silence; I mean the *circumambulation,* so prominent in primitive rites in general, and in American Indian ceremonialism particularly.

In many cases, before administering the medicine, the medicine man circumambulates the patient. The rite is, moreover, practiced as a preventive measure against the machinations of witches (see p. 13), and, with a view to facilitating delivery, at the time of parturition (see p. 123).

The dextral circuit (sunwise) seems to be the most common and original one; the sinistral circuit is, however, not unknown, and may have its origin in the symbolical reversion of that which is customary. (Compare Germ. "Rückzauber.")

To close this survey, which to the best of my knowledge is complete, it may be well to state that all of these methods are only practiced by the medicine men; all a layman may venture to do is to give a patient his medicine to drink, or to give him an additional inunction of his decoction, but all this only under the explicit direction of the worthy practitioner. (See p. 56.)

Prescriptions as to Diet, Taboos, Etc.

As will be seen in the chapter dealing with the formulas (p. 144), almost every one of these is, or should be, accompanied by an often quite extensive explanation, listing the symptoms of the ailment against which the formula should be used, its cause, the simples to be gathered, with their mode of preparation, and finally the restrictions to be observed. These restrictions, or taboos, are the object of the following lines.

Roughly speaking they may be divided into two classes: Those referring to the diet of the patient; those referring to the care of the patient and to his behavior.

As to the former, ample illustrations will be found of them in almost every formula or prescription, and I merely want to draw attention to them here, at the same time contributing a few notes toward making this custom more intelligible.

For here again, as with almost every phase in the Cherokee treatment of disease, we are dealing with entities of a purely mythological nature. Every observant reader when looking over the formulas will be struck with the so often repeated prohibition of hot food and salt. The reason for this, as for many of these restrictions, can not be given, not even by the most erudite of the Cherokee medicine men. Mr. Mooney repeatedly in his notes expresses the opinion that salt and hot food are tabooed because they have been introduced by the whites, and are therefore thought to interfere with the action of the Indian medicine. I do not quite share this opinion. Even if the use of mineral salt had not spread among the Cherokee to the same extent as it did after the advent of the whites, yet they did know lye, and lye is prohibited by the medicine men in every case where salt is forbidden.

I noticed, furthermore, that now that the food introduced by the white people, such as canned goods, coffee, sugar, etc., is easily obtainable by the Cherokee, they never abstain from these articles when under medical treatment.

It seems to me that the reason for these restrictions are to be sought in another direction: The smarting of salt in open wounds and the scalding effect of hot food have probably given the people the notion that these two articles of diet are of a pain-aggravating nature.

One disease, Gɩ·'Gö^n a`naldzi`skwskǫ·'.i ("when they spit blood '), is actually caused by "eating too much salt," Del. told me.

It also struck me that these two restrictions always most rigorously apply in cases of hemorrhage (wounds, menstruation, partus, etc.) or when there are smarting pains, even if these be internal, as in gonorrhea, pneumonia, tuberculosis, etc.

Another significant fact that I wish to present to substantiate the view here defended is that a prescription of Ms. III, the object of which is to cure a skin eruption, prescribes Gɔ.ɩNtɔ^n a·ma' v`tlɔtsö'ti nɩ`Gɛsǫ·'na ("and also grease with which (however) no salt has been mixed").

Roth, pages 348, 352, mentions two facts which of course could not prove my point of view, but which are nevertheless interesting parallels. "The Piache's (medicine man's) first prescription is to impose a general fast on the patient and his kinsfolk; the majority of the Piaches demand that no one belonging to the house should eat anything hot, anything cooked, or peppers" (p. 352).

Apart from salt and hot food, which are prohibited in the greater majority of diseases, there are some other taboos that are to be observed when suffering from some particular ailments.

So will the patient under treatment for rheumatism have to abstain from eating squirrel or rabbit meat, because of the hunchback position that is so characteristic of these animals; the one suffering from diarrhea should not eat fish or chicken, because the feces of these animals would seem to indicate that they are chronically afflicted with this very disease; the one visited with watery blisters should abstain from all juicy fruit and vegetables, etc.

Some of the taboos are to be observed during the course of the treatment only (usually four days), others "for a very long time," or "as long as possible," which may mean anything from a month to a year; others again for lifetime.

In very rare cases, not only the patient, but also the medicine man treating him, as well as the assistant of the latter, who is usually a member of the patient's household, have to abstain from certain articles; e. g., when treating anyone who has been wounded by a bullet or an arrow, the medicine man should not chew tobacco for four days; this same taboo has to be observed by the patient.

Moreover, "in all cases of sickness, the doctor abstains from all food until he is done treating the patient for the day. This usually means until about noon, but in serious cases the doctor sometimes fasts until nearly sundown. He must not eat in the house of the patient but may eat in the yard outside." (Mooney, Notes.) There is a marked tendency nowadays to abolish this custom stipulating that the treating medicine man should also observe the taboos.

Fasting is a restriction that is rather frequently imposed upon the patients, but we should have no misgivings. The proof that no sanitary consideration is to blame is obvious; the patient conscientiously fasts until sunset, or in some cases until noon, when he is allowed to gorge himself with food as if he were the most robust and healthy individual on earth.

With regard to the second group of taboos, those referring to the care of the patient and to his behavior, the most important one is the segregation of the patient. There is nothing to be added to the excellent account given of this custom by Mooney, SFC., pages 330–332. It is still alive and thriving. It more than once happened to me when I went to call on a sick member of the tribe that I was only admitted after having sustained a rigorous cross-examination as to the "conditio physiologica uxoris mcae," etc. (See p. 35.)

In some cases (documentary evidence of all this will be found in the formulas themselves) there are various injunctions to be observed such as the following:

If the disease is caused by birds, all feathers are to be removed from the cabin. (Feathers and quills are usually kept in the house to feather the arrows.)

Nor should the children made ill by the birds be taken outside, lest the shadow of a bird, flying overhead, might fall on it and aggravate the ailment.

In diseases associated with the buffalo no spoon or comb made of buffalo horn, nor a hide of that animal, was to be touched. This taboo has been gleaned from a very old prescription, the age of which is shown by its contents; the buffalo has been extinct in the Cherokee country so long that the present Cherokee do not even remember what the animal looks like.

The numerous injunctions and restrictions to be observed by a pregnant woman have been listed together. (See p. 120.)

In some diseases, especially in those of the urinary passages, sexual intercourse is prohibited. It is possible that a long time ago the medicine man himself had to observe injunctions of continence as long as he had a patient of this kind under treatment, but I have not been able to gather definite information on this score.

Attention should be drawn, finally, to the fact that the taboo may depend on the number of simples used, as in Formula No. 55, or again, on the mode of collecting them. In Ms. II a formula occurs in which the medicine man, when he goes out to gather the plants needed, states in an appropriate formula how long a period of restrictions he is going to prescribe to his patient.

A Typical Curing Procedure

We have now analyzed the different and multifarious elements and concepts which we find entangled in Cherokee ideas on disease, its causes, and its treatment. Needless to say, neither the native patient nor the medicine man ever look at the problem in such a scrutinizing and analytical way. We will therefore now present a synthetic picture of the whole as it is presented to the mind of the native. The following lines contain the account of a case of illness and of the treatment and curing of the same. The account was given me quite spontaneously and unsolicited by one (W.) who was an interested party. Apart from correcting the more flagrant grammatical lapses in it I have not changed it in any way and will give in footnotes what little supplementary information may be necessary to make it intelligible.

"Many years ago[29] my cousin, Charlie, Je.'s[30] son, was very ill; he was very poorly; he was just about to die.[31] My mother[32] was very sorry for her daughter and for her grandson, and she sent after Doctor Mink,[33] asking him to come down to see what he could do. An evening, soon after, Doctor Mink came to our house and said he would spend the night.[34] But my mother was anxious to know something about her grandson's illness and prepared the cloth and the beads.[35] Mink examined with the beads, but he found that nothing could be done. My mother cried and was sorry because of her grandson; she got some more white cloth and two more white beads, and asked the medicine man to try again. He did, but again he said the boy could not recover. And again my mother put some more cloth and two more beads down, but still there was no hope. A fourth time she got cloth and beads and the medicine man examined once more; but again he found that the boy was very poor, and that he would have to die.

"I then proposed to go over the mountain to where the sick boy lived, and to go and see him anyway. We all went, and when we got there we found the boy unconscious.

---

[29] Thirteen years ago (information given November, 1926).
[30] W.'s half-sister; cf. pp. 9, 116 and pl. 12, a.
[31] He was ill with Gŏ·'ⁿwɑni'Gιstŏ·ⁿ'.i, cf. p. 120.
[32] Ayo., herself a reputed medicine woman during her lifetime. (Cf. p. 9.)
[33] Alias Wil., son of Gad. (cf. p. 9); two medicine men (now both deceased) from whom James Mooney obtained the Mss. II and III.
[34] Cf. p. 97.
[35] Cf. p. 132.

"I asked the doctor if he would come to the river with me; we took a dipper [36] which we filled with water, and when we got back to the house, we sprinkled some of it on the boy's face; I then went back to the river and poured the rest of the contents of the dipper away exactly where we dipped the water from. When I came back, I asked Doctor Mink if he would examine with the beads again to see if the boy could be cured: I prepared cloth and the beads [37] and I went with Mink to the edge of the river. He examined with the beads, but found there was no hope. I put down some more cloth and beads, but again the doctor found there was no help. I then suggested to change the boy's name. Charlie could die, but we would give him a new name; we would call him Alick.[38] Mink then again examined with the beads, and he found that Alick was going to get better. They tried a fourth time, and again there was hope. I then got Mink to examine to see if he would be able to cure him; but he found he couldn't. Then he examined for another medicine man, and then for another, and another, and finally he found that Og.[39] could cure him. We then sent for Og. to cure him. In the sick boy's house nobody was allowed to sleep that night.[40] Doctor Mink kept busy about the fire, working against the witches.

"Og. came down every morning and every night; he did the curing, and Doctor Mink did the examining with the beads. Four days afterwards I went down to the river once more with Doctor Mink, and we found that in seven days Alick would be about, hunting. And so it was."

Surgery

As compared with the rest of their medical practice, surgery is but scantily represented in Cherokee curing methods. However, what little there is, is of sufficient interest and importance to be entitled to a short synthetic description.

As the first in importance the different methods of scarification deserve to be mentioned. Scarification is still practiced extensively, and I may add intensively, not merely by the medicine men but also by the uninitiated. The ball players are still subjected to it, as has been minutely described by Mooney.[41] The "scratching" of the ball players is usually practiced by means of the k'anv·'ɢa instru-

---

[36] Cf. p. 58.

[37] W. here plays the rôle of medicine man's assistant as his mother did in the previous ceremony (cf. p. 62).

[38] I. e., Alexander.

[39] Cf. p. 112; pl. 9, *a*.

[40] Cf. p. 31.

[41] "The Cherokee Ball Play," Amer. Anthrop., III (1890), pp. 105 seq.; cf. also Culin, "Games of the North American Indians," Twenty-fourth Ann. Rept. Bur. Amer. Ethn., 1907, pp. 575–587.

ment. This is a comblike device and is quite a remarkable specimen of primitive inventive spirit. (Pl. 7, *d, i.*)

It is made of seven splinters of bone of a turkey leg, set into a frame of a turkey quill; the quill is folded over in four parts of pretty equal dimensions, so as to form a rectangular frame 5 centimeters by 4 centimeters; where the two extremities meet they are tied together, and the seven bone splinters (about 5 cm. long and 3 mm. broad at the top; sharpened to a keen point at the bottom) are then stuck through the upper part of the quill frame, with intervals of not more than 1 or 2 millimeters; they are then also stuck through the bottom part of the frame, 1 or 2 millimeters of their cutting extremity piercing the frame at the bottom. With these seven sharp points the scratches are inflicted; and the ingenious way in which they are mounted prevents them from piercing so deep into the flesh as to inflict serious wounds.

Although only the ball players are now being scratched by this instrument there are good reasons to believe that formerly it was also used in the treatment of certain ailments, where now such objects as flint arrowheads, briars, and laurel leaves (see infra) are used.

Moreover, there seems to be a tendency nowadays for scarification to develop from a mythico-surgical operation as Mooney still found it 40 years ago in a rite of a purely symbolic nature. In many instances I observed that not only no "gashes" were inflicted, but that not even a particle of blood was drawn during the operation.

Dı'Dö·ⁿlɛ'ski (rheumatism; cf. p. 292) and ailments which from a Cherokee point of view are related to this disease, are universally treated by this "scratching" method. The scarifying is here done by means of a flint arrowhead (Daw̥ı'skŭla`), preferably of the black variety. Old medicine men assert that this is the only variety (pl. 7, *a*) that should be used, but as this kind of arrowhead is getting scarce there is a tendency to use any other kind (pl. 7, *b*). A still more curious shifting to a new position is shown in the custom which is rapidly gaining ground and according to which scratching is simply neglected, but an unworked piece of flint (also called Daw̥ı'skŭla`, pl. 7, *c*) is merely held against the sore joint, the formula for scratching being recited at the same time.

Schematically this evolution could be represented as follows:

Black flint arrowhead to scratch with

Any arrowhead to *scratch* with.   Any piece of *black flint* held against aching spot

I did not find that any articles imported by the whites, such as knives, nails, glass, etc., were in use as scratching instruments.

All kinds of briars, especially those of blackberry shrubs, nuˑGɔ̆′tlɔ̆ⁿ (pl. 7, *e*), are also used to slightly scarify the skin. By what poor means I had at my disposal I used to treat Jud. (see p. 114; pl. 10, *a*) for rheumatism in his knee. Whenever I went to see him in his cabin he stubbornly refused to be rubbed with the embrocation I used, before he had gone out, cut a thorny branch off some shrub, and scratched his knee. When he came to my quarters to be rubbed he never forgot to bring his briars!

A few leaves of the laurel (*Kalmia latifolia* L.) are also used for the same purpose. Ten or twelve leaves (originally probably seven) are plucked, kept together between thumb and forefinger (pl. 7, *f*), and a few strokes with the bristly edges are given over the skin. I was surprised to find, when I had this scarification practiced on me as an experiment, that the marks were visible and the irritation of the skin sensible for over a week.

Finally there is to be mentioned the tooth of the rattlesnake as a scarifying instrument. When used for the preparation of the members of the ball-game team it was customary until 50 years or so ago to use two of these teeth, tied together. Why this was done, and how the instrument was made, informants were unable to tell me. The scratching with one tooth, as practiced in the treatment of disease, is described by Mooney in his notes as follows: "Beginning with the right hand (the medicine man) draws the tooth from the end of the first finger [42] along the back of the hand, up the arm, across the breast, and down the left leg and foot, making one long gash. He then repeats the operation in the same way, beginning with the left hand and ending with the right foot. Next he begins at the end of the right thumb, drawing the tooth up along the arm, around the back of the neck to the left shoulder, and down again in front along the left leg and foot. Then he reverses the operation, beginning with the left thumb and ending with the right foot. He then scratches the skin at random over the affected part, or over the limbs and the body according to the nature of the sickness. . . . These scratches are not deep, being intended not to draw blood but to enable the liquid application to take a better hold upon the skin. In scratching small children, the . . . (medicine man) uses the back of the tooth." In some cases children are scratched over the tongue.

This mode of scarification seems to have died out, however; not a single instance of it came to my attention during my stay; nor was there one medicine man of the many I knew having such an instrument in his possession.

As for the scarification with such objects as flint arrowheads, briars, laurel leaves, the scratches are usually only inflicted locally—on the

---

[42] Also of the middle finger.—F. M. O.

knee, the wrist, the elbow, etc.—and are not more than 5 to 6 centimeters long. From six to a dozen of them may be applied, usually parallel, but in some cases half of them may be scratched from left to right, the other half up and down, so that the whole presents a network.

After any scarification, whatever "instruments" may have been used, an infusion of very pungent plants (see p. 53) is rubbed over the scarified area; it is undeniable that this treatment is often efficacious to allay the pains caused by neuralgia, nervous headache, and similar complaints. Similar observations have been made by W. E. Roth[43] and by Prof. J. P. Kleiweg de Zwaan.[44]

Generally speaking, scarification is performed to cure such diseases as are not permanently located in a definite part of the body, as rheumatism, which may be more pronounced in the knee joints one day and in the hip the next; or "pains moving about" (neuralgia), for neuralgia of the teeth, for "pains appearing in different places," etc.

Fractures.—The knowledge and the professional skill of the medicine men with regard to fractures is scanty indeed. The fractured member is fitted together as nicely as can be managed and one or more sticks are tied alongside of it; as soon as the patient reaches home two boards are hewn, of which a casing is made, and that takes the place of the sticks. Complete rest is prescribed and a decoction of tsɩ·yu' (*Liriodendron tulipifera* L., tulip tree, poplar, whitewood) is blown, by means of the blowing tube (see p. 58), on the fractured limb. As the medicine men put it themselves: "If everything has been fixed nicely the bones will grow together again and heal; but often they don't and then the man will not have the use of his limb again."

If a lower limb has been broken or disjointed and has failed to heal sticks and simple crutches, not different from the simpler forms known to the rural whites, are used.

A fracture which is fairly common is that of the collar bone; the rough way in which Cherokee ball players handle each other during the game often results in a player being tossed clear up into the air and falling down headforemost. To avoid falling on his head, or breaking an arm, the head is held on one side, and the arms are held horizontally extended. A broken collar bone is often the result.

Here again no other method of curing is attempted than blowing a decoction of poplar bark on the shoulder and breast. The patient is ordered to keep his arm at an angle of 45° in front of his breast, i. e., to take the position which in our hospitals is enforced by the suspension bandage. Most cases heal successfully.

---

[43] "An Inquiry into the Animism and Folk-Lore of the Guiana Indians," Thirtieth Ann. Rept. Bur. Amer. Ethn. (1915), p. 280.

[44] "Die Heilkunde der Niasser," den Haag 1913, p. 135.

Dislocation.—Cases of dislocation are treated as efficaciously as one can expect. Three or four friends get hold of the patient and simply pull long and frantically until they believe the rebellious joint has resumed its original position. As to the ultimate outcome, the same fatalistic view is taken as with regard to fractures.

Dentistry.—The art of the stomatologist is in its very prime among the Cherokee. If neuralgia is felt, it may be treated as—

(1) Dɩ`Dǫ·lɛ́'ski (see p. 292); in this case the jaw, the cheek, or the temple may be scratched by arrowhead, briars, or laurel leaves. (See p. 70.)

(2) Else the medicine man may proclaim that the pain is caused by insects. (See p. 28.) This is especially the explanation if there is any visible swelling or inflammation. If such is the case a treatment is adopted the main object of which is the sucking out of the insect. (See p. 73.)

If a tooth shows visible signs of decay the actual causes of pain are not so much believed to be of a mythical nature. The pain is combated as long as possible, by thrusting in the cavity of the aching tooth a small quid of ordinary chewing tobacco; eventually, in a fit of raging pain, the tooth is knocked out with a stone or a hammer.

A half-blood, whose scientific progress had attained the point where he pulled teeth by means of a pair of tongs, did a thriving business, people from miles around walking to his house to be "operated upon."

Wounds, boils, etc.—Wounds caused by a cutting instrument, such as an ax, a knife, a strong splinter of wood, are always treated by the recitation of a song (see p. 271) by the medicine man, or, if the case is urgent, by the patient himself or by a member of his household, if they know the formula. The infusion of tsɩ·'yu bark (see p. 71) is usually blown over the wound afterwards.

Nowadays the wound is usually bandaged in a very summary way with some stray bit of rag. It would appear that no surgical dressing, of botanical matter or of skins, was practiced before the introduction of cloth.

Severe hemorrhage, especially resulting from wounds inflicted by arrows or bullets, is stopped by a plaster of buzzard's down. The use of birds' down for this purpose is practiced by several American Indian tribes.

Contusions and internal wounds caused by falling or by being hit by heavy, blunt instruments, as by a club, a tree branch, etc., are treated by the panacea: the infusion of tsɩ·'yu bark, blown over the aching spot; no formula is recited, however.

Use of the sucking horn.—The discussion of the following practice under the caption of "Surgery" might be challenged with some reason, but the practice is undeniably of a surgical nature according to Cherokee standards. The instrument used (u‘yɔ′·nɔ̃ⁿ "horn" when off the animal; cf. u·tłuɢa′, "horn," when still attached) used to be made out of a buffalo horn: yαnsα′ u‘yɔ′·nɔ̃ⁿ it is still often called in the medicinal prescriptions. Nowadays a cow horn provides the raw material.

The top and the base of the horn are cut off, leaving a slightly tapering tube about 4 centimeters long which is shaved off on the outside and on the inside. The top opening, which is the narrower, is covered by the tightly stretched skin of a turkey's gizzard. The whole has the appearance of a small liqueur goblet. (Pl. 7, *g*.)

This contrivance is used very much as the cupping glass of the white physician is used, with this difference, that the oxygen-absorbing rôle of combustion being unknown, the air is eliminated by sucking. The horn is placed on the part of the body that is to be operated upon, and by setting it slightly at an angle, the medicine man manages to eliminate the air out of the cavity by sucking at the bottom of the horn. Although the cupping glass and the sucking horn have a very wide distribution, this is, as far as I am aware, a unique way of using this instrument.

It often happened that at the end of the operation some small object, a small pebble, a worm, an insect, was found in the horn. This the medicine man claimed had been extracted from the body and was the disease agent. The horn was used especially in ailments where a swelling was noticeable, such as toothache, boils, etc. Nowadays it is seldom used. As a matter of fact there was not one specimen to be found while I stayed with the Cherokee, and I had to have one made by Del. (see p. 115; pl. 7, *g*), one of the few medicine men who still remembered their use and who knew how to make them.

Whenever there is now any sucking to be done the horn is simply dispensed with, the medicine man merely applying his lips to the swelling.

Prophylaxis

Neither the utter neglect of hygienic precautions nor the total ignorance of measures to prevent and avert disease which we find prevailing in primitive communities should cause us any surprise.

These conditions are to be explained by the proverbial lack of foresight which seems to be the appanage of all less civilized groups. The problem of the day is enough for the mind of these happy-go-lucky people, "Let us enjoy health while we have it, and if anything goes wrong there is the medicine man to look after it."

It is explained also by the existence of a kind of prophylaxis which by ethnologists is not generally considered as such; it might be called a "mythological prophylaxis," viz, the careful observance of all injunctions and restrictions governing tribal life. If a Cherokee does not expectorate into the fire, he consciously or unconsciously observes this taboo simply that he may not be visited with toothache. If his wife is careful not to leave any offal of dressed game about the yard this again is done in order that none of the household may contract a disease.

Similarly, amulets and charms are, usually worn with the definite object of averting evil under all its multifarious forms, of which disease is by no means the least important.

Another reason for the lack of prophylactic measures among these peoples may be that the thought of a sporadic illness or ailment is not of so serious a nature as to impress their minds enough to set them to actively thinking of an expedient to avert the calamity. In this respect it is interesting to note how thoroughly and generally "prophylaxis" is practiced against all contagious diseases and epidemics, such as primus inter pares, smallpox, that terrible scourge of American Indians in general and of the Cherokee in particular.

Yet, with the Cherokee, beliefs and practice with regard to prophylaxis in disease are not quite so hopeless as we find them elsewhere; I do not mean to say that they pay such attention to rules of hygiene as we would approve of, nor that they practice certain prophylactic measures that we would consider efficacious, but we are confronted with a more pronounced exertion to forestall sickness and pain than we are wont to find; this has to be accounted for, no doubt, by the tremendous stress which is laid in Cherokee tribal life on the very problems of disease and curing.

As we have seen, according to the Cherokee theory of disease and its causes, disease preferably attacks—whether of its own accord or by the activity of a powerful disease causer—those people who are "constitutionally predisposed" as we would put it. Witches especially, and man-killers, evil wizards, attack people that are weak and in poor health, because these will far more easily fall a victim and a prey to their nefarious machinations than would the stronger, healthier, more robust individuals.

As soon, therefore, as anybody is grievously ill, one or more medicine men or lay assistants (the latter often relatives of the patient) take turns to watch in his cabin from sunset to sunrise in order to "guard against witchcraft." The smoldering ashes of the hearth are raked to one side and nicely trimmed into a neat little cone-shaped heap. A tiny pinch of crushed "old" tobacco (*Nicotiana rustica* L.) is dropped over the smoldering ashes. If a particle of the tobacco dust should flare up on any of the sides of the cone of ashes this shows that a witch is on the way to the dwelling of the sick person to aggravate his condition; should the worker of evil happen to be right overhead, or should he, though invisible, be inside the room, the sacred tobacco would land right on the top of the heap of ashes, and there flare up with a loud burst; this burst is believed to kill the witch.

Even though this rite be gone through while the person for whose benefit it is performed is already ill, it is none the less a rite which, from a Cherokee point of view, has a decided prophylactic character. It is not expected to cure the patient but to prevent any "worker of evil" taking advantage of his weakened condition to cast another and more deadly illness on the sufferer.

A variant of this rite is the smoking of the same sacred tobacco (blended, on account of its excessive scarcity, with at least 90 per cent of ordinary smoking tobacco) out of a pipe. The medicine man lights the pipe (preferably an old native carved soapstone pipe, although if such a specimen is not available a usual white trader's pipe is reluctantly substituted) and slowly walks round the patient's cabin, starting on the east side; after having inhaled a powerful puff of smoke he blows it toward the sky, then straight in front of him, then toward the east, and finally toward the ground.

This is done because some witches can not only walk on the ground (ad libitum in their human shape, or in the shape of any quadruped they choose) but they can also fly through the air, and can even travel under the surface of the earth. The smoke of the sacred tobacco prevents them from approaching in any of these ways.

Continuing his circuit, the medicine man halts at the north side, next at the west, and finally at the south side of the house, blowing the three puffs every time he halts, until the circumambulation is completed.

Contagious diseases.—It is the feeling of those who have made a special study of the problem of epidemics in pre-Columbian times that this scourge was relatively rare on the American continent. In view of this, we can easily follow the mode of reasoning of the natives, when they ascribe the origin of contagious disease to the whites. They often even go so far as to accuse the white people, and especially the white physicians, of purposely letting an epidemic loose among the Indians, in order to wipe them from the face of the continent by a quick and efficacious expedient. (See p. 39.)

With the Cherokee, as soon as there were rumors of an epidemic breaking loose—when it was known that a near-by settlement was affected, or when there was a case of illness which was pronounced by the old people, who had witnessed previous epidemics, to be a case of the disease in question—one of the most reputed medicine men announced his intention to hold a medicine dance, to safeguard the people against the coming evil. The whole community turned out at the scheduled time; the medicine dance was danced, the medicine "against all diseases" was prepared by the medicine men and drunk by the people. The medicine dance has not been staged for such a long time now that the only medicine man who knew the songs and the medicine used died during my stay with the tribe, in the spring of 1927.

Other prophylactics.—These are of an individual nature and are used not only against contagious but against any kind of diseases. They are charms prepared from the skunk (dɩᵖlaʼ) and the buzzard (sv·liʼ). "The odour of skunk . . . is believed to keep off contagious diseases, and the scent bag is therefore taken out and hung over the doorway, a small hole being pierced in it, in order that the contents may ooze out upon the timbers. At times, as in the smallpox epidemic of 1866, the entire body of the animal was thus hung up, and in some cases as an additional safeguard the meat was cooked and eaten and the oil rubbed over the skin of the person." [45]

Buzzard feathers are hung over the doorway, and I have also witnessed a case where the whole carcass was hung up in the room and was allowed to decay there; a measure the prophylactic value of which many of us will be prone to doubt.

The buzzard is used in this connection because of its habit of preying on decayed carcasses and rubbish; as he is immune from any ill effects, "caused by the bad odors," he is supposed by the Cherokee to be immune from disease-contracting propensities, and therefore to be able to communicate this valuable trait to those who keep his feathers, etc., as a charm.

Another contagious disease the Cherokee are in great dread of is whooping cough. As soon as there is known to be a case in the settlement parents prepare a decoction of vwɛtʻiʼ (*Eryngium yuccifolium* Michx., rattlesnake master, button snakeroot) and administer it to all of their children which they consider susceptible of contracting the ailment.

Various simples are used to help children grow into fine specimens of manhood or womanhood, without their deserving the privilege of being listed under the caption of prophylaxis. There is one medicine, however, in a decoction of which babies are to be bathed every new moon: kʻanɛˑsiʼ (*Orontium aquaticum* L., goldenclub).

Measures to prevent toothache are numerous. When you see a shooting star you must immediately spit, else you will lose a tooth. If you always heed this injunction you will keep all your teeth sound as long as you live.

Never throw the remains of anything you have chewed (a quid of tobacco, the skin of an apple in which you have bitten, etc.) into the fire; "else the fire will chew your teeth."

Another means, not so simple but even more efficacious: Catch a "green snake" (a snake about 50 cm. long; not poisonous) and hold it horizontally extended by neck and tail; then run it seven times back and forth between the two rows of teeth, after which turn it loose. No food prepared with salt is to be eaten for the first four days follow-

---

[45] Mooney, J., Myths of the Cherokee. Nineteenth Ann. Rept. Bur. Amer. Ethn., Washington, 1900, pp. 265–266.

ing this operation. It will keep your teeth sound as long as you live. The Tuscarora know exactly the same toothache-preventive practice.

In order not to be afflicted with boils this is the remarkable and unappetizing advice given: Swallow the body of a living daddy-long-legs (ᴅɑ·'kwsùli'), after first having pulled its legs off.

The awe-inspiring collection of Cherokee sacred and medicinal formulas contain quite a few that are to be recited to avert evil and disease; most of them are prayers of the kind which are called in German "Segen"; some of them are believed to insure a safe journey if recited before setting out; others are claimed to make the recitant invulnerable in war or strife, as one in Ms. III; others again are held to keep the feet from being frost bitten (cf. Formula No. 60, p. 258), when walking on the snow, etc.

In none of these cases is any material object used, however, and they are therefore not further discussed here.

Change From Within—Influence From Without

In the course of this chapter attention has been called to a couple of instances where the use of "surgical" instruments can actually be caught in the process of an evolution. (See p. 69.)

Also, in the paragraph sketching a few of the leading Cherokee medicine men, there will be occasion to point out a change in practice resulting from a modification in conception and outlook.

There are some more instances where Cherokee conceptions and ideas with regard to disease can be shown to have undergone, or to be in the act of undergoing, some important changes.

In this respect it has been fortunate indeed that such a keen observer as James Mooney repeatedly visited the tribe, his first visit dating as far back as 1887. At that time it was still possible to obtain information on a great many questions on which no light could now be shed by any of the present medicine men. Moreover, at that time the explanation and exegesis of the older informants was free of skepticism and sophistication.

Much of what Mr. Mooney collected could now no longer be obtained, and this in itself partly illustrates the process of change which the Cherokee, as every other of the American Indian tribes, is undergoing. Having Mooney's statements as to what conditions were like in the eighties, and comparing them with the state of things in 1926–27, it is possible to see in what respects ideas have changed, in how far opinions have altered.

Forty-five years seem a short span of time for fundamental changes to occur in the belief and the ritual of a community living so secluded a life as do the Cherokee in their mountains, but it should be borne in mind that they have been exposed to white influence for many generations, and that even more than a hundred years ago there existed, besides the traditionalists or conservatives, a lot of "progressive" Cherokee who did not look unfavorably upon the adoption of white culture.

Such being the condition, the death of every old medicine man, of every staunch traditionalist, means a blow to the culture of yore that is truly irremediable: A considerable portion of the aboriginal religion, ritual, and science dies with him; and maybe a score of myths and stories, a song or six, and a couple of dances will never again be heard. If one has had the sad experience to witness such a departure—as Mooney lived to see Ay. die and as I helped to carry Og. to his grave on a Big Cove mountain slope—only then does one realize that, if with one man so much of the aboriginal knowledge dies, how much this tribe must have lost and forgotten during the last few generations.

In spite of all this, however much of their ritual and however many of their tenets of belief they may have lost, it is remarkable how uncontaminated by white or any other influence is the bulk of Cherokee medicinal knowledge.

The following are the only beliefs and practices in the domain of medicine that can actually be traced to European influence:

A crowing hen causes a death in the family; the death can be averted by killing the animal.

This is a very general common European belief;[46] that it actually crossed the Atlantic with the European settlers appears from Bergen, Fanny D., Animal and Plant Lore, nos. 1335–38 and also Notes, p. 160.

A howling dog likewise "causes" death. (It is interesting to note that what in European folklore is considered as an omen may become a cause in Cherokee belief. (See p. 37.)[47] W. told me that his mother, Ayo., used to scold the dog, and command the animal to either stop howling or else to die itself. If the dog died, its evil-foreboding howling had no further effect.

The burning of old shoe soles in a purificatory rite against contagious disease is another practice which is undoubtedly of European origin; old shoe soles were considered an efficacious means to combat the plague in Shakespeare's time,[48] and also the Negro has borrowed this remarkable panacea from the white man's pharmacy. (Puckett, pp. 377–379.)

---

[46] Tetzner, Dr. Fr., Deutsches Sprichwörterbuch, Leipzig, (n. d.), p. 268. Eckart, R.: Niederdeutsche Sprichwörter, Braunschweig, 1893, p. 558. Le Roux de Lincy: Le Livre des proverbes français, Paris, 1842, Part I, p. 146. De Cock, Alfons, Spreekwoorden en Zegswijzen over de Vrouwen, de Liefde en het Huwelijk, Gent, 1911, p. 32.

[47] Cf. Rolland, Eug., Faune populaire de la France, Paris, 1877–1909, Part IV, pp. 66 seq. De Cock, Alfons, Spreekwoorden, Gezegden en Uitdrukkingen op Volksgeloof berustend, Antwerpen, 1920, Part I, p. 97.

[48] Cf. Wilson, T. P. The Plague in Shakespeare's London, Oxford, 1907, p. 11.

To give a dog water to drink with which cartridges have been rinsed, in order to make it a sure tracker, is another practice which only too evidently shows its pedigree.

There are, moreover, some beliefs and practices of which it is not possible to say whether they have been borrowed from European folklore or whether they have originated independently. Such are to my mind:

The vomiting into the river. (See p. 63.)

The use of spider web as a styptic.

The remarkable properties ascribed to such materia medica as stump water (see p. 57) and lightning-struck wood (see p. 54).

The saying with regard to a shooting star. (See p. 37.) It is to be noted, however, that in European folklore it is believed that when you see a star shooting you should formulate a wish, which will surely be fulfilled. So the two beliefs are not really identical; but one may easily have been transformed into the other after having passed through the oral tradition of several generations.

Not only is there this borrowing from the sources of European folklore, there is also an unmistakable influence of white scientific medical views, which, it is needless to say, are very ill digested and pretty badly mutilated.

A medicine man who had been dead some years, "Standing Deer," had told Del. that $v\text{`kayɔ}\text{`}^{\prime}\text{Dö}^n$ $v\text{`nɪsi}\text{`waskǫ}'$ (lit., "when they cough in a dry way," the Cherokee equivalent of our tuberculosis) is caused by swallowing dust, which becomes a big ball in our lungs. This view is no doubt a residue of the lessons in hygiene taught at the Government school. At one time T. gave me a similar account. When I asked him in a fitting way his views on the origin of disease he told me he could hardly answer that question—it was too difficult for him. He had heard that "some pretend that all disease is caused by very fine dust, so fine you can hardly see it, flying around in the room. It gets into our body and makes disease there, they say. Maybe it's true; maybe it isn't."

Some cases have come to my notice where these scientific medical principles are not bluntly taken over, but are happily blended with already existing aboriginal opinions. So, e. g., diseases that used to be ascribed to neglect of ritual in killing game (asking pardon, building a fire, etc.) are now often said to be caused by the hunter inhaling "bad odors" of the animal while skinning and dressing it. Another instance of this trend of ideas is the following, where it is easy to see that such explanations of the disease as by "the food having been changed" (see p. 33) has been active:

"Maybe disease results from what we eat. Whenever I went up north, to the white people's settlements, I did not like the food; I ate but little and was hungry all the time; still I always felt well; but when I came back home for a few months, I again ate all I liked, just my own business, and as much as I wanted; I suffered from stomach troubles all the time. The food we eat may have some disease in it. There may be a disease in apples, eggs, potatoes, etc." (W.)

Attitude of the Community Toward the Sick

In a community such as is here described not a thing, of however small import, happens to a member without all the others knowing about it and taking a keen interest in it.

Illness is too fickle a thing and is of too restless and shifting a nature to think or to talk lightly about it, even if it is only our neighbor who happens to be stricken just now. Who can tell whether we ourselves will not be the next to be visited?

The sick man therefore can rely on the sympathy and the commiseration of his fellows. If a member of the sufferer's houshold is met, or one of his neighbors, or any one at all who is expected to know how he is, questions as to his condition are always eagerly asked, and you can feel that these are urged by motives of sympathy and pity rather than by civility or inquisitiveness.

Nor do the people give proof of their sympathy by mere display of words—the actions are not found wanting. If the head of a family is ill, and is unable to provide for his family, all the able-bodied members of the settlement turn out on an appointed day and work all day felling trees and sawing and cutting the logs, so that the family may have firewood. If the man is still ill at corn-planting time the whole community will again rise to the occasion, plow his fields and plant his corn, etc.; even hoeing the fields of the sick and gathering their harvests is done for them free of charge, and with the most cheerful good will in the world.

This "mutual aid society," as it might aptly be called, has a chief chosen by the members, who holds office for a year. The election is a very informal affair and as a rule merely consists in the nomination of a popular individual by two or three of his friends and the oral assent of the rest; it usually takes place about corn-planting time, when as a rule the members have to meet anyway to work for some sick neighbor. The chief is assisted by a kind of messenger, who, at the former's bidding, has to call out the members whenever necessary.

This chief is at present looked upon pretty much as the chief of the settlement; it is also his duty, in times of drought, to go, accompanied by six other men, and invite a medicine man, who is expert at rain making, to use his art for the benefit of the people and their crops.

The same fine community spirit is displayed on the occasion of such a calamity as a fire. If a member of the settlement loses his cabin and all it contains by fire all the people will help him to rebuild his home, and, what is more, to refurnish it. One will be able to spare a blanket, another will donate a chair, someone else a cooking vessel, etc., until the family is fitted out again, sometimes better than before the accident.

During my stay the following rather amusing thing happened; it is a good example of the good heartedness and the generosity of these people:

On the outskirts of kʻɔ·ˈlɑnǫ·yi′, in an adjacent cove was a cluster of seven houses, one of which was inhabited by a half-blood, a very bad character, with his wife and two children.

Once while he was serving a sentence for his "moonshine" activities, and when his wife and children had crossed the mountain to spend the night at her parents', the neighbors by concerted and premeditated efforts set fire to the house, thinking that by so doing they would prevail upon the annoying family to move to some other settlement. The house burned down to the ground; not a basket was saved. But when the next day the culprits saw the despair of the poor woman they forthwith agreed that all the able-bodied neighbors (who were all directly or indirectly guilty of the arson) would rebuild her cabin on the very spot where it had stood before. Within a week the building was under construction.

Efficacy of Treatment

There are many statements in the descriptions and relations of early travelers on the American continent of the amazing skill of the native doctors and on the extraordinary results obtained by them. In many instances they are even compared to the contemporary European practitioners, and not always to the advantage of the latter.

We should, however, bear in mind that in the seventeenth and eighteenth centuries European medical practice, with its belief in such drogues and remedies as scrapings of unicorn, in mummy, human fat ("adeps hominis"), Digby's powder of sympathy, etc.,[49] in the most revolting and disgusting ingredients,[50] was still nearer the era of Plinius than that of Pasteur.

As regards the efficacy of Cherokee medical treatment the facts amply speak for themselves. In a very interesting survey Mooney has discussed this subject (SFC., p. 324 seq.), and comes to the

---

[49] Cf. Van Andel, Dr. M. A.: "Klassieke Wondermiddelen," Gorinchem, 1928. Cf. also, Lemery, Nicolas: "Dictionnaire ou Traité Universel des Drogues simples," 3d. edit., Amsterdam, 1716.

[50] Cf. Paullini, K. F.: "Heilsame Dreck-Apotheke, wie nehmlich mit Koth und Urin die meisten Krankheiten und Schaden glücklich geheilet worden," II, Franckf. 1699, but still reprinted in Stuttgart, 1847.

conclusion that only 25 per cent, or at the most 35 per cent, of the botanical materia medica used by this tribe is in accordance with the rules and principles laid down by the United States Dispensatory (14th ed.), 1877.

With the additional material collected by Mooney and by myself it will be possible to publish a more complete survey in the near future, the results of which already indicate that the tentative estimate made, based on the material then available, is altogether too optimistic.

Even the "white people's" medical knowledge has made considerable progress these last 50 years, and in the United States Dispensatory, 14th ed., 1877, properties are ascribed to many plants which the 19th edition, 1907, has not cared to reprint. The eliminatory process of reducing the some 8,000 "officinal" plants which western European official therapeutics once knew has played such havoc with these numbers that only about 300 plants are now officially recognized as officinal.[51] Thus several of the Cherokee plants the use of which was sanctioned by the school of half a century ago would now be deemed indifferent.

It should also be stressed that if a simple used by the Cherokee in the treatment of a particular disease happens to be incorporated in a Dispensatory, or listed in a Handbook of Pharmacy, this mere fact in no way confirms the efficacy of the Cherokee mode of using it.

The Cherokee rule of practically always using the bark of the trees and the roots of the weeds and herbs does not always do justice to the actual officinal parts of the simples used. Moreover, the mode of administration of a medicine, which is of such capital importance, is not deemed to be of any import whatsoever by the Cherokee practitioners. Of many simples, the curative value of which are highly extolled by the Dispensatory, if only the product be taken internally, the Cherokee medicine man will make an infusion or a decoction, and blow it on the patient sitting 3 or 4 feet distant. Finally, as has already been stated, no attention whatever is paid to dosing the patient, nor to his idiosyncrasy.

The same evaluation applies to such practices as the prescriptions relating to diet, seclusion of the patient, vomiting, etc. At first these strike us as factors that may help considerably to cause or to maintain conditions that help the patient in many cases on the road to recovery.

But here again appearances deceive. As far as diet is concerned, e. g., a particular kind of food is never proscribed because it is thought not to agree with the condition of the patient, but this taboo is simply

---

[51] von Marilaun, A. Kerner: "Das Leben der Pflanzen." Dutch translation by Dr. Vitus Bruinsma, Zutphen, n. d., Pt. IV, p. 361.

based on mythological reasons; as, for instance, when rabbit's meat is prohibited because rabbits are believed to be responsible for the disease.

Nor is the injunction of fasting of a nature that could be called hygienic; whereas the patient may stubbornly fast, and refuse to take even a particle of food all day long, immediately after sunset he will eat voraciously and gorge himself with quantities of food that might very well ruin the stomach of a perfectly healthy individual.

As for the so-called seclusion of patients, this is a taboo of the same tragico-comical nature: A visitor coming from the outside will be curtly refused admittance to the patient's bedside, or will only be allowed to enter after a most scrutinizing interrogation as to the condition of his wife, etc.; women when pregnant, or "under restrictions" for other reasons (see p. 34) are rigorously excluded. But the peace and the quietness around the patient that might thus be obtained, and that might be of benefit to him, are of no moment at all; inside the children may be carrying on as if bedlam were let loose, and I have witnessed cases of grown-up sons who would practice on a guitar in a most distracting and irritating manner for hours at a stretch within three yards of their very sick father.

Nor is the Cherokee way of purging by vomiting as efficacious a practice as we would at first be inclined to believe. Vomiting is resorted to far too frequently, and in eight cases out of ten without any plausible reason, and therefore without any beneficial result. In many cases patients take no food all day, yet force themselves to this painful procedure of vomiting several times before sunset, quite an alarming state of exhaustion often being the result.

This should be no cause of surprise to us, since we know that vomiting is practiced not so much to eliminate unwholesome or indigestible foodstuffs, but merely to "throw off our spoiled saliva" (see p. 15), or for similar reasons.

To come to a conclusion: If we marvel at it that ever a Cherokee patient recovers, we feel that we have to give the credit to his strong constitution, to the invigorating mountain air, and to the simple food he takes—lacking all spices and stimulants—much more than to the medicine man and his simples.

THE MEDICINE MAN

Having devoted the previous chapter to a fairly comprehensive survey of aboriginal beliefs concerning disease and its treatment, we will now give our attention to a most commanding figure in Cherokee life; a figure not only dominating the community in cases of disease and death but exercising its influence in almost all aspects of everyday life—the medicine man. (Pl. 8, a.)

Medicine men do not have special names, nor are they grouped in any society. Although they are sometimes referred to as aDa"nǫwǐ'ski, plur. Dɩ'ꞈDaꞋnǫ̑wɩ'ski ("he cures anyone"; "he cures people") it is more customary to call them by a name which is more discriminating and descriptive of the specialty to which the medicine man referred to devoted himself.

The overwhelming majority of the practitioners are men; sporadically there is yet a medicine woman to be found, but there are indications that lead us to believe that formerly there were far more of them than is now the case. An informant, when asked to account for the fact that there were so few female disease curers, as compared to males, told me that it was "because women do not take so much interest in it (i. e., in the study of plants, of the formulas, etc.) as men do."

Apart from midwives (see p. 122) there are now only two medicine women worth speaking of—an old person of about 80 years old, called aGʋ'ya (i. e., "it is being taken out of the liquid") and sɛ·Ꞌlɩyɛ'ni (Sally-Annie?), the wife of Og. (Pl. 8, *b*.)

A couple of the regular midwives will also occasionally go in for some curing of ailments that do not quite fall within their competence, but this is not usual.

If a woman practices at all she does not limit herself to patients of her own sex, nor to any set diseases; nor is the treatment by her of any ailments, even in male patients, considered improper. She exercises her profession on a par with her male congeners, enjoys the same rights, and if her knowledge and her skill justifies it, she may in time be held in the same reputation as one of the leading members of the faculty.

As will be seen again and again in these pages, the medicine men are the staunchest supporters of aboriginal faith, lore and custom, and with the disintegration of Cherokee material culture and social organization the medicine man has obtained a position of leadership which in many instances practically amounts to that of political head in another tribe.

Different Classes

However much the proverbial tooth of time has gnawed at Cherokee organization and tradition, it is still possible to find in the present body of medicine men traces of a differentiation which must have existed to an even greater extent at a more remote period.

It might as well be stressed right away that throughout this paper the term "medicine man" is used to cover a rather broad concept; it is used without distinction as to sex, and refers not only to those members of the tribe that treat the sick and cure diseases, but also to those that might be called "priests," "magicians," "divinators," etc.

A short discussion of these several varieties follows now, together with the names given to these practitioners and the practices they

a, TS., THE OLDEST OF THE MEDICINE MEN

b, sɛ˝lɩyɛ˝ni, a medicine woman

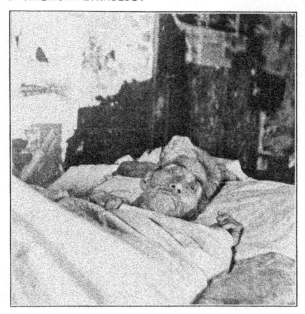

a, OG., TWO DAYS BEFORE HE DIED

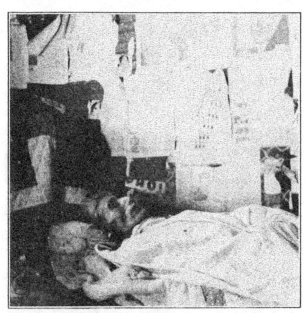

b, THE CORPSE IS PUT DOWN ON WOODEN BOARDS

specialize in. I want to warn, however, against thinking of this division as quite so rigid as it might appear to be at first: one individual may, at the same time, be a disease curer and a rain maker; or a disease curer and a divinator; or a divinator and an incantator; etc.

Dɩ·ˋDa‘nǫ̈wɩ́ski, he cures them (indef.; habit.); a curer.

This name, as already stated (p. 84), is given first to any person belonging to any of the several groups here discussed, and might therefore be considered as an equivalent of the term "medicine man" as used in this paper.

It is, however, only by a generalization that it has come to be bestowed also on such people as priests and incantators, as its meaning clearly shows that it must originally have been used to refer to disease curers only.

These are the people, men or women, that are called upon in cases of sickness to diagnose the nature of the disease, prescribe treatment, the injunctions and the restrictions, collect the plants and weeds, or whatever other kind of materia medica is to effect the cure.

Usually they proclaim to be proficient in all ailments, whatever their nature, but in some cases an individual may acquire quite a reputation for his skill in treating some particular disease. There was hardly any such case during my stay with the tribe but the names of two medicine men, lately deceased, were still fresh in everyone's memory—one, Wil., the writer of Ms. II (see p. 9) having been held in high esteem on account of his successful treatment of Dʋ·lɛ·́dzi ˙ (scrofula), and another, tsɑnʋ·́si (Leech), owing his reputation chiefly to his skill in curing unak‘ɔ·N!ǫ̈ yʋnɩyɔ·t‘ɛ́ɑ (swollen testicles).

There is one man now, yɔ·ˋnʋGǫ̈·́ⁿski (bear coming out of the water) (see p. 136 and pl. 10, b), who might in a way be called a specialist, in that he only attends to cutaneous wounds, but this, I found, was merely due to the fact that he had never been able to acquire any further knowledge.

Apart from exercising the profession of disease curer this class of medicine men will often also take patients to the river; they almost invariably perform this rite for their own family, instead of paying a regular priest to do it; they moreover generally claim some divinatory knowledge. These two qualifications, however, usually pertain to the domain of the "priest".

This class is usually called ɑmɑ·́yi Dɩ·ˋDɑdzöⁿ.stɩ·́sGi, he takes them (indef.) to, and brings them back from, the water.

The medicine men belonging to this class usually specialize in the ritual which consists in taking a client, not necessarily a sick person, to the river or the stream, and there reciting a prayer, conjuration, or incantation for the benefit of the client; for the latter's success in the ball game, in love, in hunting, for his long life; for his personal protection against disease and witchcraft, etc.; to bring about the happy delivery of a pregnant woman, etc.

The specialty which is most often combined with the one just described is that of "divinator" (see infra); more rarely they also claim to be able to command the winds and storms, to cause rain, etc. (see p. 152).

aDɔˋ·nɩˋski′, he examines and conjures (hab.).

This is the name given to the medicine men that are reputed to foretell future events, to know where hidden things are, how an absent person is getting on, etc., by means of various divinatory proceedings and paraphernalia, as, e. g., the beads, aDϵ·′lɔⁿ, also sǫnɩkt‛a, the brown stone, nɔ̃ⁿ′ya wɔˋ·Dɩgϵ·ⁿ′, several kinds of grass, the fire, etc.

The name implies not merely examining to find, or to find out the condition of a given object or person, but rather examining how a thing is, and influencing it by occult power to become as we would have it. It refers, therefore, especially to the ceremony performed by a priest, by means of which he tries to find out who our enemy or our rival is, and whether we are going to succeed against him; whether our team is going to win or lose in the ball game; whether the woman whose favors we crave is well or ill disposed toward us; whether we will get the better of a rival in a love affair; whether a relative who is very ill will live or die, etc.

At the same time as he "works" to get an answer he influences the evil thing or person against which he is acting, and strives to bring about an evolution into the matter, favorable to his client. The term "evolution" is peculiarly apt, for usually the proceeding is repeated four or seven times in succession, the pattern being that the first couple of times the chances for the client look pretty scant, but as the experiment is tried over again, and more cloth is put down, the medicine man and his patron gradually get the better of their opponent.

It frequently happens that in certain diseases, where the cause is very occult and hidden (even to the Cherokee mind), a divinator is called upon to assist the disease curer proper with his all-revealing art. Then the part of the work incumbent upon the former is first to "examine," usually with the beads, to find out which particular medicine man of the tribe is the one who will be able to cure the patient. Afterwards, while the "discovered" doctor is treating the patient, the services of the divinator are still required every day to find out, again by examining with the beads, whether the patient is progressing satisfactorily, and recovering, or whether no headway is being made. The facts here succinctly sketched are well brought out in the "Typical curing procedure," described by W. (p. 67).

About divination proper, there is yet a good deal to be said; but it has been thought that the notes relating to it, and not specifically dealing with medicine or disease, had better be withheld to introduce Ms. II, which contains several divinatory formulas, whereas not one formula of this class occurs in the Ay. Ms.

The medicine men, claiming as theirs the specialty of rainmaking, driving off storms, etc., are on the verge of extinction. The formulas used in their ceremonies are equally scanty. The Ay. manuscript does not contain a single specimen of them. There are some, however, in Mss. II and III, and since the matter does not pertain directly to the subject discussed in this paper, it is deemed advisable to go into details about it in its proper place.

Gaᴅlɪt'aᴅɪnö·'ᴅa·nḙ.a', she makes it (i. e., the baby) jump down for her (the parturiens).

This is the way in which a midwife is generally referred to. Since formerly there was an injunction that a parturient woman must be assisted by four female attendants, all the women are more or less conversant with the help to be tendered to mother and infant.

Some of them, however, perhaps a daughter of a medicine man or a woman who has married one, become more proficient in the matter, and extend their knowledge so as to be able to attend to complications and to prenatal and puerperal troubles; they may gradually come to be looked upon as regular medicine women, in which case, as already described (see p. 84), they will also treat ailments of different nature.

One of these women is usually preferred to a male doctor to assist at partus and to supervise and direct the other women attendants.

O. (pl. 12, *b*) and Je. (pl. 12, *a*) were the leading midwives at Big Cove during our stay there, sɛˑlɪyeˑni (pl. 8, *b*) and my informant, W.'s wife, also enjoying quite an enviable reputation.

Dɪ·'ᴅane·'səGɪ·'ski, he kills people by witchcraft (hab.).

This name, which can not be sufficiently analyzed—the stem may have connection with $\sqrt{}$-nɛs- "to droop"; there is, however, no causative element in the expression—is given to the medicine man who has attained the summit of occult power: he can kill a person by reciting an incantation against him, and thus "spoiling his saliva" or "making his soul dispirited." This is also done by obtaining stealthily some saliva of the victim and burning it, by shooting invisible arrowheads, sharp sticks, or pebbles into his body, even by stealing his soul. When they exert their powers in this way their activity is hardly different from that of witches. (See p. 129.)

As a rule they only harm people when asked and hired to do so by the victim's enemies. The ceremony is usually performed near the river, which accounts for the name ama·'yi Dɪ·'ᴅɑdzöⁿ.stɪ·'sGi (see p. 85) also occasionally being bestowed on these medicine men, but everybody feels that there is a black abyss between their activity and their formulas and those of the "priest."

When a medicine man has attained an advanced age and has a great reputation the laity often ascribe to him the powers of a DɩʽDanɛ`səGɩ'ski. To have this title conferred upon oneself is not exactly an honor, as it ascribes to the one to whom it is given not only the highest professional skill and occult power but also a rather jealous, fretful, and vindictive disposition. Yet a medicine man will not protest against such rumors circulating about him, nor will he do anything to hush them, as most of them do not mind being considered more powerful than they really are, even if it veneers them with a tinge of witchcraft.

It even happens that a self-sufficient medicine man appropriates and assumes the title, so as to make his influence the stronger, and to force his enemies, professional and others, to fear if not to respect him. W. told me that Ay. asserted himself to be a DɩʽDanɛʽsəGɩ'ski, but W. did not believe it. To do justice to Ay.'s memory, though, it is only fair to state that I often had the feeling that W. never liked him and was jealous of the high esteem in which Ay. was universally held.

Finally, there are several instances of a medicine man, who was an imposing and striking personality during his lifetime, being "canonized" a DɩʽDanɛʽsəGɩ'ski after his death. All sorts of rumors start circulating about his marvelous powers, the wonderful cures he effected, a journey of his during his lifetime to the Ghost Land, his prophesying his death seven days before it happened, his possessing the ʋlŏⁿʽsûDŏⁿ stone, etc. Before many years elapse his memory is recalled with the same awe and is embroidered with the same apocryphal and legendary details as that of a King Arthur or a Napoleon.

Such are, e. g., a woman, ɔ·ltaɩ·'ni, who died about 30 years ago, about 95 years old, and an old medicine man Gaᴅluʽyʽstiʼ (Ax), who died about 15 years ago.[52]

Scope of Knowledge

The brighter of the medicine men may truly be said to be walking encyclopediae as far as their knowledge of aboriginal culture is concerned.

Not only do they know all about disease and curing methods but they are also invariably very competent botanists and naturalists. Such outstanding men among them as Og. and W., and doubtless also Ay., Da`kwaDɩ''i (Catawba killer), and Ayɔ·ʽsta (she spoils is), who worked with Mr. Mooney, know at least 150 to 200 different plants, with all their peculiarities, their habitat, their time and period of blossoming, their properties and the lore pertaining to them.

They are also the curators of the myths and stories, one of them as a rule knowing more about them than four or five other members of the tribe put together.

---

[52] It has been possible to obtain the written formulas of the latter.

Having a knowledge of myths and stories in a primitive community implies being conversant with tribal history, legendary and fictional as well as actual and real, and some of the medicine men have even incorporated short historical notes in their daybooks containing their formulas.

As far as aboriginal religion is concerned, again we find the medicine men—often exercising the profession of priest at the same time as that of disease curer—remaining true to beliefs and traditions which the community at large is gradually losing, or exchanging against a slight and superficial veneer of Baptist or Methodist Christianity.

But not only do the medicine men excel in the higher intellectual, idealistic pursuits, such as those above named, but also as far as material culture is concerned they usually rate a good deal higher than even an intelligent layman. Nobody knows so much about fish traps and the way to build them and the wood to be used by preference; none knows more about the best periods for hunting different kinds of game, or all the artifices used to decoy them; nor can anybody make rattles, or wooden masks, or feather wands better than they can.

All this knowledge, however, is far from codified. I have often made a point of it to try and find out in how far it was systematized, or as we would call it, rationally ordered in their minds. This has always brought very disappointing though interesting results.

Such a medicine man who was universally acknowledged as being the one "who knew most," as Og. was, when asked to write down all the different diseases he knew, and when given five days to think it over, managed to find only 38 more or less different ones.

Another one, when asked to enumerate them offhand, could not get past a dozen, this in spite of the fact that both of them must have known upward of a hundred, since a compilation made by me from oral information obtained from several individuals, and gleaned from three manuscripts, the Ay., Ms. II, and Ms. III, revealed that some 230 different [53] diseases were known.

The same remarks hold for their botanical knowledge, and could even be made to apply to their knowledge of religion and mythology. One prominent medicine man, and at the same time the most prominent priest, T., was very anxious toward the end of my stay to act as informant, but was withheld by the fear that he would not be able to tell me anything of interest, as "he did not know much." When I had managed to convince him that anything he told me would be interesting, he came and stayed a week, telling me about fifty stories, and giving me very valuable information on sundry subjects.

Continuing an experiment along the same lines with another medicine man, this time with reference to the religion, afterlife, the spirits he invoked in the formulas, I could not get him by this method to tell

---

[53] "Different" from a Cherokee point of view.

me 5 per cent of what he knew on this score; ultimately I extracted all he knew—and a bulky lot it was—by indirect and roundabout questions.

Even a hasty perusal of the disease names (cf. the texts) and of the curing methods (see p. 60) will soon show that their anatomical knowledge is very scanty. It has been said that people living in primitive communities, especially those who have to rely on hunting for their sustenance, manage to derive pretty sound and tolerably accurate ideas about the structure and function of internal organs from analogy of the anatomy of killed and dressed animals.

This, however, does not follow. The hunter who cuts up the game in the forest, to bring home the better morsels, is not engrossed in anatomical speculation, and his wife who disembowels the rabbit or the groundhog is too anxious to have the meat barbecuing before the fire to be able to afford the time for scientific observation.

Even a people who practiced to such a considerable degree the dissecting of corpses for embalming purposes as the Egyptians are known to have long remained sadly ignorant of any anatomical knowledge worthy of such a name; yet they had the advantage of laboratory work all the time.

A medicine man who could write, and whom I asked to draw "the inside of a man" in an outline which I had sketched, put a dot about the throat, and said, "this is where our saliva is"[54]; about the height of the sternum, a small circle, with a lozenge on either side of it, which he proclaimed to be the heart with the liver around it, and the kidneys; he put the navel approximately in the right position, and drew a line above it which was to represent the diaphragm; having drawn another circle under the navel, which he pronounced to be the bowels, he laid down the pencil with a skɩ'ɢwɔ̆ⁿ nɩ'ɢa·.ɔ̆ⁿ' ("this is all there is to it") which sounded as if he were highly satisfied with his feat.

Arteries, sinews, and tendons are all held to be one and the same thing; in fact, there is only one word to refer to any of these: tsʋ'waᴅʋ·'nɔ̆ⁿ. Nothing seems to be known about the function of the blood.

A final remark I want to make on this score is, that in spite of their vast amount of erudition, and, in some cases, of their superior intelligence, these old fellows do not seem to be any more methodical than their lay congeners. Although a call is made on them three or four times a week, they will persist in walking, or rather, climbing miles and miles in the mountains each time, hunting for the herbs and roots which they need for their prescriptions, instead of transplanting a specimen near their own cabin, and laying out a garden of "officinal plants" such as Charlemagne ordered the medieval monks to do.

---

[54] See p. 15.

A poor attempt in this direction is being made by the more progressive of the medicine men, whom I found cultivating the following medicinal plants:

tsɔ·'laGayö·'ⁿli, *Nicotiana rustica* L., wild tobacco.

a·'ˡskwanɛ·'DöⁿÌ, *Veratrum viride* Ait., American white hellebore; Indian poke.

tsɔ·'lɩyʋ'ˡsti Gɩ·'GaGɛ·ⁿˋ a·'dzɩ·löⁿ'ski, *Lobelia cardinalis* L., cardinal flower.

Dʋnu·'na, *Glycine apios* L.

a·ˋt'tsɛ·'ˡi, *Alnus rugosa* (Du Roi) Spreng., smooth alder.

Gana·'Ga tsʋ·'nt'anöⁿˋ, *Scirpus validus* Vahl, great bulrush.

It is equally rare to find medicine men collecting and drying roots or other parts of simples for use in sudden emergencies. Only three items so treated have come to my attention: Powder (snuff) of the dried leaves of tsɔ·'laGayö·'ⁿli, *Nicotiana rustica* L., wild tobacco, and the root of ɔ·'DaliGa'ⁿli, *Panax trifolium* L., dwarf ginseng, and finally the roots needed for prenatal and puerperal care, and that can not be located in wintertime.

Social Status

Even if we no longer find any traces of the individual medicine man or of a body of them exercising any such politic influence as has been ascribed to the a'nɩkʋta'ˡni (see p. 97), there is no doubt but that the position of the medicine man must at one time have been one of considerable importance in the tribe.

Such hints as Adair's statement (p. 240) that Priber, forming the Cherokee "into a nominal republican government, crowned their old Archimagus emperor," seem to indicate that the political influence of the medicine men, or at any rate of the chief medicine man, was very considerable at that time.

In many of the tales relating to the war exploits of the Cherokee against the neighboring tribes it is often explicitly stated that a medicine man accompanies the party, and the success of the expedition often depends more on his skill in divination and conjuring than on the prowess and cunning of the warriors. This also must undoubtedly have resulted in strengthening their position socially, as his orders were of greater import than those of the actual leader of the party.

Even now, when two settlements are training for the ball game, a contest which with the Cherokee is as much of a social as of a sportive nature, the medicine man is exercising his influence and his personality in such a way that the whole affair takes the aspect of a contest between the occult power of the two medicine men conjuring for the teams rather than that of a match between two rival teams of players.

It is he, the medicine man, not the chief of the settlement, who addresses the team before they leave home to meet their opponents.

It is he who for the last few days has been "working to spoil the strength" and the magic power of the medicine man who is conjuring for the rival team. And the victory or defeat is laid at the door of the medicine man rather than that the players themselves are congratulated or scorned for it.

To have an adequate idea of the social status of the medicine man we should bear in mind that in his person we find cumulated such professions and pursuits which in our society would correspond to those of the clergy, the educators, the philosophers and the historians, the members of the medical profession in its widest sense, i. e., physicians, surgeons, and chemists; and finally, to a certain degree, even to those of the politicians and of the press.

His constant journeys to and fro, curing the sick, or trying to do so, gathering simples, calling on former patrons; on the other hand, his constantly being called upon by the people to assist them in their most intimate needs—a worried man asking him to make his wife's mind forget her former sweethearts, a spiteful woman demanding of him that he spoil the mind of a man she hates, all this contributes immensely toward making him the best informed person about, and nothing happens within a few miles' radius without his being aware of it.

Is it then to be wondered at that a man with such wide connections, walking in and out of so many homes, staying often with a family for days at a time, must be a most omniscient and influential individual?

Yet the medicine man should not be vainglorious about his status. All the members of the profession I have known always made a point of declaring, when asked, that they did not feel proud or haughty toward the people; they should not, because, they emphatically declared, they held their power and knowledge from une'`tlanō'`i, who had given it to them that they might help the people.

This conception is undoubtedly influenced by modern Christian views, for although une'`tlanō'`i is a powerful Cherokee deity (see p. 20), nowhere in the rest of tribal lore is he referred to as ever having granted any such gift as curing disease or the power of dispensing medicine to the people. I feel sure, therefore, that the statement here made by the medicine men refers to the Christianized une'`tlanō'`i, i. e., God, the Creator.

Whatever the medicine men may say with regard to this, I have often found evidence that their statements are not always corroborated by their actions; they do get a streak of vanity and conceit now and again, and do consider themselves as far more interesting and clever individuals than the common mortals. This, however, rarely manifests itself outwardly; they plant their corn and ply the hoe as everybody else, and do not betray by any article of dress or ornament either their profession or its importance. If this may be called any distinctive trait at all, I found most of them rather less slovenly dressed than the lay members of the tribe. Occasionally, one of them will cling to some archaic bit of garment or other, such as a pair of moccasins, a cloth turban, etc.

As to the attitude of the people toward the medicine men, this will to a considerable extent depend on the character of the latter. As a rule they are not feared, unless they profess to be, or are reputed to be Dɩ·ˋDanɛ·ˋsəGɩ·ˈski (see p. 87), these being shunned and avoided as far as possible.

The esteem in which the others are held depends chiefly on their professional skill, and on their social intercourse. Such medicine men as yɔ·ˈnɔⁿ GaᴅlɛˈGi ("the bear, he is climbing") who was Del.'s father, and Og. and W.'s brother, and who died about a score of years ago, actually managed to be respected and loved by his people, as in our villages an old clergyman or a devoted physician might be. Og. himself was held in no smaller consideration. But there are others I know who are looked upon with very different feelings and whose services would be called upon only in cases of utmost emergency.

Professional Ethics

Under this caption there are to be discussed mainly two aspects of the medicine men's profession—their sincerity, and what might be called "their desire to serve."

As to the former, I found them as a whole convinced of what they profess and teach. They practice fervently what they believe and treat themselves and the members of their own family by the same methods and means as they do their patients.

As far as sleight of hand is concerned, there are after all only four ceremonies where this is possible: When examining with the beads, when divining with the brown rock, when sucking, when scratching with the snake tooth.

In the first and in the last case I hardly think that the slight movements of the beads (see p. 132) or of the snake tooth[55] (see p. 70) should be explained by legerdemain. The tension under which the medicine man is laboring, together with a considerable dose of autosuggestion, are doubtlessly sufficient to bring about the "manifestations of life" they pretend to feel.

As for the divination with the brown rock, matters seem to be different. This mode of divination is usually resorted to when an object, an animal, or even a person has been lost. A small fragment (about the size of a thimble) of wɔ·Di' (i. e., "reddish-brown"), hematite, is tied to a thread or a bit of yarn about 30 centimeters

---

[55] The medicine man pretends that the snake tooth, prior to being scratched with, "becomes alive," as is evinced by its twitching and trembling between the fingers of the practitioner.

long. The free end of the twine is held between the thumb and index finger of the right hand, while the left hand, with the fingers stretched out, is placed over the right, ostensibly in a free, easy manner, and without any particular purpose, but actually to shield the function of the middle finger of the right hand, which is to stealthily transmit to the dangling stone its "occult" motion. The direction in which the stone starts swinging is the one in which the search is to be started. By this method often things are found, the whereabouts of which are not so completely unknown to the medicine man as he pretends.

A procedure where prestidigitation is likewise often met with is when the medicine man sucks the swollen part of a patient's body, and after much exertion usually succeeds in spitting out "the disease," viz, a pebble, an insect, etc., objects, of course, which he held hidden in his cheek before the performance began. I know of a case where Og., as a doctor, and as a man as honest a fellow as you could care to meet, produced a worm after having sucked the jaw of a man suffering with toothache.

Needless to say, just as in any other communities and as in every other professional group, there are also among the Cherokee medicine men individual differences as far as professional ethics are concerned. One of them told me the following story which throws some light on his methods of keeping up his reputation:

He once went to Yellowhill (ɛ·'lawɔ·'ᴅi) and on the way met an acquaintance who told him that he had built a fish trap but could not manage to catch more than two or three fish a day. He asked the medicine man if he did not know a formula to catch fish.

This cunning fellow said "he was sorry, he knew no such formula; as a matter of fact he would very much like to get one himself."[56] Anyhow the man insisted that the medicine man come to his house, look at the trap, and spend the night at his house.

Next morning, before breakfast, the owner of the trap went down to the river and came back with a whole washtub full of fish. There must have been more than a hundred of them; and he had to go back again, and fetch a second washtub full. He didn't doubt for an instant that the medicine man had recited a formula, and said so. The medicine man just smiled a mysterious grin, and let him continue in his belief.

(The real reason of this "prodigious catch" was, the branch by which the fish usually passed had been poisoned by a sawmill near by, letting its sawdust loose in it. This had made the fish come by another branch of the river, the one on which the trap had been set.)

Frequently, after having consulted the spirits by means of the fire or of the beads divination, the medicine man will foretell or prophesy

---

[56] This in spite of the fact that he did know at least three or four fishing conjurations.—F. M. O.

events that are to happen four or seven days afterwards, or within four or seven days. I am quite convinced that they honestly believe themselves in what they forecast in this manner, e. g., that the patron's enemy, against whom the medicine man had been asked to conjure, will die within seven days; or that a disease has been sent by a plotter, etc.

But it should be borne in mind that four or seven days (or rather four or seven "nights passed") is a ritual expression which may just as well mean the same number of years, so that the margin of error becomes very elastic. Adding to which such exegetical commodities at the command of the Cherokee medicine man as the superior magic power of the opponent, the possible neglect of the medicine man's patron to observe the necessary taboos, and all the difficulties raised by skeptics are explained away.

"A desire to serve." Such might well be the slogan of the profession, summing up its attitude toward the sick and the disabled.

There are, of course, some less worthy members who are only too anxious to convince the suffering party that a treatment of seven days would be more advantageous than one of four, thinking at the same time of the greater profit in cloth and beads which the former will bring him.

But it deserves emphasis, on the other hand, that any medicine man called upon is willing and ready to undertake the curing of a patient who is utterly destitute; although he quite well knows that he is to expect no reward for his troubles, he will dispense to him the same care, and will exert the same amount of skill to relieve him, as he would do for the benefit of a well-to-do member of the tribe.

Nor does a personal enemy of a medicine man call on his aid in vain, in his hour of need. Two medicine men told me that their mother, from whom they had inherited a great deal of their knowledge, had told them before she died that they should never make use of their knowledge to harm their enemies; they should never take vengeance of a first slight or insult, nor of a second; but if they had been abused three times (see p. 100) by the same person, then they might react by occult means against him. Should this enemy become ill, however, and call for their help, they should not refuse it, but should extend to him the benefit of their skill and knowledge with the same good will as if he were their best friend.

The Medicine Man's Fee

There is not much left to be added to James Mooney's excellent account of this in his SFC., pages 337–339.

The only main point left at issue, viz, the etymology of the word, has been subjected to a further investigation, with the following results: υGɪ′stɔ.tiʻ, the technical name for what we could call the doctor's fee or honorarium, does not seem to be etymologically connected with the verb √-Gɪʻ- "to eat something solid" ("I eat it, sol.": tsɪʻGɪʻa′) but with the rather similar sounding √-Gɪ-, "to take something" ("I take it": tsɪʻGɪ·.a′).

The literal and original meaning of υGɪ′stɔ.tiʻ would thus seem to be "for him to take it with" (υ- 3d sgl. objective pronominal prefix; -Gɪ- (stem); -st-i- causative-instrumental (cf. ayɛ·lsti "knife"; lit. "something to cut with," stem √-yɛ·l-); -ɔt- instrumental suffix.

The medicine men themselves have now lost this original meaning of the word, and when questioned about it usually render its meaning as "reward"; they all emphatically deny that the υGɪ′stɔ.tiʻ is the medicine man's pay; and this is true in so far that the value of it, e. g., the quantity or the quality of the cloth, is no factor in the cure. But they all agree that the υGɪ′stɔ.tiʻ is an indispensable prerequisite to effect the cure.

By some expressions found in the formulas some more light is thrown on the matter. A medicine man, going out to gather simples (see p. 150), recites a formula in one of the first expressions of which he says: "With the white cloth I have come to take away the medicine"

| a′nɪ̣̈ọwa′Gi | υnɛ·′Gɔ̈ⁿ | nǫ̈·ʻⁿwɔ·tʻi′ | tsɪGɪʻstɔ.tʻaʻnɪ·Ga′ |
| cloth | white | medicine | I have come to take it away with |

A formula for "when the ghosts have changed their food," in Ms. II, starts as follows: "Now then! Ha, quickly thou hast come to listen, thou red Otter, thou art staying in the Sun Land . . . Now thou hast come to rest on the white cloth, and wilt pull the disease away with it."

These two references go a long way toward proving that originally the meaning of the expression here discussed must have been either—

(1) That which is used by him (the medicine man) to take, to gather the medicine with (see p. 55), or else

(2) That which is used by (the curing spirit) to take it (i. e., the disease) away with.

I am inclined to consider the last version as the more probable, as there is still other evidence, yet to be published, which corroborates this feeling.

It is likely that in time, since the medicine man always took the υGɪ′stɔ.tiʻ away as his fee, the true meaning of the word got lost, and that it acquired that of "reward." Only after this semantic development, I think, did the use of other articles than buckskin become possible as υGɪ′stɔ.tiʻ, such as (flint) knives, moccasins, etc., since these can be considered as reward, but could hardly be used to be "spread out for the curing spirit to put his feet on, to pull the disease away with."

Cloth (since buckskin is no longer available) and beads are still now the most usual articles used as "fee." The official measure of cloth for one treatment is 1 yard, but this measure is to be taken "cum grano salis." u'tsɪ·lɔ·'Dōⁿ which may mean "a yard," "a mile," "a gallon," literally means "it has been measured" (✓-tsɪ·l-) and as used in the formulas is a term which is as vague as a period of four or seven days (see p. 95), or as a Dawɔ·'ɪlōⁿ (an "overhand"), which may mean a length from 25 centimeters to almost a meter.

The theoretical "yard of cloth" is often a gaudy handkerchief or a bit of rag 25 centimeters square.

It has not been possible to ascertain which rule prevails as to when cloth is used and when it is not. With some of the formulas this is mentioned in the directions, and although the medicine men generally know in which cases cloth is a necessary prerequisite, he is unable to state any definite rule. There are some ceremonies where cloth is invariably used: In the treatment of those ailments where the medicine man has had to go and gather medicine; in all the kinds of Dalɔ·'ni diseases; in all divination ceremonies with the beads; it also seems an indispensable item in all love attraction and incantation ceremonies.

Apart from cloth, the "fee" may be paid in garments, or in minor articles of dress and adornment, as neckerchiefs and handkerchiefs, a hat, a tie, etc. For the treatment of a menstruating woman it is invariably the undergarment of the patient. Such articles as knives or other utensils are but seldom given as "reward."

A custom which may be an innovation is to present the medicine man with eatables, such as meat, lard, salt, chewing tobacco, etc., and in very rare cases even with a nickel or a quarter coin. Some people to keep on good terms with a medicine man may offer him a present (any of the articles just mentioned) from time to time, a custom which sounds amusingly reminiscent of our medical insurance.

Finally, I should mention another method of partially paying the medicine man, viz, to have him staying as a guest at the house of the patient for two to three weeks. This is especially frequent with the more highly reputed medicine men, who are asked to go and treat patients in distant settlements.

Mutual Relations

There is no Cherokee living who remembers anything about any medicine men's society, and it is safe to regard the probability of there ever having existed such an organization with due caution and skepticism.

James Mooney (Myths, pp. 392–393) himself was very careful not to be too positive, when trying to identify the aˋnikʊta·''ni (clan?) as a society of this description; nothing has been collected, either by

Mooney or by myself, which could in any way substantiate or throw any light on the interesting but vague details given by Adair (p. 240), Haywood (p. 266), MacGowan (p. 139), or Domenech (Vol. II, p. 392).

It must therefore remain an open question whether the Cherokee medicine men were ever organized in a professional body in the past. However that may have been, at present there is no such institution, and every medicine man attends to his own pursuits.

Occasionally two medicine men may work in collaboration, one taking care of the treatment and the curing, the other devoting himself to the divination proceedings. Or again, they may call on each other's knowledge in some cases where an individual medicine man's professional accomplishments may fall short, but there is nothing organized or laid down in this respect.

Only rarely are two medicine men employed simultaneously for the actual curing, and if this should be the case a second one is never engaged without the first one knowing and approving of it.

It happens, however, that if a practitioner has worked on a case without obtaining any results, he is dropped altogether, and another medicine man is called in to see what he can do in the matter. The one thus ousted does not resent this in the least and does not consider this act an insult to his knowledge; on the contrary, he will often himself take the initiative, and if he fails to restore his patient to health in a reasonable time, will tell the sick man's relatives that evidently he is not the one who is to effect the cure and will examine with the beads, to find out which member of the profession will be successful in the matter. (See p. 68.)

If a medicine man becomes ill himself he only calls in the aid of a colleague if circumstances should make this course imperative, e. g., if he is too weak to go and gather himself the simples needed, or if the treatment calls for certain manipulations which he could not very well perform on his own person, such as sucking with the horn, blowing medicine on the crown of the head, etc.

Whenever he is taken ill with an $aye'\cdot ltgo\cdot$'gi disease (see p. 33) he invariably calls in the aid of a professional friend, and this stands to reason; for since a rival medicine man or an enemy has managed to get the better of him, this proves that the victim's power is too weak to grapple with his opponent's, and therefore the alliance of a powerful colleague is necessary to come out of the contest victorious.

There are medicine men who are always willing to cooperate with others when invited to do so; always willing to oblige with information and advice as to diagnosis, simples to be used, and the locality where these can be found, etc., and who even will volunteer the loan of a particular formula that has proved particularly efficient in the cure of a given ailment.

But others are of a jealous and miserly nature and will pretend to be ignorant and but ill-informed when they are asked for advice or counsel by a competitor. Yet I have not once heard of a case where one of these less obliging fellows purposely led an inquirer astray, or gave him information that might be deleterious to the patient under treatment. Nor has any case of "dishonest competition" come to my knowledge.

To combat the influence of the white doctor and his medicine, though, they will go to any pains, and use any means.

Initiation

There are still faint recollections of how the medicine men were initiated until three or four generations ago. The description given to James Mooney by John Ax (born about 1800) of the meetings of the "myth-keepers and priests" in the ɔ·'si (Mooney, Myths, p. 230) contains a very interesting account of the initiation of new adepts more than a century ago. The ɔ·'si is now but a dim memory of a hazy past and telling the myths is no longer the appanage of priests and elders; if 50 years ago the scratching and the "going to water" was still jokingly referred to, now it is no longer remembered that this rite was ever performed in this connection.

At present if a man wants to become a medicine man he goes to one well versed in the lore and skilled in the profession, informs him of his intention, and asks him if he is willing to teach him what he knows. The answer of the old man depends a good deal on the character of the candidate.

If he is known as a lazy individual he stands little chance of being accepted as a candidate by a conscientious medicine man, as he would be sure to neglect the care of his patients.

Nor is he likely to be favorably received if he has a reputation for being quarrelsome and jealous, as in this case he might be too prone to abuse of his occult knowledge to harm the people.

But even if the character of the candidate is without flaw or speck he is not sure to meet with an enthusiastic welcome at the hand of every medicine man, for some of these do not believe in propagating the sacred and medical lore too much, nor in diffusing it too widely, since according to those among them imbued with an idealistic outlook on the profession, the more of the lore is divulged, the less powerful every one of the adepts becomes; and again, according to others, rather more utilitarian in their views, because, the more practitioners, the less practice.

So as not to make an inveterate enemy out of an applicant by turning him down, the medicine man "examines with the beads," to find out whether the candidate is likely to make good in the profession;

"whether he has a vocation for it," as we might say. If the bead representing the applicant moves briskly, and gives ample proofs of vitality, the divination is pronounced to be in his favor. If, on the contrary, it behaves in a sluggish, lazy way, or if it does not move at all, he is dissuaded from taking up the profession.

But let us suppose that the professor in theology and medicine is willing to coach the student, then the terms and the tuition fee are discussed. He may tempt the vanity of his master by offering him a new overcoat, or a gun, or a trunk, or even a sum of money.

If the candidate comes from a settlement a few miles distant, it may be necessary for him to come and board with his master; or if the latter is able and willing to spare the time he may go and stay with the applicant. There is no rule as to the duration of this stay; it depends solely on the extent of the subject matter to be covered, and on how quickly the candidate masters it.

He may merely want to know how to cure disease; or he may even only intend to specialize in the cure of two or three ailments. On the other hand, he may be so ambitious as to desire to know all about love conjuring, hunting and fishing formulas, and even about man-killing incantations and witchcraft.

If he wants to know all this he usually leaves after 10 days or a fortnight and comes back for a similar period now and again, until he knows all his tutor can teach him.

Whatever his intentions for later life and practice may be, he must start out by mastering all the lore about disease, curing methods, and simples. This is a preliminary course every beginner must go through, even if he intends to later make his specialty in a totally different field. (See p. 84.)

But it was emphatically stressed by all informants that the very last formulas taught are those "with which to harm people," i. e., the incantations. The medicine men are very circumspect in handing out this knowledge, and very few candidates attain this step during the first few years of their "studies." Irascible or hot-tempered individuals are barred from it, as already stated. "Before they let you have that kind (i. e., incantations) they examine you, and if they find that you are a bad character, that you 'get mad' easily, that you are jealous and spiteful, they do not let you have them. A bad character will use these (incantations) even if he is insulted but once, whereas we (considerate old fellows) always wait three times [57] before we would work against an enemy to kill him." (W.)

---

[57] See p. 95. It is probable that four insults were the limit before white influence made itself felt. When I asked W. (the only one of my informants who had had a partly white education) why it should be three times he said he thought it was "because Christ had been in the grave three days, and Jonah was for three days in the fish."

Although the ɔ·'si has passed out of existence generations ago, even now the instruction is only imparted during the night. The medicine man and the candidate talk until morning, and then go to the river and bathe ritually, sprinkling water on their face, on the crown of their head, and on their breast, "where their soul is." This is done many nights in succession, whether the novice be staying with the medicine man or whether he walks in every night until he knows all his master is able or willing to tell him.

Before the instruction proper is started, however, the applicant has to drink a decoction to enable him to remember all he learns. With this end in view, he may take one or all of the following medicines:

A small cluster of leaves, rubbish, and refuse, such as is found occasionally floating on the surface of the water, must be fished out and examined. If it has any small insect, usually a spider, in it, it is cooked, insect and all, and the decoction is drunk, fasting, for four or seven consecutive days; immediately after having drank it, the candidate must go to the river and vomit.

Another much-extolled and highly esteemed medicine to obtain a never-failing memory is to drink the water found in the leaf of a pitcher plant: yv·Gwɩ'ᴅla (*Sarracenia purpurea* L., sidesaddle flower, pitcher plant, huntsman's cup).

These leaves, as is known, have the peculiar habit of keeping imprisoned anything that has fallen into them (the Cherokee say "anything that flies over them"), insects, spiders, small leaves, etc., and it is easy to see the principle of sympathy, according to which this plant is used in order to "keep the knowledge acquired imprisoned in the mind."

This plant is also called tcskɔ`·yⁱk'ɑna·'t'i "the successful (or never-failing) insect hunter," or wɑ'ɛ·'ᴅla, possibly a dialectical variant of yv·Gwɩ'ᴅla.

The different kinds of vni`stɩlɔ̃ⁿ.ɩ'sti, all the varieties of "bur plants," are also used, separately or jointly, in a decoction and drunk by the candidate. As the burs stick and cling to anything that comes in contact with them, they will also be of material assistance in keeping the acquired knowledge sticking in the mind.

The candidate has, moreover, to be more careful than ever not to eat any food prepared by a menstrual woman. (See p. 34.) A breach of this taboo is dangerous enough in everyday life and for an average individual; but for a medicine man, and even more so for a candidate medicine man who is in the act of acquiring his knowledge, it would mean a real calamity; not only would he forget all he knows, but he would be spoiled outright.

In order to avert these disasters he must, therefore, whenever he stands in any danger of coming into contact with a woman in this condition or whenever touching any object that she may have used, chew either the inner bark of ᵃtsö·ŋi' (*Betula lenta* L.; cherry birch; sweet birch; black birch), spitting the juice at regular intervals on the "place where his soul is," or even occasionally moistening his fingers and putting his saliva, under his clothes, on his breast.

Also the root of Ganɛ·'ldö︤ⁿ︥ (*Zizia aurea* (L.) Koch; Golden Alexander) is chewed as a preventive. The name of this plant means "it is pregnant." This is no doubt the reason why it is used in this connection; on the other hand, the plant owes its name to the peculiar shape of its fruit.

If then the candidate has used some or all of these potent means to make his hold on the knowledge acquired a permanent one, he will soon be ready for the last and most important communication his master has to make him. Prior to this, however, he must repair to a secluded place in the mountains or in the forest, and there prepare a decoction of all the plants mentioned above, only this time they are to be boiled simultaneously,[58] and the decoction is taken at intervals all day long; no other food or drink whatsoever is to be taken until sundown.

This is continued for four or seven days, according to the fervor and the intentions of the applicant: if he stays in the wilderness for four consecutive days and nights he will be a skillful medicine man and a priest of high repute and capacity. But if he can stand the ordeal for seven days "he will be a most powerful wizard; he will be able to fly in the air and to dive under the ground."

During this seclusion the solicitant has no dreams or visions that would seem to be specifically related to the ceremony, although this was undoubtedly the object of this four or seven days' fasting and contemplation until a few generations ago.

Before the invention of the Sequoya syllabary the instruction of the candidate must of course have been purely oral, but the possibility of committing to paper their sacred and medicinal literature has undoubtedly contributed as much to the survival of aboriginal religion and science as to the propagation of the tracts and books of the American Bible Society and to the veneer of white culture.

A medicine man may sell outright some of his written formulas to a candidate, but this is very rarely done, the usual course being that the latter be allowed to copy them. Even then a pretty high price is charged. Mooney records that Ay. told him that hunters would pay as much as $5 for a hunting song (SFC., p. 311), and W. told me that he once paid for being allowed to copy part of the formulas of Wil. an overcoat and a trunk (total value about $25), and that he sold

---

[58] In olden times they also added some others, Og. told me, but he did not know which ones.

them again, after having copied them, for a watch, a buckskin, and an overcoat.

When taking this course of instruction particular stress is laid on the explanatory remarks which should accompany each formula (see p. 158), and any ingredients, simples, and paraphernalia mentioned in these are also minutely described and explained by the tutor. This instruction is given in a truly Socratic manner, and as I found out myself, information is only dispensed so far as solicited. This is probably the reason why these medicine men are such fine informants, and why working with them is so profitable and remunerative; they have been trained in the technique of asking and giving information, and take so much interest in it, and are so visibly flattered by any one attaching so much importance to the smallest detail of their knowledge that once their initial reserve has been overcome they enjoy the work as much as the ethnologist himself.

When the candidate has learned from his master as much as he wants to know—or, as is often the case, as much as the old man is willing to tell him—he leaves him, and if his craving for knowledge and instruction is not yet satisfied, he may go to a second medicine man, and try to persuade him to impart some of his knowledge. It often happens, however, that the particular medicine man he turns to, after having completed his apprenticeship with the first one, feels slighted because he has not been given precedence and refuses to have anything to do with him.

There is no official rite of recognition or of acceptance of a new medicine man. It is soon known that So-and-so is intending to become one; that he is being instructed by Old Man X; even while he is acquiring the art, he may be asked to give his advice in matters of sickness, he may be asked to go and collect some simples, and so gradually he steps into the profession and the practice. It may soon be rumored about the settlement how successful he is in his treatment, and gradually he acquires the reputation of a skillful medicine man; in due course of time he may attain the honors of "powerful wizard."

Once the medicine man possesses the knowledge and the power it assures him, there are a few things he has to be very careful about in order not to lose these attainments.

First of all he must rigorously observe the taboo with regard to catamenial women. (See p. 34.)

Nor should he ever attend a funeral, or take any active part in any, such as making the coffin, digging the grave, etc.

Finally, he should on no account neglect, if one of his patients should die during treatment, to observe a rite of purification. As will be seen (p. 139), this purification is incumbent on every inhabitant of the settlement, but whereas with them the nonobservance at worst causes an illness, to the attendant medicine man it would mean the irretrievable loss of all power.

There are fortunately several ways of averting this calamity:

(1) All the rubbish that is found about the yard around the cabin is gathered into a heap and burned; sourwood, nö·ˋDɔ·Gwɛˋya (*Oxydendrum arboreum* (L.) DC.) twigs are boiled in a pot over this fire, and the hands are washed in this decoction.

(2) Wil. proceeded in the same way but used ka'na'sɔ''ᶜᵘlö̃ⁿ "wild parsnip" instead of sourwood.

(3) Spencer Bird, an old medicine man, now dead, used to rely on the sole purifying power of water. The informant who told me this vaguely hinted at the probability of the water being some "special water," such as that scooped out of a stump ("stump water") or even out of the stump of a lightning-struck tree.

Diffusion of Knowledge

We have just seen how an outsider may become an adept and the methods used in imparting to him the sacred and scientific lore.

But even between the medicine men and practitioners who have "graduated" years ago there is going on a constant exchange of formulas and explanations, a continual barter in hints and facts relating to the profession.

Every medicine man has either a notebook or a motley collection of miscellaneous papers of all sizes, colors, and descriptions, containing the formulas invariably written down in the Sequoya syllabary. Many of the medicine men refrain from writing down the "directions" in their books or papers, and do not write any caption to the formula, in order that, if by any chance the documents should be lost or stolen, the unlawful proprietor should be at a loss how to use them. The formulas will either want the prescriptions as to plants to be used, injunctions to be followed, the foods that are tabooed, etc., or else the title is lacking, with the result that it is well-nigh impossible to find out exactly against which disease the formula is to be used.

If two medicine men exchange any information, one of them usually gives the other one as many formulas to copy as the latter is willing to impart to his colleague. Some formulas may be rated far more important than others, however; a good love conjuration will easily sell for as much as five or six curing prescriptions. In some cases, even among medicine men, the formulas may be sold for money, or such commodities as coats, watches, etc. (See p. 102.)

In this way there is such an intense interchange of formulas and prescriptions going on that all the medicine men have a stock in trade which is fundamentally the same, only a member of the profession who specializes in a certain field, as in divination, love medicine, etc., has a totally different collection from the one who makes curing his principal pursuit.

To some extent there is also a diffusion of the medicinal knowledge from the members of the profession to the laity, to outsiders who have no intention of ever becoming medicine men, but who may want a particular formula or song because they need it so often that they can not be bothered to hire a medicine man to recite it for them on every occasion. They therefore ask a medicine man to sell them such-and-such a formula—say a hunting song or a love conjuration—which will put an end to their being dependent on the medicine man, for this emergency at any rate.

Even to his best friend a medicine man will never give a formula, excusing himself by saying that any information given free loses its power. Their motives seem to be less interested, when they state that formulas should not be propagated too much anyway, since the more they are diffused the less powerful they become. (See p. 99.)

As to the kind of formulas that are most frequently desired by laymen and communicated to them by the members of the profession, the reader is referred to the chapter on the Formulas (p. 144 et seq.).

Succession and Inheritance

There is now no definite rule as to who becomes the successor of a medicine man when he dies, and it is difficult to ascertain if ever such a rule existed.

As we have seen, a great many individuals may inherit of a medicine man's knowledge during his lifetime. The problem of the inheritance of his medicinal and ritual writings must of course be a very modern one, since it could not antedate the invention of the syllabary by Sequoya in 1821. But even so, there may have prevailed a rule prior to this, regulating the inheritance of the paraphernalia and especially of the profession, of the office. Be that as it may, there is no trace in the present beliefs or traditions that elucidates this problem.

At the death of a medicine man now, he is succeeded by any one of the members of his household who takes a sufficiently keen interest in the profession and "who is not too lazy to be continually on the road, visiting sick people, collecting medicine for them, etc."

From what has been stated (see p. 99), it is evident that anybody who succeeds him must have been officially or unofficially initiated by him, since to an outsider even the most carefully written collection of formulas would be a closed book.

His wife may succeed him, as in the case of Og.,[59] one of his children may, or again a brother or a sister, who, through having been educated with him, may know some of the ins and outs of the profession.

W. inherited a good deal of his knowledge from his mother, Ayo., and a considerable amount from his half-brother, Climbing Bear.

---

[59] Whose practice was taken over by his wife. (Pl. 8, b.)

The knowledge of Og., also W.'s half-brother, came from the same sources.

Del. is indebted for his "scientific information" to his father, again the much reputed Climbing Bear, and to his mother, O.

T. is Del.'s brother-in-law, and lives with him; he has been trained by tsι'skwa, his father.

If we bear in mind that both W.'s wife and Del.'s mother are midwives, that his half-sister, Je. is a medicine woman, and another half-brother a medicine man in another settlement; furthermore, that Og.'s wife has taken up his succession, we are bound to be struck by the endemic nature of the profession with certain families.

The group of individuals named above makes up roughly more than half of the medicine men of the settlement of which a special study was made, and the remaining number could be genealogically connected in the same way, comprising such individuals as Gad., Wil., J., Ts., and a couple more.

Skepticism

Staunch conservatives and traditionalists to the core as the medicine men are, they should not be thought of as a homogeneous body of fellows without any individuality, with nicely agreeing and tallying opinions on matters pertaining to religion and science.

Elsewhere will be found a few cases where medicine men have not feared to introduce innovations in the explanation of the cause of diseases, or in its treatment, that from a Cherokee point of view may be called truly daring.

I here want to draw attention to a couple of cases of an even more startling nature, to what might be called symptoms of skepticism and rationalism on the part of the members of the guild.

Gad., whose writings were secured by Mooney, and which are now deposited in the archives of the Bureau of American Ethnology, on two occasions gives vent to a tinge of doubt. Once he writes at the end of a prescription following a formula to attract the affection of a woman:

tsa`ndιsGє·ⁿ′  ě‛ti   tsa·`nе̤ε′ⁿi   a‛sє′   Gє·li′   yυdɔ′‛ιyυ-Gwö̈ⁿ`
they said, App. long time they lived, App. it must it seems it (is) true, Lim.

є·lι′stι-Gwö̈ⁿ`   Gє·sö̤·′
possible, Lim.   it is

I. e., "They said this a long time ago when the (old people) lived; possibly it is true, so at least it seems." And another time in similar circumstances:

a‛sє′   Gє·li′   yυdɔ′‛ιyυ-Gwö̈ⁿ`   yι′Gi
it must it seems it (is) true, Lim.   maybe

I. e., "Possibly this may be true."

The fine shades of meaning expressing doubt and even a tinge of blasphemous irony, which many of these words convey when used in this connection, are almost impossible to render in any but a very free and colloquial translation, which would run somewhat like this: "This has never been proved, but the old people, none of whom, by the way, we have ever seen, are reputed to have believed it. Maybe it isn't a joke, after all; anyway, what's the harm of trying it."

Also from personal contacts I have received similar impressions. Once I asked a medicine man whether he was absolutely sure about a particular subject I was discussing with him, and which he explained according to current orthodox and traditional views; I also asked him if he would accept another medicine man's views if they happened to be diametrically opposed to his own opinions and to tradition; he answered: "Yes, I would, if he could prove that he was right."

Good old Og. once confidentially told me that he had lost all confidence in the divinatory powers of the "brown stone"; as often as he had tried it he had been disappointed. He believed in other modes of divination and practiced them, but for "brown stone" divination he had no use at all.

Some more facts that are related to those discussed in this paragraph will be found on page 113.

Attitude Toward White Culture

Although as a rule the medicine man is strongly opposed to the influence of white culture in his domain, and very hostile to the white physician and his medicine box, this feeling is much less pronounced in some localities than in others. The Indians living in the neighborhood of the agency, who know by experience that the "white medicine" is so much superior to theirs, are breaking loose from their medicine men and their doctrines, and the medicine man feels that he is fighting a desperate and hopeless battle.

Some means he employs in this we would call hardly fair, but I am convinced that the medicine men themselves are quite honest about them, e. g., when they allege that white doctors willfully cause disease (see p. 39) so as to always have clients. "You see," one of them told me once, "your white doctors are out after money. We will treat a sick man for weeks and weeks and cure him, even though we know that he has nothing to pay us with. And if he recovers, we are just as glad as if he had been a rich man and could have given us yards and yards of cloth, and beads and money. But your doctors, if they do not get money, they will not cure; and how can they get money if the people do not become ill. So they make healthy people ill on purpose, that they may cure them and get rich."

What is there to be answered to such sound dialectics?

And yet, there are even more arguments. White medicine and Indian medicine are both good; but as Indian medicine is not good for a white man, what is the use of white medicine for an Indian? "We Indians have always used the medicine raw,[60] and have gotten used to it. But white medicine is not raw, and it does not agree with us."

Others are less dogmatic about it, and say that there are successful white doctors, just as there are skillful Indian medicine men, and that, if one of the latter has failed to cure a patient, there is no reason why the white doctor should not be given a chance. But the two should never be employed at the same time. The only exception to this rule that has come to my knowledge is a case where a child was ill, and the agency doctor, being summoned, prescribed a medicine to be drunk. The Cherokee medicine man, Wil., since deceased, who had been attending to the case, had ordered a collection of herbs to be cooked and the decoction to be sprinkled over the child. When he heard of the white doctor's prescription he did not oppose himself to the white man's medicine being used simultaneously with his own, as the former was to be used internally, whereas his was for external use only.

One point which even the most inveterate traditionalist will always be found readily willing to concede is that there are certain diseases which an Indian medicine man could not possibly cure, viz, those diseases that are of an infectious and contagious nature, and which are reputed to be imported by the white people, and more specifically, caused by the white doctors.

On the other hand, there exist ailments which even the best white physician could not cure, as the dreaded and uncanny aye·'lιɔ·'ci diseases (see p. 33) and in a general way all diseases that are held to be caused by human agency and occult means.

There are quite a few stories circulating, calculated to uphold the prestige of the native medicine men at the expense of the agency doctors. One of them, representative of the kind, follows below, almost textually (Informant W.):

One day my brother-in-law became suddenly ill on the ball field. I carried him home and went after Doctor X[61] to cure him. Doctor X came twice, but gave him up and said there was no hope of recovery. I then went to Og., who came; he said that if the sick man lived until midnight he would recover, but that he was very bad, and might die before then. So I went and warned all the relatives, and they came and stood by his bedside. About half past 10 that night he became very bad, his breath stopped, and we all thought he

---

[60] The point he wants to make here is, that our materia medica is prepared, distilled, extracted, compressed into tablets, etc. There is neither smell, taste, nor trace "of the barks and roots" left.

[61] The Government Agency physician.

had died. I straightened his legs out, and his stepmother tied her handkerchief under his chin.

But all of a sudden he breathed, and again, and again. Quickly they took the handkerchief away; he opened his eyes, and asked: "When did I come back?" (It sounded as if he thought he had been away.) His father said: "You have not been away; you have been in bed all the time."

Next day he ate, and soon he became stronger; within a week he walked about the house; he recovered.

PERSONALITIES—INDIVIDUAL DIFFERENCES

Although I have carefully avoided conveying the impression that anything applying to one medicine man likewise holds for every one of his congeners, yet I consider it necessary to specially devote a few lines to a rough sketch of the character of a few of them, bringing out such individual differences in views and behavior as struck and impressed me most.

It goes without saying that just as anywhere else, and as in any other profession, some of them are more proficient and skillful than others; that some again are less overawed and fettered by tradition and pattern than some of their colleagues; that some there are, finally, whose honesty and integrity can not be doubted, whereas others are no better than some of the vulgar and mercantile quacks that are not unknown even in our communities.

There is W. (57 years old, married; see pl. 5), who acted as my interpreter and main informant during the major part of my stay. He has a very striking personality. His mother, $ayɔ''sta$ (Mooney, SFC., p. 313; Myths, pl. xiv) was a medicine woman of high repute and a staunch traditionalist. From her W. got a lot of mythological and botanical lore when he was quite young, but after he went to the Government school at Hampton, Va., he lost, as he says himself, all faith in what the old people believed and taught. He was reconverted, however, by an experience, a detailed account of which will be given elsewhere, and during which, by some Cherokee talisman, which his half brother, Climbing Bear, had procured for him, he managed to win the affection of a white girl.

In spite of this success, the white people's settlements made him feel hopelessly homesick. He returned to his people, and it did not take him more than a few days to drop into the old life again, and to work out a quaint philosophy and outlook on life of his own, and which he occasionally teaches and advocates, with the result that these views are uttered rather frequently by other medicine men, with more or less conviction as the case may be. According to this system, "white medicine might be good, and Indian medicine might be good. There are some diseases (e. g., $ayɛ'lɩGɔ'Gi$ diseases) which a white doctor can not cure, and there are some against which an Indian doctor is helpless. But as a rule, a white man's medicine can not help an Indian, just as Indian medicine is of no use to a white man. He (W.) personally experienced this."

Although he expresses himself in such a mild way with regard to white doctors and their medicine, I know that he secretly holds the aboriginal medicine men with their paraphernalia and simples as far more successful and skilled masters, and whenever any sickness prevails in his cabin, W. will only call on the Government physician after weeks of treatment by his own and other medicine men's arts have brought no results.

Again, although he is fully convinced of the fact that a medicine man should never impose on the laymen or brag about his superior knowledge, I know that W. is very conceited, and since the death of his half brother, Climbing Bear, he considers himself second to none.

He is feared by many, despised by a few, loved by none. Yet, because of his accomplishments and his keen intelligence, he has been elected a member of the Cherokee Council so often that he has been in office for upward of a score of years. Few, if any, on the whole reserve have had a better "white education"; hardly one of his people has lived in white communities as long as W. has; yet he is the most ardent and most conscious of traditionalists.

He is fully aware of his own worth and accomplishments, and therefore extremely sensitive to mockery and slight. Unflinchingly believing in every bit of Cherokee traditional and ritual lore as he does, I am sure that many times he has by occult means tried to remove from his path and from this world, those that were his avowed or secret enemies.

In his practice he never consciously departs from ritual or tradition, and most literally and punctiliously follows and observes injunctions and prescriptions appended to the formulas.

As to his professional honesty, I found several proofs of this being scant indeed; yet I do not think that his motives were wholly or even mostly selfish. At times one would be inclined to look upon him as one who believes himself the prophet of a losing cause, and firmly convinced that all means are allowable to keep the people at large in the respect and in the awe of the beliefs and the institutions of the past.

His pronounced erotic nature, which is to be discussed later in connection with the experience mentioned above, is undoubtedly responsible for many traits in his behavior; his natural disposition for conceit, e. g., is considerably enhanced by it.

An activity and a providence, which the more surprise us as they are totally unknown to his shiftless and happy-go-lucky fellows, he owes, I feel quite sure, to his training as an adolescent in the Government boarding school, and to his subsequent stay with white families as a servant and coachman.

Altogether, W. was by far the most impressive and most important personality in the settlement at the time of my stay. If only so much antipathy had not been rampant against him he would without any doubt have been considered, implicitly if not outspokenly, the leader of the community.

This rôle, however, it has been given to T. (63 years old, bachelor, pl. 10, c) to fulfill. Vastly inferior to W., both in intelligence and knowledge, his disposition and temperament have secured for him a universal love and a public esteem, to which by the mere accomplishments of his mind he could never have attained.

His social intercourse is replete with a distinction and a nobility that would create a sensation in an aristocratic drawing-room. Children that run and scramble away into hiding when W. comes briskly stepping along the trail, approach with glee and hail with joy the person of T. as he leisurely and serenely comes strolling along. There is in the whole of his appearance, in his intercourse, in his dealings with young and old alike, a kindly amiability tempered with a dignified reserve that immediately betrays the wisdom of life.

Humbly realizing his importance, he never hurries, speaks but little and then slowly, as if he deliberately chose and weighed the value of his words; he is stoic and calm in illness and adversity as in victory and success. He not only professes to be humble, but actually considers his professional knowledge as a loan extended to him for the benefit of his people.

Although he has passed through the various grades of the profession, it speaks for his personality that he now only retains such specialties as divination, praying for long life, love attraction, etc. But anyone appealing to his medical knowledge is never disappointed—at least not by T.'s willingness.

The general consideration in which he is held has brought him the honor of preparing the Big Cove team for the ball game whenever they have been challenged by a rival team of another settlement. The meaning of this appointment has been explained (p. 91).

It will be noticed that after all, the professional aspect of T.'s character is scarcely touched upon here, and this portrays conditions exactly as I found them. To a question, which of the two, W. or T., is the better medicine man, a Cherokee answers that T. is so u·Da'nɪ́tɪ·yu', such a nice fellow.

The contrast between these two men, whose characters I have sketched as objectively as can be done by such a method as here used, is clearly brought out, and goes to prove that with the Cherokee superior knowledge in a medicine man may have to give the right of way to a more human disposition.

If all the remarkable and noteworthy persons here discussed had been born and educated in a white environment I like to think of T.

as an honorary president of a powerful amalgamation of scientific societies. W. might have built and directed a splendidly equipped and well-paying hospital; but Og. (pl. 9, a), whom we are going to present now, would have been the altruistic and devoted scientist, constantly busy in the laboratory, peering over tables and instruments, testing, measuring, and titrating, doggedly in search after methods and devices to improve the health and lengthen the life of this sorely tried and cruelly stricken humanity.

Og. was 64 years old when he died in 1927, while I was working with him. His knowledge was truly encyclopedic, and whenever the rich fund of W.'s information tarried, and no one else could supply the necessary elucidation, Og. was the last and usually happy resort.

When there was a diagnosis to be made that baffled everybody his knowledge and experience was never called upon in vain; when plants or roots were needed, the very names of which other medicine men but faintly recollected, he was always able to describe them, to find them, and to identify them.

When hoary origins of institutions and of practices were to be dug up out of the voluminous mythological lore he was the man to do it, when everybody else had failed.

If only he had had 10 per cent as much ambition as he had knowledge of tribal, ritual, and medicinal affairs he would have been as celebrated one day as that other "Oconostota" of Fort Loudon fame. But his inherent shyness, which went so far as to actually shun the company even of his friends, his passion for his profession, his truly philosophic turn of mind, made of this man a personality that in a civilized community and in an educated environment might have become an Edison or an Einstein.

Doting college juniors could not discuss the branch of their predilection with so much zeal and enthusiasm as Og. could. Hours at a stretch he could not only give information—or rather lecture on Cherokee obstetrics or semeiology, as I would much rather put it— but he could investigate a problem, ask surprisingly keen questions, that often really stimulated thought and provoked solutions.

He was practically the only medicine man of the many I have known who could be said to have a certain perspective in his knowledge and who was not hopelessly unable to connect two bits of information that came from different branches of his "erudition." If his opinion was asked regarding an obscure text in the formulas, he would of his own accord consult his fund of mythological lore, to see what he could find there that might be of any use to shed some light on the problem.

His professional devotion was edifying, and his honesty was beyond questioning. I have elsewhere drawn attention to the baffling fact that even such a character as Og. used methods which can hardly be called by any other name than that of prestidigitation. Yet I remain firmly convinced that he was in unquestionably good faith in this regard.

One of the more sinister persons in the profession is Jo. (70 years old, widower). He is looked upon by all the others not only as an outsider but as an impostor. This opinion I am rather inclined to believe as doing justice to the facts, the more so as I have never been able to induce him to work with me, in spite of his reputed greedy love of money. He is a member of the Cherokee Council and a preacher for one of the two Churches that make efforts to evangelize the people. It is quite a proposition to try to analyze Jo.'s personality, as it is very intricate. Since he is a preacher, which to him is paramount to being a full-fledged member of the intelligentsia of the white people, he considers it just as necessary to belong to the leading personalities of his own people; for this reason he becomes a medicine man, or rather pretends to be one. Since, now, being a preacher gives him the right and the authority to expound and explain the hidden and secret meanings of Holy Writ to his congregation, he thinks he also has the privilege of altering Cherokee traditional and medical lore to suit his opinion; that is where he comes in open conflict with the conservatives in general, and most of all with the ensign bearers of conservatism, the medicine men.

To give an instance: Whereas tradition teaches that the future can only be divulged by definitely specified means (beads, "brown stone," etc.), and by an elaborate ritual, Jo. pretends that he can prophecy without any such paraphernalia; that he simply sees the future happenings and events; that he has a revelation, as we would say.

Such a statement, to the mind of those of the medicine men that are sincere, is nothing short of blasphemy, and to those that are not quite so honest, it is even more odious, because when you take away from such a ceremony as divination all the mysterious uncanny, awe-inspiring proceedings, such as twisting the beads, intently watching the dangling brown stone, praying to the Ancient Fire prior to dropping the sacred tobacco over it—if all this is done away with, what remains to impress the clients?

Yet the influence which Jo. has as a preacher and as a councillor makes it possible for him to be a heretic and not be ostracized, and to be a blasphemer and not to starve.

Knowing as he does the disdain he is held in by the other medicine men, Jo. plays tit for tat, never letting an occasion pass to "make them mad." The primordial quality of a Cherokee medicine man, devotion to his patients, whether from a true moral incentive or from mere love of the fee, is absolutely foreign to Jo., and as I know him, I am honestly convinced that on the rare occasion a patient ascribes his cure to him, Jo.'s reaction is primarily, if not wholly, one of fiendish glee at the fact that he has humiliated a competing medicine man; the humane satisfaction of having rid a sufferer of his pain, which is never absent with any of the other medicine men, has no part in Jo.'s feelings.

Is it necessary to say which one, of all Cherokee practitioners, is most cordially hated by Jo.? And who most fiercely returns the compliment? W., of course. Both of them councillors and ardent with political ambition and passion, neither of them honest as a practitioner nor as a man; both of them too well educated to be good Cherokee, and neither of them educated enough to know what to take and what to leave of white culture, they often meet on the road to the same objective, and always as competitors. I personally know that drama has come near to bringing a tragic solution to their jealousy.

But all in that motley body of Cherokee medicine men is not dramatic; besides its sinister and gloomy personages, it has its Rabelais: Meet Jud. (married, no children, 63 years old, pl. 10, *a*), a most captivating and amusing personality.

To begin with, and to be quite honest, Jud. is no medicine man at all; he merely longs, languishes, dies to be one; I am sure that if only he could obtain that ardently craved honor by paying for it with 10 years of his life—if he has so much to his credit, poor old friend—he would gladly do so. If Jud. only knew, even if his compeers make sport and fun of his efforts to capture the first principles of practical therapeutics at the age of 60, that I, his adopted son, discuss him this day along with the past masters of the science, how proud he would be, and what a tremendous joke he would consider it to be.

Although I am satisfied I can show why Jud. can never be a good medicine man, I must admit my utter inability to explain why he wants to be one. He himself does not know, and considered it a very stupid question when I asked him. "Why, aren't there many people who are medicine men? And look at the old people; aren't they nearly all medicine men? Why shouldn't I become one?" And then, bethinking himself, "he was suffering so much from Dɩ'Dǫ̈lɛ·'ski (rheumatism); he needed treatment practically every day; could he afford the time and the money [62] to have a medicine man come to his house every morning to scratch him with a briar and to mumble a formula which he could learn to recite just as well?" And, finally, with a roguish twinkle in his eye that suddenly and completely seemed to metamorphize him into a lad of 18: "Moreover, if I want love medicine, do you expect me to go and ask one of those guys for it?"

---

[62] Jud. is very well off, as local standards go.

BUREAU OF AMERICAN ETHNOLOGY BULLETIN 99 PLATE 10

a, JUD., THE CHEROKEE RABELAIS

b, THE CHIEF OF THE COFFIN MAKERS

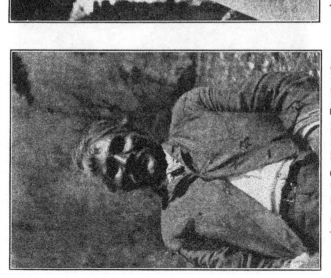

c, T., THE UNOFFICIAL CHIEF MEDICINE MAN

BUREAU OF AMERICAN ETHNOLOGY BULLETIN 99 PLATE 11

a, J., ONE OF THE LESSER STARS

b, DEL., DESCENDANT OF AN OLD LINEAGE OF MEDICINE MEN

An incorrigible jester, a side-splitting joker, Jud. is the most perfect anthropomorphized trickster you could imagine. Once as I was trying to reconstitute the Cherokee rabbit cycle, and was mobilizing all the available sources of information, Jud. came on one of his numerous visits. Brimful of the interesting subject, I asked him eagerly what he knew of the rabbit? He concentrated his thoughts on the subject, shifted his weight, looked at the ceiling, spat on the floor, and then, as I turned a keen face up from my notebook, he drawled: "All I know about the rabbit is how to eat it."

What an enormous asset this jocular disposition may be to flit through life smiling and contented, it is less desired in a medicine man. Yet, in spite of his stingy wife's protests, and unheeding the jokes and taunts of the people, Jud. goes about his plans, collecting bits of knowledge and scraps of information wherever he can, buying expensive documents, which he can neither read nor interpret. When he afterwards calls in the aid of a medicine man—whom he has to pay—to find out what his latest acquisition is all about, he learns that it is incomplete, that the "directions" are missing, or that it is worthless on account of some other defect. The whole settlement hears about it and roars, but the loudest peal of laughter comes from Jud. Somehow, he considers it a capital joke, and he could not for a moment entertain the idea that the joke is on him.

Since Jud. was politely kicked out of the door by all the members of the profession, I had the questionable privilege of being honored with his visit daily at first, and slightly less frequently afterwards. He proved second to none as far as keenness to discuss the subject was concerned. Alas, his ignorance was so manifest that the exchange of ideas proved not profitable.

There are some more medicine men with whom work was done, but they belonged to what may be called an undergraduate class, both as regards professional accomplishments and individuality.

Ts. (pl. 8, *a*), widower, 73 years old, and J. (pl. 11, *a*), his son (died 1928, 47 years old), were both very charming individuals, but had a rather narrow conception of things. They looked upon their occupation as a job or a trade rather than as an art or a profession; to dispose of his "fee" (see p. 95 et seq.; also Mooney, SFC., p. 338) was as important and as awkward a problem for J. as to cure a patient. If the other medicine men were worthy professors, these were mere Sunday-school teachers.

Del. (pl. 11, *b*), 51 years old, married, could, if he had chosen, have become a bright star in the Cherokee medical constellation. Only slightly less intelligent than Og., he is even more retiring and shy than his uncle was. He is a well-providing father for his family, and considers the medicine man's profession too unstable and precarious to support his household. I am inclined to believe, moreover, that his practical turn of mind and his active temperament have also something to do with this; thus it would be explained why, although practicing very little himself, he is the only medicine man who is still able and willing to make such "surgical" instruments as are still in use—comb scratchers, sucking horns, etc.

Je. (pl. 12, *a*), widow, 72, and O. (pl. 12, *b*), Del.'s mother, Climbing Bear's widow, 73, the two medicine women during my stay, do not call for any discussion here. Their position was devoid of any importance, and their rôle was almost limited to that of midwives. O. is far more universally loved than Je. is, which feeling I must heartily commend and sympathetically indorse.

BIRTH

Sexual Life

Since the manuscript, to which this discussion is an introduction, does not contain any formulas dealing with love matters, such as conjuration to gain the affection of a woman, to destroy in a particular woman the promiscuous tendencies she has shown, incantations to take vengeance on a woman who has scoffed at sympathies proffered, to sow discord between a couple of lovers, etc., it has not been considered necessary to go into such minute details on this score as has been done with matters pertaining to purely medical lore, which constitutes the bulk of the material offered in this manuscript.

Two more manuscripts, on which some work has already been done, and of which the publication is contemplated, will afford a far better opportunity to treat at length such topics as sense of shame, puberty, sexual life, adultery, sexual pathology, etc.

Conception

It would seem that Cherokee ideas on this subject had been considerably influenced by the views of their white neighbors. This need not, however, be the case. There are less civilized peoples whose conceptions about disease and medicine are not any more reasonable than those of the Cherokee, and whose explanation of the process of conception is even more rational (cf. Kleiweg de Zwaan, pp. 158–159).

Male and female alike "produce the matter which becomes mixed and goes to form the child in (the womb of) the mother. In some cases this matter is mixed right away, in which case they will have a baby soon; in other cases it may take several months, or even a couple of years."

"She is pregnant" is rendered Gane·'ldō^n, also 'ta'lv·li' (lit. "she carries it"?).

a, JE., A PROMINENT MIDWIFE

b, O., DEL.'S MOTHER; MIDWIFE

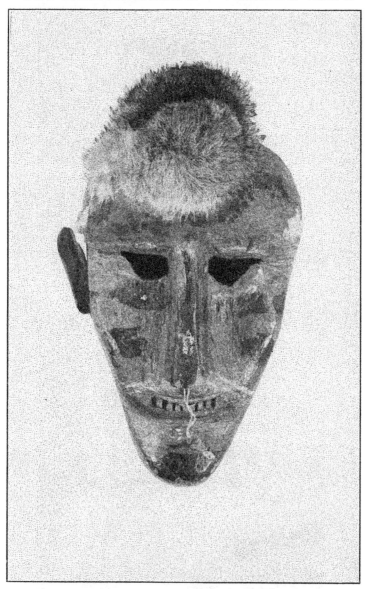

Cherokee Dance Mask

It is held that unsimultaneous detumescence can not produce offspring.

There is no clear conception as to the origin of the soul of the child. The majority of the informants say that they do not know, "they have never thought of it." The keenest of the medicine men, W., thought that it came along, with what went to form the body of the child, and was therefore secreted by both the individuals concerned in the act.

A woman knows she has conceived by the stopping of her catamenial flow.

Abortus—Contraceptives

Abortus is totally unknown; even my best informant (a man of 56, prominent medicine man, holding a leading position in the tribal organization, twice married, high school graduate), had never heard of it, and I had a good deal of difficulty in making him understand what I meant. He was horrified at the idea, and I am afraid his esteem for the white people and the ways of some of them was not improved, when he finally grasped the idea.

It does not seem to have dawned on them that the foetus can be tampered with at all, and to do so, W. thought, would be outright murder. As he put it: "You might as well cut a 5-year-old child's head off."

Of contraceptive measures, they do not seem to be quite so ignorant. They know one: tʻɩ́lɩyʋ'sti (*Cicuta maculata* L.; spotted cowbane; musquash root; beaver's poison), the roots of which are chewed and swallowed for four days consecutively by the woman who wants to put an end to her conceptive abilities. It is alleged that if a woman uses this she will become sterile forever.

From a point of view of morals, it is considered nothing less than a crime, and none of my informants knew a case where it had been used. One, W. again, said that he never knew it to be used, but that he imagines that it might be used by a woman who can not keep her children alive, or when it is considered that "partus" would endanger her life. But even then, he said, they would not do it, "for a woman will just as lief take the risk of dying with her baby, rather than to live without a child."

There is a vague hint by some of the informants at the possibility of promiscuous women using this drug, especially if they are married, so that there can be no material proof of their misbehavior. But substantial evidence to prove this impression could not be given.

When we consider their total ignorance of abortive measures and the scant and vague knowledge of contraceptives, I am inclined to think that the Cherokee hold the only means known to them from the white settlers. It is said that, at an early period of its growth, the plant resembles parsley (cf. Larousse Médical (Paris, 1922), 226), and parsley (*Petroselinum sativum* Hoffm.) has been and still is popular in several European countries as an abortive (cf. v. Hov. Kr. I 170; Lemery 417; Dodoens 1176). It is still used in official medicine as an emmenagogue (U. S. Dispensatory, p. 1393).

During Pregnancy

As soon as a woman feels she is with child she informs her husband and her friends of it. Soon the whole settlement knows about her condition, and she becomes subjected to the multifarious taboos and injunctions relating to her condition. The most important of the latter is that she be "taken to the water" every new moon.

The ceremony of going to the river to pray, to be prayed for, and to bathe, is the outstanding one of Cherokee ritual. It is now fast disappearing, and only the staunch and conservative old-timers cling to it as to one of the last vestiges of aboriginal religion.

As stated elsewhere (see p. 150), there are several occasions on which the Cherokee should perform this ceremony; as a whole, the ceremony is pretty much the same in every case; whether it be merely the monthly rite at the new moon, or whether it be to work against an enemy, or to conjure a disease away, or to "examine with the beads," the individual on whose behalf the ceremony is performed goes to the bank of the river, accompanied by the priest, who recites some prayer, conjuration, or incantation, at the end of which some water is dipped out with the hollow of the hand, and the crown of the head, the bosom ("where our soul is"), and often the face is washed.

The particular ceremony of taking pregnant women to the water is renewed at every new moon, a few months prior to the expected delivery. According to information, listed in notes of Mooney, it should be started after the third month of pregnancy; Ol. and Del. told me that it was only observed during the last three months preceding delivery, whereas W. maintained the ceremony took place every new moon, starting when the pregnant woman felt for the first time the motion of the child within her, which is said by the Cherokee to happen usually about the fifth month after conception.

The pregnant woman goes down to the river, accompanied by the priest. Two white beads (white being the color emblematic of life), or sometimes two red beads (red being the color symbolizing success), and a white thread, 50 to 60 centimeters long, are put down on the ground on a yard of white calico. All this is to be supplied by the client, and is afterwards taken away by the priest as his fee.

The couple is usually accompanied by an attendant, as a rule the husband, the mother, or some other relative of the woman, who throughout the proceedings acts as assistant, spreading out the cloth, arranging the beads and the thread. It is as a rule also the assistant who, at the end of the ceremony, makes a bundle of the paraphernalia and hands it to the priest.

The party standing on the bank of the river, facing the water, the priest recites the prayer (see Texts, Form. No. 18, p. 193), meanwhile holding a red (or white) and a black bead between thumb and index of his right and left hands (see p. 132). The lively movements of the right-hand bead spell success, those of the left-hand bead spell disappointment. At the end of the ceremony he strings the beads on the thread, deposes them on the calico, which is then wrapped up by the assistant and given to the priest to take home with him.

This ceremony, though it is understood to be gone through for the benefit of mother and child, often has as its more immediate object an aim of rather a divinatory nature, e. g., whether the child will live or will be stillborn, or again, what will be its sex, etc. The client has the right to stipulate the aim of the divination. Every time at the end of the ceremony the priest tells the woman what are the results and the prospects.

The priest takes the cloth and the two beads home with him, and at the next new moon has to bring the latter back with him. At the second ceremony the patron has to supply two more beads, which are finally strung on the same white thread along with the others, and also another yard of white cloth, which again the priest takes home as his fee.

These purely religious ceremonies are only a part of what we might term the prenatal care and treatment with the Cherokee. Even as long before delivery as this, simples are taken to induce an easy parturition.

Each time, before setting out for this river ceremony, the woman, before she leaves home, drinks a decoction of bark of ᴅaˑ'ᵘwədzɩˑ'la (*Ulmus fulva*, Michx., red, or slippery elm); stems of ᵘwalɛˑ'lu vˑ'nadzɩˑləɢɩˑ'sti (*Impatiens biflora* Walt., spotted touch-me-not); roots of ɢaˋnəɢwaᴅlɩˑ'ski niɢɔˋ'ɩlö·' ɩtsɛˊ'ïi (*Veronica officinalis* L., common speedwell); cones of nŏ.tsi,' (*Pinus pungens* Lamb., Table Mountain pine).

The first is used because of the mucilaginous nature of its bark: "It will make the inside of the woman slippery," so that the child will have no difficulty in putting in an appearance.

The second plant is alleged to frighten the child, and to entice it "to jump down" briskly.

The two last plants named are chosen because they are niɢɔˋ'ɩˑlö·' ɩtsɛˊ'ïi, i. e., "evergreens," and it is expected of them that they will convey their properties of longevity and unimpaired health to the infant.

There is no doubt but there is some symbolic significance attached to the method of selecting the ingredients—roots, barks, stems, tops. No information could be gained to elucidate this, even though all the informants agreed that there must be some cause underlying it. It may point to a symbolic way of presenting life from birth to growth, an interpretation which sounds quite orthodox in the light of what we know of Cherokee symbolism and belief.

As stated, this decoction is drunk at home prior to going down to the river; when standing near the water, the woman induces vomiting. This medicine is not only thought to be beneficial to parturition, but it also cleanses the woman from all disease germs that may be latent in her, and induces the throwing off of any "spoiled saliva." (See p. 15.)

PREGNANT WOMAN'S TABOOS

When with child, a woman not only has to be very careful lest any harm befall her; she herself is extremely dangerous to her relatives, friends, and neighbors. Beliefs relating to the latter conception have been discussed elsewhere. (See p. 35.)

As to the restrictions she herself is subjected to, there are first of all the food taboos:

She should not eat squirrel (sa'lo·li'), because if she does, the child, when about to be born, will not come down, but will "go up," as a squirrel, when frightened, climbs up a tree (Del.; O.); or because squirrels have a hump, and if she eats any squirrel meat the baby would lie in the womb in a humped position, which would make delivery very difficult (W.).

Nor should she eat t'ǫ·'ⁿdɩ·sti' ("pheasant"; ruffed grouse), as her child would not live (Mooney, Myths, p. 285).

Nor raccoon (k'öⁿ'li'), as this would give the child the gǫ·'ⁿwanɩGɩs'ti disease (see p. 67).

Nor speckled trout (a·t.tsa'), as the child would have birthmarks, black spots on the face (Del.; O.); or because this would cause undue bloodshed during partus (W.).

Nor rabbit (tcɩ·stu'), as the child would sleep with its eyes open (Del.; O.); or because it would have ridiculously large eyes.

Nor crawfish (tcɩ`stǫ·na'), which runs backward, as the child would obstinately refuse to come down at the time of delivery.

No animals are to be eaten that have been shot, either by gun or bow and arrow; in other words, no animals killed with bloodshed. But the same animals that are tabooed if killed by bullet or arrow may be eaten if caught in traps and snares, or if stunned and killed by club or adze.

There are, so to speak, no taboos with reference to plant foods. The only one I could find was the nuts of sɛ·ti' (*Juglans nigra* L., black walnut). If these nuts are eaten, the child will have a horribly broad nose.

Salt is to be used as scantily as possible. No reason for this could be given. W. said he thought it was "because salt makes meat (and therefore also flesh) swell." (See p. 65.)

No trace of the belief in the result of unsatisfied picae could be found.

Apart from the food taboos there are quite a number of restrictions and injunctions which a pregnant woman has to observe.

She should not be visited by a menstrual woman.

She should never loiter near the doorway. Whenever she has to go in or out of the cabin she must do so briskly. If she loiters at the doorway "the child will be slow in jumping down."

Every morning she should go to a near-by creek or spring, accompanied by her husband, and both should wash their faces, hands, and, some say, their feet. This custom has nothing to do with the ceremonial going to water observed at every new moon, and is of a totally different nature. It seems to be practiced solely for hygienic purposes, although there is no telling but this might be a mere rationalized explanation of an act that had formerly a religious significance. One informant, Del., gave as a reason, that it was done simply to multiply the opportunities for going out of doors. (See p. 122.)

She should not comb her hair backward, as the hair of the child, when grown, would not fall smoothly along its head, but would grow bristling and unkempt.

She should not wear a neckerchief, nor a belt of cloth or beadwork; nor should she have an apron tied around her waist. If she disregards any of these injunctions the child will have the umbilical cord twisted round its neck, and will be suffocated.

She should not see a corpse; but should she have to accompany a burial, where at the graveyard everybody is supposed to cast a last glance at the face of the deceased, any pregnant woman is given the opportunity to precede all those present; for, should others look at the corpse before she was given a chance, this would result in serious obstacles for her delivery.

"In the times of long ago," W. told me, "pregnant women were not allowed to see masks; now they are no longer so careful about this. But in olden times such powerful witches existed that they could make the unborn child look as horrible as the mask its mother had looked at. But now they are no longer so powerful." (Pl. 13.)

HUSBAND'S TABOOS

A considerable portion of the taboos that have to be observed by the future father has probably been lost. Yet some of them still exist, and are still observed by the more conservative members of the tribe.

A man whose wife is pregnant must not be a gravedigger, nor must he help in any way with a burial, else his child would be stillborn.

Nor should he put a fold or dents in his hat, since as a result of this the child would be born with dents in its head. This belief may contain an allusion to the fontanels.

As well as his wife, the husband should abstain from wearing a neckerchief, and he also should always enter and leave the house or pass through any doorway in a hurry.

If his wife has to go out of the house during the night he has to accompany her. The explanation tendered for this custom is again that it is merely done to have an opportunity for going outside (see p. 121), but it is quite possible that we are dealing here with a survival of an older belief, found among nearly all uncivilized peoples, and according to which a woman with child is a favorite victim for all kinds of marauding night sprites. Of such a belief there is now, however, no trace left.

As already stated, the husband should also accompany his wife every morning to a near-by stream or spring. (See p. 121.)

Partus

A few days before delivery the husband has to make arrangements for four women to attend to the parturient woman.

A woman acting in this capacity calls this tsiyaʻᴾliᴅaᴅɩnŏ·ʻᴅa·néːaʼ, I assist at childbirth (lit.: "I make the (child) jump down from her for her").

The woman's mother, her sister, and relatives are asked when possible, but if these are living at distant settlements, or if they are not available for other reasons, female neighbors will do just as well. It is a rule that at least one of the four is a midwife with some reputation, so that she can be relied upon to recite the necessary formulas and to indicate the simples that may be necessary if complications set in.

There is no doubt but the injunction that four women must be present is again to be explained by the respect which the Cherokee have for this number. It is interesting to note that they themselves have rationalized it; they allege that it is an official regulation of the North Carolina State authorities, that the number of female attendants should be four.

I know of cases, though, where this rule was not observed, and when a child was born at the house we stayed at, only two women were present, one of them being O. Rarely a masculine practitioner is present, but this may be the case when a difficult partus is expected, as when the woman has been ill the last few days prior to parturition, and he is invariably called in if complications set in after delivery.

As soon as the parturient feels the first pangs of pain the women who are to attend to her are summoned; they give her straightway a warm infusion of the barks of tʻaya′ ɩnɑ′Gɛ·ⁿ ɛ′ˤi, (*Prunus serotina* Ehr. (?), a variety of wild cherry).

This is probably the time when, in former times, the woman repaired to the menstruation lodge, the ɔ·′si, where she remained until 12 or 24 days after delivery. Now, however, the whole operation takes place in the cabin. All the children and the male inmates, save the husband if he cares to stay, have to leave the cabin (the cabins, as a rule, boast only of one room). If the husband or a medicine man stay they have to keep behind the patient.

At this time a medicine man or a medicine woman who has been warned a few days previously to keep ready is summoned; he or she comes, and sees to it that everything is all right; that all the precautions are taken, that the assistants are in attendance, that the necessary simples are at hand, etc. He or she, if necessary, may go out and collect the barks and roots needed.

The practitioner then walks out, stands at the eastern corner of the cabin and recites a conjuration, calling upon the child to "jump down"; the child is addressed as ′ɩ`tsʋ·′Dzõⁿ, "thou little boy."

He then slowly walks to the north-side corner of the house and repeats the formula, addressing the child as ′ɩ`Gɛ″yʋ·′Dzõⁿ, "thou little girl."

Then walking on to the west-side corner, the boy is again called upon, and at the south side, the girl.

He or she may then walk home, if satisfied that there is an old woman present who can deal with the case and who knows the formulas that may further be needed. Should this not be the fact, they stay until after parturition. Plate 12, *a*, shows the medicine woman who went through this ceremony at the birth we witnessed.

If it is deemed necessary, the house may be circumambulated once more, this time to ward off the activity of witches.

Attention has already been drawn to the belief that witches are especially active against individuals who are too weak to resist, and it is believed that they consider both the infant at birth and the woman after parturition as particularly easy prey. (See p. 33.)

The position taken by the parturient may differ considerably in different cases. One or two of these positions are undoubtedly acquired from the whites.

(1) The woman lies down until symptoms indicate that delivery is approaching. She is then taken under the axillae by one or two of the attending women, and raised to her feet, reclining backward in a slanting position; her feet are wide apart, and her legs stretched open. A third woman stands in front, stooping and ready to take hold of the child when it comes. If matters do not seem to progress,

if they think they acted upon "a false alarm," the woman who raised the patient sits down on a chair, and gently lets the woman down to the floor in a sitting position; the patient's back is supported by the seated attendant's legs.

(2) The parturient kneels on the ground, her legs wide open; she clutches the back of a chair. The attendants assist her a posteriori.

(3) The woman sits on the lap of her husband, who sits on a chair and holds his arms around his wife's waist.

(4) Parturition while lying down is almost unknown.

Whatever the position may be, the woman is always completely dressed. This does not interfere so much with the operation as one might think, as undergarments are all but unknown by the majority of the people. The dress is merely tucked up when deemed necessary.

The women arrange among themselves what particular part of the work will be performed by each of them.

The woman who first takes hold of the child, and who as a rule is tacitly agreed upon as the one in charge, is supposed to care for the child throughout the operation.

The woman standing by her side binds and cuts the navel string, while the two other women look after the parturient.

The one who stands in front of the patient, ready to catch the child, usually has a cloth spread out on her hands. Sometimes, instead of actually taking the child from the mother it is allowed to fall, with a most unhealthy sounding thud, on a cloth spread out on the floor; a few handfuls of dry leaves may be put under the cloth to mitigate the child's fall.

Prior to cutting the navel string, the blood is driven from the placenta toward the child, by running thumb and index along the funiculus; it is then bound off, about 2 centimeters from the child, and cut about 4 centimeters from its body. An odd end of string or yarn or a thin strip of calico is used for this. The cutting is now done with scissors.

Both as a prophylactic and as a therapeutic measure, a species of fungus, nɔ.kwι.'si υDι·'Gιpõⁿ (*Geaster*, puffball), is put on the navel and left on it until the withered remains of the funiculus fall off.

υ`Dι·yǫ·'ⁿDali`, navel.

υ`Dι·yǫ·'ⁿData', navel string (attached to child).

υ`Dι·yǫ·'ⁿDatǫ·nõʼi, navel string (severed from child).

No particular belief relating to the fontanel, nor any special treatment referring to it, were noticed.

Nor does there seem to exist any lore pertaining to children born with a caul.

The child is washed off with warm water and rolled in any piece of cloth that may be available, and the woman who attends to it squats down near the fire with it, her duties being now practically completed.

Complications.—As far as the partus itself is concerned there are, after all, only two kinds of complications known:
(1) The child is slow in coming.
(2) Its position in the womb prevents its delivery.

In the first case the woman's private parts are bathed with a warm decoction of ᵘwalɛ·'lu · vˋnadzɩ·ləɢɩ·'sti (*Impatiens biflora* Walt., spotted touch-me-not), which is said to scare the child.

The best means to induce partus are those where the child is "scared"; the plant just named is said to produce this result; in other cases (cf. texts, Formula No. 70, p. 273) the child is enticed to hurry as an old ugly grannie, or the terrible looking Flint, is said to be approaching. This statement, it is thought, will make the little fellow come scampering out.

Or again, the child is lured out of its mother by being promised the very playthings it likes—bow and arrows for a boy; a sieve or a loom for a girl.

Also an infusion of the simples as described on p. 119 may be administered again; if all this does not help a medicine man is called in, who will start "working" on the case. He may examine with the beads, to see what will be the ultimate outcome; he may by the same means find out that witchcraft is active against the woman and her child, in which case "old tobacco" will be smoked or burned. (See p. 31.) Or the formula calling upon the child to "jump down" may be repeated. (See above.) In this case the child is actually given a name—first a boy's name; then, if the ceremony is unsuccessful, a girl's name—so as to have a more material and coercive way of addressing it.

If a medicine man is attending to the case, and some decoction has to be applied externally, he does so in a very peculiar way. As he is not supposed to stand in front of the patient, whose garments are tucked up, and who is held by one or two of the women attendants in the slanting, semireclining position as described before, the medicine man has to stand behind these women and blow the decoction through a reed tube (see p. 58) so that the liquid descends on the stomach and the abdomen of the parturient, after having described a curve over her head.

This way of applying a medicine shows once more to what extent symbolic and mythic concepts are used in Cherokee medicine. For even if the simple used were of any therapeutic value, what result could it have when applied in such an inefficacious manner, when often more of the decoction is scattered on the attending women and on the face, arms, and legs of the patient than on the part of her body actually under treatment.

As for difficult parturition due to the inverted or otherwise abnormal position of the foetus in the uterus, the Cherokee take a more rational view of it, and apply a more efficacious if somewhat rough treatment.

A skilled midwife can ascertain the position the child is taking up, and if this is not natural, and parturition is delayed on its account, the four women take hold of the patient, each of them grasping an arm or a leg, and swing and shake her body in such a way as they consider helpful toward an easier delivery.

Afterbirth

Even while the newly born baby is being properly groomed and cared for by one of the women, the others, detailed to look after the parturiens, get busy helping her with expelling the afterbirth.

Afterbirth: vdɩ·ˋyaDõⁿ′, "that which has remained."

Also: vDzɔˋtʻanõ′ʻi, "it has had it in it." (This term is also used for "cocoon.")

This is done by reciting a formula, and at the same time rubbing the patient's abdomen with the right hand, warmed near some charcoals, taken from the fire. (See p. 62.)

A considerable amount of simples are also held to be highly efficacious in this case; the Ay. manuscript, unfortunately, does not contain a single formula or prescription for this emergency, but Ms. II has one formula and Ms. III one formula and three prescriptions. From these, and from oral information collected, it appears that the following plants are used: Gaˋnəgwaᴅlɩ′ski vˑ′tʻanõⁿˋ (*Scutellaria lateriflora* L., mad-dog, skull cap); GaDɔ′yʻti vʻstɩˑ′Ga, (*Polymnia uvedalia* L., leafcup).

A decoction of the roots is drunk, after which the patient should induce vomiting. This decoction is also used as an emmenagogue.

Another prescription lists "all kinds of Gaˋnəgwaᴅlɩ′ski." These plants are popular in this case more on account of their name, which means "it is like clotted blood," than for any other reason.

Or again a decoction of the roots of Gaˋᴅlɩwɔˑ′ti (*Smilax glauca* Walt., saw brier); nɔˑna′ (*Tsuga caroliniana* Engelm., hemlock); kʻvˋwɩyvˋˋsti (*Platanus occidentalis* L., buttonwood).

The roots should be taken shooting out toward the east. They are boiled, and the decoction is drunk by the patient.

The placenta is disposed of in the following way: The father, or should he be absent, another near relative, takes it, wrapped in some old cloth, and crosses (usually) two mountain ridges; there he makes a hole, an "overhand" (i. e., 25–30 cm.) deep, in which he buries the placenta; while doing this he whispers:

kʻa′   tʻa′ᴅli   tsvDɛʻtɩyö̆ˑ′ⁿDə   ɩˑyö̆ˑ′ⁿDõⁿ   tʻaˋᴅlɩˑnɛˑ′ⁿ   ʻɩˋDzɩGɔˋ′əʻõⁿ′
Now then!   Two   years   from now   again   I will see it

aGwɛˑ′tsi   "Well! I will want another child two years from now."
my child

Should the father be anxious to have another baby after one year he only crosses one mountain ridge, and should he want a child again only three or four years from then, he crosses the same number of ridges.

While the father is on this errand he should be careful that nobody watches him, for should anybody want to harm him they will stealthily follow him, and when he has gone, either—

(1) Dig up the placenta, bury it an arm deep and put four or seven stones on top of it before filling the earth in again. As a result of this action, never again will a baby be born to the victims.

(2) They can dig up the placenta and throw it away in the open. In this case a child is liable to be born to these people just any time; in any case before the parents wish this to happen.

The mother remains in a recumbent position for two to three days, or even less. After that, if no complications have set in, she is up and busy. In spite of the fact that she is supposed to be under restrictions for 12 or 24 days,[63] she attends to quite a number of her household duties. But she abstains from cooking, nor has she anything to do with the preparation of food, as anybody partaking of a meal prepared by her would become dangerously ill.

She should not eat any fish the first couple of days after delivery, "because fish have cold blood, and they would therefore chill the blood that has still to come out of her, and would cause it to clot." Nor should she take any hot food, or any salt. (See p. 121.) During this taboo period the woman is as dangerous as during her pregnancy or her catamenial periods.

The child is still now often given its name by one of the prominent old women of the settlement; possibly it used to be the chief woman of the clan who had the privilege of bestowing names on newly born infants, but this rule no longer obtains. As was pointed out in the previous pages, the child may be given its name even before it is born. In those cases where partus is difficult a name is bestowed on the child so as to have something "material" by which to exercise an influence upon it.

Old informants remember that in times gone by a child was endowed with its first name four or seven days after its birth. Mooney has left us a description of the ceremony in his "Cherokee River Cult," Journal of American Folk-Lore, 1900, page 2.

To this first name another name could be substituted later on; this name, that usually clung definitely to the individual for the rest of his life, was usually descriptive of one of his physical or moral

---

[63] One informant told me that he had heard that the usual taboo of 24 days could be reduced to 12 by drinking a decoction of certain simples. He did not know which ones, though.

qualities, or reminiscent of one of his feats on the war path, while hunting, etc.

CARE FOR CHILD—CHILD LIFE

The Cherokee are very fond of children and are far less loath to give vent to their affection than Indians are generally believed to be.

There are now no special cradles, nor is there any distinctive dress for children. The first few weeks it may be merely swaddled in a bed sheet, and as it grows up it is astonishingly soon considered of age to wear the cast-off garments of its elders. I saw little boys and girls of 4 and 5 years old dressed for all the world like their fathers and mothers, and at the family we stayed with, a much dilapidated black felt hat was shared by a little fellow of 6 and his married brother of 25, who borrowed it as circumstances demanded.

The child is always nourished with the mother's milk, unless it be brought up to be a witch (see p. 130), or if the mother's lactation is deficient; this is only rarely the case. If for any of these two reasons the mother does not nurse her child, it is brought up on the liquid part of k'a`nɔ'ɛ·'nŏ^n, corn hominy.

Very soon the young fellow adopts the fare of the grown-ups, and eats as they do the almost indigestible corn dumplings and the underdone venison. The results, it need hardly be said, are often disastrous.

There are various ways and means to help the child along with its growth, and to endow it with a fine physique as well as with all kinds of enviable qualities:

The very strong sinewy roots of Dɩ'stă·yö$^{n'}$ (*Tephrosia virginiana* (L.) Pers.; goatsrue; catgut) are boiled and given to the child to drink to make it strong and muscular.

It is given the eavesdrop, from where it falls in one continuous spout, to drink, so that it may be a fluent speaker. This belief is very probably borrowed from the whites.

The fleshy tubers of k'a`nɩGv·tsa'ti (*Lilium canadense* L.; wild yellow lily) are boiled and the decoction is given to the child to drink; it is also bathed in it, the object of both actions being to make it fleshy and fat. Another plant put to the same use was the *Aplectrum hiemale* (putty root; Adam-and-Eve) (cf. Mooney, Myths, p. 427). Another means to "endow the children with the gift of eloquence" is indicated by Mooney, op. cit., p. 420.

As a rule the child's hygienic condition is very bad indeed. I have known cases where infants who were born rosy, chubby little fellows had hardly made any progress two months or ten weeks after their birth, as they were literally being eaten up and worried to death by vermin and filth. There are, however, some fortunate exceptions, and some of the cleaner mothers take as much pride in their offspring as a trained white mother would, and with what scanty means they have at their disposal manage to make their babies look very clean and attractive little individuals.

Remarkably soon after its birth, often when only three or four weeks old, the child is carried about, sitting astride of its mother's back, and kept safely in this position by the carrying cloth.

As soon as it can crawl about it is left to its own resources and it starts out to discover the wonderful world.

When little boys are four or five years old they are, under the supervision of their father or elder brothers, making their first attempts at making bows and arrows and in a few weeks become remarkable marksmen. Little girls, at just as tender an age, fall into line and assist their mother and elder sisters with the household cares.

The children as a rule are quite bright, and some really astounded me by their keen intellect. Jimmy, the little 6-year-old boy mentioned before, had only once seen the train of a lumber company working in the district. When he came home he collected the empty tins of salmon and of other canned goods we threw away, and with sticks and twigs built a bridge over a 4-feet-wide rill, laid "tracks" on it, and with tins, sticks, and pebbles made the most realistic lumber train imaginable, the locomotive with funnel, the trucks loaded with "lumber," and all.

When it comes to showing acquaintance and familiarity with their own culture these children are nothing short of marvelous. At the age of 7 or 8, they know more about their fauna and flora than an average university graduate who has not made natural history his specialty. They know the dance steps and songs, are experts at making current artifacts, and if they were tested, on a fair and equitable basis, as to their faculties for observation, and for using the knowledge acquired, I feel sure that as a whole they would score at least as high, and often higher than white children of the same age.

The games played by the children are as a rule imitations of the occupations of the grown-ups—hunting and fishing, dancing, gambling, the ball game, etc. Swinging stands in high favor, and it is not sure that this was introduced by the whites, as an old informant told me that "the old people" used to get hold of a stout grapevine, securely entwined round the branches of a tall tree, on which, when cut off near the ground, they would swing to and fro.

Further notes on games, which are not here called for, are withheld for publication elsewhere.

Raising the Child to Become a Witch—Twins

A few words are left to be added on the treatment to which are subjected the children destined by their parents to become "witches." (See p. 29.)

This is alleged to be done especially with twins,[64] although a single-born baby could by the same means be brought up to become a witch.

If twins are born, and their parents intend to make witches of them, no mother's milk is given them for 24 days (i. e., the taboo period for them other, see p. 127); they are to be fed with the liquid portion of corn hominy, kʻa'nɔʻɛ'nö^n. This must be given them only during the night. Moreover, they are to be kept rigidly secluded from all visitors during the same 24 days' period. Some of these injunctions are strangely reminiscent of, and are no doubt related to, the Iroquois custom of concealing children until puberty ("down-fended" children, as J. N. B. Hewitt calls them), as practiced by the Onondaga, Mohawk, and Seneca.[65]

At the end of this period a decoction of the bark of kʻalɔ·'Gwö^0 Dɩ·'Dawɩ'skaGɛ·$^{n'}$ (*Rhus glabra* L., smooth sumac), is drunk by the mother, "to make her milk flow abundantly," and from then onward she nurses the children: the result has been obtained.

As to the power of these twin witches, the most astonishing assertions are made. Not only do they not stop at flying through the air or diving under the ground, but they can even walk on the sunrays. They can take all human or animal shapes conceivable.

Even when they are only a month old, "whatever they think happens." If they are lying on the ground in their swaddlings, and crying for hunger, and their mother should happen to be eating, and wishes to finish her meal before attending to them, her food will become undone (i. e., raw) again, and the food of all those that happen to be eating with her.

If their mother is cooking a meal while they cry for her, and she does not heed them, the food she is preparing will never get done.

When they have grown to be urchins, and happen to be playing outside, all of a sudden they will come scampering in, asking for food; if their mother says the food isn't ready yet, it will never get done. But if she gives it to them straightway, even if she had only just put it on the fire, it is ready to be eaten as soon as she hands it to them.

They often go and play with the "Little People."

They can see the Little People, and talk with them, though we can not.

But wherever they go, and however long a time they are absent, their parents are never anxious on their account, knowing as they do that they can take care of themselves.

---

[64] It is immaterial whether they are of the same sex or not.
[65] Cf. Hewitt, Iroquoian Cosmology, pp. 142, 252; Hewitt, Seneca Fiction, Legends, and Myths, pp. 510, 810.

When they are grown up they are most annoying individuals; they always know what you think, and you could not possibly mislead them. And what is worse, they can make you ill, dejected, lovesick, dying, merely by thinking you in such a condition.

A boy of twins, so reared, is a most successful hunter; he never fails or misses; not only does he get the kind of game or fish he wants, but he always bags the finest specimens and the choicest morsels to be found.

A girl in this condition is expert at all woman's work and industries. When she is preparing a meal she has but to think it is done and immediately it is ready to be eaten. Nor do such tasks as making baskets or gathering nuts, wild fruits, or vegetables mean any exertion to her.

If twins have completed their 24 days' seclusion they are more than a match for anything or anybody. The only means of preventing the calamity of the community being annoyed by such a couple of "undesirables" is to thwart their bringing up.

Og. told me that he "learned that a family were bringing up their twins to become witches. This was going to mean a lot of trouble for the settlement, so I got a menstrual woman to cook some food, and managed to slip it to the infants, without the guardians suspecting it. By so doing I 'spoiled' them, and they were never any more witch than you or I."

I asked him why it was necessary to go to so much trouble and danger to obtain this result; could he not have waited until after the 24 days' period, when he would have been able to reach the children much more easily? "Then it would have been too late," he said. "You see, by that time, they would have the full power of witches, and they would know that the food had been prepared by a woman in such a condition. They know what you think."

These people are certainly very consistent in what they believe.

DEATH AND AFTERLIFE

Death

As a sick person shows signs of losing ground, of becoming weak and despondent, of losing all interest in life, his relatives do not try to hide, neither to each other nor to the patient, their apprehension as to a fatal outcome. The care is doubled, the medicine man in charge of the treatment may be dismissed and another one may be intrusted with combating the disease; increasing attention is given to the "guard and the watch against witches."

The possibilities and probabilities, the ultimate outcome of the affair, are frequently made the subject of conversation between the patient and his friends. According to the sufferer's personal outlook on life, his attitude may be one of utter listlessness and resignation or one of hope and confidence.

In the first case he will repeatedly express to those who attend to him that they need not go to any further trouble; that he feels he is "going out west," u'sö"ï·yi', or to the settlements where the dead people live, tsù'sɑɩnɔ'ʼi. At this stage, and with this kind of patients, dreams are frequent, in which he sees some departed friend or relative, a deceased wife, his mother, etc., beckoning him to come and join them in the ghost land.

With those who have been Christianized to some extent, of whom there are only a few, this vision is often modeled on a Christian pattern: They see "our Father" calling them and telling them it is time for them to come and join Him.

Reference should also be made to visions, which the people emphatically deny to be dreams or hallucinations, but which they pronounce to be "real happenings," where the moribund sees himself setting out upon the journey toward the ghosts' country, but, upon arrival there, finds his presence undesired by the ghosts, and is sent back to his people. This vision is invariably interpreted as an omen of recovery. (See p. 142.)

As stated before, the sick man's attitude may, however, be completely different; he may feel loath to quit his settlement and his people, and will tell them very outspokenly that he does not yet want to leave them. He will himself entice them to double their efforts, to try some other means, some different methods of curing. If he is a medicine man, he will himself take charge and direction of the treatment, will send messengers to medicine men of his acquaintance, asking them to send along formulas and directions with which to cure him.

The people themselves do not attach any value or meaning to this state of mind, as is often done in some primitive and even in civilized communities, where it is considered an axiom that a man does not die as long as he gives proof of pronounced vitality, of interest in life, of attachment to all things earthly, such as are described above.

Definite and certain data as to the outcome of the illness, as to whether the patient will live or die, can always be obtained by means of divinatory methods, the most usual in this case being the "examination with the beads."

The medicine man holds a black bead between thumb and index finger of the left hand, a white or red bead between forefinger and thumb of the right hand, and, reciting an appropriate formula, examines what are the chances of the sick man. The more vitality the bead in the right hand shows, the greater are the chances for recovery.

This ceremony need not necessarily be performed at the patient's bedside, as may be seen from the description given of the typical curing procedure, page 67.

It is furthermore alleged of some powerful medicine men that they can prophesy the exact day of their death, and that they will take care themselves of the preparation of all objects that will be needed to lay out their corpse. This was reputed to have been done by old man Ax (see p. 88), and also Mooney cites a case of it in his Myths. This ability of foretelling their death these medicine men are said to possess by virtue of their keeping the ulŏⁿ'sudŏⁿ' stone.

Apart from the divination methods proper, where the future is being inquired into by active means, and apart from the very rare cases where a medicine man foretells his own death, there are some signs and omens of death which are common knowledge. Some of these have without doubt been borrowed from the whites. (See p. 37.)

When you are fishing, and you see a small fish rolling over and over in the water, dying, it is a sign one of your relatives is going to die.

If a tree is falling over near you, without any apparent cause, as a storm, lightning, etc.

If you hear something in the graveyard.

If you hear a dog howling dismally.

If one of your hens crows.

If at night a screech owl comes and perches near the house.

As it becomes apparent that no recovery is to be expected the relatives are summoned, not only those living at the settlement where the man is dying, but also those from other localities, even if they be two or three days distant. Also friends, whom the moribund may express a desire to see, are summoned.

As the end approaches the medicine man may make a last effort to turn the scales, by trying the cure for the illness generally referred to as Ga'kwe'nŏⁿ'ski, "if it wraps them up" (apoplexy). As it becomes clear that all hope is to be abandoned the moribund is made to partake of as square a meal as possible, "to strengthen him for the long journey he is about to undertake toward the Night Land."

One informant who had often been present at the decease of old people said that it was a custom for them, as they felt their end approaching, "to talk to their people, and tell them to love one another, and to love even their enemies."

Nothing that is needed to lay out the corpse should be prepared before the man has breathed his last, as "by doing this we would show that we are anxious for him to go."

As soon as the breathing stops the sufferer is pronounced dead, feeling the pulse or listening for the beating of the heart being unknown. The moment the moribund dies some one of the relatives or friends present says: aʻskwŭDɩ·Ga' (i. e., "he has ended").

In referring to the event a couple of hours after, the expression Goʼ!i' ayɔʻv‛i' ("he was lost just now") is used; whereas the next day one says vyɔʻvsö ⁿ' ("he has been lost").

BETWEEN DEATH AND BURIAL

As soon as the moribund breathes his last a relative—usually a male member of the family, as the father, the husband, or a brother—forces the legs of the corpse down to a straight position and lays the arms in such a position that the upper arms lie along the body, the forearms over the stomach, one hand lying over the other on the abdomen; it is immaterial which hand lies on top.

It is usually a female relative—a wife, a mother, or a sister—who closes the eyes and ties a (usually white) kerchief round the face and under the chin to prevent the jaw from dropping.

Then the body is washed. This is done by members of the same sex as the deceased, but never by relatives. Relatives do not take any part whatever in preparing the body for burial, or in disposing of the corpse, apart from closing the eyes, straightening the limbs, and tying the kerchief round the face.

The corpse is dressed in the best clothes that are available, and that must not necessarily have belonged to the succumbed person; a brother, a sister, a friend may bring as a present a particularly fine neckerchief, or even a valued coat or skirt, according to the sex of the deceased, to dress the corpse in.

A new hat, a new pair of shoes, a silver or gold trinket, are objects which people are especially fond of dressing the corpse with. A deceased woman is often given her favorite cup or saucer along with her. These are never "killed."

No food is put into the coffin with adults, but into that of babies a bottle of milk is placed.

If a woman dies immediately after parturition, and her baby dies with her, the baby is placed in the right arm of the mother in the coffin.

On the breast of the corpse of an adult of either sex a little vessel (a cup or a glass) of salt is placed. (Pl. 9, b.) Of this custom not one Cherokee can explain the reason; some vaguely hint that the salt serves the purpose of preventing the flesh from decaying. This explanation, however, as well as the custom itself, seems to me so foreign to the Cherokee mind that I am inclined to see in this a borrowing from the whites, either directly from traders, settlers, or mountaineers, or through the mediacy of negro slaves. (Cf. Pucket, pp. 83, 87.)

There are indications that in former times it was customary to bury with the deceased some of the property belonging to him. A case was cited by one informant: When he was a boy (about 50 years ago) the members of the tribe were still drawing an annual pension of $50 in gold from the Government. Once a girl died and it happened that her annual pension arrived the same day. Her mother insisted that the golden coins be buried with her in the coffin. And so it was done.

The body is not put into the coffin until two or three hours before burial. Prior to this the corpse, all dressed up, is laid on wooden boards (pl. 9, *b*) in a slightly slanting position, the head being raised about 60 centimeters, the feet about 30 centimeters above the ground, A sheet is thrown over the body, covering it completely. Whenever anyone comes in to see the corpse the sheet is thrown back from the face (pl. 9, *b*); the visitor just looks at the face for a few minutes; he neither addresses it nor touches it; he then goes away without speaking.

The body is kept in the house two or three days. From myths, traditions, and hazy recollections of some of the medicine men, it would appear that this period used to be a longer one—possibly seven days—in former times, but now the Government officials do not permit so long a delay.

While the corpse is still in the house, relatives, friends, and neighbors gather during the nights and in turn half of their number watch and sometimes sing, while the others sleep.

Of this watching the meaning is now lost, but the object of it must originally have been to prevent the witches from coming and "stealing the liver" of the corpse.

As for the singing, aboriginal dirges seem to have been completely lost, and when any singing is done at all some Cherokee Christian hymn (cf. Cherokee hymn book) is sung. The hymn selected depends solely on the repertory at the command of the gathering.

If this singing takes place, men as well as women may join in it.

After the death of a member of the settlement, no winter provisions, preserves, etc., are to be touched for four (others say for seven) days. As soon as it is known that a death has occurred provisions are immediately to be prepared for four (or seven) days, so that they do not have to be touched for that period; since provisions, if they are not let alone for the first few days following a death, "will be exhausted in no time."

Attention may once again be drawn to the purificatory rite observed by the medicine man who was in charge of the patient before his death. (See p. 103.)

The coffin is made by two men acting under a foreman. This "company" is elected for the term of a year, at the same time as the "grave-digging company" (cf. infra) and the chief of the settlement (see p. 80).

The election is a very unofficial affair, the members generally being volunteers. The foreman, and if necessary one of the two members, if there are no volunteers, are nominated, and usually, ipso facto, elected. The chief of this company at the time of my stay was yɔ·'nυGǫ·'ski ("bear coming out of the water"). (Pl. 10, b.)

The coffin is made of roughly hewn boards or planks and its shape shows unmistakable traces of white influence; it is sometimes covered with black cloth, nailed down by tacks.

The office of "coffin maker" seems to be on the verge of extinction, as I have known cases where they did not display any activity whatever. No particular cause could be indicated for this abstention, the reason being merely that a half-blood member of the tribe had volunteered for the job, and as he was a good carpenter, and did not charge anything, his services were readily accepted by all concerned.

Burial

As soon as it is known that someone has died, the head man of the "grave-digging company" is notified; he, in turn, gives notice to his helpers, and the same day or the next day the grave is dug.

The gravediggers are a company of six volunteers acting under a chief; the latter office at the time of my stay being held by one Gυla·'ci. They also are appointed for a year, and are elected in the same manner as the coffin makers (cf. supra).

A medicine man should never serve as a member of either of these companies, nor should he ever give assistance in anything pertaining to the laying out or burying of a corpse; he should not wash it, nor help to carry it to the grave, nor help to dig the grave.

Were he to disregard any of these injunctions he would never again be able to cure or to exert any of his other activities.

If the wife of a member of the coffin-making or of the grave-digging squad is with child he should desist from helping his fellows, as otherwise his child would be stillborn. Nor should any one help to prepare the coffin or the grave of a deceased member of his own family, as already stated (p. 134).

The cemetery is usually situated along the slope of a hill. No other reason for this custom is given but this one: That it prevents the soil and the people buried in it from being washed away, or becoming swamped, as would be the case if burial places were chosen in the lowlands. There is no preference, when choosing the site for a new graveyard, for either the "dark" or the "sunny" side of the mountain, which play so prominent a rôle in the Cherokee sacred literature.

The burial usually takes place between midday and "when the sun roosts on the mountain" (about 4 p. m.), i. e., about 2 p. m.

But as early as 10 a. m. the people of the settlement are assembling at the cabin of the deceased. Those who have not yet seen the corpse may go inside and look at it, to join afterwards those who have not entered the house and who have remained outside, squatting on the ground, or sitting on logs; as is usual at all Cherokee social gatherings, the women keep apart, and do not sit down, but keep standing in a group, some 20 or 30 feet away from the men.

It struck me that the women hardly talk, even among themselves, whereas the men did not seem to take matters quite so seriously, and they smoke and talk, and even joke in subdued tones.

All the people of the settlement, men, women and children, are present, unless prevented by serious illness, or by some other major impediment. Also from the near-by settlements many friends and all the relatives, however distant, are present.

The relatives go inside and sit on boards—improvised benches— and hardly speak a word. Female relatives do not try to hide their sorrow, but do not wail, or in any way give proof of frantic grief. It is rare to see a man weep.

An hour or so before the corpse is to be taken away a native preacher may come, whether the deceased professed to be a Christian or not, read some chapter of the Cherokee translation of the New Testament, and deliver a long speech, addressing the deceased, and stressing the main facts of his life.

At a sign of the chief of the coffin makers, four men will start hunting around for two stout poles or strong boards on which the coffin is put to be carried, and the funeral procession starts. There is not the slightest ceremonial as regards this. Five or ten men may step briskly in front or alongside of the coffin, and behind it a medley of men and women in groups, in no definite order, jostling each other, pushing and hurrying, even if there is nothing to jostle or to hurry about.

Every 200 yards or so the chief of the coffin makers, who now acts as a kind of "master of ceremonies," shouts out: anɩ`sɔ'i' nɔ·ᵘ-ɢwɔ̈ᵘ' ("other ones now"), and four other men, not necessarily belonging to this company, come out of the crowd and take the places of the coffin carriers.

The coffin is now usually carried as described above: On two poles or small beams, carried by four men, two on each side, not on their shoulders, but at arm's length.

Another way of carrying the corpse, and which may be older, but which is now disappearing, is to hang the coffin by two chains from a long pole, which is carried by two men on the shoulders. This device is still used in the lowland settlements where the cemetery is at some distance; in this case the coffin is transported by an ox-drawn wagon, but on the wagon it is fixed in such a way as to be hanging by two chains from a pole laid horizontally and lengthwise across the wagon.

When the cemetery is reached the coffin is put down near the grave which has been dug in the meanwhile by the "grave-digging company." A Christian hymn is sung in Cherokee, or maybe in English,[66] by a couple of men or women present; this again is not determined by the sex of the deceased, but depends merely on who is able and willing to sing.

The "preacher" again says a few words, bidding good-by to the departed one. Before being lowered, the coffin is opened and the cover laid back so that only the face of the corpse can be seen. Everybody passes by the coffin to cast a last look on it. The nearest relatives—father, mother, wife, children—pass first;[67] when the last person present has passed by the cover is nailed down definitely and the coffin is lowered into the grave. The grave is dug and the coffin is lowered into it in such a way that the head lies toward the west. The grave is immediately filled, and those present climb down the hill in different directions, all the people but the relatives of the deceased going to their respective homes.

After Burial

Immediately after the burial the nearest relatives of the deceased, i. e., the members of his household, have to go to the river, accompanied by the priest, who recites a prayer to purify them. If, for some reason, this ceremony is not performed immediately, before the family has gone home, it may be performed the following day; but in this case, one purification is not held to be sufficient, and the ceremony is repeated every morning for four days. The formula recited on this occasion is the same as the one used when "going to water" every new moon; white cloth and beads are also used, and the officiating medicine man also chews "old tobacco," the juice of which he sprays from his mouth into the necks of the members of the party, who stand facing the water.

Not one member of the household must go out for a period of four days (some say seven days, which is probably the older and more correct belief) for "anything which is not strictly necessary." Such essential duties as cutting wood for firewood, hunting for the daily sustenance, etc., are not prohibited, but there is to be no visiting of neighbors, no partaking in social functions, as the ball game, a dance, etc.

The belief prevails that whatever is done by the members of the household during the four days of this period will be done by them for

---

[66] "Nearer, my God, to Thee," was sung at one funeral I witnessed.

[67] Unless a woman with child be present. (See p. 121.)

the rest of their lives; i. e., if they attend only to the real necessities of life they will forever after be dutiful and reliable in whatever their occupation may be. The men will be smart, well-providing sons and husbands; the women alert and solicitous wives and mothers; whereas, were any of them to go out and gossip, or otherwise join in "unnecessary" phases of social life he would for the rest of his life be a fickle rake or a heedless hussy.

As soon as the family gets home from the burial, or from the subsequent ceremony at the river's edge, the new fire is started, after all the old ashes have been taken outside and scattered about the yard. In olden time this fire was no doubt kindled from the sacred communal fire of the council house; now the more modern match is used, although I have known cases where flint and punk were still resorted to.

The cabin is smoked with pine branches, burned in a cooking vessel; pine branches are also thrown on the rekindled hearth fire; according to some of the people, "the smell of the pine takes all away that has been left of death and disease." Pines, as all evergreens, are considered by the Cherokee to have eternal lives, and are therefore most fit to avert death and destruction.

Originally, not only the house where the death occurred had to be smoked in this fashion, but each and every house of the settlement. This custom is now rapidly falling into oblivion, but I still noticed, during my stay, that all those who had been taking any part in the care of the deceased, before and after his death, went through this purification rite with scrupulous care.

Old traditions and references to it in myths and tales establish beyond doubt that long ago, seven days after the burial a dance took place at which every member of the deceased's household and all the people of the settlement were present. This dance seems to have served the double purpose of speeding the spirit on its journey [68] and of diverting the sorrowing relatives. Such a dance is referred to in "The Daughter of the Sun" myth (Mooney, Myths, p. 254) and also in a tale collected by me, but yet unpublished.

It can not now be stated whether at these dances any special songs were sung, but if we can trust tradition on this point it would appear that those dances and songs were selected which would best suit the purpose of amusing the mourners present; it was thought that if they really enjoyed themselves on this occasion there was no fear that they would pine away with grief; but if the entertainers failed in their purpose the future looked gloomy and threatening for the mourners.

There is no visiting of graves after the burial; to do so would bring bad luck. This is easy to understand, if we recall the Cherokee

---

[68] The ghost of the deceased lingers 7 days around the settlement before proceeding on its journey "out west" (see p. 142).

belief, that thinking or dreaming of departed ones spoils the saliva, thus resulting in an uncanny but severe illness.

Likewise, if ever the small mound of earth which is piled up over a grave is scattered by rain or wind it should never be replaced. For "this would show us to be anxious for the other living persons to die and go to the graveyard."

However much this may remind us of a belief of the whites [69] there is no reason to suspect its influence on this Cherokee custom, as it is quite in keeping with their traditions and views on this subject. The basis of it is clear: Thinking or even dreaming of departed relatives is a symptom of a disease, sent by the a`nιsGι·'na or ghosts, and results in our saliva being spoiled, thus causing an uncanny but deadly illness. Any of our actions susceptible of stirring up our sorrow and affliction will, of course, again focus our attention on our loss and will make us despondent and abject, i. e., will make us ill.

This belief is still strongly, though often subconsciously, adhered to. Some half-bloods tried to prevail on their friends to tend the graves and keep them in a clean and nicely groomed condition as the white people do. They were successful for some years, the graveyard being cleared and hoed once a year (usually the first few days of August). But the aversion to this "unhealthy" work prevailed, and at the time of my visit this custom had not been observed for three years.

Not only is there no visiting of graves but the graveyard is shunned and avoided as much as possible, especially at night. There is an additional reason for this—the graveyard is constantly haunted by witches, who as soon as a new burial has taken place swoop down on the grave, exhume the corpse, and eat its liver.

Afterlife

Again and again in these pages it has been stressed how much of aboriginal belief and practice has broken down. On many problems which at one time must have been the subject of keen contemplation and of shrewd speculation, the present-day views of the people—and to but little less degree of the medicine men—are so hazy and confused that it requires a great deal of patience and much painstaking effort to gain any information on them; and great caution is to be taken when it comes to sifting, classifying, and interpreting this material.

This state of affairs is keenly realized when we endeavor to study the Cherokee conceptions regarding the soul and its survival.

---

[69] "It is bad to disturb an old grave, as by putting up a tombstone; you will thus herald a death." (Bergen, Current Superstitions, p. 133, No. 1265.)

THE SOUL

It will help our purpose materially if we briefly examine the different semantic values of the stem $\sqrt{}$-ᴅaɴᴉ̓t,[70] which we find in the word for "soul":

aᴅa`ɴᴉ̓tɔ' Soul; mind; disposition.
ɢaᴅa·`nətᴜ̓a' I am thinking.
aɢ̇waᴅa`ɴᴉ̓t'ɛtᴜ̓a' I am astonished.
aɢwaᴅa`ɴᴉ̓t'ɛta` nönï' I doubted it.
ɔ'sɩ·yu' a`ɢwaᴅa`ɴᴉ̓tatö·'ŋi I rejoice.
ʋᴅa`ɴᴉ̓tɩ·yu'· He is of a friendly disposition.

This shows how prolific has been the activity of this stem, such concepts as thinking, feeling, being conditioned, being disposed, being in a certain state of mind, and, in the ritual language, even "causing," all being rendered by it.

This points to a semantic evolution which is very similar to that of the Latin "animus."

Soul and mind are almost synonymous to the Cherokee. They are at least two closely related manifestations of the same principle. "Our soul has its seat in our heart (my heart: aɢɩ·ᴰna'u'). What we think starts in our heart, and the heart sends our mind out." Our heart is the broadcasting station, might be a very free but all the more correct version.

It is not possible to find any definite opinions as to whether the name, the shadow, or any other part of the individual is considered a part of his soul, or in exactly what relation they stand to a person. There can, however, hardly be any doubt but that the name, the shadow, the liver, the crown of the head, or perhaps a particular hair, or a particular lock (the scalp lock?) on the crown of the head, all were once believed to be intimately associated with the soul, either as parts of it or as abiding places for it.

The soul does not leave the body during sleep or dreams. Nor is sickness caused by absence of the soul; but certain psychopathological states are ascribed to this fact; the condition of utter despondency brought about by an enemy "working" against you is caused by nothing else but the fact that he has gotten hold of your soul, and has buried it "out west," in the Night Land. This does not necessarily mean instant death; it rarely does. You may live without your soul for quite a number of months, and slowly pine away; this is what happens if you can not successfully counteract the influence of your enemy.

Acute cases of lovesickness, homesickness, melancholy, and dejection are also usually explained in this way.

No definite notion is entertained as to the origin of souls.

---

[70] When the vowel becomes lengthened the nasal becomes voiced, and is followed by an obscure vowel.

SURVIVAL OF THE SOUL

At death the soul leaves the body and becomes a ghost (asgɩ·'na). It travels to the ghost country (tsü`sɑɩnɔ*'i), in the Night Land (v'sö`*'ɩ·yi'), in the west, in seven days.

It does not haunt the settlements, nor the burial places, nor does it ever return. Some informants are not so sure as to this: they claim that the ghosts sometimes return, viz, when they come to make people ill, or to come and fetch them before they die, to show them the way to the ghost country. These opinions, however, I am inclined to consider as individual beliefs, based chiefly on dreams and personal experiences.

In the Night Land the ghost people live exactly according to the native pattern; they live in settlements, have chiefs and councils, clans and families (everybody who dies goes and joins the relatives who have preceded him); they go hunting and fishing, have ball games and dances, etc.

There does not seem to exist any differentiation based upon moral conduct in this life, the Cherokee believing that morality is to be observed for its own sake, without hope of recompense or fear of punishment in the next life. These conceptions are now slowly being superseded by hazy beliefs influenced by Christian eschatology.

Some interesting facts on this score are being revealed by dreams, which indicate that some kind of a differentiation must once have been believed in, of which people now have lost all recollection.

One informant (W.) told me his mother (Ayo.) was wont to tell him of the following experience of hers:

Shortly after the Civil War the Cherokee were visited with smallpox. She was one of the many stricken, and she died (sic); she went along a road and came to a settlement where the people lived who had died; as she traveled on she came to another settlement, the chief of which had been a chief in his lifetime; she had known him. The chiefs held a council about her and decided that she could not come and live with them yet. They sent her back. So she walked back to where she lived. She recovered from the smallpox. "And it was not a dream either," the informant added.

Another, far more interesting experience was told by the individual to whom it happened, T. (Pl. 10, c.) He relates it as follows:

About 37 years ago he was very ill; all his relatives expected him to die, and they had gathered by his bedside. He became unconscious; it seemed to him as if he fell asleep. The people who were with him told him later that he actually died; he did not breathe for half an hour.

It seemed to him as if he got up from his bed, walked out of the cabin, and started traveling along a path. He climbed to the top of a mountain, where suddenly he saw a beautiful plain, a meadow, stretched out in front of him. The grass was of a fine green color, and felt very soft and nice to walk upon.

Soon he saw a building; he entered, and found it filled with children, some of them mere babies, and none of them any older than about 12 years. He asked them where the chief lived; they told him, the chief lived in the fourth building, and that, if he wished to see him, he had but to walk through the opened doors of the three first buildings.

He went through the second building and the third, and found these likewise filled with people, both men and women, but all of them older than the children he had seen at the first place.

As he came to the fourth building he found the door locked; he asked several times for admittance. "Chief, open the door for me." As he asked it the fourth time he heard somebody inside turn round on his chair; then he went in.

There was a white man, very old, with a long white beard, sitting at a desk. He did not even look up at the visitor, and shook hands with him without even turning round. He said: "Well, have you come to live with us?" T. said he had, upon which the man at the desk turned round, reached for a big account book and a pen, and made ready to write T.'s name in the book. But all of a sudden he bethought himself: "I think you had better go back home again," he said; "you will come back here again 33 days from now; then you will come to stay, and then we will write your name in the book." He closed the book and put it away.

He opened a trapdoor and gave T. a small disk-like object, like a thin sheet of tin, about the size of a silver dollar, and said: "You had better hold this in your hand, to find your way."

After that T. felt himself, still sitting on his chair, drop through the trapdoor, and falling at a terrific speed, the air rushing past him as if it were a windstorm; he soon landed on the top of a mountain near his settlement; he threw the little disk in front of him and it started rolling in the direction of his home; he followed it, went into the cabin, where he found his friends and relatives still gathered, and stretched himself out on his couch; he then opened his eyes, and found everybody very much relieved, as they had been watching him carefully, and had thought him to be dead.

In both these cases, "the different settlements," the "four different buildings," must surely have some definite meaning. In T.'s account there would appear to be a differentiation according to age, but this I suspect to be influenced by ill-digested evangelization, as another informant told me once that "all children under 12 years of age who die are happy; under 12 they do not know what is wrong."

Incidentally, I want to draw attention to a rather humorous side of T.'s account: The whole of his visit with God, in an office, with books and stationery all around, and the host's way of receiving his visitor (not answering his knocking, not looking up as he comes in, not even to shake hands, etc.), all this is strongly reminiscent of the reception accorded "Injuns" at some of the agency offices. This experience, it should be noted, was dreamed nearly 40 years ago.

I might finally state that the social status of this life is not modified in the next, chiefs remaining chiefs; medicine men, medicine men; etc.

Using such expressions as "this life" and "next life" is not quite doing justice to Cherokee conceptions; they look upon life and afterlife as different lives in space, rather than as successive lives in time. They do not, as a Christian would put it, live a mortal life, and an eternal life after that, but they move from their settlement in the Great Smokies to the "place out west." They speak of the people out west as they would of a neighboring tribe, as the Creeks, or even as they would of a Cherokee settlement some "overnights" away.

Suicide

Suicides, although not unknown, are very rare. The motives of the few cases that have come to my attention are the general human ones—to be suffering from an illness which is reputed incurable and love troubles seeming to be the two main causes.

A suicide always causes a tremendous commotion; but no special beliefs are connected with it, nor with the ghost of the victim. The burial takes place as usual.

Even old informants could not remember more than three cases of suicide; all the cases were men. Two shot themselves and one strangled himself with a rope.

Tragical Deaths

Another kind of death which arouses local interest and comment, and which is handed down to posterity along with the traditional lore and the sacred myths, is that resulting from accident, especially if it is accompanied by some uncanny details.

THE FORMULAS

Name

There are two ways in which both laity and specialists refer to the sacred and medicinal formulas and the knowledge they contain.

If one medicine man wants to broach the subject to one of his compeers, with a view of discussing their mutual knowledge, he says: Goʻṿ'sti ʻi·kt'a'ǫ·'.i, i. e., "What do you know?"; and of a medicine man who is reputed well versed in this lore, the lay community says: akt'a'ʻi·yu', i. e., "he knows a great deal."

Just as, to quote an interesting parallel, the sacred literature in Sanskrit is referred to as "veda," a term which is etymologically connected with the Indo-European stem √-wid-, "to know."[71]

Incidentally it is interesting to draw attention to the fact that the root of Cherokee aʽkt'aʽa', i. e., "he knows." is √-kt',— the original meaning of which is "to see"; cf. "eye": akt'a'.

The same semantic evolution has taken place in the Indo-European languages, where the comm.-Germanic √-wit-, "to know," and the Latin uideo, "I see," are both derived from the same Indo-European stem √-wid-. If now we go a step further, and see what a peculiar meaning this stem has acquired in Sanskrit: "veda"="the thing known"> "the knowledge" viz, "the sacred knowledge," we find the same evolution in meaning as we have in Cherokee.

Another term used, again both by the medicine men and by the uninitiated, is Gɔʽwɛ·li'.

The present meaning of this is "paper," "book," "that which has been written," as the formulas are usually kept jotted down in the Sequoya syllabary by the medicine men. It is clear from this that this name must be of comparatively modern origin, as it could of course not have been applied to them prior to the invention of the syllabary by Sequoya in 1821.

This term again throws an interesting light on the psychological principles underlying the semantic evolution in languages even so different and separated from each other in time and place to such an extent as modern Iroquois and the older Germanic dialects. The meaning "to write" of the Cherokee √-wɛl- is comparatively recent: It can not be much older than 200 years. Originally it meant "to mark," and especially "to mark wood by burning designs on it," a technique still in use among the Cherokee to mark the flat wooden dice used in gambling.

As for its parallel in the Germanic dialects, we have but to remember that our "book" traces its origin to "beech (tree)" (cf. Anglo-Saxon "boc," i. e., "beech tree"; "book." Old High German "buohha," i. e., "beech tree"). Beech boards, beech bark, and stencils made of beech wood were used by both Anglo-Saxon and Teutonic peoples as writing material.[72] So we see the material used, beech, assume the meaning of "a writing," "a collection of writings" (book), and the latter meaning has again evolved to that of "the collection of sacred lore" (cf. the Book, i. e., the Bible).

---

[71] Cf. also Kroesch, Samuel: "The semasiological development of words for 'perceive,' 'understand,' 'think,' 'know' in the older Germanic dialects." Diss. Chicago, 1911. Repr. from "Mod. Phil." VIII, No. 4, Chicago, 1911.

[72] That also to the Italic herdsmen this use of the beech was not unknown, appears from Vergil's Eclogue, V 13: "Carmina quae nuper in viridi cortice fagi descripsi."

Even though these two terms are commonly known and readily understood, the former is but seldom used now, and the latter hardly any more. Usually the formulas are referred to by a specific name, which immediately makes it clear what kind is meant, as "What do you know about curing?" or "Have you any papers for the purpose of killing (a man)?" These different names are listed below (see p. 148), where they are discussed in detail.

ORIGIN

As to the origin of the sacred formulas and songs, the laity are now almost ignorant. The medicine men themselves are gradually losing the accounts made of it in the myths, and to a question, "Where have we the knowledge of all these formulas from," they will at first superficially answer: "We know them from the people who lived a long time ago." This locution is even appended as ending clause to some of the formulas and prescriptions, and it is closely akin to a stereotyped exordium used by some informants when telling a tale: "A long time ago, this is what the people told who lived then."

On pushing scrutiny somewhat further, the older informants will vaguely remember some accounts of the origin of the bear songs and of the sacred and medicinal formulas; it is most fortunate indeed that James Mooney left us such an excellent account of these myths. (See Mooney, Myths, p. 248, for the origin of the deer songs; p. 319 for medicine and hunting songs; p. 325 for the origin of the bear songs.)

These myths were collected about 40 years ago and it would now be utterly impossible to find a Cherokee living who could give such a complete account of them.

I should not neglect to mention that sporadically a medicine man will attribute the Cherokee's knowledge of formulas and prescriptions to a revelation of une⁀'tlanö′'ti, the Apportioner, who, in this case, must undoubtedly be identified as God, the Creator, as preached by Christian missionaries. The same man on another occasion will tell you, with just as honest a conviction, that "the people inherited the knowledge from a powerful wizard when he died," referring to Stone-clad's death. (Cf. Mooney, Myths, p. 320.)

KINDS

Before going into details as to the different kinds of formulas used by the Cherokee it may not be out of place to draw attention to a sharp distinction existing between the knowledge of the laity and that of the specialists.

The average member of the tribe may know four or five formulas, but even then he usually only knows fragmentary portions of them, and mutilates them when trying to recite them, as the ritual meaning of many words is unknown to him. This scanty supply of sacred and medicinal formulas nearly always includes the song to cure the results of accidents (mostly cuts and gashes caused by ax or knife) (see p. 85); also some prayer for protection, either to be recited or sung, is usually common property; and two or three of the easier kind of medicinal conjurations may complete the lot.

There are, however, indications that until recently (15 to 20 years ago) formulas were sold to a layman by a medicine man, if the former were willing to pay the price for it. This trade was carried on especially in the domains of hunting and love conjuration, a good formula of any of these kinds commanding $3 to $5. (See p. 105.)

It is easy to understand why this practice is now on the verge of extinction: There is no game now in the Cherokee country, the killing of which would be worth such an exorbitant sum,[74] and as for the love formulas, the younger generation, which must always have supplied the main customers for this line, are fast losing faith in these practices and are relying on more material means to attract the attention and to obtain the favor of the opposite sex.

There is no objection on the part of the medicine men to selling also the more ordinary disease-curing formulas and prescriptions to the uninitiated, but there is hardly any demand for these, nor does there seem to have been in the past. A plausible reason for the popularity of the two kinds mentioned before seems to my mind to be that an individual wanted to buy love or hunting formulas mainly so as to be able to go through the necessary ritual and ceremonies without the aid of a medicine man; by acting alone he could keep his intentions and his plans in the domain of hunting and love a secret to eventual competitors.

There are some formulas, however, which a medicine man will not communicate to an uninitiated member of the tribe at any price. Even to the initiated this kind is only handed on with the utmost discrimination. (See p. 100.) These are the incantations listed below as Nos. 10–14 (pp. 148, 153).

I might add, finally, that ostensibly there seems to be some reluctance on the part of the medicine men to propagate any formulas at all. They pretend that the more the knowledge of a formula, of whatever kind it may be, is diffused, the less powerful it becomes and therefore they should be handed on to "the man in the street" with due care and moderation. This is, however, purely a theoretical, and as a rule a rather hypocritical contention; and in the practice every medicine man thinks that the occult power of the formulas

---

[74] Deer and bear are extinct on the reservation, and rabbit, squirrel, and ground hog are about all there is left on the once so richly purveyed hunting grounds of the Cherokee.

will not be tampered with to any considerable degree by what little *he* sells, if only the others would not sell so much of it.

Theoretically speaking, there are no restrictions as to the formulas a medicine man may know. But for practical reasons most of them specialize in a certain set of them, according to the subbranch of magic or curing he specializes in (as love attraction, medicine, etc.), or he may even specialize in a narrower field, according to the two or three diseases he is reputed to be an authority on.

For specialists among the medicine men see page 85; for the special sets of formulas see below.

When it comes to classifying the various formulas which the Cherokee use we can do so according to their own standards or according to ours.

They themselves distinguish clearly between "good" formulas and "bad" ones, the good ones being those the object of which is beneficial, the bad ones those with deleterious aims. Under the former they would classify those that have been listed by me as Nos. 1 to 9, pages 149–153; among the latter those which I list as Nos. 10 to 14, pages 153–155.

CLASSIFICATION

A. PRAYERS:
    1. For protection.
    2. For long life.
    3. For gathering medicine.

B. CONJURATIONS:
    4. For curing.
    5. For using tobacco.
    6. For examining with the beads.
    7. Against witches.
    8. Agricultural.
    9. For hunting and fishing.

C. INCANTATIONS:
    10. "To change."
    11. To kill.
    12. For love attraction.
    13. For making unattractive.
    14. For separating.

I feel that I should motivate in a few words this classification, as well as the terminology used.

I apply the name of "formula" as a generic term to any of the three kinds used.

Prayer.—By this name I call a formula in which a request is made or in which a desire is expressed to a power which is clearly felt as superior, and upon whom the one who prays feels himself dependent. The object is to bring about morally or materially beneficial results. The request is made, the desire expressed in a humble way; it is not felt that the result desired can be forced or extorted from the being addressed. He can not be commanded or compelled to act.

Conjuration.—This is the term I use to indicate those formulas in which a power, not necessarily felt as superior, is appealed to in a commanding, coercive, often even in a threatening, insulting tone; the object is to bring about materially beneficial results. There is an absolute certainty that our desire will materialize, if only the formula is recited and the ceremony performed without a flaw.

Incantation.—As usual in the course of this paper I define incantation as the recitation of a formula with a view to harm a person in his material belongings, in his health, or in his life.

I am quite well aware that "incantation" as generally used in English has not this exclusive meaning, and very often also covers the two other groups discussed, as indeed, etymologically, it has a right to do. But anybody who has given the subject close attention will agree that the terminology is very confusing and most inadequate. Incantation, exorcism, spell, charm, prayer, magic or sacred formula, nursery rhymes, etc., are words that often all stand for one thing, but when one particular kind of formula has to be referred to one is at a loss to know which term of the collection to use, and be sure to be understood.

The terminology as here used is adopted in German and Netherlandish as Prayer (Gm. Segen; Neth. Zegen); Conjuration (Gm. Beschwörungsformel; Neth. Bezweringsformule); Incantation (Gm. Zauberspruch; Neth. Tooverspreuk).

PRAYERS

For Protection

a·ˋDaDŭtłsö$^{n'}$ˊsti   υGǫ·ˊwŭtłiˋ
for tying oneself up   for the purpose

This kind of formulas, to which belong also many songs, are of a prophylactic nature. They are protection prayers, which are known in German folklore as "Segen."

They are recited, either by a priest on behalf of a patron, or by any one who happens to know them on behalf of himself, and are supposed to ward off evil, such as illness, ill will, witchcraft, etc. They are sung or recited especially before setting out on a journey, or when about to meet a group of people, and there is no doubt but the ferocious songs of "Ostenaco," both when setting out upon his journey and when arriving in the port of London, mentioned by Lieutenant Timberlake, were just this kind of protection songs. To quote Timberlake: "When we had got about 200 yards from the town house . . . Ostenaco sung the war song, in which was a prayer for our safety through the intended journey; this he bellowed out loud enough to be heard at a mile's distance." (Timberlake, p. 98.)

And when arriving: "While in the boat that took us to shore Ostenaco, painted in a very frightful manner, sung a solemn dirge with a very loud voice, to return God thanks for his safe arrival. The loudness and uncouthness of his singing, and the oddity of his person, drew a vast crowd of boats, filled with spectators from all the ships in the harbour . . . ," etc. (l. c., 115).

I know many Cherokee who even now would not go to a social gathering, such as a ball game, a dance, etc., without first having recited or sung one of these formulas.

Moreover, this kind of formula may be sung by a married couple at night to ward off any machinations that might be undertaken against their conjugal happiness.

There are not many of these prayers left and the Ay. manuscript does not contain a single specimen of them.

For Long Life

ama·'yi	Dɩ`·Dadzɔ͞ⁿ'st'tɔ.ti`	υGǫ·'wùtłi
water, Loc.	to lead them to, and bring them back with	for the purpose of

Since these formulas are practically used only in connection with the rite of "going to water," their name is referred to in this way.

The ritual of going to water is performed by the Cherokee with very different ends in view: To obtain long life (which is by far the more important), to cast off a disease, for the benefit of a pregnant woman and her baby, to "work" against an enemy, in love matters, not to speak of the regular ceremony at every new moon, when each family is supposed to observe it.

As a rule these prayers are the most lengthy and poetic in the collections. They are generally recited by the priests when taking patrons to the river; they are unknown to the laity. Nos. 18, 43, 83, 92, and 93 of the Ay. manuscript belong to this kind.

For Gathering Medicine

nǫ·'wɔ·t'i`	aGɩ`stɩ·yi'
to treat with	to take it

This name is given to the prayers recited when gathering medicine; they are usually addressed to υnɛ`˙tɬanɔ͞'ǐi the Apportioner, the chief deity, and ask in a humble, meek way for His permission to come and gather the medicine.

To this class might also be reckoned the formulas that are recited when putting the simples into the vessel to be boiled:

nǫ·'wɔ·t'i`	aGɔ͞`tɬanɩ`ɩ̈ɔ̈·'.i
to treat with	to put it in it

There are no specimens of this kind in the Ay. manuscript. They are unknown to the laity.

CONJURATIONS

For Curing

Dɩ·ˋDaꞌnö̧·ˊwɔ·tꞌʃˋ.tiˋ vGö̧·ˊwùtłiˋ
to treat people with   for the purpose of

This kind of formulas is the most common. Of the 96 contained in this (the Ay.) manuscript, only five (Nos. 18, 43, 83, 92, and 93) are not medicinal formulas.

Although the proportion of these curing formulas is usually quite preponderant in the manuscripts, it is almost impossible that the Ay. manuscript should not have contained more formulas for such purposes as love attraction, hunting and fishing, man killing, etc. However that may be, none were included in Mooney's transliteration of the manuscript on which this edition is based. (See p. 2.)

To this class may also be reckoned to belong those few formulas that are used to take the medicine, after it has been boiled, outside of the house: GanʋˋGɔ·wɩˋstɩ·yiˊ nö̧·ˋwɔ·tꞌiˊ

This is a welcome opportunity to say a word about the medicinal prescriptions. These are not formulas, but are nevertheless called by the same name as this class: Gɔꞌweˊˊli Dɩ·ˋDaꞌnö̧·ˊwɔ·tꞌɔ.ˋtiˋ vGö̧·ˋwùtłiˊ, i. e., "papers to cure them (indefinite) with."

They contain advice and prescriptions as to the simples that are to be used to cure a given disease, and are almost identical, both as to contents and structure, with the Dɛ·ˋGɔ·sɩˋsɩsGö̧·ˊ.i, i. e., "the directions" (lit.: "where they (the contents) have been gathered") appended to most of the formulas. (See p. 158.)

It is quite possible, not to say probable, that these prescriptions were originally the directions that went with the formulas, and that through error, neglect (or through rationalism?) of copyists, only the latter part of the formula, i. e., the directions, the prescription was copied.

For Using Tobacco

tsɔ·ˊlö̃ⁿ   Gö̃ⁿᵉ.ˊtꞌɔtiˋ   vGö̧·ˊwùtłiˋ
tobacco   it use with   for the purpose of

This name refers to the ceremony rather than to the formula used, as was the case with No. 2 (p. 150).

"Old tobacco" may be used with different formulas and with different ends in view: For curing certain diseases, for divinatory purposes, when "watching against witches," in certain incantation ceremonies.

When expressed in this way, it should always be understood as referring to one of the three ceremonies last mentioned.

Although there are three ceremonial ways of "using tobacco," viz, chewing it, burning it on a fire of charcoal, and smoking it in a pipe (see p. 75), only the second method is meant, when the action is referred to as by the title given above.

For Examining with the Beads

aDɛ·ˊlōⁿ   Dι`ḵtˋɔ.tiˊ
bead(s)   to look with them

These are the formulas that are used when conjuring with the red (or white) and black beads; this manipulation is very frequent in Cherokee magic and medicine.

It is nothing else but a kind of divination by which such hidden things are alleged to be discovered, as whether a sick man will live or die, whether we will be successful against an enemy, whether we will be successful in love, etc.

These formulas are unknown to the laity. No. 83 of the Ay. manuscript belongs to this class.

Just as the tobacco (cf. above), the beads may be used "both ways," as the Cherokee put it; i. e., they can be used to bring about beneficial or deleterious results, according to whether they are used along with a conjuration or with an incantation. But the medicine men always distinguish clearly between the two uses to which this manipulation may be put; the essence of the act does not depend on the paraphernalia used, but on the kind of formula which is recited.

Against Witches

sö·nɔˊ·yi   ɛ·Dɔˊ·ˋi   Gana·ˊyˋtɔ.tiˋ   υGö̞·ˊwŭtliˋ
at night   he walks about   to guard with   for the purpose of

This kind of conjuration is recited to ward off the evil influence or the envious machinations of witches.

As described (p. 30), witches are especially active around the dwelling of the sick and the dying. (For a full description of the activities of the witches and of the ways of thwarting these, see pp. 29–33.)

Agricultural

sɛ·luˊ
corn

The whole of the Cherokee collection of formulas is very poor in specimens of this description. This can be explained in two ways.

The fine climate and the good soil of the southern Alleghanies have made agriculture for the Cherokee a far easier proposition than it is, e. g., for the tribes of the Southwest. They are not so scantily provided with rain as the desert people are, and therefore formulas to cause rain or to make the corn grow may never have been used to any considerable extent.

The present scarcity of these formulas might also be explained in this way, that the Cherokee are now far less dependent on the native crops than they were a couple of centuries ago, when they did not have the advantages of the easy means of communication, and when they did not have traders and farmers living in their midst, or only a day's journey distant. And as with the Christians, "the fear of the Lord is the beginning of all wisdom," it may be said of the Cherokee, and of many tribes on the same level, that "the fear of drought is the beginning of a conjuration for rain."

These formulas are only known to specialists, of which there is still one living.

There is no formula of this kind in the present manuscript, but James Mooney has edited one, obtained also from Ay., in his SFC., p. 387.

For Hunting and Fishing

a′nɪnɔˑʻᶜᵗlɪDǫˑʻːi vˑntsɛˑʻlɪGa′; aGaˑʻyɪt'ǫˑ′i vGǫ·ʻwùtlïˋ
they hunt all over   (it is) theirs   fish traps   for the purpose of

By these names a variety of conjurations and songs are meant that aim at bringing success in hunting and fishing. Some of the hunting formulas are also used in divination practices, which are reputed to advise the hunter as to whether the time he has chosen to go on a hunting expedition is propitious, in which direction he has to depart, what he will kill, and when.

There is no doubt but that almost all the men knew a couple or more of these specimens some generations ago, when hunting, and even big-game hunting, were events of almost daily occurrence.

The hunters bought the knowledge of these songs and formulas from the medicine men (see p. 147), as much as $5 being paid for a bear-hunting song some 50 years ago. Now, as hunting is reduced to shooting rabbits and other small game, and with the advent of shotguns, there no longer seems to be so much call for this magic ammunition, and the formulas have therefore reverted to the custody of the medicine men.

Closely akin to the hunting formulas are those used for fishing, either by line or by trap. For reasons above stated, these also are getting scarcer from year to year, and they will undoubtedly be among the first to disappear.

No specimen of either is represented in this manuscript.

INCANTATIONS

"To Change"

With this class of formulas we enter the field of incantation. This particular kind is used by a medicine man on his own initiative, or at the invitation of a client, "to change" an enemy to a different condition with. This is only a euphemistic way of saying to change him to a bad condition with, and the worse the better.

This is the kind of incantation which, if successful, results in one of the dreaded ayɛˑʻlɪGɔˑʻGi diseases.

Just as love incantations are often alluded to by some circumlocution (see p. 158), these incantations are often written down in the collections under the innocent sounding caption of tsṿ`·ᴅalɛ‘nö·´ⁿᴅöⁿ
different sorts
ṿɢö·´wûtlï` (for the purpose of different kinds of things).
for the purpose of

To Kill

ᴅɩ‘ᴅanɛ·`səɢɩ·´sti   ṿ·ɢö·´wûtlï`
to kill people   for the purpose of

Of all the "bad" formulas, this is the worst kind, and rarely a medicine man will own that he knows one, or even that he has one in his possession.

It only results in the death of the victim if certain ceremonies are performed, as described (p. 87).

For Love Attraction

yö·ⁿwɛ´ʻi
people, living

This class of formulas is considered by the Cherokee as belonging to the most mysterious and occult of their knowledge, and to obtain information on it is quite a proposition. Even when in a secluded spot, medicine men hardly venture to give information on it, and then only by whispering, uneasily casting stealthy glances about them all the time.

The name as here given is a very general one, and may cover a horrible incantation against a rival in a love matter, as well as a pretty, innocent conjuration to gain the affection of the girl we woo.

Although yö·wɛ´ʻi is the technical name for this class of formulas, it is seldom written so outspokenly as a heading in a medicine-man's notebook. Usually some such circumlocution is used as: nö·´wɔ·t‘ï`  ᴅɩ`ɢɔsöⁿ`tɩ·yi, "to make medicine," or ᴅɩnɛ·`tsɔtiɢwö^ᵊ´, "to play with them merely." Occasionally they are even found under totally misleading captions, as

aᴅɛ·`löⁿ   ᴅɩ·´kt‘ɔti`   u^ʻ`tsöŋi´
beads   to look with,   he is ill

to examine with the beads when he is ill.

(For the terms used to clearly indicate malevolent love incantation, see p. 155.)

A thorough discussion of love incantation and the lore pertaining to it is withheld for the present, as this manuscript does not contain a single formula of this kind. The matter may be more conveniently treated when Ms. II is edited, in which quite a number of these incantations occur.

For Making Unattractive

DɩDa`skwǫ·yö ⁿ′stɔ.ti`
to cause them to become loathsome with

This is the kind of incantation which is recited by a medicine man at the request either of a scorned lover or of a jealous rival.

In the first case the patron orders the formula to be directed against the haughty object of his affections, and tries to make her so loathsome that she who spurned him will in her turn be scorned by others.

If the machinations are directed against a rival he is reviled to such an extent that no person endowed with reason could possibly think of paying any attention to him.

For Separating

Dɩ`·DaGalɛ′Nːtɔ.ti`   ʋGǫ̈·′wutłi`
to separate people with   for the purpose of

In the previous sections we discussed the kind of yǫ·wɛ′ːi formulas that are used by a spurned lover and by which he takes vengeance of an irresponsive love.

The kind we now deal with is used to kindle discord and to sow ill feeling between a married couple, or between sweethearts, so that the conquest of the party desired may be made the easier by the heretofore unsuccessful lover.

As already stated (p. 150), this is the incantation against which some protection song may be crooned by husband and wife at night that their love may not be unwrought by evil agencies.

How the Formulas Are Recited or Sung

As has been repeatedly stated in the course of this paper, some of the formulas are recited, others are sung. Although there is no definite rule as to which are spoken and which are chanted, it seems that most of the hunting formulas and a good many of the protection prayers are sung. Also some of the curing formulas, but very few of these only.

As I am not expert at recording music it was thought best to use the dictaphone to register some of the medicine, hunting, and dance songs. Fifteen dictaphone records were taken and have been deposited with the Bureau of American Ethnology, Smithsonian Institution, Washington, D. C.

Some of the hunting and protection songs are of considerable artistic value; the Cherokee sing with a high-pitched falsetto voice, and with all the singers heard, a peculiar nasal twang was noticed.

When the formulas are recited the medicine man mumbles them under his breath, and at a very fast tempo, so that neither the patient nor any one of his household manages to catch a single word.

Nowadays the medicine man does not always rely on his memory when reciting the longer formulas; he often reads the text from his ragged notebook or from the crumpled sheets of paper on which he has it jotted down.

How the Formulas are Considered by the Laity and by the Medicine Men

The layman holds the formulas of any kind in a sort of timorous respect and apprehensive awe. They are most powerful means indeed in the hands of those who know how to use them, but one who is not an expert had better leave them alone, for you never know what might happen.

To the medicine men the formulas are the means by which men are indirectly made powerful wizards; indirectly, i. e., through endowing them with the faculty to solicit or to command the services of those mighty wizards, the Spirits.

We must believe without flinching or wavering, we must have a staunch confidence in this power of the formulas. For the wizards we call on "know our mind," and if they find our conviction faltering they will not heed us, nor the words we speak.

A formula is sure to bring about the desired result, if only we are careful not to make any mistake in our choice. We may be so ignorant as to think that a patient is suffering from a disease caused by the fish, and we will consequently call on the fishing hawk to come and combat the fish. But maybe the ailment is not caused by the fish at all; possibly ghosts are responsible for it, or animal ghosts, or the birds, or the sun. It is obvious, the medicine men argue, that in this case no relief would follow, as we have appealed to a curing agent (the fishing hawk) who is absolutely powerless in this emergency.

We must also be careful not to omit a word, not a syllable, of the formula recited. It does not matter if there are words we do not understand (words, e. g., belonging to the ritual language (see p. 160) or words which, through erroneous copying, have been contaminated); the spirits we talk to understand them, as these expressions have been used in addressing them "ever since the time of long ago, when the old people lived."

Merely reciting the formula is not sufficient if we want to obtain success, though: we must also know "what is to be used with it," i. e., what simples are to be collected, how they have to be prepared, how they should be administered, etc.; and last but not least, we should also know "how we have to work." It is not difficult to recite a formula, but it is far from easy to know how to perform all the accompanying rites, to be conversant with the voluminous materia medica, and to be an expert at finding the simples and at preparing them. All this only a medicine man knows.

Technique of Writing the Formulas

Reference has repeatedly been made in the course of this paper to the sheets of paper and the notebooks in which the medicine men keep their stock of sacred and medicinal knowledge recorded.

I will now briefly describe the technique observed by them in compiling, conserving, and using this information.

The most methodic of the medicine men keep notebooks the sizes of which may differ from foolscap or quarto to 16° which they obtain from the white traders, and in which they write down the formulas they have been able to collect, without paying the slightest regard whatever to system or classification.

A conjuration to cure headache may precede a love incantation, which may be followed by a fishing song, after which a prescription for diarrhea is found.

The Ay. manuscript following is by no means the worst example of this motley topsy-turvy, as there are manuscripts in which the formulas are even interspersed with notes of an historical interest, not to speak of tribal records, such as births, deaths, accidents, etc.

It has always been a riddle to me how the medicine man finds the formula he needs for a particular occasion. This is indeed often a rather difficult proposition, but even if there are manuscripts containing nearly 300 formulas, the medicine man always knows exactly which formulas it contains. This, to my mind, is quite a remarkable feat of memory, since in such a compilation quite a few of the formulas are of necessity practically identical.

Where the formulas are kept on loose sheets of paper, of all dimensions and aspects, some of them written out in lead pencil, others in ink, others again with red or brown crayons, the confusion is even greater.

Roughly speaking, the contents of these collections may be divided into formulas and prescriptions. Usually they have a title written as a caption at the top, but this is not a rule, as very often the contents and the purpose of the formulas are briefly indicated at the end in the "directions."

Both "title" and "directions" the Cherokee call by the same name Dɛ`ɢɔ·sɩ`sɩsɢǫ̈·ʼ.i, i. e., "where they (the information, pl.) have been assembled." The directions at the end of the formula usually convey such information as the purpose of the formula, directions as to the simples or other materia medica to be used; how this is to be prepared (often even where the plants can be found), which paraphernalia are to be used, what ritual is to be gone through, and the restrictions to be observed by the patient, and eventually by the medicine man. Occasionally the fee is also listed here.

Sometimes a part of the directions of the formula, especially the passage conveying the information about the purpose it is used for, and the paraphernalia that are necessary, is prefixed to the formula as a caption.

Medicinal prescriptions may have a caption, but, as is easy to understand, usually are not followed by any directions, since they themselves contain the data which are found in the directions appended to the formula.

As will appear from the section describing the structure of the formulas, these very often are made up of four paragraphs, which, save for a couple of words, are textually identical. It does not seem to have struck many of the medicine men that they could save themselves a good deal of trouble by merely writing down one paragraph completely, and only the variants in the three following paragraphs. As a rule the four paragraphs are written out completely, this sometimes resulting in slightly varying spellings which may often be quite interesting from the point of view of the phonetician. Only when writing down certain songs in which the same expression is repeated over and over again, the copyist gives proof of a more practical turn of mind and only copies each expression once, entrusting the sequence and the repetitions to his memory.

I have already mentioned the curious practice of "camouflaging" the contents of certain of the "bad" formulas, mostly love or man-killing incantations, by captions that have nothing whatever to do with their actual purpose. (See p. 154.) This is done to deceive any outsiders or uninitiated persons, who, by accident, might get possession of the book or the papers. But considering the jealous care with which medicine men keep their writings hidden and secluded, there is really no great cause for apprehension on this score.

I finally might stress once more the importance of the "directions" of the formulas and of the prescriptions. Just as clear and explicit directions appended to them result in a value of 100 per cent, a formula without the necessary directions is almost valueless. If a medicine man acquires a new formula, and the directions to it are missing, it means that he will have to hunt for a fellow practitioner who can give him the necessary information as to its use, the simples needed, etc. This has not only the great disadvantage that he has to show his new formula to competitors and rivals, but also that he will have to pay as much and perhaps more for the "exegesis" as he had to lay out for the acquisition of the formula itself. The formula may be a gem, but the directions indicate its carat.

Although some of the directions show ample evidence of their antiquity, yet they are not bound to tradition and formalism so rigidly as are the formulas. The latter may have been handed down, as far as we are able to gather, for centuries without an iota having been altered in them; the directions, however, have been subjected to such changes, alterations, and emendations as have been rendered necessary by migration to a new habitat, by change in the material culture, or by evolution in the beliefs.

So, for instance, in a formula against bullet wounds the "bullet" is not mentioned once, and is still spoken of as an arrow; as far as the expressions used in this formula are concerned, it might have been used in the pre-Columbian period. But when we scan the directions we soon see that it has been changed with due regard to the introduction of firearms. We also find that in those directions where simples are being prescribed that are foreign to the present habitat of the Cherokee these are being gradually replaced and superseded by plants found in their present locality.

Whereas a formula loses all its power by retracting or adding as little as one syllable to it, directions and prescriptions may be improved upon, both grammatically and technically, by any one who chooses to do so.

Structure of the Formulas

Although the best way of gaining an insight into the structure of the formulas is to examine the specimens given in the text material, a few preliminary remarks will not be considered out of place here.

The general pattern according to which the formulas are built is the following:

1. An exclamation of warning, to attract the attention of the spirit addressed, as sGě', k'a, yă'.
2. The spirit's name, sometimes his color; the place where he has his abode.
3. Some expression extolling his power, as "thou powerful wizard indeed," or "thou penetratest all things," or "nothing can escape thy sight."
4. A statement as to the cause of the disease, the identity of the disease causer, or the reason for which the spirit's help is invited.
5. Some depreciatory remarks at the address of the disease, of the disease causer, of the enemy against whom an incantation is being recited, etc.
6. Some specific reason why the spirit called upon is expected to effect relief in this particular instance.
7. An emphatic statement that relief has been effected.
8. A final exclamation, usually yă', sometimes sGe', rarely k'a'.

This, as I have said, is only a general pattern; there is perhaps not one formula exactly like it, nor does it mention certain other motives, which occur occasionally, though not so regularly. For example, in many formulas the cry of the animal spirit invoked is imitated, for the fox du'; for the rabbit dĭ'st.[75]

---

[75] These imitative cries are often rather symbolic than onomatopoetic.

Again in many formulas that are used, as in love attraction, there are many motives that are quite uncalled for in the curing conjurations.

In quite a few of the formulas the name and the clan of the patient, of the patron, or of the enemy may be mentioned.

The first paragraph of the formula is often repeated three times, very slight changes being made every time; usually only the color of the spirits and their abode are modified.

Only rarely does a formula contain seven paragraphs. This is almost exclusively the case with some long-life formulas recited at the river's bank.

The Ritual Language [76]

There is abundant proof that the language as used in Cherokee religion and ritual has been checked in certain aspects of its evolution and that it has become stationary and archaic, the everyday language having followed its fatal course of development.

This process is easy to explain when we call to mind the tremendous importance which the untutored mind attaches to form and pattern. Whereas the everyday language, the tribal language as we will call it, is a tool of the community, of the man in the street, to express his views on a countless number of matters, in an almost unlimited variety of ways, the ritualistic language is usually the appanage of a chosen few, and is in any case strictly used in rigidly exclusive circumstances, and in sternly conserved, crystallized and stereotyped expressions.

Sacred formulas, whether they be conjurations, incantations, or conventional prayers, are bound to form rather than to content. The desired result is held to be brought about, not by the meaning of the words used, but merely by strict adherence to the wording and the form. This accounts for the fact that even in European folklore so many conjurations and incantations are still in use containing words and expressions so archaic that even the initiated and the adepts fail to understand them; yet not one of these adepts would dare or venture to change a word and to supply a modern, more intelligible expression for it, since to tamper with even so little as a syllable would not only seriously compromise but would render absolutely nil the power and the result of the formula. We find the same conditions prevailing with the Cherokee, only to an even greater extent.

---

[76] The following remarks have already been presented in a slightly different form in a paper read before the First International Congress of Linguists, The Hague, April, 1928.

To be systematic and methodical, I should state which, to my mind, are the sources from which the Cherokee ritual language in its present shape is derived:

1. There is first of all a substratum of what may be called the language at an earlier stage of its growth.
2. Secondly there is a layer of the Western dialect.
3. Finally there is an unmistakable influence of the rhythm in the melodies of songs.

The latter element, the influence of the song melodies, is of all the least perceptible, and from a linguist's viewpoint, of the least importance. It bears only on certain phonetic and on a very few morphologic aspects. Such are the artificial prefixing, infixing, and suffixing of particles without any semantic value, which is done with the sole object in view of filling out the meter of the melody when singing. Instances are:

(a) Prefixing (prosthesis)—'a is frequently prefixed to such words as 'a'nɔ·ᵘGwö'ⁿ, "now"; 'a'Galǫ̈·'ldi, "above"; 'a·'ʋsönʋ·'li, "quickly."

(b) Infixing (epenthesis)—ɛ'lan(a)ɒi for ɛ'ldi, ɛ'laɒi, "below"; a'Gwan(a)ɒʋ·'lɩ̇a' for a'GwaDʋ·'lɩ̇a', "I want"; nɔ'tsɩ'ɔ̈i' for nɔ'tsɩ̇i', "in the pine grove."

(c) Suffixing (paragoge; epithesis).

No instance of the suffixing of meaningless syllables to fill out the meter of a melody has come to my notice; nor is this difficult to explain: Cherokee possesses such a vast variety of emphatic suffixes (-ya, -yi, -yu, Dɩ·nö̈ⁿ', -Gɔ·Ga', etc.), that in case of emergency one or even a couple of these are called upon to bring the word or the sentence up to its necessary number of syllables.

Also the contrary of the processes just described takes place:

(a) Aphesis; aphaeresis—
Gwɛ'ɩ̇a' for aGwɛ'ɩsta'nɛɩa', "I have pain."
Gɩsɛ·'Gwöⁿ for a'Gɩ·sɛ·'Gwöⁿ, "the big bitch."
Gɛ·'iyaGʋ·'Gə for aGɛ·'iyaGʋ·'Gə, "the woman by excellence."

(b) Syncope—
tsɩsɛ·'Gɩ·.a' for tsɩ·'sɛ·Gɔ·'Gɩ·.a', "I overcome it."
ani'GaGɛ·ⁿ' for a'niGɩ·GaGɛ·ⁿ, "they (are) red."
Gwɛ'ɩ̇a' for aGwɛ'ɩsta'nɛɩa', "I have pain."

(c) Apocope—
nɔ·'GwɔDɩ·' for nɔ·'GwɔDɩ·'nö̈ⁿ', "now indeed."
wa'a'l for wa'ʻali', (name for a mountain).
tsö̧'ŋʋsɔ' for tsö̧'ŋʋ'sɔ̈i', "where the Creeks live."

As for the second layer mentioned, the evidence is as interesting to the student of psychology and history as to the linguist.

This layer, as already stated, consists of a collection of words and expressions, borrowed from the Western dialect. This is the dialect which has always been spoken by the majority of the tribe; by that fraction of the tribe, moreover, where civilizing influences during the eighteenth and nineteenth centuries made themselves felt most keenly; by that fraction of the tribe, finally, to which belonged the inventor of the Cherokee syllabary. As a result of all this, the Western dialect soon rose in importance, and in fact acquired precedence over the others, as usually happens with a written dialect. Thus, although theoretically speaking, the Central and Eastern dialects can be written just as satisfactorily by means of the Sequoya syllabary as the Western dialect, the fact that it was invented by a westerner, that it was applied to writing in the Western dialect, before it was so applied to the others, the fact that portions of biblical as well as of secular literature were translated and printed in this dialect only—all this contributed immensely toward making of the Western dialect what might aptly be called the literary tongue of all the Cherokee.

Hence the formulas written down in this dialect contained many expressions which the Central-dialect speaking Cherokee either did not understand, or else understood but would have expressed in a different way.

Since, however, a formula must be recited as written down, and since tampering with its traditional form is nothing short of sacrilege, these Western dialect expressions have been treasured and handed down ever since; needless to say, many of them have, in the course of this process, been mutilated beyond recognition, and it is quite possible that some of them may never again be satisfactorily reconstructed or explained.

It will be possible to state exactly to what extent the Western dialect has been drawn upon for the ritualistic language of the Central dialect by a thorough study of the Western dialect, which has not yet been made but which will soon be undertaken.

Finally there is the source which I mentioned first, but which I reserved for discussion until now, because it is the most important and offers more interesting material and more promising results. This source is what I called a substratum of words and expressions illustrating certain processes in the history and growth of the language.

As has been described in the previous pages, the Cherokee ritual language is used mainly in prayers, conjurations, and incantations, mostly recited, but sometimes sung, and the greater part of which are expected to prevent, cure, or cause disease; some of them are also recited in order to obtain prosperity, luck in love or in war, in hunting and fishing, and in the various pursuits of tribal life. It also may occur sporadically in songs, even if these do not belong to the ritual, and possibly in certain clan names.

These formulas are now handed down in written form, but before the art of writing was invented, about a century ago, they must have been taught to the initiated orally, and there are quite a few indications which lead us to believe that many of them must be several hundreds of years old, at least. Many of them contain references to mythical beings, spirits and animals, on which even the voluminous tribal mythology is silent. Both in the vocabulary and in the grammatical construction there occur elements which even the oldest priests and the most traditionalist of the medicine men are at a loss to elucidate. The only explanation they venture to offer is that "this was the way it was said by the people who lived a long time ago."

Knowing as we do the jealous care with which this material has been conserved, and the judgment and the discrimination used when handing it down, it will be possible to make these data serve the purpose of investigating some of the problems of historical Iroquoian linguistics. A few illustrations taken from the different fields of linguistics, viz, phonetics, lexicology, morphology, syntaxis and semantics, will show some of the results that can be obtained by this method.

Phonetics.—A˙ clan name a`nisa‘ɔ·'ni could not, so far, be identified with certainty. It is true that its relation with sa‘k‘ɔ·'ni ("blue") has been suggested, but until further evidence was brought forward, this explanation could only be called a plausible guess. It appears now, however, that the exclamatory k‘a' used in tribal language is the equivalent of the ‘a·' met with so often in the formulas; thus not only making the etymology of a`nisa‘ɔ·'ni a certainty instead of a guess, but also making it probable that once such a law as the shift from the aspirate to the aspirated velar surd occlusive must have operated initially resp. medially.

Lexicology.—With respect to the vocabulary there is a good deal to be gleaned from the material. Most, if not all, of the formulas antedating, as far as we can gather, the invasion of the whites, there are many references to aboriginal fauna and flora, to artifacts and utensils which are now obsolete, and the use of many of which has now even been forgotten. In one hunting formula the name of seven different kinds of deer are given, whereas now distinction is made between two kinds only.

The name k‘a`lɔ·gwɛ' which is now used for gun or rifle is still used in the formulas with the meaning of "bow," just as Ga^{n}ni' now meaning "bullet" or "lead" is used for "arrow" in the formulas.

^{u}wanɛ·'^{n} which is now only understood as hickory (*Hicoria alba* (L.) Britt.), is still used in the formulas as "arrow," because arrows used to be made of them.

sɛ‘"kwa which in the tribal language merely means "pig," used to stand for "opossum," in which meaning the ritualistic language invariably uses it.

There are, moreover, quite a number of concepts that are referred to in the formulas by words that are totally different from those used in the tribal language:

	Ritual language	Tribal language
Beads	sö·nɩkt'a'	aDɛ·'löⁿ
Yard (around dwelling)	tc'ɩnö·'ⁿli'	ɔ·N:ast'ǫ·.i
Disease	ʋlsGɛ·'Döⁿ	ʋ'yu'Ga

As far as morphology is concerned the most impressive fact is that in the ritualistic language the comm.-Iroq. feature of incorporation of the nominal object has been retained to a far greater extent than in the tribal language. In fact the latter seems to be losing, slowly but surely, this mode of expression altogether. E. g., such an expression as: "I am making it bigger," is rendered in the tribal language:

ʋ`t'anɩ·'Döⁿ nɩGǫ·'nɛ'a'
it-bigger-become   I make it

whereas the ritualistic language still uses the more typical Iroq.: Gat'a`nɔ'ɩ'stɩ:a' (i. e., Ga-, 1st. sgl. pronominal pref., 1st. conj. subject.; √-t'an(ɔ)-"big"; -'ɩst- causat. infix; -ɩ:a' praes. suff.). Of this there are many instances.

Another fact, equally interesting, of which only one instance has been found so far, is the prefixing of the particle expressing the possession of the object to the verb instead of to the noun, as in the tribal language:

Ritual language: a`DaN:ti' tsùDa`N:tɩ·yu'
Tribal language: tsù`DaN:ti' uDa`N:tɩ·yu'
(Both with the same meaning: "He loves thy soul.")

Syntaxis.—Adverbs of place, which in tribal language usually precede the verb, in the ritualistic language often follow it:
Ritual language: anɩ`lɔ:i' ɛ`tɫawɩ·'ni, "they pass underneath."
Tribal language: ɛ`tɫawɩ·'ni anɩ`lɔ:i', "underneath they pass."

Semantics.—This is indeed a most interesting and promising field. The stem √-DaN:t- which in tribal language only means "to think," in the ritual language invariably stands for "to cause":
ʋlsGɛ·'Döⁿ ʋ`DaN:tɛ·'lö:i`, he has caused the disease for (i. e., to) him.

The primitive notion that evil can be cast upon an enemy by thinking, wishing, saying (cf. Latin "incantare"), is hereby clearly illustrated; even more so though by the following group of words which all derive from a stem √-D(ɩ)- "to say":

ʋ`Döⁿnö'ɩ̃, "he has caused it."
a`Döⁿnɩ·Ga', "he has come to cause it"; "it has been caused."
nɩGǫ·'DɩsGɛsti', "he will continue to cause it."
nʋ·`Dət'anö·'Də, "it has been caused at the same time."

The tribal word for "disease" uʻyu'ɢa is not used in the ritual language, where it is always referred to as: "that which is important," "the important thing," ᴜlsɢɛ'ᴅöⁿ.

"Death" is referred to in the ritual language as vʻsö''ᴜᴅöⁿʻ a word which in the tribal language always has the meaning of "night-passed."

tsɩyǫ·'nɩsta·'nɛʻa' which in the tribal language means: "I hit him," in the ritual language conveys the professional idea of performing passes, of massaging.

Although many more examples could be adduced, it is considered that those given have amply proved the point; those that are held over will be worked out and incorporated in the sketch of the Cherokee grammar on which work is well advanced.

APPENDIX

With reference to the statement made on page 2, a comparative table is given in the following lines of the sequence into which the formulas had been put by Mr. Mooney. The titles and the first figures are Mooney's, whereas the figures between parentheses are those under which the formulas will be found in the texts.

Genito-urinary diseases: 1 (4), 2 (80), 3 (6), 4 (22), 5 (95), 6 (55), 7 (94), 8 (81), 9 (37), 10 (38).
Snake dreams and snake bites: 11 (5), 12 (20), 13 (47).
Indigestion and fainting: 14 (7), 15 (8), 16 (11), 17 (15), 18 (14), 19 (26), 20 (34), 21 (65), 22 (85), 23 (29), 24 (46), 25 (54), 26 (16), 27 (27), 28 (42), 29 (39), 30 (50), 31 (86).
Headache, toothache, earache, sore eyes, and throat troubles: 32 (9), 33 (10), 34 (35), 35 (13), 36 (57), 37 (82), 38 (2), 39 (89), 40 (96), 41 (63), 42 (21), 43 (56), 44 (62), 45 (61).
Chills, fever, and blisters: 46 (1), 47 (23), 48 (30), 49 (40), 50 (41), 51 (48), 52 (53), 53 (90), 54 (75), 55 (88).
Wounds and frostbite: 56 (59), 57 (60), 58 (69), 59 (87).
Worms and bowel troubles: 60 (17), 61 (49), 62 (32), 63 (52), 64 (71), 65 (72), 66 (73), 67 (74), 68 (78), 69 (79).
Childbirth, female troubles, etc.: 70 (70), 71 (76), 72 (51).
The scratching ceremony, rheumatism, and kindred pains: 73 (25), 74 (31), 75 (28), 76 (19), 77 (84), 78 (91), 79 (64), 80 (24), 81 (68), 82 (67), 83 (45), 84 (66), 85 (44), 86 (36).
Witchcraft diseases and taking to water: 87 (3), 88 (58), 89 (12), 90 (33), 91 (77), 92 (43), 93 (93), 94 (83), 95 (18), 96 (92).

1

vʽnawaʺsti	ɛ·ʹGwɔⁿ	aDăʽ	nǫ·ʽwɔ·tʼiʹ	ɫʼaʹ	
it chill	it big	the	medicine	this	

SGɛ̨ʹʹ		Galǫ̆·ʹldi	ʽɪnɛʹɫi		Galǫ̆·ʹldi	ʽɪnɛʹɫi		ʽɪnɛʹɫi	
now then!		above	thou and I are living		above	thou and I are living		thou and I are living	

ʽɪnɛʹɫi		ʽɪnɛʽɪ·-yuʹ		ʽɪʽniDaʹᵘwɛ̨ʼ		ʽɪnɛʽɪ·-yuʹ		ʽɪnɛʽɪ·-yuʹ	
thou and I are living		thou and I are living—E		thou and I (are) wizards		thou and I are living—E		thou and I are living—E]	

vtsɪʽʽnawaʹ	aDɔ̄ʽnɪ·Gaʹ		aDɔ̄ʽnɪ·Gaʹ		ʽa:yĭʹ	
beyond-it-stretched	it has become said		it has become said			

SGɛ̨ʹʹ		ǫ̆·ʽwaDɔ-ɫʹi	ʽɪnɛʹɫi		ǫ̆·ʽwaDɔʹɫi	ʽɪnɛʹɫi		ʽɪnɛʹɫi		5
now then!		storehouse—Loc	thou and I are living		storehouse—Loc	thou and I are living		thou and I are living		

ʿinéʿṣi	ʿineʿʿi-yu′	ʿiʾniDa·ʾuwéʾ	ʿineʿʿi-yu′	ʿineʿʿi-yu′
thou and I	thou and I	thou and I	thou and I	thou and I
are living	are living—E	(are) wizards	are living—E	are living—E

vtsıʿʿnawa′	aDōʿʿnıʿGa′	aDōʿʿnıʿGa′	ʿa:yï′	
beyond-it-	it has become said	it has become said		
stretched				

sGéʾʾ	nɔʿʿtsı-ʿʿi	ʿinéʿṣi	nɔʿʿtsı-ʿʿi	ʿinéʿṣi	ʿinéʿṣi
now then!	pine(s)—Loc	thou and I	pine(s)—Loc	thou and I	thou and I
		are living		are living	are living

ʿinéʿṣi	ʿineʿʿi-yu′	ʿiʾniDa·ʾuwéʾ	ʿineʿʿi-yu′	ʿineʿʿi-yu′
thou and I	thou and I	thou and I	thou and I	thou and I
are living	are living—E	(are) wizards	are living—E	are living—E

5 vtsıʿʿnawa′ aDōʿʿnıʿGa′ aDōʿʿnıʿGa′ ʿa:yï′
   beyond-it- it has become said it has become said
   stretched

sGéʾʾ	aʿmaʿ-yi′	ʿinéʿṣi	aʿmaʿ-yi′	ʿinéʿṣi	ʿinéʿṣi
now then!	water—Loc	thou and I	water—Loc	thou and I	thou and I
		are living		are living	are living

ʿinéʿṣi	ʿineʿʿi-yu′	ʿiniDa·uwéʾ	ʿineʿʿi-yu′	ʿineʿʿi-yu′
thou and I	thou and I	thou and I	thou and I	thou and I
are living	are living—E	(are) wizards	are living—E	are living—E

vtsıʿʿnawa′ aDōʿʿnıʿGa′ aDōʿʿnıʿGa′ ʿa:yï′
beyond-it- it has become said it has become said
stretched

| sGéʾʾ | ʿaʾ-nɔ·Gwōʾⁿ | ʿaʿtʿöŋaʾnıʿGa′ | aʿGəlυ·ʾGúⁿ | tsAstıʿ′Ga |
| now then | ha! | now | thou hast come to listen | whirlwind | thou little |

10 ʿıDaʾʾuwéʿi′   ɔʿʾDali′   tsυʿstıGɔ-ʿʿi   Duwaʾʾuwsat-öʿ   Dıtsōʾtłtʿɔʿʿısti′
   thou (art a) mountain(s) they small—Loc it stretched out con-   thou art staying
   wizard   tinuously—T L

ʿıDaʾʾuwéʿi′	Gɔʿυ′sti	tsúnυʾʾləʿōⁿ-ʿski	nıGeʿʾsöʿna′	ʿa-nɔʾʾuGwōᵒ
thou (art a)	something	thou failest—H	never	ha!—Now
wizard				

Dɔʾʾtʿaᴅleʿöʿŋa   vstıʿʾkʿı-yu′   vʾDıʿyaʾstanōʿʿi   ʿıʾGeʿʾseʿ′ⁿ   ʿōʾⁿʾ=
thou hast arisen small—E   it has been left over   that which is—App again—

ʿıyaləGıʿʾstʿanıʿGa′   ıGɔʿʾti   vʾstıGɔ-ʿʿi   vʾsaʿıʿlaGıʿ   ıʿGɔʿt-υʿʾłti
thou hast come to brush it swamp   it small—Loc   plateau on hillside   swamp-standing
away

nöʿʾnɔ-ʿʿi′   wi-Dɛʿʾtsatʿanöʿʿōⁿʾsi′   aʿneʿʾtsɔ·Geʿ′Dōⁿ   GeʿʾtsaᴅöʿʾNʿéʿi′
trail(s)—Loc   toward yonder they will lay   playing   they do to thee—App.
               themselves

15 nöʿʾŋōtłstʿanıʿGa′   ıGöʿʾwułstʿaʾnıdaʿʿstı-Gwōᵒ′   aʿDıʿGaleʿ′yaDōⁿʾ
   it has happened so   what is its worth as it goes about—L.   it scattered

tsaʾDöNʿeʿʾlıGa′   vtsıʿʿnawa′   nıGöʿʾDısGeʿsti′
thou hast come to do   beyond-it-   it will be said continu-
for him   stretched   ally onwards

| sGéʾʾ | ʿaʾ-nɔ·uGwōʾⁿ | ʿōⁿ-ʿaʿtʿöŋaʾnıʿGa′ | ʿaʿGalυ·′Gúⁿ | ʿeʿ′Gwɔʾʿı= |
| now then | ha! | now | again thou hast come to listen | thou whirlwind | thou (art) big— |

Gwōᵒ′   ɔʿʾDali   tseʿGwɔ-ʿʿi   Du·Daʾʾuwsat-öʿ   ıyöʿʾⁿDōⁿ   Dıʿtsōtł=
L (=E)   mountain(s)   they big—Loc   it stretching out itself   over yonder   thou art
                                       continuously—T L

tʿɔʿıʿsti   ʿaʾGalυʿ′Gōⁿ   ʿeʿʾGwúⁿ   ʿaʾ-υsənυʿ′li   Dɔʿʾtʿaᴅleʿöŋa′
staying   thou whirlwind   thou (art) big   ha! quickly   thou hast arisen

20 vstıʿʾkʿı-yu′   vʾDıʿyaʾstanōʿʿi   ʿıʿyaləGıʿstʿanıʿGa′   vlsGeʿ′Dōⁿ
   it small—E   it has been left over   thou hast come to brush it away   it important

ιGɔ·ˋt-ɛ·ˊGwö̆ⁿ   vˋsaˤιˊlaGiˋ | ιGɔ·ˋt-ɛˋGwɔˊ-ˤi   ιˋyö̆·ˊⁿDö̆ⁿ   nö̆·ˋnɔ-ˤiˋ
swamp big   plateau on hillside   swamp-big—Loc   over yonder   trail(s)—Loc

wι-Dɛˋtsatˤanö̆·ˋtö̆ⁿˋsiˊ | aˤnɛˋtsɔ·Gɛ·ˊDö̆ⁿ   Gɛˋtsɑdö̆·ˋNˤɛˋlιˋDιsɛˋstiˊ |
toward yonder they will lay   playing   they will do to thee continuously
themselves

ιGö̆·ˋwulstˤanιdaˋˤstι-Gwö̆ˊ ⁿ | vtsιˋˋnawə-Gwö̆ⁿˊ   nvˋˋDə.tˤanö̆ˊⁿDə |
what is its worth as it goes about—L   beyond-it-stretched—L(=E)   it has been said at the
                                                                    same time

nιˋGa·Giˊ yaˤ | vˋˋnawa.ˊsti   ɛ·ˊGwö̆ⁿ   v·ˋnιtlö̆·ŋö̆·ˊ.i | tˤa·yaˊ   Gö̆ⁿˤ.ˊtˤɔtiˋ
as far as all Sharply!   chill   it big   whenever they are ill   cherry   it to be used
                                                                                      with it

DιDzɔ·ˊtˤιstö̆.tiˋ | tsɔˋl-aGayö̆·ˊⁿli   yaˤɑ·ˊ   vlö̆ˊⁿkwˤɔti-Gwö̆ⁿˊ   na.skwö̆ⁿˊ   5
they to be blown   tobacco-old   if he has it   powerful   L (=E)   also
with it

(For) the Big Chill This is the Medicine

FREE TRANSLATION

Now then! Above thou and I are living,
Above, thou and I are living,
Thou and I are living,
Thou and I are living,
Thou and I are living indeed,
Thou and I (are) wizards,
Thou and I are living indeed,
Thou and I are living indeed,
Relief has been caused, it has been caused. Ha-yi!
Now then! On storehouse mountain thou and I are living,
On storehouse mountain, thou and I are living,
Thou and I are living (bis),
Thou and I are living indeed,
Thou and I (are) wizards,
Thou and I are living, indeed (bis),
Relief has been caused, it has been caused. Ha-yi!
Now then! In the pine forest thou and I are living (bis),
Thou and I are living (bis),
Thou and I are living indeed,
Thou and I (are) wizards,
Thou and I are living indeed (bis),
Relief has been caused, it has been caused. Ha-yi!
Now then! In the water thou and I are living (bis),
Thou and I are living (bis),
Thou and I are living indeed,
Thou and I (are) wizards,
Thou and I are living indeed (bis),
Relief has been caused, it has been caused. Ha-yi!

Now then! Ha! now thou hast come to listen, thou Little Whirlwind, thou wizard. Among the stretched out (tree branches) of the small mountains thou art staying. Thou wizard, thou never failest in anything. Ha! now thou hast arisen, facing us. The minute portion (of the disease) which has been left over, thou hast again come to brush away into the little swamp on the plateau along the mountain flank. Thy trails¹ lead from here to the swamp into which they disappear. They have played with thee,¹ it seems (and tossed thee about). So, indeed, it has happened. (And) who cares what happens to it?² Thou³ hast come and scattered it for him.⁴ Relief has now been caused, and will not be undone.

Now then! Ha! Now thou hast come to hear, thou Big Whirlwind, big indeed. Among the stretched out (tree branches) of the big mountains, over yonder, thou art staying. Thou Big Whirlwind, ha! quickly thou hast arisen, facing us. Only a minute portion of the disease has remained. Thou hast come to sweep it away into the great swamp on the plateau along the mountain flank. Thy¹ trails lead from here to the great swamp over yonder. They will play with thee¹ and toss thee about continually; who cares what happens to it,² now! Relief indeed has been caused at the same time, completely indeed. Sharp there!

When they are ill with the big chill, cherry is to be used to blow them with. If old tobacco is available (it is) also very efficient.

NOTES

[This formula has been edited with notes and comments by James Mooney, SFC., pp. 359–361. The plants used have been identified as tsoˑ'laGayǫⁿ'li (*Nicotiana rustica* L., wild tobacco), and tʻaya' (*Prunus virginiana* L., chokecherry; also *Prunus serotina* Ehrh., wild black or rum cherry).]

ꞌiꞌꞌa-NꞌɔⁿꞋ	Dɩꞌniskoˑli'	Duꞌnitłǫŋǫˑꞌ.iꞋ ⁵		
this-and	their heads	whenever they are ill		
ɑniꞋsGúꞌya	ɑniꞋloꞋi'	vtsɩꞋꞌnɑwaꞋ	ɑnɔꞋꞋnɩˑGɑ'	ɑꞋniDɑˑꞋᵘwɛꞋ
they men	they just passed by	beyond-it-stretched	they have come and said it	they (are) wizards
ɑniꞋloꞋi'	vtsɩꞋꞌnɑwaꞋ	ɑnɔꞋꞋnɩˑGɑ'	vtsɩꞋꞌnɑwɑ'	GɔꞋtɬtɑꞋɑⁿ'
they just passed by	beyond it stretched	they have come and said it	beyond it stretched	it (has been) rubbed
vtsɩꞋꞌnɑwaꞋ	ɑnɔꞋꞋnɩˑGɑ'	yăꞋ		
beyond it stretched	they have come and said it	Sharp!		
5 ꞋiꞋꞌa-NꞋɔⁿꞋ	naˑꞋsGwɔᵘꞋ ⁶	DɩꞋniskoˑli'	DuꞋnitłǫŋǫˑꞋ.iꞋ	ꞋiꞋaˑꞋ nɩ-vsti'ꞌ
this-and	also	their heads	whenever they are ill	this so far like
ɔꞋDali-GúꞋDli	ɑnǫꞋꞋskötłǫꞋ.i	DɩDzɔꞋˑtʻɩstoˑ.ti'		
mountain-he climbs	it (sol.) used to be held in the mouth—H	they to be blown with it		

¹ Addressing the disease.
² "It"=the disease.
³ Addressing the Little Whirlwind.
⁴ "Him"=the patient.
⁵ W. Dial. form; C. Dial.: vˑꞋnitsǫŋǫˑꞌi.
⁶ This is one of the cases alluded to on p. 2, and from which it appears that a preceding formula or prescription, "also for headache," was not included by Mooney in his transliteration of the manuscript.

AND THIS IS (FOR) WHEN THEIR HEADS ARE ILL

(FREE TRANSLATION)

The men have just passed by, they have caused relief,
The wizards have just passed by, they have caused relief,
Relief has been rubbed, they have caused relief. Sharp!
And this is also (for) when their heads are ill. This (is to be sung) like this: [9]
Mountain-climber [10] should be chewed, (and) they should be blown with it.

NOTES

This song is to cure a headache which, it is stated, is accompanied by pain in the back of the neck.

The melody closely resembles that of formulas Nos. 42 and 82.

The medicine is ginseng [10] chewed and held in the mouth. While singing the doctor rubs the forehead of the patient [with the palm of his right hand, and on finishing the song], takes a sip of water, and then blows the water mixed with the ginseng juice [on the forehead, or on the temples or on the crown of the patient's head according as to where the pain is most acute]. The song and the blowing are repeated four times, and if necessary the whole ceremony is repeated four times before noon, or at intervals of about half an hour after the first treatment. tsɔ`laGay·ö·ⁿli′ [11] may be used instead of ginseng. [There is no taboo.]

[The "men" referred to in the song are probably the "Little People" dwelling in the rocks, in the mountains, etc. (See p. 25.) It is not impossible, however, that the Thunder Boys are meant (see p. 24), but this is less likely since the latter are usually referred to as "the two Little Men," "the two Red Men," etc.]

3

ï'a′	aGɩ`tlɩ·-ya′	υni`tlönö·′.i` [12]	a`Daꞌnö·`wɔ·tꞌi′	
this	suffering—E	whenever they are ill	the medicine	

sGêˮ	ꞌa`-nɔ·ᵘGwöⁿ	ꞌa·tꞌöna·`nɩ·Ga′	Galö·`ldɩ·′-tlöⁿ` [13]	ꞌɛ·`tstꞌɔꞌɩsti′
now then!	ha! now	thou hast come to listen	above-toward	they have put thee staying

	kꞌɔ·′lanöⁿ`	öⁿ`ꞌnaGɛ·′ⁿ	ꞌɩDa·ᵘwɛ̈ɩ·-yu′		Gɔꞌυ′sti	tsúnυ·′ltᵢ
	raven	black	thou (art a) wizard—E		something	thou failest

nɩ`Gɛꞌsö·na′		ꞌa`-nɔ·Gwöⁿ′	ɛ·`DzaDzɔ·`′öⁿtꞌanɩ·Ga′	aSGɩ·′nə
never		ha! now	they have caused thee to come down	ghost

υ·`Döⁿö.′ɩ-Gwöⁿ`	ꞌɩGɛ·`sɛⁿ.i′		ꞌa`-nɩGö·`waDö·`naGwaⁿlɔ.ɛ·′stɩ-Gwöⁿ`
it has been said—L	that which is, App.		ha! a trace of trampling will be—L

[9] Follows the song, "The men have just passed by," etc.
[10] Panax trifolium L. (dwarf ginseng; groundnut).
[11] Nicotiana rustica L. (wild tobacco).
[12] W. Dial. form; C. Dial.: υnitsönö·.i.
[13] -tlöⁿ, W. Dial. suffix; C. Dial.: -tsöⁿ,-Dzöⁿ.

tsaᴾlɔ·ˈs-ǫ̈·.iˊ | ˤa-nɔ·ᵘGwɔ̈ᴅ | ᴅɛˋtˤɔ̈ˋtɫtˤanɩ·Gaˊ | ˤa·ˊ-sǫ̈ˋnəGaᴾlɔ·ˊGi
thou passed—TL   ha!—now   thou hast come to put him   ha!   it broken
                                   on his (legs)

Gɛˤsǫ̈·ˊ.i   ˋɔ·ˋstiGɔ̈ˋtɫanɩ·Gaˊ   vˋlsGɛˋᴅɔ̈ⁿˊ | ᴅvwɔ·lv·ˋwa.tɔ̈ⁿ.tiˊ   nɩˋGɛˤ-
it is, TL   thou hast come to put it   it important   it to be returned   never
                  (sol) between two ...

sǫnaˊ | nɔ̈ⁿˋˊtˤǫ̈ˋnɛˋlɩ·Gaˊ | ˤa·.vsɔ̈ˋˤɩ·-yiˊ   wɔ̈ˋⁿˊ-tˤiˋtˤɔˤɩˋstˤanɩ·Gaˊ
              thou hast come to do it   ha! night—Loo;   yonder thou hast put it to stay
              for him

ᴅaᴅv·ˋk̨tˤa̩ɔ̈ⁿˊstiˊ   nɩˋGɛ·sǫ̈·naˊ | vtsɩˤˊnawaˋ   nv·ˋᴅə.tˤanǫ̈·ˊⁿᴅə
it to look back   never   beyond it   it has been said at the
                                          stretched   same time

5 sGɛ̈ˊˊ | ˤa-nɔ·ᵘGwɔ̈ᴅˊ   ˤaˋtˤǫ̈na·ˋnɩ·Gaˊ   Galǫ̈·ˋldɩ·ˊ-tɫɔ̈ⁿˋ¹⁴   ˤɛ·ˋtstˤɔˤɩstiˊ |
   Now then!   ha! now   thou hast come to listen   above-toward   they have put thee
                                                                                  staying

kˤɔ·ˊlanɔ̈ⁿ   GɩˋGa-Gɛˤˊⁿ   (etc.)
raven   blood-like

sGɛ̈ˊˊ | ˤa-nɔ·ᵘGwɔ̈ᴅˊ   ˤaˋtˤǫ̈na·ˋnɩ·Gaˊ   Galǫ̈·ˋldɩ·ˊ-tɫɔ̈ⁿˋ   ˤɛ·ˋtstˤɔˤɩstiˊ |
now then!   ha!   now   thou hast come to listen   above towards   they have put thee
                                                                           staying

kˤɔ·ˊlanɔ̈ⁿ   saˋˤkˤɔ·niˊ   (etc.)
raven   blue

sGɛ̈ˊˊ | ˤaˋ-nɔ·ᵘGwɔ̈ᴅˊ   ˤaˋtˤǫ̈na·ˋnɩ·Gaˊ   waˤɩˊliˊ   Galǫ̈·ˋldɩ·ˊ-tɫɔ̈ⁿˋ¹⁴
now then!   ha!   now   thou hast come to listen   (south)   above

10 ˋɛ·tstɔˤɩstiˊ | kˤɔ·ˊlanɔ̈ⁿ   tsunɛ·ˊGɔ̈ⁿ   (etc.) | vtsɩˤˊnawaˋ   aᴅɔ̈ˋnɩ·Gaˊ
   they have put   raven   thou white   beyond it stretched   it has been said
   thee staying

ˋɩˋaˊ   aGɩ·ˋtɫɩ·-yaˊ   vˋnitɫǫ̈nǫ̈·ˊ.i¹⁵   aˋᴅaˤ nǫ̈·ˊwɔ·tˤiˋ | aˋskwanv·ˊˊtsˤAstiˋ
this   suffering—E   whenever they are ill   the medicine   for sucking

tsɔ·ˊᵘl-aGayǫ̈·ⁿˊli   vˋniᴅzɩ·ˋlɔ̈ˋnɔ̈ˤˊi   Gɔ̈ⁿˊtˤɔtiˋ   aˤnǫ̈ˋskutlɔ·ˊᵘ-Gwɔ̈ᴅˋ |
tobacco old   they have been   to use with   it (sol.) used to be kept in the
                        flowers   mouth

kˤaˋnasɔ·ˊᵘlə-Nˤɔⁿˋˊˊˋtsoˊl-ɩyvsˊti-Nˤɔⁿˋˊ   vstɩ·ˤGa   vˋnalɩˤˊGɔ̩aⁿˊ |
(wild parsnip)-and   tobacco-like and   it small   they together

aᴅɛ·ˊlɔ̈-Nˤɔⁿˋˊˊᴅaˤǫ̈ˊ.i | Gɔˤvˊstɩ-NˤɔⁿˋˊˊyvˋtˤAsvyǫ̈·ˊnɔ̈ⁿ   saˋwɔ·tɔ̈ⁿˊ-ˤ̩i-Gwɔ̈ᴅˋ
beads-and   they (sol)   something-and   if it united with it   mud—Loc—L
                 used to be
                 lying down

15 a.ˊti   ᴅawɔˤˋɩlə-Gwɔ̈ᴅˋ   ɩyǫ̈·ˊⁿᴅə
   put it   it over itself—L   far
   down

This is the Medicine When They are Sick With Sharp Pains

FREE TRANSLATION

(a) Now then! Ha, now thou hast come to listen, Black Raven; they have placed thee above. Thou powerful wizard, thou never failest in anything. Now they have let thee down. It is merely a ghost that has caused it. There shall only remain the traces of trampling where thou hast passed. Now thou hast come to put him on his feet. Thou hast come to put the important thing between a crevice of Broken Rock, its track never to be found; thou hast come to do

---

[14] -tɫɔ̈ⁿ, W. Dial. suffix; C. Dial.: -tsɔ̈ⁿ, -ᴅzɔ̈ⁿ.
[15] W. Dial. form; W. Dial. -tɫ->C. Dial. -ts-.

(that very thing) for him. Ha, thou hast taken it away to the Night Land, to remain. It will never return. Relief has been caused at the same time.

(b) Now then! Ha, now thou hast come to listen, Red Raven; they have placed thee above (etc.).

(c) Now then! Ha, now thou hast come to listen, Blue Raven; they have placed thee above (etc.).

(d) Now then! Ha, now thou hast come to listen, White Raven; they have placed thee above, toward the south (etc.).

This is the medicine when they are sick with sharp pains. For sucking, the flowers of old tobacco are to be used. They are just to be held in the mouth (i. e., chewed), and wild parsnip and the small tobaccolike (plant), they along with it.

And if anything be mixed with it (i. e., with the saliva, after sucking), it should be put down into the mud, as far as an overband (deep).

EXPLANATION

[This formula is the one edited under another caption (tsʋ`ⁿda-yɛ`'lɪGɔ·kt'anö́'ï a`ᴅa'nö̈·`wɔ·t'i̇̀), "the medicine (for) when they simulate (a real sickness)," by Mooney in his SFC., pp. 366–369.]

4

21   ï̈'a'   nö̈·`wɔ·t'i̇́'        tsʋ·niyɔ·`t'əGï.a` |
     this   to cure with   they have them itching

ʋni`stɪlö̈ⁿ.ɪ'sti-Gwö̈ⁿ`   sɔ.ɪ'(-nï̈ⁿ[16])   ʋstɪ·'Ga'   ʋᴅɔ·'təGwûᴅö̈ⁿ`
they came to stick to—L   other-and   it small   all day

ʋ·nᴅɪ`'t'a.sti'   |    na.'skɪ-Gwö̈ⁿ` | nɪ`Ga· ö̈·' | Ga·kt'ö̈'ᴅö̈ⁿ
they must drink it   this—L   all   it restricted

aGɔ·'nö̈ⁿ |
completely

This is to Cure With, When They Have Them Itching

FREE TRANSLATION

Merely the "they-make-them-stick-to-it" (-plant) and (also) the other small (variety). They must drink it all day. And this is all there is to it. The injunction is, fasting.

EXPLANATION

As this formula, like all the others, was written by the medicine man to assist his own memory, rather than to give any explicit information to the outside world, the wording is indefinite, as regards both

---

[16] Interpolation by editor.

the malady and the cure. [As already stated (see p. 157), the formulas or prescriptions, as written down without order by a medicine man in his notebook or on stray scraps of paper, do not always have a title, and often even lack any indication whatever as to the disease against which they are to be used.]

The disease is described as an itching of the privates, which causes the patient to scratch the parts affected, thus producing painful sores. [Women as well as men may suffer from it.] It is the result of having urinated, when a child, upon the fire, the ashes, or upon an ant hill. In the first two cases the act is a profanation of the fire, which is esteemed sacred (see p. 21), and children are frequently warned against committing such a sacrilege. In the other case the revengeful ants deposit their eggs on the privates, thus causing an irritation of these parts. [Also urinating along a trail, in the yard surrounding the house, in a place where an animal has been killed, and in the river, are all acts which may result in an ailment such as is here vaguely described as "itching." Informants do not agree as to whether the itching is internal or cutaneous. In the first case the disease is but a sympton of another illness, as, e. g.,

ᴜnɛ·ʹɢə   yᴜnɩ·ʻnənᴜʻɢɔ·tcʻɛʹ:a
ᴠ·nö·ʹⁿᴅi   tsaʻndɩ·kʻöʹ:aⁿ

and is now occasionally by "modernists" among the medicine men held to be part and parcel of a disease of venereal nature. When the itching is cutaneous it is quite possible, from the description of symptoms given, that we are dealing with a case of "itch-worm" (*Sarcoptes (Acarus) scabiei*).]

The disease may follow immediately on the commission of one of the acts mentioned above, or may lie dormant until manhood or womanhood is reached.

[The plants used are ᴠʻnɩstɩlöʹ.ɩʹsti ɛʹɢᴡöᵒˋ, *Lappula virginiana* (L.) Greene, beggar's lice, ᴠʻnɩstɩlöʹ.ɩʹsti ᴠstɩ·ʹɢa, *Cynoglossum virginianum* L., wild comfrey.]

The affected parts are bathed with a decoction of the roots, while another portion of the decoction is drunk by the patient, who, while under treatment, entirely abstains from anything else in the nature of food and drink. [The patient may drink the decoction at intervals of an hour or half an hour, from sunrise to noon, when he is allowed to break his fast, after which the treatment is considered ended for the day. In severe cases, though, he may not eat until sunset; in either of the two cases the treatment is continued for four days.]

5

ɩ·na′ᴅö̆ⁿ   ɢö̆wa`nitłö̆·`.ɩstö̆·′¹⁷   aᴅa`nö̆·′wɔ·t⁽i`   ⁽i̭′a′
snake(s)   they have made them ill   the medicine   this

¹ya⁽′ | ⁽a-`nɔ·ɢwö̆ᵛ′ ɩ·na′ᴅö̆ⁿ ɢö̆⁽`na′ɢɛ·′ⁿ ⁽a·`ɢalö̆·′ldi ɛ·`ᴅza-
Sharply   ha! now   snake   it black   ha! above   they have
there!

tło·`ö̆ⁿ′t⁽ani`lɛ·ⁿ.i′ ¹⁸ | ɩ·na′ᴅö̆ⁿ aSɢɩ·′nə-ɢwö̆ᵛ′ ɢɛ.sɛ·′ⁿ.i |
let thee down—App   snake   ghost   L   it is—App

ɛ·`ᴅzatłɔ·`ö̆ⁿ′t⁽ani`lɛ·ⁿ.i′ ¹⁷ |k⁽ɔ·′la tsö̆·Nɩ̭·`ᴅö̆ⁿ ᴅɩ`k⁽ayʋ·′ɢa` tsö̆·-
they have let thee down, App   bone(s)   they living-for-ever   teeth   they

Nɩ̭·`ᴅö̆ⁿ ᴅɛ·′ᴅʋ·ɢö̆·wa·ᵘwsaᴅaᴅɩ·⁽lɛ·ⁿ.i′ | · nö̆nɔ·′-ɭi ᴅʋ·`ᴅana·⁽- 5
living for-ever   he has advanced them toward   trail—Loc   they stretch

ᵘwaᴅɛ·ɢ-ö̆·′i | ɩ·na′ᴅə-ɢwɔᵛ′ ɢö̆⁽`naɢɛⁿ′ ɢɛ·sɛ·′ⁿ.i | ⁽a-nɔ·`ɢw·û-ᴅɩ·′
themselves out,   snake—L   it black   it is, App   ha! now -E

⁽ɩ·`tsaskö̆`tłtsɩ·`lɛ·ⁿ.i′    ⁽ɩ·`ᴅzayɛ·`lɔ·sɩ·`lɛ·ⁿ.i′ | ʋᴅɔ·`lʋ`wa·`tö̆·ⁿ.ti′
he advanced and bit thee   he has made thee like it, App   he to be retraced

nɩ·`ɢɛ·sö̆·na′ | ⁽a-`nɔ·ᵘɢwö̆ᵛ′ k⁽ɔ·′la tsö̆·Nɩ̭·′ᴅö̆ⁿ ᴅɔ·⁽ᵘsö̆ⁿ ᴅɛ·′ɢa-
never   ha! now   bone(s)   they living-forever   (weakened (?))   they have

ᴅlɔ·ᵘsɩ·ɢa′   nɩ·`tsö̆·nɛ·′ | ⁽a`-tsù·`tłö̆·wɩ·′ᴅö̆-ɢwö̆ᵛ ɢɛ·sɛ·′ⁿ.i
become broken   thou hast it so conditioned   ha thou faltering L   it is—App.

| ⁽a-nɔ·`ɢwû-ᴅɩ·′ ᴅɛ·⁽atłö̆·wɩ·`sɩ·ɢa′ | ⁽a-nɔ·`ɢwû-ᴅɩ·′ stɩ·`sɢùya′ 10
ha now E   thou hast become faltering   ha! now E   you two men

dɩ·`st⁽asɩ·tɩ·ɢa′ stɩᴅa·ᵘwɛɩ̭·`-yu′ | ⁽a-nɔ·ᵘɢwö̆·′ᵛ ʋ`sö̆nʋ·`lɩ·-yu′
you two little   you two wizards L   ha! now   quickly E

ɛ·`statłɔ·`ö̆ⁿ′t⁽a·nɩ·ɢa′ ¹⁹ | ɩ·na′ᴅö̆ⁿ ɢö̆⁽`na′ɢɛ̆·-ɢwö̆ᵛ′ ɢɛ·sɛ́·′ | ɩ·na′ᴅö̆ⁿ
they have let you two down   snake   it black -L   it is, App   snake

aSɢɩ·′na v`lsɢɛ·′ᴅö̆ⁿ ⁽ɩ·`ᴅʋnʋ·`y⁽tɛ·ⁿ.i′ | ⁽ɩ·`ᴅʋyɛ·`lɔ·sɩ·⁽lɛ·ⁿ.i′ ʋᴅɔ·`lʋ⁽-
ghost   it important   which he has put under—App   which he has made like, App   to be

wa·`tö̆ⁿ.ti′ nɩ·`ɢɛ·sö̆·na′ | ʋlsɢɛ·′ᴅö̆ⁿ ⁽ɩ·`ᴅʋnʋ·`y⁽tɛ·ⁿ.i′ | nɔ·`ɢwû-
retraced   never   it important   he has put it under—App   now

ᴅɩ·′ ⁽ö̆ⁿ-stɩ·′yö̆ⁿ`′st⁽anɩ·ɢa′ | u⁽sö̆⁽`ɩ·-yi′ wö̆ⁿ′-stɩ·′yö̆ⁿ`′st⁽anɩ·ɢa′ 15
E   again you two have come to take it (sol.) away   night—Loc   toward yonder you two have come to take it (sol.)

ɢanɛ′sa′ ᴅɩɢö̆⁽`naɢɛ·′ⁿ ᴅɔ·`ᴅɩt⁽ɔ·`ɩst-ö̆·′ wɩ·-stiskwaniɢɔ·`t⁽anɩ·ɢa′
box(es)   they black   they are being kept T. L.   toward yonder you two have come to put it stored up as you two go by

sta·sɔ·`t⁽a·ö̆·s-ö̆·′ ʋtsɩ·⁽`naᵘwa′ nʋ·`ᴅə.t⁽anö̆ᴅə·
you two have turned T L   beyond it-stretched   it has been said at the same time

ʋsɛ·⁽lɩ·t⁽i` nö̆·wɔ·t⁽i` ᴅɩᴅzɔ·`t⁽a.ɛ·⁽ti-ɢwö̆ᵛ′ | kö̆·n⁽i′ a`nskɩ·tsɢö̆·′i
it held erect   to cure with   they must be blown—L   noticeable   whenever they dream

ɩ·na′ᴅö̆ⁿ ʋ`niskö̆`tłɢɔ⁽i′ ʋ`niyɛ·`lɔ⁽ɩstɔ·`ɩ—ɢwö̆ᵛ′ | tsɩ·′yʋ-Nɭ·ɔⁿ′
snake(s)   they have bit them   they have made it like it (habit.)—L   (poplar)-and

ɢö̆ⁿ′′t⁽ɔti` ⁽ɩ·`ɢɛ·sɔ·′i
to be used with it   that which was, H

20

---

¹⁷ W. Dial. form; W. Dial. -tł>C. Dial. ts-.

¹⁸ Emendation by J. M.; instead of ɛ·statłɔ·ö̆ⁿ′t⁽anilɛ·ⁿ.i, they have let you two down.

¹⁹ W. Dial. form; W. Dial. -tł->C. Dial. -ts-.

7548°—32——13

If Snakes Have Bitten Them, This is the Medicine

FREE TRANSLATION

Ya! Ha! now, Black Snake, they have caused thee to come down, it seems. The snake (that has bitten him) is only a ghost, it seems. They have caused thee to come down, it seems.

The ever-living bones, the ever-living teeth it has advanced toward him,[20] it seems. It was only a black snake that laid itself about the trail, it seems. But right now, it feigned to bite thee,[20] it seems. Its track would never be found (it thought).

But now the ever-living bones have been made weak; thou [21] art now in such a condition. There has been hesitation (on thy [21] part) it seems. Ha! now thou [21] hast become faltering.

But at this very moment you Two Little Men, you Two Powerful Wizards, they have caused you two to come down. It was a black snake, it seems, but the snake is merely a ghost (and) it has feigned to put the disease under him,[20] it seems; (it thought) its track would never be found. But now you two have come to take it away. Where the black boxes are, you two have gone to store it up. As soon as you two have turned round, relief will have been caused at the same time.

Rattlesnake Fern is the medicine. It is merely to be blown on them. The symptoms are that they dream that snakes have bitten them. And they (the snakes) usually cause it to be the same (as if they had really bitten them); poplar should be used with it.

EXPLANATION

The sickness for which this formula is intended is a form of nightmare, resulting from some irregularity in regard to eating. The symptoms and the theory of the disease are well set forth in the formula itself, which abounds in poetic expressions. According to the theory, as is stated in the prescription, when one dreams that he has been bitten by a snake the result is just the same as that of an actual snakebite. [The treatment, however, is different (see Formula No. 47, p. 240).] If the patient does not submit himself to the treatment as here prescribed, the spot bitten in his dream will become red and ulcerate [maybe months or] perhaps years afterwards, and the victim will become ill with all the symptoms of an actual snakebite. The same rule holds good in all other cases, dreams being regarded as prophecies of coming facts. [See p. 40.] There are other formulas for treating other classes of snake dreams. These nightmare dreams are very frequent with the Indians in consequence of bad cookery, late suppers, and irregular hours.

---

[20] The patient.   [21] Disease-snake.

The medicine men explain that the ghosts of the snakes, or sometimes of the fish, in order to take vengeance on those who destroy or offend them, "spoil the saliva" of the offending ones by causing them to dream of snakes and fishes twining and crawling over them, biting them and blowing fetid breath into their faces, until the victims become disgusted with food and lose appetite and strength.

The medicine is then given to induce vomiting, by which the "spoiled saliva" is dislodged, when the patient recovers. Whatever may be thought of the theory or of the medicine actually used, the principle of the application is undoubtedly correct.

The first part of the prayer is addressed to the Black Snake above, which is evidently expected to drive out the disease snake. The second paragraph calls upon the Two Little Men—the Thunder Boys, the sons of k‘ana·'ti (see Mooney, Myths, p. 242)—to take the disease spirit to the Night Land in the West and put it away in the black boxes or coffins. The reason for invoking these "Two Little Men" here will be explained in Formula No. 20, page 196. The sick man finds relief as soon as the Little Men turn round to come back after accomplishing their task. In one place the medicine man speaks directly to the patient, who, however, has no chance to catch the meaning of the whispered words. "Black boxes" or "coffins" are frequently mentioned in the formulas. They are sometimes "buried out West in the black mud, with a black stone on top of them." The "ever-living bones," synonym of the "ever-living teeth," are referred to in most of the formulas concerning snakes. The Cherokee, like other Indians, has a great reverence for snakes in general, but for rattlesnakes in particular, and is careful never to offend one, even by word. In accordance with the principle often applied in the formulas of belittling a serious ailment, it is customary, when a man has been bitten by a snake, to announce that he has "been scratched by a brier." [See p. 14.]

The medicine used is a decoction of rattlesnake fern [*Botrychium virginianum* (L.), Sw.] root, boiled down to a sirup. The medicine man recites the whole formula, then rubs some of the decoction upon the spot where the patient dreams that he has been bitten, and finally blows his breath upon it four times. The whole ceremony is repeated four times, and, in addition, the patient drinks a small portion of the sirup.

In the absence of the plant named, the medicine man uses a decoction of poplar bark [*Liriodendron tulipifera* L.], the root being used in the same way; or he sometimes simply chews some poplar bark or a small portion of the root of v'nastɛ·ts.tɩ·'ɢa [*Aristolochia serpentaria* L.; Virginia snakeroot] and blows it upon the spot after reciting the formula. The medicine may be rubbed on at intervals by some one of the patient's family, but the blowing, with the rest of the ceremony, is performed by the medicine man, who makes the four applications the same morning, beginning soon after sunrise and ending about noon. (See No. 95, p. 307.)

The effect of drinking the sirup is to induce vomiting and thus relieve the stomach. When one dreams that he has been bitten by a snake he must be rigidly secluded and should not be seen by an outsider for four days.

6

i'a'   nǒ·'wɔ·t'i'   Dɩ'v'Dɩ'-yi'   a'ni'yɛ·'Di   v'nitłǫnǒ·'.i [22]
this   to cure with   to give it to them   they eat it   whenever they are ill
                         to drink—E   (kn.)

sGɛ̌' | 'v'u'   Dalɔ·'ni   Dv'Da·N̥t'ɛ·''lɔ̌'i' | v'lsGɛ·'Dɔ̌n   Dvnv·'y't'anɩ·'lɛ·n-
now then chat   yellow   he (E.) has thought it   it important   he (E.) has put
                                                                       it under—

[.i]   ɛ·sɔ·'tłi   Gɛ·'s-ǫ̆.i' | t'ɛ̌'Ga'   Dalɔ·'ni   tła·'wɔ·t'a'laGi'   Gɛ·'=
App   from broad   it is—T L   (frog)   yellow   ever-marshy swamp   it is,
        to narrow

sǫ̆.i'   ɩyǒ·'nDɔ̌n   v'lsGɛ·'Dɔ̌n   Dvnv·'y't'anɩ·'lɛ·n[.i]   ɛ·sɔ·'tłi   Gɛ·'sǫ̆.i' |
T L   yonder   it important   he (E.) has put it under, App from broad   it is, T. L.
                                                                       to narrow

5 vDɔ·lu·''wa.tɔ̆n.ti'   nɩGɛ·'sǫ̆'na' | Dv'Da·N̥t'ɛ·''ɛlɛ·n.i' |
  it to be retraced   never   he (E.) has thought it, App

sGɛ̌' | nɔ·u'Gwɔ̌nʼ   'a't'ǫna·'nɩ·Ga'   tsɔ̌tlɔn/ [23]   Gɩ·'GαGɛ·'n.i'
Now then   now   thou hast come to listen kingfisher   blood   like

ata'   v''staDɔ·'Gi   tsɔ̌·tłt'ɔ'ɩ·'stɩDɛ·Ga' | 'ɩDa·'uwɛ̮ɩ·'-GɔGa' |
wood   top   thou art staying, moving about   thou (art a) wizard—very E

Gɔ't'v'sti   tsúnv·'łti   nɩ·Gɛ·'sǫ̆'na' | 'v'u'   Dalɔ·'ni   vlsGɛ·'Dɔ̌n
something   thou failest   never   chat   yellow   it important

Dvnv·'y't'anɩ·'lɛ·n.i' [24] | nɔ·'uGwɔ̌n   v'sönv·'li   Dɛ''t'askɔlɔ'ɔ̌nʼt'anɩ·Ga' |
He (E.) has put it under   now   quickly   thou hast come to make him
                                                         let go his hold, as thou goest by

10 vtsɩ·''nawa'   nv·'Dɜ·t'anǒ·'Dɔ̌n |
   beyond-it   it has been said at
   stretched   the same time

i'a'   nǒ·'wɔ·t'i'   Dɩ'v'Di   a'ni'yɛ·'Di   v'nitłǫ̆·nǒ·'.i' | kǫ·N̥i'
this   to cure with   to give it   they eat it (kn.)   whenever they are ill   noticeable
                         to them to
                         drink

Dalɔ·'ni   a·'ndɩ·k'ɔ̌'ǫ̆·'.i   vnɛ·''Ga-N̥ɔ̌n   yvnɩ·''nɜnv·'Gɔtc'ɛ·'ɩa | na.ski'
yellow   whenever they urinate while   -and   if, to them, it comes out   this here

vGǫ̆·'wùtłi' | nǒ·'wɔ·t'ɩ-N̥ɔ̌nʼ   u·'G-at'asGɩ·'ski   sɔ.i'-N̥ɔ̌nʼ   Gɩ·'=
it value for   to cure with, and   coming out it oozes out, H   other, and   blood,

Gα-Gɛ·'n   v''yǫ̆·'Dv''wɩDɔ̌nʼ   tsi'kĭ   Gα'tłùD-ǫ̆·'   tsv·'iyɛGɔ·' |
like   it is covered   that which is   it has climbed—T L   they stand up, H

15 Gα·'kt'ǫ̆'nDɔ̌n   nɔ̆n.Gi'   a·ma' | vnǒ·'nDi   na''yɔ·.Gɔ̌   yɛ·li'
   restricted   four   salt   milk   however   possible

'ɩDlɔ̆nʼ   ǐGɔ'ɩ·'Dɔ̌n   v'niyɔ''ɩsti' | Dɩ·'k'anǒ·'wɔ·t'i'   v'niskwɔ·=
long   it has been   they must do   to cure them   their stomach
                made a period   without

tłɩ-'i'   ɛ·'ldi   DɩGɔ̌n.'staN̥ti' | aDɛ·'lù-N̥ɔ̌nʼ   a'niDalɔ·'nɩ-Gɛ·'nʼ
Loc   low   they must hit them   beads-and   they yellow   like

---

[22] W. D. -tł- > C. D. -ts-.
[23] Emendation by J. M.—Instead of tsɔ· lɔ̆n (=tobacco).
[24] Emendation by Editor—Instead of Dvnɩ·'y't'anɩ·'lɛ·nʼi.

t'aᴰli'	a`niGaGɛ'ⁿ	na.'skwŏᵠ`	t'a'ᴰli	ᴅa'ǫ·'i	aGɔ·'nŏᵍ	ᴠᴅɔ·'tə-
two	they red	also	two	they (sol) have been lying down, H	completely	all

ɢwŭᴅŏⁿ`	ɛ·'ldi	ts-uᵗ`ⁱx̱k'alǫ·'.i`	k'ᴅa·'ⁿ	ᴠ'nŭlsta·`y'ti`	ɢɛ·sǫ'.i
day	low	distant he perches	then	they have to take food	it was, H

THIS IS TO CURE WITH, TO GIVE IT TO THEM TO DRINK WHEN THEY
ARE SICK WITH "EATERS"

FREE TRANSLATION

Now then! The Yellow Chat has caused it, it seems. He has put the important thing under him, where his abdomen is. (And also) the Yellow Frog, yonder in the ever-muddy marsh, has put the important thing under his abdomen, his track never to be refound. He has caused it, it seems.

Now then! Now thou hast come to hear, Red Kingfisher, thou stayest, moving about, in the treetops. Thou art a powerful wizard indeed. Thou never failest in anything. The Yellow Chat has put the important thing under him. Now thou hast quickly come to make him relinquish his grasp. Relief has been caused.

This is to cure with, to give it to them to drink, when they are sick with "eaters." The symptoms are that they urinate yellow, and (also) if white (matter) comes out of it (when they urinate) this is for the purpose of it. And to cure with: The pus-oozes-out-(plant), and the other (variety) which is wrapped up in red, and grows on the hillside.

Restricted (are): four (days) salt. Milk, however, they must abstain from as long as possible. To cure them, they should be hit (i. e., rubbed) where their stomach is, low down. And two yellow beads (and) red beads, also two, should be lying down. Fasting (is to be observed) all day. When she (i. e., the sun) perches low down, going away from us, then they should eat.

EXPLANATION

This formula is for treating a urinary or kidney disease, technically known as a`nɪ'yɛ·'ᴅi "they eat it (kn.), hab."

The disease is described as first manifesting itself by a pain in the lower part of the back and abdomen, the latter also becoming swollen. Urination is difficult, and the discharge is yellow, and sometimes white and mucous.

The theory of disease has been already explained. (See p. 14.) In this instance the most obvious symptom being the yellow urine, two yellowish animals are held responsible for the trouble, and the Red (i. e. successful, powerful) Kingfisher hovering above in the treetops is invoked to drive out or break the hold of the disease spirit, figuratively called ["the important thing"].

While performing the ceremony the medicine man has four beads lying near him upon a cloth, two of these beads being yellow to represent the disease, the other two being red and respresenting the curing agent.

The medicine used is an infusion of the bruised root of uʻGatʻasGɩʻski, spurge (*Euphorbia hypericifolia* L. and of another variety uʻGatʻas-Gɩʻski GɩʻgaGeʻʻⁿ uʻiyǫ̈́duʻʻwɩdǫʻ: *Euphorbia corollata* L.; flowering spurge).

This is given in large quantities [4–5 liters] to be drunk by the patient, who remains fasting each day until about sundown. At frequent intervals the medicine man rubs the abdomen of the patient, using for this purpose only his bare hand, neither moistening it with the liquid nor warming it near the fire.

There is a characteristic and interesting correlation of ideas in the milky discharge, the "pus-oozes-out" plant application and the milk taboo.

7

sGéʻʻ	ʻaʻ-noʻᵘGwö̌ᵛʻ	uʻsö̌ʻʻi	Dǫʻtsuʻléʻnę̌ʻ	yö̌ʻwiʻ	ö̌ⁿʻⁿⁿaGeʻⁿʻ
now then	hal now	might. Loc	he has arisen, facing, us, App	human being	it black

ɩʻGa	ayéʻʻⁱli	Dalɔʻʻni	Gaʻne-ʻö̌ʻ	aʻDɩGeʻʻDö̌ⁿ	DʋDö̌ʻneʻtʻiⁿleʻⁿ.iʻ
day	middle	yellow it (liq) is in it, T L	it, moved about	he (E.) has come to do it for him, App

Dalɔʻʻnɩ-Gwö̌ᵛʻ	Geʻseʻⁿ.iʻ	uʻʻlɩsGeʻʻDö̌ⁿ	ʻɩʻDʋnuʻʻytʻanɩʻlę̌.iʻ
it yellow—L	it is—App	it important	which he (E.) has placed under, App

sGéʻʻ	ʻaʻ-noʻᵘGwö̌ᵛʻ	ʻaʻtʻǫ̈ⁿaʻʻnɩGaʻ	tsɔʻⁿstɔwaʻ	Dalɔʻʻni
now then	hal now	thou has come to listen	Killdee Bird	yellow

aʻm-ɔktʻaʻ	Dalɔʻni	DeʻstŭtsGŭʻtʻlAwʻɩstʻanɩʻGaʻ		Goʻʻt-eʻʻGwɔʻʻi²⁵
water, peeping	yellow	you two have become as one		marsh it big, Loc

Geʻs-ö̌ʻ	Dɩʻstö̌tltʻɔʻɩʻsti	uʻsönuʻʻli	Dɔʻʻtstaⁿleʻʻö̌ʻⁿaʻ	Daɩɔʻʻni-
it is, T L	you two are staying	quickly	you two have arisen, facing us	it

Gwö̌ᵛʻ	Geʻs-ö̌ʻ.i	Dalɔʻʻni	Gaʻne-ʻö̌ʻ	aʻʻDɩGeʻʻDö̌ⁿ	staʻDö̌ʻⁿɩ̌ʻeʻʻ=
yellow—L	it is—T L	yellow	it (liq) is in it, T L	it, moved about	you two have come

ɩʻGaʻ	staʻtsanö̌ʻʻⁿi-Gwö̌ᵛʻ	Geseʻⁿ.i		ʻö̌ⁿʻ-stiʻyö̌ⁿʻstʻanɩʻGaʻ
to do it for him	for your (2) adornment L	it is, App		again, you 2 have come to take it (sol) away as you 2 go by

Gɔʻʻt-eʻʻGwŭᵛʻ	aʻtsanö̌ʻʻⁿi	(uʻʻlɩsGeʻʻDö̌ⁿ²⁶)	aʻʻskwanɩGɔʻʻtɔtɩ(-ʻyǏ)²⁷
swamp it big	for his adorn	it important	it is put in store—Loc

10 stɩʻskwanɩGɔʻʻtʻanɩʻGaʻ | ɩGö̌ʻʻwŭlstɔʻtⁱ-Gwö̌ᵛʻ | vtsɩʻʻⁿawaʻ
you two have come to put it in store as you two go by | what is it worth! L | beyond-it stretched

nuʻʻDǝ.tʻanö̌ʻʻⁿDö̌ⁿ | nö̌ⁿʻstö̌neʻʻlɩʻGaʻ
it has been said at the same time | you two have come to do it for him

---

²⁵ Contraction of ɩGɔʻti (=swamp) eʻGwɔʻi (where it-big is).
²⁶ Interpolation by ayɔʻsta, a native medicine woman, recorded by J. M.
²⁷ Interpolation by ayɔʻsta, recorded by J. M.

ʇi'a'   ᴅalɔ·'ni   v'nitɫö·ŋö̌'.i [28]   v·'nəᴅi·yö̌·'ⁿᴅali`   ᴅi`k'anö̌·'wɔ·t'i` |
this   it yellow whenever they are ill   their navel   to cure them with
aᴅzi·'lɔ̈ⁿ   ᴅa'ǫ·'i   ᴅi`k'anö̌'wɔ·t'i·-yi'
fire   they (sol) used   to cure
to be lying down   them with, Loc

This is When They Are Sick With the "Yellow"

FREE TRANSLATION

Now then! Right now, in the middle of the day, the Black Man has arisen, it seems, from the night land. Where the bile is stagnant, he has come to wallow in it, it seems. It was merely bile, it seems. He had put the important thing under him, it seems.

Now then! Right now thou hast come to hear, Yellow Killdee Bird, and thou, Yellow Small Fish, you two have been caused to become united to one. You two are staying where the great swamp is. Quickly you two have arisen, facing this way.

It is merely bile. You two have come to wallow there where the bile is stagnant. It (i. e., the bile) is the very thing you two adorn yourselves with. As you two go by, you have gone to take it away to the great swamp for its adornment; you two have come to go and store the important thing as you go by, at the place where it is to be stored. Who cares what happens to it? Relief has been caused at the same time. You two have come to do it for him [the patient].

This is when they are sick with the "yellow," to treat their navel with. Fire (live coals) should be lying down while treating them.

EXPLANATION

This formula is for treating one of the many varieties of ᴅalɔ·ni or "yellow." (See p. 182.)

As stated in the introduction, various causes may be held responsible for this disease, the agent in this case being the Black Person, or the Black Man in the night land. (See p. 24.) The expression i·'ɢa ayɛ'"li` which may mean "in the middle of the sky," as well as "in the middle of the day," occurs in many of the formulas, especially in those recited against ᴅalɔ·ni and against fever, but the reason is not obvious. In one case a medicine man told [Mr. Mooney] that the illness began at noon, and that on this account the disease-spirit was referred to as arising in the middle of the day.

The animal spirits invoked as curing agents are both yellow like the disease. [In some cases (see p. 179) they are of opposite colors.]

The amǝkt'a [ama'=water; akt'a=he is peeping out from] is a fish hardly an inch in length, appearing in schools in the summer, and is simply a newly hatched individual of the common varieties.

---

[28] W. D. -tɫ=C. D. -ts-.

The color of the animal spirits being yellow explains the expression: "It is the very thing you two adorn yourselves with." The bile is supposed to have become stagnant, and these animals are expected to effect a cure by wallowing in it and thus stirring it up. It is with the same object in view that the medicine man rubs the stomach of the patient, viz, to scatter the "clotted" bile. (See p. 62.)

The symptoms of the disease are a vomiting of bile and a throbbing and soreness about the navel, so that the slightest touch is painful; [the umbilic region] also becomes much swollen. While the disease is believed to be primarily the work of revengeful animal ghosts, the doctor from whom the formula was obtained said that the immediate cause was that the gall (a·t‘a′Gŏⁿ) sometimes [by the native medicine men] confounded with the bile (ᴅalɔ·ni), gets into the veins and collects under the navel (1) He claimed this as an original discovery and prided himself upon it accordingly.

No medicine is used, the medicine man simply rubbing the sore spot with his hands previously warmed over the fire as described on page 62. The medicine man recites the formula in a whisper, while rubbing his hands together over the fire. Then laying them flat upon the seat of pain, he draws them slowly down over the place, blowing upon the spot once at the end. This operation is repeated four times at each application, and four applications complete the treatment, the first being about sunrise and the last just before noon, as already explained. In this and most other forms of ᴅalɔ·ni the tsʋ‵Gɩ·tsuyŏⁿ.′sti fish (Horny Head) is tabooed on account of its tendency to rapid decay.

Both the medicine man and his assistant, but not the patient, abstain from food until after the fourth application.

8

	v‵ndɩ·yǫ̈·′ᴅali their navel	a‵ᴅa‘nǫ̈·′wɔ·t‘i‵ to cure any one with	ʦɩ’a′ this	
sGę̈‵ʼ Now then	‘a‵-nɔ·Gwŏⁿ ha! Now	‘at‘ǫ̈ŋa·‵nɩ·Ga′ thou hast come to listen	tsɩ·‵ya′ Otter	Gɩ·‵Ga-Gɛ·ⁿ′ blood-ish
‵ɩᴅa·‵ᵘwɛ̈ʹi′ thou wizard	ǫ̈·ᴅal-ɛ-′Gwɔ‵ lake, big	ᴅɩ·tsötlt‘ɔ‵‘ɩsti′ thou art staying		‘a-‵nɔ·Gwŏⁿ′ ha, now
ᴅɔ·‵t‘a‵ᵖlɛ‘ǫ̈·ŋa′ thou hast arisen, facing us	‘a‵-Gɔ‘ʋ′sti ha, something	a‵GwAᴅɛ‵‵lɩtc‘ɛ‘ti‵ it escapes from my (sight)	nɩGɛ‵sǫ̈·na′ never	
5 tsuᴅɔ‵‵nŏʹi′ thou hast said	nǫ̈·‵nɔ-ʹi′ trail(s), Loc	ᴅɔ·‵ᴅatsana·′ᵘwaᴅi‵ they lie for thee stretched out as thou comest hither	v‵lsGɛ·′ᴅə it important	
ᴅʋ‵na‵ᴅutlǫ̈·′ where they cling to each other	‘ɩGɛ·‵sɩwi‵st‘anɩ·Ga′ thou hast come to (push it) with the crown of thy head back to where it ought to be		v‵lsGɛ·′ᴅə it important	ᴅʋᴅɔ‵‵nŏʹi′ he has said it
t‘a‵ᴅɩGɔ‵tlt‘anɩ·Ga′ thou hast come to push it away		ʋlsGɛ·′ᴅə it important	ʋ‵wɔ·Gɩ′tli from	nɩ‵Gat‘-ǫ̈·′ as high as—T L	ɩ·ˡyǫ̈′ yonder

tⁿιtʻɔʻι̒stʻanι·Gaˊ	v·lsGɛˊDə	Gǫ̑·ˋwʻAtvʻʻwιDəˋ	nǫ̈·ˋnoṭ́iˊ
thou hast come to put it staying there	it important	it all surrounded	trail(s), L
DɛˋGananvGɔ·ˊtsιDɔ⁽ʻɛ·stiˊ		vtsιʻʻnawaˋ	nιGǫ̈·ˋDιsGɛ·stiˊ
they will appear continuously in all directions		beyond it, stretched out	he will be saying it
vtsιʻʻnawaˋ	aDǫ̈ʻʻnι·Gaˋ		
	it has been said		
sGɛ̑ʻʼ	ʻaˋ-nɔ·Gwǫ̈ᵘˊ	ʻaˋtʻǫnaˋnι·Gaˊ	tsι·yaˊ	tsʻAˋska·sɛʻˋ.tιˊ-yuˊ
Now then	ha, Now	thou hast come to listen	otter	hou fearful—E
Galǫ̈·ˊldi	ayɛʻᶥliˊ	ǫ̈·ˋDalɛ·ˊGwǫ̈ᵘ	Dι̒tsǫ̈tłtʻoʻι̒stiˊ	ʻaˋ-nɔ·GwǫǏᵘˊ 5
above	middle	lake, big	thou art staying	ha, Now
Dɔ·ˋtʻaᴾlɛˋʻǫ̈·ŋaˊ		ʻι̒Da·ᵘwɛṭ́iˊ	Gɔʻvˊsti	a GWADɛ·lι̒ˋtcʻɛʻˋti
thou hast arisen facing us		thou wizard		
nι̒Gɛ·sǫnaˊ	tsu̇Dǫ̈ʻʻnǫ̈ṭ́iˊ		ʻι̒ķAtʻʻɛ·nǫ̈ṭ́i	nǫnoṭ́iˊ
			thou keen-eyed one	
Dɔ·ˋDatsana·ʻᵘwu̇Dιˋ	v·lsGɛ·ˊDə	Dvˊna·ˋDu̇tlǫ̈·ˊ	(etc.)	(with,

added at the end,:) ¹yăʻ

THIS IS THE MEDICINE FOR THEIR NAVEL

FREE TRANSLATION

Now then! Ha, now thou hast come to listen, Red Otter, thou wizard; thou art staying at the great lake; ha, now thou hast arisen facing us. "Nothing ever escapes my (sight)" thou hast said. The trails are lying stretched for thee (to allow) thee to come hither.

Where he [29] has put the important thing against him,[30] thou hast come to push it with the crown (of thy head) back to where it ought to be   What had become an important thing thou hast come to push away as thou goest by.

Where the foam is (piled up) high thou hast gone to put the important thing to stay. The trails will surround the important thing from all directions. Relief will be caused continuously; relief has been caused.

Now then! Ha, now thou hast come to listen, thou fearful Otter in the great lake in midheaven, thou art staying. But now thou hast arisen from there, facing us. Thou wizard! "Nothing ever escapes from my (sight)," thou hast said. Thou art most keen-eyed. The trails are lying stretched for thee (to enable) thee to come hither.

Where he [29] has put the important thing against him [30] (etc.).

EXPLANATION

This is another formula for the cure of navel-Dalɔ·ni, and the cure is the same as the one described in No. 7, page 180.

The medicine man was of the opinion that there was another paragraph, addressed to the Fire, and which was probably recited

---

[29] The disease-spirit.   [30] The patient.

by the medicine man while warming his hand, prior to rubbing the patient's stomach, but it does not appear in the original manuscript.

The observant habit of the Indian is shown in the reference to the watchfulness of the otter, one of its distinguishing characteristics.

The feature of quoting the words of the spirit invoked, as in this case the medicine man quotes the words of the otter, occurs frequently in the formulas, especially in those addressed to the Fire. [As students of comparative folklore will know, this feature is also often met with in European formulas, the most universally known specimen being the First Merseburger Conjuration.[31]]

9

	ï'a' this	ᴅanĭnɛʻsuʻɢǫ̈·ʼ(.i[32]) whenever.they have them drooping		
sɢɛ̌ʼʼ Now then	ʻaʻ-nɔ·ɢwö̆ᴅʼ ha! Now	v̆ʻsȯnv·ʼli quickly	akskiʼ tsö̱ʻnu̇lɩ·ɢaʼ enemy he has come to hit thee	ʻa-nɔ·ʻ= ha!
ɢwu̇-ᴅɩ·ʼnə Now—E	v̆ʻsönv·ʼli quickly	aʼkskɩ-ɢwö̆ᴅʻ enemy, L (=E)	tsö̱ʻnu̇löü̆ʼ he has hit thee	ʻɩɢɛʻʻsɛ·ⁿ.iʼ that which is—App.
ʻaʻ-nɔ·ⁿɢwö̆ᴅʼ ha! now	vtsɩʻʼnawu̇-ɢwö̆ᴅʻ beyond-it stretched—L		nv·ʻᴅə.tʻanö̆·ʼⁿᴅə it has been said at the same time	nö̆ⁿtʻö̆·nɛʻʼ= thou hast come to do
5 lɩ·ɢaʼ it for him	vtsɩʻʻnawaʻ beyond it stretched	aᴅö̆ʻʻnɩɢaʼ it has been said		sɢɛ̌ʼʼ now then!
ï'a' this	ᴅanĭnɛʻsuʻɢǫ̈·.iʼ whenever they have them drooping	na.skiʼ this here	nvʻstiʼ so far like	ɩʻɢawɛ·ʼsti it is to be said	ʻɩ·ɢiʼ that which is
ᴅɩᴅzɔ·ʻᵘtʻa.ɛ·ʼtɩ·ɢwö̆ᴅʻ they must be blown—L		aʻtʻ-tsɛʻi̇ wood green	nö̆·woʼtʻɩ-nʻǒⁿʼ to cure with-and		ᴅɩʻɢanö̆·lɩʼ= they must be
yɛʻtiʻ rubbed	ʻɩ·ɢɛsʔ·.iʼ that which used to be			

This (is for) When They Have Them Drooping

FREE TRANSLATION

Now then! Ha, just now the enemy has suddenly come and struck thee. Ha, just now indeed, the enemy himself struck thee, it appears. Ha, now relief indeed has been caused at the same time, thou hast come to do it for him. Relief indeed has been caused. Now then!

This (is for) when they have them drooping. Just like this it has to be said. It should be blown on them, alder (which) is the medicine, (or) it should be rubbed on them.

EXPLANATION

ᴅanɩ·ʼnɛʻsuʻɢǫ̈·ʼ.i is the technical name for an affection of the eyes in which the sufferer is unable to bear the strong light of the sun or of

---

[31] Cf. also some European parallels: v. Hov. & Kr. II, 77, 332, 399.
[32] Emendation by editor.

the blazing fire without pain. In treating it, the medicine man uses an infusion of alder bark, which he blows or rubs into the open eyes of the patient.

The medicine man sometimes simply chews the bark and blows out the juice upon the eyes. [The disease is caused by seeing a rattlesnake; the snake is being referred to by a circumlocution: akski′ so as not to offend it the more by calling its name. It is worthy of interest that even the common name of the rattlesnake, ᴜdzɔ·nːti′, is a euphemism, meaning "the admirable one" (√-tsɔ·nː-=admire.) (See p. 14.)]

10

Dani̇ˋnɛ·sʋˤɢǫ·.′[i] a̓Daˤnǫ̈·″wɔ·tˤi̇′ i̇ˋ’a′ |
when they have them drooping / the medicine / this

|ˤa-Dǫ̈·′ⁿtawa′ 'i·Da·ᵘwɛi̇′ | ɢalǫ̈·ˋladi′ tˤaDʋ·ˋyǫ̈·na′ | ʋtsi̇ˋˤ-
hal roller / thou wizard / above / thou hast formed thyself / beyond it

na·ᵘwa′ aDö̈ˋni·ɢa′ | tsʋ·lʋ′st | tsʋ·lʋ′st | tsʋ·lʋ′st |
it stretched / it has been said / (Onomat.)

tsʋ·lʋ′st |

WHEN THEY HAVE THEM DROOPING, THIS IS THE MEDICINE

FREE TRANSLATION

O Miller, thou wizard, thou hast originated on high. Relief has been caused.

EXPLANATION

This is another formula for the same purpose as the one last given. The medicine man uses no medicine, but simply sings the verse, and then blows his breath four times, into the eyes of the patient. The ceremony is generally repeated four times.

[The Dǫ̈·Dawa′ (really aDǫ̈·Dawa′) is a small whitish miller, which flies about the light at night. The name implies that it "playfully rolls over and over (in the flame)." A word of the same stem, "aDǫ̈Dawɪska," is used for hens curing their feathers in the dust, and also for dogs playfully rolling over in the grass or in the snow.]

On account of its affinity for the fire, the Dǫ̈·ˋDawa′ is invoked in all that the medicine men call "fire diseases." [These include this eye trouble because the patient afflicted with it can not stand the glare of the blazing fire. Curiously enough, frostbite is also considered as belonging to this class, because it affects like a burn or a scald.]

The final "tsʋ·lʋ′st" uttered four times in a sharp voice [may be] intended to imitate the sound heard when the insect singes its wings in the blaze.

11

u·ˋndɩ·yö̱ˋⁿpali` aˋpaʻnö̱·ˊwɔ·tʻi` ɩ̱·ˋaˊ
their navel   the medicine   this

sGɛ̃ˋˊ	ʻa·ˊ-wɔ·yiˊ	paloˊni	ʻɩpaˋ·ᵘwɛ̱iˊ	waˋᵘpaGuˊ	paloˋˊni
now then!	ha! pigeon	yellow	thou (art a) wizard	goldfinch	yellow
soˋᵘGwö̱ᴅˊ	ᴅɛˋstûtsGöˋtɫawʻɪstʻanɩ·Gaˊ		stɪpaˋᵘwɛ̱iˊ		sùˋlʋ·y=
one	you two have become as one		you two (are) wizards		swampy laurel-thicket
ɛˊGwö̱ᵑ	ᴅɩˋstötɫtʻɔʻɩstiˊ		uˋsənu·ˊli	ᴅɔˋtstaᴅlɛʻö̱·ŋaˊ	paloˋˊ=
it big	you two are staying		quickly	you two have arisen, facing us	it yellow
5 ni-Gwö̱ᵑ —L	Gɛsɛ̱ˊ it is, App	u·ˋlsGɛˋˋᴅöⁿ it important	ᴅʋnu·ˋyʻɪtʻanɩˋlɛ·ⁿ(.i³³)ˊ he (ᴇ.) has come to put it under		stötɫstaˋˋyʻ= it is for your (2)
tɩ-Gwùˋ-ᴅɩˋnöⁿˊ food—L (=E)	ʻɩˋGɛ·sɛ·ⁿ(.i³³)ˊ that which is, App		tʻɪstiˋskwɔ·ˊli your (2) stomachs	ᴅɛˊGɛˋstanɩsɔˋˋtʻa= you 2 have come to bury it
nɩ·Gaˊ in them		uˋkʻùwɛˋᴅəGwö̱ᴅˋ filled-up, L	ʻɩGɛˋstaᴅö̱ˋnɛ·ⁿ.iˊ they have done it for you (2), App		nö̱·ŋötɫstʻanɩ·Gaˊ it has happened so
uˋsö̱·ˊˋɩᴅöⁿ night-been	nʋˋᴅöʻnö̱ˊnə it has been said		utsɩ·ˊʻnawaˋ beyond it stretched	nʋˋᴅə.tʻanö̱·ˊⁿᴅə it has been said at the same time

(For) Their Navel, This is the Medicine

FREE TRANSLATION

Now then! Ha, Yellow Pigeon, thou wizard, (and thou) Yellow Goldfinch, you two have become united. You two wizards, you are staying where the great swampy thicket is.

Quickly you two have arisen; the important thing is merely bile; he[34] has put it under him.[35] But that is the very thing you two eat. You two have buried them in your stomachs. They have made you two filled as you go by, it has become so, and not for one night (but forever). Relief has been caused at the same time.

EXPLANATION

This formula is for the same purpose as Nos. 7 and 8, and the treatment is the same—simple rubbing with the warmed hand. The Goldfinch invoked is the American goldfinch (*Chrysomitus tristis*), known in the southern Alleghanies as the flaxbird. [The expression regarding "the food being buried in the stomach" is the formulistic equivalent for the common expression "to take food" (Gaᴅlɩsta·ˋyəʻöⁿskaˊ, I take food).]

---

[33] Emendation by W., editor's informant.
[34] The disease-spirit.
[35] The patient.

12

$aye\cdot{}^{\backprime}lιGɔ\cdot{}'Gi$	$v^{\backprime}nιye\cdot{}^{\backprime}lɔ^{\epsilon}nɔ^{n'}ʇi$	$a^{\backprime}Da^{\epsilon}nǫ^{\backprime}wɔ\cdot{}t^{\epsilon}i^{\backprime}$	$ʇι^{\flat}a'$	
simulator (s)	they have made them like	the medicine	this	

$sG\epsilon^{\check{w}\flat}$	$Gι\cdot{}tǐi'$	$wɔ\cdot{}^{\backprime}DιG\epsilon\cdot{}^{n'}$	$^{\epsilon}ιDa\cdot{}^{\backprime u}w\epsilon\ddot{\imath}'$	$nǫ\cdot{}^{n}Dɔ\text{-}Gǫ\text{-}yι\cdot{}\text{-}Dzɔ^{n}$
now then	dog	brown	thou (art a) wizard	sun, first, Loc—direction toward

$tsɔ^{\backprime}ʇt^{\epsilon}ɔ^{\epsilon}ιsti'$	$^{\epsilon}ιDa\cdot{}^{\backprime u}w\epsilon\ddot{\imath}'$	$Gɔ^{\epsilon}v'sti$	$nv^{\backprime}D\epsilon^{\epsilon}lǫ\cdot{}'nə$	$asGι\cdot{}'nə$
thou art staying	thou (art a) wizard	something	it is not overlooked	ghost

$v^{\backprime}Dɔ^{\epsilon}nɔ^{n'}ʇi$	$^{\epsilon}ι^{\backprime}G\epsilon\cdot{}s\epsilon\cdot{}^{n'}$	$Dv^{\backprime}Da\cdot{}Nɨt^{\epsilon}\epsilon\cdot{}^{\backprime}lɔ^{n}ʇi^{\backprime}$	$yι'ki$	$a^{D}l\breve{e}'$ $yǫwi'$
it has been said	that which is, App	he (E) has thought it	if it is	and human being

$D\epsilon^{\prime\epsilon}a^{D}lu^{\backprime}$	$Dv^{\backprime}Da\cdot{}Nɨt^{\epsilon}\epsilon\cdot{}^{\backprime}lɔ^{n}ʇi^{\backprime}$	$yι'ki$	$a^{\epsilon}s\epsilon'\text{-}Gwɔ^{\text{D}\backprime}$	$ι^{\backprime}Gaw\epsilon'Dəgwɔ^{\text{D}\backprime}$ 5
purple	he (E) has thought it	if it is	falsely L (=E)	it has been said L

$yι'ki$	$aye\cdot{}^{\backprime}lιGɔ\cdot{}'Gι\text{-}Gwɔ^{\text{D}\backprime}$	$Dvye\cdot{}^{\backprime}lɔ^{\epsilon}nɔ^{n'}ʇi$	$^{\epsilon}ι^{\backprime}G\epsilon\cdot{}s\epsilon\cdot{}^{n'}$	$nɔ\cdot{}^{u}\text{-}$
if it is	simulator—L	he (E) has made it like it	that which is—App	now

$Gwu\text{-}Dι\cdot{}'nə$	$Gɔ\cdot{}^{\backprime}lv^{\epsilon}nǫ\cdot{}'^{n}Də$	$aDɔ^{\backprime\epsilon}nι\cdot{}Ga'$	$Ga\cdot{}tłǫ\cdot{}sta'Gi$	$aDɔ^{\backprime\epsilon}nι\cdot{}Ga'$
—E	it has been tracked	it has been said	it untied	it has been said

$v^{\backprime}sɔ^{\epsilon}ιDɔ'^{n}$	$nv^{\backprime}Də^{\epsilon}nǫ\cdot{}'nə$	$Dι^{\epsilon}tsckwɔ\cdot{}'li$	$D\epsilon^{\backprime}GaDa^{\backprime}nιsɔ\cdot{}'tιsG\epsilon\cdot{}'sti'$
night-been	it has not been said	thy stomachs	it shall bury itself continuously in it

$v^{\backprime}k^{\epsilon}aw\epsilon\cdot{}'Də\cdot{}Gwɔ^{\text{D}}$	$G\epsilon\cdot{}^{\backprime}tsaDǫ\cdot{}n\epsilon\ddot{\imath}'$	$nǫ\cdot{}nɔtłst^{\epsilon}a^{\backprime}nι\cdot{}Ga'$	$tsɔ^{\backprime}tł\text{-}$
filled up—L	they have-done for thee, App	it has happened so	for thy

$sta\cdot{}'y^{\epsilon}ti\text{-}Gwu^{\backprime}Dι\cdot{}nə'$	$^{\epsilon}ι^{\backprime}G\epsilon\cdot{}s\epsilon\cdot{}^{n'}$	$vlsG\epsilon\cdot{}'Dɔ^{n}$	$Dvnv^{\backprime}y^{\epsilon}t^{\epsilon}anι\cdot{}l\epsilon\cdot{}^{n}.i'$ 10
food—L (=E) E	that which is—App	if important	he (E) has put it under it—App

$vtsι^{\epsilon\prime}nawə\text{-}Gwɔ^{\backprime\text{D}}$	$aDɔ^{\backprime\epsilon}nι'Ga'$
beyond it stretched—L (=E)	it has been said

$ʇι^{\flat}a'$	$nǫ\cdot{}'wɔ\cdot{}t^{\epsilon}ι'$	$tsi\text{-}Da^{\backprime}nι^{\epsilon}v^{\backprime\epsilon}ɔ^{n}ska'$	$nɔ.tsi'$ $a^{\backprime}Ganɔ^{n'}ʇi$
this	to cure with	those which have to be given them to drink—H	pine it has been boiled

$G\epsilon^{\backprime}sɔ\cdot{}.i'$	$aD\epsilon\cdot{}'lɔ\text{-}Nɨɔ^{n\backprime}$	$v^{\backprime}nιn\epsilon\cdot{}'Gə$	$a^{\backprime}nιGɔ^{\epsilon\backprime}naG\epsilon\cdot{}'^{l}\text{-}Nɨɔ^{n\backprime}$
it used to be	beads and	they are white	they are black, and

$sɔ\cdot{}^{\backprime u}Gwɔ^{\epsilon}\text{-}a\cdot{}'$
one each

This is the Medicine (if) Simulators Have Made it Resemble it (i. e., a Real Sickness)

FREE TRANSLATION

Now then! Yellow Dog, thou wizard, thou art staying toward where the sun land is. Thou wizard, nothing is overlooked (by thee).

Maybe it is a ghost that has caused it, or maybe it is the Purple Man that has caused it. But it has been said falsely—it is merely the Simulator who has made it resemble it (a real sickness).

But now its track has been found. It has been undone, and not for a night (but forever). It shall bury itself into thy stomachs. They have made thee filled; it has become so again. It is the very thing thou eatest. He has put the important thing under him, (but now) relief has been caused.

This is to treat (them) with, (and) which has to be given them to drink. Pine (tops) should be boiled. And beads, white and black, one of each (should be used with it).

EXPLANATION

[This formula is one for the cure of the mysterious variety of diseases discussed at length in the introduction, page 33.]

The symptoms are sudden pains in various parts of the body, due, it is alleged, to the fact that a conjurer has shot a stick or some other object into the body of the patient. To treat the case, the medicine man prepares a decoction of pine tops, an "overhand" ("aDawɔ'ʻɩla") long, taken from seven different trees. After the liquid has boiled, the pine tops are taken out of it and put under a piece of cloth (which afterwards becomes the medicine man's fee), while four (the formula says two) white and black beads, two of each color, are placed on top. The medicine man then takes some of the medicine in a cup in his outstretched hand, and after reciting the formula, passes the cup four times in a circle above the head of the patient, after which he gives the medicine to drink. After the ceremony the doctor carefully hides the pine tops away in a hollow log, [a rock crevice] or some other place where they will keep dry. No sucking is prescribed in this formula. Say it, merely.

13

ï'a'	aˋnɩskɔˑ'li	ʋˋneʻɩˋstaˑnḙ̃a'		DɩDzɔˑ'tʻa.ɛˑˋti˙		ɩ̈ˋ'a-Gwɔ̃'ɒ
This	their head	they ache to them		they must be blown		this L
ɩˋGawɛˑ'sti		waʻya	waʻya	waʻya'	waʻya'	Du:	a't'tɩ-Gwɔ̃ᴅˋ
it to say		wolf	wolf	wolf	wolf	(Onom.)	say it—L

This (is for) When They Have Their Heads Aching

FREE TRANSLATION

They must be blown. And merely this is to be said: Wolf, wolf, wolf, wolf. Du! Say it, merely.

EXPLANATION

Although this headache formula is from the manuscript of Ay., he said that it was not his own, and was unable to give any further information on it. It consists of a song, an invocation of the wolf, followed by blowing, but whether of medicine or of the breath alone is not stated. The final "du!" is intended as an imitation of some sound made by the wolf. The ceremony is probably repeated four times.

14

(υ'ˋndɩ·yǫ̈·ˊDali aˋDaꞌnǫ̈ˊwɔ·tꞌiˋ ꞉ɩˊaˊ)³⁶
their navel   the medicine   this

sGɛ̃ˊˊ	ꞌaˋnɔ·Gwɔ̈ᵘˋ	ꞌaˋtꞌǫ̈ŋaˋnɩ·Gaꞌ	wɔ·yiˊ	Dalɔ·niˊ	sùlυˋy=
Now then	ha now	thou hast come to listen	pigeon	yellow	swampy
ɛˊgwɔ̈ⁿ	Dɩtsɔ̈ˋtɫtꞌɔˋɩstiˊ	waˋᵘDaGuˊ	Dalɔ·ˊni	sɔ·Gwɔ̈ᵘˊ	Dɛˋstùts=
big laurel thicket	thou art staying	gold finch	yellow	one	you two
Gɔ̈ˋtɫanɩ·Gaˊ	stɔ̈tɫsta·ˊyꞌɪtɩ-Gwɔ̈ᵘˋ	Gɛsɛ·ⁿ.iˊ		Dalɔ·ˊnɩ-Gwɔ̈ᵘˋ	
have become one	it for your (2) food—L (=E)	it is, App		yellow, L	
Gɛsɛ·ˊⁿ[.i ³⁷]	υ·lsGɛ·ˊDə	ꞌɩˋDυnυˋyꞌtꞌanɩlˋɛ·ⁿiˊ		ꞌaˋ-nắꞌnaˊ	ꞌɔ̈ˋⁿꞌ=	5
it is, App	it important	which he (E) put under, App.		ha! there	again
stiˊyǫ̈ˋstꞌanɩ·Gaˊ	stɔ̈tɫsta·ˊyꞌti-Gwɔ̈ᵘˋ	Gɛ·ˋsɛ·ⁿiˊ		nɩGǫ̈·ˋwayɛˋ=	
you (2) have come to take it (sol) away	it for your (2) food, L	it is, App.		there shall be	
lənɔ̈ˋⁿꞌɔ̈ⁿsGɛ·ˋstɩGwɔ̈ᵘˊ	stɩꞌyǫ̈ˋstꞌanɩ·Gaˊ		υꞌsɔ̈ˊꞌɩDɔ̈ⁿˋ	nυˋDəꞌnǫ̈·ˊnə	
a likeness left L	you (2) have come to take it (sol) away		night, been	it has not been said	
υtsˋɩˊˊnawə·Gwɔ̈ᵘˋ	aDɔ̈ˋꞌnɩ·Gaˊ		ˊyắꞌ		
beyond it stretched, L	it has been said		Sharply!		

THEIR NAVEL, THIS IS THE MEDICINE (FOR)

FREE TRANSLATION

Now then! Right now thou hast come to listen, Yellow Pigeon; where the great swampy thicket is, thou art staying; (with) the Yellow Goldfinch, you two have become united.

It is the very thing you two eat, (for) the important thing is merely the "yellow." He [38] has put it under him.[39]

Ha, you two have taken it away again, as you two passed by. It is the very thing you two eat. There will be only a likeness of it left, where you two have taken it to, as you passed, (and) not for a night (but forever). Relief indeed has been caused. Sharply!

EXPLANATION

No medicine is used with this formula, the doctor simply applying his hands previously warmed, as explained in No. 7, page 182. The formula seems to be incomplete, and in the manuscript the latter portion is written with pencil, evidently some time after the first part had been written. The ceremony is repeated four times at each application.

---

[36] Interpolation by J. M.
[37] Correction by editor.
[38] The disease-spirit.
[39] The patient.

15

ʋ`ndɩ·yǫ̆·′ᴅali a`ᴅa`nǫ̆·′wɔ·t′i` !ɩ'a′
their navel   to cure anyone   this
           with

(a) sGě″ | nɔ·′Gwɔ̆ⁿ | ʽa`t'ǫ̆ɳa·`nɩ·Ga′ | ᵘwa·ᵘ′ᴅaGᴜ` | ᴅa`lɔ·ni′
Now then!   Now   thou hast come to listen   Goldfinch   Yellow

sʉ̀`lʋ·y-ϵ·′Gwɔ̆ⁿ   Gϵ·sǫ̆·′   tsɔ̆`tɩ̀t'ɔ`ɩ`stɩᴅϵ·Ga′ | ʽɩ`ᴅa·ᵘwɛ̀ɩ·-`Gɔ·Ga′ |
marshy thicket, big   it is, T L   thou art staying, moving about   thou wizard, E

Gɔʽʋ′sti   tsùnʋ·′łti   nɩ`Gϵ·sǫ̆·na′ | ᴅalɔ·′nɩ-Gwɔ̆ᵘ′   ʋ`IsGϵ·′ᴅə
something   thou failest   never   yellow, L   it important

5 ʽɩ`ᴅʋ·nʋ·`yʽɩt'anɩ·lϵ·ⁿ.i′ | ʽa·`.-ʋsɔ̆nʋ·′li   t'a`ᴅɩGalϵ·`ʽɩ·Ga′ | nɩGǫ̆·`wa-
it which he has put under, App   ha, quickly   thou hast come and pushed it aside   a likeness

yϵ`lənɔ̆ⁿ'ɔ̆ⁿ'sGϵ·′stɩ-Gwɔ̆ᵘˋ   ᴅʋ`·ᴅɩGϵ-ʽǫ̆·′.i | ʋ`sɔ̆nʋ·′li   ᴅϵʽt'ɔ̆tɩ̀t'a`nɩ·Ga′
of it will be left, L   he rested, T L   quickly   thou hast come to put him on his (legs)

(b) sGě″ | ʽa`-nɔ·Gwɔ̆ᵘ′   ʽa`t'ǫ̆ɳa·`nɩ·Ga′ | ᵘwɔ·′yi   ᴅa`lɔ·ni′
Now then!   ha, now   thou hast come to listen   Pigeon   yellow

Gɔ·`t-ϵ·′Gwɔ̆   Gϵ·sǫ̆·′   tsɔ̆`tɩ̀t'ɔ·ɩsti′ | ʽɩᴅa·ᵘwɛ̀ɩ·-Gɔ·Ga′ | Gɔʽʋ′sti
marsh, big   it is, T L   thou art staying   thou wizard, E   something

tsùnʋ·′łti   nɩ`Gϵ·sǫ̆·na′ | ᴅalɔ·′nɩ-Gwɔ̆ᵘ′   ʋ`IsGϵ·′ᴅə   ᴅʋ·nʋ·`yʽt'anɩ·-
thou failest   never   yellow, L   it important   it has put it under,

10 lϵ·ⁿi′ | ʽa·`ʋsɔ̆nʋ·′li   ᴅϵʽt'ɔ̆tɩ̀t'a`nɩ·Ga′ | nɩ`Gǫ̆·wayϵ·`lənɔ̆ⁿ'ɔ̆ⁿ'sGϵ·′stɩ-=
App   ha, quickly   thou hast come to put him on (his legs)   a likeness of it will remain,

Gwɔ̆ᵘˋ   ᴅʋ`·ᴅɩGϵ-ʽǫ̆·′.i
L   he moved about, lying down

(c) sGě″ | nɔ·′Gwɔ̆ⁿ | ʽa`t'ǫ̆·ɳa·`nɩ·Ga′ | yǫ̆·wi′   Ga`nəʽɩ·′'ᴅə   tsɔ̆tłɔ̆ⁿ′
Now then!   Now   thou hast come to listen   human being   long   Kingfisher

tsùnϵ·′Gə   sɔ·ᵘGwɔ̆ᵘ′   ᴅϵ`stúts.Gɔ̆`tłAwʽɩstʽa`nɩ·Ga′ | stɩ`ᴅa·ᵘwɛ̀ɩ·-
thou white   one   you two have come to be united as one   you two wizards,

Gɔ·Ga′   Gɔʽʋ′sti   stɩnʋ·′łti   nɩ`Gϵ·sǫ̆·na′ | ᴅalɔ·′nɩ-Gwɔ̆ᵘ′   ʋIsGϵ·′ᴅə
E   something   you two fail   never   yellow, L   it important

15 ᴅʋ·nʋ·`yʽt'anɩ·lϵ·ⁿ.i′ | ʋ`sɔ̆nʋ·`lɩ·-yu′   ᴅϵʽt'ɔ̆tɩ̀t'a`nɩ·Ga′ | nɩ`Gǫ̆·wayϵ·`-
it has put it under, App   quickly, E   thou hast come to put him on his (legs)   a likeness of

lənɔ̆`ⁿ'ɔ̆ⁿ'sGϵ·′stɩGwɔ̆ᵘˋ   ᴅʋ`·ᴅɩGϵ-ʽǫ̆·′.i
it will remain, L   he moved about, lying down T L

(d) sGě″ | nɔ·′Gwɔ̆ⁿ   ʽa`t'ǫ̆ɳa·`nɩ·Ga′ | yǫ̆·wi′   Ga`nɔ̆ʽɩ·′ᴅə   kʽa`nǫ̆·-
Now then   Now   thou hast come to listen   human being   long   Fish

tsʋ·′′wa   Gɩ·`Ga-Gϵ·ⁿ′   sɔ·ⁿGwɔ̆ⁿ′   ᴅϵ`stúts.Gɔ̆`tłAw'ɩstʽa`nɩ·Ga′   (etc.,
Hawk   blood, -ish

as § c. with, at the end:)   ʋ`sənʋ·′li   ᴅϵʽt'ɩstʽɔ̆tɩ̀t'a`nɩ·Ga′ [40]
                                   you two have come to put him on his (legs)

20 !ɩ″a   ᴅalɔ·′ni   ʋ`nɩtłǫ̆nǫ̆·′.i [41] | ᴅɩ`ᴅa`nǫ̆·′wɔ·′t'i`   aᴅlě′   ᴅɩ·ʽʋ·ᴅi′
this   yellow   whenever they are ill   to cure people with   and   to give it to them to drink

---

[40] Emendation by editor; instead of ᴅϵʽt'ɔ̆tɩ̀t'anɩ·Ga=thou hast come, etc.
[41] W. Dial. form: W. Dial. -tł->C. Dial. -ts-.

na.sGwö⁰′	na.`skɩ-Gwö⁰′	Gö ⁿ′′t‘ɔti`		aDɛ‘′lə	a`nɩDalɔ·`nɩ-Gɛ·ⁿ
also	this here, L	to be used with it		beads	they yellow, -ish
t‘a′ᴾli	Da‘ǫ·′.i	a`n!owa′Gi	Ganǫ̈·′Di	na.`yɔ·.Gö′	nǫ̈′wɔ.`t‘ɩ-n!ǫ`
two	they (sol) have been lying down, Hab	cloth	it (ku) let down	moreover	to cure with, and
aɣɛ·′łti	sŭlv·′yɩłGa′	a‘stǫ̈·`ŋɔsö′!i-Gwö⁰`		Gʋ·`lstanö!i-Gwö⁰`	Dɩ‘v·′Di`
made like	swamp tree	it has been scraped, L		it has been steeped, L	to give it to them to drink

THIS IS THE MEDICINE FOR THEIR NAVEL

FREE TRANSLATION

Now then! Now thou hast come to listen, Yellow Goldfinch, in the great swampy thicket thou art staying, moving about. Thou art really a most powerful wizard indeed. Thou never failest in anything. It is merely the "yellow" that has put the important thing under him. Ha, very quickly thou hast come to push it aside. Only a likeness of it will be left, where it was moving about.

Now then! Ha, now thou hast come to listen, Yellow Pigeon, in the great swamp thou art staying. Thou art a most powerful wizard indeed. Thou never failest in anything. It is merely the "yellow" that has put the important thing under him. Ha, quickly thou hast come to put him on his feet. Only a likeness of it will be left, where it was moving about.

Now then! Now thou hast come to listen, Long Human Being, (and thou) White Kingfisher, you two have become united as one. You two, most powerful wizards indeed, you two never fail in anything. It is merely the "yellow" that has put the important thing under him. Very quickly he has been put on his feet. Only a likeness of it will be left where it was moving about.

Now then! Now thou hast come to listen, Long Human Being, (and thou) Red Fish Hawk, you two have become united as one, (etc., with at the end:) Quickly you two have come to put him on his feet.

This is (for) when they are sick with the "yellow"; it is to cure people with, and (also this is what) is to be used to give them to drink. Two yellow beads should be lying down; moreover, cloth should be lying on (the ground). And to cure (them) with, swamp-tree (bark) should be scraped and steeped, (to) give it to them to drink.

EXPLANATION

In this formula for navel-Dalɔ·ni the Yellow Goldfinch and the Yellow Pigeon are again invoked (see No. 14, p. 189), together with the Long Human Being, the White Kingfisher, and the Red Fish Hawk. The Long Human Being is the formulistic name of the water in its special form as a river, considered as a giant, with his head among the mountains and his feet reaching down to the lowlands, while his arms are stretched out to embrace and protect the settlements of the tribe.

The medicine is an infusion of bark scrapings of sŭlv·'yɪlɢa' [(*Hydrangea cinerea* Small). Another specimen collected has been identified as *Clethra acuminata* Michx., white alder]. ᴀ The patient drinks it to induce vomiting, in order to throw off the disordered bile. The first two paragraphs are recited by the medicine man either while rubbing the patient's abdomen or just before giving him the medicine to drink. They then go down together to the river [or to some branch], and the patient vomits into the water. While standing by the waterside the medicine man recites the parts addressing the Long Human Being, the Kingfisher, and the Fish Hawk. It is at this part of the proceedings that the medicine man has lying upon the ground at his side a piece of new cloth, upon which are placed two yellow beads, their color corresponding with the color of the disease spirit, the goldfish, and the pigeon. The cloth [and the beads] are furnished by the patient, and are afterwards appropriated by the medicine man as his fee.

There is no taboo.

16

ɪ̆'a'	nǫ̆ˋwɔ·t'i'	k'ɔ̆ⁿ.li'	tsɪ-ɢǫ̈ˋ'wanɪtlö·ˋɪstǫ.'i [42]
this	to cure with	raccoon	it is they make them ill, H

ᴅɪˋtɬastəɢɪ·''sti	tsɪˋnᴜᴅale'ˋ'aⁿˋ	nɪɢa·ˋtɪ·-yu'	na.ski'
Gerardia	they different kinds	all	E this here

THIS IS TO TREAT (THEM) WITH IF THE RACCOON CAUSES THEM TO BE ILL

FREE TRANSLATION

This is all the different kinds of Gerardias.

EXPLANATION

The main symptom of this disease is a sudden fainting spell, in which the sufferer falls down gasping for breath in a peculiar manner. It probably results from a serious impairment of the digestive functions, or may be identified with apoplexy.

The raccoon is held responsible for the sickness, from the fact that the gasping of the fainting person somewhat resembles the cry made by that animal when cornered by the hunter. The medicine man further states that a small tuft of raccoon's hair, or a single raccoon's hair, appears on the hand, cheek, or some other part of the patient's body (see No. 42, p. 229).

The medicine consists of an infusion or a decoction of the roots of the several varieties of ᴅɪˋtɬastəɢɪ·''sti drunk by the patient while still fasting, for four consecutive mornings.

---

[42] W. Dial. -tɬ->C. Dial. -ts-.

The following varieties of this plant are known:
1. Dɩ`'tɬastəGɩ·''sti ʋstɩ·''Ga, *Gerardia pedicularia* L.
2. Dɩ`'tɬastəGɩ·''sti є·Gwȫⁿ, *Gerardia virginica* (L.) BSP.
3. Dɩ`'tɬastəGɩ·''sti ʋ`sǫ̈ⁿDɔ·''nə nɩ`Gє·sǫ̈·''Da, *Gerardia flava* L., also called Dɔ`'yi wɔ·yi', *Dasystoma flava* (L.) Wood.
4. Dɩ`'tɬastəGɩ·''sti ʋ·Ga`'tsúləGɩ·sti' (not identified).

17

sɔ'.ɩ-nʋ̈ⁿ'	Dɩ`'nɩyɔ·''tɬi	tsɩ-Dʋ`'nɩskwɔ·''ldɩ·sGǫ.'i			
other, and	they are little	it which	they from stomach, Hab		
k'ǫ̈·nʋ̈i'	Dɩtsє́'i	aᴰlє̌'	tsʋnє·''Gȫⁿ	Da·`'ndɩ·ksGǫ'	na.ski'
noticeable	they green	and	they white	they defecate, H	this here
ʋ̈``a-Gwȫⁿ'	nǫ̈·`'wɔ·t'i'	ɔ·`'Gan-a`Gǫ̈ⁿta'Gi		ts-a`nɔ·sє́ǫ·''[i⁴³]	Dɩ`'ʋDi'
this, L	to cure with	groundhog forehead		that which they call it, H	for them to drink it

And Another One if the Little Ones Have Diarrhea

FREE TRANSLATION

The symptoms of this are that they defecate green and white matter (and) merely this is to treat (them) with (the plant), which is usually called "groundhog's forehead," for them to drink.

EXPLANATION

This is a prescription for a variety of diarrhea in children ["little ones"]. The medicine is a decoction of the herb called ɔ·`'Gana`'-Gǫ̈ⁿta'Gi (ɔ·''Ganȫⁿ` = groundhog: ʋGǫ̈ⁿta'Gɩ = an animal's forehead (*Epigaea repens* L.). Another Cherokee name for this same plant is tù`ksi wɔ·yi', "terrapin paw." The decoction is drunk by the child.

Diarrhea in children is usually ascribed to the evil influence of birds.

This prescription in the manuscript follows another on the same page, which accounts for the form of the heading, "and another," etc.

18

ama·'-yi	Dɩ`'DaDzȫⁿ''st'oti`	ɩ̈'a'			
water, L	to lead people to it with	this			
¹yǎ''	'a`-nɔ·Gwȫⁿ'	a'st'i	ʋnє''Gə	aksɔ'''ᵘsɩ·Ga'	aDa·nʋ̈itɔ' 5
Sharply	ha, now	thread	white	it has come down	the soul
a`kt'oti'	aDȫ''nɩ·Ga'	ɩ·'yʋ'sti	tsʋDɔ·''ɩDə`	ʋDa·nʋ̈itɔ'	a`kt'oti'
it examined	it has been said	like	his names are	his soul	it examined
aDȫ''nɩ·Ga'	yǫ̈·wi	ʋstɩ·'	ɩ·¹yǫ̈·'Də	a'yєlɩ·'.'s-ǫ̈'	k'ɩ́·'lú-Gwȫⁿ' yɩ·'ki
it has been said	human being	little	yonder	he is driving T L	immediately, if it is L
aᴰlє́'	ɩ·Ga·'	ayє''¹'li	yɩ·'ki	nɔ·'Gwú-Dɩ·''na	ùlt'aDɩnǫ̈·'Də tsù`Dǫ̈-
and	day	middle	if it is	now E	(he has) jumped down thou hast

---

⁴³ Correction by editor.

Nɛ́ʻlɩ·ɢa´ | υ`ıtʻaDɩ·nǫ̈´Də υ`Dǫ̈nɛʻtɬɩlɩʻɩsti´ | aʻḳtʻɔti´ aDö̀ʻnɩ·ɢa´
come to do it | jumped down | it will be done so | it examined | it has been
for her | | for her | | said

¹yăʻ | ɢalǫ̈·ldi aʻstʻi υnɛ´ʻɢə Dɛ´ʻɩksɔ`ʻö̆ⁿ'tʻa`nɩ·ɢa´ | aDa`ʻNɩ́tɔ´
Sharply | above thread(s) white thou hast come to | the soul
  | let them down

aʻḳtʻɔti´ aDö̀ʻnɩ·ɢa´ | ɩyυ´sti tsυDɔ´ʻɩDə` | υDa`ʻNɩ́tɔ´ aʻḳtʻɔti´
it examined it has been said | like his names are | his soul it examined

aDö̀ʻnɩ·ɢa´ | ɩɢǫ̈·´yi´ ɢa`lǫ̈·lɔ·´ DɩGa.`skɩlöⁿ´ tsúnɛ´ʻɢə Daḳsɔ´ʻʻ-
it has been said | first above they chairs they white they have
    come to

5 ö̆ⁿ' tʻanǫ̈·´ a`Nɩ́υwa´ɢi υnɛ´ʻɢə úɩtɬǫ̈·tʻa`nɩ´ɢa´ ⁴⁴ | astʻi´ υnɛ´ʻɢə
be let T L cloth white it (kn.) has come | thread white
down   to rest on it

aDa`ʻNɩ́tɔ´ úɩɪtɬɔ·tʻa`nɩ·ɢa´⁴⁵ | ɩɢǫ̈·yi´ ɢalǫ̈·lɔ·´ aDa`ʻNɩ́tɔ´ tsυlɛʻʻ-
the soul it (sol.) has come to | first above the soul where it
  rest on it

ɩsɔʻʻtɩ·-yi´ Daᴰlɛʻɩʻsaʻnɩ·ɢa´
has arisen Loc it has been put
  up, standing on its legs

(b) tʻaᴰlɩnę̨´ ɢa`lǫ̈·lɔ·´ DɩGa.`skɩlɔⁿ´ tsúnɛʻʻɢö̆ⁿ Daʻᵘḳsɔ`ʻö̆ⁿ'tʻa=
  Second above they chairs they white they have been let
      down

nǫ̈·´ | a`Nɩ́υwa´ɢi υnɛ´ʻɢə úʻɪɪtɬǫ̈tʻa`nɩ·ɢa´⁴⁴ | astʻi´ υnɛ´ʻɢə
T L cloth white it (kn.) has come to rest on it | thread white

10 a`DaNɩ́tɔ´ úʻɪtɬɔ·tʻa`nɩ·ɢa´⁴⁵ a`Da`Nɩ́tɔ´ aʻḳtʻɔti´ aDö̀ʻnɩ·ɢa´
the soul it (sol) has come to rest on it the soul it examined it has been said

tʻaᴰlɩnę̨´ ɢa`lǫ̈lɔ´ aDa`ʻNɩ́tɔ´ Daᴰlɛʻɩʻsaʻnɩ·ɢa´
second above the same it has been put up,
    standing on its legs

(c) tsɔ·ʻɪ̈nę̨´ ɢa`lǫ̈lɔ´ (etc., as in (b), changing tʻaᴰlɩnę̨· to
  third above

tsɔ·ɩnę̨·).

(d) nöⁿ'ɢɩnę̨´ ɢa`lǫ̈lɔ´ (etc., as in (b), changing tʻaᴰlɩnę̨· to
  fourth above

15 nöⁿ'ɢɩnę̨·).

(e) ʻɩ·sɢɩ·nę̨´ ɢa`lǫ̈lɔ´ (etc., as in (b), changing tʻaᴰlɩnę̨· to
  fifth above

ʻɩsɢɩ·nę̨·).

(f) sυ`Dalɩ·nę̨´ ɢa`lǫ̈lɔ´ (etc., as in (b), changing tʻaᴰlɩnę̨· to
  sixth above

sυ·Dalɩnę̨·).

20 (g) ɢöɬkwɔ·ʻɢɩnę̨´ ɢa`lǫ̈lɔ´-.i` DɩGa.`skɩlɔ·´ tsúnɛ´ʻɢə Daʻᵘḳ=
  seventh above —Loc they chairs they white they

sɔ·ʻʻö̆ⁿ'tʻan-ǫ̈·´ a`Nɩ́υwa´ɢi υnɛ´ʻɢə úɪɪtɬǫ̈tʻa`nɩ·ɢa´ | astʻi´
have been let down, cloth white it (kn) has come to rest on it | thread
T L

υnɛ´ʻɢə a`Da`Nɩ́tɔ´ úʻɪtɬɔ·tʻa`nɩ·ɢa´ | ɢöɬkwɔ·´ɢi ɩ·´ya-ɢalǫ̈·ldi
white the soul it (sol) has come to rest on it | seven successive above

wɩ·ɢa`nanυɢɔ·ʻtsɩsaʻʻnɩ·ɢa´ aDa`ʻNʻtʻ·ɔ´ | ¹yăʻ
there, it has come to appear above the soul | Sharply!

---

⁴⁴ W. Dial. form; C. Dial.: úlsǫ̈·tʻa`nɩ·ɢa´
⁴⁵ W. Dial. form; C. Dial.: úlɪsɔ·tʻa`nɩ·ɢa´

This is to Take People to the Water With

FREE TRANSLATION

Sharply! Ha, now the white thread has come down. The soul has been examined; such-and-such are his names. The soul of the small human being has been examined, where it is growing. Either presently, or at noon, or right away thou willst come and be born to her.[46] He will be born to her.[46] He has been examined.

Sharply! from above thou hast caused the white threads to come down. The soul has become examined. Such-and-such are his names. His soul has become examined. (a) In the first upper (world) the white seats have been let down, and the white cloth has come to rest on them. The soul has come to rest upon the white thread. The soul has been lifted up as far as the first upper world, the place to where it has been raised.

(b) In the second upper (world) the white seats have been let down, (and) the white cloth has come to rest on them. The soul has come to rest upon the white thread. The soul has become examined. The soul has been lifted up as far as the second upper (world).

(c) In the third upper (world) . . .
(d) In the fourth upper (world) . . .
(e) In the fifth upper (world) . . .
(f) In the sixth upper (world) . . .

(g) In the seventh upper (world) the white seats have been let down and the white cloth has come to rest upon them. The soul has come to rest upon the white thread. At the seventh upper (world), finally the soul will appear in all splendor. Sharply.

EXPLANATION

This formula for "taking them to the water with" is practically the same as the one given in No. 83, page 289, with an additional preliminary paragraph, which is recited when the ceremony is performed for the benefit of a pregnant woman. (See p. 119.) A part of this paragraph is addressed to the child, the "little human being" itself. By leaving off this introductory paragraph the formula may be used for any of the purposes served by ordinary formulas of this kind. (See p.150.)

The ceremony may be conducted by the petitioner himself, for obtaining long life, etc., by changing the expressions to the first person where necessary.

The white threads are mentioned in a number of formulas, especially those relating to love, but the connection here is not obvious.

---

[46] The mother-to-be.

19

        ʔi'a'   nö̱·'wɔ·tʻi'   Dɩ'Dö̱·lɛ·'sGi
        this   to cure   he breaks them, H

tsɩ-Dʋ·'nɩyuwɛ·'Ga   tʻö̱Dɛ·'Ga   Gö'ɩⁿ'   nö̱'wɔ·tʻi' | Ga'ᴅlɩ-wɔ·'Dɩ-
it which they (E) feel tired   eel   oil   to cure with   he climbs, brown

Gwö̱ᵘ'   Dɩ'kʻanʋGɔ'.stʻɔti' | Dʋ·nü·'tɬawa'Dɩsö̱·' nɩGa·'Də Dɩ'kʻa-
L   they are to be scratched with   they (E) joints successively all   they

nö̱·lɩ'yɛ·ti' | nöⁿ'ki tsʋ'sö'ʻɩDə | v'sö'-ʃi ɩyʋ'stɩ̱·-aⁿ' Dɩ'kʻa-
must be rubbed   four   they nights – past   night, L   like each   they

5 nʋGɔ·'sti
are to be scratched

This is to Treat (Them) With (When) He Habitually Breaks Them (i. e., Rheumatism)

FREE TRANSLATION

When they are tired, eel oil is to treat (them) with, (and) just saw brier to scratch them with. It must be rubbed on them all over their joints. Four days they must be scratched, every time at night.

EXPLANATION

[Rheumatism is referred to by different names. (See p. 292.)]

[Scratching is almost invariably a part of the curing procedure, the instrument usually being a flint arrowhead; in this case a small portion, about 12 to 15 centimeters long, of a branch of Ga'ᴅlɩwɔ·'Di, saw brier (*Smilax glauca* Walt.), is used.]

The nighttime is chosen for the operation, in order that the patient may be the better able to rest afterwards. The same treatment is sometimes used for abdominal swelling. When the medicine man can not decide from the ordinary symptoms as to the cause of the disease, he diagnoses from the dreams of the patient, which in rheumatism are said to relate to sexual excesses, or to the commission of unnatural acts [as incest], etc.

20

  ʔi'a'   ɩ·na'Döⁿ Da'nskɩ·tsGö̱·'[i⁴⁷] nö̱wɔ·tʻi' Dɩ'ʋDɩ·[yi⁴⁷]
  this   snake(s) whenever they dream of them to cure with to give them to drink

            ɩGawɛ·'stɩ·(-yi⁴⁸)
             to say it—E

sGě'' | 'a'-nɔ·ᵘGwö̱ᵘ' sta'tʻö̱na·'nɩGa' stɩ'skùya' Dɩ'ststɩ·Ga'
now then   hal now   you (2) have come to listen you (2) men you (2) little

stɩDa·'ᵘwɛ̱'i'   v'sö'ɩ̱ Dɩstö'tɬtʻɔʻɩsti' | stü'tsanö̱'ŋɩ-Gwö̱ᵘ'
you (2) wizards night, Loc you (2) are staying   for your (2) adornment—L

10 'ɩ-Gɛ·'sɛ·ⁿ(.i⁴⁸)' | v'lsGɛ·'Döⁿ 'ɩ'-Dʋnʋ·'yʻtʻanɩ·'leⁿ.i' ɩna'Də-Gwɔᵘ'
it which is, App it important it which, he (E) put it under, App snake—L

---

⁴⁷ Correction by editor.   ⁴⁸ Interpolation by editor.

ʻɩ-Gɛˋsɛ·ⁿiʹ	aˋnisGɩˑʹnɔ̈ⁿ	vˑnəDö̞ˋnö̞ⁿ꞉iʹ	ʻɩ-Gɛˋsɛ·ⁿiʹ	
it which is, App	they ghosts	they have said it	it which is, App	
sGɛ̈ˋʼ	ʻaˋno·ᵘGwö̞ᵛʼ	staˋtʻö̞ŋaˑˋnɩ·Gaʹ	stɩˋskùyaʹ	Dɩˋststi·Gaʹ
now then	ha! now	you (2) have come to listen	you (2) men	you (2) little
stɩˋDaˑᵘwɛ̈ʼʼ	vˋsö̞ʹ-꞉i	Dɩstö̈ˋtɬtʻɔˋɩstiʹ	ɩˑʹGa	ayɛʻᵊliʹ	vˑlsGɛˑʹDö̈ⁿ
you (2) wizards	night, Loc	you (2) are staying	day	middle	it important
Dvˑnɩˋksɔʻö̈ⁿˋʼtɛˑⁿ(.i ⁴⁸)ʹ	stɩˋʻxyö̞stʻaˋnɩ·Gaʹ	stùˋtsanö̞ʹŋɩ-Gwö̈ᵛˋ
they have let it down, App	you (2) have come to take it (sol) away	for your (2) adornment—L
ʻɩGɛˋsɛ·ⁿiʹ	vˋsö̞ʹ-ʻ꞉ɩ	Gaˋnɛʹsa	DɩGö̈ˋʼnaGɛˑⁿʹ	DɔˋʼDɩtʻɔˋʻɩst-ö̞ʹ ⁵
it which is, App	night, L	box(es)	they black	they are kept, facing us, T L
wö̞ˋⁿ-ʼstɩskwanɩGɔˑˋtʻanɩ·Gaʹ	ɩGö̞ˋwùɩstɔˑʹ tɩ-Gwö̈ᵛˋ
you (2) have come to put in store as you (2) go by	what is its worth! L

This (is) to Treat (Them) With When They Have Dreamed of Snakes; (What) to Give Them to Drink, and (How) it is to be Said

FREE TRANSLATION

Now then! Ha, now you two have come to listen, you Two Little Men, you two wizards, away from here in the Night Land you two are staying.

It is the very thing you two adorn yourselves with. It is merely a snake that has come to put the important thing under him. They are but ghosts that have caused it.

Now then! Ha, now you two have come to listen, you Two Little Men, you two wizards, away from here in the Night Land you two are staying.

In the middle of the day they have let the important things down. You two have come to take it away as you two come by. It is the very thing you two adorn yourselves with. You two have put it away over there in the black boxes that are kept in the Night Land. Who cares what happens to it!

EXPLANATION

This is another formula for the same purpose as No. 5, page 175. [The reference to the Two Little Men adorning themselves with snakes, and the very reason for their being invoked in snake diseases—real or dreamed—is accounted for by a Cherokee myth. (Cf. Mooney, Myths, p. 311.)] According to this myth, the natural son of the Thunder, on arriving at boyhood, sets out toward the southwest in search of his father, who had abandoned him in infancy. After many adventures, he finally presents himself before his father, who first cures him of a loathsome skin disease, by throwing him into a pot of boiling water, and then leading him to a covered box, bids him put in his hand and take out the necklaces and other ornaments with which to adorn himself. On raising the lid, the boy finds the box full of snakes, but, undeterred, plunges his hand to the very bottom, and draws out a huge rattlesnake, which he winds about his neck for a necklace. He then takes out two copperheads, which he twists about his wrists as bracelets. Thus decked out, he takes his brother along, and goes against a celebrated gambler, who had previously insulted him, but who is now conquered by the Two Thunder Boys, and impaled at the bottom of the great lake in the west. In this myth we have another instance of the universal primitive idea of a connection between the serpent and Thunder [Lightning]. The scene is laid at The Suck, in Tennessee River, a few miles below Chattanooga.

[As previously stated, dreaming of snakes results in the patient's saliva becoming "spoiled"]; this must then be dislodged by an emetic. The medicine in this case consists of a decoction of Gana·′Ga ʋ·′tʻənö·ⁿ, *Scirpus validus* Vahl, great bulrush; Gana·′Ga ʋstɩ·′Ga, *Juncus effusus* L., common or soft rush; ůltsɔ′stə ʋ·′tʻənöⁿ, *Coronilla varia* L.; ůltsɔ′stə ʋstɩ·′Ga, *Vicia caroliniana* Walt., vetch, to which is added the inner bark of ʋᴾlö·′ⁿDə, *Rhus (Toxicodendron) radicans* Linn., poison oak, poison ivy, which grows on the east side of a poplar tree.

The decoction is boiled and drunk on four successive days, the medicine man or his assistant boiling it for but a short time the first day, adding more water and boiling it for a longer time the second day, and so on, until the fourth day, when it is boiled down to a thick sirup. While under treatment, the patient observes a taboo of salt and of hot food.

21

ʔɩ′a′   nö·̨′wɔ·tʻi′   ʋ·̀nök̓ʻɛ·̀waGǫ̈′.i |
this   to cure with   whenever they have forgotten (their voice)

ʋ·̀nanǫ̈·′wɔ·tʻì̠ | tʻa′·ya′ | Gʋlɛ̓ʻ-tsʋnstɩ·′Ga | kʻà̠nǫ̈sɩ·′′ta |
they to cure with   cherry   acorns, they are small   flowering dog-wood

söⁿktʻa′   ʋnɩ·ʻyöⁿ′stì̠ | Dɩ·̀lɩGali′ski   ɛ·′Gwöⁿ | (a·̀Ganö·′ⁿʔi
apple   they are bitter   willow   big   (it has been boiled

ʋndɩ·′′tʻastì̠)[49]
they must drink it)

This (is) to Cure (Them) with Whenever They Have Lost Their Voice

FREE TRANSLATION

These (barks) are to cure (them) with: Cherry, small acorns, flowering dogwood, bitter apples, big willow. They have to be boiled, (and) they must drink it.

---

[49] Interpolation by J. M., apparently based on information given by a′yö·̀ⁿ′ɩni′ himself.

EXPLANATION

A prescription against an aggravated form of hoarseness. The patient drinks a decoction of the inner bark of the five trees named, the decoction being intended to make him vomit the phlegm which clogs the throat passages and impedes utterance. Some of the liquid is also rubbed on his throat and neck. There is no formula to be recited in this case, nor any ceremony to be performed. The bark, as usual, is from the east side of the tree.

This prescription was written in two places in the manuscript.

The barks used are those of tʻa·ya′, *Prunus virginiana* L., chokecherry; Gʋlɛ`ʻ tsʋnstɩ·′Ga, *Quercus falcata* Michx., Spanish oak (also *Quercus imbricaria* Michx.); kʻanö·sɩʻta, *Cornus florida.* L., flowering dogwood (also *Cornus stricta* Lam., stiff cornel); sö·n̩ktʻa ʋnɩʻyöⁿ.sti, *Malus malus* (L.) Mill., apple; Dɩ·lɩ′Galɩ′ski ɛʻGwöⁿ, *Salix alba* L., white willow.

22

ɩ`ⁿa-Nɩ̃öⁿ′   ʋnö̱ⁿ′Di   ts-aˑ`ndɩ·kʻö′ɩaⁿ   ʋGö′wutłiˋ |
this, and   milk   it which they urinate for the purpose

Ga`nɛʻtʻɩ′ski | tsʋʻᵘskaʻ | tsʋ·′tʻɩnəˋ | kʻʋ`wɪyʋ′sti
water-birch   post oak   water beech   sycamore

aˋyɔ·ʋ·′tłi | na.ski′ | ʋ·ndɩ·″tʻa·stiˋ | Ga·ktʻö̱′ⁿDə | nöˋⁿ′kiˊ
crippled   this here they must drink it restricted   four

ʋ·Dɩlɛʻki aˑmaˊ ʋnö·′ⁿDi
heat   salt   milk.

And This (is) for the Purpose (of Treating Them) When They Urinate (Like) Milk

FREE TRANSLATION

They must drink (in) this (case) water birch, post oak, water beech, crippled sycamore. Restricted (are during) four (days) hot (food), salt (and) milk.

EXPLANATION

This prescription is intended for use in aggravated cases of the trouble spoken of in No. 6, page 178.

The symptoms are milky urine and pains in the hips and the lower part of the back. The medicine man prepares a strong decoction of the inner barks of the four trees named and the patient drinks this in small quantities, at frequent intervals, for four days. The sufferer abstains in the meantime from hot and salt food, whereas he has to go without milk "for a considerable period," i. e., for about a year.

The sacred four appears here in the number of ingredients and in the taboo.

As for the "crippled sycamore," see page 54.
The barks used are those of Gaʻnɛtʻɩˋsɢi, *Betula nigra* L., water-, river-, or red birch; tsʋʻskaʼ, *Quercus stellata* Wang., post oak (also hybrids of *Quercus alba* L., white oak); tsʋˑʼtʻɩnaˋ, *Carpinus caroliniana* Walt., American hornbeam, ironwood, blue-, water beech; kʻʋˋwɩyʋʼsti, *Platanus occidentalis* L., sycamore, buttonwood.

23

aˋnɩskɔˑʼli	DɩDzɔˑʼtʻɩstɔˋtiˋ	ɩ̈ʼaʼ	nǫʼwɔˑtʻiˋ	ɢöⁿʼʼtʻɔtiˋ	ɛˈldɩˑʼ-
their head	they are to be blown with	this	to cure with	to use with	down

	Dzöⁿ	tsɩˋkʻanɔˋɩ̈ɛɩ̈aⁿʼ			
	direction	it which says			

ɩɢɛ̈ʼʼyaɢiˋ	ɩɢɛ̈ʼʼyaɢiˋ	ɩɢɛ̈ʼʼyaɢiˋ	ɩɢɛ̈ʼʼyaɢiˋ	nǫˋⁿDɔɢǫ̣ˑʼyi
thou woman by excellence (?)				¦sun, direct., Loc

nǫⁿˋDɔɢǫ̣ʼyi	nǫˋⁿDɔˑɢǫ̣ʼyi	nǫˋⁿDɔɢǫ̣ʼyi	ɩɢɛ̈ʼʼyaɢiˋ	ɩɢɛ̈ʼʼyaɢiˋ	ɩyä̆ʻ
			thou woman by excellence		sharply

ɩ̈ʼaʼ	nǫʼwɔˑtʻiˋ		vˋniɢɩˑʼnə-Gaʻaʼtki	nɔ.tsɩ-ɩ̈ʼi	tsʋˋʻyɛˑɢɔʼ.i
this	to cure with		chinquapin	pine(s), Loc	they stand up, H

tsʋˋstaGaʻyɔˑʼDöⁿ	tsʋˋɢwalɔˑɢöⁿʼɩ̈i	ɢʋˋʼlstanöʼɩ̈i	ʋGaˑʼnawüⁿˋ
brittle with dryness	they have been leaves	it has been steeped	warm

DɩDzɔˑʼtʻɩsˋtɔˋtɩˋɢwöᵛʼ	Gɛˋsɔʼʼ.i
they are to be blown with it, L	they have been, H

THIS (IS) TO BLOW THEIR HEADS WITH; THE MEDICINE (WHICH IS) TO BE USED WITH IT IS TOLD BELOW

FREE TRANSLATION

Thou Woman (by excellence?) (4 times).
In the direction of the Sun Land (4 times).
Thou Woman (by excellence?) (bis). Sharply!

This (is) to treat (them) with: (of) chinquapin, which is wont to grow in the pine woods, the plucked brittle leaves, steeped warm, should be used, and they[50] should merely be blown with it.

EXPLANATION

This song and prescription are for the treatment of a feverish condition, of which the symptoms are headache, chills, and cold sweats. No special cause theory was assigned, but the song would seem to indicate that the Sun is held responsible for the disease as in No. 41.

The medicine is an infusion of the dry brittle leaves of chinquapin (*Castanea pumila* (L.) Mill.), heated by means of seven coals of fire and blown upon the head and shoulders of the patient, the blowing being done as described on page 58.

---

[50] The patients.

ʻɩɢɛʻʻyaɢi' is a vocative form, the nominative, third person single being aɢɛʻʻyaɢi', or perhaps aɢɛʻʻyaɢʋ·'ɢə. The medicine man was not certain as to the meaning of the word, but was of the opinion that it referred to aɢɛʻʻyaɢʋ·'ɢə, a formulistic name of the Sun, which in Cherokee mythology is a woman. This is probably the true explanation as the spirit is declared to dwell in the Sun Land, the East. The name ʻɩɢɛʻʻyaɢʋ·'ɢə occurs in several formulas and is probably changed here to ʻɩɢɛʻʻyaɢi' to conform to the meter. [See p. 161.]

In another formula for heat blisters it is explicitly declared that (a)ɢɛʻʻ¹yaɢʋ·'ɢə has sent the disease.

Og., who knows a different formula to cure this ailment, only uses the chinquapin infusion after a simpler treatment, in which merely water is blown on the patient, has failed.

24

ɩ'a'　　　a`nɩńɛ·'ᴅzi　　　a`ᴅaʻnǫ·'wɔ·tʻi`
this　　　their breast　　　to cure anyone with

v'sö'ɩ　askú'ya　ö^{n}naʻɢɛ　ᴅʋ`ᴅa·ɴɩtʻɛ·ʻʻlö^{n}ɩ̈　ɢɛsɛ·$^{n'}$　v·lsɢɛ·'ᴅö^n
right, Loc　man　black　he (E) has thought it　it is, App　it important
ᴅʋnʋ·`ytʻanilɛ·^{n}i'
he (E) has put it under

sɢɛ̈'᾿　　ʻa`-nɔ·ɢwö$^{v'}$　staʻtʻǫna·`nɩ·ɢa'　stɩ`skúya'　stɩ`ɢaɢɛ·'^{n}
now then　ha! now　you (2) have come to listen　you (2) men　you (2) red
nǫ̈`$^n$ᴅɔ·-yɩ·-'ᴅzö$^n$　ᴅɩ`stötɩtʻɔ`ʻɩsti'　ᴅɩɢɛ`·stɩlɔ`sɛɩ̈'　vlsɢɛ·'ᴅö^n　5
sun, Loc, direction　you (2) are staying　you two have penetrated them　it important

tʻɩ̈`staᴅɩɢö`tɩtʻanɩ·ɢa'　vtsɩ·ʻʻnawa`　aᴅö̈`ʻnɩɢa'
you (2) have come to push it away as you (2) come by　beyond it stretched　it has been said

sɢɛ̈'᾿　　ʻa`-nɔ·ɢwö$^{v'}$　staʻtʻǫna·`nɩ·ɢa'　stɩ`skúya'　saʻʻkʻɔ·ni'
now then　ha! now　you (2) have come to listen　you (2) men　blue
vʻᵗⁱyǫ̈^{n}ᴅzɔ·ʻ-yɩ-ᴅzö$^{n'}$　ᴅɩ`stötɩtʻɔ`ʻɩsti'　stɩ`ᴅa·ᵘwɛ̈'᾿　tʻʻɩstaᴅɩ`ɢaᴰ=
cold　Loc, direction　you (2) are staying　you (2) wizards　you (2) have come

lɛʻɩ·'ɢa　v·lsɢɛ·'ᴅö^n　vʻʻsönʋ·ʻli　ᴅɛʻʻtɩstɩ·skəlɔ·ʻ.ö^n'ta'　nɩ'ᴅʋ·'ᴅɛʻʻlə`ðsiᴅö$^{n'}$
to push it away　it important　quickly　cause him to let go his gripping (hands), you (2)　he has not noticed it

vtsɩ·ʻʻnawə-ɢwö$^{ñ\backslash}$　aᴅö̈`ʻnɩ·ɢa'　　　　　　　　　　　　　　　　10
beyond it stretched-L　it has been said

THIS (IS) THE TREATMENT FOR THEIR BREAST

FREE TRANSLATION

The Black Man in the Night Land has caused it. He has put the important thing under him.

Now then! Ha, now you two have come to listen, you two Red Men, you two are staying in the direction of the Sun Land. You two have penetrated them, it seems. You two have come to push the important thing away as you two go by. Relief has been caused.

Now then! Ha, now you two have come to listen, you two Blue Men, in the direction of the Cold Land you two are staying. You two wizards, you two have come to push the important thing away as you two go by. Quickly cause him to relinquish his grasp, you two, without his (even) noticing it. Relief has been caused.

EXPLANATION

This is a formula for curing sharp pains in the breast.

The patient drinks an infusion of bruised u`nastɛ·tstɩ·′Ga, Virginia snakeroot (*Aristolochia serpentaria* L.), to which a few scrapings of ɔ·ˋDalɩGa′ᴅli, ginseng root (*Panax trifolium* L.), are sometimes added, the liquid being slightly warmed by dropping four or seven live coals into it. There is no taboo.

The medicine man first recites the formula, then blows four times upon the breast of the patient, and finally gives him the medicine to drink. This is repeated four times at each treatment. The whole ceremony is repeated four times before noon, and if necessary for four consecutive days.

25

ï'a′	ɩ·na′ᴅɔⁿ	k'ayʋ′ˋGa	Gɔⁿ′'t'ɔti`	DɩˋDa·nʋGɔˋstɩ·-yi′
this	snake	tooth	to use with	to scratch them E

	k'ů′	yʋïa′ïɩ·	ïaïɩ′:
	Come on!		
		yʋïa′ïɩ·	ïaïɩ′:
		yʋïa′ïɩ·	ïaïɩ′:
5		yʋïa′ïɩ·	ïaïɩ′:

Dʋ:+	Dʋ:	Dʋ:	Dʋ:	Dʋ:
(Onom.)				

sGɛ̆′	|	Galȫ·′ldi	Dɩˋtsûnɛˋtlanȫⁿ′ïi	k'ɔ·′la	tsûnɛ·′Gɔⁿ	Dɛˋ'ak⁼
now then!		above	thou hast apportioned them	bone (s)	they while	thou

sɔ·ˋ.ȫⁿ′t'a`nɩ·Ga′	tsʋˋyɛl-ö̧′ ⁵¹	Gɛsö̧·′	Dɛˋ'ʋst'a`nɩ·Ga′	|	ʋtsɩ′'=
hast come to let them down	the body, TL	it is, TL	thou hast come to stick them (l.) in it		beyond

nawaᴅȫⁿ′	|	¹ya'
it has been stretched		Sharply!

---

⁵¹ Correction by editor, instead of tsʋGɛlö̧ (no meaning).

THIS (IS) FOR USING THE SNAKE TOOTH AT THE SCRATCHING OF
THEM

FREE TRANSLATION

Come on!
Yuhahi, hahi (four times).

Now then! Thou on high who hast apportioned them, thou hast caused the white bones to come down. Where the body is, thou hast come to stick them into. Relieved! Sharply.

EXPLANATION

The scratching operation, for which this and similar formulas are intended to be used, is a frequent preliminary to the application of medicine in the treatment of rheumatism, languor, and kindred ailments, as well as in preparing contestants for the ball game. [See p. 68.]

This formula was originally obtained by Ay. from an old man who must have been born at least as early as 1780. As the heading states, it is for scratching with the snake tooth. It consists of two parts, the first of which is sung, the second recited.

The song, the words of which are meaningless, is sung by the medicine man to a simple and pleasing tune, while standing facing the patient and holding the snake tooth, grasped between the thumb and forefinger of his uplifted right hand. As he sings, the spirit of the rattlesnake enters into the tooth, which becomes alive and moves about between the fingers of the medicine man. This is the Indian explanation of the fact, which may be accounted for on more reasonable grounds. The medicine man, while singing, labors under suppressed excitement and stands with tense muscles in a constrained position, the natural result being that before the song is ended his hand involuntarily begins to tremble and the muscles of the fingers to twitch. The peculiar hook shape of the tooth renders its slightest movement perceptible. On finishing the song the doctor brings the tooth up to his mouth with a long "du!" followed by a staccato "du, du, du, du," as he blows upon it. He then touches it to his mouth. The song is repeated four times, after which he proceeds to scratch the patient. [See p. 70.]

The skin is scratched only once, viz, before the first application of the medicine, but the medicine is applied four times. If, however, the treatment is continued for four days, the scratching may be repeated every morning.

The medicine which is rubbed on consists of a warm infusion of the leaves of ɛ·w'sö'͈i, *Leucothoë catesbaei* (Walt.) Gray, gray fetter bush; Dʋ'sʋ'Ga tsʋ·nstɩ·Ga, *Kalmia latifolia* L., mountain laurel, calico bush, spoon wood; Dʋ'sʋ'Ga tsʋ·nt'ənö^n, *Rhododendron maxi-*

mum L., great laurel; a⁻ʻskwaneʻ'ᴅo, *Veratrum viride* Ait., American white hellebore, Indian poke; ŏⁿléʻ ᴜkʻɩ́'łti, *Porteranthus trifoliatus* (L.), Britt., Indian physic.

The leaves of the three first and the roots of the two latter plants are used.

These plants are all of a pungent nature, especially the aʻskwaneʻ'ᴅo, and few persons can endure four applications of the medicine. On account of its fiery nature none of the liquid is drunk by the patient, as the experiment would be a dangerous one. While applying the liquid the medicine man recites the final formula and ends by blowing four times upon the patient, as already described.

Often a final song is added, very much like the one given in No. 42, page 229.

26

ɩ́'ⁿ'	ᴅalɔ·'ni	v̓'ⁿɩtlȫnö̇·'⁶²	aʻᴅaʻṅö́'wotʻï`
this	yellow	whenever they are ill	to cure anyone with

ᴅalɔ·'ni	ɢᴜ'ːa	ᴅalɔ·'ni	ɢᴜ'ːa	ö̇·'ᴅaliˋ	ɢᴜ'ːa
yellow	put it into it (liq.), thou	yellow	put it into it (liq.), thou	lake	put it into it (liq.), thou

ᴅalɔ·'ni ɢᴜ'ːa	ˡyaʻʻ	ö̇·'ᴅaliˋ	ᴅalɔ·'ni	ɢᴜ'ːa	ᴅaʻᴅɩɢaleʻ'ya
	sharply!	lake	yellow	put it into it (liq.), thou	come, thou, and scatter it

ᴅaʻᴅɩɢaleʻ'ya	ᴅaʻᴅɩɢaleʻ'ya	ᴅaʻᴅɩɢaleʻ'ya	ᴅalɔ·'ni
			yellow

5 ɢᴜ'ːa | ᴅalɔ·'ni ɢᴜ'ːa | aʻmaˑ'-yi ɢᴜ'ːa | ᴅalɔ·'ni
put it into it (liq.), thou | | water, Loc |

ɢᴜ'ːa	ˡyaʻʻ	aʻmaˑ'yi	ᴅalɔ·'ni	ɢᴜ'ːa	ᴅaʻᴅɩɢaleʻ'ya
		water, Loc.	yellow	put it into it (liq.), thou	come, thou, and scatter it

ᴅaʻᴅɩɢaleʻ'ya	ᴅaʻᴅɩɢaleʻ'ya	ᴅaʻᴅɩɢaleʻ'ya

This is the Treatment Whenever They are Ill with the "Yellow"

FREE TRANSLATION

Put the Yellow into it (liq.) (bis).
Put the Yellow into the lake.
Put the Yellow into it (liq.). Sharply!
Put the Yellow into the lake.
Come, thou, and scatter it (four times).
Put the Yellow into it (liq.) (bis).
Put the Yellow into the water.
Put the Yellow into it (liq.). Sharply!
Put the Yellow into the water.
Come thou and scatter it (four times).

---

⁵² W. Dial. -tl->C. D. -ts-.

EXPLANATION

This formula to cure navel palo·ni consists of a song of two verses, with a short recitation after each verse. The medicine man merely applies his hand, previously warmed near the fire, as described on page 62.

If the treatment be successful, the effect is instantaneous and the medicine man "can feel the pulsation caused by the disease scattering under his touch." The medicine man recites the formula and sings the song twice at each application, and the ceremony is repeated four times before noon, and, if necessary, the treatment is continued for as many successive days. There is nothing to indicate what spirit is expected to effect the cure.

27

u'n' u'ye·lo·'ısti˙ unıllö·ŋö·'.i [63]
this   It startles him   whenever they are ill

Gwelıa^{n'} Gwelıa^{n'} Gwelıa^{n'} Gwelıa^{n'}
Gwelıa^{n'} Gwelıa^{n'} Gwelıa^{n'} Gwelıa^{n'} 'yŭ''

THIS (IS) FOR WHEN THEY BECOME ILL SUDDENLY

FREE TRANSLATION

Gwohiha (4 times).
Gwohiha (4 times). Yuh!

EXPLANATION

This short song is to cure a fainting cramp, when the sudden intense pain makes the patient fall down as if dead. In some cases, the medicine man states, death actually follows instantaneously. It might result from indigestion, heart trouble, or some other cause.

The song consists of a single word: gwelıaⁿ [which is but an adaptation of (a)gwe'ı(stı)·n, "I have pain," to the meter of the melody.]

The treatment is equally simple: The medicine man applies his hands, previously warmed over the fire, to the seat of pain, after which he blows upon the spot. He repeats the song four times, and the whole ceremony is performed four times before noon.

28

Dı·k'anvcıo·'sti u'n' | nu·'Gıtlö^{n'} ö^{n''}t'oti˙ ne·so·'.i
to cause It to come out this   brier   to be used with it has been, Hub

sGe^{·'} | 'u·'no·Gwö^{v'} 'a·t'öŋa·'nu·Gn' k'o·'lonJ^{n'} Gı·'Gacıç·' 5
Now then   lo, now   thou hast come to listen Raven   red

hö·'Do·-Gö·'-yı·-'Dzo Dı·tsö''tlt'o'[·]sti' | u'sönu·'li Do·'t'a'[·]le^{·'}öŋa' |
sun, dir., Loo, direction thou art staying   quickly   thou hast arisen facing us

---

[63] W. Dial. -tl->C. Dial. -ts-.

206   BUREAU OF AMERICAN ETHNOLOGY   [BULL. 99

Gɔˈυˈsti   tsuDɛˈlɪtcɛ″ti nɪˈGɛˈsǫ̈ˈna′ | asGɪˈnə υˈDö̀ˈnö̀ˊ̣ˈɪGwö̃ᵘˋ   ˈɪGɛˋ-
something   it escapes thy (sight)   never   ghost   it has been said, L.   it which

sɛˈⁿ.i′   υˈlsGɛˈˊDə   ˈɪˋDυnυˈˋyˈɪtˈanɪˋlɛˈⁿ.i′ | ö̃ⁿˋˈtaˊli   υˋDö̀ˈnö̀ˊ̣ɪ-Gwö̃ᵘˋ
is, App   it important   it which he has put under, App   animal-ghost   it has been said, L

ˈɪGɛˋsɛˋ.i′   υlsGɛˈˊDə   ˈɪˋDυnυˈˋyˈɪtˈanɪˋlɛˈⁿ.i′ | tsuˋtɪstaˈˊyˈɪtɪ-Gwuˋ-Dɪˈnə′
it which is, App   it important   it which he has put under, App   it is what thou eatest, L (=E),   E

ˈɪGɛˋsɛˋ.i′ | ˋö̃ⁿˋˈyö̃ⁿˋstˈanɪˋGa′ | υsö̃ˋˈɪˋyö̃ˋ-Dzə   ɛᴰˋiaˋ-wɪˊˈnɪ-Dɪˈnö̃ⁿˋ
it which is, App   again thou hast come to take it away   night, Loc., direct   earth, under, E

5 nǫ̈nɔˊ-ˋɪ   wɪ-Dɛˋˈtsatˈanö̈ˊ″ǫ̈sɪˋ | υsö̃ˊˋɪ   ɪyö̈ˊDˋə   aDɔˋ-i   Dɛˋˊ.ɔˊᴰlυˋna-ö̈ˋ.i
trail, Loc   thither they lie stretched   night   yonder   wood, Loc   they mosses, T L.

ɪˋyö̈ˊDə   wɔˋˋstɪGö̃ˋtɬanɪˋGa′ | ɪGö̈ˋˋwuɬtö̃ˊˋtɪ-Gwö̃ᵘˋ | υtsɪˊ-na-
yonder   thou hast gone there and put it between (two)   who cares what happens to it, L.   beyond it,

wuˋ-Gwö̃ᵘˋ   aDö̈ˋˋnɪˋGa′
stretched, L   it has been said

sGɛ̌ˋ′ | ˋaˋnɔˋGwö̃ᵘˋ   ˋö̃ⁿ-ˋaˋtˋǫ̈naˋnɪˋGa′   kˋɔˊlanö̃ⁿˋ   saˋkˋɔˋniˋ
Now they   ho, Now   again, thou hast come to listen   Raven   blue

υˋˋǫ̈Dzɔˋ-yɪˊ-Dzəˋ   Galö̈ˋldɪˊ-Dzə   Dɪtsö̃ˋtɬtˋɔˊɪˋstiˋ | ˋɪDaˋᵘwɛˊ̣ɪˋ-Dɪˋnə′
cold, Loc, direction   above direction   thou art staying   thou wizard, E

10 GaDö̃″   tsunυˊlti   nɪˋGɛˋsǫ̈na′   υˋlsGɛˋDə   ˋɪˋDυnυˋˋyˋtˈanɪˋlɛˈⁿ.i′
what   thou failst   never   it important   it which he has put under, App

tsö̃ˋtɪstaˋˋyˋɪtɪ-Gwö̃ᵘˋ   ˋɪGɛˋˋsɛˈⁿ.i′ | nɪGö̈ˋˋwayɛˋlənö̃ⁿˋˋö̃ⁿsGɛˋstɪGwö̃ᵘˋ
what thou eatest (L) E   it which is, App   a likeness of it will remain, L

tsaˋᴰlɔsö̈ˊ | υsö̃ˋˋɪDə   nυˋDəˋnö̈ˊna | vtsɪˋˊ-ˋnawuˋ-Gwö̃ᵘˋ   aDö̃ˋˋnɪˋGa′
thou passed T L   night-been   it has not been said   beyond it, stretched, L   it has been said

DɪˋkˋanυGɔˊsti   ˋːˋa′ | nυˋGutla′   Gö̃ⁿˋtˋɔtiˋ   Gɛˋsǫ̈.i′ | nö̈ˋ-
to cause it to appear   this   brier   to be used with it   it has been, Hab   to

wɔˋtˋɪ-Nˈ̣ǫ̈″   kˋɔˋsDυˋˋDə   Dalɔˊnɪ-Gɛˋⁿˋ   aˋDzɪˋlö̃ⁿˋ.skiˋ   uˋɬtsɔˋᵘˋsti
cure with, and   (Everlasting)   yellow, -ish   they have been flowers   (vetch,

15 υstɪˊGa   Dɪˋkˋanö̈ˋlɪˋyɛˋDiˋ | υDɔˊˋtəGwuDə′   aDö̃ˋˋnö̀ˊ̣i   ɪˋGa-Gwö̃ᵘˋ
little   it must be rubbed on them   all day   it has been said   noon, H

ɪˋGɔˋɪˊDə | aGɔˊnə-Gwö̃ᵘˋ   Gaˋᵘktˋö̈ˊDə   ayɛˋlaˋaˋⁿˋ
as long as   fasting, H   it restricted   only

This is to Scratch Them; A Brier Should Be Used With It

FREE TRANSLATION

Now then! Ha, now thou hast come to listen, Red Raven; away from here in the direction of the Sun Land thou art staying; quickly thou hast arisen, facing us. Nothing ever escapes thy (sight).

It is merely what has become a ghost that has put the important thing under him. It is merely what has become an animal ghost that has put the important thing under him. But this is the very thing thou eatest. Thou hast once more come to take it away as thou goest along. The trails lie stretched for thee under the very earth, away toward the Night Land. Thou hast gone and put it between (a crevice) in the forests of the Night Land, where moss grows. Who cares what happens to it! Relief has been caused.

Now then! Ha, now thou too hast come to listen, Blue Raven. Thou art staying on high, in the direction of the Cold Land. Thou powerful wizard, what (is there) thou ever failest in? The important thing, which he [54] has put under him, is the very thing thou eatest. Only a likeness of it will be left, when thou will have passed. (And) not for a night (only, but forever). Relief indeed has been caused. This is to scratch them. A brier should be used with it. And to cure (them) with common everlasting (with the) yellow flowers, (and) little vetch are to be rubbed on them. "All day" has been said, but as long as noon (is) merely (meant). Fasting is the only restriction.

EXPLANATION

This formula is used for scratching with a brier, preparatory to rubbing on the medicine, in cases of local pains and muscular cramps and twitching. The patient is said also to dream of game and hunting.

Ailments of this class are ascribed to the influence of revengeful deer ghosts, possibly because the deer, like the horse and the cow, has a habit of nervously twitching the muscles while standing. The hunter always took care to ward off the evil results, by asking pardon of the slain deer according to a set formula, after having killed it. [These formulas are now no longer known. There are even many medicine men who have never heard about them. It is easy to understand that this kind of formula would soon fall into desuetude and oblivion with the extinction of the deer. (Cf. further Mooney, Myths, pp. 263–264.)]

The raven is invoked because it is accustomed to feed upon the offal left by the hunter after cutting up the game. [For the same reason the raven is mentioned in some of the hunting formulas, "because," as an informant told me, "he is as anxious to point out the deer to us as we are to shoot it, because he knows that he will get the guts (of the shot animal)."]

The formula is recited by the medicine men after each round of scratching while standing over the patient, and holding the cup containing the medicine in his uplifted hand. Having finished the formula, he brings the cup slowly down with a spiral circuit, after the manner a raven descends, imitating at the same time the raven's cry, k'a· k'a· k'a· k'a·, until he puts the cup to the lips of the patient, who then takes a drink of the medicine.

The scratching is done with a stout piece of brier, nʋ·ˈGŭtłö%n%ˈ, *Smilax glauca* Walt., saw brier, having thorns about the size of large rose thorns. The medicine which is rubbed into the scratches consists of a warm infusion of kʻɔ·ˈsDʋ·ˈDə, *Gnaphalium obtusifolium* L., common everlasting; ŭltsɔ·ˈusti ʋˈstɛ·ˈGa, *Vicia caroliniana* Walt., vetch.

---

[54] The disease spirit.

The scratching is performed and the medicine applied four times before noon. The treatment lasts but a single morning and the only diet rule observed is that the patient fasts until the whole performance is over.

[The last sentence but one illustrates in an interesting manner how in this case an error in writing the directions down was corrected. The medicine man had written that "fasting was to be observed all day," but corrects this statement later on by saying that he only means "until noon," i. e., until after the completion of the final ceremony.]

29

!ı'a' a`nɪnɛ·'ᴅzi ɢɔ·'t'ɪski` ɑᴅa'nö'wɔ·t'i`
this their breast it swells (Hab) to cure anyone with

yv'a·`.a!ɪ·.' (7 times)

¹yă'
Sharply

sɢē'' | ö`ᴅal-ɛ'ɢwɔ!i  ᴅɪᴅv·`lt'ɔ'ɪsti' vlsɢɛ·'ᴅə | v`sönv·'li ᴅɔ·`-
Now then lake, big, Loc he is staying it important quickly he

ᴅɪᴅv·`lɛ'nɛ·ⁿ.i' | v`sönv·'li ᴅvnv·`y't'anɪ·'lɛ·ⁿ.i'
has arisen, facing quickly he has put it under,
us, App App

5 sɢē'' | 'a·`nɔ·ɢwɔ̈ᵘ'  stA`t'öṇa·`nɪ·ɢa' nö·ᴅɔ·'-yi ᴅɪstötlt'ɔ'ɪsti'
Now then ha, now you two have come sun, Loc you two are staying
  to listen

stɪ`skúya'  ᴅɪ`ststɪ·ɢa' stɪᴅa·ᵘwɛ!ɪ`-ɢɔ·ɢa' | ö`ᴅal-ɛ·'ɢwɔ̈ᵘ ᴅɔ·`-
you two men you two little you 2 wizards, E lake big he

ᴅɪᴅv·`lɛ'nɛ·'  vlsɢɛ·'ᴅə | v`sönv·'li ᴅɛ·`t'ɪstö`tlt'anɪ·ɢa' vlsɢɛ·'ᴅə |
has arisen, facing it important quickly you two have come to it important
us, App   put him on his (legs)

ᴅɪᴅv·`ᴅalɛ·`nö'ɪ·-ᴅzɔ nöṇɔ!-i' wɪ-ᴅɛ·ᴅv·`t'anö·`ᴅa'si' nö·`ᴅaᴅv·`ḳt'a-
he started from, direction trail(s), Loc thither, they he stretched it to look back

'ö·sti' nɪɢɛ·`söna' | nöⁿ`ɢi' ɪ·ya-yö·lᴅaɢi`  ayɔ·`wɛ·sɔ·tlö·'ᴅɔ`
never four successive glimpsy (sights) he rested

10 ᴅɛ·`ᴅvᴅö̈·`N!ɛ'lɪ(ᴅɪ⁵⁵ᵃ)sɛ·sti'
it will be done so for him continuously along

ɢö·tsat'ta·ɢɪ·-ya' t'ɪ·staᴅɪ`ɢúᴾlö'ɪ·sɛ·sti' | ᴅɪᴅv·`ᴅalɛ·nö̈·' ö·`-
roughly E you two will push him along he started L T lake
  as you go

ᴅal-ɛ·'ɢwɔ̈ᵘ wɪ`-t'ɪstö`tlt'aᴅɪnö·t'anɪ·ɢa`  na'na''  wɪ-ᴅv·`lt'ɔ'ɪ·st'anɪ·ɢa'
big thither, you two have come to make there there, he has come to stay
  him jump

ᴅaᴅv·`ḳt'a'ö·sti'  nɪɢɛ·`sö·na' 'a·`-na'na''  wɪ-ᴅv·`lt'ɔ'ɪ·stɛ·sti'
he to look back never ha, there there, he will continue to stay

| ¹yă''
sharply!

15 !ı''a a`nɪnɛ·'ᴅzi  ɢɔ·'t'ɪsɢi` a`ᴅa'nö·'wɔ·t'i` | ö·`tlʌ⁵⁵ aᴅzɪ·'lɔ
this their breast it swells, Hab. to cure anyone with not fire

ᴅɪ''ᴅi yɪ·'ki
they (sol.) to it is
be put down

---

⁵⁵ W. Dial. form; C. Dial. ö·ts'a'.
⁵⁵ᵃ Interpolation by W; see p. 4.

This is the Medicine (for) When Their Breast Swells

FREE TRANSLATION

Yuha-ahi (7 times).
Sharply!

Now then! the important thing is staying in the great lake. Quickly it has arisen, facing us. Quickly he [56] has put it under (the patient).

Now then! Ha, now you two have come to listen, you two little men, you two powerful wizards; in the sun land you two are staying. From the great lake the important thing has arisen facing this way. Quickly you two have forced the important thing to get on its feet. His paths lie stretched toward the direction from where he started and he shall never look back again. As he stops to rest at the four successive gaps, it will happen to him that, roughly indeed, you two will push him along as you go by. You two have caused him to plunge back again into the very same lake from which he arose. There he is now lodged to stay. He will never look back. Right there he is compelled to stay. Sharply!

This is the medicine (for when) their breast swells. Fire is not to be put down, however.

EXPLANATION

[This formula has been edited with notes and comments by Mr. Mooney in his SFC, pp. 364–365.]

The only facts of interest which I found in Mooney's notes which were not incorporated in the paper just mentioned are that Da'kwa=Dṭi, to cure the same ailment, used a warm infusion of the following herbs:

DɩGa·'y'sǭ·ŋi`, *Collinsonia canadensis* L., rich weed, stone root, horse balm; ɩ·na'Dö<sup>n</sup> GaN:Ga', *Camptosorus rhizophyllus* (L.) Links, walking leaf; skwɔ·'l v·'t'önə`, *Asarum canadense* L., asarabacca, wild ginger; skwɔ·'lʊstɩ·'Ga, *Hepatica acutiloba* DC., liverleaf.

This infusion he applied four times before noon for four successive mornings, giving the patient some of the liquid to drink each time to cause vomiting. The whole plant was used, excepting in the case of the DɩGa·'y'sǭ·ŋi`, of which either the root or leaf might be taken.

---

[56] The disease-spirit.

30

ʻiʼaʼ   Duʼnɩ·tstalö·ʼ.i   Dɩʼkʻanö·ʼwɔ·tʻiʼ
this   whenever they have   to cure them with
                 blisters

(a) sGĕ̋ʼʼ | nɔ·Gwṏᵛʼ   ʻaʼtʻönaʼnɩ·Gaʼ   kʻaʼnanᴜʼsti   tsʻAstɩ·ʼGa
Now then   now   thou hast come to listen   Frost   thou Little

Galö·ʼldi   tsöʼtɬtʻɔʼʻɩstiʼ | ʻɩDaʼᵘwɛʻɩ-Gɔ·Gaʼ   Gɔʻᴜʼsti   tsùnᴜ·ʼɬti
above   thou art staying   thou wizard, E   something   thou failest

nɩGɛʻsöʼnaʼ | ᴜʼsönᴜ·ʼli   nö·nɔʼ   ʻɩksɔ·ʼʼöⁿʻtʻaʼnɩ·Gaʼ | ʻa·-ᴜʼDɩlɛʻʼGɩGwö̃ᵛʼ
never   quickly   trail   thou hast caused it   ha, Heat
                                            to come down

5 Gɛsɛ̨.iʼ   ᴜlsGɛ·ʼDə   ʻɩʼDᴜnᴜ·ʼyʻɩtʻanɩʼlɛ̨.iʼ | ʻaʼ.-ᴜsönᴜ·ʼli   ᴜkʻö̃·ʼʼataʼ
it is, App.   it important   it which he has put under, App.   ha, quickly   fog

tsʻAstɩ·ʼGa   tʻɩʼsùldɔ·ʼtʻanɩ·Gaʼ   ᴜtsɩʻ-nawù-Gwö̃ᵛʼ   nᴜʼʼDətʻanö·ʼDə
thou little   thou hast come to make him   beyond it, stretched L (=E)   it has been said
                get up   simultaneously

nöⁿʼʼtʻö·nɛʼʼlɩ·Gaʼ
thou hast come to do it for him

(b) (*Exactly as (a) but change* kʻaʼnanᴜʼsti   tsʻAstɩ·ʼGa   *and*
                                     Frost   thou Little

ᴜkʻö̃·ʼʼataʼ   tsʻAstɩ·ʼGa   *to*   kʻananᴜʼsti   ʻɛʼGwùʻɩ-yᴜʼ   *and*   ᴜkʻö̃·ʼʼataʼ
Fog   thou Little   Frost   thou Big, E   Fog

10 ʻɛʼGwùʻɩ-yᴜʼ, *respectively.*)
thou Big, E.

ɩ̈ʼa   Duʼnɩ·tstalö·ʼ.iʼ   Dɩʼkʻanö·ʼwɔ·tʻiʼ | ɩʼaʼ   nö·ʼwɔ·tʻiʼ   DɩDZɔʼʼ=
This   whenever they have   to cure them with   this to cure with   it must be
            blisters

tʻa.ɛ·ʼtɩ-Gwö̃ᵛʼ | (ᴜʼnɩ·Gɩ·ʼna   Gaʻaʼtkʼ ⁵⁷)   nɔ.tsɩ-ʼiʼ   tsᴜʼᵗⁱyɛ·Gɔ·ʼ.i
blown on them, L   (chinquapin)   pine(s), Loc   where it (Hab) ,
                                                                               grows

tsᴜʼstaGaʻlyɔ·ʼDə   tsᴜʼGwalɔ·Gö·ʼi   tsᴜGwaʼNɩ̈tɔtiʼ   tsɩ̈ʼki | nöⁿʼGiʼ
they are dry   they have been leaves   they are stuck in with it   it which is   four

Gaʼktʻö·ʼDə | ᴜʼDɩlɛʻʼGi | aʻmaʼ | waʼGɩGᴜ-Nɩ̈ɔʼ | ɩ·ʼyaʼ |
restricted   hot   salt   pumpkin(s), and   melon(s)

15 tʻᴜ·yaʼ | nᴜ·ʼnö̃ⁿ   tsaʼnɩnöʼɩ·ʼDə | nᴜ·ʼnə   tsaʼnɩsaʼGwalö·ʼ.iʼ |
bean(s)   potato(es)   they are long   potato(es)   they are round

tsuwɛ·ʼltsɩ-Nɩ̈ɔʼ | nɩGa·ʼDə   Ga·ʼGùmaʼ | Göyɩ·ʼsti | aʼnɩ-
eggs, and   all   cucumber   watermelon(s)   on-

sö·ʼŋi | nɩGa·ʼDə   Dᴜʼndɩ·wᵘskö·ʼ-ŋwö̃ᵛʼ   ɩʼGɔʻɩ·ʼDə
ions   all   they recover, L (E)   as long as

This is to Treat Them With When They Have Blisters

FREE TRANSLATION

Now then! Now thou hast come to listen, thou Little Frost, thou art staying on high. Thou powerful wizard, thou never failest in anything. Quickly thou hast caused the trails to come down. It is only Heat that put the important thing under him. Ha, quickly thou hast come, Little Fog, to lift him up. Relief has been caused forthwith, thou hast come to do it for him.[58]

---

[57] Interpolation by J. M.   [58] For the patient.

(b) Same as (a), but change "Little Frost" and "Little Fog" to "Very Great Frost" and "Very Great Fog," respectively.

This is to treat them with when they have blisters. This is the medicine which is to be merely blown on them: Chinquapin growing in the pine forests, the leaves of which are dry and crumbling while they are still on the plants. (During) four (days) are restricted: Hot (food), salt, cymlings also, pumpkins, beans, long potatoes, round potatoes, eggs also, all (kinds of) cucumbers, watermelons, muskmelons, all (these are forbidden) until they get well.

EXPLANATION

This formula is for the treatment of the burning and festering "fever blisters," which according to the medicine men are worst in the hottest part of summer and upon children. The disease theory is beautifully set forth in the formula as well as in the directions.

The disease is caused by the spirit of Heat, and is expelled by the spirits of Frost and Fog, both cooling in their nature. k‘aʻnanuʻsti, the name here given to the frost, is used only in the formulas, [and seems to be connected with the √-nanυGɔ "that which opens up"], the common word for frost being vʻyɔʻ'tɫa.

As for the treatment, through carelessness the medicine man has omitted the leading word of the name of the simple used, but there is not the slightest doubt but that it is the same as the medicinal plant prescribed in No. 23, page 200; the ceremony is also probably the same as described under the prescription just quoted.

The taboo, besides the regularly proscribed items of salt and hot food for four days, includes until final recovery: Beans and potatoes, because their skins shrivel up as from an inward heat; eggs, melons, etc., because these are watery in their nature.

The medicine men recognize a relationship in tomatoes, pumpkins, squashes, cymlings, gourds, cucumbers, and melons on account of the watery fluid they contain.

Several of the [vegetables] named have been adopted by the Indians from the whites, and are included [in the taboo] because of their resemblance to others previously known.

The avoidance of any such vegetables in all cases of blisters is a matter of common knowledge among the people; an infraction of any part of the taboo would interfere with recovery and would lead to a recurrence of the ailment.

31

ᴅɩ·ᴅa`nʋɢɔ´stĭ`   ʋɢǫ̈·´wûtlĭ` | ɩ·na´ᴅö︥ⁿ k‛ayʋ‛´ɢa ɢö︥ⁿ´´ti
to scratch them (indef.)   for the purpose   snake   tooth   to use

k‛ù yʋía´́ɩ· yʋía´́ɩ· yʋía´́ɩ· yʋía´́ɩ·
Come on!

yʋía´́ɩ yʋía´́ɩ· yʋía´́ɩ· yʋía´́ɩ·

ᴅʋ: ᴅʋ: ᴅʋ: ᴅʋ: ᴅʋ:
(Onom.)

5 sɢɛ̆´´ ɢalǫ̈·´ldi ᴅɩ`tsúnɛ·`tɬanö︥ⁿ´ɈI | k‛ɔ·´la tsúnɛ·´ɢö︥ⁿ ᴅɛ‛´ats-
Now then above thou hast apportioned them bone (s) thou white thou hast

ɔ`ö︥ⁿ´t‛a`nɩ·ɢa´ | tsʋyɛ·´lǫ̈-yi [59] ɢɛsǫ̈·´ ᴅɛ‛´ʋst‛a`nɩ·ɢa´ vtsɩ·‛-
come to let them   the body Loc.   it is, T. L. thou hast come to stick beyond it
down   them (l.) in it

nawa´ tsʋ·`ᴅö︥´nö︥ⁿ´ɈI |
stretched they have been said

a`nɩskú´ya  anɩ`ɢaɢɛ´ⁿ anɩ`lɔɈi´  |  ʋlɪsɢɛ·´ᴅö︥ⁿ  a`nɩsùla`ndɔ·t‛a`-
they men   they red   they have passed   it important   they have come to lift

nɩ·ɢa´ | a`nɩskú´ya  anɩ`ɢaɢɛ´´ⁿ anɩ`lɔɈi´ | ʋ·lɪsɢɛ·´ᴅö︥ⁿ
it up as   they men   they red   they have passed   it important
they go by

10 anɩ`sùla`ndɔ·t‛a`nɩ·ɢa´ | ¹ya‛
they have come to lift it up as   sharply
they go by

(This is) for the Purpose of Scratching People, Using the
Snake Tooth with it

FREE TRANSLATION

Come on! Yuhahi (4 times).
         Yuhahi (4 times).
         du: du: du: du: du.

Now then! On high, thou hast apportioned them. Thou hast
come to let the white bones down. Where the body is. thou hast
come to stick them [60] into. Reliefs have been caused.

The Red Men have passed.
They have come to lift the important thing up as they go by.
The Red Men have passed.
They have come to lift the important thing up as they go by. Sharply!

EXPLANATION

This formula is for the same purpose as No. 25, with the same
ceremony and application. It has as a third part the song referred
to on page 231.

The "Red Men" mentioned may be the Thunderers.

[The peculiar form: anɩsùlandɔ·t‛anɩ·ɢa is only used in songs,
and has a syllable infixed without any apparent semantic value

---

[59] Emendation by editor, instead of sɛ·lö︥·yi (no meaning).
[60] The white bones, the rattlesnake's teeth.

(-ɑn-); this is probably done to adapt the word to the meter of the song. The word, in common speech, is pronounced: anɩsùldɔ·tʻanɩ·Ga. Another instance of this same process is: ɛˑlanti instead of ɛˑldi.]

32

uˋnɩdzɩˑ′ya   DɩˋDaʻnö̱ˑ′wɔˑtʻiˋ   ɩˑ′aˊ
they (are) worms   to cure them (indef.) with   this

sGɛ̆′′	ʻaˋ-nɔˑGwö̱ᵘˋ	ʻaˋtʻö̱ŋaˑˋnɩˑGaˊ	ɩˋGayö̱ˑⁿli	tsúnɛˑ′Gö̱ⁿ
now then	ha! now	thou hast come to listen	thou old female	thou white

ɛˑl-ʋwɛʻɩstɔsö̱-′ŋwö̱ⁿ   ˋɩGɛˑsɛˑⁿ.iˊ | yɔˋˊsʋwaˋ   skanɛˑ′la
clay it has pain   L. that which is, App.   weakness(?)   it is pregnant(?)

(a) sGɛ̆′′ | ʻaˋ-nɔˑⁿGwö̱ᵘˋ   ʻaˋtʻö̱ŋaˑˋnɩˑGaˊ   Gʋwiˑ′sGʋwiˋ
now then   ha! now   thou hast come to listen   Bittern

tsúnɛˑ′Ga   ʻɩDaˑˋᵘwɛ̰ɩˋ-Gɔˑ·Gaˊ | Galö̱ˊldi   tsö̱ˋtɩ̰tɔʻɩˑ′sti | ʻaˑˋʋsö̱nʋˑ′li   5
thou white   thou wizard—E.   above   thou art staying   ha! quickly

uˋtɬawɔˑtúˊtɬi   ⁶¹   Gɛsö̱ˑ′i   ɛˑˋDzaksɔˑˋˊö̱ⁿʻtʻaˋnɩˑGaˊ | uˋsö̱nʋˑ′li   Dɛˋ=
where the mud is   it is, T. L.   they have let thee down as   quickly   they
solid in it   they went by

tsakʻanɔˑtʻanɩˑGaˊ   ʻaGö̱súnʋˋˋyʻtʻanɩˑGaˊ | ʋtsɩˑ′ya=Gwö̱ᵘˋ   ɩˋGɛˑsɛˑⁿ.i
made thee look at it as   thou hast come stuck thy bill   worm, L.   that which
thou wentst by   under it as thou wentst by   is, App.

uˋlsGɛˑ′Dö̱ⁿ   ɩˋDʋnʋˋˋyʻtʻanɩˋlɛˑⁿ.iˊ   tʻaˑˋsɛsö̱ˑɩˑGaˊ | tsúˋtɩ̰staˑ′yʻti=
it important   that which he put under   thou hast come to   it for thy food,
                    it, App.   pull it out

Gwö̱ᵘˋ   Gɛsɛˑ′ⁿ | tsʻAskwɔˑ′li   DɛˑˋGaDanɩˑsɔˑtʻanɩGaˊ   ⁶²   uˋkəwɛˑˋDə=
L.   it is, App.   thy stomach   it shall bury itself in it as it goes by   craving(?)

Gwö̱ᵘˋ   Gɛˑˋtsa̰Dö̱Nɛ̰ɩˊ   nɩGö̱ˋtɩ̰stʻanɩˑGaˊ | ʋtsɩˑ′nawaˋ   nʋˋdə=   10
L.   they have done   it has happened so   beyond it stretched   it has
    it so for thee, App.   been said

tʻanö̱ˑ′Dö̱ⁿ | nö̱ⁿˋtʻö̱nɛˑˋlɩˑGaˊ | nɩGö̱ˑˋwayɛˑˋlənö̱ⁿˋˊö̱ⁿsGɛˑˋstɩˑGwö̱ᵘˋ
at the same   thou hast done it   a likeness of it will remain   L.
time   for him

(b) sGɛ̆′′ | ʻaˋnɔˑGwö̱ᵘˋ   ʻaˋtʻö̱ŋaˑˋnɩˑGaˊ   kʻaˋnö̱ˑstʋˋwa
    now   ha! now   thou hast come   Sandpiper
    then   to listen

tsúnɛˑ′Gö̱ⁿ . . . (etc.).
thou white

(c) sGɛ̆′′ | ʻaˋnɔˑGwö̱ᵘˋ   ʻaˋtʻö̱ŋaˑˋnɩˑGaˊ   tsaGɔˑ′ᵘsta   tsúnɛˑ′Gö̱ⁿ . . .
    now   ha! now   thou hast come   Mud Snipe(?)   thou white
    then   to listen

(. . . etc., and add:)   ʋtsɩˑ′ˋnawa-Gwö̱ᵘˋ   aDö̱ˑˋnɩˑGaˊ | uˋnɩdzɩˑ′ya 15
            beyond it stretched, L.   it has been said   they (are)
                        worms

DɩˋDaʻnö̱ˑ′wɔˑtʻiˋ   ɩˑ′aˊ | nö̱ˋwɔˑtʻɩ-Nö̱ⁿˋ   GɩˑˋGa-Gɛˑⁿ   aˋDzɩlö̱ⁿˋski
to cure them (indef.)   this   to cure with, and   blood, like   it is a flower
with

DɩˋˋʋDiˊ   ᵘwaˑˋᵘDalʋˑ′si   aˋsʋˑyiˊ   Gɛˑsɔˑ′i | ɩGö̱ˑ′yi   DɩˋˋʋDiˊ |
to give   honey   it mixed   it has   first   to give
them to   with it   been, H.   them to
drink   drink

kʻɩlaˊ   kʻanö̱ˑwɔˑtʻiˊ   Dɩskɔˑˋlɩˑ′yɛtə-Gwö̱ᵘˋ
then   to cure him   they must be rubbed, L.
    with it

---

⁶¹ W. Dial. form; C. Dial.: uˋsawɔˑtúˊtɬi.
⁶² This word is queried by J. M. in his transliteration of Ay.'s original.

This (is) to Treat Them with (for) Worms
FREE TRANSLATION

Now then! Ha, now thou hast come to listen, thou Old White One. The body has been made very painful; it is pregnant with (weakness?).

(a) Now then! Ha, now thou hast come to listen, thou White Bittern, thou real wizard, staying on high. Ha, quickly they have come to let thee down to where the marsh is. Quickly they have made thee look at it, as thou wentst by. Thou hast come to stick thy bill under it. The important thing which he has put under him is merely a worm. Thou hast come to pull it out; it is indeed the very thing thou eatest. It shall bury itself into thy stomach; they have made thee insatiable (?). It has happened so; relief has been caused at the same time; thou hast come and done it for him; [63] only a mere likeness of it [64] will remain.

(b) Now then! Ha, now thou hast come to listen, thou White Sandpiper, *etc.*

(c) Now then! Ha, now thou hast come to listen, thou White Mud Snipe, *etc.*

(*And add at end:*) Relief has been caused.

This (is) to treat them with (for) worms. To treat with, Indian pink, mixed with honey, should be given them to drink. First it should be given them to drink, then it should merely be rubbed on them.

EXPLANATION

This formula, which seems to have lost [its fourth paragraph], is for the treatment of intestinal worms. These betray their presence by the following symptoms: yellowness of the patient's skin, redness of the fingertips, fever and diarrhea.

The medicine is a decoction of Gu'Gaqɛ' a'dzu'löⁿ'ski', *Spigelia marilandica* L., Indian pink, sweetened with honey, to be drunk both night and morning for four days, or until the worms are dislodged. If this result should not follow within that period, the medicine man tries a different medicine or concludes that the sickness is due to some other cause.

In applying the treatment, the medicine man first gives the medicine to the patient to drink, then warms his hands over the fire, while addressing "the Old White One," and then rubs the abdomen of the patient with his hands thus warmed, reciting in the meanwhile the second part of the formula, addressed to the bird. The final rub with both hands is in a downward direction, along the abdomen, typical of the downward passage of the expelled worms. In conclusion, he blows four times upon the stomach of the sick man. The

---

[63] The patient.   [64] The disease.

blowing is also from the breast downward along the abdomen. The whole operation should be repeated four times at each treatment, but as the formula as here given consists of but three parts, it seems probable [that a fourth paragraph has been lost in the course of time].

While under treatment the patient only drinks soup or the decoction, but no water, which for some reason unexplained is believed to bring the worms to life again, when they are said to be more troublesome than at first. Eggs are tabooed for the same reason, and all greasy food is prohibited.

The formula opens with a short address to the Fire, "The Old White One," in which the medicine man declares that the patient's body, spoken of under the figurative term of "clay," is filled with pain, and pregnant with yo‶svwa‵ a word which the medicine men can not now explain [but which is very probably connected with dɔ‶su, "weak"].

The word for worms v‵nιDzι·′ya (sgl. υDzι·′ya) is also applied to the common earthworm, which renders peculiarly appropriate the use of the figurative term "clay" to designate the body.[65]

After having addressed the Fire, while warming his hands the medicine man goes on to invoke various long-billed swamp birds, which feed upon worms, telling each in turn to put his bill into the muddy ooze and pull out the intruder, which "is just what you eat." In this case the mythic color of the birds is white, which is not to be understood as their actual color.

[Og. told Mr. Mooney that he used a similar formula but a slightly different prescription to cure this ailment; in addition to Indian pink he used vnι′skwüDö ⁿ‵ tsvnstι·′Ga (small buckeye). This does not grow on the Cherokee Reservation, but somewhere in Tennessee, and only one old medicine man, v‛sa′wi(?), who lived about 15 years ago, knew where to find it, and was sent for it whenever it was needed. No informant was able to identify the plant during my stay in 1926–27.]

33

⁀ı′a′	Gananv·‵Go·tsιDǫ·′⁀ıi	vnɛ‵ιsta·‵nɛ⁀ıi	yι′ki	a‵Da‵nǫ′wo·t‛i‵	
this	it appears about, H	they have pain, App.	if it is	to cure anyone with	

sGɛ̌‵′		‛a‵-no·ᵘGwö⁰′	‛a‵t‛ǫna‵nι·Ga′	tsι·ya′	wo·‵tιGɛ·ⁿ′
Now, then!		ha! now	thou hast come to listen	Otter	brown

v‵ǫDzɔ·‵-yι·-Dzö ⁿ′	Dιtsö‵tĭt‛ɔ‛ιsti		sɔ·Gwö′⁰	Dɛ‵nutsGö‵tłanι·Ga′	
cold, Loc, direction	thou art staying		one	thou and I have become one	

[65] E·lvwɛ‛ιstɔsö⁀ıi may be a contraction of: ɛ·la (=clay) vwɛ‛ιstɔsö⁀ıi (it has been made painful), as Mr. Mooney interprets it. During my stay no medicine man was able to give any information on this expression, nor did anyone remember whether the body was ever referred to by this metaphor. None of the myths throw any light on the question. I am inclined to believe that the ɛ·l- prefix is not an abbreviation of ɛ·la, clay, but a contamination of ayɛ·lö ⁿ, body.

υ`sönυ·´li	Dɔ·`t‛aᴰle‛`ǫŋa´	‛ιDa·`ᵘwɛ̡i´	Gɔ‛υsti	tsúnυ·´lti	nι̒·ⁿ
quickly	thou hast arisen, facing us	thou wizard	something	thou failest	never
Gɛ·sǫ̈·na´	υ`lsGɛ·´Dö̃ⁿ	υ`Danυ·`y‛t‛anι·`lɛ·ⁿ.i´		asGι·´nə	υ`Dö̃‛-
	it important	he has put it under, App.		ghost	it has
nö̃´ⁿι̒-GWö̃ᵛ`	Gɛ·sɛ·ⁿ.i´	aᴰlɛ´	υ`´y-ιGawɛ·´ski	Dυ`Da·N̥ıt‛ɛ·‛´lö̃!i	yι´ki
been said, L	it is, App	and	different he speaks, H	he has thought	if it is
sGɛ̌´’	nɔ·ᵘGWö̃ᴅ´	t‛ι`nasɛ`sö̃‛ι·Ga´		υsö̃´-!i	nǫ̈nɔ-!´i	Wι`-Dɛ·ⁿ
now then!	now	thou and I come to pull it out		night, Loc	trail, Loc	yonder
5 Dυ`tanǫ̈`´ö̃ⁿ’si´		υsö̃!´i	ιyǫ̈·ᴅ´Də	ǫ̈´Dali	ɛ·GWɔ!-i	wö̃´ⁿ’-t‛ι`t‛ɔ‛ι`st‛aⁿ
they lay themselves for him		night, Loc	yonder	lake	big, Loc	yonder thou hast
nι.Ga´		ιGǫ̈`wúlstɔ·´ti-GWú`-Dι·nə´			vtsι‛´nawú-GWö̃ᴅ`
come to put it		what its worth, L (=E) E			beyond it stretched
nιGǫ̈`DιsGɛ·´sti					
it will be said continuously					

THIS (IS) THE MEDICINE, IF THEY HAVE (PAINS) APPEARING ABOUT IN DIFFERENT PLACES

FREE TRANSLATION

Now then! Ha, now thou hast come to listen, Brown Otter; in the direction of the Cold Land thou art staying. Thou and I have become united as one, quickly thou hast arisen. Thou wizard, thou never failest in anything. It is merely what has become a ghost that has put the important thing under him,[66] or maybe a speaker of evil (words) has caused it.

Now then! Now thou hast come to pull it out. The paths lay themselves out toward the Night Land. Thou and I have come to put it at rest in the Great Lake, away in the Night Land. Who cares what happens to it! Relief will be caused continuously! Sharply!

EXPLANATION

This is another formula for the cure of ayɛ·‛lιGɔ·´Gi or simulator-diseases, and the general ceremony is the same as already described. (See p. 73.)

The medicine used is a warm infusion of the roots of tsɔ·`lιyυ´sti υ`nιkw‛t‛ɛ·´nöⁿ, *Verbascum thapsus* L., common mullein; Gι·´GaGɛ̡` a`Dzι·lö̃ⁿ´ski, *Lobelia cardinalis* L., cardinal flower; and of the bark of ιtsɛ!i, *Alnus rugosa* (Du Roi) Spreng., smooth alder.[67]

The cup containing the infusion is placed on the floor upon a piece of cloth, about one or two yards in length, together with four beads—red, blue, black, and white. The cloth [and the beads] are kept by the medicine man as his pay after the ceremony.

---

[66] The patient.

[67] Another specimen was identified as *Alnus serrulata* Willd.

Having recited the prayer, the medicine man takes a sup of the liquid, and applying his lips to the sore spot, sucks the place and then discharges the liquid from his mouth into another empty bowl kept ready for the purpose. This is repeated four times, after which the medicine man examines the liquid in the bowl to find the intrusive object which has caused the trouble. When found it is carefully hidden away as already described. (No. 3, p. 173.)

If necessary, the whole ceremony is repeated four times before noon, by which time, the medicine man asserts, the hidden coal, splinter, or pebble is always brought to light and relief accomplished.

34

ï'a'	Dalɔ·'ni	Dɩ'kstɔ.ti`				
this	yellow	to make them vomit				
sGé͞''	'a-'nɔ·Gwɔ͞ⁿ'	'a`t'ǫŋa·'nɩ·Ga'	tcɩ·'stɛ·	Dalɔ·'ni'	ɩ`Da·ˡᵘ=	
now then!	ha! now	thou hast come to listen	rat	yellow	thou	
wɛ̀ɩ·-yu'	sGé͞''	'a`nɔ·ᵘGwɔ͞ⁿ'	a`nìowa'Gi	vnɛ·'Gɔ͞ⁿ	Dɛ'ʿAla.=	
wizard, E	now then!	ha! now	cloth	white	thou hast	
sɩ'ʿt'anɩ·Ga'	nɔᵘGwɔ͞ⁿ'	Dalɔ·'ni	'ɔ͞ⁿ'-t'a·'sɛsɔ͞'ɩ·Ga'	'a`nɔ·ᵘGwɔ͞ⁿ'		
come to put thy feet on it	now	yellow	again-thou hast come to pull it out	ha! now		
ǫ̀·ⁿDal-ɛ'Gwɔ'ɪ̀-i	ɩ·yǫ̀·'ⁿDə	wɔ̀ⁿ'-t'ùtlGɔ·'t't'a`nɩ·Ga'	'ɩDa·ˡᵘwɛ̀ɩ'-Dɩ·nə'			5
lake, big, Loc	yonder	yonder thou hast come to scatter it	thou wizard, E			
vtsɩ·ʿ'nawa`	nǫ̀`DɩsGɛ·stì'	ⁱyǎ`ɩ̀				
beyond it stretched	he will say continuously	Sharply!				
ï'a'	Dalɔ·'ni	Dɩ'kstɔ.ti`	vnɩ·ʿ'kwa'-nìɔ͞ⁿ`	sùlv·'yɩ·-ɬuGa'	a`t'tsɛ'ʿi	
this	yellow	to make them vomit	(±black gum), and	swampy laurel tree thicket	(red alder)	
v'uyv'Gɩtɔ͞ⁿ`	v·'nalɩ`Gɔ̀ʿaⁿ'	aDɛ·'lə	nɔ̀`ⁿ'ki'	ɩyv·'nəDalɛ·'Gi		
(hazelnut)	they together	beads	four	they are so many kinds		
a`nɩDalɔ·'nɩ-Gɛ·ⁿ'	a`nɩGaGɛ·'ⁿ	a`nɩGɔ͞'naGɛ`	v'nɩnɛ·'Gɔ͞ⁿ			
they yellow, like	they red	they black	they white			

THIS (IS) TO MAKE THEM VOMIT BILE

FREE TRANSLATION

Now then! Ha, now thou hast come to listen, Weasel, thou powerful wizard.

Now then! Ha, now thou hast come to put thy feet upon the white cloth. Now thou hast come and pulled out the bile. Ha, now thou hast come to take it far away, and to scatter it in the Great Lake.

Thou art a wizard indeed. Relief has been caused. Sharply! This (is) to make them vomit bile. Black gum, white alder, red alder, hazelnut (are used) all together. Beads, as many as four different kinds: Yellow ones, red ones, black ones, white ones.

EXPLANATION

This formula is used for a form of Dalɔ·'ni in' which the whole abdominal region becomes swollen and painful, while the patient loses appetite and becomes unable to retain food in his stomach.

The medicine man invokes the weasel, called by the Cherokee "yellow rat," tcɪ·ste·Dzi, here abbreviated to tcɪ·ste· being the generic name for rats, mice, and weasels. Here again we have the color correspondence between the disease and the curing spirit.

The medicine man induces vomiting to dislodge the bile, by giving the patient to drink a warm decoction of the inner bark of the four small trees named vnɪ·'kwa, *Nyssa multiflora* Wang, black gum; sûlv·yɪłGa, *Clethra acuminata* Michx.,[68] white alder; a`t'tsɛ́'ɬi (or ɪtsɛ́'ɬi), *Alnus rugosa* (Du Roi) Spreng., red alder; v'yu'GɪDə`, *Corylus americana* Walt., hazelnut.

It will be noted that the inner bark of all these trees has a peculiar yellowish color, this again carrying out the theory of color symbolism.

The medicine man first recites the formula and then gives the patient a drink of the medicine. This is repeated four times, after which he allows the patient to drink as much of the decoction as he can swallow. The whole ceremony and application is performed four times before noon.

After the patient has drunk the decoction the medicine man "takes him to the water"; he gives the sufferer some warm water to drink, which causes him to vomit the bile, after which he finds relief. This vomiting sometimes weakens the patient considerably, so that the medicine man has to give him some sour corn gruel "kʻa`nɔʻɛ́'nə" to drink, to keep up his strength. Although not noted in the manuscript, it is probable that the medicine man addresses some formula to the "Long Man" (as in No. 15, p. 190) and that the beads mentioned are used only at this part of the ceremony. The beads are deposited on a piece of cloth and the whole is taken after the ceremony by the medicine man as his fee. The yellow bead typifies the disease, the red denotes the powerful spirit which conquers it, the black signifies the great lake in the Night Land into which the disease spirit is cast, and the white is emblematic of the happiness which comes with recovery.

[It is deemed necessary to draw attention to the fact that as a rule medicine men are unable to explain the symbolism of the beads and of their colors as is here done by Mr. Mooney.]

---

[68] Another specimen was identified as *Hydrangea acuminata* Small.

35

Daʽnιnɛˑ′svʻGǫ̈ˑ′   aʽDaʽnǫ̈ˑ′wɔˑtʻi̔ˋ
whenever they have   to cure anyone with
them drooping

sGé̯'' | ʻa-ˋnɔˑGwö̆ⁿ′   vˋsönvˑ′li   akski′   tsǫ̈ˑˋNi̭li̭ˑGa′ | Galɔ′s̭i
now then   ha! now   quickly   evening   he has come and   he passed
                                                       hit thee

Galɔ′s̭i   Galɔ′s̭i   Galɔ′s̭i | ʻaˋ-vsönvˑ′li   a′kski̭-Gwö̆ⁿˋ   Geˑsɛˑⁿ′
                                     ha! quickly   enemy—L   it is, App

tsǫ̈ˑˋNi̭ˑtli̭ˑleˑⁿ.i′ ⁷⁰   Galɔ′s̭i   Galɔ′s̭i   Galɔ′s̭i   Galɔ′s̭i
he has hit thee, App.   he passed

(This is) the Treatment When They Have Them Drooping

FREE TRANSLATION

Now then! Ha, now swiftly the enemy has come and hit thee. He has passed by *(four times)*.
Ha, it is but the enemy (who) swiftly came and hit thee, it seems. He has passed by *(four times)*.

EXPLANATION

This formula is for the same purpose as No. 10 and is very similar to it; the treatment also is about the same. The medicine man recites the first paragraph, and then rubs into the eyes of the patient a little of the ιtsɛ′s̭i (*Alnus rugosa* (Du Roi) Spreng.; also *Alnus serrulata* Willd., alder) infusion, the bark being used, after which he blows into the eyes, holding the eyelids apart as he does so.
The same is done after the recitation of the second paragraph, and the whole ceremony is repeated two or four times.

36

vnɛʻˋιstaˑˋnɛˑlιDɔˑö̆ˑ′   vGǫ̈ˑ′wutli̔ˋ   s̭i′a′   5
whenever they have pain about   for the purpose   this

(a) sGé̯'' | ʻaˋnɔˑᵘGwö̆ⁿ′   ʻaˋtʻǫ̈ŋaˑˋnι̭ˑGa′   awɔˑʻaᵖli̔ˋ   wɔˑˋtιGɛˑ′ⁿ
     now then!   ha! now   thou hast come to listen Eagle   brown

ʻaGalǫ̈ˋldι̭ˑ-Dzə   tsö̆ˋti̭tʻɔʻι̭ˋstιDɛˑGa′   a′Da   tsvˋʻstaDɔˑ′ˑGi   ιyǫ̈ˑⁿ′Də |
ha! above, direction   thou art staying, moving about   wood   they are tops   yonder

ʻιDaˑʻᵘwɛs̭ι̭ˑ-yu′ | asGι̭ˑ′nə   vˋDö̆ˋnö̆ⁿs̭ι̭ˑ-Gwö̆ⁿˋ   Gɛsɛˑⁿi′   (ö̆ⁿᶜ)⁷¹   talvˑˋDö̆ᶜ-
thou wizard, E   ghost   it has been said, L.   it is, App   animal-ghost, it has

nö̆′ⁿι̭ˑ-Gwö̆ⁿ′   Geˑsɛˑⁿ.i′ | vˋsönvˑ′li   ι̭ˑʻᵃyǫ̈ˑstʻanι̭ˑGa′ | tsutsɛˑ′lι-
. been said, L.   it is, App   quickly   thou hast come to   it (is) thine,
                                                  take it away

Gwö̆ⁿˋ   tsu̔ˋti̭staˑyᶜˋItι̭-Gwö̆ⁿ   Gɛsɛˑⁿi′ | vtsι̭ˋnawə-Gwö̆ⁿ′   nvˑˋdə.- 10
L (=E)   it (is) for they food L (=E)   it is, App   beyond it stretched, L.   it has

tʻanǫ̈ˑ′ⁿDə   nö̆ⁿˋtʻǫ̈ˑnɛˋlι̭ˑGa′ | tsuᶜ′ | tsuᶜ′ | tsuᶜ′ | tsuᶜ′
been said at the   thou hast done it for him   (Onom.)
same time

(b) sGé̯'' | ʻaˋnɔˑᵘGwö̆ⁿ′   ʻaˋtʻǫ̈ŋaˑˋnι̭ˑGa′   uwɔˑʻaᵖli̔ˋ   saʻkʻɔˑ-
                                                       Eagle   blue

ni′ . . . (*etc.*).

⁷⁰ Correction by editor; instead of tsǫNι̭ni̭ɛⁿi, an evident slip of the pen.
⁷¹ Emendation by editor.

(c) sGǽ'ʼ | ꞌaꞌnɔ·ᵘGwɔ̃ᵛʼ ꞌaꞌtꞌǫ̇ŋaꞌ·ꞌnɩ·Gaʼ úwɔᵗʼaᴅliꞌ ɔ̃ⁿᵗna-
Gɛ·ⁿ . . . (etc.)   Eagle   black

(d) sGǽ'ʼ | ꞌaꞌnɔ·ᵘGwɔ̃ᵛ ꞌaꞌtꞌǫ̇ŋaꞌnɩ·Gaʼ úwɔᵗʼaᴅliꞌ tsúnɛ·ʼ-
Gɔ̃ⁿ . . . (etc.)   Eagle   thou white

5 Dᴜ·sᴜᶜʼGa   tsᴜ·ʼntꞌəꞌnɔ̃ⁿ· | Dᴜ·sᴜ·ʼꞌGa   tsᴜ·ꞌnstiꞌGa   aꞌꞌəskwa-
   (laurel)   they are tall   (laurel)   they are little (Indian poke)
nɛ·Dɔ̃ⁿʼ   nǫ̇·ꞌwɔ·tꞌiʼ | ɛ·ᵘwsɔ̃ꞌii   DɩkꞌaꞌnᴜGɔ.ʼstɔ.tiꞌ
to cure with   (Fetter Bush) to scratch them with

This (is) for the Purpose of It, Whenever They Have Pain
        in Different Places

FREE TRANSLATION

(a) Now, then! Ha, now thou hast come to listen, Brown Eagle. Ha, thou art staying, moving about, yonder in the treetops.
Thou art a powerful wizard. It is only what has become a ghost (that has put the important thing under him); it is only what has become an animal ghost (that has put the important thing under him). Quickly thou hast come to carry it off. It is thine; it is thy food. Relief has happened at the same time. Thou hast come to make it so for him.[72]
Tsuh! (*4 times*).
(b) Now, then! Ha, now thou hast come to listen, Blue Eagle (*etc.*) . . .
(c) Now, then! Ha, now thou hast come to listen, Black Eagle (*etc.*) . . .
(d) Now, then! Ha, now thou hast come to listen, thou White Eagle (*etc.*) . . .
Great laurel, mountain laurel, Indian poke (are) to treat (them) with; fetter bush (leaves) to scratch them with.

EXPLANATION

Another formula for the treatment of shifting pains. (No. 33, p. 215.) It consists of four paragraphs addressed to the eagles. The medicine consists of a warm infusion of the leaves of DᴜsᴜᶜʼGa tsᴜ·ʼntꞌə-nɔ̃ⁿ·, *Rhododendron maximum* L., great laurel; DᴜsᴜᶜʼGa tsᴜnstɩ·ʼGa, *Kalmia latifolia* L., mountain laurel, calico bush, spoonwood; aꞌꞌəskwanɛ·ʼDə, *Veratrum viride* Ait., American white hellebore, Indian poke, making a very pungent application, which is rubbed upon the sore spot by the medicine man, after having scratched the skin with the prickly serrated edge of a bunch of the leaves: ɛ·ᵘwsɔ̃ꞌii, *Leucothoë catesbaei* (Walt.) Gray, fetter bush.

---

[72] The patient.

The medicine man scratches only over the aching part, no matter how small it may be, and repeats the operation and the application at each spot in turn as the pain shifts about, until it disappears, or, as the medicine man says, "until the important thing is driven out."

When the pain extends over a larger area, as over a whole side of the body, the whole surface is scratched.

Each paragraph of the formula is recited while rubbing on the medicine, and at the end the medicine man imitates four times the cry of the eagle: tsuh, tsuh, tsuh, tsuh, after which he blows four times upon the spot. The ceremony is repeated four times before noon for four mornings, the scratching being performed only at the first application each day.

37

nǫ·wɔ·t'i'	k'anɔ'ʟɛ(ʟaⁿ⁷³)	'ʟ'a'	Dalɔ·'ni	ya'ndɪ·k'ɔ̈'ʟaⁿ
to cure with	it tells	this	yellow	if they urinate

tsʊ'waDʊ·'nə	ʊstɪ·'Ga		sɔ.'ɪ-Nɔ̈ⁿ'	ʊ·'t'únɔ̈ⁿ'	tsʊ'waDʊ·'nə
they have arteries, sinews	it small		other, and	tall	they have arteries, sinews

Gʊ·'lstanɔ̈ɪ-Gwɔ̈ⁿ'	ʊGa·'nəwa'	Gɛ·.sɔ.'i		ʊDɔ·'təGwúDɔ̈ⁿ'	ʊ'n-
it has been steeped, L.	warm	it has been, H.		all day	they must

dɪ't'a.sti'		nɔ̈ⁿ'ki'	Ga·kt'ǫ·'ⁿDə	a'ma'	ʊGa·'nəwù-Nɔ̈ⁿ'
drink it		four	restricted	salt	warm-and

THIS TELLS (ABOUT) WHAT TO TREAT (THEM) WITH IF THEY URINATE YELLOW

FREE TRANSLATION

Small sinews and the other (kind:) Large sinews should merely be steeped warm; they must drink it all day. Four (days) restricted: Salt and warm (food).

EXPLANATION

[It appears from Mr. Mooney's notes that this prescription is one of those which Ay. obtained from ʊ·'tɬanǫ·'ⁿDə. (See p. 3.) Ay. copied them in his book, but in some cases did not get the oral dircetions along with them, so that in several instances he was not able to tell Mr. Mooney any more than the written formulas or prescriptions actually contained. (See p. 157.)]

In this case the patient drinks a warm infusion of the herbs named and abstains from salt and hot food during the period of the treatment, viz, four days.

---

[73] Interpolated by editor.

38

	υʽndɩ·ksti'	yυʽnủstυN!ɛ·ʽ!aⁿ	nǫ̈ʽwɔ·tʽi'		
	they to urinate with	if they are stopped up to them	to cure with		
sɔ.ʽɩ-N!ȫⁿ'	naʽskɩ-Gwȫᴅ	na.sGwȫᴅ	|	a·sḙ̌'	nǫ̈·ʽⁿDɔGwɛʽ ya
other, and	this here—L	also		it must	sourwood
Dɩ·Gɩ·'GaGɛ·ⁿˋ	Gȫʽlkwɔ·Gi'	Dɩ·ʽGaᴅlDɩ·'sti		Gɛsɔ.'i	
they (are) red	seven	they (l.) to be put into		it has been, H.	

(This is) to Treat (Them) With, if They have Their Urinary Passages Stopped up

FREE TRANSLATION

And this one right here is another one also: But seven red sourwood twigs should be put along with the rest into (the infusion).

EXPLANATION

This is likewise a prescription against a urinary trouble but against one of a different order, viz, suppression of the urine. A warm infusion of the same simples as those prescribed in the previous recipe is to be made, but in addition, seven sourwood twigs are to be added to the other ingredients.

[It is clear why the sourwood twigs, nǫ̈·ⁿDɔ·Gwɛʽlya, *Oxydendrum arboreum*, (L.) DC. (also *Nyssa sylvatica* Marsh) are chosen to effect relief: the disease is thought to be caused by the urinary passages being twisted, kinked, coiled, clogged up; the smooth, even twigs are considered the very best means to restore them to their original straight, smooth condition.

Sourwood twigs are also the favorite material for making arrow shafts.]

39

	!ɩ'a'	Dalɔ·'ni	ȫⁿʽnaGɛ·ⁿ'	aʽDaʽnǫ̈·'wɔ·tʽiˋ		
	this	yellow	black	to cure anyone with		
(a)	ʽa:yǐ'	| SGḙ̌'' |	ʽa·Gȫⁿtsa'Gȫⁿ	Dayɛ·'nə	| Dayɛ·'nə |	5
	(Excl.)	now then!	ha! roughly	he comes towards us		
	aDaʽᵘwɛ!i'	Dayɛ·'nə |	Dayɛ·'nə |			
	he wizard					
	aDɔ'!-ɩ!aⁿˋ	Dayɛ·'nə |	Dayɛ·'nə |			
	wood, Loc					
	υtsɩʽʽnawa'	axyɛ'!i	Dayɛ·'nə |			
	beyond it stretched	he holds in his hands				
	υtsɩʽʽnawa'	Gǫ̈Dɩ'ski:+				
		it will be said				

(b) ʻa·yĭ̆′ | sGɛ̆′ʼ | ʻa·Gǭⁿtsa′Gö̆ⁿ | Dayɛ′nə | Dayɛ′nə |
    (Excl.)   now then!   ha!   roughly   he comes toward us

    aDaˋⁿwɛ̓i′   Dayɛ′nə | Dayɛ′nə |
    he wizard

    nö̆ⁿʼyɔ′-ȟ̓aⁿˋ   Dayɛ′nə | Dayɛ′nə
    rock, Loc

    vtsɩˋⁿawa′   axyɛ′ȟi   Dayɛ′nə |
    beyond it stretched   he holds in his hand

    vtsɩˋⁿawa′   Gǭdɩ′ski:+   5
                 it will be said

(c) ʻa·yĭ̆′ | sGɛ̆′ʼ | ʻa·Gǭⁿtsa′Gö̆ⁿ | Dayɛ′nə | Dayɛ′nə |
    (Excl.)   now then!   ha!   roughly   he comes toward us

    aDaˋⁿwɛ̓i′   Dayɛ′nə | Dayɛ′nə |
    he wizard

    amaˋˋ-yɩˋ-Dzö̆ⁿ′   Dayɛ′nə | Dayɛ′nə
    water, Loc, direction

    vtsɩˋⁿawa′   axyɛ′ȟi   Dayɛ′nə |
    beyond it stretched   he holds in his hand

    vtsɩˋⁿawa′   Gǭdɩ′ski:+   10
                 it will be said

(d) ʻa·yĭ̆′ | sGɛ̆′ʼ | ʻa·Gǭⁿtsa′Gö̆ⁿ | Dayɛ′nə | Dayɛ′nə |
    (Excl.)   now then!   ha!   roughly   he comes toward us

    aDaˋⁿwɛ̓i′   Dayɛ′nə | Dayɛ′nə |
    he wizard

    vʻǭˋⁿDzɔ·-yi′   Dayɛ′nə | Dayɛ′nə
    cold Loc

    vtsɩˋⁿawa′   axyɛ′ȟi   Dayɛ′nə |
    beyond it stretched   he holds in his hand

    vtsɩˋⁿawa′   Gǭdɩ′ski:+   15
                 it will be said

ȟ̓ʼa   aˋDaˋnǭ′wɔ·tʻiˋ   aˋnɩskɔ·′li   yvˋnalö̆·tʻɛˋȟaⁿ |
this   to cure anyone with   their head   if they faint

vˋnastɛ·ts.sti′Ga   nǭ′wɔ·tʻi′ | tsɔ·′lə-Gwö̆ⁿˋ   na.′skwö̆ⁿ
(Virginia snakeroot)   to cure with   tobacco, L   also

ɔˋsɩ·-yu′
it (is) good, E

This (is) the Medicine (for) the Black "Yellow"

FREE TRANSLATION

(a) Ha-yi! Now then! Ha, boldly he comes toward us.
    He comes toward us.
    He, the wizard.
    He comes toward us (bis).
    From the forest.
    He comes toward us (bis).
    He holds relief in his hand.
    He comes toward us.
    Relief will be caused.
(b) Ha-yi! Now then!...... *From the rocks..:...::*
(c) Ha-yi! Now then!...... *From the direction of the water........*
(d) Ha-yi! Now.then!...... *From the Cold Land.......*

This (is) the medicine (for) their head, if they faint. Virginia snakeroot (is) to cure (them) with; (or) merely tobacco is also very good.

EXPLANATION

This is a formula for the cure of dizziness or fainting fits accompanied by headache and sometimes also by pains in the back of the neck and in the breast; the collection of these symptoms is known to the medicine man as "black Dɑlɔ·ni," or literally "black yellow." The patient feels faint and giddy on rising suddenly from his seat. The medicine man further states that as the disease progresses the lips and circles round the eyes turn black, and in extreme cases red blotches appear on the face, especially about the mouth. Ay. calls it a variety of Dɑlɔ·ni, while another medicine man, Dɑ`kwɑDɛ´ĭ (Mooney, Myths, Pl. XLII), ascribed it to sunstroke. The medicine is an infusion of ɛ´nɑstɛ·tstɛ´ɢɑ, *Aristolochia serpentaria* L., Virginia snakeroot, warmed by dropping into it seven live coals, and blown upon the head, breast, and back of the neck of the patient. When the snakeroot can not be procured the medicine man blows the juice of ordinary chewing tobacco upon the patient in the same way. While he chews the tobacco he takes a sup, before each blowing, from a cup of pure water, into which seven live coals have been dropped as just described. An infusion of snakeroot is said to be frequently used as a wash in cases of headache.

The patient is placed sitting, facing the east, while the medicine man stands a short distance away holding in his uplifted hand the cup containing the medicine. He then sings the first verse, after which, without approaching any nearer, he blows the liquid four times upon the head of the patient. This operation is repeated with each of the four verses; when coming nearer, he blows his breath four times upon the head of the sick person. If there be pains also in the breast or back of the neck, the operation is repeated in the same way, blowing upon the part affected.

The song is addressed to four different classes of invisible "Little People" [see p. 25], the spirits of the forest, of the cliffs, of the water, and of the Cold Land, or the North, the last being invoked probably on account of the feverish condition of the patient, or because, as the other medicine man (DɑkwɑDɛ´ĭ) asserted, the sickness is due to the heat of the sun.

40

ṳ'a' this	tsʋnɩt'ᴇ·lɔ'ᴇ̗aⁿ' they have them shaking	a`ᴅa'nö̟·wɔ·t'i` to cure anyone	
sɢḗ'' Now then	v'sö̗i night Loc	a`skúya' man	ö̟ⁿnaɢᴇ·ⁿ' black	v`ᴅa·nɩ̗t'ᴇ·''lö̟i' he has thought it	ɢᴇ·sᴇ·ⁿ- it is,
(.i'⁽¹⁾) App	a`ɢᴜ·s-ᴇ·'ɢwö̟ᵘ female animal, it big	ᴅᴜᴅa·nɩ̗t'ᴇ·''lö̟i' he (E) has caused it	ɢᴇ·sᴇ·ⁿ(.i⁷⁴)' it is, App	
sɢḗ'' Now, then,	nɔ·ɢwö̟ᵘ' now	'at'ö̟na·`nᴜ·ɢa' thou hast come to listen	nö̟ⁿᴅɔ·-yi sun, Loc	stö̗`tɩ̗t'ɔ̗`ɩsti' You (2) are staying	

stᴜ̗`skúya'   stᴜɢᴜ·`ɢaɢᴇ·ⁿ'   stᴜ̗`ᴅa·ᵘwḗ''   | a`ɢᴜ·s-ᴇ·'ɢwö̟ᴅ   ᴅᴜ·ᴅa·-   5
you (2) men   you (2) red   you (2) wizards   female animal, big   he (E)

nɩ̗t'ᴇ·''lö̟i'   ɢᴇ·sᴇ·ⁿ(.i⁷⁴)' | v'sö̟nʋ·'li   ᴅᴇ·`t'ɩsta`skɔlɔ·''ö̟ⁿ.t'anᴜ·ɢa'
has thought it   it is, App   quickly   you (2) have come to cause him to let
                                                  go his grip(ping hands)

ʋtsᴜ`'nawú·ɢwö̟ᴅ'   nʋ·`dɔ.t'anö̟'ᴅɔ | nö̟ⁿ't''ɩstö̟·nᴇ`·lᴜɢa'
beyond it stretched,   It has been said at the   you (2) have come to do it
L (=E)   same time   for him

ᴅᴇ·`ɢɔ·sᴜ̗`sisɢ-ö̟·'.i | ṳ'a'   tsʋ·nᴜt'ᴇ·'lɔ̗ᴇ̗aⁿ'   a`ᴅa'nö̟·wɔ·t'i` |
They have been gathered   this   they have them shaking   to cure anyone with
together, T L

tsɔ·'l-ᴜyʋ''sti   ʋsti·'ɢa   ɢaᴅʋ·`s-ᴇ̗`i   ʋsti·`k'ᴜ-ᴅᴜnö̟ⁿ'   nö̟`wɔ·t'i' |
tobacco-like   small   mountain, it lives   very small, E   to cure with

ɢʋ·'lstɔ·ti`   | wa·'lɢᴜɢʋ'   ʋstɩ·'ɢa   ᴅᴜᴅzɔ·t''ɩstɔ·'tᴜ-ɢwö̟ᴅ`   10
to make a   cymling   small   to blow them with, L
steep with

THIS (IS) THE MEDICINE WHENEVER THEY HAVE THEM SHAKING

FREE TRANSLATION

Now, then! It is the Black Man from the Night Land who has caused it. Surely, it is the Big Bitch that has caused it.

Now, then! Now you two have come to listen, you Two Red Men, you wizards, you are staying in the Sun Land. It is the Big Bitch that has caused it. Swiftly you two have come to cause him to relinquish his grasp. Relief itself has been caused at the same time. You two have made it so for him.

This is the medicine whenever they have them shaking. (Of) the small mountain-growing tobaccolike (plant), a very small portion steeped in a small cymling is to treat (them) with. It is just to be blown on them.

EXPLANATION

This formula is for the treatment of a disease in which the arms shake and tremble violently, as in some forms of paralysis. The ailment is, however, stated to be of a temporary character.

No explanation as to the cause could be given beyond what is contained in the formula itself, according to which the "Black Man" in the Night Land is held responsible for the trouble. [The identity of the Black Man is discussed on page 24.

---

[74] Interpolated by W., recorded by editor.

This is the only instance where the Black Man is identified with the aGɩ·sɛ·Gwɔ͞ⁿ or Big Bitch.

From what has been said (p. 24) it results clearly that the Two Red Men are without any possible doubt to be identified as the Two Thunder Boys.]

The medicine is a little of the root of tsɔ·ˋlɩyʋ′sti ʋstɩ·′Ga Gatʋ·ˋsɛ′ˊi (*Lobelia spicata* Lam.), steeped in cold water, in a small fresh cymling gourd. The cymling thus used in medical practice is always procured from out-of-doors just when wanted, and is put safely away again outside the house when the operation is over. This precaution is taken, as was explained to Mr. Mooney on a subsequent visit, to prevent the medicinal virtues of the cymling being spoiled by the presence of a menstrual woman in the house.

The medicine man first scratches the skin of the patient over the seat of pain as described elsewhere, and then, after reciting the formula, blows the liquid four times upon the spot. The formula and blowing are repeated four times at each application, and the whole ceremony, without the scratching, is performed four times before noon and if necessary also for four consecutive days. At the conclusion of each application the patient drinks a little of the liquid. As he is usually very weak, no fasting or other taboo is enjoined.

41

ˊɩ′a′	ʋˋⁿawa.′sti	aˋDaˋnö·′wɔ·t′iˋ
this	chill	to cure anyone with

(a) sGɛ̌′′ | nö·ˋDɔ·-Gö·-yi | ˊɩˋskuya′ | Gɩ·ˋGaGɛ·ⁿ′ | ʋˋsönʋ·′li
Now then | Sun, Loc. | thou Man | thou red | quickly

ˊaˋt′öⁿaˋⁿɩ·Ga′ | Gɔˊʋ′sti tsünʋ·′łti nɩGɛ·ˋsö·na′ | aˋnɩDa·ᵘwɛˊ
thou hast come to listen | something thou failest never | they wizards

tcʋ·ˋⁿˊAstɩ·Ga′ | Dɛtsȫˋtłtʋᵘwɩstɩ·ˋDɛ·Ga′ | Gɔˊʋ′sti ˊɩˋDzɩnʋˋlə′ö·ⁿ′′ski
they little | they surround thee as thou goest about | something you all fail (Hab.)

5 nɩGɛ·ˋsö·na′ | GaˋnɩsöˋˋwA Gɛ·sö·′ tsʋˋDʋ·ˋkt′anö́ˊˊi Gɛsɛ·′ⁿ(.i [75])
never | underneath it is, T. L. it has been decided it is, App.

GaˋnɩsöˋˋwA Gɛ·sö·′ DaDʋ·ˋkt′anɩ·Ga′ | GaˋnɩsöˋˋwA Gɛ·sö·′
underneath it is, T. L. it has become decided | underneath it is, T. L.

ʋtsɩ·′′-nawaˋ nö·ˋDɩsGɛ·sti′ |
beyond it, stretched it will be said continuously

(b) sGɛ̌′′ | ʋˋö·Dzɔ·′-yi ˊɩˋskuya′ saˋk′ɔ·ni′ (*etc*.).
Now, then! | Cold, Loc. thou Man Blue

(c) sGɛ̌′′ | ʋsö̌′′ɩ· ˊɩˋskuya′ ö̌ⁿˋⁿnaGɛ·ⁿ′ (*etc*.).
Now, then! | Night thou Man Black

---

[75] Emendation by editor. \

(d) sGĕ´'ⁱ | wa'ɩ'l-ɛ·Gwɔ'ʇi | dɩtsö'tɪt'ɔ'ɩs'ti | 'ɩ'skùya' tsûnɛ·'Gə
Now, then! Measure worm, big, Loc. thou art staying thou Man thou White

v'sönv·'li 'a't'ǫ·ŋa'nɩ·Ga' | Gɔ'v'sti tsûnv·'ɩti nɩGɛ·'sǫ·na' |
quickly thou hast come to listen something thou failest never

a'nɩpa·ᵘwe" tsv'n'Astɩ·' dɛ·tsöt'ɩtv'ᵘwɩstɩ'dɛ·Ga' | Gɔ'v'sti
they wizards they little they surround thee as thou goest about something

ɩ'dzɩnv·'ɩti nɩGɛ·'sǫ·na' | Ga'nɩsǫ·'wa tsvdv'kt'anö'ʇi Gɛ'sɛ·ⁿ(i ⁷⁶) |
you all fail never underneath it has been decided it was, App.

Ga'nɩsǫ·'wa Gɛ'sǫ·' dadv'kt'anɩ·Ga' | GaNɩsta' dɩGɩ·'GaGɛ·'ⁿ 5
underneath it is, T. L. it has become decided switch(es) they are red

dù'lsɛ·Gɔ·'Gɩsɩ·Ga' | vtsɩ·'-nawa' adö·'nɩ·Ga'
they have come to conquer him beyond it, stretched it has been said

dɛ·'Gɔ·sɩ'sɩsG-ǫ·'.j | ʇɩ'a' v'ⁿnawa.'sti a'da'nǫ·'wɔ·t'i' |
they have been gathered, this chill to cure anyone with
T. L.

nǫ·'wɔ·t'ɩ-nʇö·ⁿ' ɩGöⁿ'li' | sɔ.i' ɩGöⁿ'li vyɛ·'lə'a·'ⁿ tsɩ'ki |
to cure with, and fern the other fern it naked it which is

vwɔ·'sGɩlɩ-nʇöⁿ' tsɩ'ki | k'ɔ·'G-askǫda'Gɛ | yɔ·'n-vdzɛ·stöⁿ' |
soft and it which is ground hog, his forehead bear for him to lay on

Gɔ·'tsötɪti' 10
it put in (along with the others)

This is the Medicine for the Chill

FREE TRANSLATION

Now, then! Thou Red Man of the Sun Land, quickly thou hast come to listen. Thou never failest in anything. The Little Wizards surround thee as thou goest about. You all never fail in anything. It has been decided underneath, it seems. (And it is the truth:) it has been decided underneath. Underneath relief be caused constantly.

Now, then! Thou Blue Man of the Cold Land (etc. . . . .).

Now, then! Thou Black Man of the Night Land (etc. . . . .).

Now, then! In the South thou art staying, thou White Man; quickly thou hast come to listen. Thou never failest in anything. The Little Wizards surround thee as thou goest. You all never fail in anything. Underneath it has been decided, it seems; (and it is a fact:) it has been decided underneath. They have come to conquer him with the red switches. Relief has been caused.

Where (the directions) have been assembled: this is the medicine for the chill. And the medicine is fern; (and also) the other fern, the one that is naked; and the one which is soft; the ground hog's forehead (fern) and the bear's bed (fern); this all put together.

EXPLANATION

This is another formula for the cure of chills, a disease which, although attributed to the ghosts, is said to rise up "from under-

---

[76] Emendation by editor.

neath," which is another way of saying that it has its origin in malarial exhalations in the vicinity of the house. This explains the expression so often repeated: "It has been decided underneath.' The same word (Ganɩ·tłi) is now used for both a bedstead and a board floor, but in former times the Cherokee cabins had no floor but the ground, and the "bed" was a raised platform running around next to the wall on the inside. As the Indians never dreamed of keeping the premises clean it was the universal custom among the eastern tribes to occupy a house until the accumulated filth rendered the site unhealthy, when the site was abandoned and the inmates removed to a new location.

The formula consists of four paragraphs differing but slightly except as regards the color and location of the spirit invoked. Each one is named in the regular order, east, north, west, and south, with the corresponding color, red, blue, black, and white. Each one is also said to be surrounded as he goes about by a number of subordinate and auxiliary spirits, probably the "Little People" so often invoked, the countless spirits that dwell in the air, the forests, the cliffs, and the water. The great Measure Worm (waʽɩ'li ɛ'Gwōⁿ), figuratively used in the formulas to denote the south is said to be a mountain on the border of South Carolina, perhaps the same known as Cæsar's Head. It is quite possible, however, that the mythic waʽɩ'li had no real existence, and that the modern Cherokee have simply confused the name with that of Walhalla, a town in upper South Carolina.

The medicine consists of a warm infusion of the roots of several varieties of fern; [ɩGōⁿʽ'li is a name given to any variety of fern; without any more definite description it is not possible to identify it; it may be one of the following species: ɩGōⁿ'ʽli ʋwɔ·'skɩli` ʋstɩ·'Ga, *Osmunda cinnamomea* L., cinnamon fern; ɩGōⁿ'ʽli ʋwɔ·'skɩli` nöyɔ'ʽi ɛ'ʽi, *Cystopteris fragilis* (L.) Bernh., bladder fern; ɩGōⁿ'ʽli ʋyɛ·'laʽa·ⁿ', *Dennstaedtia punctilobula* (Michx.) Moore, hay-scented fern (also ɩGōⁿ'ʽli Dawɩ`s=kaGɛ·'.i); kʽɔ·Gaskö̈ⁿDaGɛ, *Adiantum pedatum* L., maidenhair fern; yɔ·'nə ʋDzɛ`'stɔ', *Polystichum acrostichoides* (Michx.) Schott., Christmas fern].

The medicine man holding a cup containing part of the decoction in his hand, stands on the east side of the patient, who faces him. The medicine man then recites the first paragraph, addressing the Red Man, after which he takes a draught of the liquid and blows it four times upon the head and the breast of the patient. Then moving around successively to the north, west, and south of the patient, he recites in order the remaining three paragraphs, blowing the medicine on the patient after each one as described. The ceremony is repeated four times before noon, and for four days, if necessary.

[For the reason why the ferns are used, see page 54.]

42

	u'sönu·li' quickly	u·'n'ta·ne'ö·'[.i⁷⁷] they attack him	a'Da'nö·wɔ·t'i' to cure any one	ï'a' this
(a)	a'nɩskú'ya they men	anɩ'lɔïi' they just passed		
	ɛ·'tɬawɩ·'ni under the earth	anɩ'lɔïi' they just passed		
	vtsɩ'ᵋ-nawa' beyond it, stretched	aDɔ̈''nɩ·Ga' it has been said		
(b)	a'nɩskú'ya they men	anɩ'lɔïi' they just passed		5
	ɛ·'tɬawɩ·'ni under the earth	anɩ'lɔïi' they just passed		
	vtsɩ'ᵋ-nawa' beyond it, stretched	aDɔ̈''nɩ·Ga' it has been said	'a:yï'	
(c)	ɛ·Dɔ·'Dǝ ⁷⁸ my father	aDa·'Nïti' the soul	tsaGɛ'ᵋ¹yu'ɩ·-yu' he loves thee, L.	Galö̈·'ldi' above
	aDa·'Nïti'	tsaGɛ'ᵋ¹yu'ɩ·yu'	ɛ·Dɔ''Dǝ'	
	aDa·'Nïti'	tsaGɛ'ᵋ¹yu'ɩ·yu'	Galö̈·'ldi'	10
	aDa·'Nïti'	tsaGɛ'ᵋ¹yu'ɩ·yu'	'a:yï'	
(d)	ɛ·Dv·'tsi ⁷⁹ my maternal uncle	aDa·'Nïti' the soul	tsaGɛ'ᵋ¹yu'ɩ·-yu' he loves thee, E.	Galö̈·ldi' above
	aDa·'Nïti'	tsaGɛ'ᵋ¹yu'ɩ·yu'	ɛ·Dv'tsi'	
	aDa·'Nïti'	tsaGɛ'ᵋ¹yu'ɩ·yu'	Galö̈·'ldi'	15
	aDa·'Nïti'	tsaGɛ'ᵋ¹yu'ɩ·yu'	'ǝ·:yï'	
(e)	nö̈·'ŋwɔ·na'	sö̈·'nɩlaGɩï¹ ⁸⁰	(4 times).	
(f)	sGɛ̌'' Now, then!	sv'sa' ?	Gɛ'sɛ̨·' it is, App.	v'lsGɛ·'Dǝ it important Dunv·'y't'anɩ·'lɛ·ⁿ.i' he has put it under, App.
	ɛ·'Dzalɩ·.ɩ-Gwɔ̈ᴅ' ? L.	'ɩGɛ·'sɛ·.i' it which is, App.		

sGɛ̌'' Now, then,	'ɩ·'skúya' thou Man	ts'A'stɩ·Ga' thou Little	'ɩ·Da·ᵘwɛ'' thou wizard	vDɔ'ᵋ'aᴅlɛ' sunny side
Gú'tɬaDɔ·'Gɩ hill-side	Gɛ'sǫ̈·' it is, T. L.	'ɛ·'Dzaksɔ''ö̈ⁿ't'anɩ'lɛ·ⁿ.i' they have let thee down, App.		aDa·'Nïtɔ' 20 the soul
'asö̈'ⁿ'Gatɬɩ·'sɩski' thou art continually gripping back	Gɔ'v'sti something	tsö̈·sö̈ⁿ''Gatɬɩ·'sɩ·ta' thou art taking a firmer grip		ɩ·'Gă-Ga·ta' light, it hangs on
ɩ·'ǫ̈·'nɛɩi' thou art doing, App.	aDa·'Nïtɔ' the soul	'asö̈ⁿ''Gatɬɩ·'sɩski' thou art continually gripping back	vsö̈'ᵋɩDǝ' night-been	nu·'Da'nö̈·'nǝ it has not been said
vtsɩ'ᵋ-nawú-Gwɔ̈ᴅ' beyond stretched, L.	aDɔ̈''nɩ·Ga' it has been said	¹yă' sharply		

---

⁷⁷ Emendation by editor.
⁷⁸ W. D. form; C. D.=aGɩDɔ·'Dǝ
⁷⁹ W. D. form; C. D.=aGɩ·'Dv·'tsi.
⁸⁰ ? ? Very probably contaminated, from sǫnɩGalɔ·Gɩïi=where Broken Rock is.

This is the Medicine When they Attack Him Suddenly

FREE TRANSLATION

The men have just gone by,
Under the earth they have just gone by,
They have caused relief.

The men have just gone by,
Under the earth they have gone by,
They have caused relief. Sharply!

My father on high loves thy soul,
Thy soul my father loves.
Thy soul, he on high loves,
Thy soul he loves. Ha-yi.

My uncle on high loves thy soul,
Thy soul my uncle loves.
Thy soul, he on high loves.
Thy soul he loves. Ha-yi.

Nö̆'ŋwɔ·na' sö̆'ⁿɹla'ɢʌ̈ï' (4 times).

Now then! It is merely su'sa that has put the important thing under him; it is merely ɛDzɑlɩ'.i.

Now then! Thou Little Man, thou wizard, on the sunny side of the mountain slope you have been let down. When the soul slips out (of thy hand), thou art continually gripping it back; thou art doing as one who takes a firmer grip of something (when it is about to escape from his grasp). Thou art continually gripping the soul back, (and) not for one night (only, but forever). Relief has been caused indeed, sharply!

EXPLANATION

This peculiar formula is intended for the treatment of what, from the description given of the symptoms, appears to be apoplexy. The patient is stricken suddenly, becomes black in the face, and falls to the ground struggling and gasping for breath. The attack is frequently fatal. The sickness closely resembles that described in No. 16 and is attributed to the same cause: the raccoon, on account of the gasping sound made by the struggling victim. The raccoon theory in connection with gasping attacks seems to be held by the medicine men generally.

The formula consists of a song of four verses, followed by a recited part. The medicine used is an infusion of the root of ɔ'Dɑlɩɢa'ᴅli, *Panax trifolium* L., dwarf ginseng, groundnut, to which the leaves of: tsɔ'laɢayö̆'ⁿli, *Nicotiana rustica* L., wild tobacco, may be added. The ginseng may be used by itself, but the other herb can not be used without a small piece of ginseng root.

The liquid is heated by dropping into it four or seven coals of fire.

Sometimes also the arms of the patient are scratched and some pungent decoction is rubbed into the scratches.

The medicine man facing the patient and holding the cup in his hand begins by singing the first verse, after which he takes a draught of the liquid and blows it four times upon the head and the breast of the sick man. The same operation is repeated with each of the other three verses. Finally he recites [the "parlando" part of] the formula, after which he blows his breath four times on the top of the head [the crown], the back of the neck, and the face of the patient. The ceremony is repeated four times if necessary. [If the attack is considered so serious that immediate action is necessary, no time is lost in procuring ginseng or wild tobacco, and the medicine man merely blows water on the stricken man.]

The formula contains a number of expressions which the medicine man himself from whom it was obtained [Ay.] could not explain, as he in turn had obtained it from his grandfather. In fact, he was completely in the dark as to the meaning of the formula, and when pressed for an explanation became sullen and asserted that he recited the formula as it had been handed down to him, and that it was not for him to question its authority. The same difficulty was experienced in connection with formulas obtained from other medicine men, and goes to show the antiquity of the formulas, while it also proves how much of the sacred knowledge has been lost. As Ay. was born about 1830, his grandfather was probably a boy when Adair wrote his account of the Cherokee and the other southern tribes in 1775.

The words ɛ·dɔ·'dǝ and ɛ·dʋ·'tsi show that the formula was originally written by a Cherokee speaking the Western Dialect, the corresponding forms in the Middle Dialect being a'gɩdɔ·'dǝ and a'gɩdʋ·'tsi. [I noticed during my 1926–27 stay, however, that among the Central Dialect speaking Cherokee these two Western Dialect forms are quite frequently used.]

[As to the persons or spirits meant by "my father" and "my (maternal) uncle" no information could be obtained, neither by Mr. Mooney nor by me. As is known, it is common for American Indians to call a powerful protecting spirit by some name denoting relationship, and this is also frequently done by the Cherokee: they will address the moon as "grandfather," and will proclaim themselves the children of the "Old White One," i. e., the Fire, or of the "Long Human Being," i. e., the stream, the river, the flowing water. No doubt the meaning of these expressions has to be looked for in that direction.]

The expression "a'nɩskú'ya anɩ'lo·ï'," "The men have just gone by," occurs also in a song to cure headache. (No. 2, p. 170.) Who the men referred to are, the medicine men can not tell. Ay. was of the opinion that they were the Thunder Boys, commonly spoken of as the Two Little Men, or the Little People, i. e., the spirits inhabiting the cliffs, the mountain caverns, etc. The latter explanation is more probable, as the Little Men here referred to are spoken of as "going by under the earth."

[sʋ″ʽsa and ɛʽDzalɩ′.i are the same names as given to the disease spirits of No. 45, but as already stated no light can now be thrown on the meaning of the word, nor on the identity of the spirits meant. The same refers to the expression nǫ̈ʽŋwɔ·′na sǫ̈·ʽnɩlaʽGɩ̓ʽi′. The latter part of this might possibly be connected with an expression which is rather common in the formulas, sǫ̈·ʽnɩGaʽlɔ·Gɩ′ʽi, "where Broken-Rock Mountain is."

This formula furnishes a good illustration of the difference between the colloquial language of the people and the archaic language of the formulas, this difference being so great that [the vocabulary of] the medicine man is almost unintelligible to the laity.

The "Little Man" addressed in the last part of the formula and who "has been let down on the sunny side of the mountain slope" is none other than the ginseng plant. (See p. 171.)

43

ʽɩ′a′ ama·′-yi Dɩ·ʽDa·Dzɔ̌ⁿ′stʽɔti′ ʋʽnDanɩ·′yuDǝ′
this   water, Loc   to take people there with it   they have been left

(a) sGě″ | ʽɩ·Gayǫ̈·li tsúnɛ·′Gɔ̌ⁿ aDa·ʽNɩ̓ti′ Dɛ·tsckalɔ·ʽsǫ̈·′
   Now, then!   thou old   thou While   the soul   thou hast relinquished
                                                      thy grasps, T L

ɩGǫ̈·ʽwulstʽanɔ̌·ʽɩ-Gwɔ̌ᴅ | ɔ·ya′ tsu·Dɩ·yaʽstʽanɛ·ʽlɩ·Ga′ | ayɛ·ʽ=
it has become worthless, L   Fire   it has been left for thee   years-passed

GaᴅlɔʽɩstiʽGɛsɛ·sti′ | kʽǔ′
         it will be   Come on

5 (b) sGě″ | yǫ̈·wi Gaʽnɔ̌ʽɩ·Dǝ nɔ·′Gwɔ̌ᴅ aDa·ʽNɩ̓ti′ Dɛ·ʽtsck=
   Now, then!   Human Being   long   now   the soul   thou hast

alɔ·ʽs-ǫ̈·′ (etc., as in a.)
relinquished thy
grasps, T L

(c) ɩGǫ̈·yi′ Galǫ̈·l-ǫ·′ Gɛ·ʽʲya-Gʋ·′Gǝ DɩGa·ʽskɩlɔ̌ Dɩtsǫ̈·yɛ·a′ |
   first   above, Loc   woman, E (?)   tables   thou hast laid them

a′Gɩsti′ ʋnɛ·′Gǝ ú·tɬaʽɛ·Dǝ aʽDɔ̌ʽnɩ·sɛ·sti′ | Gǫ̈·ʽDasawɔ·ʽɩlɩyɛ·′Dǝ
food (sol)   while   moved   it will be said   it covered over

aʽDɔ̌ʽnɩ·sɛ·sti′ | sɩGúᴅlta aɔ̌Dɔ̌ʽnɩ·sɛ·sti′ ɔ·ya′ | tsu·Dɩya·ʽ=
it will be said   pushed away (?) it will be said   fire   it has been left

10 stanɛ·ʽlɩ·Ga′ ayɛ·ʽGaᴅlɔ·ʽɩsti′ Gɛ·ʽsɛ·sti′
    for thee   years-passed   it will be

(d) tʽaʽDlɩ·nɛ·′ Dɩ·Galǫ̈·ʽlDɩ·-yǫ̈·′ Gɛ·ʽʲya-Gʋ·′Gǝ (etc., as in c.)
    second   above T L   woman, E

(e) tsɔ·ʽɩ·nɛ·′ Dɩ·Galǫ̈·ʽlDɩ·yǫ̈·′ Gɛ·ʽʲyaGʋ·′Gǝ (etc., as in c.)
    third

(f) nɔ̌ⁿ·′Gɩ·nɛ·′ (etc.).
    fourth

(g) ʽɩ·skɩ·nɛ·′ (etc.)
    fifth

15 (h) sʋ·ʽDalɩ·nɛ·′ (etc.).
    sixth

(i) Gɔ̌łkwɔ·ʽGɩ·nɛ·′ (etc., with at the end:) ¹yăʽ
    seventh   Sharply

This Is To Take Those That Have Been Left (Alive) To the Water With

FREE TRANSLATION

Now, then! Thou Old White One, (the moment) thou hast taken thy (protecting) grasp away from the soul, it has become worthless. (But, do not despair:) the Fire of the hearth has been left in its place for thee;[81] thou[81] wilt (yet live to) be old. Come on!

Now, then! Long Human Being, now thou hast withdrawn thy (protecting) hand from the soul, (*etc.* . . . .).

In the first upper world, thou Woman by excellence, thou hast prepared the white tables. The white food will be circulating. It will be covered over (by the hands of the ghost?) but the covering (hands) will be pushed away. The fire (of the hearth) will be left in its place for thee;[81] thou wilt yet live to be old.

In the second upper world, thou Woman by excellence (*etc.* . . .).
In the third upper world, thou Woman by excellence (*etc.* . . .).
In the fourth upper world, thou Woman by excellence (*etc.* . . .).
In the fifth upper world, thou Woman by excellence (*etc.* . . .).
In the sixth upper world, thou Woman by excellence (*etc.* . . .).
In the seventh upper world, thou Woman by excellence (*etc.* . . .), (*with, at the end:*) Sharply!

EXPLANATION

This is a typical example of a formula "for taking them to the water with." [It has been discussed at length by Mr. Mooney in his "Cherokee River Cult," pages 4 et seq.]

This is the most impressive of all the ceremonies of the Cherokee and is performed only on important occasions, such as the birth of a child, the death of a relative or a very close friend, to obtain long life, in preparing for the ball game or for the green corn dance, at each new moon, to counteract the evil conjurations of an enemy, and in connection with some of the more important love formulas. A similar but less elaborate ceremonial may be performed for the less important of the purposes enumerated above, by a layman, without the intervention of the medicine man.

The various formulas for taking patients or clients to water usually differ but slightly from one another, the principal feature of all of them being the lifting up of the client's soul by successive stages to the seventh upper world.

The one here given is performed for the joint benefit of all the members of a family, who are all present, after the death of a near relative, for the purpose of making them forget the deceased (see p. 26).

---

[81] Addressing the patron.

The first paragraph is addressed to the Old White One, the Fire. It is recited by the medicine man inside of the house of his clients, while standing in front of the hearth and looking down into the fire. He has his back turned to the members of the family, who stand in line with their backs turned toward him, and facing the open door [of the cabin]. The medicine man has with him an assistant, who, at the conclusion of the paragraph, ejaculates: "k‘ŭ" ("Come on!"), and precedes the family, who start in procession to go down toward the stream, the medicine man following.

On arriving at the stream, the persons for whose benefit the ceremony is intended stand in line, side by side, close to the water's edge, with their eyes intently fixed upon the water rushing by, while the priest stands behind them, with his hands outstretched and looking straight ahead; he then recites the paragraph addressed to the Long Person, the River, followed by the seven others addressed to (a)Gɛ`ᵗ-ʼyaGᴜ·ʼGo, the Woman by excellence, the Sun, represented as the owner of tables covered with "white" [or success-bringing food. The recital ends with the assurance that the clients will not die, that they will yet occupy their place at the hearth, that they will live to be old.]

During this part of the ceremony the attendant is closely watching the appearance of the water in front of the clients for the distance of an "overhand" from the bank. Should a stick, a fish, or any object whatsoever come within this limit during the recitation of the formula, it is a sign that the death in the family was caused by witchcraft. By certain signs in connection with the appearance of the object, the medicine man is enabled to guess the whereabouts, or even the name, of the enemy, who must then be proceeded against in another ceremony to annihilate the influence of any further activities of his. Should the water appear clear and undisturbed, the death was not due to human machinations and no other ceremony is necessary.

As the priest mentions in turn each of the seven upper worlds—each of which is figuratively said to be an "overhand" above the last—he gradually raises his hands higher and higher, until at the concluding paragraph they are stretched high above his head. At the final "yă‘", his clients of one accord bend down, and, dipping out the water with their hands, they lave their faces, heads, and breasts, or else, wading out into the stream, they duck under completely seven times in succession.

Each upper world represents a definite period of life, usually a year, sometimes a month. In ceremonies for long life it usually stands for a year. Should the omens in the water be propitious up to the mention of the third, fourth, or fifth upper world, the client will live in peace three, four, or five years longer. If all goes well until he is raised up to the seventh or highest upper world he may expect at least a seven years' lease of life. Beyond this the prophetic ability of the Cherokee medicine man never goes.

Should, on the contrary, an unfavorable omen be perceived in the course of, let us say, the paragraph relating to the fifth upper world, the priest knows that some great danger, possibly death itself, threatens the man in five days, five months, or five years to come. This necessitates the immediate performance of another ceremony, accompanied by fasting and going to water, to turn aside the impending peril. The final result is usually successful, as the priest seldom ceases from his labors until the omens are propitious. If, however, all his efforts prove to be without avail, he frankly informs his client of this, who is often [impressed to such an extent by the medicine man's suggestive prophesies and by his own autosuggestion that he not infrequently loses all courage, becomes despondent and listless], believing himself doomed by an inexorable fate, finally sickens and actually dies, thus fulfilling the prediction.

44

ᴜnɛ`'ɩsta·`nɛ'ǫ·' Ga·na`nᴜ·ɢɔ·`tsɩᴅǫ·'.i
whenever they have   it is appearing about (Hab.)
pain

(a) sɢɛ̌'' | 'a`-nɔ·ɢwɔ̃ᴅ' | 'a`t'ǫ·ŋa·`nɩ·ɢa' | tsɩ·ya' | ɢɩ·`ɢaɢɛ·ⁿ'
Now then   ha, now   thou hast come to listen   Otter   red

nǫ·ᴅɔ·''-yi ᴜᴅzɩ·`-ᴅzə.ɛ·''-yi a`m-ɛ·ɢwɔ·̈-i ᴅɩ`tsö̆tɩt'ɔ'ɩ'sti | ᴜ'sönᴜ·'li
sun, Loc   beyond, direction, Loc   water, big, Loc   thou art staying   quickly

ᴅɔ·`t'aᵖlɛ·'ǫŋa' | asɢɩ·'nə | ᴜ·`ᴅö̆`nö̆'ɩ-ɢwɔ̃ᴅ' | ɢɛ·`sɛ̣.i' | tsù`tsɛ·'li
thou hast arisen,   ghost   it has been said, L   it is, App.   it is thine
facing us

ɢɛ·`sɛ̣.i' | ɩ·''yǫ·`st'anɩ·ɢa' | ᴅɩtsaᵖlɔsǫ·-ŋwɔ̃ᴅ w-ö̆ⁿ-ɩ''yǫ·`st'anɩ·ɢa' 5
it is, App. thou hast come to take   where thou hast passed, L   thither, again, thou hast
              it away   gone to take it away

ö̆·`ᴅal-ɛ·'ɢwɔ·̈i` w-ö̆ⁿ-`ɩ`skwanɩɢɔ·`t'anɩ·ɢa' ɩɢö̆·`wùlstɔ·'ᴅɩ-ɢwɔ̃ᴅ' |
lake, big, Loc.   thither, again, thou hast gone to store it up   who cares what happens to it L

ᴜ'sö̆''ɩ-ᴅə` nᴜ·`ᴅə`nö̆·'na | ᴜtsɩ·''nawa` nᴜ·`dət'anö̆·'ᴅə | nö̆`ⁿt'ǫn-
night, been   it has not been said   beyond it, stretched it has been said simul-   thou hast
                                                           taneously

ɛ·`lɩ·ɢa' | 'yă`'' | tsu'' | tsu'' | tsu'' | tsu''
come to do   sharply   (onom.)
it for him

(b) sɢɛ̌'' | nɔ·ᵘ'ɢwɔ̃ᴅ | 'a`t'ǫŋa·`nɩ·ɢa' tsɩ·ya' wɔ·`ᴅɩɢɛ·'' nö̆·'-
now, then!   now   thou hast come to listen Otter   brown   sun,

ᴅɔ·-yɩ·''-ᴅzə ɛ·`skɩ·'-ᴅzə  ö̆·`ᴅal-ɛ·'ɢwɔ·̈-i` ᴜ`wɔ·ɢɩ·'tli nɩ`ɢat'ö̆·' 10
Loc, direction this side, direct lake, big, Loc   foam   as high as

ɩ·yö̆·'ᴅə ᴅɩtsö̆·tɩt'ɔ'ɩ'sti | ɢɔ·'ᴜ'sti tsúnᴜ·'lti nɩɢɛ·`sönə·' asɢɩ·'nə
yonder   thou art staying   something   thou failest   never   ghost

ᴜ·`ᴅö̆`nö̆·̈i ᴜ·`ᴅa·nìt'ɛ·''lö̆·̈i  ɢɛ·`sɛ̣.i' | 'ö̆ⁿ-'iyö̆·`stanɩ·ɢa' ö̆·'ᴅa-
it has been said he has thought it   it is, App.   again, thou hast come to   lake,
                                                    take it away

l-ɛ·'ɢwɔ·̈-i ᴜ`wɔ·ɢɩ·'tli  nɩ`ɢat'ö̆·'.i' t·`t'ɔ·'ɩ`st'anɩ·ɢa' | 'yă'' |
big, Loc   foam   as high as   thou hast gone to put it to stay   sharply

tsu'' | tcu'' | tcu'' | tsu''
(Onom.)

(c)⁸² sɢɛ̌'' | nɔ·ɢwɔ̃ᴅ 'at'ǫ·ŋa·nɩ·ɢa tsɩ·ya sa`k'ɔ·ni · (etc.). 15
                                        Otter   blue

(d)⁸² sɢɛ̌'' | nɔ·ɢwɔ̃ᴅ 'at'ǫ·ŋa·nɩ·ɢa tsɩ·ya ö̆ⁿnaɢɛ̣· (etc.).
                                        Otter   black

⁸² Added by J. M., based on information given by Ay.

WHEN THEY HAVE PAINS APPEARING ABOUT IN DIFFERENT PLACES

FREE TRANSLATION

Now then! Ha, now thou hast come to listen, Red Otter, in the Sun Land beyond the great water thou art staying. Quickly thou hast arisen, facing us. It is merely what has become a ghost (that has caused it). It is thine. Thou hast come to take it away, merely by passing, (and) thou hast taken it away over yonder, and thrown it into the great lake. Who cares what happens to it? (There it shall remain) not for one night (only, but forever). Relief has been caused forthwith, thou hast come to do it for him. Sharply! Tsuh!

Now then! Now thou hast come to listen, Brown Otter, in the direction of the Sun Land, on this side of the great lake yonder where the foam is (piled up) high, thou art staying. Thou never failest in anything. It is what has become a ghost that has caused it. Thou hast come to take it away; thou hast gone to put it into the great lake where the foam is (piled) high. Sharply! Tsuh!

Now then! Now thou hast come to listen, Blue Otter (etc. . . .)

Now then! Now thou hast come to listen, Black Otter, (etc. . . .)

EXPLANATION

This formula is for the treatment of shifting or moving pains, called technically by a name which means "when they have pains appearing about in different places." The ceremony and treatment is the same as described under No. 66, with the addition that the medicine man imitates the cry of the animal addressed as he presses his thumb upon the sore spot. He also blows upon the place after each pressure.

The ailment in this case is ascribed to the influence of a ghost. The medicine man explained that the formula to be complete should have two more paragraphs, which he forgot to write down, addressing the Blue and the Black Otter, dwelling in the Cold Land and in the Night Land, respectively.

'ɪ·k'ȼwɪ·pɘ'ɪ·ɢɑ` | ʋlsɢɛ·'pɘ ʋ'`sönʋ·'li pɛ't'ŏ`tlt'ɑnɪ·ɢɑ' | ʋtsɪ''-
hast come and   it important   quickly   thou hast come to put   beyond it,
lifted them   it on its (legs)
nɑwɑ` ɑpö''nɪ·ɢɑ'
stretched   it has been said

'ɑ·`ɑ·.yĭ 'yă'
ʋ`sö'ɪ`pɘ'ɑ·' ʋtlɔ'ɑ' (4 times)
'ɑ'ɑ·.yĭ 'yă'   5

sɢȼ'' | sʋ''sɑɢwö⁰` ɢɛ'sȩ' ʋ'lsɢɛ·'pɘ 'ɪ`pʋnʋ·'y't'ɑnɪ'lȩ·.i'
now then   L   it is, App   it important   it which he has put
                                                    under, App
ɛ`pzɑlɪ·'.ɪ-ɑwŭ`-pɪ·nɔ' 'ɪɢɛ`sȩ·.i'
?   L (E),   E   it which is

(b) sɢȼ'' | 'ɑ-`nɔ·ɢwö⁰' 'ö''.stɑt'ö·`ŋɑ·`nɪ·ɢɑ' stɪ'skŭyɑ'
    now then   ha, now   again, you two have   you two men
                               come to listen

stɪɢɪ·`ɢɑɢȩ' pɪ`ststɪ·ɢɑ' | nö·pɔ·-'yi pɪ`stö`tlt'ɔ'ɪ'sti | stɪ-
you two red   you two little   sun, Loc   you two are staying   you

pɑ·'''wȩ't`-ɢɔ·ɢɑ' ʋ'sönʋ·'li pɔ·`tstɑᵖlȩ''öŋɑ' | ɢɑnisstɑ' pɪ·ɑɪ·'ɢɑ- 10
two wizards, E   quickly   you two have arisen   switch(es)   they
                     facing this way

ɢȩ' pɛ`stötlskɛ`wᵘst'ɑnɪ·ɢɑ' | ɢö·tsɑ`t'ɔtɘɑɪ·-'yɑ' pɛ`stɪk'ɑwɪ'-
red   they have come as a bunch   roughly, E   you two have come
      in your (hands)

pɔ'ɪ·ɢɑ` | ʋ'lsɢɛ·'pɘ nɪpʋ·'lt'ɑnö·'pɑɢwŭ·-pɪ·nɘ' nö''t'ɪ·stönɛ'-
and picked   it important   (he has) gotten up simultaneously   you two have come to
them up   L (=E), E

lɪ·ɢɑ' ʋsö''ɪ-yɪ·'-pzɔ` nö·nɔ' wɪ·pɛ·pʋ·`pɑnö·`pɑ·si' nö·`pɑpʋ·`k t'ɑ-
do it for   night, Loc, direction   trail(s)   they will lie stretched out   he never to look back
him

'ö·sti' nɪ·ɢɛ`sö·nɑ' | nö''t'ɪ·stönɛ`lɪ·ɢɑ' | ʋsö·ɪ·' ɪ·yö·'pɘ
again   never   you two have come   night, Loc   yonder
               to do it for him

nɪ-'t'ɪt'ɔ'ɪ·st'ɑnɪ·ɢɑ' [83] pɛ·t'ɑskɔlɔ·''ö'''t'ɑnö·' [84] ɔ·'nɪɛyi' | ʋtsɪ''- 15
there, thou hast put him   thou hast caused him to relinquish   after   beyond it,
there to stay   his grasps   T L
nɑwŭ-ɑwö⁰' nɪɢö·pɪsɢɛ`sti'
stretched, L   it will be said continuously

'ɑ`'ɑ·.yĭ 'yă'
ʋtsɪ'-nɑwɑ` ɢö`tltɑ'ɑⁿ' (4 times)
beyond it, stretched   It rubbed (?)

'ɑ''ɑ·.yĭ 'yă'
(c) sɢȼ'' | 'ɑ·-sʋ''sŭ-ɢwö⁰' ɢɛsȩ' ʋ'lsɢɛ·`pɘ pʋnʋ·`y't'ɑnlȩ·.i' 20
    now then   ha, L   it is, App   it important   he has put it under, L
ɛ`pzɑlɪ·'.ɪ-ɑwŭ`-pɪ·nɑ' 'ɪ·ɢɛsȩ'
   L (=E), E   it which is, App

sɢȼ'' | 'ɑ·-nɔ·ɢwö⁰' 'ö''stɑt'ö·ŋɑ·'nɪ·ɢɑ' stɪ'skŭyɑ' stɪ`sɑ'-
now then   ha, now   again, you two have come to listen   you two men   you two
k'ɔ·'ni pɪ`ststɪ·ɢɑ' ʋ''ö·pzɔ·'-yi` pɪ`stö`tlt'ɔ'ɪ'sti ɢɑnisstɑ' pɪ`sɑ'-
blue   you two little   cold, Loc.   you two are staying   switch(es)   they
k'ɔ·'ni pɛ`stötlskɛ`wᵘst'ɑnɪ·ɢɑ' (etc., as in b) | 'yă'
blue   they have come as a bunch   sharply
       into your (hands)

---

[83] A better form would be: wɪt'ɪst'ɔ'ɑst'ɑnɪɢɑ=you two have put him there, etc.

[84] A better form would be: pɛt'ɪstɪskɘlɔ ö''t'ɑnɪ·ɢɑ=you two have caused him, etc.

This is the Medicine for Their Sides

FREE TRANSLATION

> Ha-ha-yi! Sharply!
> All night it has been in it (?) (4 times).
> Ha-ha-yi! Sharply!

(a) Now, then! Ha, now thou hast come to listen, thou (who) art staying in the Sun Land, Red Man, thou powerful wizard! The red switches have become bundled in thy hands, roughly thou hast come and picked them up. Quickly hast thou come and put the important thing on its feet. Relief has been caused.

> Ha-ha-yi! Sharply!
> All night it has been in it (?)
> Ha-ha-yi! Sharply!

Now, then! It is merely sv$^{u\prime}$sa that has put the important thing under him; it is merely e$^\cdot$'dzalɩ'.i.

(b) Now, then! Ha, now you two in your turn have come to listen, you Two Little Red Men, you are staying in the Sun Land, you powerful wizards. Quickly you have arisen, facing this way. The red switches have become bundled in your hands, roughly you have come and picked them up. The important thing has gotten up forthwith, you have come to do it for him; his paths will stretch out toward the Night Land, never again he will look back; you have come and done it for him. You have taken him to the Night Land, and have put him there to stay, after you had forced him to let go his hold. Relief will be caused constantly.

> Ha-ha-yi! Sharply!
> Relief by rubbing (?).
> Ha-ha-yi! Sharply!

Now, then! Ha, it is merely sv‘sa that has put the important thing under him; it is merely e·dzalɩ·.i.

(c) Now, then! Ha, now, you two in your turn have come to listen, you two Little Blue Men, you are staying in the Cold Land. The blue switches have become bundled in your hands (*etc., as in (b)*). Sharply!

EXPLANATION

This is for treating a pain in the side. The medicine man from whom it was obtained could assign no particular cause for the sickness but another practitioner declared that it was due to tc‘skɔ·'ya or insects which might have been put into the sick man's body by a hostile conjurer. In accordance with this theory the second medicine man called upon the birds to come and eat the [insects].

Neither of them could explain the words sv‘sa or ɛdzalɩ·i, the names given to the disease spirit [see p. 232, nor could any of the medicine men consulted during the editor's stay with the tribe give any information on this subject].

The disease spirit is driven out by the Red Man, the Two Little Red Men, and the Two Little Blue Men, all of whom carry threatening switches in their hands, with which to thrash the intruder. The formula as here given consists of three parts, each containing a song and a prayer. It is quite probable that it had originally a fourth part, which has been lost [in the course of tradition]. The treatment, in regard to which both authorities agreed, consists of a simple rubbing with the warm hands, as indicated in the last song. The medicine man sings each verse while holding his hands over the fire, and recites the following paragraph while rubbing the sore spot on the patient's body, blowing four times upon the place at the close of each paragraph.

46

Ï'a'	nǫ·ˊwɔ·t꞉i'	υˋnaDzɛˋnōˋɩsɛˋō'.[i 85]	tsaˋndɩskɔⁿ(.i' 85)
this	to cure with	when it does it to them	that which they call, H

k꞉ŭ́lsɛˊDzi'	υˋskwa-ye·lōⁿˊꞌi	υ·skwat꞉iˋ
(Honey locust)	short body—Loc	they have it (sol) at the top

This (is) to Treat (Them) with When "It Affects Them in Such a Way," as They Usually Call It

FREE TRANSLATION

Honey locust; venus looking-glass; red buckeye.

EXPLANATION

This is a prescription to cure an aggravated form of dyspepsia or indigestion caused by overeating. The abdomen becomes swollen and the patient has an insatiable appetite, but constantly loses flesh.

The medicine used is the bark of k꞉ŭ́lsɛˊDzi, *Gleditsia triacanthos* L., honey locust, and the roots of υˋskwayɛ·lōⁿꞌi, *Specularia perfoliata* (L.) A.DC., Venus looking-glass; υˊskwat꞉iˋ, *Aesculus pavia* L., Red buckeye, steeped in warm water overnight. Early next morning the medicine man goes to the stream with the patient, who bathes himself all over, and then drinks a little of the infusion, bathing himself from head to foot with the remainder. The operation is probably repeated, if necessary [according to the regular pattern].

---

[85] Emendations by W.; recorded by editor.

47

ṣ'a'   ɩ'na'Dŏⁿ   v'nɩskŏtltsŏ''ḷi   aDa'nö·'wɔ·t'ḭ'
this   snake   they have bitten him   to cure anyone with

sGě''' | 'a·'nɔ·ᵘawŏᵘ' 'a't'öṇa·'nɩ·Ga' | Gɩ·na' tsune·'Gŏⁿ |
Now, then!   Ha, now   thou hast come to listen   Fawn   thou white

(ɩ·na'Doawŏᵘ') Gese'⁸⁶) Dɩ·k'ayɪGa' tsö·Nɩ̣ɩ̣·'Dɔ De·'Dɪ·Göwe·'ᵘw'sù-
snake, L   it is, App. tooth   they everliving   he has advanced them

Dadɩ·'lę̣·i' | nöɪɔ-ṣi' Dɪ·'Dana·'ᵘwuDe·Gö·' | Dɩ·k'ayɪ·'Ga' Dɔ'ᵗᵘsŏⁿ
towards him   trail-Loc   it has laid itself about   tooth   weak
App.

5 De·'Galɔ·'tsɩ·Ga' | 'a-'nɔ·awŏᵘ' Gɩ·'na tsune·'Gŏⁿ v'sönɪ·'li
they have become   Ha, now   Fawn   thou white   quickly
broken

a'ˢskwanɪ·'tsaDŏⁿ tsu'Döṇɩ̣e'lɩ·Ga
It sucked   thou hast come to
                   do it for him

sGě''' | 'a-'nɔ·awŏᵘ' 'a't'öṇa·'nɩ·Ga | t'ɩ·'yɔʷ'aᴅ'li tsune·'Gɔ |
Now, then!   ha, now   thou hast come to   lizard   thou white
                          listen

'ɩDa·'ᵘwęɩ̣' | ɩ·'na'Dɔ·awŏᵘ' Gesę' Dɩ·k'ayɪ·'Ga' tsö·Nɩ̣ɩ̣·'Dɔ De·'DɪGö-
thou wizard   snake, L   it is,   tooth   they everliving   he has
                                 App.

we·'w'sù'Dadɩ·'lę̣.i' | nönɔ-ṣi' Dɪ·'Dana·'ᵘwuDe·Gö' | Dɩ·k'ayɪ·'Ga'
advanced them toward   trail, Loc it has laid itself about   tooth
him, App.

10 Dɔ'ᵗsŏⁿ De·'Galɔ·'tsɩ·Ga' | 'a·'nɔ·awŏᵘ' t'ɩ·'yɔ·'aᴅli tsune·'Gŏⁿ
weak   they have become   ha, now   lizard   thou white
         broken

v'sönɪ·'li a'ˢskwanɪ·'tsaDŏⁿ aDŏ'nɩ·Ga'
quickly   it sucked   it has been said

This is the Medicine if Snakes Have Bitten Them

FREE TRANSLATION

Now then! Ha, now thou hast come to listen, thou White Fawn-Imitator. It was but a snake (which) has advanced its everliving teeth to (bite) him, as it was lying stretched out about the path. The teeth have been broken and made weak. Ha, now Thou White Fawn-Imitator, quickly thou hast come to suck it for him.

Now then! Ha, now thou hast come to listen, thou White Lizard, thou wizard. It was but a snake (which) has advanced its everliving teeth to (bite) him as it was lying stretched out about the path. The teeth have been broken and made weak. Ha, now, thou White Lizard, quickly it has been sucked.

EXPLANATION

This is a formula to cure an actual snakebite with, not a "dreamed" one. (See p. 176.) Ay. had procured it originally from another medicine man, who had died some years previously. He was unable to give the meaning of the word Gɩ·na' [but this was held by other

---
[86] Interpolated by J. M.

medicine men consulted to be an abbreviation of Gɩ‵na aʽⁿˈyɛˑlɩˑsGi, a mythic kind of serpent which owes its name to its habit of imitating (aʽⁿˈyɛˑlɩˑˈsGi = he imitates, Hab.) the bleat of a fawn ((a)Gɩˑnaˈ) so as to ensnare its mother.

On hearing the bleating, the doe, believing her young calls her, hurries to the spot, and the mythic serpent catches the artless animal, by merely striking out its huge tongue, and swallows it. [The extraordinary "licking" powers of this monster is without any doubt the reason why it is being appealed to in this formula to come and lick or suck the wound.]

The Lizard meant is the alligator lizard (*Sceloporus undulatus*) which has the habit of alternately puffing out and drawing in its throat, as though sucking, when basking in the sun. There is an obvious consistency in calling upon these two animals, in accordance with their nature to suck the wound.

The medicine is tobacco juice [ordinary chewing tobacco being used]. The medicine man recites the first paragraph while chewing the tobacco, and then applying his mouth to the wound, sucks out the poisonous matter or Daloˑˈni, "yellow." Then, taking a fresh quid, he recites the second paragraph, and again sucks the wound in the same manner. The whole ceremony is then repeated, so as to make four suckings, which are said to be sufficient in ordinary cases. The medicine man holds the tobacco in his mouth while sucking, and does not, as might be supposed, suck out the poison first, and then apply the tobacco juice. Before chewing tobacco, as it is now used, was introduced by white traders, the medicine men probably used tsoˑˈlaGayǫ̈ˑˈⁿli, *Nicotiana rustica* L., wild tobacco [which has now become so scarce with the Cherokee that it is only used in minute quantities in certain of the more important ceremonies. (See p. 75.)].

48

ɩˈaˈ	vˑˈndɩlɛˈˈöⁿˈsGö̤ˑˈ	aˈDaˈnö̤ˑˈwɔˑtˈiˈ				
this	whenever they have it hot	to cure anyone with				

sGɛ̤̈ˈ	ˈaˑ.ʋsöˑˈ-i	tsöˈtɩtˈɔˈɩˈsti	aˈtsutiˈ	ö̈ˈnaˈGɛ̨ˑ		Dɔˑˈtsʋlɛˈ̌-
Now then	ha, night, Loc	thou art staying	fish	black		he has got up,
nɛ̨ˑ.iˈ	ɩˈG-ayɛˈˈˈli	vˈsöˈˈ-ɩDəˈ	vˈDö̤ˑNɩˑˈlɛ̨ˑ.iˈ		nö̤Dɔˑ,ˈ-yi	Dɩˈtsötɬ-
facing us, App	day, middle	night, been	he has come and done it, App		sun, Loc	thou art
tˈɔˈɩˈsti	aˈtsutiˈ	vnɛˈˈGə		DɔˑˈDɩyʋˈlɛˈnɛ̨ˑ.iˈ [87]	ɩˈG-ayɛˈˈˈli	
staying	fish	white		he has arisen, facing us, App	day, middle	
ˈtˈsɔⁿ.iˈ	vˈlDɩDɩˈ-tlə-Gwö̈ⁿˈ [88]		ayɔˑˈwɛˈsɔˑtłö̤ˑˈDə	DɔˑˈDzʋlɛˈnɛ̨ˑ.iˈ	5	
this other	near by, direct., L		he resting as he goes along	he has got up, facing us, App		

---

[87] Archaic form; same meaning as DɔˑDzʋlɛˈnɛ̨ˑ.i (line 5).

[88] W. D. form; C. D.=vˑlɩɩˑDzəGwöⁿ.

ɩ‵ᴳ-ayɛ‵′ˡli	v‵‵ᴅɩlɛ‵′ᴳi	ᴅɛ.v‵‵natsɔ‵ɩ‵st‵anɩ‵lɛ‵.i′	‵a‵‵-na‵na′
day, middle	Heat	they caused them to come together, App	ha, there
v‵sɔ̈‵′-ɩᴅə‵	v‵ndǫ̈‵‵nɛ‵tlɩ‵lɛ‵.i′	yö‵′wi a‵ᴅayö‵′lt‵awa‵	v‵ndǫ̈‵‵nɛ‵-
night, been	they have come to do it, App	human being glimpsy view	they have come
tlɩ‵lɛ‵.i′	vᴅzɔ‵‵nǫ̈ᴅzɛ‵′ᴅə-ᴳwɔ̈ⁿ‵	v‵ndǫ̈‵‵nɛ‵tlɩ‵lɛ‵.i′	v‵ᴅɩlɛ‵′ᴳi
to do it, App	he full of admiration, L.	they have come to do it, App	Heat
v‵nᴅzɔ‵‵ɔ̈ⁿ′t‵anɩ‵lɛ‵.i′	tsvyɛ‵‵tlɩlɔ̈‵′ɩ-ᴳwɔ̈ⁿ‵	‵ɩᴳɛ‵‵sɛ‵.i′	
they have let it down, App	he has been overcome, L	it which is, App	

5 sᴳɛ̈‵′ | v‵‵ǫ̈‵ᴅzɔ‵′-yi | ᴅɩtsɔ̈‵tlt‵ɔ‵ɩs′ti | ‵ɩ‵skuya′ | sa‵k‵ɔ‵′ni
Now then | cold, Loc | thou art staying | thou man | blue

‵ɛ‵ᴳwɔ‵ɩ‵′	a′tsutɩ-ᴳwɔ̈ⁿ‵	ᴳɛ‵sɛ‵′ v‵‵ᴅɩlɛ‵′ᴳi	ᴅv‵ksɔ‵‵ɔ̈ⁿ′tɛ‵.i
thou big	fish, L	it is, App Heat	he has let it down, App
‵a‵-nɔ‵‵ᴳwú-ᴅɩ‵′nə	ᴅɛ‵‵t‵askəlɔ‵‵ɔ̈ⁿt‵a‵nɩ‵ᴳa′		vsɔ̈‵‵ɩ-yɩ‵′-ᴅzə
ha, now, E	thou hast come to make him relinquish his grasps		night, Loc., direction
nǫ̈‵nɔ‵i′	wɩ‵ᴅɛ‵ᴅv‵‵ᴅanǫ̈‵′ɔ̈ⁿ′si′	‵ɩ‵lɔ̈‵ɩ‵′tlə⁸⁹	ɩ‵yǫ̈‵′⁹⁰	aᴅayǫ̈‵′l-
trail(s)	they lie stretched out toward the distance	somewhere	yonder	glimpsy
t‵awa‵	ᴅö‵‵ᴅö‵ɴ‵ɛ‵‵ɛ‵sti′	na‵′na-ᴳwɔ̈ⁿ‵	v‵sɔ̈-‵ɩᴅə‵	wɩ‵-ᴅö‵ᴅö‵‵ɴ‵ɛ=
view	he will do it for him	there, L (=E)	night, been	there he will do it

10 ‵ɛ‵sti′ | ‵a‵-nɔ‵ᴳwɔ̈ⁿ′ | wɔ̈‵tlt‵ɔ‵ɩ‵st‵anɩ‵ᴳa′ | | ᴅɛ‵t‵askəlɔ‵‵ɔ̈ⁿ-
for him | ha, now | it has gone there to stay | | thou hast made him relinquish his grasps

t‵an-ö‵′.i	vtsɩ‵′nawú-ᴳwɔ̈ⁿ‵	nɩᴳö‵‵ᴅɩsᴳɛ‵sti′	vsɔ̈‵′-ɩᴅə‵	nv‵‵ᴅə‵-
T L	beyond it, stretched, L	it will be said continuously	night, been	it has not
nö‵′nɔ	vtsɩ‵′-nawa‵	aᴅɔ̈‵‵nɩ‵ᴳa′	¹yǎ‵′	
been said	beyond it, stretched	it has been said	sharply	

This is the Medicine When They Have it Hot

FREE TRANSLATION

Now, then! Ha, in the Night Land thou art staying, White Fish. He has arisen, facing us, in the middle of the day, and at night he has done it. In the Sun Land thou art staying, White Fish. He has arisen, facing us, in the middle of the day. Quite near this other one he was resting, it seems, (as) he rose up, facing us, in the middle of the day. They have caused the Heats to come together. There at night they have come to do it. Where human beings (live) and move about flittingly, they have come to do it, it seems. They have come and done it, full of envy. He has been overcome by the Heat which they caused to come down.

Now, then! In the Cold Land thou art staying, thou great Blue Man. It is a mere fish that has caused Heat to come down. Ha, but now thou hast come to force him to let go his hold. His paths lie stretched out toward the Night Land. Somewhere in the distance he will be (seen) flittingly carrying on (his activity), but there it will be doing it for a night (only). Ha, now, (in the Night Land) it has gone to stay; thou hast come to force him to let go his hold. Relief

---

⁸⁹ W. D. form; C. D.: ‵ɩlɔ̈‵‵ɩᴅzɔ̈ⁿ′.   ⁹⁰ Abbreviation for ɩyǫ̈‵ᴅə.

indeed will be caused constantly, (and) not for one night (only, but forever). Relief has been caused. Sharply!

EXPLANATION

The medicine used with this formula to cure fever attacks is a decoction of ᴅaleꞌᴅa tsv·ʻntʻənõⁿˋ, *Linum usitatissimum* L., common flax, with which the patient is washed, the medicine man pouring the liquid upon the head and allowing it to run down over the body of the sick man.

The medicine man first recites the whole formula, then applies the liquid, and finally blows his breath four times upon the head and shoulders of the patient. This is repeated four times at each application, and the ceremony is repeated four times before noon, and for four days, if necessary. The Cherokee medicine men are said to be skillful in treating fevers, and the patient commonly experiences speedy relief.

This formula is again a beautiful exemplification of the Cherokee disease theories: the fever is caused by the fish, i. e., the fish-ghosts, not by the living fish, which are harmless. The Black Fish rises up from the great lake in the west, or "Night Land," and is joined by the White Fish from the east, or "Sun Land." The two go along side by side until they come to the abodes of men, or in the words of the formula ["where human beings (live) and move flittingly about"]. Here they pause overhead and look down, filled with envious admiration. From the east and from the west they bring two spirits of Heat, and send them down upon the people to parch and wither them as with a hot blast.

But now the medicine man calls upon the spirit of Cold, the Blue Man of the Cold Land or north, to drive out the Heat. He comes at once and breaks the hold of the disease spirit upon the sick man, and drives him on toward the great lake of the west, where all disease is banished. This result is not attained by one effort, for the disease spirit is seen ["flittingly, carrying on his activity in other places"]. But finally it is pushed into the great lake by its pursuer, where it must forever remain.

49

ï'a'	ᴅawɩ·ˋnéꞌïi⁹¹	v·ˋnɩtłö̞·ŋö̞·ˋ.i⁹²			
this	they living in the wood	whenever they are ill			

ᴅa·ᵘwəᴅzɩ·ʼlə	kʻv̓ˋwɩyv·ʻsti	ɩ·ᴅéꞌïa	ᴅɩ·ˋtłastəɢɩ·ʼsti		
(Slippery Elm)	(Sycamore)	(limetree)	(foxglove)		

| sɔ.iⁿʼ | sɔ·ᵘɢwõ̞ᵘʼ | v̓ˋlyɛˋnö̞·ʼⁿᴅə | wɔ·ʻtɩɢɛ·ⁿʼ | nɔ.tsɩ·ʼ-ïi | tsv·ᵗⁱyɛꞌɢɔ·ʼ |
| other | one | it has grown up | brown | pine, Loc | they stand up (II) |

---

⁹¹ Contracted out of ăʼtă-aʻwɩ·ni-anéꞌïi wood, underneath, they are living.
⁹² W. Dial. form; W. Dial. -tł->C. Dial. -ts-.

Dɩ·ʻtɫastəGɩ·ʼsti | Dɔ·ʻᵘlatʼsi aʻʻwɩ·-ˡyaʼ tsɩDɛʻʻGa·.Gẃuʼtʻa ɩyʋʻsʼti
(foxglove) (Red oak) meat real that which they are like
sticking on it (l)

tsɩʻGɛ·sǫʼ sɔʻ.ɩ-Nǚⁿʼ tʻaᵖlaʼ tsɩDʋ·ʻwɛʻDaʻtɫalǫ·ʼ tsʋ·ʻnstɩ·ʼGa
that which other and (white oak) it which lying along, H they small
is, H

tsɩʻki | na.skiʼ Gɔ·ʻtsötɫtiʼ |
it is this it (sol) put in
with it

This (is) When They Are Ill (by) Those Living in the Forest

FREE TRANSLATION

Slippery elm, sycamore, limetree, foxglove, another (of this kind) which has one brown stalk (and) which grows in the pine woods, red oak which is the one that (looks as) if pieces of meat were sticking to it; and furthermore, the white oak that (looks) as if it had little (blowgun) arrow tufts; this (all together) has to be put into it.

EXPLANATION

This is a prescription for the treatment of diarrhea or dysentery; this, the medicine men assert, is caused by "those living in the forest," i. e., the bear, deer, rabbit, and other game; [only quadrupeds are held responsible for this disease, in adults. If, however], children suffer from it, it is ascribed to the influence of birds. (See No. 78, p. 281.) The prescription here given furnishes a good illustration of the connection between the disease theory and the treatment as regards selection of the medicine and the taboo.

The symptoms are described as a frothy discharge from the bowels, accompanied by griping pains in the abdominal region. The patient is required to drink for four days a decoction compounded of seven ingredients—another instance of the combination of the sacred numbers 4 and 7—which completely purges the system, after which recovery follows.

The purgative elements of the decoction are Da·ʻᵘwəDzɩ·ʼlə, *Ulmus fulva* Michx., slippery elm, red elm; kʻʋʻwɩyʋʻʻsti, *Platanus occidentalis* L., sycamore, buttonwood; ɩ·Dɛʻ̓a, *Tilia americana* L., limetree, whitewood, basswood, of all of which the inner bark is used; while the two varieties of Dɩ·ʻtɫastəGɩ·ʼsti, *Dasystoma virginica* (L.), Britton, smooth false foxglove, are said to have a sedative and healing effect.

The two varieties of oak, Dɔ·ʻᵘlaʼtsi, *Quercus rubra* L., red oak, tʻaᵖlaʼ, *Quercus alba* L., white oak, are used solely on account of their connection with the mythic disease agents, the game animals of the forest. The red oak, "which looks as though pieces of meat are sticking on it," is one of which the twigs have numerous excrescences or knots, resulting from the stings of insects, and suggesting to the Indian the idea of pieces of venison or bear meat strung upon a stick to be barbecued.

By the "little (blowgun) arrow tufts" on the white oak are meant the swellings or buds on the suckers which grow up from around the base of the tree, as compared to the thistledown at the end of a blowgun arrow. These suckers are considered to resemble in appearance the jointed sections of a rabbit's intestines, and thence to have an occult influence over a disease which may have been caused by the rabbits. The medicine man selects seven of these suckers and three or four of the knotty red oak twigs, each about a foot long, and puts them into the vessel with the decoction.

The taboo includes salt and hot food as usual, together with greasy food of any kind, for the reason that grease, being derived from animal sources, would neutralize the effect of the medicine, intended to counteract the influence of those animals.

50

υyǫ·'.i   v·`nɩ‛a`yö̞·ⁿlö̞'‛i   nö̞·`wɔ·`t‛i'   ‛ï'a'
different   they have inhaled   to cure with   this

sɛ·`lɩkwɔ·'ya    Gö̞`lkwɔ·'Gi   nυ·‛¹yɛ‛Gö̞·'   ɩyυ`stɩ̲‛aⁿ'    sɔ·`Gwɔⁿ'-‛i
(eryngo)   seven   full grown   like, each   one, Loc

THIS (IS) TO TREAT (THEM) WITH (WHEN) THEY HAVE INHALED BAD (ODORS)

FREE TRANSLATION

Eryngo, seven full-grown (stalks) each (having) one (stalk) where (it grows).

EXPLANATION

This prescription is for the cure of nausea or stomach disorder caused by disagreeable inhalations, as from a dead body (human or animal) or any fetid matter.

The patient drinks a warm infusion of seven sɛ·`lɩkwɔ·'ya, *Eryngium virginianum* Lam., Eryngo plants, which produces vomiting.

The infusion is strained before use, and drunk once every morning for four days. Hot food is prohibited during this period.

There is no ceremony, but a peculiar injunction that the seven plants selected must each have but a single stalk. Such plants are rather difficult to find, as the Eryngo usually sends up a number of stalks from each root. (See p. 54.)

51

tsaꞌⁿdaʔkt'ꞋeꞋGöⁿNˑŝⁿ   tsʋꞌⁿalɛꞋnöˑꞋⁿDo   tsaꞌⁿskɩˑtsGaꞋ
it which they are restricting   they are (different)   they dream them
themselves, and   kinds

ᴅɩꞋⁿᴅaɴɛˑꞋlowɔˑꞋⁿski   k'ʋꞋw'yʋꞋꞌsti   söˑⁿtiwüꞋⁿli   tsɩˑwʋᴅɛˑt'ɔˑꞋ.i
(wild Hydrangea)   (sycamore)   (raspberry)   it which, it has
                                                        come down, it

ɩꞋt.tsɛꞋꞋi   tsʋꞋⁿnastɛˑⁿöꞋꞋi   aɪnaꞋ-yi   ɴɩGaꞋꞋᴅᴏ | aꞋNꞏowaꞋGɩ-Nˑŝⁿ
(red alder) they have roots   water, Loc all   cloth   and

aꞋwɩˑꞋni   ʋꞋNꞏʋwʃⁿ   ꞋꞋwaꞋsöⁿ   aˑꞋ.sɛꞋꞋiꞋ   tsʋˑꞋꞋyɔꞋɩstiꞋ
underneath her dress   itself   it must   she will do without

And ('This is for) When They are Under Restrictions (and)
They Dream of All Sorts (of Things)

FREE TRANSLATION

Wild hydrangea, sycamore, raspberry (a branch of which) has come down (and taken root again), red alder, all having their roots in the water.

And she will have to give up her own undergarment (as a fee).

EXPLANATION

This prescription is for use when a woman, during her catamenial period dreams of bringing forth a bear, a litter of puppies, or something of a similar kind, out of the ordinary course of nature. tsaꞌⁿdaʔkt'ꞋeꞋGöꞋ.i literally: "when they are restricting themselves," is the technical term for being subject to the taboo rules (cf. GaˑktꞋöⁿᴅo, "restricted"); although it is also used to indicate the restrictions to which either a male or a female patient may be subjected in case of illness, it is, in this connection, understood to refer to the injunctions to be observed by a woman during her menstrual periods.

No formula is used, but the prescription introduces several interesting features of Cherokee medical practice.

The patient drinks a decoction of the roots of ᴅɩꞋⁿᴅaɴɛˑꞋlowɔˑꞋⁿski, *Hydrangea arborescens* L., wild hydrangea; k'ʋꞋw'yʋꞋꞌsti, *Platanus occidentalis* L., sycamore, buttonwood; ɩꞋt.tsɛꞋꞋi, *Alnus rugosa* (Du Roi) Spreng., smooth alder, to which is added the root of an "inverted" raspberry branch söˑtawüꞋⁿli, *Rubus strigosus* Michx., wild red raspberry. Also, *Rubus occidentalis* L., black raspberry; thimbleberry.

As stated, not the root of the main plant is used but that of a branch that has taken root a second time. (Pl. 6, *a*.) Such a double-rooted raspberry is an important factor in a number of prescriptions, although the medicine man was unable to assign any reason for the fact. [From information obtained at a later date by Mr. Mooney, it appears that a medicine man thought this kind of root was used], "because it is more bitter than the main root." [I did not find this view confirmed and would be inclined to think that it owes its popularity merely to such considerations as are discussed on page 54.]

The roots selected are such as dip into the water from trees and shrubs overhanging the stream. Such water-growing roots are also frequently specified in the prescriptions [especially in those dealing with troubles of the urinary passages and related ailments. Medicine men can not now advance any explanation of this peculiar injunction; the idea is probably that the unimpeded contact of these roots with the water renders them effective in the treatment of organs in which the flow of liquid (urine, catamenial blood, etc.) is laborious and defective.]

By a loose wording of the sentence this provision ("all having their roots in the water") is made to apply also to the raspberry, which is not intended.

All the roots, however, have to be taken from the east side of the tree.

The decoction is drunk several times during the day, in doses of about half a pint at a time, for four days, and affords relief by acting as an emetic and a purgative.

The patient abstains from all food the first day until sunset, the second day until noon, the third day until late in the morning, and on the fourth morning eats breakfast with the rest of the household. She abstains also from salt and hot food while under treatment.

For his pay it is specified that the medicine man shall receive the undergarment of the patient. [This may be some article of dress which we also would call an undergarment, such as a petticoat, a chemise, etc., but these luxuries are not yet generally introduced among the Cherokee, so that the undergarment is generally an older dress. Some girls and women wear three or four dresses, one on top of the other.]

52

ï'a'	ʋ`nιDzι·'ya	Dι`Da'nö·'wɔ·t'i`
this	they (are) worms	to cure people with

sGë̌·''	'a`-nɔ·Gwö⁰'	ʋ`sɘnʋ·'li	'a`t'ö̤·'ŋa·'nι·Ga'	Dawι'skula`
Now then!	ha, now	quickly	thou hast come to listen	Flint

tsAstι·'Ga	ɔ·'Dali`	tsɘ`stιGɔ'-ï	Dι`tsö`tłt'ɔ'ι'sti`	'ιDa·'ᵘwɛ:li'
thou little	mountain(s)	they are little, Loc	thou art staying	thou wizard

GaDɔ'	tsunʋ·'łti	nιGɛ·'sö̤·na'		ʋ`sö̤nʋ·'li	'ι`ksɔ'ᵘsι·Ga'
what	thou fallst	never		quickly	thou hast come down

ʋ`tławɔ·tu'tłi ⁹⁴	ast'ö̤·'	Dɛ·'ιDɔ'ᴶᵒsι·Ga'		tsckɔ·'ya	ʋ`ska·sɛ'ᵘti·	5
swampy marsh	edge	thou has come and halted		insects	frightful	

⁹⁴ W. D. form; C. D.=(ʋ)sawɔ·tu'tłi.

248 BUREAU OF AMERICAN ETHNOLOGY [BULL. 99

u'nanυGɔ·'tsɛ̈i' | υDzu·'ya-Gwɔ̈ ᵘ' Gɛ'sɛ̈.i' | tsɔ̈'tIsta·'y'tu-
he has come out, App   it worm, L   it is, App.   (it is) what
                                                           thou eatest
Gwu-'Dι·'nɔ` 'ιGɛ'sɛ̈.i' | nιGȍ'wayɛ·'lənɔ̈ ᵘ'ɔ̈ ᵘ'sGɛ·'stι-Gwɔ̈ ᵘ'
L (=E), E   it which is, App   a likeness of it will be left, L
tsa'lɔs-ȍ·'.i` | ɔ̈ ⁿⁱ'pali u·'ndɔ̈'nɔ̈"ιGwɔ̈ ᵘ' 'ιGɛ'sɛ̈.i' | u'nιDzι·'ya-
thou hast   animal-ghost(s) they have said it, L it which is, App they (are)
passed, T L

Gwɔ̈ ᵘ'   Gɛ'sɛ̈.i' | t'a`ᵖlιnɛ·'ˡGwɔ̈ ᵘ'   'ȍ-ɲɛ·'t'ɔ̈tIsta·'y't'anιGa'
worms, L it is, App.   second, L   again, thou hast come and eaten
                                         them as thou goest by

5 nιGȍ·'wayɛ·'lənɔ̈ ᵘ''ɔ̈ ᵘ'sGɛ·'stι-Gwɔ̈ ᵘ' tsa'lɔs-ȍ·'(.i⁹⁵) υtsι'-'nawu-Gwɔ̈ ᵘ'
  a likeness of it will be left, L   thou has passed, T L   beyond it, stretched, L

nιGȍ·'DιsGɛ·sti' | υtsι'-'nawa` aDɔ̈"nιGa'
it will be said   beyond it, stretched it has been said
continually

(b) sGɛ̈" | 'a`-nɔ·Gwɔ̈ ᵘ'  u'sȍnu'li  'a`t'ȍɲa·'nιGa' Dawι'skulə`
   Now then   ha, now   quickly   thou has come to listen   Flint
sa'k'ɔ·'ni tsɔ̈'tIti su'lυ·y-ɛ·'Gwɔ-'ⱡi Dι'tsɔ̈'tIt'ɔ'ι'sti` (etc. . .).
blue   thy abode swampy laurel thicket, thou art staying
                      big, Loc

(c) sGɛ̈" | 'a`-nɔ·Gwɔ̈ ᵘ'  u'sȍnu'li  'a`t'ȍɲa·'nιGa' | Da'Gȍtlɢa'
   Now then   ha, now   quickly   thou hast come to listen   Goose
10 sa'k'ɔ·'ni | Galȍ'ldi tsɔ̈'tItɔ'ι'sti` (etc. . . .).
blue   above   thou art staying

(d) sGɛ̈" | 'a`-nɔ·Gwɔ̈ ᵘ'  u'sȍnu'li  'a`t'ȍɲa'nιGa' | u·'tli'
   Now then   ha, now   quickly   thou hast come to listen   Swan
tsune·'Gə | Galȍ'ldi tsɔ̈'tItɔ'ι'sti (etc. . . .)
thou white   above   thou art staying

(e) sGɛ̈" | 'a`-nɔ·Gwɔ̈ ᵘ'  u'sȍnu'li  'a`t'ȍɲa'nιGa' | Gυwι's-
   Now then   ha, now   quickly   thou has come to listen   Bit-
kυwi` sa'k'ɔ·'ni | Galȍ'ldi tsɔ̈'tItɔ'ι'sti (etc. . . .).
tern   blue   above   thou art staying

15 (f) sGɛ̈" | 'a`-nɔ·Gwɔ̈ ᵘ'  u'sȍnu'li  'a`t'ȍɲa'nιGa' | k'a`-
    Now then   ha, now   quickly   thou has come to listen   Sand-
nȍ'stυ"wa sa'k'ɔ·'ni Galȍ'ldi tsɔ̈'tItɔ'ι'sti (etc. . . .).
piper   blue   above   thou art staying

THIS IS THE MEDICINE FOR WORMS

FREE TRANSLATION

Now then! Ha, now thou hast come to listen, thou Little Flint!
where the little mountains are thou art staying. Thou wizard;
what dost thou ever fail in? Quickly thou hast come down. At
the edge of the ever-swampy marsh thou hast come to halt. It
came out (as a) terrible insect (but) it was a mere worm. But
that is the very thing thou eatest. A mere likeness of it will be
left when thou wilt have passed. They are merely what have
become animal ghosts. They are mere worms. (And) a second
time thou hast again come and eaten them as thou goest by; a mere
likeness of it will be left when thou wilt have passed. Relief will
be caused constantly. Relief has been caused.

---

⁹⁵ Emendation by editor.

Now then! Ha, now thou hast quickly come to listen, Blue Flint, thou art staying at thy abode, the big swampy laurel thicket (*etc.* . . .).
Now then! Ha, now thou hast quickly come to listen, Blue Goose, thou art staying above (*etc.* . . .).
Now then! Ha, now thou hast quickly come to listen, thou White Swan, thou art staying above (*etc.* . . .).
Now then! Ha, now thou hast quickly come to listen, Blue Bittern, thou art staying above (*etc.* . . .).
Now then! Ha, now thou hast quickly come to listen, Blue Sandpiper, thou art staying above (*etc.* . . .).

EXPLANATION

This is another formula for removing worms and closely resembles No. 32 (p. 213), both in principle and treatment.

It consists of six paragraphs, the first two being addressed to the Flint and the other to four varieties of birds. The wording of the six paragraphs in the original is almost identical, the only differences, except as regards the spirits invoked, being such as might easily arise in transcribing. The complete formula occupies a considerable time in the recital. The goose, Daˋgōˋtlɢa' addressed in the third paragraph is the American white-fronted goose (*Anser albifrons gambeli*). The medicine man could give no reason for invoking the flint, but this was explained by another practitioner, who stated that in a worm formula used by himself he put a flint arrowhead into the decoction and prayed to it under the name of Flint to cut the worms to pieces with its sharp edge. In Irish folklore a prehistoric flint arrowhead is used in the same way.

The medicine used is a decoction of the roots of ɢɩˑ'ɢaɢę`ˋ aˋdzɩˑlōⁿ'ski, *Spigelia marilandica* L., Indian pink; k'kwę̌'' ʋˋlasʋˋla, *Cypripedium parviflorum* Salisb., Small yellow ladyslipper; and of the bark of ʋ'skwùtaˋ ʋstɩˑ'ɢa.

The decoction is sweetened with honey or with the pods of the honey locust, k'ùˋlsę'dzi, *Gleditsia triacanthos* L. (See p. 56.)

The medicine is given for four consecutive days, in the morning and at night, the general ceremony being the same as described in No. 32. The final pass is around and then downward. The effects of the medicine usually make themselves felt on the second day. The taboo consists of water, eggs, and greasy food. The patient drinks nothing but the decoction while under treatment.

53

ʔi'a'   υ'N̥awa'tṏⁿ'ṏⁿ'ski'   a'Daʻnö·'wɔ·tʻi'
this   it makes them as if   to cure anyone with
        clothed, Hab

sGě̆'' | ʻa'-nɔ·Gwȫᴅ' Gᴇʻ'¹yₐ-Gυ·'Gə' Dυ'Da·N̥tʻᴇ''ɛlȫ̥'   'ι-'Gᴇ'sᴇ'i' |
Now then | ha, now   woman, E   she (E) has thought it   it which is, App

υ'Dιlᴇ''Gι-Gwȫᴅ'   ʻι-Dυ'ksɔ·'ȫⁿʻtʻanι'lᴇ·.i' | ayᴇ·'lιGɔ·'Gι-Gwü'-Dι·nə'
Heat   L   it which she (E) has   simulator,   L   E
                   let down, App

υyᴇ·'lȫ'nȫ'ʻi   Gᴇ·'sᴇ·.i' |
he has made   it is, App.
it like

5 sGě̆'' | ʻa'-nɔ·Gwȫᴅ'   ʻa'tʻǫ̈na·'nι·Ga'   (ʻι'skuya'   saʻkʻɔ·ni'⁹⁶)
   Now then | ha, now   thou hast come to listen   thou Man   Blue

υ'ʻǫ̈ⁿDzɔ·'-yι·'Dzə   Dι'tsȫtɪtʻɔ·'ʻιsti' | υ'sunυ·'li   Dɔ·'tʻaᴅlᴇʻǫ̈na' |
Cold, Loc., direction   thou art staying   quickly   thou hast arisen,
toward   facing us

Gᴇʻ'¹yₐ-Gυ·'Gə'   Dυ'Da·N̥tʻᴇ·''lȫ̥'   Gᴇsᴇ·.i' | υ'Dιlᴇʻ'Gι   Dυ'ksɔ·'=
woman, E(?)   she (E.) has thought it   it is, App   Heat   she has

ȫⁿtʻᴇ·'ⁿ | ayᴇ·'lιGɔ·'Gι-Gwü'-Dι·na'   υyᴇ·'lȫ'nȫ'ʻi   ʻι-Gᴇ'sᴇ'i' |
let it down | simulator, L, E   he has made   it which, it is, App
                                           it like

naʻna'   tʻι'tʻɔʻlə'stʻanι·Ga'   υ'ʻkəʻaʻtə-Gwȫᴅ'   tsιDaᴅlᴇʻȫⁿski   ι·'Ga-
right there thou hast come to   fog, L   when it rises (Hab.) light,
             cool it off

10 Ga·tʻa'   Daᴅlᴇʻȫⁿska' | υ'sȫʻιDȫⁿ   nυ'Dəʻnö·'nə | υtsι·''-nawə-
   it hangs it rises   night-been   it has not been   beyond it,
   on   said   stretched,

Gwȫᴅ'   aDȫʻ'nι·Ga'   ¹yă̆ʻ''
L   it has been said   Sharply!

This is the Medicine when They have Blisters

FREE TRANSLATION

Now, then! Ha, now it is the Sun who has caused it. That is the one who has caused Heat to come down. And she has made it (appear) as if it actually were a simulated disease.

Now then! Ha, now thou hast come to listen, thou Blue Man, in the direction of the Cold Land thou art staying. Quickly thou hast arisen, facing this way. It is the Sun who has caused it. She caused Heat to come down, but made it (appear) as if it actually were a simulated disease.

Now thou hast come to cool it off. As the fog, when it arises, so does it arise, not for one night (only, but forever). Relief has been caused. Sharply!

EXPLANATION

This is a formula for the cure of watery blisters which break out on the body in summer, and are caused, according to the medicine man, by the heat of the sun.

---

[96] Interpolated by J. M.

The medicine used is a warm infusion of the bark of kwaᴾlɔ·`ɢə, *Rhus hirta* (L.) Sudw. (also *Rhus glabra* L., smooth sumac); ᴅalɔ·′ni, *Rhus copallina* L., dwarf sumac, which the medicine man pours over the affected part, after reciting the formula, the whole ceremony being similar to that described in No. 48. Whenever the water ceases to run from the blisters the cure is considered as effected, one application being sometimes sufficient for this purpose. There is a taboo of salt, beans, potatoes, eggs, pumpkins, and cymlings for reasons already explained. (See No. 30, p. 210.)

The sickness is ascribed to ɢɛ`ᶥyaɢʋ·′ɢə, the Sun (see p. 20), which sends the disease spirit, Heat, into the body of the patient. It is said to counterfeit ayɛ·`lɩɢɔ·′ɢi, a disease brought about by evil conjurers, because the blisters resemble the swellings caused in ayɛ·`lɩɢɔ·′ɢi diseases by the cinders or sticks put under the skin of the victim by the conjurer's arts. The name of the relief spirit was inadvertently omitted in the manuscript, but he is brought from the North, or the Cold Land, and is probably the Blue Man as in Formula No. 48, page 241. He cools the Heat, and compels it to rise "like the fog when it arises."

54

ṭ‛a′	a`nɩnɛ·′ᴅzi	a`ᴅa‛nǫ̈·′wɔ·t‛i`		tùḳsi′	nɩɢǫ̈·`wanǫ̈·`N̈aᴅɛ`ɢɔⁿ·.i′
this	their breast	to cure anyone with		terrapin	it does it to them as they go about

sɢɛ̈́·′		‛a`-nɔ·ɢwɔ̈ⁿ	ɔ·′ᴅali`	tsʋ`stɩɢɔ̈·-i′	ʋ‛sö̈`‛ɩ-ᴅɩ·′tɬə	97
Now then		ha, now	mountain(s)	where they are little, Loc	right, direction toward	

nǫ̈·nɔ	ᴅɩɢǫ̈·`wanaˋᵘwùᴅɛ·ɢa′		tù′ḳsi	ᴅʋ·`ᴅa·N̈t‛ɛˋᵉ]ɔ̈‛i′	ɢɛ·sɛ̈·.i′
trail(s)	they are lying (stretched) about		terrapin	he (E.) has thought it	it is, App

ayɛ‛li′	ᴅɛɢǫ̈·`watǫ̈·`tc‛ɩlɛ·ⁿ.i′		t‛ᴀsɢɩ·′nə-ɢwɔ̈ⁿ	ɢɛ·sɛ·ⁿ.i′
in the middle	they have come to hang on, App		ghost (E), L	it is, App

nɔ·′ɢwɔ̈ⁿ	‛a·′ɢwɔ̈ⁿ	‛ɩ`ɢayǫ̈·′li	tsùnɛ·′ɢə	t‛ɩ`yɛ·l-ǫ̈·′	ᴅast‛ǫ̈·′-	5
Now	however	thou old	thou White	thy body—T L	edge, limit	

ŋwɔ̈ⁿ	tsùᴅɩ·ˋʸustí′		tùksi′	ɢɛ·sɛ̈[.i′ 98]	ʋ·lsɢɛ·′ᴅə	ᴅʋnʋˋy‛=
L (=E)	thou surroundest him		terrapin	it is, App	it important	he has

t‛anilɛ·‛i′		asɢɩ·′nə-ɢwɔ̈ⁿ`	ɢɛsɛ̈·‛i′		‛ɩ`ɢayǫ̈·′ⁿli	tsùnɛ·′ɢə
put it under,App		ghost, L	it is, App		thou Old	thou White

ᴅɛ`t‛askəlɔ·`‛ɔ̈ⁿ′t‛a`nɩ·ɢa′		ʋ·lsɢɛ·′ᴅɔ̈ⁿ	ʋ‛sö̈`‛ɩ-yi′	ɩ·yǫ̈·′ⁿᴅə
thou hast come to make him relinquish his grasps		it important	night, Loc	yonder

tɬa`wɔ·t‛a·ᴾlaɢi` ⁹⁹	ɢǫ̈·`waᴅanʋˋy‛tɩᴅɛ·`ɢɛ·sti′		ᴅɔ‛`sö̈ⁿ′lɔ·tsö̈‛i
marsh	ever (muddy)	they will place him under as he moves about		he has been made weak

ʋ‛sö̈′‛ɩᴅə`	nʋ`ᴅə‛nǫ̈·′nə		ʋtsɩ·″-nawa`	nɩɢǫ̈·`ᴅö̈‛nö̈`ⁿ‛ö̈ⁿ′sɢɛ·sti′	10
night-been	it has not been said		beyong it, stretched	it will be said again and continuously	

[97] W. D. form; C. D.=ʋ‛sö̈′‛ɩᴅɩ·ᴅzə.
[98] Emendation by editor.
[99] W. D. form; C. D.=sawɔ·t‛-.

This is the Medicine for Their Breast, When the Terrapin Affects them as They go About

FREE TRANSLATION

Now then! Ha, now he has his trails stretched about toward the little mountains in the direction of the Night Land. It is the Terrapin that has caused it. He has come to hang in the middle (of the body). It is but a ghost.

Now, however, thou Old White One, at the very edge of thy body he[1] is sitting. It is the Terrapin that has put the important thing under him. It is but a ghost. Thou Old White One, thou hast come to make the important thing relinquish its grasp. Let him err about under the swamp, yonder in the Night Land. He has been made weak, and not for one night (only, but forever). Relief will be caused continuously.

EXPLANATION

This is a formula for the cure of an abdominal pain, probably due to the violation of some one of the rules of digestion, although the medicine man asserts that it is caused by the Terrapin, which in some way "spoils the saliva" of the patient. This diagnosis is based exclusively upon the fact that in the disturbed sleep which accompanies the illness, the sick man dreams of terrapins. Precisely the same disease would be ascribed to the evil agency of the snakes or of the fish, or of any other animal, if the sufferer happened to dream of them.

In the formula the Fire is addressed as the Ancient White One, and is asked to drive out the important thing, the disease which has come from the little mountains in the Night Land, the West, and to put it away under the mud, so that it may not get out again to do any further mischief. The fire is generally invoked against the terrapins, snakes and fishes, for the reason that these cold-blooded animals are unable to withstand the heat.

The treatment consists of rubbing the abdomen and administering a strong herb decoction to cause vomiting so as to dislodge the "spoiled saliva." The plants used are skwɔ·'l vʼt'ənö"·', *Asarum canadense* L., asarabacca, wild ginger; skwɔ·'l ustʋ·'Ga, *Hepatica acutiloba* DC., liver leaf; tú'ksi wo·yi', *Epigaea repens* L., mayflower.

The last name means "terrapin's paw," a fact which doubtless has something to do with its selection in this case. The decoction is boiled four times, as already explained, until it becomes a thick sirup. On each of the four days the patient drinks the liquid until he vomits, when no more is drunk until next day. The medicine must not necessarily be prepared by the medicine man, but may be

---
[1] The patient.

concocted and administered by members of the patient's household. The formula is recited by the medicine man, while rubbing the abdomen of the sick person. The rubbing is repeated four times before noon and for four days if required.

55

ĭ'a'	nö̆·ˋwo·t'i'	ᴅalɔ·ˋnɩ-ɢɛ·'ⁿ	ts-a·ˋndɩ·k'ö́ˤta	ɪya-nɔ·ɢwö̆ᴅ'
this	to cure with	yellow-ish	it which, they urinate	successively, now

tsa·ˋndɩ·k'ö́ˤɔ·.i |
it which they urinate (Hab)

t'ɛ·lö̆·ldi'	ɛ·'ldi	a`ɢʋ'alö̆·'ᴅə	k'anɛ·'lska	ʋ·ˋtɫanö̆'ˤi	sûl=
it hangs down	low	if has been cut off	(Calycanthus)	it has been in it	squirrel,
ɔ·'l-akt'a'	ʋ·ˋna'stɛ·'ᴅzi	w-a·ˋ.ɩs-ö̆·ⁿ'	aɢɩ·'ᴅə		tsʋ·ˋwaᴅʋ·'nə
eye-ball	they (are) roots	thither, it goes T L	it has been taken		they have sinews, arteries
ɛ·'ɢwö̆ᴅ	kwaᴅlʋ·'si	ɛ·'ldi	a`ɢʋ'alö̆·'ᴅə	ʋ·ˋna'sʋ'.ɢa	ɛ·'ldi 5
it big	blisters	low	it has been cut off	toes in the liquid(?)	low
a`ɢʋ'alö̆·'ᴅə	ɢɩ·'ɢə	tsʋ'ˤya·'.i	ɩɢö̆·'yi	ɢa·yɔ·'tɫi	ʋ·ˋlĭˤtɫö̆·'=
it has been cut off	blood	it has them in it	first	a little	it has been
ᴅə ²	ɢɛˋsǫ.i'	ʋnᴀdɩ·''t'asti`		ɢa·k̇t'ö̆·'ᴅə	ɢö̆`ɫkwɔ·'ɢi
boiled	it has been, Hab	they must drink it		it restricted	seven
a`ˋk'alɩ·'.i	yĭ'ki				
it is full	if it is				

This is to Cure (Them) With, if What They Urinate is Yellowish

FREE TRANSLATION

(A piece of) summer grape, cut off low down; a calycanthus tuber; dewberry roots, where it goes away (i. e., a runner); strawberry bush; (a piece of) northern foxgrape, cut off low down; (a piece of) ampelopsis, cut off low down; loosestrife. It (all) should first be boiled a little, (then) they must drink it. There are restrictions, if the seven be complete.

EXPLANATION

The symptoms of this disease are at first frequent and excessive urination, gradually decreasing in quantity, until it goes to the other extreme. According to the medicine man's statement, if the flow should stop, the patient dies. The remedy is to drink a decoction of the barks of the following plants:

t'ɛ·ˋlö̆·'ldi, *Vitis aestivalis* Michx., summer grape, pigeon grape; k'anɛ·'lska, *Calycanthus fertilis* Walt., calycanthus, bubby root; sûlɔ·ˋlakt'a', *Rubus nigrobaccus* Bailey (also *Rubus villosus* Ait.), dewberry; tsʋ·ˋwaᴅʋ·'nə ɛ·'ɢwö̆ᴅ, *Evonymus americanus* L., strawberry bush; kwaᴅlʋ·'si, *Vitis labrusca* L., northern fox grape; ʋ·ˋna'sʋ·'ɢa,

---

² W. D. form; C. D.=ʋ·lɩˤtsö̆·ᴅə.

Ampelopsis cordata Michx.; and of the roots of ɢɩˑ′ɢətsv⁽ˡ'ya·′.i, *Lysimachia quadrifolia* L., loosestrife.

The loosestrife, [as well as the different varieties of grape prescribed are often met with in recipes] to cure urinary ailments.

No rubbing nor any ceremony accompanies the treatment.

When all seven of the plants prescribed are used there is a taboo of salt, hot food, and of sexual intercourse, but when, as sometimes happens, less than seven are used, there is no regular taboo.

56

	ï'a'	aˋnɩyö̧·tsɛ·′ni	aˋpaˈnö̧·′wɔ·tˈiˋ	
	this	their throat	to cure anyone with	
(*a*) sɢɛ̌″	tˈɛ̌″ɢa	wɔˋʰDɩɢɛˑⁿ′	nö̧ˋpɔˑ-yɩˑ′-ᴅzə	ö̧·ᴅal-ɛˋɢwɔ-ï′
Now, then,	Frog	brown	sun, Loc. direct	lake, big, Loc.
ᴅɩˋtsö̧tltˈɔˈɩˋsti	vˋsunvˑ′li	ᴅɔˋtˈaᴰlɛˈö̧ŋa′	vˋlsɢɛˑ′ᴅə	ˈɩˋᴅvnvˑˋy'-
thou art staying	quickly	thou hast arisen, facing us	it important	it which he (E.) has
tˈanɩˋlɛˑⁿ.i′	ɛˈɩˋsti	ɢɛsɛˑⁿ.i′	nɔˑˋᵘɢwuˑ-ᴅɩˑnə′	ᴅɛˋtˈaskəlɔˋ-
put under	pain	it is, App.	now, L	thou hast come
5 ï̧ⁿtˋanɩˑɢa′		vtsɩˋⁿawa′	aᴅö̧ˋnɩˑɢa′	ˈya″
to make him relinquish his grasps		beyond it, stretched	it has been said	Sharply
(*b*) sɢɛ̌″	tˈɛ̌″ɢa	saˋkˈɔˑni′	vˋʰyö̧·ᴅzɔˋ-yɩˑ-′ᴅzə	ö̧·ᴅal-ɛˋ-
Now, then,	Frog	blue	cold, Loc., dir	lake,
ɢwɔ̈-i′	ᴅɩˋtsö̧tltˈɔˈɩˋsti (*etc.*).			
big, Loc	thou art staying			
ï'a'	aˋnɩyö̧·tsɛˑ′ni	aˋᴅaˈnö̧·′wɔ·tˈiˋ		tsɩˋᴅanɩˋyö̧·tsɔˑˋtˈɩska′
this	their throat	to cure anyone with		it which, their throats are swollen
tcɪskɔˑ′ya		ᴅɩᴅzɔˋtˈa.ɛˋtɩ-ɢwö̧ᴰ′		nö̧·wɔˑtˈi-nï̧′	tsɔˋl-ɩyvˋsti
insects		they are to be blown, L		to cure with, and	tobacco-like
10 vˋnɩkwɔtˈɛˑ′nə				
it has down				

This is the Medicine For Their Throat

FREE TRANSLATION

(*a*) Now, then! Brown Frog, in the great lake in the direction of the Sun Land thou art staying. Quickly thou hast arisen, facing us. It is Pain that has put the important thing under him. But now thou hast come and caused him to relinquish his grasp. Relief has been caused. Sharply!

(*b*) Now, then! Blue Frog, in the great lake, in the direction of the Cold Land thou art staying (etc.).

This is the medicine for their throat, when their throat is swollen on account of insects. They are to be blown. And to cure (them) with the tobaccolike (plant), (which) has down.

EXPLANATION

This formula is for the cure of an ailment which, from the symptoms as described by medicine men, seems to be diphtheria. According to the theory, it is caused by the insect ghosts, which effect an entrance into the throat, where they multiply, causing the throat to swell and producing a choking sensation.

The curing spirit addressed is the tʻɛ'Ga', a small species of frog, which is represented as living in the great pond, and is expected to come and devour the mischievous worms and insects, as is the habit of the frog. The medicine is a poultice of tsɔ·'lɩyɩ'sti vʻnɩkwʻtʻ-ɛ'nə, *Verbascum thapsus* L., common mullein leaves, beaten up in warm water and applied to the throat with the hand of the medicine man, who recites the formula at the same time, blowing once at the end of each paragraph. The operation is repeated, thus making four blowings in all.

While under treatment the patient is forbidden to eat the larvae of the yellow jacket or locust, both of which are roasted as food [and considered a great delicacy] by the Cherokee, or to taste honey, the reason being that both larvae and honey are derived from insects, and would consequently serve to aggravate the disease. Pumpkins, cymlings, tomatoes, and all other juicy fruits and vegetables must also be avoided, for the reason stated (p. 65), these same insects being held responsible for all kinds of boils, blisters, and similar complaints.

57

ı̵'a'	aʻnɩskɔ·'li	aʻDaʻnö̜·'wɔ·tʻïʻ		
this	their head	to cure anyone with		

sGé̵''	|	nɔ·ᵘGwö̃ᵛ'	ʻaʻtʻö̜ŋaʻnɩ·Ga'	ʻɩʻskuya'	tsAsti·'Ga
now, then!		now	thou hast come to listen	thou man	thou little

DɩGɛʻʻdɔ.'sé̵·ⁿ.i'	|	ʻaʻnɔ·Gwö̃ᵛ'	vʻlsGɛ·'Dö̃ⁿ	tʻaʻDɩGaʻlɛʻɩ·Ga'	|
thou penetratest them, App.		ha! now	it important	thou hast come and pushed it away	

vtsɩ·ʻʻnawaʻ	aDö̃ʻʻnɩ·Ga'	|	¹yă̵ʻ	GaᴰIɛ̵̌ʻ	|	GaᴰIɛ̵̌ʻ	|	GaᴰIɛ̵̌ʻ
beyond it stretched	it has been said		Sharply!					

GaᴰIɛ̵̌ʻ |

5

This (for) Their Head (is) the Medicine

FREE TRANSLATION

Now, then! Now thou hast come to listen, thou Little Man, thou penetrator. Ha, now thou hast come to push away the important thing. Relief has been caused. Sharply!
Galeh. (Four times.)

EXPLANATION

This short formula for the cure of headache is addressed to the Little Man, [possibly] one of the Thunder Boys. The title of "penetrator" is frequently bestowed on a spirit invoked, and implies that he has the power of going irresistibly through all obstacles.

[The final ɢaᴰlɛ̌" could not be satisfactorily explained either to Mr. Mooney or to me by any of the medicine men; the word may have some connection with ɢaᴰlɛni', his ear.]

No medicine is used. The medicine man recites the formula while warming his hands over the fire, after which he lays them upon the temples or the back of the neck of the patient, or wherever the pain is most acute. He ends by blowing four times at the words ɢaᴰlɛ̌". The ceremony is repeated four times.

58

ǐ'a' vnιyɛ·'lɔ·skö·'[.i ³] a`ɴa'nö·'wɔ·t'ǐ'
this   when they have become   to cure anyone with
              thlike it

sɢɛ̌" | 'a`-nɔ·ɢwɔ̆ᵘ  'a`t'ö·ɢa·'nɩ·ɢa' vɴa'ti sa`"k'ɔ·ni' ɛ̆"lιstɛ̌'-
Now then!   ha, now   thou hast come to listen watersnake   blue   head of

ni ɢɛ·sö·' ɴιtsö`tlt'ɔ'ιsti'  |  'ιɴa·'"wɛ'ι-ɴι·no'  |  'a`-nɔ·ɢwö̆ᵘ
streamlet it is, T L thou art staying   thou (art a) wizard, IC   ha, now

v`sönv·'li ɴɔ·'t'aᴰlɛ'öɢa' | ɢɔ'ɩ'sti tsιnv·'lti nι'ɢɛ·sö·na' |
quickly thou hast arisen, facing us   something thou failest   never

5 ┤ ┤   tsvɴɔ·'ιɴo | nö̆'nɔ-ǐ' ɴaγv·'taɴö̆"ö"si' | v`lsɢɛ·'ɴo
(such-and-such) his names are   trail, Lee it lies toward this direction   it important

'ι`ɴvnv·'y't'anι'lɛ·ⁿ.i'  vɴɔ·'lv'wa'.tö̆ⁿ·ti'  nιɢɛ·'sö·na'  |  vyɛ·'lɔ·sι`-
it which he (IC) has put under it   its track to be refound   never   he has been

lö̌'ι-ɢwö̆ᵘ   ɢɛ·'sɛ̣.i' | asɢι·'no ɴv·'ɴö̆"nö̌i' ɢɛ·'sɛ̣.i' | aᴰlɛ'
made like him, L it is, App   ghost   he (IC) has said it   it is, App   and

v·'y-ιɢawɛ·'sɢi ɴv`ɴa·ɴ̣t'ɛ·"lö̌i' yǐki' | aᴰlɛ' yö·'wi ɴɛ̆"aᴰlu'
different he speaks (Hab.) he (IC) has thought it   if it is   and   human being   purple

ɴv`ɴa·ɴ̣t'ɛ·"ölö̌i'  yǐ'ki  |  'a`-nɔ·ɢwö̆ᵘ 'ö̆ⁿ-t'a`sɛsö̆'ι·ɢa' vlsɢɛ·'-
he has thought it if it is   ha, now   again, thou hast come   it impor-
                                            to pull it out

10 ɴo | vsönv·'li dɛ̆"t'ü'tlt'anι·ɢa' | vtsι'"-nawa` aɴö̆"nι·ɢa' |
tant   quickly   thou hast come to put   beyond it, stretched   it has been said
                    him on his legs

'yx̣̆"
sharply!

This is the Medicine When They Have Become as Though (They Were Really Ill)

FREE TRANSLATION

Now then! Ha, now thou hast come to listen, Blue Watersnake, thou art staying at the head of the streamlet; thou powerful wizard! Ha, now thou hast arisen, facing us; thou never failest in anything. He is called so-and-so. The path lies toward our direction. He has put the important thing under him, its track never to be found. It has made him as though (he were really ill), it seems. It is a ghost that has caused it, it seems; or maybe it is a speaker of incantations that has caused it; or maybe it is the Purple Human Being that has

---

³ Emendation by editor.

caused it. (Anyway), now thou hast come to pull out the important thing. Quickly thou hast come to put him on his feet. Relief has been caused. Sharply!

EXPLANATION

This is another formula for the treatment of ayɛ`ˊlɑɔ·ˊɑi diseases. It is couched in such terms as if the reciter were in doubt as to who caused it: a ghost [a "speaker of different (i. e., evil) things," viz, an incantator, or by the Purple Person. The probable explanation is that all the possible causes are enumerated, so as not to take any chances; a process which is very common in conjurations the world over].

The ᴠ·ˊᴅati` or watersnake (*Natrix sipedon*) is regarded as an especially crafty animal fit to combat the cunning of a secret enemy. The symptoms are described as sudden keen pains in the arm, the shoulder, etc., and shifting from one place to another. The pain is caused by the moving about of the object which has been shot into the victim's body. (See p. 87.)

The medicine used is a cold infusion of the bark of ɩtsɛ́ˊʟi, *Alnus rugosa* (Du Roi) Spreng., smooth alder; with this in his mouth, the medicine man sucks the different sore spots in turn, afterwards spitting the liquid into another bowl [so as to make possible the discovery of the intrusive object].

The formula is recited four times, the medicine man sucking after each recital; the whole ceremony is repeated four times before noon. There is no taboo.

59

ʟi'a'	tsᴠ·`ˋnastaɢɔ̆ˊli	a`ᴅa'nö·ˊwɔ·t'ı`
this	whenever their feet are frostbitten	to cure them (indef.) with

'ɛ́ɩ·ˊ-yu·   'ɛ́ɩ·ˊ-yu·   'ɛ́ɩ·ˊ-yu·   'ɛ́ˊɩ-yu·
thou art living—E

'aɴa`-ʟi-yu·ˊ   'ɛ́ɩ·ˊyu·   'ɛ́ɩ-ˊyu·   'ɛ́ɩ-ˊyu·
There thou art living—E

'ɩᴅa`·ⁿwɛ́ʟi'   tsö·`ˋtăᴅzi'   ɢɩ·`ˋɢaɢɛ·ˊⁿ   'ɛ́ɩ·ˊyu
thou wizard   mountain lion   red   thou art living, E

'ɩ`ᴅa·ⁿwɛ́ʟi   tsö·`ˋtăᴅzi'   ɢɩ·`ˋɢaɢɛ·ⁿˊ   'ɛ́ɩ·ˊyu   'ɛ́ɩ·ˊyu   5

THIS, WHENEVER THEIR FEET ARE FROST BITTEN, (IS) THE TREATMENT

FREE TRANSLATION

Thou art living, indeed. (Four times.)
There thou art living, indeed.
Thou art living indeed. (Three times.)
Thou Wizard, red Mountain Lion, Thou art living indeed (bis).

EXPLANATION

This song, for the cure of frostbite, has a very pleasing tune, and is addressed to the mountain lion, which is supposed to have power over this ailment, because, according to the medicine men, its feet are never frostbitten. The red indicates its power.

The treatment consists of the application of snow water to the frostbitten parts. The snow is first melted over the fire, and the water thus obtained is again warmed in a vessel into which the patient puts his feet. The medicine man now sings the song, after which he takes some snow or a small piece of ice in his mouth and sucks the affected part.

The ceremony is repeated four times before noon. Snow is preferred to ice for sucking.

60

ʔi'a' tsʋ·ˋnastaGöⁱ̓i a`Da'nö·'wɔ·t'i'ˋ
this whenever their (feet) are frostbitten to cure anyone with

(a) sGĕ'' | ʽa`-nɔ·Gwö⁰'  ʽa`t'öŋa·ˋnɩ·Ga' tcɩ·'stu wɔ·ˋDɩ-Gɛ·'ⁿ |
Now then ha, now thou hast come to listen Rabbit brownish

k'anɛ·'skə-wɔ·ˋDi Gɛsö·' tsù·Danʋ·'y't̓ɩDɛ·Gö·ˋ | ʋGa·ˋnəwɔ·ˋtöⁱ̓i
grass, brown it is, T L thou stayest under them, moving about where it is warmed

Gɛsö·' Gaˋᴅlnasùnʋ·ˋy't'anɩ·Ga' | ʋtsɩ·ˋ-nawə-Gwö⁰' aDö̀ˋnɩ·Ga'
it is, T L I have come to put my toe under beyond it, stretched, L it has been said

5 (b) sGĕ'' | ʽa`-nɔ·Gwö ⁿ'  ʽa`t'öŋa·ˋnɩ·Ga' tcɩ·'stu sa'k'ɔ·ni' |
Now then! ha, now thou hast come to listen Rabbit blue

(etc.).

(c) sGĕ'' | ʽa`-nɔ·Gwö⁰'  ʽa`t'öŋa·ˋnɩ·Ga' tcɩ·'stu öⁿ''naGɛ·ⁿ' |
Now then ha, now thou hast come to listen Rabbit black

(etc.) dɩ·st dɩ·st dɩ·st dɩ·st ⁱyă·'
(Onom.) Sharply!

THIS IS THE MEDICINE WHEN THEIR FEET ARE FROST BITTEN

FREE TRANSLATION

Now then! Ha, now thou hast come to listen, Brown Rabbit, thou art staying under the (sheltering) broom sedge, (and art there) moving about. I have come to put my feet under it where it is warm. Relief indeed has been caused.

Now then! Ha, now thou hast come to listen, Blue Rabbit (etc.).

Now then! Ha, now thou hast come to listen, Black Rabbit (etc.).

(with at the end:) dist! dist! dist! dist! Sharply!

EXPLANATION

This formula is intended to prevent frostbite as well as to cure it. It is addressed to the Rabbit, for the same reason as explained in

No. 59, because this is one of the animals that is thought to be immune from frostbite. The Rabbit is represented as hiding under the warm kʻanɛʽskəwɔʽᴅi, *Andropogon virginicus* L., broom sedge, and the patient obtains relief by putting his frozen foot under the same warm cover.

The final "dist," repeated four times in a slow way, is intended to imitate the cry of the rabbit when startled.

As a preventive, the formula is recited on starting from the house in winter, and [is believed to] enable one to walk barefoot on the snow without injury.

61

ɩ̓'a' ᴅʋnɩʽala'ɢɔ!ǫ̈·ʼ[i⁵] ᴅɩʽᴅaʻnǫ̈wɔ·tʻɩ̓ʽ
this whenever their mouths are sore to cure people with

sɢé̌ʼ | ʻaʽ-nɔ·ɢwɔ̈⁰ʼ ʻa̓·tʻǫ̈ŋa·ʽnɩ·ɢa' ǫ̈·ʼN!atsi' tsastɩ·ʼɢa |
Now ha, now thou hast come to listen Snow thou little
then

υ·ʽᴅɩlɛʻʻɢɩ=ɢwɔ̈⁰ʼ ʻɩ·ɢɛ·sɛ̣·ʼ[.i⁵] υ·lsɢɛ·ʼᴅə ʻɩ̓ʽ-ᴅʋnυ·ʽyʻtʻɛ·ⁿʼ | υʽsönυ·ʼli
Heat, L that which is, App it important it which he has put under quickly

tʻa̓ʽᴅɩɢalɛʻʸɩ·ɢa' | υtsɩʽʽnawəɢwɔ̈⁰ʼ nυ·ʽᴅətʻanǫ̈·ʼᴅə nɔ̈ⁿʽʻtʻǫ̈·=
thou hast come to beyond it stretched, L it has been said at the same time thou hast
scatter it

nɛ·ʽlɩ·ɢa' | ʼyǎ̓ʽʻ 5
come and Sharply!
done it for
him

ɩ̓'a' ᴅʋ·nɩʽʽalə'ɢɔ!ǫ̈·ʽ[.i⁵] ᴅɩʽᴅaʻnǫ̈·ʼwɔ·tʻɩ̓ʽ | ᵘwanɛ·ʼⁿɢwɔ̈⁰
this whenever their mouths are sore to cure people with (hickory) L

ɢɔ̈ⁿʼʼtʻɔti' ᴅɩᴅzɔ·ʽtʻɩstɔ·ʽtɩ-ɢwɔ̈⁰ʼ | ɢa·ktʻǫ̈·ʼᴅə nɔ̈ⁿʽʼɢi' tsʋsɔ̈=
it (is) to be used they must be blown with it, L it restricted four they
with it nights

ʻʼɩᴅə̓ʽ υ·ʽᴅɩlɛ·ʼɢi a·ma' aᴅlɛ̌·ʼ tʻυ·ya'
been hot salt and beans

THIS IS THE MEDICINE WHEN THEIR MOUTHS ARE SORE

FREE TRANSLATION

Now then! Ha, now thou hast come to listen, thou Little Snow. It is but Heat that has put the important thing under him.[6] Quickly thou hast come to scatter it. Relief has been caused forthwith, thou hast come to do it for him. Sharply!

This is the medicine when their mouths are sore. Hickory (bark) is merely to be used for blowing them with. (Are) restricted (for) four days: Hot (food), salt, and beans.

EXPLANATION

This formula is used for thrush in children and for a similar coating of the inside of the mouth in adults, no matter from what cause originating. According to the medicine men's theory, the disease is

---

[5] Emendation by editor.   [6] The patient.

caused by fever, personified under the name of vʽˈᴅɩlɛʽʽɢi or Heat. In accordance with the theory, Little Snow is invoked to dislodge the disease. The medicine is the inner bark of the ⁿwanɛʽ, *Hicoria alba* (L.) Britt., hickory, chewed by the medicine man, and blown by him into the mouth of the patient, after having recited the formula. He then blows his breath into the patient's mouth, the whole operation being repeated four times at each treatment, according to the regular practice. The patient can not chew the hickory bark for himself, but is sometimes given another medicine to chew in addition.

The ceremony may be performed either in the morning or in the evening, or [if the seriousness of the complaint demands it], both. If in the morning, it is performed while the patient is still fasting. The medicine man, however, is not obliged to fast as in some cases.

Hot food and salt are tabooed as usual, and also beans. The latter are prohibited in all fever diseases, because their skins sometimes shrivel up as from an interior heat; [according to other medicine men], because they resemble boils, or because they are watery. The same reason probably accounts for the prohibition of beans and potatoes in a similar ailment of the throat, noted in No. 48.

62

tcɪskɔˑʽya	amaˑʽ-y-anɛʽʽi	ᴅɩˋᴅaʽnö̆ˑʽwɔˑtʽiˋ	ʽi'a'
insect(s)	water, Loc, they are living	to cure people with	this

(a) sɢɛ̆ʽʽ | ʽa'-nɔˑɢwö̆ⁿ' | vˋsönvˑ'li | ʽa'tʽö̤ŋaˑˋnɩˑɢa' | tsvlɩʽsta-
now then | ha now | quickly | thou hast come to listen | (cat-fish)

nalaˋ | ᴅɛʽʽaᴰluˋ | aˋm-ayɛʽʽ'li | ᴅɩˋtsötɪtʽɔʽɩˋsti | ʽa'ˋ.-tcskɔˑʽyaˋ
purple | water, middle | thou art staying | ha, insect(s)

aˋnɩᴅɛʽʽaᴰluˋ | ɢɛˋsɛʽ[.i⁷] | vˋlsɢɛˑ'ᴅə | ᴅvˋnɩnvˑʽyʽtʽanɩˋlɛˑi' | ʽa'ˋ-nɔˑ=
they yellow | it is, App, | it important | they have put it under him, App | ha,

5 ɢwö̆ⁿ' | vˋsönvˑ'li | ɢɛˋtʽaᴅɩˋɢalɛʽʽ'yɔˑwʽɩstʽaˋnɩˑɢa' | vsö̆ʽʽɩᴅəˋ
now | quickly | thou hast come to scatter it as thou comest | night, been

nvˑʽᴅəʽnö̆ˑʽna | vtsɩʽʽ-nawú-ɢwö̆ⁿ | aᴅö̆ʽʽnɩˑɢa' | ¹yă̆ʽ
it has not been said | beyond it stretched, L | it has been said | Sharply

(b) sɢɛ̆ʽʽ | ʽa'-nɔˑɢwö̆ⁿ' | vˋsönvˑ'li | ʽa'tʽö̤ŋaˑˋnɩˑɢa' | ɔˑ'lɩˑɢaˋ
now then | ha, now | quickly | thou hast come to listen | Red Horse

wɔˑˋᴅɩɢɛˑ'i | aˋm-ayɛʽʽ'li | ᴅɩˋtsötɪtʽɔʽɩˋstɩᴅɛˑɢa' | ʽa'ˋ.-tcskɔˑyə-ɢwö̆ⁿˋ
brown | water, middle | thou art staying, moving about | ha, insect(s), L

aˋnɩwɔˑʽᴅɩɢɛˋʽ[i⁷] | ɢɛˋsɛʽ[i⁷] | vlsɢɛˑ'ᴅə | ʽɩᴅvnɩnvˑʽyʽtʽanɩˋlɛˑi' | ʽa'ˋ-nɔˑ=
they brown | it is, App | it important | it which they have put under, App | ha,

10 ɢwö̆ⁿ' | vˋsönvˑ'li (*etc., as in a.*)
now | quickly

ʽi'a' | tcskɔˑ'yö̆ⁿ | ᴅɩˋᴅaʽnö̆ˑʽwɔˑtʽiˋ | aˋnɩyö̤ˑⁿtsɛˑ'ni | tsvˋnɩyö̤ˑˋ=
this | insect(s) | to cure people with | their throat | when their

tsɔˑtʽɩska' | vˑˋntʽasɢɩˑ'ᴅə | yɩˋki | ʽi'ʽa-ɢwö̆ⁿˋ | ɩɢa'ˑ.i'
throat swells | it oozes out from them | if it is | this, L | it (is) all

---

⁷ Emendation by editor.

nǫ·'wɔ·t'ɩ-Nɩ̈ǫ̈'	k'ɔ·stʋ·'Də	ʋnɛ·'Gə	ù`tlGɔ·Dö ⁿ'skì`	tsɩ̈'kì	Gö ⁿʲ't'-
to cure with, and	(everlasting)	white	it scatters (Hab.)	it which is	it to be
ɔti	DɩDzɔ·t'a.ɛ·tɩ-Gwö ⁿ'		yɛ·lɩ·'Ga	Gaḳt'ǫ·'Də		sö ⁿkt'a'
used with	it must be blown on them, L		much	it restricted		apple(s)
kwanö ⁿ'	nʋ·nö ⁿ'	t'ʋ·'ya-Nɩ̈ǫ̈'	Ga·Dʋ'	na.'sGwö ⁿ	k'ǫ·'Nɩ̈ɩ	Gɛ·sǫ·'
peach(es)	potato(es)	bean(s), and	bread	also	noticeable	it is, T. L
ʋ·`wa·nsö̈'ɩ̈		yɛ·lì'	'ɩDlö ⁿ'	ɩ'Gɔ'ɩ·'Də	ʋ·'nùlsta·'y'tì'	nɩ·Gɛ·`sǫ·na'
it is done		possible	somewhere	as long as	for them to eat	never

THIS IS THE MEDICINE FOR THE INSECTS LIVING IN THE WATER

FREE TRANSLATION

Now then! Ha, now thou hast come to listen, Purple Blue-Catfish, in the middle of the water thou art staying.

Ha, it is the purple insects that have put the important thing under him.[8] But now thou hast quickly come and hast caused them to scatter, (and) not for one night (only, but forever). Relief has been caused. Sharply!

Now then! Ha, now thou hast quickly come to hear, Brown Red-Horse, thou wizard, in the middle of the water thou art staying, moving about.

Ha, it is the brown insects that have put the important thing under him.[8] But now thou hast quickly come (*etc.*).

This is the medicine for insects, when their throat swells and if (pus) oozes out from the (swellings). This now is all, namely, the medicine is the common everlasting (from which) white dust scatters itself; they are merely to be blown with it. There are considerable restrictions: apples, peaches, potatoes, beans besides (all this); also bread that has been cooked in plain (sight). They should not eat any of these as long as (they can) possibly (abstain from them).

EXPLANATION

This is a formula for the cure of a disease which is described as a clogging up of the throat passages so as to seriously interfere with breathing and utterance, and which seems to be diphtheria or some similar ailment.

The formula was carelessly written in the original and hence the two paragraphs do not correspond as closely as they should.

The disease is ascribed to the tɔskɔ·'ya ghosts, which "form a settlement" under the membrane of the throat as explained in No. 56. In this particular case they are stated to be water insects, and the large fish which prey upon these animals are called from the great water to come and disperse them. The fish named are locally known as the blue catfish and the red horse.

---

[8] The patient.

The medicine is a warm decoction of kʽɔ·stʋ·ˈDə ʋnɛˈGə ùˋtłGɔ·Dōⁿˈski, *Gnaphalium obtusifolium* L., common everlasting, the liquid being blown down the throat of the patient by means of a tube made from the stalk of ămaDιˈˈtɔ.tìˋ ʋ·tʽənōⁿˋ, *Eupatorium purpureum* L., Joe-pye-weed, trumpet weed.

The medicine man recites the first paragraph, and then blows the liquid in this manner, after which he blows his breath through the tube in the same way. The operation is repeated at the end of the second paragraph, and the whole ceremony is repeated twice, so as to make up four applications of the medicine. [As usual,] the treatment is repeated four times before noon, and for four consecutive mornings.

The taboo includes apples and peaches, [because, some medicine men say their watery and juicy nature shows that they are of the same nature as boils and watery blisters, and would therefore only aggravate the complaint; others hold that they are forbidden, as well as the dumplings (see below), because their shape is like that of the malignant swellings that are to be cured. The reason for the prohibition of beans and potatoes is evident from the explanation given in No. 56, page 254, which deals with a similar illness in the mouth.

"The bread which has been made visibly" is the name the Cherokee give to a peculiar kind of dumplings they make; unlike their common corn bread, which is baked under the ashes of the hearth, and is therefore not "visible" while it is being done, these dumplings, made out of corn meal and beans, are cooked in an uncovered vessel, i. e., "visibly."]

63

ιˈaˊ DʋnιˈˈˡyʋGwùˋtιsGö̱·ˊ[.ìˋ ⁹] aˋDaʽnö̱·wɔ·tˈìˋ
this   whenever their teeth ache   to cure anyone with

sGḗˈˈ | nɔ·ˊGwō̱⁰ ʽaˋtʽö̱ŋa·ˋnιˊGaˊ sùˋlɔ·ˈᵘli tsùˋnɛ·ˊGə nö̱·Dɔ·ˊ-yi
Now, then! now   thou hast come to listen Squirrel thou white sun. Loc.

Dιˋtsötłtʽɔˋιˈsti | ʋˋsönʋ·ˈli Dɔ·ˋtʽaᵖlɛˈˈö̱ŋaˊ | ʋlsGɛ·ˊDə ɛˈˈιstìˋ
thou art staying   quickly   thou hast arisen, facing us   it important pain

Dʋwaˋˈᵘwsùnʋ·ˋyˈtʽanιˋlɛ·ⁿiˊ | tsötłsta·ˊyʽtι-Gwō̱ᵛˋ ʽιGɛ·ˋsɛ·ⁿ.iˊ |
he has come to put it inside, from the   it is what thou eatest, L   it which is, App.
bottom up

5 asGιˈˊnə ʋ·ˊDö̱ˋnö̱ˋ!i | aGιˈˊsti ʋˈˈˡyùˋkt’anō̱ʽˈι-Gwō̱ᵛˋ Gɛ·ˋsɛ̨·.iˊ |
ghost   it has been said   food (solid) it has been changed, L   it is, App.

ʽιˈˈˡyō̱ⁿ·ˋstʽanιˊGaˊ ʋˋsönʋ·ˈli ʋlsιˈˈGιnɛ·ˋˈι-Dzəˊ Dɛ·ɔᴅˋlʋˋG–ö̱·ˊ ιˊyö̱·ˊDə
thou hast come to take it   quickly   dark   direction   they moss   T L   yonder
away as thou goest by

ʽιˋskwanιGɔˋˋtʽanιˊGaˊ | ιGö̱·ˋwōłstɔ·ˊtι-Gwùˋ-DιˊDəˊ | ˡyă̌ˈˈ Gʋ·ˊ
thou hast gone to store it up   who cares what happens to it L. (=E), E   Sharply (Onom.)

Gʋ·ˊ   Gʋ·ˊ   Gʋ·ˊ

---

⁹ Emendation by editor.

This is the Medicine When Their Teeth Ache

FREE TRANSLATION

Now, then! Now thou hast come to listen, thou White Squirrel, thou art staying in the Sun Land. Quickly thou hast arisen, facing us. The important thing has put Pain into (the tooth) from the bottom up, and all around it, it seems. It is the very thing thou eatest.

What has become a ghost, has merely changed the food. (But now) thou hast quickly come to take it away in the direction of the dark mountain slope. Over yonder, where moss grows, thou hast gone to store it away. Who cares what happens to it! Sharply.

Gu, gu, gu, gu.

EXPLANATION

The toothache theory as shown in this formula is that a ghost transmutes the particles of food lodged about the teeth into tcskɔ·′ya or worms, which burrow into the tooth, and thus cause the pain. The theory, as will be noticed, is not so very far wrong.

The disease is represented as penetrating into the tooth from underneath and as completely surrounding it with pain. The cure is effected through the agency of the squirrel, which pulls out the intruder, and takes it to the dark (i. e., north) side of the mountain, where, in accordance with the habits of the squirrel, it hides it away in a moss-covered (hollow) log.

In performing the ceremony the medicine man spits into his left palm and rubs his right thumb upon it while reciting the formula. He then holds his thumb a moment over the fire, after which he presses it firmly upon the jaw of the sufferer over the aching tooth, repeating at the same time the final "gu!" four times in succession. This is intended to represent the cry of the squirrel when alarmed. The operation is repeated several times, there being no strict rule as to the number in ailments of this temporary character.

64

a`nιneˑDzι′.-i`	yυneˑ′ιsta·`neˑa′	a`Da`nǫ̈·′wɔ·t‛i`	
their breast, Loc.	if they have aching	to cure anyone with	

sGe̽′′		nɔ·′Gwö͡ᵔ	‛a`t‛ǫ̈na·`nι·Ga′		Galǫ̈·′ldi		Dιtsö̍`tĭt‛ɔ‛ιsti′
Now, then!		now	thou hast come to listen		above		thou art staying

‛ι`skùya′	Gι`GaGeˑ′ⁿ		‛ιDa·ᵘweˑ̤i′		DιGeˑ‛dɔ`.seˑ̤i′		asGι′nɔ
thou man	red		thou wizard		thou penetratest them,		ghost

v`Dö̍‛nö̍ˑ̤i′	v`Dιleˑ‛Gι-Gwö͡ᵔ`		Geˑ`sę·.i′		nɔ·′Gwö͡ᵔ	v`sönv·′li	vlsGeˑ′Dǝ
he has said	Heat	L	it is, App.		now	quickly	it important

t‛a`DιGö̍`tĭt‛anιGa′		‛ιDa·ᵘweˑ̤ι-′Dι′nǝ′		v`sönv·′li	Deˑ‛t‛ù`tĭt‛anιGa′		5
thou hast come to push it away		thou wizard, E		quickly	thou hast come to put him on his (legs)		

ʋtsɩꞌ`-nawə-ɢwȫⁿꞌ       aDȫ`ꞌnɩ·ɢaꞌ | ʋsȫꞌꞌɩDəꞌ   nʋ`ꞌDətꞌanö̧·ꞌⁿDə
beyond it, stretched, L   it has been said   night been   it has not been said

nö̧ⁿꞌtꞌö̧·nɛꞌꞌlɩ·ɢaꞌ   +   +   tsʋDɔ·ꞌɩDə
thou hast come to do it (such-and-such)   his names are
for him

This Is the Medicine When Their Breast Aches

FREE TRANSLATION

Now then! Now thou hast come to listen, thou (who) art staying on high, Red Man, thou Wizard, thou Penetrator! What has become a ghost is merely Heat. Now thou hast quickly come and pushed the important thing away. Thou powerful wizard, quickly hast thou made him get up. Relief has been caused, (and) not for one night (only, but forever). Thou hast come to make it so for him.[10] He [10] is called so-and-so.

EXPLANATION

[This formula is for the same purpose as No. 24, page 201.
The cause, medicine used, application, and treatment are likewise identical. It appears from Mr. Mooney's notes that this formula was very carelessly written in the original and that he reconstructed it. It is not possible to state exactly in how far the emendations are Mr. Mooney's.]

65

ꞌɩꞌaꞌ   ʋ·ꞌndɩyö̧·Dalɩ`      Dɩ·ꞌDaꞌnö̧·ꞌwɔ·tꞌɩ`
this   their navel   to cure people with

sɢɛ̈̌ꞌꞌ | ꞌa·ʋsȫꞌɩꞌ | a·ꞌm-ɛ·ɢwɔꞌꞌi   Dɩtsȫꞌtɬtꞌɔꞌɩsti   tsɔ·ꞌᵘstȫwa`
now then!   Ha Night, Loc   water, big, Loc   thou art staying   killdee bird

5 Dalɔ·ꞌni | ꞌaꞌ-nɔ·ɢwȫⁿꞌ Dɔ·ꞌtꞌaᴰlɛꞌö̧ŋaꞌ | Dalɔ·ꞌni ɢɛ·s-ö̧·ꞌ Dɛꞌaꞌsɛ=
yellow   ha, now   thou hast arisen, facing us   yellow   it is, T L   thou hast

Dɔ·ꞌsɩ·ɢaꞌ | ʋꞌsönʋ·ꞌli ʋtsɩꞌꞌ-nawa`   nö̧·ꞌDɩsɢɛ·stiꞌ   ꞌiyă̌ꞌꞌ
come to fan it   quickly   beyond it, stretched   it will be said con-   sharply
                                                    tinuously

sɢɛ̈̌ꞌꞌ | ꞌaꞌ-nɔ·ɢwȫⁿꞌ   ʋsȫ-ɩ̧ꞌ   a·ꞌm-ɛɢwɔꞌꞌi   Dɩtsȫꞌtɬtꞌö̧ꞌɩsti
Now then   ha, now   Night, Loc   water, big, Loc   thou art staying

nɔ·ꞌɢwùDɩ·ꞌ   Dɔ·ꞌtꞌaᴰlɛꞌö̧ŋaꞌ | ɢɔꞌʋꞌsti   tsúnʋ·ꞌɬti   nɩꞌɢɛ·sö̧·ꞌna |
now, E   thou hast arisen,   something   thou failest   never
              facing us

ꞌɩDa·ꞌᵘwɛꞌiꞌ | Dalɔ·ꞌni   ɢɛ·sö̧·ꞌ   ayɛ̌·ꞌli   DɛꞌaꞌsiDɔ·ꞌsɩ·ɢaꞌ | Dalɔ·ꞌni
thou wizard   yellow   it is, T L   middle   thou hast come to fan it   yellow

10 ɢɛsö̧·ꞌ   tꞌùꞌtɬkɔ·ꞌtꞌtꞌanɩꞌɢaꞌ | ʋtsɩꞌꞌ-nawa`   aDȫꞌꞌnɩɢaꞌꞌ
it is, T L   thou hast come to scatter it   beyond it, stretched   it has been said

This Is the Medicine for Their Navel

FREE TRANSLATION

Now, then! Ha, in the Great Water in the Night Land thou art staying, Yellow Killdee Bird. Now thou hast arisen, facing us. Where the Yellow is, thou hast come to fan it away with thy two (wings). Relief will forthwith and continuously be caused. Sharply!

---

[10] The patient.

Now, then! Ha now, in the Great Water, in the Night Land thou art staying; (thou art staying) where the foam is piled high, thou Yellow Killdee Bird. Right now thou hast arisen, facing us. Thou never failest in anything, thou wizard. Where the Yellow is, thou hast come to fan in its very center with thy two (wings); where the Yellow is, thou hast come to scatter it. Relief has been caused!

EXPLANATION

This is another formula for a mild form of navel Dalɔ·'ni. The medicine consists of a warm infusion of the bruised bark of tsv·'t'ɪnɔ̃ⁿ', *Carpinus caroliniana* Walt., American hornbeam, blue beech, water beech, ironwood, which is drunk by the patient after the medicine man has recited the formula. There are usually four applications, the effect usually being to relieve the patient without vomiting or purging. In preparing the medicine the medicine man bruises the bark with a stone or club before stripping it from the tree, and then putting the bark into a vessel of cold water dipped from the stream, returns to the house and warms the liquid over the fire.

66

ïʼa′	vnɛʻɪstaʻnɛ·lɪʻDɔʻọ̈·′[.i¹¹]	aʻDaʻnǫ̈·′wɔ·tʻi̯ʻ			
this	whenever they have pain in different places	to cure anyone with			

sGẽ″′	ʻaʻ-nɔ·GWɔ̃ᴅ′	ʻaʻt'ǫ̈·ŋaʻnɪ·Ga′	tsɪ·ya′	saʻk'ɔ·ni′	aʻm-ɛʻGWɔ′-ii
now then	ha, now	thou has come to listen	Otter	blue	water, big, Loc

Dɪʻtsɔ̃ʻtɪt'ɔʻɪ′sti		GaDʌ̌′	tsùnv·′łti	nɪGɛʻsǫ̈·na′	ʻaʻ-nɔ·GWɔ̃ᴅ′
thou art staying		what?	thou failist	never	ha, now

Dɔ·ʻt'aᴰlɛʻǫ̈ŋa′	vʻstɪʻkʻɪ-Gwù-Dɪ·nə′	vʻlsGɛʻDə vʻDanvʻyʻɪt'anɪʻlɛ·.i′	
thou hast arisen, facing us	very little, L (=E), E	it important he has put himself under him, App	

vʻy-ɪGawɛ·′sGi	yɪ̆′ki	ʻa-nɔ·GWɔ̃ᴅ′	ʻɔ̃ᴅ'tʻɪnvʻyʻDɛsɪ·Ga′	saʻk'ɔ·′= 5
different, he speaks Hab.	if it is	ha, now	again thou hast come and taken it away from under him	blue

nɪ-GWɔ̃ᴅ	nɪGǫ̈·ʻDɪsGɛ·′sti	vʻsɔ̃′ʻ-ɪDə	nvʻDaʻnǫ̈·′na	vtsɪ·″na=
L	it will be said continuously	night, been	it has not been said	beyond it,

wùGWɔ̃ᴅ	nɪGǫ̈·ʻDɪsGɛʻsti	ʻⁱyă̆ʻ′		
stretched, L	it will be said continuously	Sharply		

sGẽ″′	ʻaʻ-nɔ·GWɔ̃ᴅ′	ʻaʻt'ǫ̈·ŋaʻnɪ·Ga′	sɔ̃ᴅ'Gi′	tsùnɛ·′Gə	aʻm-ɛʻ=
now then	ha, now	thou hast come to listen	Mink	thou white	water,

GWɔ′i̯	Dɪʻtsɔ̈tɪt'ɔʻɪ′sti	Gɔʻv′sti	tsùnv·′łti	nɪGɛʻsǫ̈·na′	
big, Loc	thou art staying	something	thou failist	never	

ʻa-nɔ·GWɔ̃ᴅ′	Dɔ·ʻt'aᴰlɛʻǫ̈ŋa′	vstɪʻkʻɪ·yu′	vlsGɛʻDə vʻDanvʻyʻ= 10		
ha, now	thou has arisen, facing us	very little, E	it important he has put		

tɛ·.i′	ʻaʻ-nɔ·GWɔ̃ᴅ′	ʻɔ̃ᴅ'tʻaʻsɛsɔ̃ʻɪ·Ga′	vtsɪ·′nawù-GWɔ̃ᴅ aDɔ̃ʻ=
himself under him, App	ha, now	again, thou hast come to pull it out	beyond it, stretched, L.

nɪGa′	ⁱyă̆ʻ	
it has been said	sharply	

¹¹ Emendation by editor.

sɢǽ''	ʻa`-nɔ·ɢwɔᵑ'	ʻa`tʻǫ̈ŋa·`nɩ·ɢa'	kʻa`nǫ̈·tsʋ''wa	saʻkʻɔ·'ni'
now then	ha, now	thou hast come to listen	Fish-Hawk	blue

ɢalǫ̈·'ldi	tsö`tɬtʻɔʻɩ'sti	v`sönv'li	dɔ·`tʻaᴰlɛʻöŋa'	v`stɩ·kʻɩ·'
above	thou art staying	quickly	thou hast arisen, facing us	very little

v`lsɢɛʻ'Də	v`danv·`yʻtʻanɩ·`lɛ·.i'	v·`y-ɩɢawɛ·'sɢi yɩ̈'ki	nɔ·`ɢwu̇-
it important	he has put himself under him, App	different, he speaks, if it is (Hab.)	now

Dɩ·'nə	ʻö'tʻa`sɛsö'ɩ·ɢa'	vtsɩ''-nawu̇-ɢwöᵑ	aDö'`nɩ·ɢa'	¹yắ''
E	again, thou hast come to pull it out	beyond it, stretched, L	it has been said	Sharply

5
sɢǽ''	ʻa`-nɔ·ɢwöᵑ'	ʻö·-ʻa`tʻǫ̈·ŋa·`nɩ·ɢa'	tsötɬɔⁿ'	tsu̇nɛ·'ɢə
now then	ha, now	again, thou hast come to listen	Kingfisher	thou white

a`m-ast-ʻǫ̈·'	Dɩ·`tsö`tɬtʻɔʻɩ'sti	ʻɩDa`ᵘwɛʻɩ-`Dɩ·nə'	v·`y-ɩɢawɛ·'sɢi
water, edge, T. L	thou art staying	thou wizard, E	different, he speaks (Hab)

Dv`Da·Nɩ̈tʻɛ·''əlö̤·i yɩ̈'ki	nɔɢwöᵑ' ʻö'`tʻa·`sɛsö'ɩ·ɢa'	vtsɩ''nawu̇--
he has though it, App if it is	now again, thou hast come to pull it out	beyond it stretched,

ɢwöᵑ' aDö'`nɩ·ɢa'	¹yắ''
L it has been said	Sharply

ʻɩ'a'	vn`ɛɩsta·`nɛʻlɩ·dɔʻǫ̈·'[.i¹²]	a`Daʻnǫ̈·'wɔ·tʻi`	Dɩɢǫ̈nɩ̈·-
this	whenever they have pain in different places	to cure anyone with	they must be hit for them, L

10 stanɛ·`lɩDa.'stɩ-ɢwöᵑ

This is the Medicine When They have Pains (Shifting) About

FREE TRANSLATION

Now, then! Ha, now thou hast come to listen, Blue Otter; in the Great Water thou art staying. What dost thou ever fail in? Now, thou hast arisen, facing us. Just a very small quantity of the important thing has come to put itself under him.[13] Maybe a speaker of incantations (has caused it). Now thou hast come to take it away from under him;[13] blue indeed it will become (and remain) not for one night (only, but forever). Relief will be caused continuously. Sharply!

Now, then! Ha, thou hast come to listen, thou White Mink; in the Great Water thou art staying. Thou never failest in anything. Ha, now thou hast arisen, facing us. Just a small quantity of the important thing has come to put itself under him.[13] Ha, now thou hast come to pull it out. Relief has been caused. Sharply!

Now, then! Ha, now thou hast come to listen, Blue Fish Hawk; on high thou art staying. Quickly thou hast arisen, facing us. Just a small quantity of the important thing has come to put itself under him.[13] Perhaps a speaker of incantations (has caused it). But this very moment thou hast come and pulled it out. Relief has been caused. Sharply!

---

[12] Emendation by editor.   [13] The patient.

Now, then! Ha, now thou hast finally come to listen, thou White Kingfisher; near the edge of the water thou art staying; thou powerful wizard! Perhaps a speaker of incantations has caused it; now thou hast come and pulled it out. Relief has been caused. Sharply! This is the medicine whenever they have pains (shifting) about. They should be rubbed in different places.

EXPLANATION

This formula is for the same purpose as No. 44, page 235.

According to an expression repeated in every paragraph, the sickness seems in this case to be caused by the [incantations of a] witch, who maybe has, by magical means, shot some invisible sharpened stick, a pebble, or some similar small object into the body of the victim. The pain shifts about as the intrusive object moves from place to place. The ailment is probably connected with rheumatism or pleurisy.

The animals invoked to pull out the disease are all of the class designated in the formulas as "penetrators," from their manner of seizing and holding their prey, or sucking its life blood. The weasel and the leech are put into the same category. The otter seems to be regarded as the chief of these, on account of its diving ("penetrating") abilities, combined with its extreme bloodthirstiness and its real or fancied cunning. The "penetrators" are commonly invoked in ayɛ`ˋlɩGɔ·ˊGi or witchcraft diseases, to pull out the intrusive object which has been shot into the body of the patient.

The treatment consists of simply pressing the sore spot with the warm hand or thumb, according to the size of the place. The medicine man recites the first paragraph while warming his [right] thumb over the fire, occasionally rubbing it in the palm of his left hand, after which he presses it gently upon the seat of pain. The same ceremony is repeated with the other paragraphs, the medicine man eventually following up the pain as it moves about from place to place, until, according to the theory, he finally chases "the important thing" out of the body.

67

ʔi'a´	Dʋ·ˋnătsö·ˋwalö·ˋnɛˤö·ˊ[.i ¹⁴]	aˋDaˤnö·ˊwɔ·tˤi̇ˋ			
this	whenever they have it along both sides	to cure anyone with			
sGɛ̆ˊˀ	|	nɔ·ˊGwö ⁿ	ˤa`tˤöŋa·ˋnɩ·Ga´	yö·ˊwi ö ⁿˊˤnaGɛ·ⁿˋ	vˤsö´vɩ̇
Now, then,		now	thou hast come to listen	human being black	Night
tsö`tɩ̆tˤɔˤɩ´sti	|	vlsGɛ·ˊDə	v`sənv·ˊli	Dɔtsv·ˊlɛˤnɛ·ˋⁿ.i | ɩ·ˊnə	
thou art staying		it important	quickly	he arose from there, facing us, App. far	
Gö·lɛ´ʔi	DɩˋDv`nɛ·ˊDzə	v·lsGɛ·ˊDə			
he standing yonder	he has spoken	it important			

¹⁴ Emendation by editor.

(a) sGɛ⁽⁾ˀ | ʿaˋ-nɔ·Gwɔ̃ᴅˊ sta`t‛ǫ̈ŋaˋni·Ga´ sti`skúya´ Dɩ`ststɩ·-
Now, then! ha, now you two have come you two men you two
to listen

Ga´ sti`GaGɛ·⁽ⁿ | sǫ̈Dv·´li ɩyǫ̈·´Də wɩDɛˋstɔy‛a´naGiˋ | GaNɩ̣sta´
little you two red (Place name) yonder you two lead him by switches
the hands toward

Dɩ·Gɩˋ GaGɛ·⁽ⁿ Daᴅlɩˋk‛əwɩ·ˋtə‛ɩ·Ga´ Gǫ̈ˋDzat‛ɔtaGɩ·-ⁱya´ Dɛ‛t‛ɩstɔ̃ˋ-
they red they have become bundled you two handle roughly, E you two

tɬt‛anɩ·Ga´ | t‛iˋstaDɩˋGalɔ̃‛ɩ·´Ga | tcɩnǫ̈·´li Gɛˋs-ǫ̈·´ wɔ̃ⁿˋʾt‛-
have made him you two have pushed him yard it is, T L you two
get on his (legs) away

5 ɩsta`Da.vGa´ nɩDɔˋDaDv·ˋk‛anɔ·ti´ nɩ·ˋGɛ·sǫ̈·na´ | wǫ̈ŋɛ·ˋtsaDa.vGa´
have thrown him he to look back never they have thrown thee
over there again over there

‛ɩGɛ·ˋtsútɬstɔ.t´ɩ-Gwɔ̃ᴅˋ
who cares what happens
to thee, L

(b) *Change* tcɩnǫ̈·´li Gɛˋsǫ̈·´ *to* nvnǫ̈·ˋDatɬ-ɔ̃·´ [15] vDzɩ·ˋDzə.ɛ·ⁿ´
as far as hill, T L yon side

(c) *Change to* sɔ.i´ nvnǫ̈·ˋDas-ǫ̈·´[.i] [16] ɩyǫ̈·´Də
other as far as hill, T L yonder

5 (d) *Change to* a·ˋm-ɛ·Gwɔ-´ɩ̣ sk‛ɔ·´nɔ̃ⁿ ɩyǫ̈·´Də
water, big, L beyond yonder

This is the Medicine When They Have it Along Both Sides

FREE TRANSLATION

Now, then! Now thou hast come to listen, Black Human Being thou art staying in the Night Land. The important thing has quickly arisen from there, facing us. From yonder where he stood the important thing has spoken (i. e., incantated the patient).

(a) Now, then! Ha, now you two have come to listen, you Two Little Red Men; you two lead him by the hands to faraway sǫ̈·Dv·li. You two (thrash) him roughly with the bundled red switches; you have made him get up; you have thrown him out into the yard, he never to look back again; over there you have thrown him; who cares what happens to him!
(b) *Change* "out into the yard" *to* "beyond yonder hill."
(c) *Change* "out into the yard" *to* "beyond yonder further hill."
(d) *Change* "out into the yard" *to* "beyond yonder great water."

EXPLANATION

This is to treat what is described as a very painful ailment, akin to rheumatism, in which the pains dart from the base of the spine around the hips to the front, and up the breast in parallel lines. The pain is also sometimes accompanied by a swelling of the parts most affected.

The treatment consists of a simple rubbing with the warm hands. The medicine man recites the formula during the rubbing, and blows

---

[15] W. D. form; C. D. nvnǫ̈·Dasǫ̈ (cf. § *c*.). [16] Emendation by editor.

his breath four times upon the body at the end of each paragraph. The rubbing at first is easy on account of the soreness of the patient, but the medicine man gradually increases the pressure of his hands.

The first or preliminary statement of each paragraph serves the purpose of an introduction conveying information as to the cause of the ailment, the whereabouts and the origin of the disease causer. (See p. 159.)

The second part of each paragraph calls upon the Two Little Red Men, the Thunder Boys, to cast out the disease. Here again we find the regular four stages in the cure: In the first the Red Men with the red switches chase out the intruder and drive him out into the yard; in the next they drive him across the mountain ridge; in the third they pursue him across the other ridge; and in the fourth they throw him beyond the great lake (in the west?), where all disease is banned.

sǫ·Dʋ·ʼli is a place name, probably somewhere in nǫ·Dɔ·ʼyi, the abode of the Thunder Boys, but the meaning of it has now been lost.

68

ꞈıʼaʼ	aˋnιneˊʼDzi	ʋneˋʻιstaˋneʻǭˊ	aˋDaʻnǫ̈ˊwɔʻtʻiˋ
this	their breast	whenever it aches to them	to cure anyone with

sGéˇʼ	sö ⁿʼGiˊ	ʻa-Giˊ 17	ʻa-GιˋʻGaGeʻ ⁿʼ
now, then	Mink	ha,	ha, red

sö ⁿʼGiˊ   ʻaGiˊ   ʻaGιˋʻGaGeʻ ⁿʼ

ʋˋlsGeˊDə	ʻιGiˊ 18	ʻιGaˊ
it important	take it	eat it

sö ⁿʼGiˊ	ʻa-GιˋʻGaGęˊ	ʻιDaˋʻᵘweꞈiˊ	ʋˋsönʋˊli	5
Mink	ha, red	thou wizard	quickly	

ʋtsιʻʻ-nawaˋ	aDöˋʻnιʻ-Gaˊ	ꞈyaˋʻ
beyond it, stretched	it has been said	Sharply!

sGéˇʼ	nɔˑGwöⁿʼ	ʻaˋtʻǫna·ˋnιˋGaˊ	tsιˑyaˊ	ʻιGιˋʻGaGęˊ	ʻιDaˋʻᵘ=
now, then	now	thou hast come to listen	Otter	thou red	thou

weꞈiˊ	ʋˋlsGeˊDə	ʻιˋ-Dʋnʋˋʻyʻtʻanιˋlęˊ.iˊ	aˋsGιʻʻn-ʋˋDöˋnöˋꞈi	ʻιGeˋsęˊ
wizard	it important	it which, he has put under, App.	ghost, it has been said	it which, App.

ʋˋlsGeˊDə	ʻιˋDʋnʋˋʻyʻtʻanιˋlęˊ.iˊ	ʋDɔˋʻlʋʻwaˋ.töⁿˋ.tiˊ	nιGeˋˋsǫ̈naˊ	
it important	it which he has put under, App.	to be found	never	

sGéˇʼ	nɔˑGwöⁿʼ	ʻaˋtʻǫˋnaˋnιˋGaˋ	tsιˑyaˊ	tsAˋskaˋseʻtiˊ	10
now, then!	now	thou hast come to listen	Otter	thou frightful	

DιGeˋʻəlɔˋʻseꞈiˊ	ʋˋlsGeˊDə	DëˋʻtʻöˋtɬtʻanιˋGaˊ	ʋtsιʻʻ-nawaˋ
thou penetratest them	it important	thou hast put him on his (legs)	beyond it stretched

aDöˋʻnιˋGaˊ	ʋsöʻʻ-ιDəˋ	nʋˋDəʻnǫ̈ˊna	ʋtsιʻʻ-nawù-Gwöⁿʼ	aDöˋʻnιˋGaˊ
it has been said	night, been	it has not been said	beyond it, stretched, L. (=E.)	it has been said

ꞈyăʻʻ
Sharply

sGéˇʼ	tcιˋʻsteˑ	Dalɔˋʻni	ʻιDaˋʻᵘweꞈiˊ	ʋˋsönʋˊli	nǫ̈ˋnɔˊ	Dɔˋʻ-
now, then	rat	yellow	thou wizard	quickly	trail(s)	thou

Datsùnaˋʻᵘwatiˋ	ʋlsGeˊDə	aˋsGιˋʼn-ʋˋDöˋꞈnöꞈˊi	ʻιGeˋsęˋ.iˊ	15
hast them lying stretched toward us	it important	ghost, it has been said	it which is, App.	

---

[17] Abbreviation of following word.

[18] Emendation by editor; instead of ʻaGi=he takes it.

ᶜa`-noˑGwŏᵛ'     Dᵉ̆`t'ŏ`tɫt'anɩˑGa'     |     nɩGǫ̆`ʷwayɛ`lǝnǫ̆`'ŏⁿ'sGɛ`stɩ'
ha, now   thou hast put him on his (legs)   a likeness of it has been left

tsa`lɔsǫ̆ˑ'.i     |     vtsɩ`'-nawu̇-Gwŏᵛ'   aDŏ`ᶜnɩˑGa' | ¹yă̆ᶜ
thou has passed, T. L.   beyond it, stretched, L.   it has been said   Sharply

sGᵉ̆'' | nɔGwŏᵛ'   ᶜa`t'ǫˑɳa·`nɩˑGa'   tɫanv·'si ¹⁹   saᶜk'ɔˑ'ni   ᶜɩDa·`ᵛᵘ-
now, then   now   thou hast come to listen   Leech   blue   thou

Wɛ̆ḯ' | v`lsGɛ'Dǝ     a`sGɩ'n-v·Dŏ`'uŏ'ᴸi     ᶜɩGɛ`sᶓ'.i' | v·`Dɩlɛ'ᴸGi
wizard   it important   ghost, it has been said   it which is, App.   Heat

5 ᶜɩDv·`ksɔ'ŏⁿ`tᶓˑi' | v`sŏnv·'li     t'a·`sɛsŏ'ɩˑGa' | nɩGǫ̆`ʷwayɛ`lǝnǫ̆`'-
he has let it down, App.   quickly   thou has come to pull it out   a likeness of it

ŏⁿ'sGɛ·'stɩ-Gwŏᵛ' | vtsɩ`'-nawa`   aDŏ`ᶜnɩˑGa' | ¹yă̆ᶜ
will remain, L.   beyond it stretched   it has been said   Sharply

THIS IS THE MEDICINE WHENEVER THEIR BREAST ACHES

FREE TRANSLATION

Now, then! Mink, ha, red (one).
Mink, ha, red (one).
Take the important thing and eat it.
Mink, ha, red (one), thou wizard, quickly relief has been caused
Sharply!

Now, then! Ha, now thou hast come to listen, Red Otter, thou wizard. It is what has become a ghost that has put the important thing under him.[20] He has put the important thing under him,[20] that it might never be found again.

Now, then! Ha, now thou hast come to listen, thou terrible Otter, thou penetrator. Thou hast come to make the important thing get up (from under the patient). Relief has been caused (and) not for one night (only, but forever.) Relief has been caused. Sharply!

Now, then! (Ha, now thou hast come to listen), Weasel, thou wizard, quickly thou hast thy paths stretched out in our direction. The important thing is merely what has become a ghost. Ha, now thou hast come to make it get up. A mere likeness of it will only remain where thou hast passed. Relief has been caused at the same time. Sharply!

Now, then! Now thou hast come to listen, Blue Leech, thou wizard. The important thing is merely what has become a ghost; it let Heat down, it seems. Quickly thou hast come and pulled it out. A mere likeness of it will remain. Relief has been caused. Sharply!

EXPLANATION

This peculiar formula, the initial paragraph of which is sung, is for treating pains in the breast, which are due, according to the formula itself, to Heat having been let down by a ghost.

The Mink, the "yellow rat" or Weasel, and the Leech are invoked, on account of their sucking powers, to pull out the disease. The

---

[19] W. E. form; C. D., tsanv·'si.   [20] The patient.

Otter, here, as often, styled a "penetrator," is probably classed with the mink and the weasel on account of its general resemblance to them in form, and in the wariness of its movements, which causes it to be regarded by the Indians as an especially subtle animal. Another medicine man used for the same purpose a similar formula addressed to the mink, the weasel, the otter, and the kingfisher, the latter of which is also regarded as a "penetrator" on account of its long, strong bill. This medicine man was of the opinion that the disease was caused by hostile conjurers.

The treatment consists of a simple application of the hands, previously warmed over the fire. The medicine man stands up, and spits in his hands at "sGĕ'" then rubs them together while chanting the first verse. Then, stooping down, he warms his hands over the fire and lays them upon the breast of the patient, drawing them downward with a steady pressure. He then blows his breath over the aching part once. The same ceremony is repeated with each of the four paragraphs.

In some cases, instead of applying the hands, the medicine man blows warm water four times upon the head and breast of the patient after each verse, the water being warmed by means of four or seven live coals dropped into it, as described.

69

Gɛʼˋtsɩyɔˑwlŏ́ɩ̭ Dɩˋkʻanŏ̜ˑ′wɔˑtʻɩˑˋ-yi |
when they have   to cure them with,   E
been shot

ɩ̭ʼaʹ   DɩˋkʻanɔˑⁿGɩˑ′Dǝ-Gwŏ̜ŏ̜ˋ   tsaᴰlɛˋnɩ̭ɩ̭aʹ   ɩGǫ̜̇ˑyiʹ |
this   they have been sung, L   where it begins   first

Gʋˑyaʹ (4 *times*) nŏⁿˋlyɔ-ɩ̭ʻi   ayɛʻʼli   Gʋˑyaʹ   Gʋˑyaʹ
                  rock(s) Loc   middle

Gʋˑyaʹ (3 *times*) GaDɔ-ɩ̭ʻi   ayɛʻʼli   Gʋˑyaʹ   Gʋˑyaʹ   Gʋˑyaʹ
                  earth, Loc   middle

Gʋˑyaʹ (3 *times*) aDɔ-ɩ̭ʻi   ayɛʻʼli   Gʋˑyaʹ   Gʋˑyaʹ   Gʋˑyaʹ   5
                  wood(s), Loc middle

Gʋˑyaʹ (3 *times*) amaʼ-yi   ayɛʻʼli   Gʋˑyaʹ   Gʋˑyaʹ   Gʋˑyaʹ
                  water, Loc   middle

ɩ̭ʻʼa-Nɩ̭ǫ̜ʻˋ   nɔˑʻGwŏ̜ᴰ   kʻaˋnɔʻɛˋDɩˑ-yiʹ
this, and   now   it has been told, E

sGɛ̆ʼʼ | ʻaˋGalŏ̜ˑʻlǝDiˋ   ayɛʻʼlɩˑʼ-yuʹ   tsŏˋtɩ̆tʻɔʻɩ̭sʻtiˋ
now, then! ha, above   middle (E)   thou art staying

Gɩˑtliʹ   wɔˋDɩGɛ̣.iʼ | ʻa-ˋnɔˑGwŏ̜ᵛʼ   nŏ̜nɔ-ɩ̭ʼ   ʻɩksɔˋʼŏ̜ᴰʼtʻaˋnɩˑGaʼ |
dog   brown   ha, now   path(s), Loc   thou hast come to let it
                                                        down

GɩˑʼGŏ̜ᴰ   Gǫ̜̇ˑwaˑʼᵘwaDiˋ   Gɛˑsǫ̜̇ʼ   ayɛʻʼli   DɛʻˋɩDɔˑˋᵊSɩˑGaʼ | nɔˑGwŏ̜ᴰ 10
blood   it is spouting   it is, T L. middle   thou hast come to halt now
          continuously

7548°—32——19

tsaˑ⁽ᵘwaᴅzɩˑ'lə	aᴅö'nɩˑGa'	ʋtsɩ⁽'-nawa`	nʋ`ᴅətᶜanö̜ˑ'ᴅə	sGȩ̈''
thy saliva	it has been said	beyond it, stretched	it has been said simultaneously	now then

Gɛ`tsɩyɔˑwlö̆'ɩ̈	ᴅɩ`kᶜanö̜ˑ'wɔˑtᶜɩˑ'-yi'	sʋˑ'li	ʋ`Gɩˑᴅu'tɬi	Gaˑ`sə-
when they have been shot	to cure them with, E	buzzard	feather	it cut off at

Gɩˑ'ᴅə	aᴅzɔtᶜastɔˑ`tiˋ	ᵘwaˑ'nɛ̣ᶜ-¹Gwü-ⁿnǫ̈ˋ	a`nǫ̈ˑskötᶜɩ̈ti
ends	to blow him with	hickory, L, and	to have it (sol) in the mouth

nɔˑ`Gwɔ-nǫ̈̆'	Gaᴅni'	uwaˑ`nɩ̈l-ö̜ˑ'.i	atcᶜɩˑ'la	uˑwaᴅnö̜ ⁿ'	ʋ`Gɩᴅu'tɬi
now, and	bullet	it has hit T L	down	soft	feather

5 | sʋˑ'li | Gaˑ'yilö̜ˑ'-ᴅə | Gaˑktᶜö̜ˑ'ᴅö̜-ya' | tsɔˑ'lə | nö̜ⁿ'Gi' | tsʋsö̆ᶜ'-ɩᴅəˋ |
|---|---|---|---|---|---|
| buzzard | plastered | it restricted E | tobacco | four | nights, been |

ʋ`ndaᶜnö̜wɩˑ'ski	naˑ'sGwɔˑᵘ-nǫ̈̆'	aˋkᶜanö̜ˑwɩ'ski	naˑski'	ɩˋGɔᶜɩˑ'ᴅə
they cure them (indef.) (Hab)	also, and	he is being cured (Hab)	this	as long as

ʋ`ᴅɩyɔ⁽'ɩstiˋ	aˑ'ma-nǫ̈̆'ˋ	naˑ'sGwö̜ᵑ	nö̜ⁿ'Gi	ʋGaˑ'nəwa`
they must abstain from	salt, and	also	four	warm

naˑ'sGwö̜ᵑ	nö̜ⁿ'Gi	tsʋ'sö̆ᶜ'-ɩᴅə	ʋ`yɔ⁽'ɩstiˋ	Gɛ`tsɩyɔˑwlö̆'ɩ̈-Gwö̜ᵘˋ
also	four	nights, been	he must abstain from	they have been shot, L

ᵘwaˑ'sö̆ⁿ	naˑ`yɔˋGɔ'ⁿ	sʋˑ'lɩnǫ̈̆'	yɩˋkᶜanɩˑ`Gö̜ˑŋa'	ᴅɩ`tɬastəGɩˑ'stə-
by himself	however	buzzard, and	if there is none	(Gerardia)

10 | Gwö̜ᵘˋ | ʋᶜsö̜ˑⁿᴅɔᶜ'nə | aᴅzɔˑ'tᶜastɔˑ`tiˋ |
|---|---|---|
| L | hollow | to blow with |

To Cure Them With, When They Have Been Shot

free translation

This, in the beginning, has to be sung:

Gʋˑya' (4 *times*), in the middle of the rocks Gʋˑya', Gʋˑya'.
Gʋˑya' (3 *times*), in the middle of the earth Gʋˑya (3 *times*).
Gʋˑya' (3 *times*), in the middle of the woods Gʋˑya (3 *times*).
Gʋˑya' (3 *times*), in the middle of the water Gʋˑya (3 *times*).

And this now has to be recited: Now, then! Ha, on high, in the center thou art staying, Brown Dog. Ha, now, thou hast come to let thy path down. Thou hast come to halt in the middle of the spot where the blood is spouting. Now, it has become thy saliva. Relief has been caused forthwith. Now, then!

To cure them with when they have been shot. A buzzard feather cut off at both ends (should be used) to blow with. And hickory (bark) should be chewed. Where the bullet has hit him,[21] down and soft feathers of the buzzard should be plastered. Rigorously restricted are: Tobacco during four days; (both) they who cure and also they who are being cured should abstain from it for a considerable time; and from salt also (during) four (days); and from warm (food) he [21] must also abstain for four days (this latter restriction referring only to) those who have been shot. Should no buzzard feather be available, the hollow Gerardia is (to be used) to blow them.

---

[21] The patient.

EXPLANATION

[This is another of the Ut. formulas, so that the explanation must be gathered from the text itself.]

It is for the cure of wounds made by a bullet or arrow, both being called by the same word, and the application consists of the inner bark of ᵘwănɛ‛, *Hicoria alba* (L.) Britt., hickory, chewed and blown through a buzzard quill, or the hollow stalk of a species of Gerardia. The directions specify that both the medicine man and the patient must abstain from tobacco for four days ["because the juice of chewing tobacco irritates wounds"].

The song of four verses at the beginning is an invocation of the spirits of the rocks, the earth, the forest, and the water, and is sung by the medicine man prior to blowing the hickory juice on the wound. The part addressing the brown dog is recited after the medicine man has blown the chewed bark into the wound. The expressions are somewhat obscure, but the purpose seems to be for the dog to lick up the blood as it flows from the wound. The buzzard, as stated elsewhere, is held to have a mysterious power over disease.

The treatment here prescribed is that usually followed in cases of bullet wounds, especially where the bullet remains in the wound. The application has no very pronounced effect, but acts rather as an emollient and sedative.

The word Gaᴾni' originally meant arrow, but by a natural evolution has now come to signify bullet and lead, just as the original word for bow, k‛alɔ·Gwĕ', now means also gun and rifle.

The whole formula is carefully written out, as is usually the case with the Ut. manuscripts.

70

ʟ'a'	tsʋnstɩ·'Ga	DɩDö̆`tɫt‛aDɩ·`nöDaNɩ̓tɩ·'-yi'
this	they are little	to make them jump down for them, E

sGĕ̌''		‛ɩskúya'	ts‛Astɩ·'Ga	‛a`-nɔ·'Gwö̆ᴺ	Dɔ·`t‛aᴾlɛ‛ö̯·ŋa'	kɩ́lú-
Now then!		thou man	thou little	ha, now	arise, facing us	then,

Gwö̆ᴺ`		ɩ·yö·'De	a`Gayöɫɩ-'nasɩ`	Da`ya·.i'		ɛ·ska·`Nɩ̓·-yu'	ʋnayɛ‛ɩsti'
L		yonder	the old one, E (?)	she is coming this way		close by, E	they fearful (things)

nö̯·Dayʋ`Dö̆‛ə`nti'		sGĕ̌''		Dɩnö̆`lt‛ɔGɩ·'	tɫɛ·`kɩ·-yu'[22]	
she does as she comes this way		Now then		let thou and I run	rightaway, E	

tsù`Dzɛstɔ·'Gi	w‛ɩ`nə`Gi'		¹yă̌‛'			5
for thee to lie on	take it over there		Sharply			

---

[22] W. D. -ts-; C. D. -s-.

sGë̆⁽ʸ⁾' | ʽιGε⁽ʸ⁾'ya tsʽastι·'Ga ʽa`-nɔ·Gwö̆ᵛ' Dɔ·'tʽaᵖlεʽọ̈ŋa'
Now   thou woman   thou little   ha, Now   arise, facing us
then

(*etc.*, *but change* a`Gayö̆lι-'nasi` *to* tsûDᴜ·`Dᴜ·nasi').
                        the old one, E (?)   thy (maternal)
                                               grandfather, E (?)

This is to Make (the) Little Ones Jump Down from Them, for Their (Mothers)

FREE TRANSLATION

Now then! Thou little man, ha, now! get up right away. Yonder the old grannie is coming. She is approaching, behaving frightfully as she comes. Now then! Let us both run off forthwith. Take thy mattress over yonder. Sharp now!
Now then! Thou little woman, ha! now, get up right away. Yonder thy (old) maternal grandfather is coming (etc.).

EXPLANATION

This formula for childbirth has been edited and commented by Mr. Mooney in his SFC., pages 363–364.
The decoction is made of the root of Da·'lɔ·'ni ʋnastε·'Dzi (also called Dalɔ·'ni a`mayᴜ·'ltë̆'ǐi), *Xanthorrhiza apiifolia* L'Her., shrub yellow root. (See p. 123.)

71

ːtʽ'a-nɪ̆ʃ̆' ʋ·`nιskwɔ·`ldισaō̆·' ʋ⁽ʸ⁾yö̆ⁿ`skιlö̆·'Də ιyᴜ'sti yɪ̆'ki
this, and   whenever they (let) down it made to slime   like it   if it is
             from stomach

nö̆·`wɔ·tʽi'  kʽa`ndjιstû'Ga ʋnι·'tli tsɔ̆'ki   Ga`tłaDö̆·'   εʽ'i
to cure with (Agrimony)   tuber   it which is   hillside, T L   it is
                                                                      living

Gᴜ·`lstanö̆'ʽιGwö̆ᵛ`   ʋ·ndιʽ'tʽasti`
it has been steeped, L they must drink it

And This (is for) When They Discharge Slimy (Matter) from Their Bowels

FREE TRANSLATION

The medicine is the agrimony (which) has a tuber (and which is) growing along the hillside; it should merely be steeped and they should drink it.

EXPLANATION

The medicine used is a cold infusion of kʽa`ndjιstû'Ga ʋnι·'tli Ga`tłaDö̆·' εʽ'i, *Agrimonia parviflora* Ait., agrimony.
[It is drunk by the patient at regular intervals; there is no ceremonial administration nor any taboo.]

72

<table>
<tr><td>Gɪ·'Gṏⁿ</td><td>ʋ`nɪskwɔ·`ldɪsGö·'</td><td>nö·'wɔ·t'i`</td></tr>
<tr><td>blood</td><td>whenever they (let) down from stomach</td><td>to cure with</td></tr>
</table>

<table>
<tr><td>kw'a`n-ʋnstɪ·'Ga</td><td>sú'lɪnɪ̇ŝ`</td><td>na.'sGwö⁰</td><td>Gɪ·'Gɔ</td><td>ʋ`nɪskwɔ·`ldɪsGö̇[.i²³]</td></tr>
<tr><td>peach(es), they little</td><td>persimmon, and</td><td>also</td><td>blood</td><td>whenever they (let) down from stomach</td></tr>
<tr><td>nö̇·'wɔ·t'i`</td><td>|</td><td>a`Ganö̇ː́i</td><td>ʋ·`ᵖlɔsö̇ː́i</td><td></td></tr>
<tr><td>to cure with</td><td></td><td>it has been boiled</td><td>it has passed</td><td></td></tr>
</table>

(This is) the Medicine When They Discharge Blood from Their Bowels

FREE TRANSLATION

Small peaches and persimmons are the medicine when they discharge blood from their bowels. It should be boiled and boiled down.

EXPLANATION

This prescription for flux would undoubtedly be efficacious when drunk by the patient, as it has a pronounced astringent effect. kw'a`nʋnstɪ·'Ga, *Prunus pennsylvanica* L. f., wild, red, bird, fire, or pin cherry; súli', *Diospyros virginiana* L., common persimmon.

73

<table>
<tr><td>Gɪ·'Gṏⁿ</td><td>ʋ`nɪskwɔ·`ldɪsGö̇'(.i ²³)</td><td>|</td></tr>
<tr><td>blood</td><td>whenever they (let) it down from stomach</td><td></td></tr>
</table>

<table>
<tr><td>·ʋ·Gu'G-ʋskɔ'ː́-i</td><td>Gɪ·'Gṏⁿ</td><td>ʋ`nɪskwɔ·`ldɪsGö̇·'</td><td>na.'sGwö⁰`</td><td>nö̇·`wɔ·t'i'</td><td>|</td></tr>
<tr><td>hooting owl, its head, L</td><td>blood</td><td>whenever they (let) it down from stomach</td><td>also</td><td>to cure with</td><td></td></tr>
<tr><td>ᵘwa.''sə-Gwö⁰`</td><td>Gʋ·`lstanö̇ː́ɪ-Gwö⁰`</td><td>ʋ`ndɪ·''t'asti`</td><td></td><td></td><td></td></tr>
<tr><td>by itself, L</td><td>it has been steeped, L</td><td>they must drink it</td><td></td><td></td><td></td></tr>
</table>

Also a Medicine When They Discharge Blood from Their Bowels

FREE TRANSLATION

Goldenrod should merely be steeped by itself. They must drink it.

EXPLANATION

Another of the Ut. prescriptions on which no additional information could be obtained. The infusion is made with the root of ʋ·`Gucʋskɔ', a species of *Solidago* L., goldenrod. A specimen collected by another informant was identified as *Pedicularis canadensis* L., common lousewort.

---

[23] Emendation by editor.

74

ιGŏⁿʻʻlι-Nɪ̨́ʼ	Gədʋʻsi	ɛʻɿ̈i	nŏⁿʼGiʼ	nʋʻⁱyɛGǫʼ	əGιʼDə	ʋʻna=
fern and	mountain	it is living	four	as far as it grows up	it taken	they are at
tʻŏⁿʻιstιʼ-yι-Gwŏⁿʻ	Dιʻx̧tsúGιDəʻ	aGɔʻstə=Gwŏⁿʻ		naʻ.sGwŏⁿ		
the top, Loc, L (-E)	they have been cut	it raw, L		also		
ʋʻskɔ·lǫ̈́ʼ	Gιʼ Gə	yʋʻnιskwɔʻləDιʼaʼ	ʋʻʻiyŏⁿʼskιlö̧ʼDə	ιyʋʼsti		
pale color	blood	if they (let) down from stomach	it made to slime	like		
yɪ́ʼki	naʻskiʼ	nö̧ʼwɔ·tʻiʼ		Gʋʻlstanŏ́ʼι-Gwŏⁿʻ	aDzιʼlə-Nɪ̨́ʼ	
if it is	this here	to cure with		it has been steeped, L	fire, and	
5 nŏⁿʻGiʼ	DιGŏʼtɪti	ʻιGɛʻsɔʻ.iʼ				
four	they (sol.) put in	it which has been (Hab)				

Also a Medicine When They Discharge Pale Blood (and) Slimy Matter from Their Bowels

FREE TRANSLATION

Four stalks of the fern growing on the mountain, the very tops being taken and cut off; (this is) also a medicine, when they discharge pale blood (and) slimy matter from the bowels. This medicine should be steeped, and four (coals of) fire should be put into (the infusion).

EXPLANATION

[This is another one of the Ut. prescriptions on which even Ay. was not able to give any more information to Mr. Mooney. ιGŏⁿʻʻli is the generic name for all the varieties of fern, and the classifying expression "Gədʋʻsi ɛʻɿ̈i" "growing on the mountain," is too vague a one to allow of the exact identification of the species.]

75

ʋʻnawaʼʼsti   nö̧ʼwɔ·tʻiʼ
chill   to cure with

10 ʋʼlιʼDa.stiʻ	ʋstιʼGa	sɔʻι-Nɪ̨́ʼ	naʼsGwŏⁿ	ʋstιʼGa	sɔʻι-Nɪ̨́ʼ
he-deceives	it (is) little	the other, and	also	it (is) little	the other, and
ʋʼtʻanŏⁿʻ	ʋʼlιʼDa.stiʻ	tʻaʼya-Nɪ̨́ʼ	GəDʋʼs-ɛʻɿ̈i	tsʋʻwaDʋʼnə	
it (is) tall	he-deceives	cherry-and	mountain, it is living	it has sinews arteries,	
ʋstιʼGa	DʋʻsʋʼG-ö̧ʼ[.i²⁵]	ɛʻɿ̈i	ᵘwɪ́skι-Nɪ̨́ʼ	GaʻnιGwaᴰlιʼski	
ʻit small	laurel, T L	it is living	whisky, and	(Speedwell)	
nιGɔʻʻdö̧ʼ	ιtsɛʻɿ̈i tsɪ́ʼki	ʋʻnɛʻləGiʻ	Gʋʻlstɔ.tiʻ	ʋnaDιʻʻtʻaʻstι=	
all the time	green it which is	by itself	to be steeped with	they must	
Gwŏⁿʻ	ʋnιʻtʻaDɛʻGιskö̧ʼi	naʼski	nö̧ʼwɔ·tʻiʼ		
drink it, L	whenever they are thirsty	this here	to cure with		

---

²⁵ Emendation by editor.

To Cure the Chill With

FREE TRANSLATION

White bugbane and another small (variety) also; and another tall (i. e., black cohosh); and the cherry growing in the mountain; and the small (plant that) has arteries, growing among the laurels: and whisky; common speedwell, the one which is all the time green; is to be steeped by itself, and they must drink this whenever they are thirsty; this is to cure them with.

EXPLANATION

An infusion is made of v·lɩ·′ᴅa.stiˋ ᴠstɩ·′ɢa, *Actaea alba* (L.) Mill., white bugbane; v·lɩ·′ᴅa.stiˋ sɔ·i′ ᴠstɩ·′ga, *Actaea alba* (L.) Mill., white bugbane; v·lɩ·′ᴅa.stiˋ v·′tˤənöⁿˋ, *Cimicifuga racemosa* (L.) Nutt., black cohosh, black snakeroot, rattleweed; tˤaya′, *Prunus virginiana* L., chokecherry; tsᴠˋwaᴅᴠ·′nə ᴠstɩ·′ɢa ᴅᴠˋˤsᴠ'ɢö·′ ε′ˤi, *Phlox stolonifera* Sims, and this is blown on the patient with the usual four repetitions.

A separate infusion of ɢaˋniɢwaᴾlɩ′ski, *Veronica officinalis* L., common speedwell, is drunk by the feverish patient whenever he feels thirsty.

76

ˤɩ′a′	ᴅɩˋnɩyɔ·′tˡi	ᴅɩᴅö̈ˋtɩ̆tˤaᴅɩˋnəᴅaˋNˤtɩ·′-yiˋ		ˤɩ″a-ɢwöⁿ	nɩˋ.-ᴠsti′
this	they (are) small	to make them jump down, for them, E.		this, L.	so far, like

	kˤanɛˋɩstɩ·-yi′				
	it to be said, E.				

sɢĕ″		ˤɩtsᴠ·′ᴅzə	ɢɛ·sö̈·′-ŋwöⁿ	kˤɩ′lû-ɢwöⁿ	ɩ·yö̈·′ᴅə	ᴠ'söˋ-′ˤi
Now, then		thou boy	it is, L	soon, L (=E)	yonder	right, Loc

ᴅɔ·ˋᴅaᴾlɛˤö̈·ŋa′	ᴅawɩ′skûlaˋ	ᴠˋskaˤsɛˤ′ti		nö̈·ˋᴅayᴠ·′ᴅöˋˤöⁿ'tiˋ
he has arisen, facing us	Flint	it frightful		he is doing as he comes hither

nö̈·ˋnɔ-ˤi′	ᴅɔ·ˋᴅayᴠ·′na·ᵘwatiˋ	ᴠˋskaˋsɛˤti′	ᴅaya′.i		ˤɩtsᴠ·′ᴅzə	5
trail(s), Loc	they lie stretched hither	frightful	he comes hither		thou boy	

kˤɩnᴠ·ˋɢɔ·ⁿ.i′	kˤɩ′lû-ɢwöⁿˋ		ɩ·yö̈·′ᴅə	ᴅɩnû′ɩ̆tˤɔɢiˋ	nö̈·ᴅɔ·-′yi
come out, thou!	soon, L (=E)		yonder	let thou and I run	Sun, Loc

wɩnɩˋlɔˤi′		ˤa·ˋ-ˡyă″
thou and I will pass to there		ha, Sharply!

sɢĕ″		ˤɩˋɢɛˤˡyᴠ·′ᴅzə	ɢɛ·sö̈·′-ŋwɔ-ᵘNˤʠ̌		kˤɩ′lû-ɢwöⁿˋ	ɩ·yö̈·′ᴅə
Now then,		thou girl	it is, L, and		soon, (L=E)	yonder

ᴠˤsöˤˋ-i	ᴅawɩ′skûlaˋ	ᴠˋⁿayɛˤˤɩstiˋ	nö̈·ˋᴅayᴠ·′ᴅəˋˤöⁿ'tiˋ		ᴅɩˋᴅɔ·′lə-
night, Loc	Flint	he frightens them	he is doing as he comes hither		they walking

nö̈·′sti′	ᴅɩˋɢɩ·ˋɢaɢᴇˤ′	ᴅɩɢö̈·ˋkˤawɩˋᴅə.ɛˤ.i′	ᴠˋskasɛˤ′tɩ·yi′		ˤɩˋɢɛˤˡ-	10
sticks	they red	he rises them, App	he frightful, E		thou	

yᴠ·′ᴅzə	kˤɩ·ˋnᴠɢɔ·ˋtsö̈·′-ŋwɔᵘNˤʠ̌	kˤɩ′lû-ɢwöⁿˋ	ɩ·yö̈·′ᴅə	ᴅɩnû′l-
girl	come out	L (=E), and	soon, L	yonder	let thou

tˤɔɢiˋ	nö̈·ˋᴅɔ·-yɩ·′-ᴅzəˋ	wɩnɩˋlɔˤi′		ˤa·ˋˡyă″
and I run!	Sun, Loc, direction	thou and I will pass to there		ha, Sharply

sgĕ⁽ˀ⁾ | ˤa-ˋnɔˑgwŏᴅ′ ˤaˋtˤǫnaˑˋnɩˑGa′ nŏˑˋDɔˑ-yɩˑ′-dzə ˤɩˋskůya′
Now, then | ha, now thou hast come Sun, Loc, direct thou man
 to listen

tsůneˑ′Gə ˤɩDaˑ⁽ᵘweˤɩˋ-Dɩˑnŏ ⁿ′ + + Gŏˋlstú′tłi | yŏˑwi′ ʋstɩˑ′Ga
thou white thou wizard, E like his clan human being it little

ˤɩˑ′a′ tsútseˤˋlɩ-Gwůˋ-Dɩˑnə′ nɔˋᵘGwů-Dɩˑnə′ ˤŏⁿˤɩnaˑGɩˋˋsɩˑGa′
this it is thine, L (=E), E now, E again, thou hast come
 to get it (Kn.)

ʋˋDanʋˑˋlŏˋnŏˋˤɩ | nŏˑˋDɔˑ-yɩˑ′-dzə wŏⁿˤɩˋnˤǫsta′ tsˤaˋskalɔˑ⁽ˤɩstɩˋ
he has failed to do Sun, Loc, direction carry it (Kn.) relinquish thy grasp
 it himself

↘5 nɩGeˑˋsǫ̈ˑna′ | deˤˤaᴅleˤɩˋsɔˤtˤanɩˑGa′ ʋˋDaˑNˤtɔ′ deˑGŏˋˋleˤɩˋsaˤ-
 never thou hast come to put his soul it will rise up as
  him on his legs

nɩˋseˑsti′ | aˋNˤǫwa′Gi ʋneˑ′Gə Daˋᴅlaˑ′sɩˋtˤanɩˋseˑsti′ | Gŏˋłkwɔˑ′Gi
he goes it cloth it white he will put his feet on seven
 as he goes

ɩˑˋya-Galǫ̈ˑ′ldɩˋ wɩˋDaᴅleˤɩˋsaˤnɩˑGa′ aˋDaˑNˤtɔ′ | ˤyăˤˤ
in succession, above he has arisen there the soul Sharply

THIS IS TO MAKE THE SMALL ONES JUMP DOWN FROM THEM FOR THEIR (MOTHERS)

FREE TRANSLATION

Now, then! Thou art a boy, no doubt.
Yonder in the Night Land, Flint hast arisen this instant.
He is behaving frightfully as he is coming hither; his paths lie stretched hither; he is coming hither, (behaving) frightfully.
Come out at once, thou boy! Let us run quickly to over yonder (out of reach of Flint). Let us pass (to the direction) of the Sun Land, sharply!
Now, then! Thou art a girl then, no doubt. (From) yonder in the Night Land Flint (is coming) this instant. He frightens (everybody) as he is coming hither. He raises his red walking sticks threateningly. Come out this instant, thou girl. Let us quickly run to over yonder. Let us pass (to the direction) of the Sun Land, ha! sharply!
Now, then! Ha, now thou hast come to listen, thou White Man from the Sun Land, thou powerful wizard. He is of such-and-such a clan. The little human being is thine, be sure of it. Now thou hast come to get him; he has failed to (come out) by himself. Carry him to the Sun Land, and do not withdraw thy hand from him. Thou hast come to put him on his feet, his soul will ascend (to happiness and prosperity) as he walks along the path (of life). He will place his feet on white cloth as he walks along. His soul has ascended to the supreme seventh upper world. Sharply!

EXPLANATION

This formula is, like No. 70, page 273, for childbirth. The prescription and the ceremony are the same, and but little additional explanation is required.

Dawɩ`skúla´ or Flint is personified in Cherokee mythology as a terrible and an aggressive individual, the dreaded enemy of all the mythic animal world because it was with flint that man pointed his deadly arrows. [Cf. Mooney, Myths, pp. 234, 274, 451.] He is here represented as advancing threateningly shaking his red walking sticks.

The final paragraph is recited only when the preceding ones fail to produce any effect. It is sometimes recited at the house immediately after the others, but usually the medicine man goes down to the stream for this purpose, using the beads during the recital, in the manner described elsewhere, in order to learn from their motions whether the child is alive or dead. The medicine man stated that it was not always possible to ascertain this by the ordinary means. The bead ceremony is sometimes repeated seven times, the rest only once.

After having recited this paragraph at the water he returns to the house and repeats it without the beads, while standing by the side of the mother-to-be. According to the medicine man's statement, the result is always successful.

The final paragraph resembles the formulas used when "going to water" described in other places. The cloth referred to is perhaps the cloth upon which the beads are placed during the ceremony [or may be the cloth which used to be spread out for the child to fall upon. (See p. 124.)]

77

꞉ɩ'a´	u`ɪsta·y'ti`	v·`tɫɩyu`ḳt'anɔ̄´꞉i	a`Da'nǫ̈·´wɔ·t'i`
this	it is eaten	it has changed itself	to cure anyone with

sGe̋''		a`Gawɛ·´la	v'ⁱyuḳt'anɔ̄´꞉i	Gɛsę´(.i [26])	a´Gɩstɩ`	Gɛ·`t'A=
now then		the Old Woman	has changed it	it is, App	it (Sol) to eat	within

GǪ·´ vt'ɔ̈´ⁿsę·.i´
it has grown, App

(a)	sGe̋''		Gɩ·tɫi´	wɔ·`DɩGę´	nǫ̈·`Dɔ·-yɩ·´-Dzə	Galǫ̈·´ldi
	now then		Dog	brown	sun, Loc, direction	above

tsɔ̄`tɪt'ɔ·ɩ́sti	v`sɔ̄nv·´li	tsa·'ᵘwutsɩ·´lə [27]	Dɛ·`aDɔ'꞉ɔ̄ⁿt'a`nɩ·Ga´		5
thou art staying	quickly	thy saliva	thou hast come to let them down		

a´Gɩstɩ`	Gɛ·`t'AGǪ·´	vt'ɔ̈´ⁿsɔ̄ⁿ´		'a`-nɔ·Gwɔ̄ⁿ´	t'a·`sɛsɔ̄'꞉ɩ·Ga´	
it (sol) to eat	within	it has grown, App		ha, now	thou hast come and pulled it out	

tsɔ̄`tɪsta·´y'tɩ·-Gwɔ̄ⁿ`	Gɛ·sę´(.i [26])		Dɩtsckwɔ·´li	Dɛ·`Ga'a`Danɩsɔ´=
it what thou eatest, L	it is, App		thy stomachs	they have come to

ɔ̈ⁿ't'anɩ·Ga´		nɩGǪ·`wayɛ·`lə.nɔ̄ⁿ'ɔ̈ⁿ'sGɛ·´stɩ-Gwɔ̄ⁿ`	tsa`ᵖlɔsǫ̈·´	
bury themselves in it		a likeness of it will be left, L	thou passed, T L	

vtsɩ·''-nawa`	nv·`Dət'anǫ̈·´Də	nɔ̄ⁿ'´t'ǫ̈·nɛ·`lɩ·Ga´		ⁱiyă'
beyond it, stretched	it has been said simultaneously	thou hast come to do it for him		Sharply

---

[26] Emendation by editor.
[27] Emendation by J. M.; instead of Dv·`watsɩ·´lə=*his* saliva.

(b) sGĕ́⁄' | Gɪ·tlĭ' sa'k'ɔ·ni' ʋⁿ'ö̱·Dzɔ·-yɪ·'-Dzə Galö̱·'ldi (etc.).
   now   Dog   blue   cold, Loc, direction   above
   then

(c) sGĕ́⁄' | Gɪ·tlĭ' ö̱ⁿ'naGɛ·' ʋ'sö̱'ɪ-yɪ·'-Dzə Galö̱·ldi (etc.).
   now   Dog   black   Night, Loc, direct.   above
   then

(d) sGĕ́⁄' | a'Gawɛ·'la ʋⁿ'yu̧kt'anö̱'̱·i Gɛ·sɛ̨·('́i ²⁸) a'Gɪstɪ̀'
   now   the Old Woman she has changed it   it is, App   it (sol) to eat
   then
Gɛ·'t'AGö̱·' ʋt'ö̱·'sɛ̨·.ĭ'
  within   it has grown,
              App

5 sGĕ́⁄' | Gɪ·tlĭ' Dɪ'st'Astɪ·'Ga' stɪ·Gɪ·'GaGɛ̨·' Galö̱·'ldi nɪ'Dö̱'-
   now   Dog(s) you two Little   you two red   above   right
   then   above
lö̱ⁿ' ɪ·yö̱·'Də stö̱·tɪ̨lt'ɔ'ɪ·'sti ʋ'sönʋ·'li ts'Ast'iwaDzɪ·'la ²⁹ Dɛ'sta=
 us   yonder you two are staying   quickly   your (²⁹) saliva   you two
Dɔ·'ʼö̱ⁿ'tanɪ·Ga' | a'Gɪstɪ̀' Gɛ·'t'AGö̱·' ʋ't'ö̱ⁿsö̱·' | 'a'-nɔ·Gwö̱ⁿʋ'
 have come to let them   it (sol) to   within   it has grown,   ha, now
       down   eat   App
t'ɪsta·'sɛsö̱'ɪ·Ga' | ayɪ'xsɪsu̧'Də-Gwö̱ⁿʋ' Gɛ·'staDö̱·'Nɛ̱·lɪ·Ga' |
 you two have come and   it looked over repeatedly, H   you two have come and done
   pulled it out   it for him
nɪGö̱·'wayɛ·'lə.nö̱'ö̱ⁿ'sGɛ·'stɪGwö̱ⁿʋ' stɪᵖlɔ's-ö̱·.i' | ʋtsɪ·'-nawu̧-Gwö̱ⁿʋ'
 a likeness of it will remain, L   you two passed   beyond-it, stretched, L
                                             T L

10 aDö̱ⁿ'nɪ·Ga' | 'yă'
   it has been said Sharply

THIS IS THE MEDICINE WHEN THEIR FOOD IS CHANGED

FREE TRANSLATION

Now, then! the old Woman has changed it; the food within has grown.

Now, then! Brown Dog, on high, in the direction of the Sun Land thou art staying; quickly thou hast come to let thy saliva down. The food within has grown. Ha, now thou hast come and pulled it out. It is the very thing thou eatest. It has come to bury itself into thy stomachs. A mere likeness of it will remain, when thou wilt have passed. Relief has been caused forthwith, thou hast come to do it for him. Sharply!

Now, then! Blue Dog, on high, in the direction of the Cold Land (etc.).

Now, then! Black Dog, on high, in the direction of the Night Land (etc.).

Now, then! The Old Woman has changed it; the food within has grown.

Now, then! You two Little Red Dogs, yonder on high, right above you two are staying. Quickly you have come to let your saliva down. The food within has been changed. Ha, now you have come and pulled it out. You two have come to look it over carefully. Scarcely

---

[28] Emendation by editor.
[29] Emendation by editor; instead of Dʋ·'watsɪ·'lə=*his* saliva.

a likeness of it will remain when you will have passed. Relief has been caused. Sharply.

EXPLANATION

This formula is used when the medicine man suspects from the soreness of the abdominal region of the patient that some enemy has "changed the food" in his stomach, and caused it to sprout or become a living thing inside of the man's body. The sickness is evidently a digestive trouble.

The treatment consists of a simple rubbing of the abdomen with the hands of the medicine man, previously warmed over the fire. This is said to ease the pains and induce action of the bowels, thus dislodging the metamorphosed and unwholesome food.

The medicine man warms his hands at the fire and then recites the first paragraph while rubbing the patient's abdomen, blowing upon it at the end of the recital. This is repeated with each of the four paragraphs, and if necessary the whole ceremony is repeated four times before noon.

Each paragraph starts out with a statement that the trouble is due to a metamorphosis or change caused by "the Old Woman" a`Gawɛ·'lə. This is a formulistic name for the new corn which is the chief food staple of the Cherokee, and which according to one of their myths originally sprang from the blood of an old woman (Mooney, Myths, p. 242).

The common word for corn is sɛ·lu'.

78

ï'a'	nö̢·`wɔ·t'i'	tsv·`nɩskwɔ·`ləDɩ·.a'	nv·`ndɩ·wᵘskö̢·'nə
this	to cure with	they (let) them down from stomach	they do not recover

sGe̋·'		tsanɛ·`tɬanö̋·'i	tsötɬskɔ·`lt'a(nö̋³⁰)ː'i		nɔ·ᵘGwö̋ᵛ
now then		thou hast apportioned	thou hast given permission		now

nö̢·`wɔ·t'i'	vnɛ·'Gə	Gʋ̀·.nɩ·Ga'
to cure with	it which	I have come and put it into it (liq)

sGe̋·'		tsanɛ·`tɬanö̋·'i	tsötɬskɔ·`lt'a(nö̋³⁰)'i		nɔ·ᵘGwö̋ᵛ'
now then		thou hast apportioned	thou hast given permission		now

nö̢·`wɔ·t'i'	vnɛ·'Gə	Gö̢·DaGɩ·`sɩ·Ga'		nɔ·Gwö̋ᵛ'	nö̢·`wɔ·t'i'	vnɛ·'Gə	5
to cure with	it which	I have come to take it out of the fire		now	to cure with	it white	

ʽö̋ⁿ`'-skɩnɛ·`Gwɔ.ɛ·`lɩ·Ga'
again, thou hast come to increase it for me

t'ɛ·lö̢·'ldi	nö̢Dɔ·'-yi	tsɩ-`wʋktɔ·'.i	ɛ·'ləDi	tsɩ̀·-GanQ.'i	
(summer grape)	sun, Loc	it which, it comes out (Hab)	low	it which, it lies (Hab.)	

v̋·'nasv.'Ga-N!ö̢	nö̢·Dɔ·'-yi	tsɩ̀·-wʋktɔ·'.i	ɛ·'ldi	tsɩ̀·-GanQ·'i	
they have claws, and	sun, Loc	it which, comes out (Hab.)	low	it which, lies (Hab.)	

---

[30] Emendation by W., recorded by editor.

kʻaʻnö̆ʻsɩ́ʻtʻa-nɪ̣̈́ʻ (flowering dogwood), and	na.ʻsGwö̆⁰ also	nö̆ʻdɔʻ-yi sun, Loc	uʻwʊktö̆ʻ.i it comes out (Hab.)	ʋnɩʻkwanɪ̣̈́ʻ (black gum)
na.ʻsGwö̆⁰ also	nö̆ʻdɔʻ-yi sun, Loc	uwʊktö̆ʻ.i it comes out, (Hab)	ʋdɔʻlanö̆ⁿʻ-nɪ̣̈́ (service berry), and	nö̆ʻdɔGwɛʻⁱyaⁿ-nɪ̣̈́ (sourwood) and
dɩʻʻdaGę̈ʻ.i they sprout	dɩʻGɩʻʻGaGę̈ʻ.i they red	Gö̆tkwɔʻGi seven	ʋʻʻnastɛʻtɬö̆ⁿ³¹ they roots	aʻGɩsti` they to be taken
ɩyʋʻstɩ́ʻaʻⁿʻ like each	nɩGaʻʻdə all	ɬɩʻʻa-nɪ̣̈́ʻ this, and	aGö̆tɬanɩʻʻɩ̈ö̆ʻ.i when it (sol) is put into it	
5 nö̆ⁿʻʻGi four	ɩʻyʋʻᴅlɔʻɩsti´ it passed, successive times	amaʻʻ-yi water, Loc	ɩyö̆ʻʻdə yonder	aʻⁱyö̆ʻʻsti it to be carried	Gö̆ʻ-dáⁿ it taken out
Gɩʻʻdə of the fire	na.ski´ this	waʻkʻʋGɩʻstɔʻtiʻ it dipped out with it	ɩyʋʻstɩ́ʻaʻⁿʻ like, every	Gaʻ tɬɔ.sk-ö̆ʻ.i it has boiled down, T L
amaʻʻ-yi water, Loc	uwadzö̆ⁿʻʻsti to go there	tsutʻaʻʻGə chicken	atsʊdʻɩ-nɪ̣̈́ʻ fish and	ʋyɔʻʻuɩ-yu´ different, L

This is to Cure (Them) With, When They let Them Down From Their Stomach, (and) They Do Not Recover

FREE TRANSLATION

Now, then! Thou (who) hast apportioned (all things) thou hast given (me) permission; now I have come to put the white medicine into (the boiling vessel).

Now, then! Thou (who) hast apportioned (all things), thou hast given (me) permission; now I have come to take the white medicine out of (the pot on the) fire; now thou hast come to increase (the virtue of the medicine) for me.

Summer grape trailing low down (on the ground, shooting) out toward the Sun Land, an ampelopsis (vine) trailing low down (on the ground, shooting) out toward the Sun Land, flowering dogwood also (going) away toward the east; and service berry; and seven red sourwood sprouts. The roots are to be taken in every case and this (i. e., the first paragraph) is to put it into (the boiling vessel).

It has to be boiled down four times in succession. When it is taken from the fire it has to be carried down to the stream, (to add more water to it); and this here (i. e., the second paragraph) is to dip (the water) out with. Every time it has boiled down, one has to go down to the stream. Chicken and fish are very bad (for the patient).

EXPLANATION

[This formula to cure an obstinate case of diarrhea is a very interesting one in that it introduces two of the prayers that are still often used by the medicine man to invoke the blessing of some mighty spirit, usually ʋnɛʻʻtɬanö̆ʻʻi himself, on the medicine and on the operations of boiling and administering it.

---

[31] W. D. form; C. D.=ʋʻnastɛʻdzi.

The medicine is a decoction of the following plants:]
tʻɛ·lǫ·ˊldi, *Vitis aestivalis* Michx., summer grape, pigeon grape.
vˋnasv.ˊGa, *Ampelopsis cordata* Michx.
kʻaˋnǫsɩˊˊtʻa, *Cornus florida* L., flowering dogwood.
vnɩˊˊkwa, *Nyssa multiflora* Wang., black gum.
vDɔˊlanö^{n}ˋ, *Amelanchier canadensis* (L.) Medic., shadbush; serviceberry.
nǫˋˋDɔ·Gwɛˊˊ^{i}ya, *Oxydendune arboreum* (L.) DC., sorrel-tree, sourwood.

The roots are taken from the east side in the case of the trees; from the vines, runners that grow out toward the east are chosen.

The roots are put into a vessel of water [which has been dipped out of the stream], and the whole is boiled down until the liquid is nearly evaporated, when the vessel is taken from the fire and taken down to the stream to be filled again. The roots are then boiled down once more, and so on for four consecutive times, after which the medicine is administered to the patient. Chicken and fish are rigorously tabooed in [all diarrhea cases, as these animals, judging from their loose feces, seem to be chronically suffering from this very ailment].

79

	aˋnatlɔ·yɩˊˊi	vˋnAstɩˊGa	vGǫˊwutłiˋ	ɩˋaˊ	
	they cry, (Hab)	they little	it for the purpose	this	
sGɛ̈ˊˊ	Gölkwɔ·ˊGi	ɩGölsta^{D}ˊlaGiˋ	aʻˋnɛ·Dzɔ·ˊGi	tsöˋtlɔsɩˊlöˊˊi	
Now then	seven	they clans	ball-game	it has assembled	
tsvˋlawɩtsöˊˊi	ɔ·ˊDali	anɛˊˊi	Gɛˋˊsɛ̨.iˊ	nǫˋˋDɔ·-Gǫ̈-yi	(ˊi^{32})c-
it has met	mountain	they are living	it is, App	sun, Loc	thou
kùyaˊ	Gɩˋ'GaGɛ̨ˊ	tsöˋtɫtʻɔˋɩˊsti	ʻaˋtʻǫˋŋaˋˋnɩ·Ga		Galǫ̈·ˊldi
Man	red	thou art staying	thou hast come to listen		above
Döʻɩˋloˊˊi	ˊö^{n}ˋaˋnɛsvˋnɩ·Gaˊ	Dɛʻʻ aDaGalɛˊˊNɩtʻanɩ·Gaˋ		vˋsönvˊ·	5
thou comest from	again, thou hast come down	thou hast come to separate them		quickly,	
lɩˋ·yuˋ	vsöˋˋɩ·-yiˊ	nǫˋnɔˊ·ˊi	wɩ·DaˋˋDanö^{n}ʻʻǫŋaˊ	sɩyaǫ̀ˋDaGwa	
E	night Loc	trail(s), Loc	thither, they have laid themselves	a noise of thunder	
^{D}lɔˊski	vsöˋˋɩ·-yiˊ	ˋˋwaˋDzɩtʻɔˊɩˋstʻanɩ·Gaˊ	nǫˋDayvˊˋktʻaʻǫ·stiˋ	nɩGɛˊˋ·	
der	night Loc	he has come to put it to stay there	it to look back	never	
sǫˋnaˊ	vtsiˊˊnawaˋ	nɩGǫ̈ˋˋDɩsGɛ·stiˊ			
	beyond it, stretched	it will be said continuously			
DɛˊˋGɔ·sɩˋsɩsG-ǫ̈·ˊ.i	yǫ̀·wiˊ	Gǫ̈·ˋwanɩskaˋˋstaˋnɛʻǫ̈·ˊ.i		aˋndɩskɔ^{n}ˊ.i	
they have been assembled repeatedly T L	human being	they are scaring them (Hab)		they say (Hab)	
ts-aˋnatlɔ·yɩˋaˊ	vˋnAstɩˊGa	ɔ·ˊDali	anɛˊˊi	yǫ̀·wi	tsɔˋl-aGa- 10
when it is, they are crying	they little	mountain	they are living	human being	tobacco, it
yǫ̀ˋlɩ-Gwö^{D}ˋ	DɩDzɔˊtʻɩstɔ·ˋtiˊ	nɩGaˊDə	aˋnɩyɛl-ǫ̈·ˊ.i		aˋnɩGɛn-ǫ̈·ˊ.i
old, L.	they to be blown with it	all	their body, T L		their crown of the head, T L

---

[32] Interpolated by J. M.

ιGö·yi′ DιDzɔ·′t'ιstɔ·'ti` | nö<sup>n</sup>'Gi′ a`skwůDι·′sti ιyυ`stiḷaⁿ′
first   they to be blown with it   four   it ended   like, each

υsö!′i | Da`k'anö·′wιskö·′.ι-N!5^t′ nöⁿ'Gi′ tsυsö-"ιDə ιyö·′Də
night   while they are being cured and   four   they nights, been   yonder

υnε`·Da.sti′ nιGε`sö·na′ | !ι′′a-N!5^t′ Gɔ'υ′sti tsυ`GιDů′tli y'′ki
they to walk   never   this, and   something   they feathers   if it is
about

nιGa·′Də 5ⁿ'Dɔ·′yi a'ti′ Gε`sɔ·.i′ Gö·`wanι·`Gιstö·′.i ι·Dzυ·′lə'a·′-
all   outside   it to be put   it was, Hab   whenever they are eating   both, each
down   them

5 -Gwö^v` Dιk'anö·′wɔ·t'ι·-yi` | a^blě′′ k'a`nε·Ga′ Gɔ'υ′sti nιGa·′Də
L   to cure them with, E   and   skin   something   all

GanυGɔ′^uwιsti` | nö·`wɔ·t'i′ tsɔ·′l-aGayö·′lι-Gwö^v`
it has to come out   to cure with   tobacco, it old, L

This is for the Purpose of (Curing) Children When They Constantly Cry

FREE TRANSLATION

Now, then! The seven clans have assembled for a ball game; they have met. They are the Mountain Dwellers.

Thou (who) art staying in the Sun Land, O Red Man, thou hast come to listen; thou comest from above; again thou hast come down, thou hast come to separate the (ball players). Their paths have laid themselves in the direction of the Night Land. With a noise as of thunder, he[33] has taken it[34] to the Night Land to stay, it never to look back. Relief will be caused constantly.

Where the (directions) have been assembled: The people are scaring them, they say, when the children are constantly crying, the people living in the mountain (that is). Old tobacco should be blown on them,[35] all over their bodies. Their[35] crown should be blown first. The (operation) should be repeated (lit., "ended") four (times), each time at night. While they[35] are being cured (that is) four nights, they should not walk about. And this (you ought to be careful about): If there are any feathers (inside the house), put them all outside (just) like when they are being treated for the (disease that is called) "they are eating them." And any skin that (might be inside the house) all has to come (outside). The medicine is just old tobacco.

EXPLANATION

This prescription is for a stomach or bowel complaint common to very young children, and which causes them to cry constantly. According to Cherokee views, this ailment is sent by the ɔ·′Dali anε!i or Mountain Dwellers, a class of invisible fairies. (See p. 25.)

---

[33] The Red Man.   [34] The disease.   [35] The patients.

The medicine man makes the rather startling assertion that the crying of the child is due to the fact that seven fairy clans are playing a ball game in its stomach, and he calls upon the Red Man to swoop down upon them like a hawk upon its prey and drive them out into the Night Land.

The Red Man is probably the Thunder, and this would explain the reference to "the noise as of thunder" with which he takes them out west.

The medicine consists of an infusion of tsɔ·ˈlaGayǫ̈·ˈli, *Nicotiana rustica* L., wild tobacco, blown over the body of the child for four consecutive nights. Any feathers in the house must be put outside during the course of the treatment, and the child itself should be kept indoors for the four days during which the treatment lasts. These precautions are taken, as the medicine man stated, because the disease closely resembles Gȫ·ˈwanι·ˈGιstǫ̈·ˈ.i,[36] another children's complaint, which is believed to be caused by the birds, and which may be communicated from their feathers or from their shadow falling upon the child as they fly overhead.

Ay. could not explain the restriction with regard to the articles of skin, since this is one of the Ut. formulas.

80

vnιyɔ·ˈtʻəGιsGǫ̈·ˈ[.i [37]]   aˈDaʻnǫ̈·ˈwɔ·tʻiˑ   ˑιˈaˈ
Whenever they have an   to cure anyone with   this
itching

v·ˈnasteˑˈt-s·tι·ˈGa   v·ndι·ˈˈtʻastι·-yiˈ | Gȫⁿˈˈtʻɔtiˑ   DιDzɔ·ˈtʻa.ɛ·ˈtι=
root, little   they must drink it, E.   to be used with it   it must be blown
                                                                        on them,

Gwȫᵘˑ
L

ɔ·ˈya   Dalɔ·ˈnιGɛ·ⁿˈ   (*4 times*).
(Fire) yellow

ˈyăʻ   5
Sharply!

ɔ·ˈya (*4 times*).
(Fire)

tcι·ˈstu   Dalɔ·ˈnιGɛ·ⁿˈ   (*4 times*).
Rabbit   yellow

ˈyăʻ.
Sharply!

teι·ˈstu (*4 times*).
Rabbit

[36] When they (i. e., the birds) eat them (the children).
[37] Emendation by editor.

This is the Medicine When They Have the Itching

FREE TRANSLATION

They must drink Virginia snakeroot; it is also to be used to blow them with.
Yellow Fire (*4 times*). Sharply!
Fire! (*4 times*).
Yellow Rabbit (*4 times*). Sharply!
Rabbit! (*4 times*).

EXPLANATION

[This song is to treat the same ailment as described in the notes following prescription No. 4, p. 173.

In this case the disease is believed to be caused by the patient having urinated on the ashes. This doubtless explains why the fire is addressed under its formulistic name of ɔ·ya' but it has not been possible to learn why the Rabbit was called upon. Both to the fire and to the rabbit a yellow color is ascribed, to correspond with the color of the urine.]

The medicine used is the root of vˋnastɛˋtstu·'Ga, *Aristolochia serpentaria* L., Virginia snakeroot, which is chewed by the medicine man and blown by him into the urethra by means of a grass stalk or a small tube of cane, according to the sex of the patient. A portion of the snakeroot is also steeped in water and the infusion drunk by the patient, who is forbidden to eat potatoes or beans while under treatment. As this disease has its theoretic origin in the Fire, the reason for this taboo is probably the same as that given in No. 45.

The bark of tsɩ·yu', *Liriodendron tulipifera* L., tulip tree, poplar, whitewood, is sometimes used as a substitute for the snakeroot.

In making the ceremonial application, the medicine man sings the first line of the song, addressed to the yellow Fire, and then blows the medicine four times into the urethra. He then repeats the line in the same manner, after which he calls four times upon the Fire in a quick, sharp tone of voice, and blows his breath four times into the urethra as the medicine was blown into it before. The same alternate blowing of the medicine and of the breath is repeated with the second part of the song addressed to the Yellow Rabbit. The ceremony thus consists of four stages, as is usually the case in the medical formulas, viz.:

1. Song to the Fire; medicine blown four times.
2. Song to the Fire; breath blown four times.
3. Song to the Rabbit; medicine blown four times.
4. Song to the Rabbit; breath blown four times.

[During my stay with the Cherokee the practice of blowing the medicine into the urethra of the patient was no longer known.

The medicine was blown from a distance of 3 to 4 feet in the direction of the patient's bare abdomen by the medicine man, a tube of aˋmadɩˊʻtɔ.tiˋ vˑʼtʻənöⁿˋ being used for this purpose.]

81

ɩˊaˊ	Dalɔˑˋni-Gɛˑʼⁿ	ts-aˑˋndɩkʻəʻǫˑʼ[.i ³⁸]	nǫ̈wɔˑtʻiˊ	DɩʻυˋDɩˑyiˊ
this	yellow-ish	that which they urinate (Hab.)	to cure with	to give it them to drink—E.

¹yăˑʼ		ʻaˋ-nɔˑGwöⁿˊ	skwAtʻǫ̈ˑˋŋaˑnɛˑˋlɩˑGaˊ	Galǫ̈ˑʼldi	ayɛˑˋlɩˑ-yuˊ
Sharply!		ha, now	thou hast come to listen to me	above	middle, E.

tsö̈ˋtɩtʻɔʻɩstiˊ	skwanɛˑˋtłanö̈ːʼi		ʻa-nɔˑˋGwù-Dɩˑnəˊ	nǫ̈ˋwɔtʻiˊ
thou art staying	thou hast apportioned for me		ha, now, E.	to cure with

υnɛˑˊGə	ʻaˑˋ-tʻaˋᴰlskɔˑłtʻaˊ		ʻaˋ + +	Göˋłstúˑtłi	ɩˑˋyυDɔˑʼtali + +
it white	ha, thou hast given permission		ha, so and so	his clan	heaped up so and so

tsυDɔˑʼɩDə		tsυˋłtʻɔʻɩst-ǫ̈ˊ	vˋłtɛˑ-yɩˑʼDzö̈ⁿ	tɩˋtʻɔˋɩstʻanɩˑGaˊ		5
his names are		where he stays T. L.	near, Loc., Direction	thou hast come to put it to stay		

ʻaˑˋ-Goˋυsˊti	stɩnυˋləʻöⁿˊski	nɩˑGɛˑsǫ̈ˋnaˊ		ʻaˋ-nɔˑˋGwù-Dɩˑnəˊ
ha, something	you two fail (Hab.)	never		ha, now, E

ǫ̈ˋDal-öⁿˊnaˋGɛ-stǫ̈ˑ-yiˊ	ʻaˑˋwɩkʻυˋsɩˑGaˊ		+ +	Göˋłstútˊłi		+ +
lake, black, edge, Loc.	ha, it (sol.) has been thrown in (liq.)		so and so	his clan		so and so

tsυDɔˑʼɩDəˋ		ʻaˋʼ-ayɛˑłǫ̈ˊ	Gɛˑsǫ̈.iˊ	ɛʻɩsti	vˋDöˋnɩˑʻᶿlɛˑⁿ.iˊ	
his names		ha, his body, Loc.	it is, T. L.	pain	it has been said, App.	

ʻaˋ-nɔˑGwöⁿˊ	vˋsönυˋlɩˑ-yuˊ	DɛGǫ̈ˋlɛˑʼɩsɩsGɛˑstiˊ	Nɩˋɩstǫ̈nɛˑˋlɩˑGaˊ
ha, now	quickly, E.	he shall arise continuously	thou hast come to do it for him

This is the Medicine to Give Them to Drink When They Urinate Yellowish (Urine)

FREE TRANSLATION

Sharply! Ha, now thou hast come to listen to me, on high in the center thou art staying, thou (who) hast apportioned (the things) for me. Ha, now indeed thou hast given me permission (to use) the white medicine. Ha, he is of such and such a clan, he is called so-and-so. Thou hast come to put it to stay near the place where he is staying. Ha, you two never fail in anything. Ha, but now it [39] has been thrown into the black lake, near its shore. He is of such-and-such a clan, he is called so-and-so. Ha, his body [40] has been caused to become pain(ful). But now he will quickly and constantly arise; you two have come to do it for him.

EXPLANATION

This formula, which was noted down by the medicine man at a later time than most of the others, is carelessly written and evidently

---

[38] Emendation by editor.   [39] The disease.   [40] The patient.

incomplete. The first part of it is addressed to ʋnɛ`'tɬanɔ̈'ʃi, the Sun, one of the greatest divinities of the Cherokee pantheon.

The two spirits called upon in the second paragraph are not named, evidently through forgetfulness in writing out the formula, but they are probably the Two Thunder Boys, or Little Men.

The medicine used is a decoction of the roots of ʋ·yɔ·'ᴅali` ʋstɩ·'ɢa ɢaᴅʋ·'sɛ'ʃi, *Iris verna* L., dwarf iris; ʋ·yɔ·'ᴅali ʋstɩ·'ɢa a'mayʋ·'ɫt'ɛ̣i, *Acorus calamus* L., sweet flag, calamus; ʋ·ᴅa·'.i ʋstɩ·'ɢa, *Clematis virginiana* L., virgin's bower, together with chips of the stalk of ʋ·ᴅa·'.i ʋ·'t'ɘnɔ̈'ⁿ, *Aristolochia macrophylla* Lam., pipe vine, Dutchman's pipe.

The decoction is drunk by the patient after the formula has been recited by the medicine man. The ceremonial [administration] takes place two or four times, but the patient drinks the medicine at intervals as often as desired, abstaining from other food or drink in the meantime. There is no bathing or blowing of the medicine.

82

ʃɩ'a'   a`nɩskɔ·'li   a`ᴅa'nö·'wɔ·t'ï` |
this   their head   to cure anyone with

ʃɩ'a'   ᴅɩ`k'anɔ·ɢɩ·'ᴅɘ |
this   they have been sung

'a:yi' | a`nɩsku'ya   a`nɩᴅa·'ᵘwɛ   anɩ'loʃi' |
            they men   they wizards   they have
                                         gone by

ʋtsɩ·''-nawa`   anö̈`ⁿ'nɩ·ɢa' |
beyond it, stretched they have said it

5 ɛ·`tɬ-awɩ·'ni   anɩ'loʃi' |
   earth, under   they have
                  gone by

ʋ`lɩsɢɛ·'ᴅa   anɩ`sala`ndɔ·t'a`nɩ·ɢa' |
it important they have come and lifted it
              up as they went by

ʋtsɩ·''nawa`   anö̈ⁿ·'nɩ·ɢa' |

a`nɩᴅa·'ᵘwɛ   tsʋ`nasᴅɩ·ɢa' |
              they are little

anɩ'loʃi'   ɛ·`tɬawɩ·ni' |

10 ʋ`lɩsɢɛ·'ᴅa   anɩ`sala`ndɔ·t'a`nɩ·ɢa' |
    ʋtsɩ·''nawa`   anö̈ⁿ·'nɩ·ɢa' | ¹ya·''

sɢɛ̈·'' | a`nɩsku'ya   anɩ·ɢaɢɛ·ⁿ'i   anɩ'loʃi' | ayɛ·lö̧·'   ayɛ·''li
                          they are red   they have   his body   center
                                         gone by

anɩ·k'atö̧`ᴾleʃi'   |   ʋ·`lsɢɛ·'ᴅɘ   'a`nʉlkɔ·`t't'a`nɩ·ɢa'   |   ʋtsɩ·''nawa`
they have forced   it important they have come and scattered it
through App.

anö̈·''nɩɢa' | ¹ya·''

15 sɢɛ̈·'' | nɔ·'ɢwö̈ᴅ   a`nɩsku'ya   a`nɩᴅɛ·''aᴾlu`   'anɩ'loʃi'   ɢalö̧·`l-
                                         they purple   above

dɩ·'ᴅzɘ | ʋ·`lsɢɛ·'ᴅɘ   a`nʉlkɔ·`t't''anɩ·ɢa'   |   ʋtsɩ·''nawa`   anö̈··-
nɩ·ɢa' | ¹ya·'

This is the Medicine (for) Their Head

FREE TRANSLATION

This has to be sung:
>Ha-yi! The Men, the Wizards have gone by,
>They have caused relief.
>
>Under the earth they have gone by.
>As they went they lifted the disease up.
>They have caused relief.
>
>The Little Wizards
>Have gone by under the earth.
>As they went they lifted the disease up.
>They have caused relief. Sharply!

Now, then! The Red Men have gone by. They have forced their way through the center of his body. They have come to scatter the important thing. They have caused relief. Sharply!

Now, then! Now, the Purple Men have gone by on high. They have come to scatter the important thing. They have caused relief. Sharply!

EXPLANATION

The medicine used with this headache formula is [ordinary chewing] tobacco, with a little ginseng (*Panax trifolium* L.) root, [if available]. These are chewed by the medicine man and the juice is blown upon [the forehead, the temples, the crown of] the head and the back of the neck of the patient.

The medicine man stands erect while singing the preliminary song. He then recites the first paragraph of the formula and blows the juice on the patient four times. This is repeated after the second paragraph, and the whole ceremony may be repeated. As usual, the patient sits facing the east. In most headache formulas the ceremony is about the same.

[The Red Men and the Purple Men mentioned belong probably to the class of the "Little People." (See p. 25.)]

83

ɪ'a'	aDɛ·'lə	Dɩ'kt'ɔti'
this	bead(s)	to look at them with

sGɛ̈''	'a-'nɔ·Gwŏⁿ'	'a`t'ǫŋa·'nɩ·Ga'	yǫ·wi'	Gan'ŏ'ɩ·'Də
Now, then	ha, Now	thou hast come to listen	human being	long

tsŏtɩtɔ'ɩ·'sti	Go'ʋ'sti	tsanʋ·'łti	nɩ·Gɛ`'sǫ'na'	'ɩyɛ`'l-ast-ǫ·'
thou art staying	something	thou failest	never	thy body, edge, T L

nǫ·'nɔ'i'	Dɛ`'tsɩGasɔ·''ŏⁿ't'a`nɩ·Ga'	DɩGa`skɩlɔ·'Gi	tsùnɛ·'Gə	a'N'ǫ-
trail(s), Loc	I have come to bring them down	they chairs	they white	it cloth

wa'Gi	ʋnɛ·'Gə	a'łtłǫ·'t'anɩ·Ga' 41	sǫ·nɩk't'a	tsùnɛ·'Gə 5
	it white	it (kn.) has come to lie on it	beads	they white

---

41 W. Dial. form; C. Dial. aᶦlsǫ·'t'anɩ·Ga'.

aˡⁱtłɔ·ˋtʻanɩ·ɢa′ ⁴² | ɩˋɢö·yi′ ɢalö·lɔ·′ⁿ aᴅa·ni̥tɔ′ tsʋᴅlɛˋɩsɔtɩ·-yi′
it (sol) has come to lie on it | first | it above | it soul | it has arisen, Loc

ɢɛ·s-ö·′ ᴅaˋᴅlɛʻɩˋsaʻnɩ·ɢa′ |
it is, T L   it has risen

tʻaˋᴅlɩ·nɛ̨′ ɢaˋlö·ldi′ ᴅɩɢaˋskɩlöⁿ′ tsûnɛ·′ɢə ᴅa·ksɔ″öⁿ′tʻanö·′ |
second above they chairs they white it has been let down, T L

aˋni̥ǫwaˋɢi ʋnɛ·′ɢə aˡⁱtłǫ̈ˋtʻanɩ·ɢa′ ¹ | sǫ̈·ˋnɩ̨kt‘a′ ʋnɛ·′ɢə
it cloth it white it (kn) has come to lie on it bead(s) it white

5 aˡⁱtłɔ·ˋt‘anɩ·ɢa′⁴² | tʻaˋᴅlɩnɛ̨′ ɢaˋlö·ldi′ aᴅa·ni̥tɔ′ tsʋlɛˋɩsɔtɩ·-yi′
it (sol) has come to lie on it | second above it soul it has arisen, Loc

ɢɛ·sǫ̈·′ ᴅaᴅlɛʻɩsaʻnɩ·ɢa
it is, T. L it has risen

tsɔ·ˋɩnɛ̨′ ɢaˋlö·ldi′ (etc.).
third above

nöⁿˋɢɩnɛ̨′ ɢaˋlö·ldi′ (etc.).
fourth above

ʻɩˋsɢɩnɛ̨′ ɢaˋlö·ldi′ (etc.).
fifth above

10 sʋ·ˋᴅalɩnɛ̨′ ɢaˋlö·ldi (etc.).
sixth above

ɢöłkwɔ·ˋɢɩnɛ̨′ ᴅɩˋɢalǫ̈·ˋldɩ-y-ö·′.i ᴅɩɢaˋskɩlɔ·ⁿ′ tsûnɛ·′ɢə ᴅaksɔ″-
seventh they above, Loc, T L they chairs they white it has

öⁿ′t‘an-ö·′ | aˋni̥ǫwaˋɢi ʋnɛ·′ɢə aˡⁱtłǫ̈·ˋtʻanɩ·ɢa′ ⁴¹ | sǫ̈nɩkt‘a′
been let down, T L it cloth it white it (kn.) has come to lie on it bead(s)

ʋnɛ·′ɢə aˡⁱtłɔ·ˋtʻanɩ·ɢa′ ⁴² | + + tsʋᴅɔ·′-ɩᴅə | ʋˋᴅa·ni̥tɔ′
it white if (sol) has come to lie on it so and so his names are his soul

ʋwɔ″ɩsɔˋnö·i̥′i aˋkt‘oti‘ aᴅö″nɩ·ɢaˋ | ɢöłkwɔ·ˋɢɩnɛ̨′ ɢaˋlö·ldi′
it has been made completely beautiful if looked into it has been said seventh above

15 wɩˋɢananʋɢɔ·′tsɩsaˋnɩ·ɢa′ aᴅa·ni̥tɔ′ ᴅɛɢǫ̈·ˋlɛʻɩˋsaʻnɩˋsɛ·sti′ | ¹yǎʻ
it has appeared up there it soul he will arise continuously Sharply

This is to Examine with the Beads

FREE TRANSLATION

Now, then! Ha, now thou has come to listen, Long Human Being, thou art staying (right here); thou never failest in anything. I have come to bring my paths down to the edge of thy body. The white cloth has come to rest on the white chairs; the white beads have come to rest on (the white cloth). The soul has risen to the first upper world, the place of its ascension.

In the second upper world the white chairs have been let down; the white cloth has come to rest on them; the white beads have come to rest on (the white cloth). The soul has risen to the second upper world, the place of its ascension.

---

⁴² W. Dial. form; C. Dial. aˡⁱsɔ·ˋtʻanɩ·ɢa′.

In the third upper world (*etc.*).
In the fourth upper world (*etc.*).
In the fifth upper world (*etc.*).
In the sixth upper world (*etc.*).
In the seventh upper world the white chairs have been let down; the white cloth has come to rest on them; the white beads have come to rest on (the white cloth). He is called so-and-so. His soul, made pleasing, has become examined. In the seventh upper world it has appeared, the soul will ascend constantly. Sharply!

EXPLANATION

[This is one of the three formulas published by Mr. Mooney in his interesting account of the Cherokee River Cult (p. 8).] It is recited when "going to water," for obtaining long life, before eating the new corn, etc. The general ceremony is the same as the one described in Nos. 43 and 93, but in this case the medicine man also uses the beads.

When the medicine man takes a whole family to the water he performs the whole ceremony for each member in turn. Should the movements of the beads foreshadow sickness for any member of the party he afterwards performs another ceremony to learn whether that person will recover or die, and also, if possible, to avert the threatened evil.

[According to the oral directions given by Ay.] the beads must be laid down upon a yard of cloth; [both] cloth [and beads] afterwards become the fee of the medicine man.

84

Ɪⱻ'a'   Dɩˋdǭ·lɛ́'sGi   a`Da‛nǭ'wɔ·t‛Ɪˋ
this   it breaks them,   to cure anyone with
                Hab

sGɛ̈́'ᵎ | ‛a-`nɔ·Gwö̆ ᴅ'   Ga`nɩ·tɬi ⁴³   Ga`nɩtɬǭ'wa ⁴³   Gɛ·sǬ·'
Now, then!   ha, now   bedstead   under the floor   it is, T L

nǭ·`waᴅᴜ·`yǭnö̆'Ꞻi | ᴜlsGɛ·'ᴅǝ   ᴅᴜnᴜ·`y‛t‛anɩˋlɛ·ⁿ.i'    wa‛ɩl'ɩGwö̆ ᴅ`
it has formed itself it important he has put it under, App   Measure-worm

(a) ᴜˋsönᴜ·'li   GaNꞮsta'   tsᴜnɛ·'Gǝ   Gɛ·ˋsɛ·ⁿ.i'   ᴅaᴅɔˋᵘltsɩ·Ga' |
    quickly   switch(es)   they are   it is, App   they have come and
                                      white   recognized each other

a`nɩᴅa·'ᵘwɛ        tsᴜˋnstɩ·'Ga     ᴅɛ·`Gɛ·tsᴜ`tɬtɔ·t‛anɩ·Ga` | GaNꞮsta'   5
they wizards   they little   they have come to make thee get up   switch(es)

tsᴜnɛ·'Gǝ   ᴅɛ·Gɛ·`GasǬ·`Gö̆ldɩst‛anɩ·Ga' | a‛ᶥyɛ·'lsti   ᴜnɛ·'Gǝ   Gɛ·ts‛=
they are white they have come to take them   knife   white   they
                into their (hands)   have

ska·sɛ·`taᴅɩ·Ga'       |   nɩᴅᴜ·`lt‛anǭ·ᴅǝ   nǭnɛ·`tsǭnɛ·'lɩ·Ga'      |   nǭ`ᴅɔ·=
come to frighten thee   arisen at the same time   they have come and made   sun,
                                                     it so for thee

---

⁴³ W. Dial. form; W. Dial. -tl->C. Dial. -s-.

yɩ-ʹdzə	wɩ`dɔ·Gɛ`'tsötłtɔ·ʹtʻanɩ·Ga'		wɔ·`ᴅal-ǫ·ʹ	tsu`ckɔ̇-iʹ	Galǫ̈`ldɩ·=
Loc, Direction	they have come to make thee stand there		the mountain, Loc, yonder	post oak, Loc	above,
ᴅze	wǫ̈ŋɛ`ʹtstʻɔ`ʹɩstʻa`nɩ·Gaʹ				
direction	they have come to make thee stay there				

(*b*, *c*, and *d exactly the same, with each a final* ¹yăᵛ.)

ᴅɛ`'Gɔ·sɩ`sɩsG-ǫ̈.ʹi		ǃɩʼaʹ	ᴅɩ`ᴅǫ̈·léʹsGi	ᴅɩ`ᴅaʻnǫ̈·`wɔ·tʻiʹ	
they have been gathered		this	he breaks them, Hab	to cure people with	

súʻli	Gö ⁿʹʹtʻɔtiˋ	ᴅɩGǫ̈`ⁿ!stanɩʹᴅa.stiˋ		υᴅɔ·ʹtəGwüᴅə`ˋ	ᴅɩkǃa=
(persimmon)	to use with it	they must be struck		all day	to cure

5 nǫ̈·ʹwɔ·tʻiˋ	Gɛsɔ·ʹ.i		uˋGɩstɔ.tiʹ	aᶜʹyɛ·ʹlsti	aˋᴅɩ.stiʹ
them with it	it has been, Hab		for him to take it (sol) away with	knife	to be put down

This is the Medicine (When) it Breaks Them

FREE TRANSLATION

Now, then! Ha, now, it is under the floor, under the bedstead that it has formed itself. It is only a measure worm that has put the important thing under him, it seems.

Quickly the white switches have come to act in unison (lit., they have come and recognized each other). The little wizards have come and have forced thee [44] to get up with them. They have come to take the (switches) into their hands. They have come to frighten thee [44] with the white knife. They have come and forced thee to arise forthwith; they have come to make thee stand up in the Sun Land; in the post oak, on the mountain above, they have come to put thee staying.

Where the (instructions) are gathered: This is the medicine when it breaks them; a persimmon (stamper) must be used to massage them with; they should be treated all day with it; as fee, a knife should be paid.

EXPLANATION

This formula for rheumatism consists of four paragraphs, differing only in minor points and evidently intended to be the same. [For the measure worm as cause of rheumatism, see p. 293.]

[Medicine men are now unable to explain the expression, according to which the disease "has formed itself under the floor, under the bedstead." Cherokee cabins are usually built on some stout corner stones, a foot or more high, as a support. This caused the floor to be somewhat elevated as a platform, and under it all sort of refuse and rubbish is generally thrown. It is not impossible that the expression under discussion is a vague hint at this hearth of infection as the abode

---

[44] Addressing the disease.

of disease. To the rubbish of the yard is also often imputed such a rôle.]

The measure worm is driven out with white switches by the little wizards, who finally dispose of him by putting him in the branches of a post oak (*Quercus stellata* Wang.) upon the mountain. Throughout most of the formula the medicine man speaks directly to the disease spirit.

The meaning of the sentence with regard to the white knife is obscure and could not be satisfactorily explained by either of the two medicine men who were familiar with the formula.

The ceremony was described jointly by two medicine men. The medicine man first prepares a sort of pestle or stamper of the wood of sûli', *Diospyros virginiana* L., common persimmon, about 3 or 4 inches long and an inch in diameter at the large end. The stamper must be newly made in every case, but why this should be so, or why the wood selected should be persimmon, the medicine man could not explain. One of these instruments [collected by Mr. Mooney] forms part of the Cherokee collection in the United States National Museum, Washington, D. C.

The medicine man recites the first paragraph while warming the stamper over the fire. He then presses the broad end upon the several aching places a number of times. The same operation is repeated [during the recitation of] every one of the three [next] paragraphs, after which he blows four times upon each of the sore spots. The whole ceremony is repeated four times before noon, the expression ʋDɔ·'təGwûDə` ("all day") in the prescriptions [often] being understood to mean until the completion of the fourth and final ceremony about noon. After this final application the medicine man scratches the patient about the joints with a brier (see p. 70) and rubs into the cuts a warm infusion of four varieties of fern (ιGɔ̈ⁿ·'li) (see p. 71).

The taboo list for a rheumatic patient as given by the two medicine men includes the aGɔ·'ᵘlə or sun perch; the Gɑ·`sûDə' or drumfish, also called buffalo fish; the tsʋ`nιGι·`tsιyɔ̈ⁿ·'sti or hornyhead; the a`ndûtsa' or speckled trout; the squirrel, sûlɔ·'ᵘlə; and the buffalo, yaN̈sa'. The taboo extends through life, and with the exception of the tsʋ`nιGι·`tsιyɔ̈ⁿ·'sti which is prohibited in a number of diseases on account of its tendency to rapid decay (see p. 182), is owing to a mythic connection between the disease and the tabooed animal. This formula in fact furnishes a perfect illustration of the ideas underlying the whole theory and practice of medicine among the Cherokees. The disease, rheumatism, is caused by the measure worm, because the cramped movements of the patient resemble those of the worm. The remedial herbs used are ferns, because, as these plants grow, their fronds unroll and straighten out, just as the medicine man wishes the contracted muscles and limbs of the patient to do.

The patient is forbidden to taste of the sun perch or the buffalo fish, because both of these have rounded backs which convey the impression as if they were drawn up or cramped, as though [afflicted with] rheumatism. The squirrel is tabooed on account of its habit of "humping" itself at times, and in another rheumatism formula from a different medicine man the patient is forbidden to stroke or to touch a dog or a cat for the same reason.

The buffalo is tabooed because of its hump, and the rheumatic must not even touch a buffalo hide or a comb made of buffalo horn. Neither medicine man could say why the trout is forbidden, as it is also in the other formula just referred to, but the reason doubtlessly lies in some similar peculiarity of shape or movement.

The mention of the buffalo in this connection possesses a special interest for the light it throws upon the age and traditional character of the formulas. The buffalo was probably never very numerous in the southern Alleghanies, the old country of the Cherokee, and according to a tradition still current on the reservation, was last seen on Buffalo Creek, in western North Carolina, about the beginning of the Revolution. Neither of the medicine men who commended this formula had ever seen a buffalo, or even a picture of one, and had no idea at all of its shape. They were consequently unable to state why the animal was so strictly tabooed, even to its hide and horns, but simply said that thus the rule had been handed down to them along with the rest of the formula. When shown a picture of a buffalo they saw at once the reason for the prohibition. It is safe to assert, therefore, that this formula at least dates back to a time long prior to the Revolution when the buffalo was comparatively common in the mountain valleys and in the lower regions occasionally visited by the Cherokees. In a collection of over 100 Cherokee myths obtained [by Mr. Mooney] the buffalo is introduced but once [Mooney, Myths, p. 293].

85

Dalɔ·'ni   v·'ndɩyö·'Dali`    ʋGö·'wŭtli`   ʇɩ'a'
it yellow   their navel   it for the purpose   this

sGɇ̌'ˀ | Dalɔ·'ni   Ga`·ta-Gɛ̨'.i   aDö̌``'nɩ·Ga' | Dalɔ·'ni   Gɛ`sɛ̨'.i'
now, then!   it yellow   clay-ish   it has been said   it yellow   it is, App

sGɇ̌'ˀ | k'ɔ·'lanö̌ⁿ`    ö̌ⁿ`'naGɛ·ⁿ`    ʋ`sönʋ·'li   'a·t'öŋa·'nɩ·Ga' |
now, then!   Raven   black   quickly   thou hast come to listen

ʋsö̌'ʇ-i   D`ɩtsö̌`tlt'ɔ'ɩ·'sti   'ɩDa·'ᵘwɛ̨ɩ`-Dɩ·'nə'  |  Dalɔ·'ni    Ga`ta-Gɛ̨'.i
night, Loc   thou art staying   thou wizard, E   it yellow   clay-ish

5 ʋ`Dö̌'nö̌'ʇi-Gwö̌ⁿ`   Gɛ`sɛ̨'.i'.  |  ʋ`sönʋ·'li   'ö̌ⁿ't`a·sɛsö̌'ɩGa' |
it has been said, L   it is, App   quickly   again, thou hast come to pull it out

tsötlsta·'y't́ɩ-Gwö̌ⁿ`    Gɛ`sɛ̨'.i' | nɩGö̌·'waDö̌·'nɩGwa`ᴅlɔ.ɛ·'stɩ-Gwö̌ⁿ`
it what thou eatest, L   it is, App   it will be trampled down continually, L

*v*ˈIsGɛˈˈDə-GWɔ̆ᴅˋ	DᴜˈˋDɩGɛˈ-ö̯ˑˈ.i		ᴜsöˈˈ-ɩ	ɩˈyö̯ˑˊDə	wöˋᴅˈtˈɩˑˊtˈɔ-
it important, L	he was moving about, T L		night, Loc	yonder	thither, thou hast
ˈɩˋstˈanɩˑGaˊ	ᴜsöˈˈ-ɩDə	nᴜˈˋDəˈnö̯ˑˊna		ᴠtsɩˈˈ-nawu̇-GWöᴅˋ	aDö̆ˋˈ-
gone to put it to stay	night, been	it has not been said		beyond it, stretched, L	it has
nɩˑGaˊ		¹yăˈ			
been said		Sharply			
sGɛ̆ˈˈ		Daloˑˊni	GaˋtaˑGɛˈˈ	aDöˋˈnɩˑGaˊ	Daloˑˊni	Gɛˈˈsɛˈ.iˊ
now, then!		it yellow	clay-ish	it has been said	it yellow	it is, App
sGɛ̆ˈˈ		sᴜˋliˊ	ö̯ᴅˋˈnaGɛˈˈ	ᴠˋsönᴜˑˊli	ˈaˋtˈö̯ŋaˑˋnɩˑGaˊ	ᴜsöˈˈ-i 5
now, then!		Buzzard	black	quickly	thou hast come to listen	night, Loc
ɩˈyö̯ˑˊDə	Dɩˋtsöˋtɩtˈɔˈˈɩsti		Gɔˈᴠˊsti	tsanᴠˑˊɩti	nɩGɛˈˋsö̯ˑnaˊ	
yonder	thou art staying		something	thou failest	never	
Daloˑˊnɩ-GWöᴅˋ	Gɛˈsɛˈˈ	ᴠIsGɛˈˈDə	Dᴜnᴜˑˋyˈtˈanɩˋlɛˈ.iˊ		tsötɩstaˑˈ-	
it yellow L	it is, App	it important	he has put it under, App		it what	
yˈtɩGwöᴅˋ	Gɛˈˋsɛˈ.iˊ		nɩGö̯ˑˋwaDö̯ˑˋnɩGwaᴅlɔ.ɛˈstɩ-GWöᴅˋ		tsaᴅlɔs-ö̯ˋˈi	
thou eatest, L	it is, App		it will be trampled down continually, L		thou passed, T L	
ᴠsö-ˈˋɩyɩˋˈDzə	wɩNˋtö̯ˈˊNˋAtˈaˋ	ᴠsöˈˋɩˈ	ɩˈyö̯ˑˊDə	wöᴅˋˈ-tˈaDɩˋGalɛˋˈ.-	
night, Loc, direction	thou hast driven him	night, Loc	yonder	thither, thou hast	
ɩˑGaˊ		nɩGö̯ˑˋwayɛˈˋlə.nö̯ˈˋöᴅˈsGɛˈˈstɩ-GWöᴅˋ	tsaᴅlɔs-ö̯ˑˊ	ᴜsöˈˈ-ɩDə 10
scattered it		a likeness of it will remain, L	thou passed, T L	night, been
nᴜˑˋDəˈnö̯ˑˊnə		ᴠtsɩˈˈ-nawu̇-GWöᴅˋ	aDöˋˈnɩˑGaˊ		¹yăˈ
it has not been said		beyond it, stretched, L	it has been said		Sharply
sGɛ̆ˈˈ		Daloˑˊni	wɔˑˊDɩGɛˈˋ	Gɛˈsɛˈˊ.i	ᴠIsGɛˈˊDa	
Now, then!		it yellow	brown	it is, App	it important	
sGɛ̆ˈˈ		awɔˈˈɩli ⁴⁵	ᵘwɔˑˊDɩˋGɛˈˋ	Galö̯ˋˊldi	Dɩˋtsöˋtɩtˈɔˈɩˈsti	
Now, then!		Eagle	brown	above	thou art staying	
Gɔˈᴠˊsti	tsaDɛˈˋlɩˋtcˈɛ̆ˋˈti	nɩGɛˈˋsö̯ˑnaˊ		Daloˑˊni	Gɛˈsɛˈˈ	ᴠIsGɛˈˊDə
something	it escapes thy (sight)	never		it yellow	it is, App	it important
Dᴜnᴜˑˋyˈtˈɛˈ.iˊ		nɩGö̯ˑˋwaDö̯ˑˋnɩGwaᴅlɔ.ɛˈstɩ-GWöᴅˋ		Dɩtcˈskwɔˑˊli 15
he has put it under, App		it will be trampled down continually L		thy stomachs
DɛˑGɛˈˋstaDanɩsɔˈˈtˈanɩˑGaˊ	ᴠsö-ˈɩDəˋ	nᴜˑˋDöˈnö̯ˑˊna		ᴠtsɩˈˈnawaˋ	
thou hast come to bury it in them	night, been	it has not been said		beyond it, stretched
aDöˋˈnɩˑGaˊ		¹yăˈ			
it has been said		Sharply			

This is for the Purpose of (Curing) the "Yellow" of Their Navel

FREE TRANSLATION

Now, then! It has become clayey Yellow. It is Yellow, it seems. Now, then! Black Raven, quickly thou hast come to listen; thou art staying in the Night Land, thou powerful wizard. It seems it is only what has become clayey Yellow. Quickly thou hast again come and pulled it out. Where the important thing was moving about, only the traces of trampling will remain. Thou hast gone to put it staying yonder in the Night Land, (and) not for one night· (only, but forever). Relief has been caused. Sharply!

---

⁴⁵ Emendation by editor, instead of wạˈɩˈli=1/Measure-worm, 2/South.

Now, then! It has become clayey Yellow. It is the Yellow, it seems.

Now, then! Black Buzzard, quickly thou hast come to listen; yonder in the Night Land thou art staying. Thou never failest in anything. It is merely the Yellow that has put the important thing under him. (But) that is the very thing thou usually eatest. Where thou hast passed, only the traces of trampling will remain. Toward the direction of the Night Land thou hast driven it, in the Night Land thou hast scattered it. A mere likeness of it will remain where thou hast passed, (and) not for one night (only, but forever). Relief has been caused. Sharply!

Now, then! The important thing is the brown Yellow.

Now, then! Brown Eagle, thou art staying on high. Nothing ever escapes thy (sight). It is the Yellow that has put the important thing under him. Only the traces of trampling will remain; thou hast come to bury it into thy stomachs, (and) not for one night (only, but forever). Relief has been caused. Sharply!

EXPLANATION

In this, as in most other formulas for this disease, the whole treatment consists of the application of the warm hands of the medicine man. The ceremony, however, is peculiar. The medicine man recites the part referring to the raven while rubbing his hands together over the fire, bringing them around in a circular sweep in imitation of the raven's manner when hovering over its prey. Then imitating the raven's cry, he utters a rapid k‘a· k‘a· k‘a· k‘a· and brings his hands down upon the abdomen of the patient. He goes through the same motions while repeating the paragraph addressing the buzzard, but ends with a prolonged su:+ su:+ to imitate the swishing noise made by the wing of the buzzard in its ordinary flight, followed, as he brings his hands down, by a rapid Gwšⁿ Gwšⁿ Gwšⁿ to imitate the sound on rising. In the same way, while addressing the eagle, he imitates its movements and its cry. The ceremony is repeated four times before noon; there is no taboo.

This formula consists of three paragraphs only, rather an unusual number in Cherokee ritual; it is probable that in the course of repeated copying it has lost a fourth paragraph. This has happened to more than one formula.

86

	ᏥᎥ'a-Nʟ̣ʃ̣'	ᏀᎣ·t'ᵢ'sᏀi	tsᴜ'nᵢtłö̇·ŋa' [46]		
	this, and	it swelling, Hab	they are sick with them		
a't'-tsε'ʟ̣i	ᴜstᵢ·'Ꮐa	súli'	k'ᴜ'wa	ᴜnε·'Ꮐə	t'aya'
wood, green	it little	(persimmon)	(mulberry)	it white	(cherry)
tsᵢ·yu'	tsᴜ'ᵗ¹yön.'stᵢ-Nʟ̣ʃ̣		ama·.-'yi	ᏀᴜᏀᵢ·'Ꭰə	nönya'
(poplar)	they are bitter, and		water, Loc	it taken out of the (liq)	rock
Ꮆön'ᵗ'ᴐti	aᎠᏃᴐ·'lət'ᵗ'ᏚᏖi'		a'Ꮐa·nö'ʟ̣i	ᴜnε·'ləᏀᵢ-Nʟ̣ʃ̣'	sᴐ.i'
to use with it	to smoke with		it boiled	by itself, and	the other
na.sᏀwöᴅ'	na·'skᵢ-Ꮐwöᴅ'	ᏀᎣ·'ᵘtsalε·'Ꭰə	ᴠ·'lᵢkstᴐ.'ti'		Ꭰᵢlε·'nᵢsᏀ-ọ̈' 5
also	this here, L	a part of it has been taken	he to vomit with it		they begin T L
ᴜᎠᵢ'ᵗt'a'stᵢ-Ꮐwöᴅ'	sᴜnalε·'ⁿ.i		ᵢ·Ꮐa'	k'ᵢla'	ᴠ'lᵢkstᴐ.'ti'
he must drink it, L	in the morning		noon	then	he to vomit with it
ᴜsö'(ᵢ̣ [47])-Nʟ̣ʃ̣	ᴠ·'Ꭰatsᴐ·'lət'ᵗ'ᏚᏖi'		ᴜnε·'Ꮐə	nönya'	Ꮐε·yọ̈.'i
night, and	he should smoke himself with it		white	rock	(river-) branch
ᏀᴜᏀᵢ·'Ꭰə	Ꮆön'ᵗ'ᴐti'	k'ọ̈Nʟ̣i'	Ꭰalᴐ·'nᵢ-Ꮐε'	Ꮐε·sᴐ·.i'	ᴠ'nᵢnε·Ꮐᴐ'-ʟ̣i
it taken out of the (liq)	to use with it	clearly (noticeable)	yellow-ish	it has been	their skin L
na.ski'	nọ̈·'wᴐ·t'i'	tsi'k'anᴐ'ε̣ʟ̣a'	Ꮐalọ̈·'kwᴐᎠᵢ·-yu'		
this here	to cure with	it which tells	remarkable	E	

THIS IS (FOR) WHEN THEY ARE SICK WITH A SWELLING

FREE TRANSLATION

Small alder, common persimmon, sycamore, chokecherry, poplar, cucumber tree, when boiled (poured) on a rock taken out of the water, to smoke (i. e., to steam) (the patient) with; and (just this) by itself. Another (way) also (to cure) this, is (to drink it) to vomit with it; at the beginning he must drink it in the morning and vomit with it at noon; in the evening, then, he should steam himself with it, using a white rock taken out of the stream. The symptoms are that their skins are yellow. This medicine here described is a remarkably (efficacious one) indeed.

EXPLANATION

This is a prescription for the treatment of a form of indigestion or biliousness, attended by a swelling of the abdomen and yellowness of the skin. The remedy is a sweatbath. A decoction is prepared of six varieties of barks, and is poured upon one or more stones (the number depending on their size), taken out of the river. The stones are heated in a fire, and the decoction poured on them produces an abundant steam. (See p. 61.)

---

[46] W. D. form; W. Dial. -tł->C. Dial. -ts-.
[47] Emendation by editor.

For some ritualistic reason it is specified that the stones used must be white. In some cases a portion of the decoction is first drunk as an emetic. Ay. stated that the sickness is caused by tcsɢɔ·'ya or insects, which were formerly parasites of snakes and are sent into the body of the patient in revenge for some offense given to those reptiles.

The barks used are those of ɩtsɛ'ⁱi ʋstɩ·'ɢa, a variety of *Alnus serrulata* Willd., red alder; sůli', *Diospyros virginiana* L., common persimmon; t‛aya', *Prunus virginiana* L., chokecherry; k‛ʋ·'wa ʋnɛ·'ɢə, *Platanus occidentalis*, sycamore, buttonwood; tsɩ·yu', *Liriodendron tulipifera* L., tulip tree, poplar, whitewood; tsʋ‛ⁱyo̊ⁿ.'sti, *Magnolia acuminata* L., cucumber tree.

87

tsʋ·`na.stəɢo̊'ⁱi    Dɩ`k‛anȯ·'wɔ·t‛i`
whenever they have   to cure them with
their (feet) frostbitten

tcɩ`-tsɩ.-ᵘwa‛ya'   (*4 times*).
I,   I   wolf

tcɩ`-tsɩ-‛tsʋ‛la'   (*4 times*).
I,   I   fox

tcɩ`-tsɩ-.a‛wɩ·ya' (*4 times*).
I,   I   deer

5   tcɩ`-tsɩ‛-sɩ‛kwa' (*4 times*), kwa:'
I,   I, opposum

a‛ⁱyɛlɩ·'sti   ᵘwa'(‛so̊ⁿ ⁴⁸)   tsɩ`nɩɢəwɛ·ⁿ'.a    ɩ`ɢawɛ·‛ɛsti   o̊ⁿ`skw-
to imitate it   by itself   that what it calls   is to be called   every time
ůtɩ.sȯ·'.i | na.sɢwo̊ⁿ'   o̊ⁿ`skwůtɩ.sȯ·'.i    Dɩskwanʋ·`tsa.ɛ·ti'
when it is   also   every time when it is   they must be sucked
ended   ended

tsʋ·`na.stəɢȯ·'i    ʋ`staɢȯ·.'i
where they have their   whenever he has
(feet) frost bitten   frost bitten (feet)

To Cure Them When They Have Their Feet Frost Bitten

FREE TRANSLATION

I, I am a wolf (*4 times*).
I, I am a fox (*4 times*).
I, I am a deer (*4 times*).
I, I am an opossum (*4 times*).

Each time, at the end, the cry of each (animal) is to be imitated and cried; (and) also every time, at the end, they [49] must be sucked at their feet where they are frost bitten.

EXPLANATION

This is another formula for the cure of frostbite. (See Nos. 59, 60.) [As it was obtained by Ay. from Ut. no additional information could be obtained on it.] The treatment is probably the same as previously

---

[48] Interpolated by editor.   [49] The patients.

described, the sucking being done by the medicine man, who holds ice or snow water in his mouth.

"I am a wolf" is properly tsɩwaᵘya′ the initial syllable being doubled to fill in the meter of the song. "Deer" is properly aʻwi′, the final ya being added for the same reason.

The opossum has now two names: vʻi`yö̆·sv′′ɢa, and sɩ′′kwa ᴜᴅᴢᴇ‵′tsti, the latter meaning literally "grinning hog." It seems probable, however, that sɩ′′kwa was originally the name of the opossum alone, and that, on account of the resemblance of the two animals, the name was applied to the hog on its introduction by the whites, thus rendering an [epithet] necessary to distinguish [the former from the latter].

88

(ɩ̈′a′   ᵘwa·sŏ′′la   tsa`nŏ.sɛ̀·ɔ·′   a`ᴅa`nö̆·wɔ·t̒i` [50])
 this   "cocoon"   as they call it   to cure anyone
                        (Hab.)   with

waɢu′ (4 times).
(moth)
larva

ɢa·ᵘwu′ (4 times).
it is pul-
verized

sa·nă′ (4 times).

This is the Medicine (for) What They Call "Cocoons":

FREE TRANSLATION

Cocoon! (4 times).
Pulverized! (4 times).
sana (?) (4 times).

EXPLANATION

ᵘwa·sɔ·′′la is the name of a small species of "horned" caterpillar, and also of the tobacco worm, as well as of a butterfly or moth originating from one of the larvæ named. The name is also applied by medicine men to a peculiar chilling boil or swelling, because it resembles the same chilling or shuddering effect as that resulting from contact with the larvæ. Presumably the worm so constantly trodden and crushed under the careless foot of man is held responsible for the boil. The treatment consists in merely pressing the previously warmed thumb upon the swelling, repeating four times each of the words of the formula. [It has taken considerable effort to get the meaning of the first two words. As for sa·nă′, it has not been possible to find out its meaning or to analyze it, the most erudite medicine men themselves being in the dark about these three words.]

---

[50] Interpolated by J. M., probably based on information by Ay.

89

Ŭ'a'   a'nɩskɔ·'li   a'ᴅa' nǫ·'wɔ·t'ĭ'
this   their head   to cure anyone
                     with

(a) Ga̲lǫ·'ldi ᴅanɩ'la·ᵘwɩ.a' | 'a'-nɔ·ɢwɔ̈ⁿ v'sönv·'li vtsɩ''-nawa̲
    above   they are assembling   ha, now   quickly   beyond it,
                                                              stretched

aᴅö''nɩ·ɢa' | ¹yă''
it has been said   Sharply!

(b) ε·'ləᴅĭ'   ᴅanɩ'la·ᵘwɩ.a' (etc.).
    below   they are assembling

This is the Medicine for Their Head

FREE TRANSLATION

On high they are assembling; ha, now relief has quickly been caused. Sharply!

Below they are assembling; ha, now relief has quickly been caused. Sharply!

EXPLANATION

The medicine man from whom this formula was obtained had in turn procured it from a medicine woman, and was unable to tell much about it. It is therefore impossible to say what spirits are referred to as being assembled, or whether they are the disease curers or the remedial agents. In many formulas the spirits are represented as having assembled as in council, sometimes under the couch of the patient, sometimes even in his body.

No medicine is used, the treatment merely consisting in rubbing the forehead of the patient after every paragraph, and afterwards blowing the breath four times over the aching part. This, repeated a number of times—[no rigid rule is followed]—is said to be effective.

90

Ŭ'a'   t'v·'yA-stĭ'   aᴅa''nǫ·'wɔ·t'ĭ'
this   beans, (like)   to cure anyone
                       with

EXPLANATION

The formula bearing the heading "This is the medicine (for) a beanlike (boil)" is too evidently incomplete in the original to be given here, but deserves notice for the spirits invoked and the treatment prescribed.

The former are the Rattlesnake and the Puffing (Spreading) Adder, and the fragmentary expression of the formula seems to imply that the festering boil is the result of a bite from some disease snake, which must be driven out by the more powerful snakes invoked. The rattlesnake is mentioned under its proper name, v·ᴅzɔ·'nꞏti, but the spreading adder, commonly called tʻalɩ́ksta, "the vomiter," is spoken of here as kwaʻndayɔʻ́ɪa, which literally means "he has just shot the plums (or peaches)." The meaning is plain but the Cherokee are unable to give any reason for the name, which may have a mythic origin. The medicine man had obtained the formula in an accidental manner from another man, which accounts for its incompleteness.

The medicine prescribed was tobacco juice rubbed on the boil by the medicine man while reciting the formula, when the swelling first made its appearance. The swelling was said to go down before dark.

91

ɪʻaʻ   Dʋnǫ̈ʻlɛstǫʻ[.i]   ʻɪʻʼandɩʻskǫʻ.iʻ
this   it causes them to   it which they call (Hab)
           be broken

sGɛ̌ʻʼ | nɔʻGwɔ̈ⁿ   ʻaʻtʻǫ̇naʻˑnɩˑGaʻ   ʻɩˑskuyaʻ   (saʻkʻɔˑni ⁵¹)
Now, then! now   thou hast come   thou man   blue
                      to listen

ʻɩDaˑʻᵘwɛɪ̌ʻ-Dɩˑnɔ̃ⁿʻ | DɩGɛʻʻdɔʻsɛɪ̌ʻ | kʻɔˑlaʻ   ʋwɛʻʻɩstɔsɔ̈ʻɩ-Gwɔ̈ⁿʻ
thou wizard, L   thou penetratest them, bone   it has been made L (=E)
                        App   painful

Gɛʻsɛˑⁿ.iʻ | ʋʻDɩlɛʻʻGɩ-Gwɔ̈ⁿʻ ʋʻDətʻanɔ̈ʻ́i Gɛˑsɛˑⁿ.iʻ | nɔʻGwu-
it is, App   heat, L   it has been said it is, App   now

-Dɩʻʻnə Dɛʻtʻaskəlɔʻʻɔ̈ⁿʻtaʻnɩˑGaʻ   kʻɔˑlaʻ Gɛˑsǫ̈ʻ | DɛGǪʻlɛʻɩsaʻ-   5
E   thou hast come to make him   bone   it is, T L   he will get on his
         relinquish his grasps

nɩˑsɛˑstiʻ | ʋtsɩʻ-nawə-Gwɔ̈ⁿʻ   nʋʻDətʻanǫ̈ʻDə   nɔ̈ⁿʻtʻǫ̇nɛʻʻlɩˑGaʻ |
(legs) as he goes beyond it, stretched, L (=E) it has been said at thou hast come to do
                                                 the same time   it for him

sGɛ̌ʻʼ | nɔʻGwɔ̈ⁿ   aᴰlɛ̌ʻ   ʻɔ̈ⁿʻstatʻǫ̇ˑnaˑnɩˑGaʻ   stɩˑskuyaʻ   stɩˑGaGɛˑⁿʻ
Now, then, now   also   you 2 have again come   you 2 men   you two red
                                to listen

ʋʻsönʋˑliʻ DɛʻstɩdɔʻʻsɩˑGaʻ | ʋʻlsGɛʻʻDə   tʻɩˑstaˑsɛʻsɔ̈ʻɩˑGaʻ   kɔˑlaʻ
quickly   you two have come and   it important   you two have come and bone
            halted   pulled it out

Gɛˑsǫ̈ʻ | tsʋʻlɛʻɩˑsatǫ̈ʻ   aʻDɔ̈ʻnɩˑsɛˑstiʻ   uwɔʻʻɩsɔʻnɔ̈ʻ́i   aDaˑNɪ̌toʻ |
it is, T L   he has been lifted up   it will be said   it has been made   the soul
                                     all along   pleasing
                                                                                10
ʋtsɩʻʻ-nawə-Gwɔ̈ⁿʻ   aDɔ̈ʻʻnɩˑGaʻ
beyond it, stretched, it has been said
L (=E),

THIS IS (FOR) WHAT THEY CALL "IT CAUSES THEM TO BE BROKEN"

FREE EXPLANATION

Now, then! Ha, now thou hast come to listen, thou Blue Man, thou powerful wizard, thou penetrator. The fact is that the bone has been made painful. It is merely Heat that has caused it, it seems. But now thou hast come to force him [52] to give up his hold from the bone. He [52] will get on his feet (and will not stop walking). Relief has been caused forthwith; thou hast come to do it for him.[53]

---

[51] Interpolated by J. M.   [52] The disease.   [53] The patient.

Now, then! (and) now you both in your turn, you have come to listen, you Two Red Men; quickly you have come and halted. You have come and pulled out the important thing from the bone. He has been raised up, and will remain in that position. The soul has been made pleasing. Relief has been caused.

EXPLANATION

This formula is for the cure of pains in the limbs, resembling rheumatic pains, but ascribed to the influence of the Heat spirit.

By an oversight [of a copyist in the course of transcription] the color of the spirit invoked in the first paragraph is not given, but as the [disease causer] is Heat, the remedial spirit is probably the spirit of Cold, viz., the Blue Man of the Cold Land.

No medicine is used; the medicine man merely rubs the limbs of the patient with his hands previously warmed, while reciting the formula, blowing four times at the end of each paragraph. The ceremony is four times repeated.

92

ɨ'a'	vyɔ·'ⁿ.i	v·'nskɩ·tsö·'.i
this	different	they have dreamt

sGɛ̈''	+ +	Gö`ɪstûtli	+ +	tsυdɔ·'.ɩdə`	tsɔ·'ᵘstə aGa`-
Now, then,	(such-and-such)	his clan	(such-and-such)	his names	they are good he

nɛ·la·'nɛ'ɛ·.i' | Ga·tlɔ̃ⁿ/⁵⁴ | Gö·'wûtlt'ɔ'ɩ'sti | tsɔ·'ᵘstə | anɛ·'lɩski' |
has apportioned for him, App. | where | he is staying | they good | he apportions (Hab)

sGɛ̈''	'a-'nɔ·Gwɔ̃ᵛ'	'a't'öŋa·'nɩ·Ga'	Dɔ·'yi	wɔ·'DɩGɛ·'ⁿ'
Now, then,	ha, now	thou hast come to listen	Beaver	brown

5 tsɔ·'ᵘstə aGa`nɛ·la·'nɛ'ɛ·.i' | nɔ·'Gwû-Dɩ·nə' | Ga`nəGɩ·'Də aDö̃'`nɩ·Ga' |
they good he has apportioned for him, App. | now, E | it taken up it has been said

+ + tsυdɔ·'.ɩdə` | ayɛ·'la tsɔ·'ᵘstə Ga`nəGɩ·'Də aDö̃'`nɩ·Ga' |
(such-and-such) his names are | the body they good it taken up it has been said

yö·wi' tsυ`tsat-ö·' ɩyö·'Də wɛanɛ·'tlanɩ·Ga' tsɔ·ᵘ'stə | + + |
human beings | they are many T L | yonder | there, thou hast apportioned for him | they are good | (such and such)

tsυdɔ·'.ɩdə | υDa·N:tɔ' | a`stυdɛ·'Də aDö̃'`nɩ·Ga' | υDaN:tɔ' |
his names are | his soul | it released it has been said | his soul

Daᴾlɛ'ɩ`sa'nɩ·Ga' | aDaN:tɔ' | astɛ·'Dalɩyö·'Də aDö̃'`nɩ·Ga' |
it has been lifted up | it soul | it has been changed it has been said

10 aDaN:tɔ' Daᴾlɛ'ɩ`sa'nɩ·Ga'
it soul it has been lifted up

sGɛ̈''	+ +	Gölstû'tli	+ +	tsυdɔ·'.ɩdə`	tsɔ·'ᵘstə aGa`-
Now, then,	(such and such)	his clan	(such and such)	his names are	they good he has

nɛ·la·'nɛ'ɛ·.i' | Gatlɔ̃ⁿ ⁵⁵ | Gö·'wûtlt'ɔ'ɩ'sti | tsɔ·'stə | anɛ·'lɩski' |
apportioned for him | where | he is staying | they good | he apportions (Hab)

---

⁵⁴ W. D. form; C. D.: Ga·ts5ⁿ   ⁵⁵ Cf. Note 54.

sgĕ·'		Dɔ·'yi	tsúnɛ·'Gə	tsɔ·'GιDι·'tɫ̃ɔⁿ [56]		Dι'tsö'tɫt'ɔ'ι'sti
Now, then,		Beaver	thou white	at head of stream		thou art staying
υ'sönυ·'li	Dɔ't'aᴰlɛ'‛öŋa'		tsɔ·'stə	aGa'nɛ·la·'nɛ‛ɛ·.i'		nɔ·‛ᵘGwù-Dι·nə'
quickly	thou hast arisen, facing us		they good	he has apportioned for him		now, E
	Ga'nəGι·'Də	aDö'‛nι·Ga'		anɛ·‛tɫanö'‛i	tsɔ·'ᵘstə	a'stυDɛ·'Də
	it taken up	it has been said		it has been apportioned	they good	it released
	aDö'‛nι·Ga'		yǫ·wi'	tsυ·'Dzat-ǫ·'	aDι'Galɛ·'yaDǫ·'	aDö'‛nι·Ga'
	it has been said		human beings	they are, many T L	it has been scattered	it has been said
ιGǫ·'wùlstɔ·'tι-Gwöⁿ'		aDa·Nιtɔ'		astɛ·'Daliyǫ·'Də		aDö'‛nι·Ga'	5
who cares what happens to it, L		it soul		it has been changed		it has been said
υwɔ·‛ιsɔ‛nö'‛i	aDa·Nιtɔ'		Daᴰlɛ‛ιsa‛nι·Ga'		Gölkwɔ·'Gι	ι·'ya·Ga-
it made completely beautiful	it soul		it has been lifted up		seven	successive,
lǫ'ldi	w‛ιt'aᴰlɛ‛ι'sa‛nι·Ga'		aDa·Nιtɔ'		¹yăʽ	
above	thither, thou hast lifted it up		it soul		Sharply	

This Is (For) When They Have Bad Dreams

FREE TRANSLATION

Now, then! He [57] belongs to such-and-such a clan; he [57] is called so-and-so. He [58] has apportioned evil [59] for him; [57] where is the (one who) usually apportions evil staying?

Now, then! Ha, now thou hast come to listen, Brown Beaver. He [58] has apportioned evil for him. [57] But now it has been taken; he [57] is called so-and-so. The evil has been taken away from his [57] body. Yonder where there is a crowd of human beings thou hast gone to apportion the evil. He [57] is called so-and-so. His [57] soul has become released. His soul has been lifted up. The soul has become changed. The soul has been lifted up.

Now, then! He belongs to such-and-such a clan; he is called so-and-so. He has apportioned evil for him; where is the (one who) usually apportions evil staying?

Now, then! Thou White Beaver, at the head (waters) of the stream thou art staying; quickly thou hast arisen, facing us. He has apportioned evil for him. But now it has been taken away. The evil (which) has been apportioned for him has been released. It has been scattered where there is a crowd of human beings (living). Who cares what happens to it! The soul has been changed. The soul, made pleasing, has been lifted up. Up to the seventh upper (world) the soul has been raised. Sharply!

---

[56] W. D. form; C. D. tsɔ·'GιDι·'Dzöⁿ
[57] The patient.
[58] The apportioner of evil.
[59] Literally "good."

EXPLANATION

This formula [edited and discussed by Mr. Mooney in his article on Cherokee River Cult, p. 9] is for going to water to avert the consequences of bad dreams, such as of falling from a cliff, drowning in the river, or being crushed under a log. Such dreams are generally regarded as the result of hostile conjurations of some secret enemy, and it is held that the calamity thus shadowed forth will actually befall (the victim) unless some ceremony be performed to avert it.

The medicine man mentions the name and clan of his client and endeavors to send the evil fortune from him, to "where [there is a crowd of] people," i. e., to some distant settlement.

The medicine man and his client go down to the water at daybreak and stand at the edge of the stream as already described. The medicine man then recites the formula, after which his client, stripped with the exception of his shirt, wades out into the water and ducks under seven times. At the seventh plunge he tears the shirt from his body while still under water and lets it float down the stream. It is afterwards secured and taken by the medicine man as his fee if it is worth the trouble. If of no value the client gives other cloth instead. After this preliminary ceremony the client remains standing in the water while the medicine man, on the bank, takes out his beads and proceeds to banish the impending calamity.

He first asks [his client] to what [settlement] he wishes to send the evil foreshadowed in the prophetic dream, for it is held that such dreams must be fulfilled, and that all the medicine man can do is to divert their accomplishment from the intended victim. The client names some distant settlement as the place where he wishes the blow to fall and the medicine man at once begins the ceremony to send the tsɔ·'stə to that point. Should the medicine man find himself unable to send it so far his client names some nearer settlement, and a second attempt is made, and so on, until a resting place is found for the calamity, even if it be necessary to send it to another clan or family within the settlement of the client himself. These successive trials are made by "working [with] the beads": [The medicine man holds a black bead representing the evil between thumb and forefinger of one hand, and a red or white bead, representing the client, between thumb and index finger of the other hand. Should the black bead prove the more lively and vivacious in its movements, the client's bead remaining motionless, or moving only very slowly, the chances for banishing the evil to the settlement in question are very scanty, and another settlement has to be named and the operation has to be started over again.]

After each successive trial the client stoops down and laves his face [sometimes also the crown of his head and his breast with water dipped out with his hand]. Should the medicine man [after all his efforts] not succeed in sending the evil fortune to some other victim it is believed that his client must suffer.

Each trial with the beads necessitates the laying down of additional cloth, all of which is taken by the medicine man at the conclusion of the ceremony [as his fee]. To make assurance doubly sure [to check up, as if it were, on the results of the first day], the ceremony is sometimes performed for four consecutive mornings; in each case the client fasts until noon, although it is not necessary to keep awake throughout the preceding night as in some other ceremonies of a similar nature.

Should all other means fail there still remains one resource: the dreamer kills [a hog, or some poultry] belonging to himself, and has it cooked to be eaten by his family and friends. He himself, however, must not partake of it. In former times, [if it proved not possible] to send the calamity away from his own settlement, [the one who dreamed] went hunting and killed a deer or a bear, with which he made a feast in the same way for his friends and neighbors of the settlement.

[These latter means of averting the evil consequences of bad dreams are no longer known.]

93

ï'a'	ama·'-yi	a`dzō$^n$.sï'.sŏ.tï`	a`gŭwa'sə-gwō$^{v}$`	ŭlstɛ·'ĭtŏ`.ti'
this	water, Loc.	to take one there repeatedly	oneself—L.	to help one with

sgĕ̆·'		'a·`nɔ·gwō^{v}'	'a`t'ọ̈ŋa·`nɪga'	yọ̈·'wi	ga`nə^{c}ɪ·'də
Now, then		ha, now	thou hast come to listen	human being	long

tsō`tɪ̆t'ɔ^{c}ɪ·'sti		yọ̈·wi'	ɪ`stɛ·lɪ·'ski'		ts^{c}A`ska$^D$lɔ`^{ɔc}ɪsti'	nɪgɛ·`=
thou art staying		human being	thou helpest (Hab.)		thou relinquishest thy grasp	never

sọ̈·na'		aDa·`Nɪ̆tɔ̃`	ts^{c}A`ska^{D}lɔ^{ɔc}ɪsti'	nɪgɛ·`sọ̈·na'		gɔ^{c}ʋ'sti
		the soul	thou relinquishest thy grasp	never		something

ts^{c}Asō^n`gōtlɪ.`si'	ɪ·`ga-ga·Dọ̈·'	ɪ`ọ̈'nɛ^{c}i'		ama'	ga^{D}lɔ·'lɛ·g-ọ̈·'	5
thou wilt take a firmer grasp	light, it hangs on, T. L.	thou hast made		water	it slides, T. L.	

nọ̈Dọ̈·`gwaDʋ·`yō'nō̆i'	ɪ·`nō̆^{n}	nɪgɛ·`sọ̈·nə'		nọ̈Dọ̈·`gwaDɔ^{c}ya=
I originated in the distance	far away	never		I will stretch out my

nō̆^{c}ɪ·Dɪsti'		'ɪ`yɛ·lọ̈·'	gɛ·sọ̈·'	aDʋ^{c}ɪlɔ^{u}st^{c}anɪ·ga'		ʋ`wɔ·=
hand		thy body	it is, T. L.	it has come to wash itself		foam

gɪ·'tlɪ	ʋnɛ·'gō^n	gọ̈ŋwŭ·`tlstɪlaw$^{c}$ɪstɪ·`Dɛ·gɛ·sti'		aDɔ·`lanọ̈·'	ʋnɛ·'=
	white	it will cling to my head as I go about		walking stick	white

gə	gọ̈·^{n}kwsō̆^{n}gʋ^{D}ldɪ·'tsɪ·^{c}ɪsti'	gɛ·sɛ·sti'		ɔ·^{u}ya'	agwat^{c}ɪ·ya=
	it to come into my extended (hand)	it will		Fire	it will be

stanɛ·lɪ·`sɛ·sti'		gō̆lkwɔ·'gi	ɪ·`yagalọ̈ldi`		wɪ-Da^{D}lɛ^{c}ɪsa·'nɪ·ga`	10
left over for me continuously		seven	above-in-succession		over there he has come to rise up	

a`Da·Nɪ̆tɔ'		^{1}yă^c
the soul		Sharply

This is to Take Oneself to the Water with, to Help Oneself

FREE TRANSLATION

Now, then! Ha, now thou hast come to listen, thou Long Human Being, thou art staying (right here?) thou Helper of human beings. Thou never lettest go thy grasp; thou never lettest go thy grasp from the soul. Thou hast, as if it were, taken a firmer grasp upon (the soul). I originated at the cataract, not so far away. I will stretch out my hand to (where thou art). (My soul) has come to bathe itself in thy body. The white foam will cling to my head as I walk (along the path of life), the white staff will come into my extended hand. The fire (of the hearth) will be left (burning) for me incessantly. The soul has been lifted up successively to the seventh upper (-world).

EXPLANATION

[This formula for going to water was tentatively edited by James Mooney in his discussion of the Cherokee River Cult, p. 2.]

It is for the purpose of obtaining long life, and the ceremony may be performed either by the medicine man for the benefit of his client or by the client himself on his own behalf. It may be performed [whenever] desired, the favorite time being at each new moon. The patient, often accompanied by all the members of his household, goes down to the stream before sunrise, and while still fasting. Whether he recites the formula himself, or whether this is left for the medicine man to do, the ceremony is the same. The client [and those accompanying him, dip out water with the hollow of their hand. This is the action referred to in the expression: "I will stretch out my hand to where thou (Long Human Being, i. e., the stream, the Water) art."] They wash [their face, the crown of] their head and their breast ["where their soul is"] and may even step into the stream and completely duck under seven times, if they so desire.

The formula is addressed to the "Long Human Being," the stream, the river, the flowing water, and who is called the "helper of mankind." [In many of the formulas the "Long Human Being" is referred to as having originated at the cataract, and this is doubtlessly the reason why the reciter claims for himself the same origin; this establishes a close and intimate relationship between him and the spirit invoked, and all but forces the latter to pay heed to the requests of his relative.]

The idea to be conveyed by the latter part of the formula is that the suppliant, having bathed in the stream, comes out with the white foam [i. e., gray hairs, old age] clinging to his head, and taking the white [walking stick], or staff [an attribute of old people or chiefs?], in his hands, starts on his journey to the seventh upper-world [i. e., the summum of human happiness, prosperity, and success. Surely, he will live to be old, for "the fire of the hearth will be left for him (until his old age), to warm and to protect him"].

The expression wιDa‛ᴅlɛ‛ι`sa‛nι·Ga´ implies that the subject [now has been lifted up to the seventh upper world] after having lain [supine as sick or tired for some time]. From this stem the missionaries have [formed the expression expressing the Christian concept] of resurrection.

94

ːι'a´	nö̜·`wɔ·t'i´	ʋnɛ‛´Gə	ⁱya`ndι·k‛ɔ̈‛ːa ⁿ		
this	to cure with	white	if they urinate		
ʋ`‛st‛AGaᴅli´	ʋ`‛G-at‛asGι‛´sGi	ʋ`nιskɔ-ːi´		sɔ.ι´	ʋstι‛´Ga
if leaning against	pus, it oozes out (Hab)	their heads, Loc		the other	it little
ʋ`‛st‛AGaᴅli´	sɔ´ˡ-´lɛ‛‛wɔ̈ⁿ´	ʋstι‛´Ga	tsϊ´ki		
it leaning against	the other, however also	it little	it which is		

This is the Medicine When They Urinate White (Matter)

FREE TRANSLATION

Flowering spurge, spurge, viper's bugloss, and the other small flowering spurge; the other one (i. e., the first one) is also small.

EXPLANATION

In this prescription we are given only the names of the plants used, four in number, viz, ʋ`‛st‛AGaᴅli´, *Euphorbia corollata* L., flowering spurge; ʋ`‛st‛AGaᴅli´ ʋstι‛´Ga, (?); ʋ`‛Gat‛as=Gι‛´sGi, *Euphorbia hypericifolia* L., spurge; ʋ`nιskɔːi´, *Echium vulgare* L., viper's bugloss, blueweed, blue devil.

In severe cases Gι‛´Gə tsʋya‛´.i, *Lysimachia quadrifolia* L., loosestrife, is added to the prescription.

Ay. explained that the roots are steeped in warm water and the infusion drunk. The infusion is kept warm near the fire.

95

	ːι'a´	nö̜·`wɔ·t'i´	ʋnö̜´ᴅi	tsa`ndι·k‛ɔ̈‛ːa ⁿ		
	this	to cure with	milk	it which they urinate		
ʋnι‛kwa´	ιtsɛːi´		Gʋ‛ɬstɔ.ti`	ʋGa`nəwɔ·´Də`		ʋ`ndι‛´- 5
(purple?)	green		to steep it with	warm		they must
t‛a.sti`	ʋDɔ·`təGwùDə´		t‛a`ᴅlι·ne·´	ι·Ga´		tsɔ·`ι·ne·´ⁿ-nϊɔ̈`
drink it	all day		second	noon		third and
ʋ`ᴅalʋ·lö̜.´i`	ι·Ga´		nö̜ⁿ`Gιnɛ·´ⁿ	a‛sɛ̈´	tsι`ᴅùtɬsta·`yəːɔ̈ⁿ´skəGwɔ̈ⁿ`
it has not completed itself	noon		fourth	it must	when the meal is being taken, L
ʋ·´nùɬsta·`ˡy‛ti´		Ga·k̜t‛ö̜·´Də	nö̜ⁿ´Gi´	tsʋ‛sɔ̈´ιDə	ʋ`ᴅιlɛ‛´Gi
let them partake of the meal		restricted	four	they nights-been	hot
aᴅlɛ‛	a·ma´	a`skùya´	aᴅlɛ̈‛´	a`Gɛ‛ⁱyö̜ⁿ`	ʋ·yɔ·´.ι-Gwö̜ⁿ`
and	salt	man	and	woman	different, L(=E)

This is the Medicine When They Urinate Milky (Substance)

FREE TRANSLATION

Black gum (and) alder steeped with it, warm; they must drink it all day; the second (day, until) noon; and the third (day until) noon has not completed itself; the fourth (day), let them eat along with the others; restricted (are during) four nights hot (food) and salt; (intercourse between) the man and the woman is very bad.

EXPLANATION

The characteristic symptoms of this sickness were given as a discharge of milky urine, preceded or accompanied by frequent discharges of dark red urine, together with pains in the lower part of the back and pelvic region, and perspiration about the private parts. It is considered a more serious form of urinary disease than any previously mentioned. The patient drinks a warm infusion of the inner bark of *unɩ́ʻkwa*, *Nyssa multiflora* Wang., black gum; *ɩtsɛ́ʻɨ*, *Alnus rugosa* (Du Roi) Spreng., smooth alder, the bark being taken from the root just above the ground on the east side of the tree. The patient drinks the medicine at intervals [ad libitum] during the whole of the first day, until noon on the second day, until about 10 a. m. the third day, and until just before breakfast the fourth day, which completes the course of treatment.

The taboo includes salt, hot food, and sexual intercourse.

96

ɩ̈ʼaʼ   yu`Da·Nɩ̈tɛ·ʼksɔ̆ⁿ   aʼskwanɩGɔ·ʼtɔ.tɩ·-yiʼ | ɩ̈ʼʼaGwɔ̆ᴅʼ   naʻnɩ-
this   if a tooth comes off   to store it up with, E   this, L   they have

wɛʻskɔ·ʼ.i | ᴅɔ·ʼyi   skɩnɩ̈tɔ̆ⁿʼ   *(4 times)*
been said (Hab)   beaver   put a tooth
                             into my (jaw)

This is, When a Tooth Comes Out, to Throw it Away With

FREE TRANSLATION

This is all that has to be said: "Beaver, put a tooth into my jaw!" *(4 times)*.

EXPLANATION

The knowledge of this bit of folklore was first obtained [by Mr. Mooney] through a young mixed blood from the Cherokee Nation in the west, who said that when, in early childhood, his milk teeth were being replaced by permanent teeth his Cherokee mother had told him to throw the loosened teeth upon [60] the roof of the house, asking the beaver at the same time to give him a new one instead. He could not remember the details, but on asking Ay. about the matter he at once confirmed the statement, giving the words as above, which the child repeats four times while running around the house, after which he throws the old tooth upon[60] the roof. He had not the formula written down, as it is a well-known folklore custom, and in no way a secret matter. As the beaver is noted for its gnawing powers, there is a good Indian reason for asking it for a set of new teeth.

[Although a similar belief and formula is very common through almost all Europe (where, however, mice and rats are addressed instead of the beaver), there is no necessity to consider this Cherokee practice as borrowed from the whites.]

---

[60] "Over the roof," my informant told me.—EDITOR.

INDEX

	Page
ABORTION, attitude toward	117
ACCIDENTS, belief concerning	17
ACORUS CALAMUS, use of	288
ACTAEA ALBA, use of	277
ADIANTUM PEDATUM, use of	228
AESCULUS PAVIA, use of	239
AFTER LIFE, beliefs concerning	140–144
AGRIMONIA PARVIFLORA, use of	274
AGRIMONY, use of	274
ALDER—	
cultivation of	91
medicinal use of	185, 216, 218, 219, 246, 257, 298, 308
ALNUS RUGOSA—	
cultivation of	91
use of	185, 216, 218, 219, 246, 257, 308
ALNUS SERRULATA, use of	185, 219, 298
AMELANCHIER CANADENSIS, use of	283
AMPELOPSIS CORDATA, use of	254, 283
AMULETS, sickness averted by	74
ANATOMY, lack of knowledge of	90
ANIMAL GHOSTS, disease caused by	27, 182, 207
ANIMAL SPIRITS, belief in	25
ANIMALS, beliefs concerning	27
ANTS, belief concerning	174
APLECTRUM HIEMALE, use of	128
APOPLEXY, formula for	230
ARISTOLOCHIA MACROPHYLLA, use of	288
ARISTOLOCHIA SERPENTARIA, use of	177, 224, 286
ARROWHEAD used for scarifying	69
ASARUM CANADENSE, use of	209, 252
BABIES, medicated bath for	76
BALL GAME, part taken in, by medicine man	91
BARK—	
decoction of, used in sweat-bath	297
medicinal use of	185, 198, 199, 200, 218
BATHS, sweat and vapor	61
BEADS—	
use of, in diagnosis	41
use of, in divination	59, 152, 304
used in prognosis	42
BELIEFS—	
changes in	77–78
traced to white influence	78–79
BETULA LENTA, use of	102
BETULA NIGRA, use of	200
BIG COVE, work conducted at	7
BILIOUSNESS, formula for	297
BIRTH, customs connected with	116–127
BLACK GUM TREE—	
use of bark of	218
use of roots of	283, 308
BLACK MAN, belief in	24
BLISTERS, formulas for	167, 210, 250
BLOWING TUBE, use of, in medicine	58, 60
BLUE MAN, power of	24
BOAS, FRANZ, acknowledgment to	xv
BOILS—	
preventive of	77
treatment for	299, 300–301
BOTANY, medicine man's knowledge of	88, 89
BOTRYCHIUM VIRGINIANUM, use of	177
BOWEL TROUBLES, formulas for	167, 274, 284
BUGBANE, WHITE, use of	277
BULRUSH—	
cultivation of	91
medicinal use of	198
BURIAL CUSTOMS	121, 122, 134–140
BURS, symbolic use of	101
BUTTON SNAKEROOT, use of	76
BUZZARD, dead, used as a prophylactic	76
CABINS, CHEROKEE, manner of building	292
CALAMUS, use of	288
CALYCANTHUS FERTILIS, use of	253

311

INDEX

CAMPTOSORUS RHIZOPHYLLUS, use of.................... 209
CARDINAL FLOWER—
  cultivation of............ 91
  use of................... 216
CARPINUS CAROLINIANA, use of. 200, 265
CASTANEA PUMILA, use of...... 200
CATAMENIAL CUSTOMS.......... 34–35, 97, 101, 246
CEMETERY, location chosen for. 136
CEREMONY—
  for pregnant women. 195, 118–119
  of going to the water..... 118–119, 233–235, 291, 306
CHARMS, sickness averted by... 74
CHEROKEE DIALECTS............ 10
CHEROKEE INDIANS—
  attitude of, toward whites.. 8
  present life of............ 8
CHEROKEE LANGUAGE, study of. 10
CHEROKEE MANUSCRIPTS AND MATERIAL, loss of.......... 1
CHEROKEE TEXT, method of reconstituting............... 3–5
CHERRY, WILD, use of........ 170, 275
CHILD LIFE................... 128–131
CHILDBIRTH—
  complications in.......... 125
  customs connected with.. 122–127
  formulas to aid in........ 167, 274, 278–279
  medicine used in......... 53, 119
CHILDREN—
  clothing of............... 128
  food of................... 128
  formula for............... 284
  games of.................. 129
  hygienic condition of..... 128–129
  intelligence of........... 129
  method of carrying........ 129
  naming of................. 127
  trained to become witches. 129–130
CHILLS, formulas for......... 167, 169, 200, 227, 277
CHINQUAPIN, medicinal use of. 200, 211
CHOKECHERRY, use of......... 170, 199, 277, 298
CICUTA MACULATA, use of..... 117
CIMICIFUGA RACEMOSA, use of.. 277
CIRCUMAMBULATION in treatment of disease.............. 63–64
CLEMATIS VIRGINIANA, use of.. 288

CLETHRA ACUMINATA, use of... 192, 218
CLOTHING—
  of a corpse............... 134
  women's, manner of wearing............... 247
COFFIN MAKER, office of..... 136
COHOSH, BLACK, use of....... 277
COLLINSONIA CANADENSIS, use of.................... 209
COLOR SYMBOLISM............. 51
COMMUNITY SPIRIT among the Cherokee................. 80–81
CONCEPTION, Cherokee belief concerning............. 116–117
CONJURATIONS—
  against witches........... 152
  agricultural.............. 152–153
  for curing................ 151
  for hunting and fishing... 153
  for using tobacco......... 151
  formulas used in, with beads................. 152
  use of the term........... 149
CONTRACEPTIVES—
  attitude toward........... 117
  Cherokee knowledge of... 117–118
CORNUS FLORIDA, use of..... 199, 283
CORONILLA VARIA, use of..... 198
CORYLUS AMERICANA, use of... 218
COWBANE, use of............. 117
C. R. B. EDUCATIONAL FOUNDATION (INC.), NEW YORK, acknowledgment to......... xv
CUCUMBER TREE, use of....... 298
CULTURE, CHEROKEE, loss of knowledge of.............. 78
CURING—
  methods used in.......... 60–64
  procedure in............. 67–68
  See also DISEASES; FORMULAS; MEDICINE; SURGERY.
CYNOGLOSSUM VIRGINIANUM, use of....................... 174
CYPRIPEDIUM PARVIFLORUM, use of....................... 249
CYSTOPTERIS FRAGILIS, use of.. 228
DANCES after burials........ 139
DASYSTOMA FLAVA, use of..... 193
DASYSTOMA VIRGINICA, use of.. 244
DEATH—
  customs connected with.. 131–134
  foretelling of............ 133

INDEX

	Page
DEER, diseases caused by ghost of	28
DEL., a medicine man, characterized	115–116
DENSTAEDTIA PUNCTILOBA, use of	228
DENTISTRY—	
among the Cherokee	72
See also TOOTHACHE.	
DEWBERRY, medicinal use of	253
DIAGNOSIS of disease	39–41
DIARRHEA—	
diet for	65
formula for	193, 244, 282
DIOSPYROS VIRGINIANA—	
pestle made of wood of	293
use of	275, 298
DIPHTHERIA, formula for	254, 261
DIPPER, GOURD, use of, by medicine man	58
DISEASES—	
causes of	15–16, 17–39
change in conception of	77–80
Cherokee conception of	14–16
contagious, cause of	39
contagious, safeguard against	75
curing methods in	60–64, 67–68
efficacy of treatment of	81–83
number of, known to the Cherokee	89
prevention of	73–77
transferring of	62–63
treatment of	39–83
See also FORMULAS; MEDICINE; SICKNESS.	
DISLOCATIONS, treatment of	72
DIVINATION—	
by means of beads	132
procedure in	93–94
DIVINATOR, activities of	86
DOGS, medicine given to	30
DOGWOOD, medicinal use of	199, 283
DREAMS—	
as a cause of disease	35–37, 40
belief concerning	15
formula for	246
interpretation of	36–37
nightmare, remedy for	176–177
of ill omen, formula for	304
snake, formulas for	167
taboo concerning	178

	Page
DUTCHMAN'S PIPE, medicinal use of	288
DWARF IRIS, use of	288
DYSENTERY, formula for	244
EARACHE, formulas for	167
ECHIUM VULGARE, use of	307
EDMUNDS, MR. AND MRS. J. R., JR., acknowledgment to	xv
ELECTION of coffin makers and grave diggers	135–136
EMETICS, use of	23
EPIDEMICS, Cherokee belief concerning	39
EPIGAEA REPENS, use of	193, 252
ERYNGIUM VIRGINIANUM, use of	245
ERYNGIUM YUCCIFOLIUM, use of	76
ERYNGO plants, use of	245
ETHICS, professional, of medicine men	93–95
EUPATORIUM PURPUREUM, use of	262
EUPHORBIA HYPERICIFOLIA, use of	180, 307
EVERGREENS, belief concerning	139
EVONYMUS AMERICANUS, use of	253
EYES, formulas for treatment of	167, 184–186, 219
FAINTING, formulas for	167, 192, 205, 224
FASTING—	
by medicine man	66
by patient	66
efficacy of	83
FEE of medicine man	95–97
FERNS—	
medicinal use of	54, 228
symbolism of, in medicinal use	54, 293
FETTER BUSH, use of	220
FEVER, formulas for	167, 200, 243
FEWKES, J. W., acknowledgment to	xv
FIRE—	
associated with sun	21
association of, with disease	21
curative properties of	21
prayers offered to	20
profanation of	174
FLAX, medicinal use of	243
FLINT, place of, in Cherokee mythology	25
FLOWERING SPURGE, use of	180
FLUX, formulas for	275–276

FOLKLORE, EUROPEAN, beliefs
    traceable to_____ 78-79
FOOD—
    buried with the dead_____ 134
    for children_____ 128
FORMULAS—
    age of_____ 163, 294
    attitude toward_____ 156, 162
    beliefs concerning_____ 147, 156
    classification of_____ 148
    directions for using__ 157-158, 159
    exchange of_____ 104
    kinds of_____ 146-155
    method of keeping_____ 104, 157
    method of writing_____ 158
    origin of_____ 146
    recited or sung_____ 155
    sale of_____ 147, 102-103, 105
    structure of_____ 159
    term used for_____ 144-146
    to avert evil_____ 77
    vocabulary used in_____ 163-164
    western dialect in_____ 162
FOUR, the sacred number_____ 52, 199
FOXGLOVE, medicinal use of____ 244
FOX GRAPE, use of_____ 253
FRACTURES, treatment of_____ 71
FROSTBITE—
    formulas for_____ 167, 258, 298
    treatment for_____ 258
FUNGUS, use of_____ 124
GALPIN, P. C., acknowledgment
    to_____ xv
GAMES of children_____ 129
GENITO-URINARY DISEASES, formulas for_____ 167
GERARDIAS, use of_____ 192, 193, 273
GHOSTS—
    animal, activities of_____ 26-27
    conception of_____ 142
    human, activities of_____ 26
    See also SPIRITS.
GINSENG—
    collected and dried_____ 91
    use of_____ 171, 230, 289
GLEDITSIA TRIACANTHOS, use of_ 239, 249
GLYCINE APIOS, cultivation of___ 91
GNAPHALIUM OBTUSIFOLIUM, use
    of_____ 207, 262
GOATSRUE, use of_____ 128
GOLDEN ALEXANDER, use of____ 102
GOLDENCLUB, use of_____ 76

GOLDENROD, use of_____ 275
GOURD DIPPER, use of, by medicine man_____ 58
GRAVEDIGGERS, office of_____ 136
GRAVES, beliefs concerning___ 139-140
GREAT LAUREL, use of_____ 204, 220
GROUNDNUT, medicinal use of___ 230
HAZELNUT, medicinal use of____ 218
HEADACHE—
    Cherokee belief concerning_ 17
    formulas for_____ 167, 171,
        188, 200, 224, 255, 289, 300
HELLEBORE, AMERICAN WHITE—
    cultivation of_____ 91
    use of_____ 204, 220
HEMORRHAGE, treatment of____ 72
HENDERSON, J., acknowledgment to_____ xv
HEPATICA ACUTILOBICA, use of_ 209, 252
HICKORY BARK, medicinal use
    of_____ 260, 273
HICORIA ALBA, use of_____ 260, 273
HOARSENESS, remedy for_____ 199
HODGE, F. W., acknowledgment to_____ xv
HONEY LOCUST, medicinal use
    of_____ 239, 249
HORNBEAM, medicinal use of
    bark of_____ 200, 265
HORSE BALM, use of_____ 209
HUSBANDS, taboos for_____ 121-122
HYDRANGEA ARBORESCENS, medicinal use of_____ 246
HYDRANGEA CINEREA, use of____ 192
IMMORTALITY. See SOUL.
IMPATIENS BIFLORA, use of__ 119, 125
INCANTATIONS—
    for love attractions_____ 154
    to cause separation_____ 155
    to change an enemy_____ 153
    to kill_____ 154
    to produce unattractiveness_____ 155
    use of the term_____ 149
INDIAN PHYSIC, use of_____ 204
INDIAN PINK, use of_____ 214, 249
INDIAN POKE, use of_____ 204
INDIGESTION, formulas for_____167,
        181, 186, 189-192, 217, 239,
        281, 297.
INFANTS, medicated bath for____ 76
INFORMANTS, Cherokee_____ 9
INHERITANCE of office_____ 105

INDEX

INITIATION of medicine man___ 99–104
INSECTS, belief concerning_____ 29
IRIS VERNA, use of_____ 288
IRONWOOD BARK, use of_____ 200, 265
ITCHING, formula for_____ 173, 286
Jo., a medicine man, characterization of_____ 113–114
JOE-PYE-WEED, use of_____ 262
JUD., a medicine man, characterization of_____ 114–115
JUGLANS NIGRA, taboo concerning_____ 120–121
JUNCUS EFFUSUS, use of_____ 198
KALMIA LATIFOLIA, use of____ 203, 220
KIDNEY DISEASE, formula for_ 179, 199
KNIVES, STONE, Mohammedan use of_____ 59
LADYSLIPPER, medicinal use of__ 249
LAMBERT, JESSIE, acknowledgment to_____ xv
LANGUAGE—
    Cherokee, study of_____ 10
    ritual_____ 160–165
LAPPULA VIRGINIANA, use of___ 174
LAUREL, used for scarification__ 70
LEGERDEMAIN, use of, by medicine men_____ 93, 94
LEUCOTHOË CATESBAEI, use of_ 203, 220
LILIUM CANADENSE, use of_____ 128
LIMETREE, medicinal use of____ 244
LINUM USITATISSIMUM, use of__ 243
LIRIODENDRON TULIPIFERA, use of_____ 177, 286, 298
LITTLE PEOPLE—
    beliefs concerning_____ 25
    the cause of accidents_____ 18
LITTLE RED MEN, belief in____ 23, 24
LIVERLEAF, use of_____ 209, 252
LOBELIA CARDINALIS—
    cultivation of_____ 91
    use of_____ 216
LOBELIA SPICATA, use of_____ 226
LOOSESTRIFE, use of_____ 254, 307
LOUSEWORT, use of_____ 275
LOVE ATTRACTION, formulas used for_____ 154
LYSIMACHIA QUADRIFOLIA, use of_____ 254, 307
MAGNOLIA ACUMINATA, use of__ 298
MALUS MALUS, use of_____ 199
MAN-KILLERS—
    conception of_____ 29
    methods of_____ 33
MASSAGE, use of, in illness_____ 62

MAYFLOWER, use of_____ 252
MEASURE WORM, disease attributed to_____ 293
MEDICAL PRACTITIONERS, number of, among Cherokee_____ 7
MEDICAL TREATMENT, efficacy of_____ 81–83
MEDICINAL KNOWLEDGE, uncontaminated by whites_____ 78
MEDICINE—
    administration of_____ 56–57, 60
    animal elements in_____ 52, 57
    Cherokee_____ 52–59
    disposal of, after use_____ 57
    external application of_____ 60–61
    mineral elements in_____ 57
    of the whites, Cherokee attitude toward_____ 108
    use of water in_____ 57
    See also DISEASES; FORMULAS; SICKNESS.
MEDICINE DANCE, object of____ 75
MEDICINE MEN—
    activities of_____ 85
    anatomical knowledge of__ 90
    assistance of, in childbirth_ 123, 125
    attitude toward_____ 93
    botanical knowledge of____ 88, 89
    canonization of_____ 88
    classes of_____ 84–88
    fees of_____ 95–97
    importance and influence of_____ 83, 92
    instruction for career of__ 100–103
    paraphernalia of_____ 58–59
    personalities of, described__ 109–119
    place of, in warfare_____ 91
    professional ethics of_____ 93–95
    qualifications for_____ 99
    relations between_____ 98
    scope of knowledge of_____ 88–91
    sincerity of_____ 93, 95
    social status of_____ 91–93
    status of, in ball game_____ 91
    succession to office of_____ 105
    supernatural power of_____ 18
    use of the term_____ 84, 85
    See also DIVINATORS; PRIESTS.
MEDICINE MEN'S SOCIETY, existence of, doubtful_____ 97–98
MEDICINE WOMEN, scarcity of__ 84

316 INDEX

MEMORY, medicine to aid — 101
MENSTRUAL CUSTOMS — 34–35, 97, 101, 246
MIDWIFE, activities of — 87
MILK TABOO — 179, 199
MOON, diseases caused by — 22
MOONEY, JAMES—
    paper dedicated to — XVII
    work of — XVII, 2, 5, 6
MOUNTAIN LAUREL, use of — 203, 220
MOUNTAIN PEOPLE, the cause of accidents — 18
MULLEIN, use of — 216, 255
MYTH of the Two Thunder Boys — 197–198
NAMES, change of, to cure disease — 63, 68
NAMING CUSTOMS — 127
NAUSEA, formula for — 245
NICOTIANA RUSTICA—
    cultivation of — 91
    use of — 170, 171, 230, 241, 285
NUMBERS, SACRED — 52
NYSSA MULTIFLORA, use of — 218, 283, 308
NYSSA SYLVATICA, use of — 222
OG., a medicine man, characterization of — 112–113
OLBRECHTS, MARGRIET, acknowledgment to — XV
OMENS—
    belief in — 37
    of death — 133
ORIENTATION in burials — 138
ORONTIUM AQUATICUM, use of — 76
OSMUNDA CINNAMOMEA, use of — 228
OWL, belief concerning — 29
OXYDENDRON ARBOREUM, use of — 222, 283
PAINS, formulas for — 172, 202, 205, 216, 220, 238, 252, 257, 266, 268, 302
PANAX TRIFOLIUM—
    collected and dried — 91
    use of — 171, 202, 230, 289
PARAPHERNALIA of medicine man — 58, 59
PARSLEY, used as an abortive — 118
PARTURITION. *See* CHILDBIRTH.
PEDICULARIA CANADENSIS, use of — 275
PERSIMMON, medicinal use of — 275, 298
PERSIMMON WOOD, stamper made of — 293
PETROSELINUM SATIVUM, use of — 118
PHLOX STOLONIFERA, use of — 277

PHONETIC SYMBOLS and abbreviations — 11–13
PICKERING, JOHN, loss of manuscript by — ⊥
PINE—
    medicinal use of — 119, 188
    use of, to purify dwellings — 139
PINUS PUNGENS, use of — 119
PITCHER PLANT, use of — 101
PLACENTA—
    disposal of — 126
    means for expelling — 126
PLANTS, MEDICINAL—
    collection of — 55
    cultivation of — 91
    gathering of — 90, 91
    preparation of — 55–57
    use of — 53–54, 82
PLATANUS OCCIDENTALIS, use of — 200, 244, 246, 298
POISON IVY, medicinal use of — 198
POLYSTICHUM ACROSTICHOIDES, use of — 228
POPLAR, medicinal use of bark of — 177, 286
PORTHERANTHUS TRIFOLIATUS, use of — 204
PRAYERS—
    for gathering medicine — 150
    for long life — 150
    for protection — 149–150
    use of the term — 148
PREGNANCY—
    beliefs concerning — 35
    customs connected with — 118–122
    formula of ceremony for — 195
    taboos connected with — 18, 120–122
PRIBER, CHRISTIAN, lost manuscript by — ⊥
PRIEST—
    activities of — 85–86
    use of the term — 85
    See also MEDICINE MEN.
PROGNOSIS, CHEROKEE — 41–42
PROPERTY, buried with the dead — 134–135
PRUNUS PENNSYLVANICA, use of — 275
PRUNUS SEROTINA, use of — 170
PRUNUS VIRGINIANA, use of — 170, 199, 277, 298
PUFFBALL, use of — 124

INDEX

317

PURIFICATION RITES, observance of _____ 103–104, 138, 139
PURPLE MAN, associated with magic _____ 24
PUTTY ROOT, use of _____ 128
QUERCUS ALBA, medicinal use of_ 244
QUERCUS FALCATA, use of _____ 199
QUERCUS MIBRICARIA, use of ___ 199
QUERCUS RUBRA, medicinal use of _____ 244
QUERCUS STELLATA, use of ____ 200
RABBIT, taboo concerning _____ 120
RAINMAKERS, almost extinct ___ 87
RASPBERRY, medicinal use of ___ 246
RATTLE, restricted use of _____ 59
RATTLESNAKE, teeth of, used for scarification _____ 70
RATTLESNAKE FERN, use of __ 176, 177
RATTLEWEED, use of _____ 277
RED BUCKEYE, medicinal use of_ 239
RED OAK, medicinal use of _____ 244
REINCARNATION of animals ____ 27–28
RESTRICTIONS, observance of, to prevent sickness _____ 73–74
RHEUMATISM—
    diet for _____ 65
    food taboos for _____ 293
    formulas for _____ 167, 196, 292
    remedy for _____ 53–54
    treatment for _____ 196
RHODODENDRON MAXIMUM, use of _____ 203, 204, 220
RHUS COPALLINA, use of _____ 251
RHUS GLABRA, use of _____ 130, 251
RHUS HIRTA, use of _____ 251
RHUS (TOXICODENDRON) RADICANS, use of _____ 198
RICHWEED, use of _____ 209
RITE OF PURIFICATION, observance of _____ 103–104
RITUAL LANGUAGE—
    sources of _____ 161–162
    use of _____ 160–165
RIVER—
    beliefs concerning _____ 22–23
    disease sent by _____ 23
    ritual connected with _____ 85
    symbolic conception of ____ 191
ROOTS—
    collected and dried _____ 91
    water-growing, medicinal use of _____ 247

RUBUS NIGROBACCUS, use of ___ 253
RUBUS OCCIDENTALIS, use of ___ 246
RUBUS STRUGOSUS, use of _____ 246
RUBUS VILLOSUS, use of _____ 253
SACRED NUMBERS—
    discussed _____ 52
    in formula _____ 199
    reference to _____ 244
    use of, in medicine _____ 54
SALIVA, belief concerning _____ 15
SALIX ALBA, use of _____ 199
SALT—
    belief concerning _____ 121
    placed in burials _____ 134
    tabooed in sickness _____ 64–65
SARRACENIA PURPUREA, use of __ 101
SCARIFICATION—
    in treatment of ailments ___ 69
    instruments used for _____ 69–71
    of ball players _____ 68–69, 70
    See also SCRATCHING CEREMONY.
SCIRPUS VALIDUS, use of _____ 198
SCRATCHING CEREMONY, formulas for _____ 167, 203, 207, 212
SEQUOYA SYLLABARY, use of ___ 3–4
SERVICEBERRY, use of _____ 283
SEXUAL TABOOS _____ 66
SHADBUSH, use of _____ 283
SHALER, MILLARD H., acknowledgment to _____ XV
SHELL, TERRAPIN, use of _____ 59
SICKNESS—
    Cherokee attitude toward_ 80–81
    seclusion in _____ 83
    See also DISEASES; MEDICINE.
SINGING, CHEROKEE, characteristics of _____ 155
SKUNK, use of, as a prophylactic _____ 76
SLIPPERY ELM, medicinal use of 119, 244
SMALLPOX, preventives used against _____ 76
SNAKE BITES, formulas for ____ 167, 176, 240
SNAKE DREAMS, formulas for ___ 167
SNAKE TOOTH, used in scratching operation _____ 203
SNAKEROOT, BLACK, use of ____ 277
SNAKEROOT, VIRGINIA, use of_ 177, 286

318 INDEX

SNAKES—
  attitude toward 185
  belief concerning 185
  reverence for 177
SOLIDAGO, use of 275
SORE EYES, formulas for 167
SORREL-TREE, use of 283
SOUL—
  beliefs concerning 16, 117
  Cherokee conception of . 140–141
  survival of 142–143
SOURWOOD, use of 222, 283
SPECK, FRANK G., acknowledgment to xv
SPECULARIA PERFOLIATA, use of . 239
SPEEDWELL, common, use of ... 277
SPIGELIA MARILANDICA, use of . 214, 249
SPIRITS—
  animal, belief in 25
  anthropomorphic, of the Cherokee 19–25
  belief in power of 19–29
  disease-causing 42–50
  eliminating disease 43–50
SPOTTED COWBANE, use of 117
SPURGE, use of 180, 307
SQUIRREL, taboo concerning ... 120
STAMPER, persimmon-wood, use of 59, 62
STANDLEY, PAUL C., acknowledgment to .... xv, 6
STIRLING, M. W., acknowledgment to xv
STOMACH TROUBLE—
  baby's, formula for 284
  See also INDIGESTION.
STONE KNIVES, Mohammedan use of 59
SUCKING HORN, use of 72–73
SUICIDE rare among Cherokee .. 144
SUMAC, medicinal use of 130, 251
SUMMER GRAPE, use of 253, 283
SUN—
  association of, with disease . 20–21
  beliefs concerning 19–21
  prayers offered to 20
SURGERY in Cherokee curing methods 68–73
SWANTON, JOHN R., acknowledgment to xv
SWAYNEY, work conducted at .. 7

SWEATBATH—
  bark decoction used in 297
  described 61
  object of 61
SWEET FLAG, use of 288
SWELLINGS, treatment for 299
SWIMMER, brief account of 7
SWIMMER MANUSCRIPT, loss of .. 1
SYCAMORE, medicinal use of .. 200, 244, 298
SYMBOLISM—
  in medicinal plants 53–54
  in medicine 63, 120
  of color 51
SYMPTOMS OF DISEASES, value attached to 16–17
T., a medicine man, characterization of 111–112
TABLE MOUNTAIN PINE, use of .. 119
TABOOS—
  belief concerning 15
  concerning birds 66
  concerning corpse 136
  connected with pregnancy . 120–122
  diet, in sickness 64–65, 179, 199
  food, basis for 82
  for husbands 121–122
  for medicine men 103, 136
  for mother, after childbirth . 127
  for rheumatic patients .. 293–294
  in treatment of sickness .. 64–66
  menstrual 34, 101
  results of violation of 38
  sexual 66
  See also RESTRICTIONS.
TEETH, custom concerning 308
TEPHROSIA VIRGINIANA, use of . 128
TERRAPIN SHELL, use of, for medicine 59
THOMAS, W. H., loss of manuscript by 1
THROAT TROUBLES, formulas for. 167
THRUSH, formula for 259
THUNDER—
  association of, with disease . 24
  beliefs concerning 23–24
TILIA AMERICANA, use of 244
TITHYMALOPSIS COROLLATA, use of 180, 307

INDEX

TOBACCO—
- ceremonial use of........ 151
- chewing, medicinal use of. 224, 241, 289, 301
- cultivated by Cherokee.... 91
- use of, against witches..... 31, 32, 74–75
- wild, medicinal use of..... 170, 171, 230, 241, 285

TOOTHACHE—
- formulas for............ 167, 263
- means of preventing...... 76
- See also DENTISTRY.

TRICKS. See LEGERDEMAIN.

TROUT, SPECKLED, taboo concerning.................... 120

Ts., a medicine man, characterized.................... 115

TULIP TREE, medicinal use of bark of................ 286, 298

TWINS—
- as witches............. 130–131
- customs concerning..... 129–131

ULMUS FULVA, use of........ 119, 244

URINARY DISEASES, formulas for. 179, 199, 221, 222, 153, 287, 307, 308

VAPOR BATH, object of........ 61

VENUS LOOKING-GLASS, medicinal use of.................. 239

VERATRUM VIRIDE—
- cultivation of............ 91
- use of................ 204, 220

VERBASCUM THAPSUS, use of.. 216, 255

VERONICA OFFICINALIS, use of 119, 277

VETCH, medicinal use of....... 198

VICIA CAROLINIANA, use of... 198, 207

VIRGINIA SNAKEROOT, use of... 177, 202, 224

VITIS AESTIVALIS, use of..... 253, 283

VITIS LABRUSCA, use of........ 253

7548°—32——22

VOMITING—
- efficacy of.............. 83
- to transfer disease........ 63

W., a medicine man, characterization of.............. 109–111

WALNUTS, taboo concerning.... 121

WARFARE, medicine man in.... 91

WATER, use of, in medicine.... 57

WATSON, MRS. ALLAN, acknowledgment to................ xv

WHITE OAK, medicinal use of.. 244

WHITES—
- attitude toward........ 8, 39, 99
- attitude toward culture of 107–108

WHOOPING COUGH, preventive used against.............. 76

WILD GINGER, use of........ 209, 252

WILLOW, WHITE, use of........ 199

WITCHCRAFT—
- as a cause of illness....... 41
- precautions against....... 31
- use of, by medicine man... 87–88

WITCHCRAFT DISEASES, formulas for................ 167, 187–188

WITCHES—
- activities of.............. 33
- conception of............ 29–30
- diseases caused by........ 29–33
- preparation for profession of. 30

WORCESTER, S. A., loss of manuscript by................... 1

WORMS, formulas for.......... 167, 214, 248–249

WOUNDS—
- formulas for........ 167, 272–273
- treatment of............ 72

XANTHORRHIZA APIIFOLIA, use of........................ 274

ZIZIA AUREA, use of........... 102